Tessa Hare

The Shell Guide to Ireland

The Shell Guide to Ireland

Lord Killanin and
Michael V. Duignan

Revised and updated
by Peter Harbison

M

Published 1989 by
MACMILLAN LONDON LTD
4 Little Essex Street London WC2R 3LF
and Basingstoke

Published simultaneously by Gill and Macmillan, Dublin

Associated companies in Auckland, Delhi, Gaborone, Hamburg, Harare, Hong Kong, Johannesburg, Kuala Lumpur, Lagos, London, Manzini, Melbourne, Mexico City, Nairobi, New York, Singapore and Tokyo

ISBN 0-333-46957-7

A CIP catalogue record for this book is available from the British Library

This book was edited, designed and produced by
Swallow Publishing Limited,
260 Pentonville Road, London N1 9JY

Editor: Anne Yelland
Designers: Stephen Bitti and Mick Keates
Indexer: Helen Litton
Maps: Swanston Graphics, Derby
Typeset by Graphicraft Typesetters, Hong Kong
Origination and printing by Imago Publishing Ltd
Printed in Italy

Photographic acknowledgments
The photographs reproduced in this book were kindly supplied by:
Bord Failte 2, 8, 20, 35, 37, 50, 55, 56, 62, 65, 67, 68, 74, 78, 79, 80, 82, 92, 95, 100, 103, 107, 119, 121, 127, 143, 145, 146, 151, 153, 158, 163, 164, 168, 173, 181, 185, 188, 190, 192, 196, 218, 221, 228, 230, 233, 235, 236, 240, 253, 267, 269, 272, 279, 289, 307, 308; Peter Harbison 99, 136; Northern Ireland Tourist Board 19, 73, 75, 85, 88, 115, 129, 132, 171, 178, 201, 223, 259, 261, 263, 264; Office of Public Works 1, 40, 43, 44, 49, 57, 71, 81, 84, 87, 91, 109, 123, 128, 135, 167, 169, 182, 183, 187, 195, 197, 199, 200, 206, 209, 213, 214, 217, 225, 227, 241, 242, 243, 249, 250, 251, 282, 283, 288, 292, 295, 298, 300; Imogen Stuart 285, 286

Page 1 South Cross, Ahenny, Co. Tipperary (see page 94); page 2 Lough Key, Co. Roscommon (see page 81).

CONTENTS

EDITOR'S PREFACE

The Shell Guide to Ireland must surely be the most comprehensive guide to modern Ireland ever written, and I feel it an honour to have been asked to edit this, its third edition. I have great pleasure in expressing my gratitude for all the assistance and co-operation I have had in this venture from the two authors of the *Guide*, Lord Killanin and Professor Michael V. Duignan, though it is with regret that I must record the death of Michael Duignan in March 1988.

This third edition has tightened up the text of the second edition, in order to bring out more clearly the material which is likely to be of greatest cultural value. In the process, some monuments – including standing stones, holy wells, earthworks and, occasionally, even megalithic tombs, churches, castles and houses – have been omitted, particularly if they are not easily accessible. But so many surveys of particular localities, and types of structures (such as megalithic tombs), have been published since the completion of the second edition, that the dedicated specialist should be able to discover by other means what he may find missing here. In addition, opening times have been omitted in this edition as they tend to change from year to year. By editorial agreement, the distances in miles have been allowed to stand, rather than adopting the metric system (which will be found on signposts on trunk roads, but not on minor roads, in the Republic). Where possible, the authors' original text and flavour have been retained and the book remains, therefore, a general guide which pays particular attention to antiquities and to things of historic, artistic and literary interest. Since the *Guide* was last revised in 1967, many things have happened in Ireland, some good, some not so good. This edition has laid special emphasis on two major developments in the intervening period. These are, first, the emergence of many small museums throughout the country and, second, the blossoming of interesting church architecture in the wake of the Second Vatican Council. This has brought with it a new flourish of fine church furnishings. Together, these will surely be seen by future generations as an outstanding contribution to Irish art and architecture in the twentieth century.

The main part of this *Guide* is presented in the form of a gazetteer; that is to say, the items are grouped under alphabetically ordered principal centres – usually towns and villages. Under each principal centre will be found not only a description of the noteworthy features of the place itself, but also references to places (usually townlands) within convenient reach of it. These sub-entries are arranged in order following the points of the compass, normally from north to east, south and west, about the chosen centre. In some cases it has seemed convenient to group some of the sub-entries under a sub-centre, working clockwise round the sub-centre. Where this has been done, the sub-entries have been 'paragraphed' by means of dashes. It should be noted that the compass-bearings are, for the most part, approximations, and that the mileages, with certain self-evident exceptions, represent distances by road or track, not straight across country.

The maps in the *Guide* are included as a visual index of the main entries in the gazetteer. It is assumed that each user of the *Guide* will have maps of a scale suited to his or her purpose, but even the possessor of the Ordnance Survey six-inch sheets must be prepared to invoke local guidance when looking for some of the lesser-known monuments. Maps to various scales can be obtained from booksellers or from the Government Publications Office in Molesworth Street, Dublin 2, and H.M. Stationery Office, 80 Chichester Street, Belfast 1.

In the spelling of place-names, the forms used by the Ordnance Surveys have usually been adopted. In the spelling of personal names, whose orthography has fluctuated through the centuries, absolute consistency has not been attempted. In the English rendering of surnames beginning with O, the misleading apostrophe has been omitted, as in O Neill, not O'Neill. When such names are given in their Irish form the mark of length is included, for example, Ó Néill.

Monuments in State ownership or care are 'National Monuments' in the Republic, 'Historic Monuments' in Northern Ireland. These terms have been somewhat loosely applied not only to monuments in State care, but also to those in the ownership or custody of local authorities and those for which Preservation Orders have been issued by the State. Mention of a building, garden, monument, or anything else, in private ownership does not imply public right of access.

For brevity, and in accordance with long-established usage, the dioceses, cathedrals, parish churches, etc., of the Roman Catholic Church are referred to simply as 'Catholic', and those of the Church of Ireland (Anglican Communion) are usually referred to as 'Protestant'. Since the Church of Ireland is the only Protestant Church in the country with a diocesan-parochial organization, and since non-episcopalian Protestant churches and institutions are named specifically Methodist, Presbyterian, etc., as the case may be, no confusion should arise.

Information about particularly scenic areas, the location of beaches, as well as golf and fishing activities, and details of accommodation, travel, local events, and so on, can be obtained from Bord Fáilte – The Irish Tourist Board, Baggot Street Bridge, Dublin 2, or from the Northern Ireland Tourist Board, 48 High Street, Belfast 1, or from the local tourist offices.

The authors have not hesitated to give free rein to personal opinions and foibles in respect of things social, political, historical, religious and artistic; it should be emphasized that the sponsors of the *Guide* are in no way responsible for such opinions and foibles.

In addition to those thanked in the second edition, I would like to express my gratitude to the following who, in the twelve months allowed for the revision of the *Guide*, assisted in checking and/or partially re-writing the entries mentioned in brackets after their names: Canon Bradley (St Patrick's Cathedral); John Bradley (Kilkenny and Moynagh Lough); Dr Seamus Caulfield (Belderg and Ballycastle area); Dr George Cunningham (Roscrea); Liam de Paor (Inishcaltra); Dr Pat Donlon (Chester Beatty Library and Gallery of Oriental Art); Dr Tom Fanning (Galway City); Allen Figgis and the Dean of Christ Church (Christ Church Cathedral); Nicky Furlong (Wexford Town); Jack Johnston (Co. Tyrone); Helen Lanigan-Wood (Co. Fermanagh); Brian Lacy (Co. Derry); Dr W.A. Maguire and Richard Warner (Belfast and Co. Antrim); Con Manning and Klaus Ungert (Dublin Castle); Muriel McCarthy (Marsh's Library); Pat Mackey (Waterford City); Dr Edward McParland (Dublin City); Prof. Frank Mitchell (Valentia Island); Dr Harman Murtagh (Athlone); Dr Seán O Nualláin (megalithic tombs); Aodh O Tuama (Cork City); The Earl of Rosse (Birr); Grellan Rourke (Skellig Michael); Martin Timoney (Sligo); Dr John Waddell (Aran Islands); Roger Weatherup (Co. Armagh) and Anthony Weir (Co. Down). I would particularly like to thank the following artists/craftspeople who compiled lists of their works for me: Seán Adamson, Margaret Becker, Michael and Frances Biggs, Ruth Brandt, Cliodna Cussen, Bernadette Madden, Patrick McIlroy, Patrick Pollen and his wife Nell (née Murphy), Patrick Pye, Veronica Rowe, Christopher and Elizabeth Ryan, Imogen Stuart and Benedict Tutty, O.S.B. A special word of thanks to Wilfrid Cantwell who supplied me with an invaluable list of modern churches and their architects, and to Joy McCormick who kindly produced a list of the churches built by her husband Liam and his various partners, and also to Dr Maurice Craig and the architects Daíthí Hanly, D.J. Kennedy, Paul McMahon and Anthony O Neill for clarification of certain points.

In compiling a *Guide* of this type, one turns to so many people for help that it would be very difficult to list them all here individually. I hope that they will all accept my most grateful thanks for what they have contributed to the success of this volume. Nevertheless, I would not like to conclude the acknowledgements without mentioning the photographic assistance I have received from the two Tourist Boards, North and South, and also from the Office of Public Works in Dublin. Finally, my most grateful thanks to Noel Tierney of Irish Shell, Michael Gill of Gill and Macmillan, and Stephen Adamson and Anne Yelland of Swallow Books in London, whose experience and help have ensured the smooth production of this *Guide*.

In a work of this kind, some inaccuracies and discrepancies are perhaps inevitable. Corrections and suggestions for future editions should be addressed to the Editor, c/o Noel Tierney, Irish Shell House, 20–22 Lower Hatch Street, Dublin 2.

Peter Harbison 1988

Poulnabrone dolmen, Ballyvaghan, Co. Clare (see page 68).

HISTORICAL INTRODUCTION

Prehistoric Ireland

The Middle Stone Age – The First Settlers

From the time of the onset of the last great cold period in Ireland about 75,000 years ago, the Ice-Age glaciers ebbed and flowed over the face of Ireland, undulating with the relative severity of the temperature. That which expanded southwards from the great north-European ice-body sometime around 15 000 B.C. proved to be the last (for the moment!), for by 12 000–11 000 B.C. the worst was over, and warmth-loving plants and animals could gradually spread across the country. The scientists are still debating the date when the last land-bridge between Britain and Ireland was finally washed away by the sea, but it is unlikely to have been any later than 6000 B.C. We still cannot be sure, therefore, whether the first men and women who set foot on Irish soil were able to reach the country by dry land, or whether they had to risk their lives in making the voyage by sea. But what we can be fairly sure of now is that they had reached the country by 8000 B.C. and perhaps even some time before that.

They were mesolithic (Middle Stone Age) hunters and fishers, who penetrated up the rivers from the coast into the interior of a virgin country which was already covered by fairly dense wood and scrubland. We come upon what are among the first known traces of human activity in small temporary camp-sites such as those discovered at Mount Sandel in Co. Londonderry and Lough Boora in Co. Offaly. Excavations at Mount Sandel suggested the existence of the earliest-known round houses in these islands, made of interwoven branches clad with sod, and made sometime around 8000 B.C. by a small number of pork- and salmon-eating fisherfolk. Their ancestors had probably come from Scotland, northern England or the Isle of Man, attracted to the north-east coast of Ireland by the abundant presence of flint from which they could make their primitive stone tools and arrow-heads.

Their temporary settlement at Lough Boora, however, opens up the possibility that small population groups may have crossed (by land or sea) an area of the Irish Sea further south, possibly from Wales, at about the same time. Beneath the layers with traces of human activity at Lough Boora were found the bones of the giant Irish deer, suggesting that this splendid animal had become extinct not through hunting activity but possibly because it could no longer negotiate its giant antlers through the dense growth of trees in an effort to reach its natural feeding grounds.

Although there is a gap of around 1000 years in the record of human activity during the seventh and sixth millennia B.C. in Ireland, there is little evidence so far to suggest that there were any (or many) new arrivals between the earlier mesolithic peoples of Mount Sandel and Lough Boora, and those whom we find spread over much larger areas of the country in the fifth and fourth millennia, extending as far south as the Munster Blackwater in counties Cork and Waterford, and the Dingle Peninsula in Co. Kerry. These later mesolithic peoples, well exemplified from their remains discovered at Sutton and Dalkey Island at the mouth of Dublin Bay, had a life-style which differed little from that of the earliest inhabitants, but this began to change, possibly as early as the fifth millennium B.C., with the arrival of the first farmers.

The Neolithic (New Stone Age) Farmers

The new wave of agriculturalists brought with them across the sea the necessary livestock and a store of seeds for sowing crops, both of which allowed them to relax from the eternal problem of having to be constantly on the move in search of food, and to remain in the same spot to raise their cattle and till their newly created fields. By the fourth millennium B.C., we pick up traces of their first houses, as at Ballynagilly, Co. Tyrone, and Tarkardstown South, Co. Limerick.

Neolithic houses were either round or rectangular, as at Lough Gur, Co. Limerick, or Ballyglass, Co. Mayo. Some were constructed with upright planks, and others had stone foundations and walls of wattle-and-daub, topped probably by thatched roofs. Even at this early stage, the houses were isolated (as they still are in the Irish countryside today), and not grouped into villages, which are known to have existed at this period on the continent of Europe. Nevertheless, the feeling of a community spirit is visible in the miles of parallel stone walls built in the Behy/Glenulra region of north Mayo before the bogs had begun to form around 2000 B.C. These walls formed extensive strips of land, designed in one operation, apparently to enclose livestock rather than necessarily to divide up the land.

Megalithic Monuments

The houses of these neolithic peoples have left no obvious traces above ground, and their discovery has usually had to await the digging of archaeologists' spades. The earliest visible traces of human building activity in the Irish landscape are the great stone tombs, of which around 1200 are now known. Called megaliths, from the Greek words *megas* (great) and *lithos* (stone), they can be divided into a number of clearly defined types, though the relative order in which each type was built is still imperfectly understood.

The simplest of these is the portal-tomb, better known as the dolmen (from the Breton, meaning a stone table), which consists of between three and seven upright stones, two of which form a door or portal, and carrying one or two capstones, which, in the case of Browneshill, Co. Carlow, has been estimated to weigh 100 tons. They were sometimes placed in a long or rectangular mound, and human remains placed in them were usually cremated first.

More complicated in ground plan is the court-tomb (or court cairn), so-called because stones forming an almost semi-circular forecourt were placed at the entrance to the flat-roofed burial gallery, originally covered in a number of instances by a long mound of stone and earth. This chamber consisted of up to four separate sections, subdivided by jambs and low sills. This basic form, as found for instance at Ballyalton, Co. Down, and Browndod, Co. Antrim, could be varied to provide more extensive tombs. An example at Cohaw, Co. Cavan, has two such tombs placed back-to-back. Others, including that at Creevykeel, Co. Sligo, have a forecourt which forms an enclosed open-air oval in front of the entrance to the tomb, and they have been shown by excavation to have contained both inhumed and cremated remains of the dead. The inhumed bones, however, were frequently found in a disarticulated condition, suggesting that they were placed elsewhere before burial in the court-tombs. In fact, there is very little evidence to show that court-tombs were used as primary places of burial, suggesting that they may have served initially as ritual 'temples' for the creation of sympathetic magic to ensure good harvests, and only secondarily as places of burial. They are distributed largely in the northern half of the country, usually in upland areas and isolated from one another, unlike the third major type of megalithic tomb, the passage-tomb. The presence in a small group of court-tombs of transeptal chambers – which were more typical of the passage-tombs – suggests that the builders of both types of tomb had some contact.

The passage-tombs are often grouped together in cemeteries, and get their name because a passage leads in from the periphery of the tumulus to a burial chamber at or near the centre. The major concentrations of passage-tombs are found in counties Meath (Boyne Valley) and Sligo (Carrowkeel and Carrowmore). Carrowmore includes monuments which, if themselves not actually passage-tombs, are in a cemetery which includes passage-tombs and, on excavation, they produced radiocarbon dates which are many centuries earlier than the great passage-tombs of the Boyne Valley. It is not possible, however, to say that the oldest passage-tombs were built in Co.

Sligo. The earlier examples in the east of the country, such as Townley Hall, Co. Louth, are simple structures, and the great examples of Newgrange, Knowth and Dowth, can now be seen to be the climax of passage-tomb development in Ireland, and not its beginning.

Newgrange and Knowth are the most famous passage-tombs, and – together with other examples on the Loughcrew Hills – they are decorated with a variety of geometrical motifs which may reflect those in other materials that possibly decorated the houses of the living. Newgrange has become internationally famous since the discovery that the rising sun on the shortest day of the year, 21 December, casts its rays along the gradually rising passage into the very centre of the burial chamber. Knowth, too, produced its surprises on excavation, not only because of the richness of its decorated stones, but also because its large mound covered two separate chambers placed back-to-back, each showing a different kind of chamber construction – one with a flat roof, the other of corbel type, somewhat similar to that at Newgrange. Both tombs had a number of 'satellite' tombs surrounding them, though two of those at Knowth have proved to be earlier than the main mound. Other than fragments of cremated bone and inhumed burials, the primary finds from passage-tombs are meagre (bone pins, stone balls and pendants, as well as primitive pottery), and these stand in contrast not only to the quality of the decoration on the stones of the tombs, but also to the size of the monuments, with mounds of diameters of up to 300 ft. The people who built these tombs seem to have belonged to a hierarchical society which showed great faith in the 'Afterlife', a considerable knowledge of structural engineering and a use of the annual calendar. They can be said to have produced some of the earliest specimens of true architecture known anywhere in the world. But while one section of the population was burying its dead in megalithic tombs, others were using a much simpler form of single burial, and placing with the dead a much more decorative type of pottery than that used in the passage-tombs.

The Bronze Age

The fourth type of megalithic tomb that has been found was built later than the others, during a period when bronze was becoming the dominant material in the making of tools and weapons. These tombs are called wedge-tombs, since they have a long burial gallery placed in a wedge-shaped mound, which was broader at the end where the entrance to the tomb-gallery lay. These tombs survive in larger numbers than the other three types and, unlike them, are scattered widely over most parts of the country.

The Bronze Age, which began sometime before 2000 B.C., is characterized by new types of pottery known as Beaker, Food Vessel and Urn, and by the increasing popularity of single inhumation or cremation burials, often in cists unmarked above ground. Axes, which had been made of stone during the Neolithic Age, now came to be made of metal – copper at first, and subsequently, with the addition of 10 per cent tin, bronze. Halberds, and also daggers of increasing length, were also made during the earlier part of the Bronze Age, when the country's reserves of river gold were also being exploited to provide ornaments of thin sheet gold, of which the lunulae are the best known. Ireland became one of north-western Europe's greatest producers of copper and gold, and a portion at least of the raw material – and probably some of the finished products as well – were probably exported to Britain and the continent of Europe.

The Bronze Age is best studied through its products, the finest of which are on display in the National Museum in Dublin. Other than the wedge-tombs, the best-known Bronze Age monuments in the countryside are the stone circles, notable concentrations of which are found in west Cork and Kerry, and central Ulster. Their round shape could suggest their use as places of ritual connected with the worship of the round orb of the sun, but they may also have been used as places where the movements of celestial bodies could be studied and recorded, though the evidence for this is by no means conclusive. Equally uncertain is the function of the standing stones found singly or in lines in many parts of the country.

Both Bronze Age pottery and single-grave burials come to an unexplained end sometime around 1400 B.C., and for our knowledge of the remainder of the Bronze Age, up to about 500–300 B.C., we have to rely largely on its metal products, of which new forms – such as bronze swords and cauldrons – seem to emerge around the eleventh century B.C. While ornaments of massive gold were being made about a century before that, the production of both gold ornaments and bronze objects reached its zenith in the period around 700 B.C., when a number of hoards or ritual deposits, notably that at Dowris in Co. Offaly, display a great richness and variety in the forms used. These include bronze swords, spear-heads, cauldrons, horns and shields, as well as socketed axes, and brilliantly executed ornaments using a massive amount of gold. The great extent of metal production is reflected in trade connections with areas as far away as Spain, and probably Scandinavia as well.

Deterioration in weather conditions led to an increasing concentration of settlement in the lowland areas of the country during the later part of the Bronze Age, although hilltops – sometimes those used for burial purposes during the stone and earlier Bronze Ages–were utilized for the construction of hill-forts. These, however, may have been more tribal meeting-places than permanent habitations. It is now becoming increasingly apparent that construction of these hill-forts began during the later phases of the Bronze Age, when the growing use of the sword, and possibly the deposition of a number of hoards, may hint at an increasingly war-like society having to defend its ancestral territories. But the lack of hard evidence for new arrivals of peoples during the Bronze Age does not mean that defence was necessarily against foreign invaders, although many scholars place the first use in Ireland of an Indo-European Celtic language sometime during the later phases of the Bronze Age, and certainly before 600 B.C. The great royal site of Emhain Macha near Armagh, which began life around 700 B.C. and grew to become one of the most important sites in Ulster before the dawn of recorded history, demonstrates a continuity in society between the Bronze Age and the ensuing Iron Age.

The Iron Age: Kings and Heroes

Gaelic epic, which mirrors the Ireland of the closing centuries of the prehistoric Iron Age, shows us a country of chariot-riding kings and heroes whose aristocratic culture displays many of the features reported in Classical accounts of the Continental Celts. The archaeological evidence, such as it is, of the Irish Iron Age proper, is consistent with the testimony of the Heroic tales.

Although the Irish Iron Age lasted several centuries – perhaps from the third century B.C. to the firm establishment of Christianity, say about A.D. 500 – it is only meagrely represented in the archaeological record. Once again we are hampered by the paucity of known dwelling places and burials. Once again there is no unambiguous evidence of significant immigration.

Archaeologically speaking, the outstanding feature of the period is the highly sophisticated abstract ornament applied to fine metalwork and to a few stone carvings. This ornament is in the La Tène style characteristic of the specifically Celtic phase of the European Iron Age. Some of the La Tène manifestations in Ireland, notably the decorated cult-stones of Turoe, Castlestrange, Killycluggin, and Mullaghmast (the last two now in the National Museum), have no counterpart in Britain and may represent direct connections between Ireland and Europe – conceivably only Continental craftsmen working for native clients. But the Turoe stone, and other details of ornamental metalwork, could be interpreted as showing people arriving in Ireland from Britain around the first century B.C.

The so-called ringfort, the classic farmstead of early Irish history, was perhaps known in the prehistoric Iron Age, though the great majority date from the Christian period. The same may also be said of the crannóg, an artificial island habitation.

In the course of the centuries Irish traditions and the Irish environment combined with external stimuli to modify and attenuate the La Tène elements in the later Iron Age material. By the close of the Iron Age the Gaelic-speaking nation of early history had evolved, a nation with a distinctive civilization that is all the more fascinating because it is archaic in so many respects. Major roots of that civilization lie in the Celtic Iron Age, whence its distinctive social and political institutions, its art, its epic literature, derive. Its patriarchal warrior aristocracy, only finally overthrown by the Tudors, preserved to the last something of the heroes of Emhain and Cruachu. Its poets, maintained to the end by that aristocracy, were in a real sense the heirs of the *druides, vates,* and *bardi* of La Tène Europe.

Gaelic Ireland, *c.* 500–1165

The Coming of Christianity and Primitive Monasticism

The Romans omitted Ireland from their conquests. No Germanic migrants violated her shores until the Viking age. Gaelic Ireland, therefore, presents us with the unique example of an archaic, Iron Age, Celtic society operating unchanged – save in so far as it has been affected by Christianity – in the light of history. Therein lies much of its fascination.

By the opening of the historic period Ireland is substantially Christian, the first country outside the Roman world to be won for the new faith. There were probably British missionaries in Ireland before St Patrick, but he is the one usually given credit for the Christianization of the country, traditionally during the years between 432 and 461. According to ancient tradition Patrick established his principal church at Armagh, close to Emhain Macha, the capital of the prehistoric Fifth of the Ulaid.

The coming of Christianity was of tremendous cultural consequence. The remote, peripheral, island was reintegrated into the fabric of Western Europe. The artistic repertoire was enlarged with new media and enriched with new motifs and new techniques that stimulated the last, and finest, flowering of insular Celtic art. To the church, Ireland owes her first true architecture, her introduction to the treasury of Mediterranean thought and letters, and that early written literature in the Gaelic vernacular which is one of the boasts of her heritage.

When, in the seventh and eighth centuries, the Irish Church emerges into daylight, we find that a wave of monasticism has well-nigh obliterated all traces of the primitive Patrician episcopal framework, and that the typical focus of regional jurisdiction is no longer the episcopal see but the monastery ruled by a priest-abbot. These monasteries had been founded in the sixth and seventh centuries by men such as Enda of Aran, Finnian of Clonard and Columba of Iona, some of whom had studied the monastic way of life in Britain. But the Irish Church adhered to an outmoded method of computing the date of Easter, and to an outmoded tonsure. Curiously enough, it is these minor eccentricities of the computus and the tonsure which roused the ire of the orthodox abroad.

'Exiles for Christ'

For the Gaelic saints, passionately attached to home and kindred, to go into exile 'for the love of Christ' was to make the supreme sacrifice, to suffer martyrdom. And so we find them sailing away in their frail boats to the Orkneys, to the Faroes, and even to distant uninhabited Iceland, as well as to Britain, France, the Germanies, and Italy. The best-known names in the countless roll of these 'exiles for Christ' are those of Columcille (Columba) of Iona, Colmán (Columbanus) of Bangor, Luxeuil, and Bobbio, Aidan of Lindisfarne, Fursa of Cnoberesburgh and Péronne, Gall (Gallus) of St Gallen, Fergal ('Vergilius') of Aghaboe and Salzburg, and Cilian (Kilian) of Würzburg. Such men brought or revived Christianity wherever they went, often leaving a monastic foundation in their wake to continue their work. In the ninth and tenth centuries, their footsteps were followed by scholars celebrated for their knowledge; men such as Dicúil the geographer, teacher at Charlemagne's palace school; Sedulius Scottus the poet, active between 848 and 858 at Liège, Metz and Cologne; and – greatest of them all – the philosopher, poet, grammarian, and theologian Johannes Scotus Eriugena.

'Island of Scholars' – Monastic Culture

The Irish monasteries quickly won international renown for their scholarship. Princes, nobles, prelates, priests, and monks flocked from overseas for training in the several branches of Christian learning as well as in the religious life. Students from Anglo-Saxon England were particularly numerous, among them several whose names were to become famous in English history.

Since the texts and treatises studied were in Latin, a good grounding in that language was a primary requirement; some of the Irish scholars have to be numbered among the foremost Classical scholars of their time, while others rank among the finest Latin poets of the Carolingian age. The attainments of such men are fully appreciated only when we recall that Ireland, unlike Britain and France, had never formed part of the Roman Empire and thus had no tradition of Latin culture.

A unique feature of the Latin culture of the Irish monasteries was the fact that it proved in no way inimical to the development of a written literature in the Gaelic vernacular. On the contrary, it was monks who adapted the Latin alphabet and Latin verse-forms to Gaelic requirements and who created the vernacular written literature. St Columcille was a famous protector of the *filí,* and an elegy on him by one of them, Dallán Forgaill, is the oldest securely dated (597) Irish poem we have. That lovely ancient tale, *The Voyage of Bran*, was first committed to writing in the monastery of Bangor. The *céle Dé* movement of the eighth and ninth centuries has left us a body of personal lyrics, intimate nature poems which still delight. Clonmacnois and Terryglass have left us the oldest of our collections of secular tales. Only in the twelfth century did Gaelic secular written lore finally pass into the guardianship of the famous secular families who conserved it throughout the rest of the Middle Ages.

The arts, too, owed much to the monasteries. Most of the finest metalwork of the period, exemplified by such masterpieces as the Ardagh Chalice (National Museum, Dublin), was produced for them and, like the other manifestations of ecclesiastical art, reflects their foreign connections. The same is true of the stone-carving exemplified by cross-slabs, and High Crosses (*below*). Book-painting, an essentially monastic art, produced its supreme masterpiece in the *Book of Kells* (Trinity College, Dublin).

The early monastery usually consisted of an enclosure ringed by one or more ramparts of earth or stone; within it one or more tiny churches or oratories, of the simplest form and, at first, of timber wherever possible; a series of rude huts for the monks; similar structures for kitchen and refectory, and for library, workshops, and school, where such existed; a series of crosses and cross-pillars and slabs, whose inscriptions are normally in Irish, not Latin; from the tenth century onwards a lofty, free-standing, conical-roofed, circular belfry (Round Tower) whose impregnable strength and remote doorway made it also a convenient refuge when danger threatened. In time the timber churches were translated into stone, to give small, ill-lit, and usually single-chamber, buildings whose remains are normally devoid of ornament. However, a seventh-century description of the church at Kildare, with its glowing shrines, its painted pictures, and its hangings, reminds us that such remains are but fleshless skeletons of the dead.

Some monastic sites are noteworthy for their High Crosses, great free-standing crosses of stone whose elaborate carvings were doubtless picked out in colour. One group, exemplified at Ahenny near Carrick-on-Suir, is characterized by predominantly abstract, overall ornament. A second group, nobly represented at Monasterboice, dates from the ninth or tenth centuries; it is characterized by panelled figurations of scriptural themes.

Monastic Decay: The *céle Dé* Movement

The ideals of the early monastic movement were endangered by an increasing degree of secularization during the eighth century. One effort to stem the tide was the *céle Dé* ('culdee') movement, which came to the fore in the eighth and ninth centuries. The movement was characterized by anchoritic asceticism, puritanical idealism, and strict supervision by spiritual superiors. With these were combined choral duties and care of the poor, of the sick, and of travellers. The Viking wars arrested the natural development of the movement and, by the time they had subsided, few culdee houses survived.

Norse Pirates and Traders

Ireland's freedom from serious foreign aggression ended in 795 with a Viking raid on Rathlin or Lambay Island. Two centuries of devastation and destruction followed.

At the outset the heathen ravagers came in small independent bands, and confined their 'tip-and-run' forays to the seaboard. The attack entered on a more serious phase with the arrival, in 837, of a large fleet on the Boyne and Liffey, which became bases for plundering expeditions deep into the heart of the country. In 841, Dublin was founded as a permanent base. One notorious Viking, Thorgestr (Turgesius), united the Viking marauders and pillaged most of the midland monasteries. Further devastation was prevented only when Maelsechlaill, King of Meath, captured and drowned him in 845. Maelsechlaill (847-62) often successfully defeated alliances between Gaelic king and Norse raider, and raised the Uí Néill kingship of Tara to its greatest height, compelling Munster in 859 to concur in the transfer of the important kingdom of Ossory to the hegemony of Meath and to acknowledge for the first time the supremacy of a king of Tara (*see pp. 297–8*).

By this time, Dublin was on the way to finding a place in Gaelic polity, and alliance – often by marriage – with the heathen was becoming a normal feature of the policy of the Gaelic kings. The forty years after 876 were marked by a comparative lull in major Norse activity, a fresh phase of which opened with the arrival in 914 and 915 of fleets which set up a new raiding base at Waterford. Plunderings followed partially based on new settlements (Limerick, Cork, and Wexford) but, luckily for Ireland, about this time (918–54), the Dublin Norse were dissipating their strength in efforts to get control of the Scandinavian kingdom of York.

Although they contributed considerably to Ireland in terms of trade, knowledge of boat-building and the introduction of coinage, and influenced art styles, the Norse wrought untold harm to Ireland. Mercilessly efficient, they were tramelled in their search for lands and booty by neither Christian principle nor Gaelic convention, but slaughtered and laid waste all about them. Having learned to counter like with like, the Irish kings soon began to apply Viking methods to their traditional quarrels. From the ninth and tenth centuries onwards Gaelic battles too became ruthless; the old Gaelic order was wrecked, and the strongest king in the country could make himself high-king of all.

Organized religion suffered too: the monasteries, treasure-houses of art and nurseries of Latin learning and of Gaelic civilization, were foremost among the victims of the Scandinavian plunderers – and of their Irish emulators; at the same time, secularization of the greater foundations was intensified.

One of the first signs of a serious break in the established Gaelic tradition was the successful challenge to Norse Limerick and the declining Eóghanacht power in Munster by the obscure Dál Chais (eastern Clare), particularly under Brian Boru. Brian defeated Maelsechlaill II, King of Tara, in 997 but, combined, they marched on Dublin the following year. By 1005 Brian was strong enough to go to Armagh, the ecclesiastical capital, there to present himself in the great church as *Imperator Scottorum*, 'Emperor of the Irish'.

Brian was the most famous king in early Irish history, and the legends which grew around him make him first and foremost a life-long leader of resistance to the Norse. They also credit him with active measures to restore religion, learning, and civilization, and with endeavouring in every way to undo something of the damage the Scandinavians had wrought. In the political sphere his one innovation was the nominal high-kingship. He was constantly being challenged by a variety of shifting alliances, both Irish and Norse. At Clontarf, in 1014, he defeated Norse Dublin and the King of Leinster in a famous battle, in which he lost his life.

Reorganization of the Church

In the eleventh and twelfth centuries, Irish kings, as well as ecclesiastics, made contact on the Continent with the Cluniac and Hildebrandine movements which were reorganizing monasticism and freeing bishops and popes from subservience to secular rulers to raise them to unprecedented heights of authority. Irish participation in the movements quickly followed, kings and churchmen uniting to improve private morals, to cleanse and revive monasticism, and to provide the country with a normal diocesan system. To help in the undertaking they invited the assistance of the great European orders of monks, notably of the Tironian, Savigny, and Cistercian Benedictines and of the Canons Regular of St Augustine, who arrived in the decades following 1125.

Giolla Easbuig ('Gilbert'), who became bishop of the Norse diocese of Limerick in 1105, appears to have been the initiator of Hildebrandine reforms in Ireland. As papal legate, he initiated a number of synods which were destined to set up a new diocesan organization in Ireland. But the greatest of the Irish Reformers was St Malachy of Armagh, who obtained the co-operation of his friend, St Bernard of Clairvaux, to introduce the Cistercians into Ireland.

This eleventh- and twelfth-century reformation made a distinctive contribution to the arts, the most important development being in architecture. The need for diocesan cathedrals stimulated the adoption of the Romanesque style – in a distinctively Irish guise. At first the churches were small in size, but both monastic and diocesan churches grew greatly in dimensions during the course of the twelfth century.

Closely related to the Romanesque churches was a new style of sculpture well represented (at such places as Cashel, Kilfenora, and Tuam) by High Crosses, which are characterized by large figures and by Scandinavian-style ornament. Scandinavian influence is also a feature of the art-metalwork of the time, outstanding examples of which are the Cross of Cong (National Museum, Dublin) and St Manchán's Shrine (Boher Church).

The vitality of the contemporary literati is also well attested. Secular and religious literature was gathered into great bibliotheca like the so-called *Book of Leinster,* compiled by an abbot of Terryglass, and *Lebor na hUidre* ('The Book of the Dun Cow'), compiled at Clonmacnois. In this period, too, ballad poems made their first recorded appearance, Finn tales found their way into the canon of upper-class literature, and early Gaelic story-telling reached its culmination in *Acallamh na Senórach* ('The Colloquy of the Ancient Men').

The Close of the Gaelic Epoch

Brian Boru's high-kingship marked the end of the old Gaelic order. For a century, the Dál Chais and O Neill kings battled indecisively with one another for hegemony. Then a new actor, Turloch Mór O Conor, imposed his domination on Munster, Leinster and Ulster kings in turn, and presided as High-King over the national Synod of Kells in 1152 (*see p. 209*). When Turloch died in 1156, Tír Eóghain claimed the high-kingship, but by 1166, Turloch's son Rory became not only King of Connacht but High-King as well. As such, he presided in 1167 over the national Synod of Tlachtga (Hill of Ward, near Athboy) and in 1168 over a national assembly at the site of Aonach Tailteann. The downfall of Gaelic Ireland was at hand.

Medieval Ireland, 1165–1690

The Coming of the 'Franks'

By his misdeeds and his ambitions Dermot Mac Murrough of Leinster had made many enemies. Of these the most dangerous were the O Conors of Connacht. The accession of Rory O Conor led inevitably to Dermot's dethronement, and in 1166 he fled to Henry II of England, his mind full of a childish project for recovering Leinster and seizing the high-kingship.

For Henry, Dermot's naïve appeal for help was indeed timely. A decade or so previously, within a couple of years of the Synod of Kells, the Norman bishops and 'religious men' of England had combined with the magnates to get ready an army for the purpose of invading Ireland and making Henry's brother king. Henry had had the project deferred, but in 1155–6 had himself sought papal permission to conquer Ireland, professing a desire to proclaim the truths of religion among a rude and barbarous people. Over-zealous Irish reformers had already reported to Rome the 'enormities of the vices' of their people. Not surprisingly, therefore, Pope Adrian IV had readily acceded to Henry's request and had invested him with the government of Ireland.

Though Henry II had not published his papal commission, he now gave Dermot leave to recruit volunteers. These Dermot found in south Wales, at that time full of Normans of broken (or no) fortune. For his principal lieutenant he chose Richard de Clare, Earl of Pembroke, better known as Strongbow. To him he promised the hand of his beautiful daughter, Aoífe, and the succession to the kingship of Leinster, this latter in utter disregard of Gaelic law. In the history books Dermot's allies are conventionally labelled 'Anglo-Normans'. To the Irish chroniclers, they were 'Men from overseas', 'Foreigners' or, more precisely, 'Franks'. And Franks, i.e. French, their leaders were in language, customs, and institutions, if not wholly in blood. Royal officials in Ireland were to remain French until well into the fourteenth century. The rank and file of Dermot's allies were mostly Welsh and Flemings.

In 1167 Dermot returned home with the foreign vanguard. The obtuse High-King was content to accept his hostages and leave him in possession of Hy Kinsella, his ancestral kingdom in south Leinster (capital, Ferns). Dermot, of course, was merely biding his time, while Rory's attention was absorbed by the Synod of Tlachtga and by the revival of the Aonach (Fair of) Tailteann. It was the coming of Strongbow in 1170 with 200 armoured knights and 1000 men-at-arms which first spurred him to action. But even then the enemy struck faster.

Dermot and his allies had promptly stormed Waterford, where Aoífe was married to Strongbow. Dublin was their next objective. King Rory had meantime blocked the normal route to Dublin from the south. Dermot simply came another way, and on 21 September 1170 the vital seaport was in Leinster-Norman hands.

Dermot now announced his intention of making himself High-King, but he died suddenly on 1 May 1171. Backed by Dermot's adherents in Hy Kinsella, Strongbow set about making good his own illegal claim to Leinster, and was able to outwit the Norse mercenaries and keep Rory from capturing Dublin.

In the meantime, Henry II of England, alarmed at the easy success of his barons in Leinster, had rushed across to thwart any notions they might have of setting up an independent kingdom. His first act on reaching Ireland was to confirm Strongbow's title to Leinster, but as a fief of the Crown of England. At the same time he reserved to the English Crown the vital Norse seaports. Dublin was to remain the seat of England's power in Ireland until 1921.

Almost at once the Gaelic kings began to come in and make their submission, influenced, no doubt, by Adrian's Bull and by the naïve belief that they were simply exchanging one high-king for another. Only the High-King himself and the Northern Uí Néill kings of Tír Eóghain and Tír Chonaill held aloof. Acceptance of their submissions bound Henry to respect the rights of the

Gaelic kings himself and to protect them against attack by others. Henry, however, had his own concept of honour.

The Irish Church too, at a synod held in Cashel, obeyed the papal instructions and acknowledged Henry's authority. The following year Pope Alexander III commended the Irish rulers for submitting peacefully to Henry, instructed the bishops to support his authority, and formally conferred on him the Lordship of Ireland.

Before leaving Ireland Henry appointed one of his followers, Hugh de Lacy, to be Justiciar (that is, representative and principal law officer of the English Crown) of Ireland. At the same time, in defiance of law and honour, he granted to him the whole of the former kingdom of Meath. The Irish kings were having their first lesson in English statecraft, a lesson that they were singularly slow to learn.

The Conquest, 1171–1280

Henry's bad faith in regard to Meath, soon to be repeated in the case of other kingdoms, was promptly emulated by the invading barons. And so began a long-sustained policy of deceit, aggression, and murder which in eighty years was to make the invaders masters of three-fourths of Ireland. At the outset, the credulous Irish – lightly armed, occasional fighters who wore no armour, and whose foolish custom it was to disperse their short-term levies once a battle had been won or a fortress overthrown – were no match for the seasoned forces of the enemy, an enemy who employed murderous bowmen as well as mail-clad cavalry and men-at-arms, and promptly secured every foothold by erecting a motte castle. The persistence of Irish credulity is well exemplified by the Treaty of Windsor, 1175, whereby King Rory at last submitted to Henry who, for his part, undertook to maintain Rory in the high-kingship as well as in kingship of Connacht.

In the long run, the speed and extent of the conquest were to prove its undoing. At first, however, all seemed more than well, with great tracts of the richer lands quickly falling to the invaders. These they promptly organized into feudal manors, planted with castles, monasteries, villages, and towns, and colonized with tenants lured from England with the offer of special privileges and easy tenures.

In 1177 Henry II created his younger son, John, Lord of Ireland and, shamelessly disregarding his obligations, he granted most of Munster to his barons, while reserving to the Crown the cities of Cork and Limerick. But Donal Mór O Brien of Thomond proved too strong to be disturbed. That same year, 1177, John de Courcy, a young freebooter, over-ran the little kingdom of Ulster (Cos. Down and Antrim) and set himself up as more or less independent Prince of Ulster and, with future conquests in mind, 'granted' the Tír Eóghain seaboard (in Co. Londonderry) to the Norman Lord of Galloway.

Eight years later the young Lord of Ireland paid his first visit to his new dominion, and trusting Gaelic rulers came to him to reaffirm their submissions. John's entourage included three men who were to found great Anglo-Irish families and lordships: Bertram de Verdun, John's Seneschal; Theobald Walter, his Butler; and Walter de Burgo. They, and others, were granted vast territories including south-east Uriel, as well as Ormond (East Munster) and parts of the kingdom of Thomond (North Munster). The attack on Thomond was resumed when Donal Mór died in 1194. Among those who shared in the spoil were Theobald Walter, ancestor of the Butlers of Ormond, Thomas fitz Gerald, ancestor of the Earls of Desmond, and Walter de Burgo (ancestor of the Burkes), who was already planning the conquest of Connacht.

When he succeeded his father, John endeavoured to secure effective authority for the English Crown in Ireland. With this object in view, he set up a royal administration and courts of law; tried to create a new, subservient baronage; conceded Connacht to King Cathal Crovderg O Conor, Rory's successor, and what was left of Thomond to Donnchad O Brien; sought to make the Church an instrument of state by the appointment of non-Irish, feudal

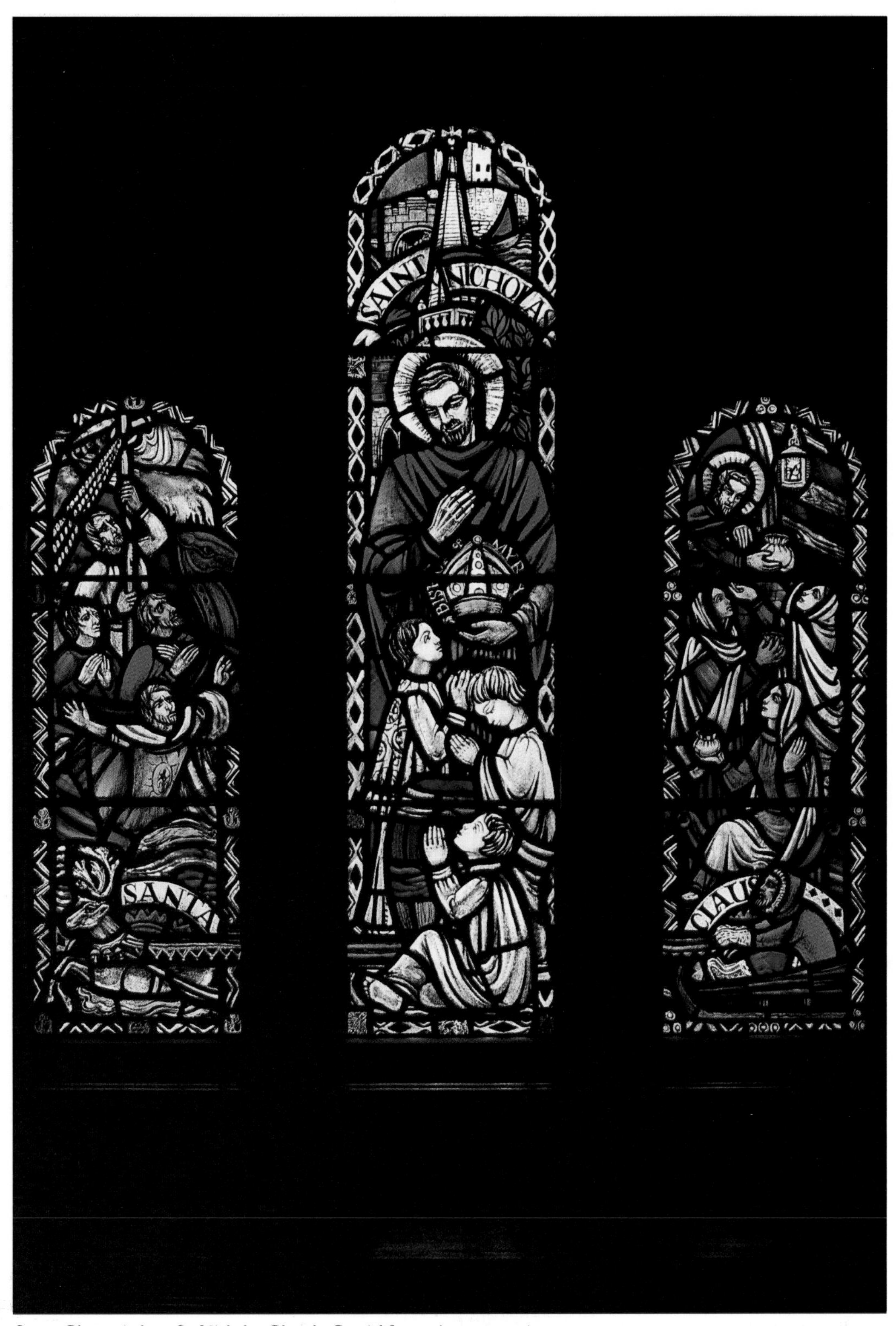

Santa Claus window, St Nicholas Church, Carrickfergus (see page 93).

Dun Oghil, Inishmore, Aran Islands (see page 41).

prelates; clipped the liberties of the Norman lordships of Leinster and Meath; and expelled de Courcy from Ulster, which he made into an earldom for Hugh II de Lacy.

This policy inevitably aroused discontent among previously unbridled magnates, and drove some of them into rebellion. In 1210 John held a council of his barons, at which English law was extended to Ireland and many Gaelic rulers made formal submission. But the kings of Tír Eóghain and Tír Chonaill were not among them, and the O Neills and O Donnells were to maintain their ancestral kingdoms for another 400 years.

With the aid of castles, the Normans were gaining control of large tracts of the country, so that, by 1215, only Thomond, Connacht, Tír Chonaill, Tír Eóghain, and western Uriel remained outside the 'English land'.

In 1227, Richard de Burgo obtained a shameful grant of Connacht, and King Felim O Conor salvaged what he could of the wreckage by submitting to de Burgo, who left him the O Conor domain in Roscommon. The rest of the Connacht lowlands was at once parcelled out among the victors, de Burgo retaining for himself the limestone plains of Galway and Mayo. On the conquered lands the usual manors, villages, and towns were founded, and colonies of Welshmen, Flemings, and other foreigners established. In less than a century the countryside was to revert to the Gaelic order, but towns like Galway were to remain enduring citadels of English royal authority and of foreign speech.

After Brian O Neill overthrew the last Mac Lochlainn to rule Tír Eóghain in 1241, the proud names of Tír Eóghain and O Neill were to remain synonymous until 1605. After some unsuccessful invasions of Tír Eóghain from Connacht, the Irish King began to employ armies of galloglas (*gall-óglách,* foreign soldier), mail-clad Norse-Gaelic mercenaries from the Kingdom of Argyll and the Isles (the Lordship of the Isles), whose hereditary captains received estates by way of payment. The importation of Hebridean fighting men was to continue for three centuries, so that they came to form an appreciable element of the Gaelic-speaking population. In time, the Norman magnates too, and the Dublin government itself, saw fit to employ them.

In 1258 Tír Eóghain moved into the forefront of the Gaelic resistance, for in that year Aodh O Conor of Connacht and Tadhg O Brien of Thomond formally acknowledged the ancestral claims of Brian O Neill to the high-kingship of Ireland. O Conor and O Neill invaded Ulster in 1260, only to be disastrously routed in the epic First Battle of Down (14 May 1260). Despite this setback, O Neill power continued to grow and in 1264 Brian's successor, Aodh Buidhe, ancestor of the Clann Aodha Bhuidhe ('Clannaboy') O Neills, extended Tír Eóghain sovereignty over Uriel (the Monaghan-Fermanagh region). After this time O Neill of Tír Eóghain calls himself *Rex Ultoniae – Rí Uladh,* 'King of (Great) Ulster', i.e. king of the whole of the prehistoric Fifth, not just of the tiny historic Ulster.

The year after the Battle of Down, Finghin (of Rinn Róin; *see p. 228*) MacCarthy won a resounding victory in Desmond. At Callan near Kenmare, on 24 July 1261, the MacCarthys routed the Norman host with heavy loss. Nine years later Aodh O Conor and Turloch O Brien won a comparable victory over de Burgo and the Justiciar at Athankip near Carrick-on-Shannon. Eight years after that King Donnchad again routed the invaders of Thomond at Quin. The tide was on the turn at last.

Decline of the Colony and Gaelic Resurgence, 1280–1400

The first attempt to conquer the whole of Ireland had resulted in a threefold division of the island which was to endure until the Tudor conquest: an ever-shrinking 'English land', or 'land of peace', i.e. the few shires effectively controlled by Dublin; the Liberties of the feudal magnates who acknowledged the English Crown, but were opposed alike to encroachment on their privileges and to government from England, and who inclined more and more to Gaelic speech and ways; and the unconquered Gaelic kingdoms which, during the next two centuries, were to recover much ground at the expense of both the feudal Liberties and the 'English land'.

A variety of causes had contributed to this stalemate, among them the speed and thinness of the conquest, the absorption of the English Crown in domestic strife and Continental wars, the thwarting of English Crown policy by the self-seeking Anglo-Irish baronage, the repeated passing by marriage of great feudal fiefs to absentee lords unable to defend them, the revolt of cadets against such transferences, the impossibility of extinguishing any Gaelic ruling stock because the *derb-fine* always provided heirs capable of continuing the kingship, and the creation of Gaelic standing armies.

A considerable stir was caused on the Irish scene by the arrival first of Edward (1315), and two years later Robert Bruce in an attempt to foment a Scottish-Irish-Welsh alliance after Scotland's victory over England at Bannockburn. But hopes of an independent Irish monarchy were dashed with the defeat of Edward Bruce at Faughart in 1318. Norman power in Thomond had been shattered at the Battle of Dysert O Dea in 1317, but the Bruce episode shook the whole Anglo-Norman colonial fabric. Many inland towns and settlements were destroyed for ever. Great areas were recovered for Gaelic civilization, a fact well exemplified by the restoration in 1327 of the Mac Murrough kingdom of Leinster that had been in abeyance since the death of Dermot II in 1171. The Norman magnates too were enlarging their privileges by maintaining standing armies of native Irishmen. The growing power of the magnates is reflected in the creation of the Earldom of Ormond (1328), with great privileges, for James Butler, Earl of Carrick, and of the Earldom of Desmond (1329). The Earls of Desmond were to lead the Home Rule Party of the 'Middle Nation' and to incline more and more to Gaelic culture. The Earls of Ormond, on the other hand, were eventually to lead the English Party among the colonists.

The year 1333 was marked by a grave blow to the English interest. William de Burgo, 'Brown' Earl of Ulster and Lord of Connacht, was murdered in the course of a family feud. The title to his vast possessions passed to his infant daughter and, ultimately, to the English Crown. In the meantime the Earldom of Ulster was leaderless against the northern Irish, whose great hour came in 1375, when Niall O Neill of Tír Eóghain, great-grandson of Brian of the Battle of Down, routed the feudal levy of Ireland at the Second Battle of Down. Of the Norman supremacy established in Ulster by John de Courcy, only Carrickfergus now remained. In less than fifty years after the 'Brown' Earl's death, the ancient Uí Néill stocks dominated the whole of the North as never before, and Tír Eóghain had pushed its eastern frontier across the Bann into Ulster itself, where the Clannaboy O Neills were to remain the foremost stock until the seventeenth century.

In Connacht too the Gaelic order made a spectacular recovery. There, semi-Gaelicized de Burgo cadets seized the 'Brown' Earl's lordship and the whole of the West, apart from the town of Galway, was won back to Gaelic speech and culture. Even in the Midlands the Gaelic tide was turning. Here the most notable successes were won by the O Mores of Laois, the O Connors of Éile, and the O Kennedys of north Ormond.

In 1361 Lionel, Duke of Clarence and husband of the 'Brown' Earl's heiress, came to Ireland as Lieutenant of the English king. The sole enduring relic of his five years of effort to hold back the tide were the notorious, unenforceable, Statutes of Kilkenny designed to prevent the colony, its laws, language (now largely English), and culture from succumbing to Gaelic arms and Gaelic civilization. The statutes were an admission of the threefold division of the island between the 'Irish enemies', the 'degenerate English', and the 'land of peace'. By implication, four-fifths of the island were abandoned to the 'Irish enemies' and 'English rebels', though the feudal titles to them were not surrendered and, centuries later, were resurrected as opportunity offered.

The reign (1375–1418) of Art Óg Mac Murrough of Leinster, with its widespread assaults on the dwindling 'land of peace', presented English authority with a crisis of such magnitude that Richard II felt impelled to resolve it himself. But neither of Richard's two campaigns in Ireland (1394 and 1399) had any long-lasting impact: Art Óg, indeed, had 'wrecked English unity for a hundred years'. The English king's Lordship of Ireland collapsed, not to be restored until Tudor times, for from 1399 to 1534 the effective authority of the English Crown in Ireland was hedged into the little Pale, outside of which Gaelic kings and Norman magnates ruled the land. A succession of these magnates nominally represented the Lord of Ireland, but they behaved as independent princes.

Anglo-Norman Home Rule: Gaelic Resurgence Continues, 1400–1534

Fifteenth-century England's preoccupation with foreign and dynastic wars played into the hands of the Irish potentates, Gaelic and Norman. Some of the more spectacular manifestations of Gaelic resurgence were in the North. Hand in hand with political recovery went a religious revival exemplified by the Observant movement among the Augustinian, Franciscan, and Dominican friars, for it was the Gaelic lands which first, and most widely, adopted the Observant reforms.

Among the Normans, by now speakers of English (and Irish) rather than French, the counterpart of the Gaelic resurgence was the Home Rule movement which had manifested itself as far back as 1326, when – so his enemies later alleged – Maurice of Desmond had engaged in the first of many conspiracies to make himself King of Ireland. From the Fourth Earl of Ormond's viceroyalty of 1441–4 onwards, it was the Home Rule Party that ruled Ireland, controlled its parliament, shared the offices of state, and exercised the prerogatives of the Lord of Ireland.

In the Wars of the Roses the Earls of Desmond and Kildare, backed by their Gaelic relatives and allies, actively espoused the Yorkist cause, and when Richard of York fled for refuge to Ireland, the colonial parliament constrained him (1460) to acknowledge the independence of the 'land of Ireland', save only for the personal link with the English Crown. When Richard returned in triumph to England, he left Kildare as his Deputy in Ireland.

By 1465 the English Pale had shrunk to Dublin and the nearer parts of Louth, Meath, and Kildare. To forestall some feudal magnate or any other setting himself up as King of Ireland Edward IV sent over Sir John Tibetot to assert the royal authority in 1467. Tibetot shocked the Anglo-Norman colony by having Desmond and Kildare attainted for treason, felony, and alliances with the Irish. Desmond was at once beheaded, but Kildare made his escape to England.

This shrewd blow at the Home Rule party proved premature, for the Yorkist cause was still in need of support from Ireland. Three years later Kildare was appointed Justiciar, not by the English government, but by the colonial parliament of Ireland. In the days of their supremacy (1470–1534), the Earls of Kildare were Kings of Ireland in all but name, clothing their doings with legality by acting with the authority of a subservient parliament. The zenith of their power, and the zenith of colonial Home Rule, was attained under the Eighth Earl, Gearóid Mór – Gerald the Great – whose sister and daughters allied him by marriage with three great Norman and four great Gaelic stocks, among the latter the O Neills of Tír Eóghain. With such backing he was safe even from Lancastrian Henry VII. Nevertheless, the advent of the Tudors and the introduction of firearms spelled the doom of feudal earl and Gaelic king alike.

It was Yorkist conspirators and impostors who opened Henry VII's eyes to the dangers threatening the new absolute monarchy of England from a Home Rule and Yorkist Ireland, and from the continuing erosion of the English Pale. Clearly the immediate necessity was to secure the English bridgehead and to nullify the colonial parliament. Both objectives were secured in the brief Deputyship (1494–6) of Sir Edward Poynings, whose 'packed' parliament adopted the necessary measures, including a sweeping Act of Resumption (which gave the Crown the appointment of all officers of state) and the notorious 'Poynings' Law'. The latter was to hamstring every Anglo-Irish parliament until 1782 by providing that no parliament could thereafter assemble without prior English approval of its proposed enactments and unless it was summoned under the Great Seal of England.

Poynings' task completed, Kildare was restored, and retained in office until his death (1513).

He was succeeded as Lord Deputy by his heir, Gearóid Óg (Young Gerald), third successive Earl of Kildare to hold the chief governorship. After numerous trumped-up complaints against the Earl's rule, Henry VIII replaced him for two years (1520–2), but later reinstated him. In 1534 Kildare was summoned to London, for the third time, to answer the charges of his enemies, leaving as his deputy his eldest son, Silken Thomas. Thomas was goaded into rebellion by false rumours of his father's death in the Tower. Though O Conor Faly and O Carroll of Éile rallied to their kinsman's support, the rebellion was speedily crushed by a great English army equipped with heavy guns. The Earl died, Silken Thomas and his five uncles were executed, and the sole survivor of the ancient and powerful house of Kildare was a fugitive boy of ten.

The Tudor Conquest, 1534–1603

With much of Leinster subjugated and, by a legal fiction, forfeit to the Crown, more active policies directed to the subjugation of the whole island seemed feasible. Their implementation was to prove slow, arduous, and costly.

The first steps were to give Henry VIII control of the Church and to provide him with capital by dissolving the monasteries; the next to make him King of Ireland, free from the shackles of papal grants of simple lordship. And so the state 'Church of Ireland' was called into being in 1537, the 'Kingdom of Ireland' in 1541. From first to last (1541–1800) the Kingdom of Ireland was governed from England through English viceroys and officials responsible to London. From first to last (1537–1869) the state Church of Ireland was the church of a minority, for Protestantism was something alien introduced by new English officials and planters.

His legal titles acknowledged, Henry VIII was, on the whole, content to let events drift to their logical outcome. He was normally content to allow the Gaelic magnates (once they had acknowledged the Crown by treaties of surrender and regrant) to rule their countries by Gaelic law. Not until the reign of Mary was the next major step taken, the adoption of the long-debated plantation policy.

In 1556 the inland Leinster territories of Laois and Uí Failghe were shired as Queen's County and King's County, and the eastern two-thirds granted to English and Welsh settlers. The victims fought desperately to retain their ancestral lands and only finally laid down their arms in 1603.

English attention was next directed to Tír Eóghain. Elizabeth I gave orders that Seaán the Proud, King of Tír Eóghain, should be crushed. Seaán gave arms to the common folk – 'the first that ever did so of an Irishman' – and could not be brought to bay. But, in the end, it was the O Donnells who broke Great O Neill, the Mac Donnells of Antrim who murdered him (1567). The English at once had him attainted, the title O Neill pronounced extinguished, and – somewhat prematurely – the land of Tír Eóghain declared forfeit to the Crown.

In the meantime the attack was switched to the old earldom of Ulster. About the same time Desmond was attacked, and the possessions of the Old English in Munster (and elsewhere) began to be threatened by Devon-Somerset adventurers like Sir Peter Carew and Sir Walter Ralegh. In 1569 the Pope at long last excommunicated Elizabeth I for her share in making England Protestant, whereupon Desmond's cousin, Sir James Fitzmaurice, headed an Old English revolt in defence of the Catholic religion and of ancestral property. But after several Munster castles had been taken with merciless slaughter, the revolt died away, Fitzmaurice surrendering in 1573 and departing for the Continent.

In 1579 Fitzmaurice returned and tried to rally the south in defence of Catholicism, joined only by a few of the Old Irish in Leinster. In Munster the rising was countered with horrifying savagery, the whole land laid desolate, and the hapless, hunchback 15th Earl of Desmond driven to rebellion and destruction. Abandoned by Philip II of Spain, on whom they had pinned their hopes, the insurgents were overwhelmed. All was over by 1583.

The way now seemed clear for the plantation of Munster. Accordingly 210,000 acres of the best land were confiscated for settling with Protestant English owners and tenants. (The opportunities for swindling on a grand scale were eagerly seized. Sir Walter Ralegh, for example, ended up with 40,000 ill-gotten acres.) Nevertheless, as an effort at colonization, the Plantation proved a failure.

By this time the English Governor of Connacht was steadily encroaching on the southern marches of Tír Chonaill and Tír Eóghain. For twenty-five years, against a background of widespread plotting to organize a national, Catholic confederacy supported by Spain, Great Hugh O Neill (Earl of Tyrone, 1587) had cunningly, patiently, and tortuously maintained a minimal loyalty to the English Crown. The English seizure (1594) of Enniskillen and the Gap of the Erne forced him at last to choose between open war and surrender. So began the Nine Years' War. Having no artillery with which to reduce the English towns, O Neill adopted Fabian tactics, engaging the enemy only when compelled to do so.

The first five years of war gave O Neill and Red Hugh II O Donnell a series of spectacular victories; victories which brought most of the country over to them, including Munster, where the Plantation was swept away. But in 1600 Lord Mountjoy arrived with the greatest army ever sent from England. His savagely effective policy of repression and devastation soon crushed the revolt in the south. Within eighteen months O Neill and O Donnell had been hemmed into their own territories by a chain of forts and entrenchments; but they still held out, their hopes on Spain. At long last the Spanish aid arrived – at the opposite end of Ireland. The English and Irish armies hurried south to Kinsale, and there the issue was decided by a resounding English victory on Christmas Eve, 1601.

Thereafter Mountjoy harried the North until Tír Eóghain and Tír Chonaill surrendered at last on 30 March 1603. Gaelic Ireland had made its greatest effort and had failed.

The Final Conquest, 1603–90

Though the vanquished were pardoned by James I, the earldom of Tyrone restored to O Neill, and the earldom of Tyrconnell conferred on Red Hugh's successor, Rory, the Northern princes were no longer independent Gaelic rulers. Their territories were shired (as Cos. Donegal, Tyrone, Derry, and Armagh) and subjected to English law; Gaelic law and Gaelic tenures were abolished. In addition, the Dublin junta never ceased to plot Tyrone's destruction. Only by flight could he and O Donnell hope to save themselves and their families, and so, on 14 September 1607, they sailed away, never to return.

The 'Flight of the Earls' was promptly declared to be treason and made a pretext for finding the six western counties of the modern Province of Ulster forfeit to the Crown. By chicanery of every kind nearly 500,000 acres of the best land were taken from their owners and thrown open for planting with Protestants from England and Scotland, the City of London Companies obtaining large estates. Similar, if smaller, plantations were carried out in parts of Leinster and Connacht. In the long view, however, perhaps the worst feature of these plantations was the enlargement of the agrarian proletariat by the depression of a substantial body of ancient freeholders. It was in these confiscations and plantations that the oppressive features of the landlordism of eighteenth- and nineteenth-century Ireland had their roots.

Despite the plantations, the great majority of Irish landowners, as of the population at large, was still Catholic. But it had grave causes for fear: Protestants, aliens by birth and speech as well as by religion, had control of parliament and the state; further confiscations were in the air, imperilling even Old English magnates who had become Protestants; Munster was falling into the clutches of English 'carpet-baggers' like Robert Boyle, 'Great' Earl of Cork; Catholics were barred from public office, the legal profession, and the university, and were forbidden to keep schools. In general, however, James I, and after him Charles I, adopted a policy of 'connived indulgence' towards the majority, and all might have ended well enough but for the rise of Nonconformist parliamentarianism in Britain and the repeated cheating of the Irish Catholics in the matter of royal Graces (i.e. the amelioration of injustices) promised by Charles I in return for subsidies. In 1638 the Scottish Presbyterians rose against Charles and the following year the Dublin government fell into the clutches of Puritan Lords Justice, who finally blocked the Graces and seemed bent on driving the country to rebellion so as to justify further spoliation of the natives. And rebellion came. It started in October 1641 with the rising of the Old Irish of Ulster and Leinster, but soon spread to the Old English lords of the Pale, to Munster, and to Connacht. Tragically, if understandably, the first upsurge of those so recently and so cruelly wronged was the occasion of atrocities on the planters, particularly in the North. The insurgent demands appear to us today as scarcely excessive: civil and religious rights for all, redress of injustices arising from the confiscations, the freeing of parliament from the shackles of Poynings' Law.

The course of the ensuing Eleven Years' War was bedevilled by a complexity of sometimes shifting interests: Royalist *v.* Parliamentarian, Catholic *v.* Protestant, Episcopalian Protestant *v.* Dissenting Protestant, Old Irish and Old English *v.* New English, Old Irish *v.* Old English. The Old Irish provided the best Catholic army, that of Ulster, and the best Catholic general, Eóghan Rúa O Neill, nephew of Great Hugh. Nevertheless, the Old English faction dominated the government and parliament of the Catholic Confederacy (Confederation of Kilkenny).

In 1649–50, O Neill being dead, Cromwell butchered his way through Leinster and Munster and the Confederation dissolved. Thereafter the Catholic-Royalist armies were beaten one by one, the war coming to a close in 1652. By the time it had ended famine, plague, and the sword had reduced the population to a mere 500,000.

The victors allowed the Irish leaders and troops to take service abroad, and then set about crushing the defenceless nation for ever. The Catholic Church was suppressed; thousands of common folk were shipped to the West Indies practically as slaves; the 'Irish Papist' landowners – save those who took to the hills and woods as 'rapparees' – were herded into parts of Connacht and Clare; 11,000,000 acres of land were apportioned out among new Protestant settlers; the towns, too, were colonized with new Protestants. In this way a substantial Protestant and English minority was added to the population and Protestants came to dominate, not only the landowning classes, but also the urban, commercial, industrial, and professional life of the country.

The restoration of Charles II (1660) merely confirmed the Cromwellian settlers in power and possessions. The King had been well served by the Catholic Irish exiles, but only a minority of these recovered anything of their estates. However, the King's policy of 'connived toleration' meant that the worst anti-Catholic laws were seldom enforced.

Under James II the 'Old English' Catholic party came to power, and in 1687 a member of that party, Richard Talbot (Earl of Tyrconnell, 1685), became Lord Lieutenant. Civic rights were restored to the majority, the army and the legal profession opened to them. Such elementary justice awakened the resentment of the newly come Protestants, and when Talbot proceeded to raise a Catholic army to maintain the Stuart Crown, they began to fear for their rights as well as for their privileges. Accordingly, when the Williamite rebellion broke out in England, most of the Protestants in Ireland sided with the rebels. Catholic Ireland, on the other hand, naturally rallied round King James against the Protestant ally of the Pope. In 1689 James came to Ireland and summoned the Patriot Parliament, whose Catholic majority proceeded to disendow the Church of Ireland and to undo the Cromwellian Confiscation in such a way as to cause injustice to some Protestants. James then took the field against the northern rebels, who had seized Derry and Enniskillen. His attempt on Derry failed, and a Williamite army landed at Carrickfergus to outmanoeuvre him on the Boyne (July 1690). Though James then left the country, his adherents continued the struggle with French help. The decisive action took place at Aughrim, near Ballinasloe (12 July 1691), where the Jacobite field army was broken, with heavy losses among the Old Irish and Old English aristocracy. The war ended with the Treaty of Limerick, on 3 October 1691. The Jacobite army sailed away to France. The English conquest of Ireland was complete.

Modern Ireland, 1691–1921

The Rise and Fall of the 'Protestant Nation', 1691–1801

The Williamite victory was followed by further confiscations, so that by 1700 only one-seventh of the land remained in Catholic ownership. Even this small fraction was to be further whittled away by the operation of the Penal Laws enacted against Catholics between 1695 and 1727, in violation of the Treaty of Limerick. The worst aspect of the revolution thereby completed was not the transfer of the land to a small minority, but the replacement of a patriarchal system, in which the lord was primarily the lord of dependants who looked to him for protection, by a system in which he was an absolute lord of land to be exploited solely in his own interest.

The population was by now quite a medley: Old Irish, Old English, Elizabethan and Stuart Planters, Cromwellians, and Williamites, with the Catholic (Gaelic and Old English) element much the largest. The victorious Protestant minority was divided into two hostile halves, the episcopalian Church of Ireland on the one hand, the Nonconformists on the other. From 1691 onwards the Episcopalians constituted that 'Ascendancy' whose plebeian aristocracy aroused the contempt of the blood-conscious Gael, the hostility of the democratic Nonconformist.

The Catholic majority was deprived of political and civic rights and was excluded from public office, the legal profession, the army, and several branches of trade and manufacture. Its Church was forbidden by law. It was not permitted to educate its children either at home or abroad. The Catholic peasant was among the most oppressed in Western Europe. The old aristocracy, the leaders of the people and the patrons of the poets and poetry that had so long fanned the flame of Gaelic resistance, was gone. For a time the bardic schools and the bardic profession managed, indeed, to survive by the liberality of the countryside; but soon the polished literary language, the classical metres, and the traditional themes ceased to be cultivated, their place taken by a new literature in the peasant language, a literature whose themes were the unfortunate 'Dark Rosaleen' (Ireland) and the joys and sorrows of the oppressed. In some districts the poets continued for a while to vie with one another in 'Courts of Poetry' meeting in farmhouse or inn, but their normal stage was the market-place or, preferably, the peasant's fireside, where captive listeners absorbed their outpouring into the fibre of their being. In this way the last Gaelic struggle for the soul of the nation was prolonged into the nineteenth century, when the advice of political leaders and the struggle for survival in an age of hunger and emigration induced the masses to jettison the last treasure of their Gaelic heritage, a treasure which had come to seem a badge of servitude at home and which proved an impediment to advancement.

The democratic Nonconformists, too, turned towards combination with the majority, to the alarm of the English interest. Unfortunately for Irish democracy – so it was to prove – Ulster custom gave the Presbyterian tenant rights denied to his Catholic neighbour. Moreover, the starveling Catholic was often tempted to outbid the Presbyterian when leases came to be renewed. Selfish landlords, therefore, had good reasons for replacing Presbyterian by Catholic tenants. The natural resentment of the dispossessed occasionally found expression in outbursts of anti-Catholic violence.

More important at first, however, than such sectarian conflict, was the stream of Presbyterian emigration to New England. From their American havens of religious and political equality, the exiles passed back democratic ideals to their kinsfolk in Ulster, and it was among these that Irish republicanism first took root. In the outcome sectarianism was to triumph in Ulster, and the story of Irish democracy is largely the story of the slow, agonizing resurrection of the indomitable explosive older peasantry which broke in succession sectarian tyranny, landlordism, and the entire English system in Ireland. The nation as a whole – including the non-Catholics – has benefited by the victory.

The episcopalian oligarchy had its own grievances. Foremost among its champions was a Dublin-born Englishman, Jonathan Swift (1667–1745), who to personal disappointment added a bitter indignation against social wrong. His indignation was not, however, typical of episcopalian Protestants, and the oligarchy's complaints were primarily concerned with its own pocket. The oligarchy's venal, unrepresentative parliament had no real power. Neither had it a voice in appointments to the great offices of Church or State, which were filled with English-born nominees of the London government. In addition, Irish trade, largely in Protestant hands, was hampered by restrictions imposed in the interests of England. Towards the middle of the eighteenth century there began to emerge among the Protestants a Patriot Party which by 1770, under the leadership of Henry Grattan, was agitating in the name of the 'Protestant Nation' for a 'free Constitution and freedom of trade'.

The rising tide of rebel successes in America prompted limited concessions (1774, 1778) to the Catholic middle class as well as to the few surviving Catholic landowners, and the admission (1780) of Nonconformists to public office. When France, Holland, and Spain joined in the American war against England, fear of invasion was added to the dread of risings by the Presbyterian and Catholic peasantry. England therefore consented to the raising of Protestant volunteers to defend the country. The Patriot Party lost no time in employing these volunteers to wring from her a relaxation of the restrictions on trade (1779) and the acknowledgement of legislative independence (1782).

The Protestant colony now had its free parliament, 'Grattan's Parliament', but that parliament had no control over the Dublin government, which continued to be a junta manipulated from London. Moreover, the parliament was as venal as it was unrepresentative, and it resisted every attempt at electoral reform. It is true that the period of Grattan's Parliament was one of great prosperity for the upper and middle classes, but the masses continued to be exploited in the same old evil way. Small wonder if the Catholic peasantry proved indifferent to the fate of the legislature, or sought to defend itself against local tyrants by terrorist societies. Small wonder if the competition for farms called forth rival secret societies among the Presbyterians.

In the meantime increasing agitation for parliamentary reform and for Catholic emancipation, and the spread of French and American republicanism, were turning the thoughts of the Dublin junta to complete union with Great Britain as the only hope of preserving the power and privileges of the Ascendancy. At the same time disagreements between the Dublin and London parliaments were awakening English fears for the link between the two kingdoms, fears which were magnified by the rapid growth of the Irish population and the outbreak of war with the French Republic (1793).

It was about this time that the democratic movement found a leader in Theobald Wolfe Tone, a young Protestant lawyer who had been attracted by the French doctrines of liberty and equality. In 1792 Tone became secretary of the Catholic Committee – a timid organization for pleading the Catholic cause – and he helped it to secure the parliamentary vote for Catholics and other concessions (1793). In 1791 he and other Protestants founded in Belfast the secret Society of United Irishmen. It was the continued rejection of the demands for parliamentary reform and Catholic emancipation which turned the United Irishmen into a revolutionary organization and sent Tone to France to seek the aid of the new republic there.

The United Irishmen had become particularly strong among the Presbyterians of Ulster. And yet it was now that sectarian feuds in the North began to come to a head with the 'Battle of the Diamond' (Co. Armagh) and the foundation of the 'Orange Order', pledged to maintain Protestant ascendancy.

In December 1796 Tone set sail from France with a large French army which was only prevented by ill luck from putting ashore in Bantry Bay. The Dublin junta now took steps to disarm the United Irishmen and to set off the threatened revolution at half-cock by provoking premature risings. Yeomanry and militia were let loose on the countryside to disarm the peasantry and to cow them by flogging, burning, torture, and other atrocities. In this way Ulster was substantially disarmed in 1797. Despite these set-backs, the Directory of the United Irishmen made plans for a national rising on 23 May of the following year, 1798, under young Lord Edward FitzGerald, son of the Duke of Leinster. But it was betrayed, FitzGerald alone evading arrest. Nevertheless, on 24 May, sporadic, unco-ordinated risings of poorly armed peasants took place in parts of Leinster and of north-east Ulster. Two days later the only formidable rising broke out – among the Old English peasantry of Wexford. Here too the insurgents displayed desperate courage, and the fighting lasted into July. Though the Wexfordmen had chosen a Protestant landlord to lead them, their rising was represented to Ulstermen as essentially a Catholic affair, and this contributed to the ultimate estrangement of Ulster from the democratic cause.

The Rising also played into the hands of those who were bent on the Union. The entire oligarchy took fright. Through Pitt's unfulfilled promises to the Catholic hierarchy, and substantial payments to those in favour of abolishing the Parliament, the Act of Union was passed in 1800 and Henry VIII's (and Pope Paul IV's) 'Kingdom of Ireland' came to its shameful end on the following New Year's Day, 1801. Simultaneously the Church of Ireland was united to the Church of England.

The Rise of Irish Democracy, 1801–1921

The expectations of the Catholic bishops were disappointed, and Ireland's entry into the United Kingdom had to be marked by renewal of the agitation for the emancipation of the majority. At this juncture Catholic Irish democracy found its first great leader in Daniel O Connell, the Liberator. O Connell, a Gael of the Gaels, found the Irish peasants slaves. He left them men.

The close of the Napoleonic wars brought widespread poverty, unemployment, and evictions. Partial famines in 1817 and in 1821–2 added to the misery of the fast-increasing population. The proud, harassed victims of landlordism knew but one means of self-defence: agrarian crime and counter-terror. The government knew but one cure for social ills: further oppression. And indeed from 1796 to 1837 the whole social-political fabric was sustained by an uninterrupted, official, reign of terror; the shadow of the gallows hung over every parish; the oligarchy snatched at every device, including sectarian strife, to retain its power.

It was under these conditions that O Connell, aided by the parish clergy, set to disciplining the tortured explosive peasantry, to organizing them within the law so that they might bring overpowering weight to bear on the law without risking the law's brutality. He spoke to their hearts, and to their hearts they took him while he guided their steps in the tortuous, alien paths of constitutional agitation and English party politics.

The first demonstration of their new-found manhood came at the Waterford election of 1826, when the electors, heedless of the vengeance of their landlords, returned a liberal Protestant. Two years later the peasants of Clare elected O Connell himself. The law barred his entry to the House of Commons, but the Claremen sent him back a second time. And behind them stood the millions of Catholic peasants! The British Government capitulated; Catholic emancipation was grudgingly conceded in 1829.

O Connell's victory automatically freed the Presbyterians from their civic and political disabilities. Nevertheless, by now anti-Papist agitators had worked their will on the instinctive fears of the Presbyterians, and the Liberator, whose struggle against oppression won the admiration and support of enlightened opinion everywhere else in Europe, found himself unwelcome in Ulster.

By alliance with the Whigs, O Connell began to secure some measure of social justice for his people, including the ending of Protestant terrorism (1837). When, however, the Tories ousted the Whigs (1841) it quickly became clear that Ireland had little hope of even elementary social justice under the Union. O Connell, spurred on by the rise of the Young Ireland movement, therefore embarked on a gigantic campaign for 'Repeal of the Union', i.e. for the setting up of an Irish legislature with limited powers. His efforts to overawe the Government by a series of 'Monster Meetings' quickly raised national feeling to fever pitch, but the Government called out troops and artillery to prevent what was to be the greatest meeting of all (8 October 1843). O Connell called off the meeting to save his followers from slaughter. The Repeal movement collapsed. Four years later the Liberator himself was dead.

For a brief space his place was taken by Young Ireland, a militant movement of romantic nationalists – Protestants and Catholics – whose *Nation* newspaper gave Ireland her first romantic, nationalist literature in the fast-spreading English tongue.

At this stage the peasants were overwhelmed by catastrophe, the famine of 1845–7. Hundreds of thousands perished of hunger and cholera; hundreds of thousands fled to penniless safety in Britain and America. Between 1845 and 1850 the population fell from 8½ million to about 4½, and since that time the drain of emigration has scarcely ever ceased.

This disaster, the greatest of its kind ever to befall a European nation in a time of peace, was the final condemnation of the Union, and in 1848, a year of European revolutions, Young Ireland made a futile despairing effort at insurrection under the leadership of William Smith O Brien, a Protestant aristocratic landlord of ancient Gaelic lineage. With this fiasco, the Young Ireland movement in turn collapsed, but it passed on its ideal of the union of 'Orange' and 'Green' in a sovereign nation, a union symbolized by its republican tricolour flag – which today flies over twenty-six of the Irish counties.

While the Tories refused any substantial redress of Irish grievances, they did make some minor concessions, among them the Queen's Colleges (1845) of Belfast, Cork, and Galway, designed to answer the Nonconformist and Catholic demands for university education. The Catholic bishops and O Connell rejected the colleges as 'Godless', and only the Belfast foundation prospered.

The four or five decades after the famine saw continuing distress, with much rural unemployment and wholesale evictions. The peasantry sought to defend themselves by their traditional terrorist combinations, only to provoke the inevitable Coercion Acts. To add its sectarian poison to the witch's brew, the Orange Order had by now become firmly entrenched in the North. Nationalist efforts to secure moderate concessions by constitutional means continued to prove unavailing, and republicanism, aimed both at the abolition of the landlord system and at complete separation from Britain, raised its head once more. In 1858 exiles in America founded the Irish Republican Brotherhood, a secret oathbound society dedicated to the principles of Wolfe Tone. Under the name 'Fenians', its members set about preparing for a revolution to which veterans of the American Civil War (in which Irish-born generals and soldiers had played brilliant and heroic parts on both sides) would make expert contributions. Though the movement succeeded in recruiting a great number of adherents, the rising (1867) was easily crushed. But the Irish Republican Brotherhood survived to organize the underground, physical-force arm of the later constitutional movement for land reform and Home Rule.

About this period the Irish cause found a noble English champion in Gladstone, whose liberal principles were grounded in a Christian sense of justice. In 1869 Gladstone disestablished the Protestant state church which, resuming its pre-Union name, Church of Ireland, has ever since governed itself. The following year he carried a Land Act ameliorating the peasants' condition.

That same year an Ulster Protestant lawyer, Isaac Butt, founded the Home Rule Association to press for Home Rule within the United Kingdom. In 1873 a strong Home Rule party entered the House of Commons. Four years later the leadership of the party passed to Charles Stewart Parnell, a young Protestant landlord from Wicklow. Parnell proved to be the second great leader of Irish democracy. No suppliant pleading for favours, but a proud aristocrat asserting his people's rights, his personality and tactics won the love and veneration of the nationalist majority. He had able lieutenants, most notable of them Michael Davitt, who in 1879 founded the Land League and forged the weapons of the boycott and 'No Rent'. Under Parnell and Davitt the constitutional movement for peasant proprietorship and Home Rule filled the stage, with distress, evictions, and peasant violence supplying a lurid backcloth. In the wings, ready to intervene should constitutional agitation fail yet again, stood the Irish Republican Brotherhood. In 1881 Gladstone, in alliance with Parnell's Irish Party, succeeded in carrying through an Act securing the tenant's right to fixity of tenure and substantially reducing his rent. Even the landlords now began to see the wisdom of selling out to their tenants, and a series of later Land Acts (1887, 1891, 1903) effected the social revolution.

In 1885 Gladstone embarked on his last great crusade. His Home Rule Bill was, however, rejected by the House of Commons, and the Conservatives returned to power. In 1890 tragedy overtook Parnell: he was convicted of adultery. Gladstone's Nonconformist supporters were shocked and he was compelled to refuse further co-operation with the Irish leader. The Irish nationalist movement thereupon split into two factions; and then Parnell died suddenly at the age of forty-five (1891). In 1892 Gladstone introduced his second Home Rule Bill, only to have it defeated in the House of Lords. In Ireland there followed a decade of political stagnation, during which the Irish Republican Brotherhood maintained its secret revolutionary organization.

In non-political fields, on the other hand, there were at this time many signs of renewed life. In 1893 the Gaelic League was founded to stem the rapid decay of the Irish language. About the same time a new generation of writers in English was beginning to write the most brilliant chapter in Anglo-Irish literature. About this time, too, the ill-paid workers of the towns began to organize trade unions to protect themselves from exploitation. In 1899 Arthur Griffith began to propound the gospel of Sinn Féin (We Ourselves): passive resistance to British rule, the revival of Irish industry, and abstention from the Westminster Parliament. His aim was 'government by the King, Lords, and Commons of Ireland'.

The return of the Liberals to power at Westminster in 1906 made Home Rule a live issue once more. In 1911 the power of the House of Lords was curtailed, and the way at last seemed clear for the third Home Rule Bill, which passed the Commons in 1912 and was due to come into effect in 1914. But the British and Irish opponents of Home Rule found a most effective leader in Sir Edward Carson, M.P. for Trinity College, Dublin. Carson worked on the fears of the Protestants, raised the Ulster Volunteers to resist the law, and named a 'Provisional Government' which would take over Ulster if the Home Rule Act were put into operation. Nationalist Ireland countered these seditious illegalities by raising the Irish Volunteers 'to secure and maintain the rights and liberties common to the whole people of Ireland', the Irish Republican Brotherhood (which itself included Ulster Protestants) having a hidden hand in the business.

The outbreak of the First World War gave the British Government an excuse for putting the Home Rule Act into abeyance. Most Nationalists supported the 'struggle for the freedom of Belgium and small nations', but a minority, including the Republican Brotherhood, held aloof in anticipation of an opportunity to strike for Irish freedom. Among the Republican leaders were Patrick Pearse (Dublin-born son of an English father), James Connolly (leader of the Socialist wing of the trade-union movement then emerging from the testing fires of a series of great lockouts and strikes), and Bulmer Hobson (a Belfast Quaker). In alliance with Connolly's Irish Citizen Army, the Republican Brotherhood prepared for a widespread insurrection. The insurrection broke out on Easter Monday 1916, but was more or less confined to Dublin, and was crushed in less than a week. But thirty months later a new (Sinn Féin) republican party swept the polls. The Sinn Féin members of parliament constituted themselves a national assembly (Dáil Éireann), ratified the 1916 proclamation of the Irish Republic, and set up a 'government' claiming *de jure* authority over the whole island. Guerrilla warfare soon broke out between the Irish Republican Army and the forces of the Crown. In 1920 the British amended the Home Rule Act so as to establish two Irish parliaments with limited powers, one for the six north-eastern counties ('Northern Ireland'), the other for the remaining twenty-six counties ('Southern Ireland'). Dáil Éireann rejected this solution of the Irish Question and the struggle continued until the following year. Britain then improved her offer by conceding full Dominion Status to the 'Twenty-six Counties' ('The Irish Free State') while insisting on allegiance to the Crown and on the maintenance of the special position of the 'Six Counties' as an integral part of the United Kingdom (but with a local parliament and government in control of agriculture, social services, education, police, etc.). The partitioning of the country – and of Ulster itself – was hateful to Nationalist Ireland. There was strong dislike also of the British Crown. In the event, Dáil Éireann ratified the Anglo-Irish Treaty, but by so slender a majority that civil war proved inevitable. Peace finally came when the Republicans cached their arms (1923).

As a part of the United Kingdom, the 'Six Counties' were actively involved in the Second World War, whereas the independent 'Twenty-six Counties', though at one in heart and principle with the democracies, remained neutral. But neutrality was no obstacle to prompt assistance for bombed Belfast, or to generous post-war succour for the hungry and homeless peoples of devastated Europe.

In 1948 the 'Twenty-six Counties' seceded from the British Commonwealth and became a sovereign republic calling itself 'Ireland' (*Éire* in Irish). Thanks to its traditions of nationalism, democracy, and individual liberty, the republic has been able to play a valuable role in the councils and affairs of the United Nations. It joined the European Community in 1973, and broke the link with sterling in 1978 when it created its own currency, the Irish punt. During the 1960s, new industries were created, partially attracted from outside, and this laid the foundations for an economic boom which continued well into the 1970s. But, in providing a sophisticated welfare state, and at a time when the world economy moved into recession, successive Governments showed themselves to have been living beyond their means, and the 1980s have been characterized by a painful tightening of the nation's belt in order to balance the financial books. In the process, many social and environmental needs have, inevitably, remained unfulfilled.

During the past twenty years, Northern Ireland has been going through a period of crisis. What began as a justifiable campaign for civil rights in 1968, was soon overtaken by the extreme Republican forces of the IRA, who, in their terrorist struggle against their equally militant Unionist counterparts, have polarized the Catholic/Nationalist and Protestant/Unionist communities. These make up the vast majority of the population who make every visitor welcome and who desire nothing more than to live in peace with one another. The British Government continues to uphold the North's union with Britain as long as this is the wish of the majority – those same Unionists who feel betrayed by the Anglo-Irish Agreement signed at Hillsborough in November 1985, which permitted the Republic a consultative role in the affairs of Northern Ireland.

There is no short-term resolution to the problems of Northern Ireland which have, in effect, permeated the whole island of Ireland. The only certainty is that the use of violence postpones the day when Irish people of all communities can live together in the peace and harmony which the vast majority desire.

USEFUL TERMS

The more unfamiliar terms which occur throughout the book are explained briefly below.

Ambry, aumbry A wall cupboard.
Antae Pilaster-like projections of the side walls of buildings.
Bachall A short, crozier-like staff.
Bailey A ward or enclosure of a castle.
Barge-boards Boards or rafters finishing off a gable immediately beneath the roof edge.
Batter The sloping inwards, from bottom to top, of a wall face.
Bawn A fortified enclosure.
Bivallate Having two ramparts.
Bohereen A country lane, or minor road.
Boulder burial Burials covered by a large boulder resting on three or more low stones.
Buaile Milking place, particularly of summer hill pastures.
Bullaun An artificial, basin-like hollow in a boulder, used for grinding.
Caoine A traditional mourning lamentation.
Cashel A ringfort of dry masonry; the vallum or rampart of such a ringfort.
Céle Dé see p. 15
Chamber tomb A prehistoric burial chamber large enough to enter, covered by or buried in a tumulus or cairn. See **Court-tomb**, **Passage-tomb**, **Portal-tomb**, **Wedge-tomb**.
Chantry A chapel or altar endowed for masses.
Chevaux-de-frise A defence zone made of close-set stakes or comparable obstacles.
Chi-rho A monogram formed from the initials X (chi) and P (rho) of the Greek form of Christus; in simple form represented by a cross with a small lateral hook or loop at the top right.
Clochán A corbel-roofed hut of dry masonry, usually beehive-shaped.
Collegiate church One staffed by priests living in community.
Court-tomb A segmented wedge-tomb set in a long cairn and entered from a forecourt at or towards the end of the cairn.
Crannog In archaeology, applied to lake-, river-, and marsh-dwellings, which often present the form of artificial islands.
Cross-pillar A pillarstone or standing stone with one or more crosses.
Cross-slab A stone slab with one or more crosses; often an early gravestone.
Currach A primitive type of keel-less sea boat.
Dolmen see **Portal-tomb**
Erenagh Originally a monastic official, later a hereditary farmer of parish lands.
Gaeltacht A district where Irish survives as the vernacular.
Gallo(w)gla A foreign soldier.
Garderobe Latrine.
Halberd A dagger-like blade mounted at right angles to its handle.
Henge monument A ritual enclosure with a ditch inside the rampart.
High Cross A tall ring-headed cross of stone, usually with figure and/or other carving.
Hill-fort A fort whose defences circle the top of a hill.
Lughnasa A harvest-time festival. In early times Aonach Tailteann (*see p. 130*) was one of the major public assemblies connected with it. In more recent folk practice, it took place at traditional hill sites and other places. Some of the surviving gatherings take the place of Christian pilgrimages, the best-known of which is to Croagh Patrick (*see p. 130*).
Motte-and-bailey The earthwork remains of a primitive castle: the motte is a steep-sided, flat-topped, round mound; the bailey an enclosure at the foot of the mound.
Multivallate Having multiple ramparts.
Ogham A 4th/5th c. adaptation (lines and notches) of the Latin alphabet originally for cutting inscriptions on sticks, later on memorial stones.
Orthostat A stone set on end.
Passage-tomb A chamber tomb with a passage (sometimes used for burials) leading to the chamber(s).
Pátrún Celebrations of the festival of a patron saint.
Pillarstone A prehistoric single large upright stone.
Piscina A basin for washing liturgical vessels, usually in a wall-niche close to the altar.
Plantation castle A type of stronghouse and bawn characteristic of the Ulster Plantation; features of the Scottish variety are crow-shaped gables and conical-roofed turrets corbelled out on the angles of the towers.
Portal-tomb A simple-chamber, megalithic tomb whose entrance is flanked by a pair of tall portal stones.
Promontory fort A promontory or hill spur protected by defences across the neck from one cliff to another.
Ring barrow A (usually low) burial mound encircled by a low earthen ring.
Ringfort An enclosure, commonly ring-shaped, bounded by one or more ramparts and (usually) ditches.
Round Tower A tall, free-standing circular belfry-cum-stronghouse with a conical stone roof.
Sedilia Wall seats for use by the celebrant, deacon and sub-deacon during High Mass.
Sheila-na-gig An obscene female figure of uncertain significance.
Souterrain An underground series of chambers of undetermined purpose.
Sweat-house A stone structure (usually small, simple and with a single opening) used for sweat baths.
Trabeate Having a straight, single-stone lintel.
Transitional Transitional from Romanesque to Gothic.
Trivallate Having three ramparts.
Turas The making of 'rounds' of prayers and penitential exercises at stations often marked by ancient monastic (or comparable) remains.
Urnes style An art style characterized by distinctive interlaced beasts, often in pairs or enmeshed in serpents.
Voussoir One of the wedge-shaped stones of an arch.
Wedge-tomb A rectangular or wedge-shaped chamber tomb without a passage.
Weepers The figures of mourners, angels or saints on a tomb-chest or other monument.
Zoomorphic Of animal form.

GAZETTEER

A

ABBEY, Co. Galway (Map 6, J3), on the Portumna (8 m.)–Gort (22 m.) road, takes its name from the adjacent Franciscan friary of Kinalehin. A monastery founded before 1252 by John de Cogan for Carthusians was abandoned *c.* 1340 and was taken over by the Franciscans *c.* 1370.

3½ m. WSW., in the former Burke demesne of Marble Hill, are two wedge-tombs and a portal-tomb.

ABBEYDORNEY, Co. Kerry (Map 5, F1), is a village on the Tralee (5 m.)–Ballyduff (8 m.) road. The Catholic church of Our Lady and St Brendan (1967), by D.J. Kennedy, has attractive furnishings by Benedict Tutty (tabernacle, crucifix, etc.), Ray Carroll (stonework), Brian Clark (monstrance), and Ian Stuart (Stations of the Cross).

N. of the village are remains of the small Cistercian abbey, Mainistir Ó dTórna, from which it takes its name; it was colonized from MELLIFONT in 1154. Gilla Críst O Conairche, first abbot of Mellifont, afterwards Bishop of Lismore and Papal Legate, died there in 1186. The remains are largely 15th c.

ABBEYFEALE, Co. Limerick (Map 5, H1), is a small market town on the Newcastle West (13 m.)–Castleisland (14 m.) road. It takes its name from a Cistercian abbey founded beside the Feale by Brian O Brien in 1188, and annexed to Monasternenagh (*see p. 123*) in 1209. The derelict, 1846, parish church and churchyard occupy part of the site. In the market-place is a statue of the Rev. William Casey (1844–1907), parish priest and leader of his people in the grim struggle against landlordism.

ABBEYKNOCKMOY, Co. Galway (Map 7, J9), a hamlet on the Galway (18 m.)–Mountbellew Bridge (8 m.) road, takes its name from the nearby Cistercian abbey of Collis Victoriae (Knockmoy, *see p. 188*) founded in 1190 by King Cathal Crovderg O Conor of Connacht. The abbey remains (Nat. Mon.) comprise 13th c. church and chapter-house and 15th c. cloister arcade. The aisled church was a Transitional–Early Gothic structure on the Cistercian cruciform plan, with rib-vaulted chancel (roof modern) and with two E. chapels in each transept. On the N. wall of the chancel are traces of paintings which included the *Holy Trinity, Martyrdom of St Sebastian*, and *The Three Dead and Three Living Kings*. Traces of medieval graffiti and colouring are still discernible in various parts of the church.

ABBEYLEIX, Co. Laois (Map 3, E7), is a village on the Portlaoise (13 m.)–Durrow (6 m.) road. It takes its name from vanished Mainistir Laoighse, the Cistercian abbey of Lex Dei dedicated to the Virgin Mary, which was founded as a colony of BALTINGLASS in 1183 by Conor O More.

The village was built by Viscount de Vesci about the middle of the 18th c. and provides a good example of the work of an 'improving' landlord of the period. Like many other places, it decayed after the Union. The Protestant church has windows by A.E. Child (*Dove*, 1907; *The Good Samaritan*, 1929) and Catherine O Brien (*St James and St Martha*, 1942).

Immediately SW. of the village is the beautiful demesne (private) of Abbeyleix House, home of Viscount de Vesci. The house has been attributed to Sir William Chambers and to James Wyatt. In the garden are the effigy (Ossory armour) of Melaghlin O More, Lord of Laoighis (1502), and the grave slab (by William O Tunney, 1531) of William O Kelly.

ACHILL, Co. Mayo (Map 7, C4), is a large, mountainous island – joined to the mainland by a bridge across Achill Sound – between Blacksod Bay and Clew Bay, 17½ m. NW. of Newport. Its fine cliff scenery, excellent beaches, and colourful moors make it a holiday resort of singular beauty.

Achill Sound has given its name to the chief shopping village. Bathing, boating, and fishing may be had there. Motor and sailing boats may be hired for viewing the spectacular cliffs of the W. Coast, visiting Achillbeg, and for deep-sea fishing (tunny and porbeagle shark).

Form Achill Sound village: 4 m. NW., in Bunacurry, a by-road leads N. to Valley (3¾ m.), a lake-ringed settlement near Ridge Point, the N. extremity of the island.

6¾ m. NW. a branch road leads N. to Doogort on the N. coast at the foot of Slievemore. Doogort comprises Doogort village proper, at the E. end of Pollawaddy cove, and the Missionary Settlement to the SW. of it. The former is an old island village, the latter now primarily a holiday resort. The name of the settlement recalls its origin (1834) in the unhappy campaign of the Rev. E. Nangle to proselytize the poverty-stricken Catholic islanders. There is a good bathing beach at Pollawaddy. Slievemore (2,204 ft) is a picturesque cone of quartz and mica, which rises abruptly from the ocean. A splendid view is to be had from the summit (most readily reached from the graveyard on the E. slope). On the southern slopes of Slievemore are about a dozen prehistoric chamber-tombs. Close to the old village of Slievemore is Keel East Giants Grave, a ruined cairn with elliptical court. Slievemore village serves as a *buaile*, i.e. is occupied only during the summer pasturing season.

9 m. WNW., at the NW. end of Trawmore, a very fine 2 m. strand, is Keel village. Boating, bathing, and sea fishing may be had there. At the SE. end of the strand begin the Cliffs of Menawn (highest point, 800 ft), best viewed by boat. Behind them rises Mweelin (1,530 ft), which affords excellent views of the Galway-S. Mayo coast. It may be climbed from Dookinelly near the SE. end of Trawmore. The walk S. along the cliffs and moors in the direction of Dooega Head (318 ft) is very fine.

11 m. WNW. is Dooagh, a village beside Dooagh Strand. 1½ m. W., on the slope of Croaghaun, is Corrymore House, once occupied by Captain Boycott (*see p. 57*). 1¾ m. W. is beautiful

little Keem Bay, with an excellent small beach sheltered on the S. by Moyteoge Head, on the N. and W. by the great mass of Croaghaun. The ascent (two hours) of Croaghaun (2,192 ft) from Corrymore House is simple enough, but should not be attempted in stormy or misty weather, and the seaward edge of the mountain should always be treated with caution. Near the summit the whole mountain has been shorn away by the Atlantic and falls very steeply for 1,950 ft to the water.

2½ m. S., beside Achill Sound itself, is the well-preserved tower of a small castle (Nat. Mon.) associated with Gráinne Ní Mháille (*see p. 104*); a fragment of the miniature bawn survives.

4½ m. S. is Achillbeg Island. Half-way down the W. coast is Doon Kilmore, one of the most elaborate of Irish promontory forts, within which is Kilmore, a rounded enclosure with graves, remains of huts, and a bullaun; presumably the remains of an early hermitage. To the W. are two smaller promontories with defence works across the necks. The larger, SW., promontory, the Dún, is trivallate. The smaller promontory, the Daingean, has remains of a medieval castle.

ADAMSTOWN, Co. Wexford (Map 4, K3), is a village on the Clonroche (6 m.)–Taghmon (7 m.) road. There are remains of a castle and a church.

ADARE, Co. Limerick (Map 6, H8), is a model village in a setting of rich, quiet beauty where the Limerick (10 m.)–Rathkeale (7 m.) road crosses the Maigue at the head of the tideway. The village owes its attractive, if exotic, appearance to Edwin, 3rd Earl of Dunraven (1812–71), an Oxford Movement convert to Catholicism, one of the best of the 'improving' landlords of his time, and an authority on early Irish architecture.

Nothing is known of the history of Adare prior to the early-13th c., when the Norman Geoffrey de Marisco had a manor there. Subsequently a small town grew up in the shelter of the Kildare Castle (*below*). Tomás Ó Glasáin, poet, lived in the 18th c. village, while between 1733 and 1759 another poet, Fr Nioclás Ó Domhnaill, was five times guardian of the Penal-times Franciscan community, presided several times over the Croom 'Court of Poetry' and was 'Sheriff' of the Cork 'Apollonian Court'.

Holy Trinity Church incorporates the nave, crossing (with low tower over), chancel, and N. transept of the church of the White Monastery, a house of Trinitarian Canons of the Order of the Redemption of Captives. The only certain house of the Order in Ireland, the monastery was allegedly founded *c.*1226 by Lord Ossory and restored, or enlarged, in 1272; it was dedicated to St James. The church ruin was re-edified for the Catholic parishioners by the 2nd Earl of Dunraven in 1811. In 1852 the 3rd Earl had the nave lengthened, the E. end of the chancel

Keem Bay, whose beach is sheltered by Moyteoge Head, and Mt Croaghaun, Co. Mayo.

rebuilt, the Lady Chapel, sacristy, and S. porch added, and battlements (modelled on those at Jerpoint Abbey) placed on the tower, all to the designs of Philip Charles Hardwick. Subsequently he added the new nave and N. aisle (also by Hardwick) which fill most of the medieval cloister court. Hardwick also designed the Convent of Mercy and the school which incorporate the remnants of the W. cloister range. The Lady Chapel altar incorporates medieval alabaster roundels: *Annunciation, Visitation, Crowning of the Virgin*. SW. of the convent is the monastery columbarium.

The Tudor Gothic Adare Manor, former seat of the Earls of Dunraven and opened as a luxury hotel in 1988, was erected from 1831 onwards to the designs of the 2nd Earl (1782–1850); from 1850 onwards to the designs of Hardwick (S. and W. fronts, garden terraces, a geometric garden, etc.); Augustine Webby Pugin designed (1846–7) a couple of fireplaces and a scheme of decoration for the dining room. The Earls of Dunraven descend from Thady Quin, who leased the castle and lands of Adare from the Earl of Kildare in 1683. The poet, Seán Ó Tuama (1706–75, *see p. 123*), fallen on evil days, was a servant ('keeper of hens') to the then Mrs Quin; he wrote a satire on her, *Bean na cleithe caoile*.

In the middle of the golf course, on the N. side of the Maigue, are the now neglected ruins of a Franciscan friary dedicated to St Michael the Archangel, in 1464. In 1466, church, sacristies, cloister, and cemetery were consecrated for friars of the Strict Observance. The completion of the friary extended over many years, Anglo-Norman and Gael contributing to every phase. A tablet E. of the chancel marks the spot where John Wesley, founder of Methodism, preached.

400 yds W. of the friary are the overgrown remains of 'Desmond's Castle' (Nat. Mon.). The first builder is unknown, but in the 14th, 15th, and 16th c. the castle belonged to the Earls of Kildare. Forfeited by Silken Thomas's rebellion (1536) and granted to the Earl of Desmond (1541), it was recovered by the Kildares. It was dismantled by the Cromwellians. The inner ward was defended by a water fosse and – like the outer ward – by a crenellated curtain. Adjoining the main gate (*c.* 1200 and later) of the outer ward is a Great Hall (cellar basement) of *c.* 1200 (Transitional windows) with 15th c. S. wing (latrine). E. of the hall was its kitchen, etc. Further E. are the ruins of a second (later 13th c.?) Great Hall (aisled; buttery at E. end); it had its own kitchen further E. The square keep was a characteristic Norman work of its period (*c.* 1200). Taken as a whole, the castle is one of the most interesting examples of feudal architecture in the country, which makes its present condition all the more regrettable.

N. of the castle are the overgrown, neglected remains of the manorial, parish church of St Nicholas of Myra. This was a much altered, nave-and-chancel structure of various 13th c. (chancel) to 16th c. (E. end; priest's residence) dates. N. of it are situated the densely overgrown remains of a 15th c. chantry chapel (undercroft); the chaplain's quarters were over the E. end.

NE. of the village are the Protestant parish church and school, re-edifications (1807–14 by the Ecclesiastical Commissioners; 1852–4 by Caroline, dowager Countess of Dunraven) of the Black Abbey, an Augustinian friary founded *c.*1316 by the 1st Earl of Kildare and which adopted the Observant reform in 1472. Noteworthy details of the church are: the sedilia and aumbry, the W. window and the cornice (figures of beasts, etc.) of the aisle. The tower is a 15th c. insertion. The beautiful small cloister, too, is 15th c.; the N. and E. ambulatories are 1831 rebuildings by the 2nd Earl of Dunraven. The E. and W. ranges have disappeared. W. of the site of the W. range is an 1826 Dunraven mausoleum. The N. range had vaulted apartments below. In 1814 the upper floor (dormitory) was re-roofed for use as a school. At the NE. angle of the claustral buildings are remains of the friary gatehouse.

2½ m. S. (by the Croom road) of Adare, in Dunnaman, are the remains of small Teampall na Tríonóide (Trinity Church). Nearby is the stump of a 16th c. castle tower with a sheila-na-gig.

The road SW. to Rathkeale passes through the Palatinate, so called from Calvinist refugees planted there early in the 18th c. by Lord Southwell, after the French conquest of the Rhenish Palatinate. Their descendants still retain their German surnames (pronounced with an Irish twist), but have been largely absorbed by the Catholic majority.

1½ m. SW. the road passes the small manorial castle of Clonshire with a twice-enlarged tower. Nearby are the ruins of Templenakilla, a small, early church with trabeate W. door and Transitional E. window. ½ m. further W. are the ruins of 15th c. Garraunboy castle (small tower in a rectangular bawn with D-shaped angle turrets).

ADRIGOLE, Co. Cork (Map 5, E7), is a seaside village on the Glengarriff (11 m.)–Castletown Bearhaven (9 m.) road.

The roads N. to LARAGH via the Tim Healy Pass (1,084 ft), NE. to Glengarriff, and SW. to Castletown Bearhaven are noted for their splendid scenery. The Castletown Bearhaven road skirts the lower slopes of Hungry Hill (2,251 ft), which gave its name to Daphne du Maurier's novel.

AGHABOE, Co. Laois (Map 3, D7), is situated on the Borris-in-Ossory (4 m.)–Durrow (8 m.) road.

St Cainneach, companion of Columcille and the 'Kenneth' of Scottish churches, founded a celebrated monastery there, where he died and was buried (599/600). In time this monastery supplanted Seir Kieran (*see p. 78*) as the principal church of Ossory, and it was not until the synod of Ráth Breasail (1111) that it, in turn, was supplanted by KILKENNY. Destroyed several times, the monastery was rebuilt as an Augustinian priory in 1234. In 1346 Aghaboe was burnt by Dermot Mac Gillapatrick (Fitzpatrick), on which occasion the shrine and relics of St Cainneach were destroyed. A turret of the medieval priory church survives at the Protestant parish church, which occupies the site of the Augustinian choir and incorporates windows from the church of the nearby Dominican friary, which was founded in 1382 by Mac Gillapatrick. The remains of the friary include a late-15th c. aisleless church and the small Phelan's Chapel. Some of the church windows are at Heywood House, BALLINAKILL. 150 yds from the Protestant church a square earthwork marks the site of the Anglo-Norman castle. Nearby is the hill-top motte of Monacoghlan.

Ledwich, the renowned 18th c. antiquary, was for a time vicar of Aghaboe.

The ruins of the Franciscan friary in Adare, Co. Limerick.

AGHAVANNAGH, Co. Wicklow (Map 3, J7), is a remote mountain hamlet at the junction of roads from Baltinglass (16 m.) and Aughrim (7 m.) with the old Military Road (not for cars) from GLENMALURE to Tinahely. Gaunt Aghavannagh House, now an An Óige (Youth) Hostel, was one of the chain of posts guarding the early-19th c. Military Road into the heart of the mountains. It was later the shooting lodge of Charles Stewart Parnell (1846–91), and later still the country residence of John Redmond (1858–1918), leader of the Irish Party at Westminster. Aghavannagh is a good place from which to climb Lugnaquilla (3,039 ft), highest mountain in Leinster. Climbers should take precautions against losing their way in the mists which can descend unexpectedly on the mountain.

AGLISH, Co. Waterford (Map 4, E7), is a village on the Cappoquin (7 m.)–Ardmore (11 m.) road.

3 m. N., at Kilmolash, are the remains of a church of various dates; it is called after St Mo-Laisse. In the chancel step is a broken, defaced, ogham stone with three inscribed crosses.

1 m. NE. are the ruins of Clogh Castle, a square bawn with angle-turrets. 5 m. NE. is Kilgreany cave where traces of Stone Age habitation were found.

2 m. W., in Dromore townland, 1 m. S. of Villierstown, is Kiltera, an ancient cemetery with two ogham stones. A third ogham stone has been removed to the National Museum.

3½ m. NW. is Dromana House, seat of the Villiers Stuarts. Demesne and gardens are justly famous. At the historic Waterford election of 1826 the Catholic voters elected Henry Villiers Stuart of Dromana, a liberal Protestant, in place of Lord George Beresford. In revenge the Beresfords evicted hundreds of their tenants. Dromana Castle was the birthplace of the celebrated Old Countess of Desmond, said to have been 140 years of age at her death (1604). Sir Walter Ralegh was entertained at the castle by Sir James Fitzgerald. The former Protestant church in the village of Villierstown, presented to the Catholic parish in 1965, dates from 1748.

Antrim Round Tower, in State care, is situated in the grounds of Steeple House.

AHASCRAGH, Co. Galway (Map 7, L9), is a village on the Ballinasloe (7 m.)–Mountbellew Bridge (9 m.) road.

3 m. E. are the partially restored remains of Eglish 'Abbey', a Carmelite friary founded about 1396 by Uilliam Ó Cormacáin, Bishop of Elphin.

ALLENWOOD, Co. Kildare (Map 3, H4), 8 m. W. of Clane and 10 m. SE. of Edenderry, has a peat-fired power station exploiting the great Bog of Allen.

3 m. W., in Lullymore East, on an 'island' in the bog is an early monastic enclosure. Old cross-slabs from the site have been built into the nearby 1978 roadside memorial (by Niall Meagher) to Captain John Doorley, a native of Lullymore, who was hanged for his part in the 1798 Insurrection.

ANASCAUL, Co. Kerry (Map 5, D3), is a hamlet on the main Tralee (20 m.)–Dingle (11 m.) road. The name of South Pole Inn commemorates the participation by a former owner in Scott's expedition to the South Pole.

3 m. NNE., attached to the E. gable of a house in Ballinahunt, is a cross-inscribed ogham stone.

1½ m. NE., at an ancient church site in Ballinvoher, Rathduff, are two ogham stones, one with three crosses.

1¼ m. E., in Ballintermon, is a cross-inscribed ogham stone.

3 m. SE., at Inch, is a beautifully situated 3 m. beach backed by dunes.

3 m. SW. are the remains of Minard castle (Knights of Kerry). Thomas Ashe, the patriot (1885–1917; *see p. 47*) was a native of Minard East.

¾ m. W., at a well in Ballinclare, is an early cross-slab.

2 m. W., in Gortacurraun, is an early cross-pillar.

2 m. NW., in Knockane, are the remains of a large tumulus in which can be found cist graves; to the SE. is a boulder with a chi-rho cross.

ANNAGHDOWN, Co. Galway (Map 7, H9), on the shore of Lough Corrib, 12 m. N. of Galway, is the site of a monastery attributed to St Brendan of Clonfert who, it is said, died there in 577 after setting his sister, St Brigid, over a nearby nunnery. In the 12th c. the monastery adopted the rule of the Canons Regular of St Augustine. In the same century there was also a convent (St Mary's) of Arrouasian Augustinian nuns. It is possible that this may have become a house of Premonstratensian canons before 1224.

About 1188/9 Annaghdown became the see of a diocese, which was reabsorbed by Tuam *c.* 1325/6, but a succession of English and Irish titular bishops is recorded in the 15th c.

The remains at Annaghdown comprise cathedral, 'nunnery', Augustinian priory (Nat. Mons.), castle, and holy wells.

The cathedral, perhaps rather a Premonstratensian church, is a simple, rectangular building. It has a Gothic doorway in the N. wall and a Late Romanesque-Transitional E. window purloined from the chancel of the nearby priory. The high quality and delightfully delicate carvings of this window reward examination.

The scant remains of the 'nunnery' lie NW. of the cathedral, and may, in fact, represent the *Cella Parva* of Premonstratensian canons established at Annaghdown before 1224. The featureless remains include a relatively long nave-and-chancel church of Premonstratensian type.

The ruins of the priory are by the lake shore, W. of the cathedral. The remains are, for the most part, those of a 15th c. monastery. Sheltered in a garderobe on the S. side may be seen excellent Romanesque pilasters from a doorway or chancel arch. The church, on the N. side of the cloister garth, is of at least three periods. The small chancel was an excellent Transitional structure.

The 15th c. tower of the castle rises above the lake to the SE. of the priory. Nearby are St Brendan's Well and St Cormac's Well.

ANTRIM, Co. Antrim (Map 1, J7), the little town which gives its name to the county, lies at the NE. corner of Lough Neagh (where the Six Mile Water enters the lake), 17 m. NW. of Belfast and 11 m. S. of Ballymena. The place gets its name from Aentrebh, an early monastery, of which little is known.

In 1643 the town was burned by Scottish Covenanters under General Munroe. In 1798 it was attacked, unsuccessfully, by insurgent United Irishmen led by Henry Joy McCracken. The Protestant parish church of All Saints, in Church St, began as an Elizabethan rectangular structure with S. transept (1596). It was enlarged in 1816, when the tower was added, and again in 1869. A small window in the old transept has rich Continental glass, put there in the 18th c. The monuments include one by Flaxman to the 4th Earl of Massereene (d. 1816).

At the W. end of the main street is the small, but good, Town Hall of 1726. Nearby is the entrance to Antrim Castle demesne. There are a motte-and-bailey; the ruins of a house built in 1602, rebuilt in 1816, and burned down in 1922; and also what remains of formal gardens with canals, in the Versailles manner (supposedly designed by Le Nôtre).

1 m. N., in the grounds of Steeple House (now Borough Council offices), is a fine Round Tower (in State care), 93 ft high, with a relief cross over its trabeate doorway; the cap is modern. This and a nearby 'bullaun' stone are all that visibly survive of the early monastery.

2 m. E., near the motorway interchange, is Rathmore Trench, probably the *Ráith Mor* ('great fort') of Magh Líne which was a seat of the kings of Dál nAraide in the 6th and 7th c. William Orr, United Irishman (hanged 1797), was born in Farranshane nearby. 2 m. ENE. of Rathmore is Donegore, where a church and graveyard mark an ancient ecclesiastical site. Sir Samuel Ferguson (1810–86), poet and antiquary, is buried there, and the graveyard contains a fine collection of early-18th c. headstones depicting symbols of mortality. NE. of the churchyard is a huge, partly natural mound, Donegore Moat, which seems to have been originally a Neolithic passage tomb (one of a number in the valley of the Six Mile Water) reused as an Anglo-Norman motte. 1 m. NE. is Donegore Hill, around whose summit is a Neolithic enclosed settlement, from which another on Lyle's Hill (*see p. 291*) is clearly visible. ½ m. NE. is Ballywee ringfort (in State care), in which early historic house foundations and souterrains can be seen as excavated. 2 m. N. of the hill, on Browndod Hill, is a fine four-chambered court-tomb, as well as other monuments of many periods.

1½ m. SE., Muckamore cemetery marks the site of an early

monastery founded *c.* 550 by St Colman Eala, joint patron of the diocese of Connor.

1 m. WNW., on the road to RANDALSTOWN is the entrance to Shane's Castle Park (and Nature Reserve). A 2½ m. avenue (or, in summer, a narrow-gauge railway with steam locomotive) takes the visitor to the lakeshore remains of O Neill castles and of a later mansion. A splendid conservatory (by Nash) on a parapet overlooks Lough Neagh.

ANTRIM, THE GLENS OF, Co. Antrim, noted for their scenery, are the coastal valleys between Larne Lough and the Bush. Most of them debouch on the famous Antrim Coast Road, while five of them may also be reached by roads across the hills from Ballymena to Glenarm, Carnlough and Cushendall. In this *Guide* the relevant particulars will be found under the nearest town or resort: BALLYCASTLE, Carnlough, CUSHENDALL, and GLENARM.

The region of the Glens or Glynn(e)s was a large part of the little kingdom of Dál Ríada, whose 5th c. rulers united the Gaelic colonies of SW. Scotland under their sway, so laying the foundation for the future kingdom of Scotland. The narrow seas made repeated comings and goings of settlers in both directions easy, the more so because the inhabitants on both shores of the North Channel shared a common Gaelic speech and culture, as well as a common Catholicism. From 1242, the Norman Bisets dominated the area. The MacDonnells came later as galloglas recruited by Irish rulers to resist the Normans, and in the 16th c. their hold on the Glens was confirmed by Alasdar Carrach MacDonnell, who also annexed the MacQuillan (de Mandeville) country known as the Route (from the Glens to the Bann). Alasdar's son, James, became chief of the MacDonnells of the Isles in 1540, leaving his brothers – one of whom was the redoubtable Somhairle Buidhe ('Sorley Boy') – in charge of the Antrim lands. Somhairle's son, Raghnall (Randall), like his father, resisted the spread of English power in Ulster and for a time supported his kinsman and father-in-law, Hugh O Neill. He forsook O Neill after the battle of Kinsale, however, and James I rewarded him with a grant of the Glynns, etc., in 1603, and the earldom of Antrim in 1620. At the end of the 17th c., despite having supported James II against the victorious William of Orange, the 3rd Earl managed to avoid confiscation of his vast estates, which survived more or less intact until they were fragmented by extravagant living and multiple inheritance in the late-18th c.

Temple Benan (or Benen) on Inishmore.

ARAN ISLANDS, Co. Galway (Map 6, C–D3–4), three in number – Inishmore, Inishmaan, Inisheer – lie NW.–SE. across the mouth of Galway Bay. They are most readily reached by air or steamer from Galway, but may also be reached by boat from Rossa Veal and DOOLIN.

The islands consist for the most part of exposures of limestone karsts, continuations of those of Burren, Co. Clare (*see p. 68*). They have long been celebrated in antiquarian and folklore circles. More recently they have become popular with those in search of pleasant, restful vacations. Accommodation, simple but good, is available. There are several good, small beaches.

The relative isolation of the islands has preserved something of the traditional way of life: Irish is the normal speech of the majority (though the non-Irish-speaking visitor will find sufficient English for his needs); the canvas-covered currach, handled with superb skill, is still the standard boat; traditional costume is now rarely worn. Noteworthy items of local costume were the rawhide shoes (*brógaí urleathair*; tourist literature calls them by the exotic name 'pampooties') admirably adapted to the island rocks; the superb, hand-knitted, white sweaters of infinitely varied pattern and the finger-braided *crios* or girdle of coloured wools (now, sadly, made with synthetic fibres).

In archaeological circles the islands are famous for their prehistoric forts of dry-stone masonry. In Irish literary legend these are associated with the Fir Bolg (Belgic Celts).

In Irish history the islands are celebrated for their early eremitical settlements, most notably that founded by St Éanna (Enda; d. *c.*530), who appears to have introduced monasticism, in the strict sense, into Ireland, and who numbered among his disciples several of the most famous of the early Irish saints.

The civil history of the islands is obscure. During the Middle Ages the O Briens and O Flaherties contended for them. In 1587 they passed into effective English control.

John Millington Synge (1871–1909) drew the attention of the literary world to the islands (*Aran Islands*, 1907); his play *Riders to the Sea* is derived from an Inishmaan story.

In 1934 Robert Flaherty, distinguished American film director, made his splendid *Man of Aran* on the islands, the entire cast being island folk. The island life depicted was that of an older generation.

Liam O Flaherty (1896–1986), the distinguished author, was a native of Gortnagapul, Inishmore.

INISHMORE

Kilronan, capital and port of the islands, is a village on the NW. side of Killeany Bay, near the E. end of Inishmore. The village takes its name from the monastery of St Rónán, of which the only relic is Toberonan, a holy well. There is a small museum there displaying items relevant to the history and crafts of the island. There are small beaches to the E. and S.

1 m. NW. is Monasterkieran (St Ciarán's Monastery), alias Mainistear Chonnachtach – Connacht Monastery, with ruins of a Transitional church, several early cross-pillars, cross-slabs and St Kieran's Well; all Nat. Mons.

1½ m. WNW. is the village of Oghil. 800 yds NE. are the fragmentary remains of Templesoorney (Teampall Assurnaidhe, Assurnaidhe's Church, a small primitive structure), and St Soorney's Bed (Nat. Mons.). 150 yds NW. of these is St Soorney's Well, to the W. of which is St Soorney's Bush (Nat. Mons.). – ¼ m. SSE., to the E. of the old lighthouse, is Oghil Fort (Nat. Mon.), with two concentric, dry-masonry ramparts, the inner one terraced. In the inner enclosure are remains of two clocháns.

½ m. W. of Oghil is Cowrugh village. To the SSW. is a holy well. To the S. of this is the small 15th c. church (Nat. Mon.), Teampall an Cheathrair Álainn, Church of the Four Comely Saints (SS Fursa, Brendan of Birr, Conall, and Bearchán). At the E. gable is the Leaba, or Bed, of the four saints (Nat. Mon.). S. of the church is a holy well (Bollán an Cheathrair Álainn). A couple of fields W. are graves marked by plain pillarstones. 300 yds S. of the church is ruinous Clochán a' Phúca; 400 yds SW. is a wedge-tomb (Nat. Mon.).

2 m. W. of Cowrugh is Kilmurvy village. To the E. is the excellent small strand of Portmurvy. (The two cottages by the pier were built by Robert Flaherty when making *Man of Aran.*) A short distance SW. of Kilmurvy are Templemacduagh (Nat. Mon.), an early cross-pillar, Tobermacduagh holy well, and a fragment of an enclosing cashel (Nat. Mon.). Church and well are dedicated to St Colmán mac Duach (*see p. 224*). The church is a small, pre-Romanesque structure with *antae*; its chancel a plain Transitional addition. The battlemented chancel parapet is a 15th c. addition. In the N. face of the N. nave wall is the figure of a horse. 100 yds S., on the E. side of the bohereen leading to Dún Aonghus, is little Templenaneeve, Church of the Saints (Nat. Mon.). ½ m. SW. of Templenaneeve, spectacularly sited on the edge of a 300 ft cliff, is Dún Aonghus (Nat. Mon.), one of the finest prehistoric monuments in W. Europe. For all its size and interest, it does not figure in island folklore, and 100 years ago only one old man could be found who remembered its name (pronounced Doon Eeneece); today the islanders call it Dún Angus, a name they have learned from antiquarians and tourists ignorant of Irish. (Aonghus was a chief of the Fir Bolg in medieval literary legend.) The fort, which covers some 11 acres, comprises three 'concentric' enclosures defended by stout walls of dry masonry: outer enclosure, 1,174 × 650 ft; middle enclosure, 400 × 300 ft; inner citadel, 150 ft in diameter. The middle wall is defended by a remarkable abatis (or *chevaux-de-frise* of jagged, limestone uprights), which also embraces an outwork at the NW. gateway through the wall. The terraced innermost wall, built in three sections and 12 ft 9 in. thick, is now 18 ft high. (The outer part rose above the inner.) Much of the walls had collapsed when conservation was undertaken by the Office of Public Works in 1881. Unfortunately, the work was carried out without judgement, and no records were made of the fort as it then stood. Many of the flights of steps, etc., date from that time. The innermost rampart affords a splendid view of the island and of the Connemara coast. – 2 m. N. of Kilmurvy, to the N. of the Onaght road near Sruffaun, is Clochán na Carraige (Nat. Mon.), a late clochán, oval without, rectangular within. The disposition of the doors and other features link it with the traditional Irish peasant house.

1¾ m. NW. of Kilmurvy is Onaght village. Here the miscalled Seven Churches (Nat. Mons.) mark an ancient site dedicated to St Breacán. There are remains of two small churches, Temple Brecan and Teampall an Phoill. Temple Brecan is a nave-and-chancel structure of various dates. Built into the W. wall (inner face) is an early gravestone inscribed: OR[ŌIT] AR II CANOIN ('A prayer for two canons'). Re-erected near the SE. of the church, on the NE., is Leaba an Spioraid Naoimh ('Holy Ghost Bed'), a penitential station with fragments of a figured High Cross (*Crucifixion,* interlacing, etc.). Nearby, to the SE., is Leaba Bhreacáin, another 'station' and portion of an early cross-slab inscribed S[AN]C[T]I BRE[CA]NI. N. of the church are the ruins of late-15th c. monastic houses. In the SE. corner of the churchyard are some early graves; the cross-slabs include one inscribed TOMAS AP[STAL] ('Thomas the Apostle'), moved from elsewhere on the site. Another cross-slab here is inscribed UII ROMANI, presumably referring to the seven martyr sons of Symphorosa; their cult was known in Ireland. Prostrate on the rock in the field to the SE. is a fractured High Cross (Nat. Mon.) with elaborate interlaces, etc. E. of the monastery are another *leaba* and fragments of an ornamented cross with a rude *Crucifixion* (Nat. Mons.). ½ m. SSE. of Onaght village is Dún Onaght (Nat. Mon.), a massive, univallate, stone ringfort (restored) with terraced rampart and three house-sites. ENE. of the fort is the ancient ecclesiastical site of Kilcholan (Nat. Mon.); in the enclosure are the remains of a slab-built shrine or reliquary.

1½ m. SE. of Kilronan is Killeany village, with the island's airstrip. Nearby are the ruins of Arkin Castle (Nat. Mon.), a Cromwellian fort. 150 yds S. is the ancient monastic site of Cill Éinne, from which the village takes its name. The scant remains (Nat. Mons.) include the stump of a Round Tower, parts of a High Cross with zoomorphic and other ornament, an 'altar', and Dabhach Éinne (alias St Eany's Well). On a rock-terrace 200 yds SW. is Temple Benan (St Benignus's Church), a diminutive structure with trabeate N. door. A stone at the SE. angle is inscribed CARI. – ½ m. ESE. of Killeany, by Trawmore, is Tighlagheany (Teaghlach Éinne, Enda's Household), holiest place in Aran with, says tradition, the graves of 120 saints. All that remains there is a small early church (Nat. Mon.) with E. *antae* and some 15th c. features. In it are part of a figured High Cross, and early gravestones. Two of the latter are inscribed: BEN[DACH]T DIE F[OR] AN[MAIN] S[AN]C[T]AN ('The blessing of God on the soul of Sanctán') and OROIT AR SCANDLAN ('A prayer for Scannlán'). Nearby is St Enda's Leaba. 400 yds SW. are remains of a clochán. – 1½ m. SE. of Killeany, are 'puffing holes' in the rock surface.

1½ m. W. of Killeany (via the cliffs), at Bensheegipson, is the great promontory fort called Doocaher (Nat. Mon.); it, too, has been restored. Outside the massive stone rampart are remains of *chevaux-de-frise* with traces of hut-sites. In the shelter of the rampart are remains (restored) of several clocháns.

INISHMAAN

Near the slip at the middle of the E. coast, SW. of Trawletteragh, are the ruins of Kilcanonagh church (Nat. Mon.) and Tobercanonagh holy well; the church is a small, primitive structure with trabeate W. doorway. Nearby is the triangular end-stone of a slab-shrine. On a rock-terrace to the W. is Doonfarvagh (Nat. Mon.), a stone ringfort; the rampart is terraced.

The first village to the W. of the landing place is Moher (Mur). 300 yds NNE. is a collapsed wedge-tomb (Nat. Mon.).

About the centre of the island, at the W. end of Ballinlisheen village, are: Templemurry, a small 15th c. church which was incorporated in the 19th c. church; traces of Templeshaght-macree (Church of the King's Seven Sons, Nat. Mon.); Labbanakinneriga (St Cinneirge's Bed, Nat. Mon.); and Tober-nakinneriga (St Cinneirge's Well).

400 yds W. of Templemurry is Doonconor, Dún Conchuirn (Nat. Mon.), a magnificent oval stone fort with an outer bailey and a small forework at the entrance. The massive rampart (restored) of the fort proper is terraced and has wall chambers; it encloses a number of hut-sites (restored).

INISHEER

Close to the landing place is Knockgrannia, an ancient circular cemetery (Nat. Mon.).

In the sands SE. of the landing place are the ruins of Teampall Chaomháin (Nat. Mon.), an early church with later W. chamber and Gothic chancel. A pátrún is held on 14 June.

On the rocky hill S. of the landing place is fragmentary O Brien's Castle, alias Furmina Castle (Nat. Mon.), a 15th c. tower set in a stone ringfort (Great Fort, Nat. Mon.). ¾ m. S. are remains of Cill na Seacht nInghean (Nat. Mon.), a cashel with the 'Grave of the Seven Daughters'; there is an early cross-slab there.

800 yds W. of the landing place are the ruins of Cill Ghobnait (Nat. Mon.), a small church with trabeate W. door. In the enclosure are remains of a clochán and two bullauns.

ARDAGH, Co. Limerick (Map 6, F9), is a village on the Newcastle West (4 m.)–Shanagolden (7 m.) road, at the foot of Slieveluachra.

At the W. end of the village, beside the road in Reerasta South, is a large, overgrown, and partly defaced ringfort (Nat. Mon.). The celebrated Ardagh chalices and brooches, now in the National Museum, were discovered there in 1868.

1½ m. NE. is Cahermoyle House, 1870 successor (by J.J. MacCarthy, Ireland's foremost Gothic Revival architect) of the home of William Smith O Brien (1803–64), leader of the abortive Young Ireland rebellion of 1848. The house is now a novitiate of the Oblates of Mary Immaculate.

1 m. NW. is Ballylin, one of Ireland's largest hill-forts.

ARDARA, Co. Donegal (Map 8, C6), is a village on the Killybegs (12 m.)–Glenties (5 m.) road, noted for its homespun tweed, embroidery, and knitting industries. The Church of the Holy Family has a rose window (1954) by Evie Hone: *Christ, David, Moses and the Evangelists' Symbols.*

5½ m. W., in Maghera on Loughros Beg Bay, are caves accessible at low tide; nearby is Eassaranka, a waterfall. Foot-paths follow the coast to Glencolumbkille. Others cross the summits of Slievetooey (1,515 ft, 1,458 ft and 1,500 ft).

3½ m. WNW., in Newtownburke, are three early cross-slabs, one 20 yds S. of the road to Loughros Point, the second 50 yds N. of the road, the third 400 yds away on a hillside. 1½ m. NE., in Kilcashel graveyard, to the N. of Lough Aleen, is St Conall's Cross, a primitive stone cross with a cross incised on it.

ARDEE, Co. Louth (Map 2, H7), is a market town where the Drogheda (15 m.)–Carrickmacross (12 m.) road crosses the little Dee River.

Ardee takes its name from Áth Fhir Diadh, Fear-Diadh's ford, now crossed by the bridge. The name has inspired the well-known story of the mythical Cú Chulainn's single combat with Fer Diad, interpolated into *The Cattle Raid of Cooley.*

About 1186 Prince John of England, as Lord of Ireland, granted the barony of Ardee to Gilbert Pipard, but by 1302 the Pipards had given up hope of retaining Ardee against the Irish. In the period 1402–25 the town, however, remained in English hands. In 1539 Conn O Neill and Manus O Donnell burned the place. From October to November 1689, James II had his headquarters there.

The principal monument in the town is Ardee Castle, now the Court House (Main St), the largest fortified medieval town house in Ireland. This square keep is reputed to have been built by Gilbert Pipard's brother, Roger, but it is scarcely earlier than the 15th c. In its day it was an important border-fortress of the English Pale. After the Restoration it was granted to Theobald Taafe, Earl of Carlingford (1639–77; *see* Smarmore Castle *below*, and *p. 89*).

In Market St in Hatch's Castle, so called after the Cromwellian family that lived there until 1940. This, too, is a 15th c. structure.

St Mary's Protestant Church (1789, 1812) incorporates the S. nave arcade and other fragments of a medieval church. The church has a medieval font (from Mansfieldstown near Castle-bellingham). In the churchyard is part of a 16th c. stone cross with a *Crucifixion* on the W. face and a *Virgin and Child* on the E. face.

Near the railway station is a fragment of the medieval town wall, known as Cappock's Gate.

¾ m. S. of the town is Castleguard, alias Dawson's Fort, motte of Gilbert Pipard's castle of Ardee.

4½ m. N. is much altered and enlarged 17th c. Louth Hall, until recently the seat of Baron Louth (Plunkett family; *see p. 134*). St Oliver Plunkett (1629–81), martyred Archbishop of Armagh, found refuge there with his kinsfolk; his hiding-place is still pointed out. In the demesne are the shattered remains of a figured cross set up in 1601 in memory of Oliver, 4th Baron Louth, by this widow, Ienet Dowdall (*see also p. 167*). ¾ m. N. of Louth Hall is Tallanstown motte.

3½ m. NE. is Mapastown motte with nearby remains of a manorial church.

3 m. ENE., via the Castlebellingham road, is Roodstown Castle (Nat. Mon.), a small 15th c. tower with two angle turrets.

2 m. SSE., in Kildemock, are remnants of medieval St Catherine's church, sometimes known as the Jumping Church. A storm in February 1715 caused part of the W. gable to shift inwards from its foundation, but popular belief soon explained the 'jump' as a miracle to exclude the grave of a heretic who had been buried within the church.

4 m. SSW. is Smarmore Castle, former seat of the Anglo-Norman Taafes. Several members of the family sought refuge abroad with the 'Wild Geese'; two of them (Francis, 1639–1704, and Nicholas, 1677–1769) became Austrian field marshals, while the 12th Viscount was Prime Minister of Austria (1879–93). John Taafe (1787–1862), poet and commentator on Dante, was also a member of this family. The castle is a 14th c. square keep with modern wings. ¼ m. N. are remains of a medieval manorial church.

6 m. NW., Aclint bridge (motte nearby) crosses the Lagan, alias the Glyde, at the ford where Elizabeth's ill-starred favourite, Robert Devereux, Earl of Essex, parleyed with Great Hugh O Neill, 7 September 1599. The ensuing truce was signed at Lagan Castle 2 m. SW. The castle was the birthplace of Christopher Fleming, who published the *Life* and *Works* of St Columbanus and other early Irish ecclesiastical documents. Sent to Prague in 1630 as first superior of the Irish Franciscan college there, he was murdered by Hussites in 1631.

ARDFERT, Co. Kerry (Map 5, E1), on the Tralee (5 m.)–Ballyheigue (6 m.) road, was the site of a monastery founded by the celebrated St Brendan the Navigator (d. 577; *see p. 107*). In the 12th c. it became the see of a diocese now absorbed into that of Kerry. The medieval remains are among the most interesting in Co. Kerry. St Brendan's Church (1853–4) is by J.J. McCarthy.

The principal monument is the scandalously neglected St Brendan's Cathedral (Nat. Mon.), a mid-13th c. rectangular structure (details excellent) with S. nave aisle, to which a S. transept (with E. chapel) and a NE. chapel, or sacristy, were added in the 15th c. Interesting features are the incorporated fragment (doorway flanked by blind arcading) of the W. wall of a 12th c. Romanesque church, the fine lancet windows of the choir and two episcopal effigies of *c.* 1300. There was a Round Tower near the NW. angle of the church until 1771.

NW. of the cathedral are the ruins (Nat. Mons.) of Temple-na-Hoe, a small, Late Romanesque, nave-and-chancel church, and Temple-na-Griffin, a small, simple, 15th c. church. Opposite the graveyard stile is an ogham stone (partly defaced) which formerly stood in a field opposite the Protestant church.

¼ m. E. are the ruins (Nat. Mon.) of a Franciscan friary founded in 1253 by Thomas Fitzmaurice, 1st Baron of Kerry. The remains include late-13th c. nave and chancel, 14th/15th c. S. transept, W. tower, cloister, etc.

2¾ m. E., in Tubridmore, is Tobernamolt, alias Wethers' Well, the most frequented holy well in Kerry today (Sat. before Midsummer). Nearby is St Íde's Grave. Íde's prayers called forth the well, in whose waters St Erc baptized St Brendan. The arcaded tomb slab with three weepers (popularly SS Erc,

St Brendan's Cathedral in Ardfert, Co. Kerry.

Ardmore Cathedral and Round Tower, Co. Waterford.

Brendan, and Íde) came from Ardfert friary. Sufferers from rheumatism, etc. used to bathe in the well; hence the little 'dressing house'.

1 m. SW. is Mc Kenna's Fort, a univallate ringfort where Sir Roger Casement (1864–1916) was arrested on Good Friday, 1916, after landing at nearby Banna strand from a German submarine. A monument (by J.E. MacCanna) was erected near the landing site to commemorate the event.

ARDFINNAN, Co. Tipperary (Map 4, E5), is a market village where the Clonmel (10 m.)–Mitchelstown (17 m.) road crosses the Suir. The name of the village commemorates St Fíonán Lobhar, who founded a monastery here in the 7th c. (the Protestant church stands on the site). On a precipitous rock commanding the river-ford are remains of a strong castle of 12th–13th c. origins, but with 19th c. additions.

2 m. NW., in Rochestown, are the ruins of a medieval church. The recently stolen sheila-na-gig in the E. gable was the first of these curious carvings to be published and has given its name to the entire series.

2 m. S., in Raheen, are the ruins of Ballybacon 13th c. church. There is a medieval carved font there.

5 m. SE., near the mouth of the lovely Nire valley, are remains of New Castle and its manorial church. 1 m. NE. of the village is a remnant of Molough 'Abbey': remains of the church and traces of the conventual buildings. A nunnery dedicated to St Brigid was founded there in the 6th c. by the daughters of Cinaed, King of the Déise.

ARDGLASS, Co. Down (Map 2, M3), is a fishing village and small resort 7 m. SE. of Downpatrick. Its importance in medieval times is attested by the remains of five 14th–16th c. fortified merchants' houses: King's, Margaret's, Cowd, Horn (incorporated in 1790 Ardglass Castle, now the Golf Club), and Jordan's, this last restored by the antiquarian F.J. Bigger, who had bought it in 1911.

¾ m. NNE., in Ardtole, are the ruins (Hist. Mon.) of the medieval church of St Nicholas of Myra. A cross-slab from there is preserved at the Catholic church at Chapeltown, 1½ m. NE.

2½ m. WSW. is Killough, a well-laid-out fishing village. Some 2 m. SSW., near St John's Point, St John's Well and remains (Hist. Mon.) of a pre-Romanesque church mark an early monastic site. 5 m. W., in Rathmullan, is a motte-and-bailey.

ARDMORE, Co. Waterford (Map 4, E8), is a pleasant, small seaside resort with a good strand, 14 m. SW. of Dungarvan and 6 m. E. of Youghal.

The 'pre-Patrician' abbot-bishop, St Déaglán (Declan), founded a monastery there, which became one of the principal ecclesiastical centres of the kingdom of the Déise (Decies).

In 1495 the vanished Ardmore Castle was seized by Perkin Warbeck, who left his wife there when he marched on Waterford. In 1642 the castle was taken by Lord Broghill, who hanged 117 of the defenders.

On the hill-slope S. of the village, St Declan's Cathedral, St Declan's House (alias Tomb), and the Round Tower (Nat. Mons.), mark the site of Déaglán's monastery.

The three-period Cathedral, said to have been erected by Máel-Ettrim Ó Duibherathra (d. 1203) before he became bishop, is a nave-and-chancel church. The Romanesque arcading (with figure carvings) of the W. gable is unique in Ireland. The subjects include *The Fall, The Judgment of Solomon,* and *The Adoration of the Magi*. The arch of the early-13th c. chancel has Transitional capitals, etc. In the chancel are two ogham stones; the S. stone, which was found used as a building stone in St Declan's Tomb, has two inscriptions. The basin and base of an octagonal, 15th c. font from the cathedral are preserved in the nearby Protestant church.

St Declan's House (modern in parts), which is said to contain the saint's grave, is an important 'station' of the annual pilgrimage (24 July). St Declan's Grave, a stone-lined pit in the floor, was covered by a flagstone which, like the filling of the grave, has vanished as a result of centuries of relic-collecting.

The beautiful Round Tower (95 ft 4 in.) is perhaps the finest, and latest, in Ireland. Five of the corbels have grotesque carvings.

On the lawn of the local Doctor's house is Cloch Daha, the base of a stone cross which formerly stood by the roadside opposite the Protestant church.

At the S. end of the strand is St Declan's Stone, a conglomerate erratic which, the tale goes, carried the saint's bell and vestments across the waves from Menevia in Wales and, by coming ashore at Ardmore, indicated Declan's place of resurrection. To crawl under the stone, a feat impossible to those in a state of sin, is held to cure rheumatism.

½ m. SE. of the village is a fragment of Dysert Church, successor of the *desertulum* ('little hermitage') mentioned in Déaglán's *Life*. Nearby is St Declan's Well, repaired in 1798. The remains here include a rudely built stone chair, two rude stone crucifixes, and a shallow tank in which pilgrims used to bathe their limbs.

ARDPATRICK, Co. Limerick (Map 4, A4), a hamlet on the Kilmallock (5½ m.)–Fermoy (18¾ m.) road, 3 m. SW. of Kilfinnane, is situated at the foot of the Ballyhoura Mountains which are associated with legends of Fionn MacCumhail and his son Oisín (the Fingal and Ossian of Macpherson's famous 18th c. literary forgeries). St Patrick is said to have founded a church there, whose monastic successor is represented by the stump of a Round Tower, remnants of a contemporary church with *antae* and a plain, Romanesque S. door (with Gothic insertion), etc. This monastery was the seat of 'Patrick's *maor*' for Munster, whose function was to collect Munster contributions to Armagh; the O Langans were hereditary coarbs. On 1 April 1129, Ceallach, reformer and 1st Archbishop of Armagh, died there (he was buried at Lismore). Nearby are Rian Bó Phádraig (the 'Slug of St Patrick's Cow's Horn'), an ancient, entrenched roadway; also remains of an ancient field system.

2 m. SE., in Glenosheen (Gleann Oisín), is the demesne of Castle Oliver. Nothing remains of 18th c. Castle Oliver, birthplace of Lola Montez (Marie Gilbert, 1818–61), who danced her way into the lunatic affections of Ludwig I of Bavaria, got control of the country, and provoked the revolution of 1848.

2 m. W., at Mount Russel, is Oscar's Bed, a wedge-tomb of unusual construction.

ARDRAHAN, Co. Galway (Map 6, H3), is a hamlet on the main Galway (17 m.)–Limerick (44 m.) road, 8 m. N. of Gort. The surrounding countryside is rich in ancient remains of all periods. On an earthwork (*bretesche*) beside the village stand the fragmentary remains (Nat. Mon.) of a square-keep castle of *c.* 1250, one of the fortresses of the Anglo-Norman invaders of Connacht. The nearby churchyard occupies an early monastic site with the stump of a Round Tower (outside the W. wall of the graveyard) and fragments of a medieval church.

3 m. ENE. are the remains of Isertkelly (Díseart Cheallaigh) church; about 600 yds SE. of the church, in Castlepark, is the 16th c. tower (Nat. Mon.) of a Mac Hubert Burke castle; noteworthy interior details.

1¼ m. S is Laban. The nondescript parish church has its place in the story of 20th c. Irish church art. When Edward Martyn of Tullira (*below*) wished to commission family windows for the church, he discovered that Continental and English factories had a monopoly of the 'art' of the resurgent Catholic Church in Ireland. For Martyn it was self-evident that art is the function of artists, and that 'the artists of Ireland should decorate the churches'. Accordingly, he commissioned the English artist Christopher Whall, a disciple of William Morris, to do windows for Laban and for LOUGHREA Cathedral, stipulating that the 'actual work' on the Loughrea windows should be done in Ireland. Whall sent A.E. Child over to Dublin to execute the Loughrea windows. Martyn's zeal helped to have Child appointed (1903) teacher of stained glass in the Dublin Metropolitan School of Art, and stimulated Sarah Purser to found the famous Túr Gloine (Tower of Glass) studio (*see p. 162*). The Laban windows in question are five single lights: *St Anna* (?), *St Robertus, Naomh Peadar* (the poorest; reset when the church was reconstructed in 1965), *Naomh Eilis and Naomh Andrís*; the first two are undated and may really be by Selwyn Image (1849–1930), the others are 1910–12. The altar baldachino looks like a William Scott design, its capitals and bases like the work of Michael Shortall (*see pp. 240 and 284*).

1¼ m. SE. is Tullira Castle (appointment to view necessary), home of Edward Martyn (1859–1923; *see also p. 229*), playwright, poet, author, and admirable patron of the arts, who figures prominently in the lives and writings of his contemporaries, W. B. Yeats, Lady Gregory, George Moore, *et al* (e.g. George Moore's *Hail and Farewell*). The house, incorporating a 16th c. tower-house, was rebuilt in a 'Tudor' style at a time (1882) when Martyn was very much under the influence of William Morris.

1¾ m. SW., in Drumharsna, is Seán Ballach's Castle (Nat. Mon.); it served as a British outpost (1920–1). 4½ m. SSW. (via Laban) is the tower of Lydican Castle (Nat. Mon.).

ARKLOW, Co. Wicklow (Map 3, L8), is a fishing port and popular seaside resort on the estuary of the Avoca (properly the Avonmore), 16 m. S. of Wicklow and 11 m. NE. of Gorey. The town has long been noted for the building of small wooden ships and boats, including the Arklow 'nobbies' and the naval training vessel *Asgard*. In more recent times it has developed a flourishing pottery.

In Viking times the Norse had a settlement at Arklow.

In 1185–9 Prince John granted the town, castle, and manor of Arklow to William Marshal and Theobald fitz Walter, ancestor of the Butlers. The town was burned by Edward Bruce in 1315. By the beginning of the 16th c. the towns of Arklow and Wicklow were the only parts of E. Wicklow remaining in English hands. In 1641 the castle was taken by Confederate Catholics, who held it until 1649, when they burned it down on the approach of Cromwell. On 9 June 1798, the Wexford Insurgents, incompetently, if bravely, led by Fr Michael Murphy, made a reckless assault on the town in their effort to link up with the United Irishmen of Dublin. Fr Murphy was killed at the head of his men, who were dispersed with heavy loss. It was the decisive battle of the Rising.

The Catholic church is by Patrick Byrne (1783–1864). In a field adjoining the parish priest's house are remains of a Dominican friary founded in 1264 by Thomas fitz Walter. Of the 13th c. Butler castle only fragments of the curtain and of one corner tower survive. The only modern building of note is the large, English-looking, Protestant church (1900) by Sir Arthur Blomfield; it has a three-light window (*Ascension*, 1922) by Harry Clarke. In front of the Catholic parish church is a 1798 memorial. There is a small Maritime Museum in the town.

2 m. NE. is Ennereilly. The Protestant church has a three-light window (*The Ascension* or *Ecce Homo*) and an abstract window with slab-glass by Harry Clarke (1924).

2¼ m. NW., on the N. bank of the Avoca, are Shelton Abbey and its beautiful demesne (noted for rhododendrons), formerly seat of the Earls of Wicklow, now an open prison. The Tudor-style house is by Sir Richard Morrison (1767–1849) and his son, William Vitruvius Morrison (1794–1838). A chemical factory has recently been erected in the demesne by Nitrigín Éireann, which has played havoc with the fine woods.

6 m. NW. is Woodenbridge. Nearby the Avoca and Aughrim (Gold Mine) rivers unite in a beautiful 'meeting of the waters' beneath the wooded heights of Kilcarra and Ballyarthur. To the SW. rises Croghan, alias Croghan Kinsella (1,995 ft), whose streams have yielded placer gold from time to time. Some gold mining was carried out there round the turn of the 18th c.

ARLES, Co. Laois (Map 3, G7), is a village on the Carlow (6 m.)–Stradbally (10 m.) road.

The Grace family, descended from Raymond le Gros who accompanied Strongbow to Ireland, has a curious mausoleum there.

ARMAGH, Co. Armagh (Map 2, G3), primatial city of Ireland, is an important road junction on the Belfast (40 m.)–Enniskillen (50 m.) and Dundalk (28 m.)–Derry (73 m.) roads.

The name of this historic town, Árd Macha ('Macha's Height'), derives from the goddess Macha, but its enduring fame rests on its choice by St Patrick to be the site of his principal church (445?). Bishop Cormac (d. 497) made the church of Armagh monastic, and for some centuries thereafter the offices of bishop and abbot were united in the same person, with the episcopal functions being, as elsewhere in Ireland, subordinate to the abbatial. From at least the 8th c. onwards the bishop-abbots of Armagh, as the heirs of Patrick, claimed primatial authority over the whole Irish Church. Armagh suffered from Viking raids and during these disturbed centuries the abbatial office separated from the episcopal, falling in 957 into the hereditary possession of the Sinaich family. When Cellach ('Celsus') Ua Sinaich succeeded to the abbacy in 1105 he was a layman, but promptly took holy orders. On the death of the bishop in the following year, he had himself consecrated in his stead, thereby re-uniting the episcopal and abbatial offices. As his successor he nominated the celebrated St Malachy Ua Morgair, who broke the Ua Sinaich family hold on Armagh. His successor, Gilla-meic-Liag ('Gelasius'), received at the Synod of Kells (1152) his pall as first Archbishop of Armagh and Primate of All Ireland from the papal legate Cardinal Paparo.

Armagh had a monastic school from an early date, and played its part in the post-Viking renaissance, so that in 1162 a national synod decreed that no-one not an alumnus of Armagh might be a master of studies in any Irish monastic school.

From the 14th c. on, the English Crown contrived the appointment of archbishops only of non-Gaelic stock. Such archbishops could only exercise restricted jurisdiction outside the English Pale, and therefore made TERMONFECKIN their normal place of residence. It was not until the 16th c. campaigns against the O Neills of Tír Eóghain that Armagh came under effective English control, so that few relics of either the ancient or medieval ecclesiastical capital now remain, and the most important of these are elsewhere. The *Book of Armagh* (*see p. 261*) is in the library of Trinity College, Dublin, the Bell of St Patrick's Will and its superb shrine in the National Museum in Dublin, and the *Gospels of Máel-Brigte Úa Máel-Úanaigh* (1138) in the British Library, London.

St Patrick's Protestant Cathedral occupies the site of St Patrick's principal church, which had been erected inside a bivallate hill-fort. The cathedral, though its walls have a much mutilated and altered medieval core, is the work of the English architect L.N. Cottingham, who between 1834 and 1837 restored the fabric for Archbishop Lord John George Beresford.

Inside the cathedral are monuments to Sir Thomas Molyneux (1661–1733) by Roubiliac, to Dean Drelincourt (d. 1722) by Rysbrack, to Archbishop Stuart (d. 1822) by Sir Francis Chantrey, and to Archbishop Robinson (Lord Rokeby, d. 1749) by Nollekens; also 17th c. monuments of the Caulfeilds of CHARLEMONT. At the W. end of the N. aisle are the shaft and broken head of a High Cross (in fact, fragments of two separate High Crosses placed one on top of the other), which formerly stood in Market St to the E. of the cathedral. (It is said to have been brought to Armagh from Raphoe in 1441.) A slab on the W. wall of the N. transept records the burial of King Brian Boru, whose body was brought to Armagh after the Battle of Clontarf in 1014. In the churchyard are fragments of a stone cross which was at one time known as St Patrick's Chair. Medieval Armagh had many stone crosses – at least six in 1166.

NW. of the cathedral is the Public Library (1771) with its valuable collection of manuscripts and books. Founded by

Archbishop Robinson, the original building by Thomas Cooley – a librarian's residence and a long hall with a gallery – was completed in 1771, with the W. staircase entrance being added in 1848.

SE. of the cathedral off Friary Road is the entrance to the former Archbishop's Palace, now the offices of Armagh District Council. Just inside the gate are the remains (Nat. Mon.) of a Franciscan friary founded in 1264 by Archbishop O Scannail. The first buildings are attributed to a Mac Donnell leader of the galloglas of O Neill of Tír Eóghain. The Palace was designed about 1770 for Archbishop Robinson by Thomas Cooley; Francis Johnston (1761–1829), Armagh's distinguished architect son, added the third storey and built the chapel. This is an excellent little Classical temple, the sensitive interior being typically Johnston. An obelisk in the demesne commemorates Primate Robinson's friendship with the Duke of Northumberland.

The former Bank of Ireland, Scotch Street, was designed by Francis Johnston (1812); it occupied the legendary site of Tempall na Fearta, St Patrick's first church, and, according to some, his burial place. To the E. is the Mall, an early-19th c. promenade with, at its N. end, the Classical County Courthouse (1809) also by Johnston, and, at the south end, the former Prison (1780). On the E. side there is a good late Georgian terrace by Johnston's nephew, Mulvany, and Armagh County Museum incorporating a Classical school house of 1833.

The NE. corner of the Mall opens on College Hill, called after the Royal School founded by James I in 1608. In 1774 the school was removed from Abbey St to its present site. Across the road is Armagh Observatory, founded in 1793 by Primate Robinson. The original buildings with their telescope dome were designed by Francis Johnston; the Planetarium, opened in 1968, provides regular exhibitions on astronomy and space travel with the most modern computer facilities.

St Patrick's Catholic Cathedral was begun in 1840, and completed only in 1873. The original architect, T.J. Duff of Newry (*see pp. 168 and 259*), had designed a perpendicular church with a central tower as well as two W. ones. The resumed work was entrusted to J.J. McCarthy, who gave us the existing decorated building with its twin W. towers housing a carillon of 39 bells. The lavish interior decorations and appointments (designed by J.J. McCarthy, 1887–1904) were entrusted to Italian artists, but in recent times the sanctuary has been reorganized to conform to modern liturgical requirements, and the large crucifix (1984) is by Imogen Stuart.

2¼ m. N., at Allistragh, is the Yellow Ford, scene of Hugh O Neill's victory over Marshal Sir Henry Bagenal in 1598 (*see p. 78*).

6 m. NE. is Richhill Castle, an interesting gabled house of 1655–96. The superb wrought-iron entrance gates of about 1745, thought to be the work of the Thornberry Brothers of Richhill, were removed to Government House, HILLSBOROUGH in 1936.

1¼ m. SW., by the River Callan in Tullymore, is Niall's Mound, reputedly a cenotaph marking the place where King Niall Caille was drowned in 846.

2 m. W., in Navan (An Eamhain), is Navan Fort (Nat. Mon.), an 18-acre hill-fort enclosed by a bank (largely defaced) set (as at Tara and Knockaulin, Kilcullen) outside its ditch, and encroached by a stone quarry. On the summit of the enclosure is a univallate tumulus (excavated 1963–71), the evidence from which revealed a residential site subsequently used for ceremonial purposes. These remains are all that survive of the Isamnion of Ptolemy's *Geography,* the Emhain Macha of Irish mythology and heroic literature, and the seat of the kings of the ancient 'Fifth' of the Ulaid destroyed by the 5th c. (?) expansion of the Uí Neill. Thereafter Ulster was confined to Cos Antrim and Down. In the celebrated *Ulster Cycle* of heroic tales, the King of Emhain is the mythological Conchobar mac Nesa, who dwells and feasts here with his heroes, Cú Chulainu, Cú-Roí, and the rest.

ARMOY, Co. Antrim (Map 1, I3), is a village 6½ m. S. of Ballycastle, 1 m. W. of the main road to Belfast (49 m.). Close to the Protestant church is the stump of a Round Tower (in State care), all that survives of a monastery which succeeded a church attributed to St Patrick.

5 m. E., in Drumaqueran, is a rare early cross on which is carved a form of the chi-rho.

2 m. ENE. are two ancient stone crosses.

ARVAGH, Co. Cavan (Map 2, C6), is a small village on the Cavan (8 m.)–Longford (17 m.) road, 2 m. N. of pretty Lough Gowna.

2½ m. NE., near the foot of Bruse Hill (856 ft), with its fine panoramas, is Coranea Mass Rock, a relic of Penal times.

3½ m. NW. is Drumhart court-tomb.

ASHBOURNE, Co. Meath (Map 3, J2), is a village on the Dublin (13 m.)–Slane (16 m.) road.

In 1916 a sharp skirmish took place 1 m. N. between a strong party of Royal Irish Constabulary and local insurgents led by Thomas Ashe, the village schoolmaster (1959 memorial by Peter Grant). The following year Ashe died in Mountjoy Prison, Dublin, as a result of forced feeding when on hunger strike.

> But down the pale roads of Ashbourne
> Are heard the voices of the free
>
> Francis Ledwidge

1¼ m. S. is an 1880 obelisk (interesting panels) to the memory of Charles Brindley of Stafford, for 35 years (1843–78) Huntsman of the Ward Hounds. The Huntsman's House is noteworthy.

It is from Ashbourne that the Gibson barons take their title. William, the 2nd baron (d. 1947), always wore a saffron kilt – in the fond belief that it was Ireland's national costume – and insisted on speaking Irish in the House of Lords.

ASHFORD, Co. Wicklow (Map 3, L6), is a small village beautifully situated by the River Vartry on the Newtown Mount Kennedy (8 m.)–Wicklow (4 m.) road. Beside the village is Mount Usher, whose noted gardens are open to the public in spring and summer.

2½ m. NNE., in Courtfoyle, is a medieval square fortification with a water-ditch and traces of a masonry revetment. It was an O Byrne stronghold in the 16th–17th c.

3 m. SW. is Glenealy State Forest.

2 m. NW. is the beautiful Devil's Glen, a rugged 2 m. defile where the Vartry tumbles down a fine fall. The glen was one of Joseph Holt's retreats after 1798.

1½ m. NNW. is classical Ballycurry House (1805) by Francis Johnston, owned by Charles Tottenham.

ASKEATON, Co. Limerick (Map 6, G8), is a small market town on the Limerick (16 m.)–Tarbert (19¼ m.) road. After the Anglo-Norman invasion the place was among those granted to Hamo de Valognes, who built a castle *c.* 1197/9. Early in the 14th c. the manor was acquired by the Earls of Desmond, whose great castle, on an island (the ancient Inis Geibthine) in the River Deel, adjoins the bridge. The remains (Nat. Mon.) comprise two courts or wards. The upper ward is on a limestone outcrop scarped into a sort of motte in the 13th c.; in it are a lofty, narrow tower and remains of a tall 16th c. house. On the W. side of the lower ward are ruins of a splendid 15th c. Great Hall raised on the remnants of an older one by the 7th (?) Earl of Desmond; the S. end has remains of a chapel. In 1579 Malby, the English Governor of Connacht, failed to dislodge Garret, 15th (rebel) Earl of Desmond, but Pelham succeeded in gaining the castle for the English the following year. It fell to the Confederate Catholics in 1642, and ten years later to the Cromwellians, who dismantled it.

On the E. bank of the river are remains of the medieval parish church of St Mary and of Rock Abbey (Nat. Mon.). The 'abbey' was a Franciscan friary founded before 1400, probably by Gearóid *file*, 4th Earl of Desmond, and restored in the 15th c. by James, the 6th earl. The original friary consisted of a rectangular church and the usual buildings round a cloister (on the S. side). Additions included a sacristy, aisled N. transept, belfry (removed), and a large refectory to the S. of the cloister. The cloister is a beautiful example of the friary type; at the NE. angle (N. ambulatory) is a carving of St Francis, showing the stigmata. In the chancel are fine sedilia, 15th c. tombs, and the figure of a bishop (16th c.).

The remains (fragments of belfry and chancel) of St Mary's Augustinian priory are close to the Protestant parish church. Aubrey de Vere (*see below*) is buried in the churchyard.

5 m. SE. is Currah Chase, ancestral home of the de Vere family, and now part of a forest park. The fine late-18th c. house was destroyed by fire in 1941. It was the birthplace of Aubrey de Vere (1814–1902), poet.

ATHBOY, Co. Meath (Map 3, G1), is a market village on the Trim (8 m.)–Oldcastle (16 m.) road.

In the Middle Ages Athboy was a small walled town, a strongpoint of the English Pale. In 1643 it was captured by Eóghan Rúa O Neill.

The Protestant parish church stands on part of the site of a Carmelite friary, whose 15th c. W. tower it incorporates. At the church door, exposed to the elements, is an early-16th c. tomb with effigies of an armoured knight and his wife; the panels include Christ as Judge. Nearby are fragments of the town wall.

3 m. NE., on the Navan road, are the ruined early-15th c. castle and manorial church (Nat. Mon.) of Rathmore. The church, which was dedicated to St Laurence, was built *c.* 1420–40 by Sir Thomas Plunkett or by the father of his wife, Mary Cruise. It is a nave-and-chancel structure with a small bell-tower at the SW. angle, a three-storey sacristy-cum-priest's house, and a N. porch. The E. window is good. Parts of the base of the high altar survive; the figures include one of St Laurence the Deacon, and the coats of arms include those of Plunkett, Fleming, Bellew, Bermingham, and Cusack. In the sacristy is the mensa of an early-16th c. double tomb with the effigies, in high relief, of an armoured knight and his lady. These probably represent Sir Thomas Plunkett (d. 1471) and Mary Cruise. Near the N. porch is a medieval labyrinth stone and the figured shaft of a 15th c. font: *Baptism of Christ, Ecce Homo, St Peter, St Paul, St Brigid.* The porch was erected in 1519 by Sir Christopher Plunkett and Katherine Preston, as was the sculptured cross of which a portion (Nat. Mon.) may be seen to the N. of the church. The subjects on the latter represent SS Patrick, Laurence, and Brigid.

1 m. E. is the Hill of Ward, formerly called Tlachtga and the meeting place of an *aonach*, or great public assembly, which met at Samhain (31 October). The site of the assembly is presumably marked by the much disturbed multivallate ring-work (Nat. Mon.). In 1168 High King Rory O Conor presided over a national synod of kings and prelates which enacted 'good decrees regarding veneration for churches and clerics and for the good government of the tribes and túatha'; 13,000 horsemen are said to have thronged the roads leading to the hill on that occasion.

1½ m. SSE. is Ballyfallon, birthplace of Father Eugene O Growney (1863–99), author of a celebrated Irish primer. He had learned his Irish from local native speakers, and is commemorated by a statue (1956) in front of the Catholic church in Athboy.

ATHENRY, Co. Galway (Map 6, H2), is a small market town on the N. road from Ballinasloe (25 m.) to Galway (15 m.), 11 m. NW. of Loughrea. It is the best centre for hunting in the County Galway Hunt ('Galway Blazers') area. (The Blazers' kennels are at Craughwell, 5 m. S.)

The town was founded by Meiler de Bermingham, to whom William de Burgo, Anglo-Norman conqueror of much of Connacht, granted the place about 1235. Meiler also built the first castle and founded the Dominican friary. On 10 August 1316, a great battle was fought outside the town between young King Felim O Conor, ally of Edward Bruce, and the Anglo-Normans of Connacht and Meath, led by William Liath de Burgo and Richard de Bermingham. The Irish were routed in the end, and the victors walled the town out of the profits of the arms and armour taken from the fallen. In 1596 the town was stormed and sacked by Red Hugh II O Donnell.

Considerable lengths of the town wall survive, also five of its flanking towers, but only one of its gates.

At the NE. corner of the old town stands the imposing de Bermingham castle (Nat. Mon.). The great three-storey keep of *c.* 1235–7 is well preserved. The ground floor is vaulted on three square pillars; the floor above, the hall or principal apartment of the castle, was entered by a handsome Early Gothic doorway which was approached by an outside flight of steps; the roof-gables are medieval additions.

Nearby to the S. are the once fine, but now much disfigured, ruins (Nat. Mon.) of the church of the Dominican friary of SS

The Bermingham castle in Athenry, Co. Galway.

Peter and Paul, founded in 1241 by Meiler de Bermingham, who made it the family place of burial. Though an Anglo-Norman foundation, it owed much to native Irish patronage: the refectory was built by Felim O Conor (d. 1265), son of Cathal Crovderg; the dormitory by Eóghan O Heyne; the chapter-house by Conor O Kelly. In the early-14th c. the choir was extended and the N. aisle and transept added. A disastrous fire of 1423 entailed large-scale rebuilding (notice the inferior character of the alterations to the aisle and transept arcades and of the 16th c. E. window inserted inside the remains of its nobler predecessor). Being in the land of the Irish, the friary was specifically exempted from Henry VIII's dissolution of the monasteries. In 1574, however, it was dissolved and granted to the town. That very year, town and friary were sacked by Clanricard's sons. Early in the 17th c. the friars returned, and remained in possession until the Cromwellian victory of 1652. About 1750 the conventual buildings were demolished to make way for a military barracks, whose occupants wrecked the funerary and other monuments.

The Protestant parish church, SW. of the castle, occupies the site of the chancel of St Mary's Church founded in the 13th c. Fragments of the medieval nave and transepts survive, while two nave columns serve as churchyard gateposts. Outside the gateway, on a modern stepped pedestal, is the head of a 15th c. cross with *Crucifixion* and *Virgin and Child*. Nearby, in Nicolroe St, is the ruined N. gate of the medieval town.

6 m. SE., Kiltullagh parish church has notable Stations of the Cross by Evie Hone.

ATHLEAGUE, Co. Roscommon (Map 7, L8), is a village 5 m. SW. of Roscommon on the Ballygar (5 m.) road to Galway. There are ruins of a 13th c. castle, and a trench across the middle of this 'Fort of the Earls' is evidence of a partition between rival claimants who had failed to settle the issue with the sword.

2 m. NW., beside the avenue in derelict Castlestrange demesne, is the Castlestrange Stone (Nat. Mon.), a granite boulder covered with incised Iron Age spiral patterns.

ATHLONE, Co. Westmeath (Map 3, B3), is a thriving commercial, industrial and communications centre, on the main Dublin (78 m.)–Galway (56 m.) road. A strong castle commands the river-crossing from the W. bank. The town has long been an important garrison post and, because of its strategic position, has figured prominently in Irish wars. In 1129, Turloch Mór O Conor, King of Connacht and High-King of Ireland, 'the Augustus of the west of Europe', built a fort to protect the bridge he had constructed across the river to provide ready access to Meath. Bridge and fort were repeatedly destroyed and replaced by rival interests during the following 30 years. The Anglo-Norman invaders had seized the vital crossing by 1199 when their castle was plundered and burned by Cathal Crovderg O Conor. In 1210, Bishop John de Gray, the English Justiciar, built a stone castle to guard the bridgehead into Connacht. This is probably the decagonal *donjon* still standing, which now houses a small local museum. The curtain walls and drum-shaped towers overlooking the river date from the late-13th c. Following the construction of a new bridge, 1566–7, the castle became the headquarters of the newly established English Presidency of Connacht, 1569–72. During the Eleven Years War (1641–52), it changed hands several times, finally surrendering to the Cromwellian Sir Charles Coote II in 1650. In 1690, the town was attacked by 10,000 Williamites. The following year it was severely damaged by a Williamite bombardment. Williamite preparations for an attack across the bridge were thwarted by the bravery of a detachment led by Sergeant Custume (who has given his name to the nearby military barracks). Athlone finally fell when the Jacobites defending the Connacht town were surprised by a courageous Williamite assault across a ford below the bridge. Ginkel, the Dutch general who commanded the Williamite army, was made Earl of Athlone for his success. Subsequently, the castle continued to be used by the English army, and shortly after 1800, when a Napoleonic invasion was feared, it was heavily remodelled to serve as one of the strongpoints guarding the River Shannon, along with those at SHANNONBRIDGE and BANAGHER.

The earliest reference to a town wall is in 1251, but the portion which survives, with its bastions, at Railway View dates from the 17th c. The military barracks, some of which dates from 1697, consists in the main of interesting 18th and 19th c. buildings. John Wesley, who visited Athlone on many occasions, preached in the barrack riding school. The handsome Classical Watergate on Grace Rd was erected in 1852.

The former existence of an early monastery in Athlone is suggested by some cross-slabs in the Castle Museum. In the Middle Ages there were religious houses of Cluniac monks and Franciscan friars; nothing remains of their buildings.

After the Dissolution, the Franciscan friars found a place of refuge in Coillan Inbhair (Villenure) near Glassan where, in 1630, Brother Michael O Clery, one of the famed Four Masters, completed his *Succession of the Kings of Ireland* and his *Naomhshenchas Érenn*. By 1750, the friars were back in permanent residence in the town. The unfortunate parish church of SS Peter and Paul, W. of the river, is Italianate in inspiration (by Ralph Byrne, 1937), with a stained glass window by A.E. Child (*Sacrifice*, 1936). St Mary's Protestant church (1826) replaces an earlier structure of 1622, of which the taller of the two towers is now the only remnant. The interior of the church contains some interesting monuments, the earliest being a fragment of the tomb of Sir Mathew de Renzi (d. 1634), a native of Cologne, who 'gave a great perfection to this nation by composing a grammar dictionary and chronicle in the Irish tongue.'

The lock, dock and town bridge, all constructed by the Shannon Navigation Commissioners, are an impressive monument to the durability and ingenuity of Victorian engineering. The same may be said of the railway bridge (by G.W. Hemans, 1850), and the recently renovated Southern Station.

Among the natives of Athlone who have achieved celebrity were Richard Rothwell (1800–68), the painter; T.P. O Connor

White's Castle in Athy, Co. Kildare.

('Tay-Pay', 1848–1929), journalist and Nationalist M.P.; and John, Count McCormack (1884–1945), the noted tenor, who was born in The Bawn, off Mardyke Street. Cartron, in the parish of St Peter's, was the home of Tadhg Ó Neachtain, Gaelic poet (d. 1729).

5 m. NE., near Glassan, are the ruins of Waterstown House, by Richard Cassels; an octagonal, spired dovecot raised on arches survives.

3 m. ENE., on the hill N. of Bealin post office, is a High Cross (Nat. Mon.) said to have come from an ancient well near Twyford House. The carvings consist for the most part of spirals and interlaced zoomorphs, but include a figured panel with a hunting scene. The inscription OROIT AR TUATHGAIL LAS DERNATH IN CHROSSA ('A prayer for Túathgal by whom this cross was made') is thought to date the cross to *c.* 800.

ATHY, Co. Kildare (Map 3, G7), is a market town where the Kilcullen (15 m.)–Castlecomer (17 m.) road – the old highway from Dublin to the South – crosses the Barrow.

Though the ford from which it takes its name was always an important passage, the town is a Norman creation, the first lords of the feudal manor being the de St Michaels. In the late-13th c. the manor, along with that of Woodstock (*below*), passed by marriage to the House of Kildare. In 1420 James 'White', Earl of Desmond and Lieutenant of the King of England, slew 'many of the kin and the terrible army of O More' at the Red Moor of Athy. The partisan sun stood still for three hours to facilitate the slaughter of the Irish. The town fell to the Cromwellians in 1650.

There are some remains (E. end of town) of the 14th c. parish church of St Michael. The Court and Market House (now a fire station) is a good late-18th c. building. The Dominican church (1963–5, by John Thompson and Associates) is of unusual interest: a pentagon with hyperbolic paraboloid roof; statues and high-altar crucifix by Bridget Rynne, high-altar plaque by Breda O Donoghue, and windows and Stations of the Cross designed by George Campbell, R.H.A.; the Stations are rather spoilt by the windows. White's Castle (Nat. Mon.), on the bridge, is a 16th c. replacement of Sir John Talbot's fortification.

½ m. N., on the W. side of the river, are the remains of 15th c. Woodstock Castle, badly damaged by Confederate Catholic besiegers in 1649.

3¾ m. NE., on the Kilcullen road, is the great Moat of Ardscull, 55 ft high; there are remains of Cromwellian fortifications. 1½ m. NNW. is Skerries where, on 26 January 1316, Edward Bruce defeated the army of the English Crown.

4 m. SW. are the ruins of the castle of Ballyadams. At the Tudor plantation of Laois–Uí Fáilghe the manor was leased to John ap Thomas Bowen (Ap Owein). Called Seón an Phíce (John of the Pike) by the Irish, Bowen was notorious for his cruelty. In 1643 Castlehaven, the Royalist general, summoned the castle to surrender under threat of bombardment, but Sir John Bowen, Parliamentarian provost marshal of Leinster and Meath, dissuaded him: 'I will cover that part, or any other your Lordship shoots at, by hanging both my daughters in chairs.' The remains of the castle comprise turreted tower and post-1550 Bowen wings. ¾ m. WSW. are the remains of a nave-and-chancel church which served the Protestant parish until about 1780. In the chancel are: the fragmentary remains of a 1631 altar-tomb of Sir Robert Bowen (d. 1621) and his wife, Allis Harpole (d. 1634) – the weepers represent the children and two daughters-in-law of Sir Robert; also the broken tombstone of Thomas and Walter Hartpoole, 'Brittanes born'. Walter, whose low-relief effigy fills the slab, was Protestant Deãn of Leighlin and died in 1597.

AUBURN, Co. Westmeath (Map 3, C2), properly Lissoy, is a hamlet on the Ballymahon (6 m.)–Athlone (9 m.) road. It is the 'Sweet Auburn' of Goldsmith's *Deserted Village*, for it was here, where his father was rector, that the poet first went to school.

A short distance NE. is The Three Jolly Pigeons, a pub named after the inn in *She Stoops to Conquer*. Although Goldsmith nominally set his works in England, there can be no doubt that he had his boyhood Irish home always in mind: 'If I go to the opera, I sit and sigh for the Lissoy fireside and Johnny Armstrong's 'Last Goodnight' – or if I climb Hampstead Hill, I confess it is fine, but then I had rather be placed on the little mount before Lissoy Gate, and there take in, to me, the most pleasing horizon of nature.'

3 m. NW., at Bethlehem, are the remains of Ireland's first Poor Clares' nunnery. A wooden statue of the Virgin and Child from Bethlehem is still preserved in the Poor Clares' convent in GALWAY.

AUGHER, Co. Tyrone (Map 2, E2), is a small village on the Enniskillen (25 m.)–Dungannon (18 m.) road, about 2 m. NE. of Clogher.

At the W. end of the village is Spur Royal Castle, built by Sir Thomas Ridgeway *c.* 1611 on the site of an O Neill fortress. It is a square Plantation castle with a triangular tower at the middle of each side. Two mock-Tudor wings were added in 1832. Of the original bawn, only the circular SW. tower survives.

5 m. SE., in Altadaven, are St Patrick's Chair and Well, set on an eminence in a picturesque glen. 1 m. SW., on the side of Cullamore, is Cullamore court-tomb. In the same area, in Ballywholan townland, is well-preserved Carnagat dual court-tomb (Hist. Mon.) in a long cairn, while at Carnfadrig, also in Ballywholan, is a long cairn with an unroofed portal-tomb at the E. end and conjoined lateral chambers 12 yds to the W. (Hist. Mon.).

2 m. S., in Ballynagurragh townland, is St Macartin's Catholic church, or 'The Forth' chapel, built on the site of a ringfort. The novelist William Carleton (1794–1869) lived for a time at Springtown, ¾ m. to the SW., where his cottage is marked by a plaque (*see also p. 156*).

2 m. NW, near the summit of Knockmany (770 ft), is Annia's Cove passage-tomb (Hist. Mon.), with a number of decorated stones which feature concentric circles, spirals and zigzags. The grave has recently been given a protective heavy glass roof, and access to it is possible at all times (get key beforehand from Clogher police station).

AUGHNACLOY, Co. Tyrone (Map 2, F2), is a small market town on the Monaghan (12 m.)–Omagh (21 m.) road. St James's Protestant church was built in 1736 by Acheson Moore (spire added in 1796). A stained glass window *Mary of Bethany* (1909) is by Ethel Rhind.

3 m. NE. is Carnteel, a small village with the ruins of a late-16th c. church.

1½ m. W. is Garvey House, in ruins, a great square block built for Nathaniel Montgomery Moore by Francis Johnston. Here, too, is a spa well.

3 m. WNW. is Lismore Bawn, built in 1611 by George Ridgeway. Close by is Favour Royal, a mock-Elizabethan mansion built for the Moutray family in 1825. The datestone of the old house (1670) is incorporated in the new house.

AUGHRIM, Co. Galway (Map 6, K2), is a small village off the main (i.e. S., or Loughrea) road from Ballinasloe (4 m.) to Galway (37 m.). It takes its name from the nearby ridge, scene of the battle of 12 July 1691, which decided the Jacobite-Williamite war and the course of Irish history. The memorial cross erected in the 1960s at the site of the castle had lain incomplete for half a century or more at the edge of a street in Ballinasloe, the promoters having fallen out at the time of the 'Parnell Split'!

After the fall of ATHLONE, St Ruth drew up the Jacobite army on an admirably chosen and prepared position. His lines followed the high ground from the castle, whose fragmentary remains stand beside the road at the N. end of the village, as far S. as the neighbourhood of Tristaun bridge (1¾ m.). The Jacobites stood up well to several assaults, but a series of blunders and mischances, including St Ruth's death at the crisis of the battle, turned expected victory into complete rout.

William J. Mac Nevin (1763–1841), member of the United Irishmen and father of American chemistry, was a native of Ballynahown, in Aughrim parish.

Some historical and archaeological items of local interest are displayed in the village National School.

¾ m. S., on the highest point (338 ft) of Attidermot Hill (Gallows Hill), is Gen. St Ruth's Fort, a small ringfort (Nat. Mon.); 250 yds NE. is the spot where St Ruth was killed.

AUGHRIM, Co. Wicklow (Map 3, K8), is a village on the Rathdrum (9 m.)–Tinahely (8 m.) road. It is a convenient road junction for the explorer of the S. Wicklow mountain region.

B

BAILIEBOROUGH, Co. Cavan (Map 2, F6), is a market town on the Virginia (9 m.)–Carrickmacross (16 m.) road. The parish church has Stations of the Cross by George Collie.

6 m. SW., in Beagh (Glebe), are the remains of the cottage birthplace of Gen. Philip Sheridan (1831–88), Commander of the United States Army and one of the great generals of history.

BALBRIGGAN, Co. Dublin (Map 3, K1), is a small manufacturing town and minor seaside resort on the Dublin (20 m.)–Drogheda (11 m.) road. It was at the estuary of the Delvin River that St Patrick is said to have met and christened his disciple and successor, St Benignus. The Catholic parish church has two two-light windows by Harry Clarke: *Raising of Lazarus* (1921) and *Visitation* (1922).

To the NNW. are the remains of the chapel and outbuildings of Bremore Castle, a Barnewall stronghold. ½ m. N. of the castle, on a low headland by the sea, are the remains of five tumuli (a passage-tomb cemetery?).

2 m. SSW. is Balrothery, where the Protestant church has a bell-tower of *c.* 1500.

6 m. WSW. is The Naul, a hamlet on the S. side of the Delvin. The parish church has a two-light Harry Clarke window: *Sacred Heart, Our Lady* (1926). 1 m. NW., in Fourknocks, Co. Meath, are three tumuli (Nat. Mons.). The largest (Fourknocks I), of layered turves and shingle, covered a cruciform passage-tomb, some of whose passage and chamber stones have typical passage-tomb scribings (including anthropomorphs). In passage and side chambers were the remains, cremated and uncremated, of more than 65 individuals. (Passage and chambers have been skilfully re-roofed by the Office of Public Works.) Fourknocks II had a cremation trench, while Fourknocks III covered a Bronze Age burial.

3 m. NW. is Gormanston, from which the Prestons, Viscounts Gormanston, took their title. Sir Robert Preston, Chief Justice of the Common Pleas in the English colony, purchased the manor in 1363. The Prestons always supported the interests of their ancestral England, but adhered to the Old Faith at the Reformation and, until the advent of O Connell, were usually numbered among the leaders of the oppressed Catholic majority. Thomas Preston, uncle of the 6th viscount and a distinguished soldier in the Spanish service, was appointed general of the Confederate Catholic Army of Leinster in 1642. His failure to co-operate wholeheartedly with Gen. Eóghan Rúa O Neill was responsible for the failure of the Confederate siege of Dublin (held by the royalist Ormonde) in 1646. After various vicissitudes, the Preston properties were given back in 1800 to the 12th viscount, who restored the castle. In 1947 the castle was purchased by the Franciscans, who built (1955–7) the large boarding school by John Thompson. 1¾ m. SW. of the castle is the village of Stamullin, Co. Meath. It takes its name (Techmeic Mellén) from an early monastery founded by Mellén's Son. There are ruins of a medieval nave-and-chancel parish church dedicated to St Patrick. On the S. side of the chancel is the roofless chantry chapel of St Sylvester, founded by the 2nd Viscount Gormanston (d. 1532) with cadaver effigy and Preston double effigy of *c.* 1540; beneath it is the Preston family vault.

BALLA, Co. Mayo (Map 7, G5), is a village on the Castlebar (7 m.)–Claremorris (8 m.) road. A broken Round Tower (Nat. Mon.) and a medieval altar mark the site of a monastery founded in the 7th c. by St Crónán. To the W. of the graveyard are Tobar Mhuire, alias the Blessed Well, and the ruins of a 17th c. shelter for the blind and lame who resorted to the well on Patron Day (15 August).

3 m. S. is Mayo, from which the county takes its name. Now a mere hamlet, it occupies part of the site of a famous early monastery. When the Irish party was defeated at the Synod of Whitby, Bishop Colmán of Lindisfarne withdrew from the English mission to Iona, and thence to Ireland. Disputes having

arisen between the Irish and English brethren who had accompanied him, Colmán transferred the latter to a new monastery at Mayo, thereafter called Mag nEó na Sachsan (Mayo of the English). The monastery, which won the praise of Bede, retained its English character for a considerable time. All that remains today are fragments of ecclesiastical buildings and the trace of a great circular enclosing wall or vallum.

BALLAGHADERREEN, Co. Roscommon (Map 7, J5), is a small market town on the Roscommon (25 m.)–Charlestown (10 m.) road. St Nathy's Cathedral (Catholic diocese of Achonry) is a mediocre Gothic Revival structure. Ballaghaderreen was the home of James Dillon (d. 1987), minister and orator.

1 m. W. are the remains of Castlemore Castle and, opposite, a small early monastic site. – 4 m. W. is Kilmovee. ½ m. NE. are the ruins of Kilmovee parish church, where a Gothic chancel arch was inserted under a Romanesque one. ½ m. S. of the village is Kilmovee cashel (Nat. Mon.).

4 m. SW. at Lisacul Catholic church is a late *Crucifixion*.

BALLINA, Co. Mayo (Map 7, G3), is a busy market town and small seaport on the estuary of the Moy (Killala Bay), 37 m. SW. of Sligo, 10 m. N. of Foxford, and 39 m. ESE. of Belmullet. The largest town in the county, it is also the cathedral town of the Catholic diocese of Killala. At Ardnaree, on the Co. Sligo bank of the river, are the ruins of an Augustinian friary founded by the O Dowds *c.* 1375 (?).

¾ m. SW., by the roadside beyond Cockle St, is Cloghogle, remnant of a megalithic tomb (Nat. Mon.).

4 m. N. via a minor road (5½ m. via the main Killala road) are the ruins of Rosserk 'Abbey' (Nat. Mon.), the best-preserved Franciscan Tertiary friary in Ireland. Founded before 1441 by one of the Joyces, it was burned in 1590 by the English Governor of Connacht, Sir Richard Bingham. The remains comprise a typical friary church (with two-chapel S. transept; note the miniature round tower carved on the sedilia) and conventual buildings; the cloister garth has no ambulatories.

4 m. SE., on the W. shore of Ballymore Lough, are the remnants of little Kildermot church (Nat. Mon.), of *c.* 1200.

4¾ m. WNW. are the ruins of the Mac William (Burke) castle of Rappa.

1 m. NNW. is the ancient site of Kilmoremoy, where St Patrick's disciple, Olcán, founded a church. There are remains of an ancient church and of an enclosing rampart. Near the centre of the enclosure is the Liag, a cross-inscribed rock-surface.

BALLINAFAD, Co. Sligo (Map 7, K4), is a village on the Boyle (6 m.)–Sligo (20 m.) road.

The small four-towered Castle of the Curlieus (Nat. Mon.) was built about 1610 by Captain St John Barbe. It was captured in 1642 by the insurgent Irish. The medieval Red Earl's Rd passes to the E. of the castle.

2 m. N., by the shore of Lough Arrow, are Hollybrook House and demesne. Hollybrook is the setting of the romantic adventures of Carleton's *Willy Reilly and His Fair Colleen Bawn*.

4 m. N. is Castle Baldwin (Nat. Mon.), a small, L-shaped, 17th c. fortified house. From Castlebaldwin crossroads, a road leads 4 m. W. and S. to the Carrowkeel passage-tomb cemetery on the Bricklieve Mts (highest point 1,057 ft). There are an ancient village site, and 14 chambered cairns. The chamber-tombs constitute one of the most important passage-tomb cemeteries in Ireland; some of the tombs may be entered, but all are in a dangerous condition. One of the tombs, Cairn E, is of exceptional interest, in that it combines the long cairn and ritual forecourt of the court-tomb with a cruciform passage grave. The burials in the tombs were mostly cremated remains. The village site is on the NE. spur of the mountain, in Mullaghfarna; if the stone footings of about 70 circular huts, 20–42 ft in diameter, were the dwellings of the cairn builders, they would represent the only known village of their period in Ireland.

BALLINAGH, alias **BELLINAGH**, Co. Cavan (Map 2, D6), is a village on the Cavan (5 m.)–Granard (12 m.) road.

4½ m. E., in Carrickboy, the foundations of a church and an early cross-slab mark the site of an early monastery and of the medieval parish church of Denn. At the Protestant church in Denn Glebe (1 m. NE.) is the shaft of a medieval cross with interlacing, etc.

4½ m. ESE. (1½ m. S. of Denn) the Worm Ditch, a bank and ditch, marks a mile-long quarter-circle on the W. and S. slopes of Ardkillmore hill.

BALLINAKILL, Co. Laois (Map 3, E8), is a village on the Abbeyleix (3½ m.)–Ballyragget (7 m.) road.

The important castle there (slight remains) was taken by the Confederate Catholic general Thomas Preston (*see p. 52*) in 1646, and later severely battered by Fairfax's Cromwellians.

The Market House was built for Lord Stanhope, a former proprietor.

1 m. NNE. is Heywood House (1773; rebuilt after a fire, 1950). Formerly home of the Trenches, it is now a Salesian missionary college. The Italianate sunken garden is by Sir Edward Lutyens. By the avenue is a 19th c. folly with windows from the Dominican friary at AGHABOE and part of a 1522 tomb.

BALLINAMORE, Co. Leitrim (Map 2, B5), is a village on the Killeshandra (13 m.)–Drumshanbo (15 m.) road. A collection of folk and historical items is displayed in the County Library.

¼ m. N., in Fenaghbeg, are a portal-tomb, the remains of three simple passage-tombs, and a pillarstone. Longstones townland, to the NE., takes its name from a series of pillarstones.

3 m. SW. is Fenagh, site of an early monastery of St Caillín's, patron of the O Rourkes of Breany. In 1516 Tadhg O Roddy had the *Book of Fenagh* (now in the Royal Irish Academy) copied out of 'an old book of Caillín's'. It contains a catalogue of the lands, privileges, etc., of the monastery, as well as a collection of wonders, alleged to have been performed by the saint. The O Roddys were hereditary coarbs and also hereditary custodians of St Caillín's Bell (12th/13th c.), which is now preserved in Armagh Library. The remains at Fenagh comprise two churches (Nat. Mons.). One is an aisleless, rectangular structure with a good 14th/15th c. E. window and sculptured gable-brackets. The W. end is barrel-vaulted, and presumably had living-quarters above. The second church, 150 yds NE., is also barrel

vaulted at the W. end and has a curious 'corridor' along the S. side. $\frac{1}{4}$ m. SW. of Fenagh, to the W. of the road, in Commons, is Giants Graves, a two-court cairn.

BALLINAMUCK, Co. Longford (Map 2, B7), is a village $\frac{3}{4}$ m. NE. of the Arvagh (8 m.)–Newtown Forbes (9 m.) road.

Here took place the last encounter of the daring French invasion of 1798. Gen. Humbert, having marched the 160 m. from Castlebar with his small force of French troops and untrained insurgents, was forced to accept battle here with superior British forces under Lord Cornwallis. The French surrendered after a brief engagement, but the Irish fought with desperate bravery. The battle is commemorated by a statue near the village. 3 m. N., in Tubberpatrick graveyard, are memorials to Gunner Magee and his cousins, who manned Humbert's two guns, and to Gen. Blake, executed after the battle.

BALLINASLOE, Co. Galway (Map 6, K1), at the crossing of the River Suck, on the Athlone (15 m.)–Galway (40 m.) road, is the principal market town of E. Galway. Its great October Fair is still the largest livestock fair in Ireland. In the days of cavalry and horse transport it was also the largest horse fair in Europe.

Though there was previously a small O Kelly settlement in the shadow of the castle (*see below*), the town is essentially an 18th c. creation of the Trench family.

At the E. end of Church St (on the E. side of the Suck) are the remains of Creagh medieval church. The nearby Church of Our Lady of Lourdes has two early single-light porch windows (*Annunciation, Nativity, St Joseph,* etc.) by Patrick Pye and two others, *Noli Me Tangere* and *Gethsemani* (1987), in the nave. Nearby, to the W., is the Mental Hospital for Cos Roscommon and Galway (1838). A short distance W., beside the Suck, a 19th c. dwelling, Ivy Castle, masks the towered bawn of the medieval castle. In 1579 it was made the residence of the English Governor of Connacht, Sir Anthony Brabazon, and in 1651–2 it was held against the Cromwellian Ireton by another Anthony Brabazon, who had espoused the Confederate Catholic cause.

The Catholic parish church of St Michael (1852–8) is by J.J. McCarthy, whose 1846 design was revised by Pugin. The high altar (with *Dead Christ*) is by Albert Power; it has an excellent tabernacle door (*Christ at Emmaus*) in gold, silver, and enamels, by Mia Cranwell. The chancel mural paintings (1921), *SS Brendan and Greallan*, are by Joseph Tierney. The painting (on canvas) of the *Holy Trinity* over the chancel arch was by Harry Clarke, who was awarded an Aonach Tailteann prize. (Having deteriorated, its 'restoration' was later entrusted to a housepainter.) The church has three good windows: one of two lights, *St Rose of Lima* and *St Patrick*, by Harry Clarke (1925); *The Holy Family* and *The Daughter of Jairus* by Patrick Pollen (1958). The church also has Dun Emer Guild vestments, banners, and carpets.

On the W. side of the town is Garbally, formerly seat of the Trenches, Earls of Clancarty, now St Joseph's College. The house (1824) is a late Georgian mansion of local limestone. The school collection of paintings includes works by modern Irish artists. The library has some rare books and manuscripts. The altars in the chapel (former ballroom) are by Albert Power as is the garden statue of St Joseph.

4 m. SSE., via the Portumna road, in Clontuskert, are the interesting remains of St Mary's Priory (Nat. Mon.), of the Canons Regular of St Augustine (Arrouaisian Congregation). The principal patrons were the O Kellys. In 1404 the priory and its contents were destroyed by fire, and it was rebuilt in its present form. Its final destruction doubtless dates from the Cromwellian victory. Excavations in 1971–2 revealed the extent of the poorly preserved cloister and the buildings adjoining it, but the church is better preserved. In its original form this was a rectangular Transitional structure. Additions and alterations included a 14th/15th c. rood-screen of Sligo 'Abbey' type (reconstructed; note the mason's name JOHES – for Johannes – on the SW. respond), a 15th c. N. transept or chapel, a Perpendicular W. door of 1471 (with figures of SS Michael, John the Baptist, Catherine of Alexandria, and St Augustine), and an interesting holy water stoup. The inscription over the door commemorates Bishop Maitiu Mac Craith of Clonfert and Pádraic Ó Neachtain, 'canon of this house'. Restorations in 1637 include the wall shutting off the chancel (date over doorway) and the oven at the NE. corner of the claustral buildings, often reusing older material.

BALLINCOLLIG, Co. Cork (Map 5, L5), is a village and former British artillery depot in the beautiful valley of the Lee, $5\frac{1}{4}$ m. W. of Cork (Macroom road).

Gen. Patrick Roynane Clebourne, one of the greatest Confederate commanders of the American Civil War, was born (1828) in Ballincollig, where his father was a physician. He advocated emancipation of the American slaves and was a member of the Fenian Brotherhood.

1 m. SW. are the ruins of Ballincollig Castle, a large rock castle of the Barrets, dating from the reign of Edward III. It was garrisoned both by Cromwell and by James II.

3 m. WSW., on the River Bride, is Ovens, which takes its name (Uamhanna) from a 670 yd labyrinthine limestone cave in a quarry near the bridge. $3\frac{1}{2}$ m. WSW. of the bridge are the ruins of Kilcrea Castle and 'Abbey', both built by Cormac Láidir Mac Carthy (d. 1495, *see p. 79*). The castle ruins comprise tower, small court, and turret; the moat has been partly obliterated by the railway. The 'abbey', a Franciscan friary, dates from 1464; it was dedicated to St Brigid. In 1650 the friary was turned into a strong-point by the Cromwellians. The remains (Nat. Mon.) represent a typical Irish medieval friary: on the N. the conventual buildings grouped around a small cloister (sacristy-scriptorium unusually well lit); on the S. a church comprising nave with S. aisle, bell-tower (inserted), choir, and aisled S. transept with two E. chapels. In the SE. angle of the nave is the tomb of Art O Leary of Raleigh, Macroom, sometime officer of the Hungarian army. He was slain as an outlaw by English troops near Carriganimmy, 4 May 1773, and for some years his remains were forbidden burial in any churchyard. His widow, Eileen Dubh O Connell of Darrynane (*see p. 86*), aunt of the great Liberator, mourned him in a celebrated *caoineadh* which has been finely rendered into English by 'Frank O Connor'.

BALLINDERRY, LOWER, Co. Antrim (Map 1, I8), lies on the Lurgan (7 m.)–Glenavy (5 m.) road, near the SE. corner of Lough Neagh.

Top: Glin, Co. Limerick (see page 194); Foot: Ballynahinch, Co. Galway (see page 66).

The Blasket Islands, Co. Kerry (see page 79).

1 m. WNW., by Lough Beg, alias Portmore Lough, are the remains of Ballinderry first church, alias Portmore church, where Jeremy Taylor (1613–67), afterwards Protestant Bishop of Dromore, often preached when he found refuge from the Cromwellians in Lord Conway's nearby house of Portmore.

1½ m. E. is Ballinderry Middle Church, built (1666–8) for Jeremy Taylor. Thanks to an 1896 restoration, this is an unusually well-preserved example of Irish Protestant church architecture of the time; noteworthy pulpit, pews, etc.

BALLINEEN–ENNISKEAN, Co. Cork (Map 5, J6), are twin villages on the Cork (29 m.)–Dunmanway (8 m.) road.

3 m. NW. of Enniskean, in Sleenoge, is the unusual, 68 ft (topless) Cloigtheach, or Round Tower, of Kinneigh; the first 18 ft are hexagonal, the doorway trabeate. It marks the site of a monastery founded by St Mo-Cholmóg.

3 m. NNW. of Kinneigh, in Capeen West, is Cahervaglier (Nat. Mon.), a bivallate ringfort with a collapsed trabeate gateway in the inner stone-faced rampart; it contains a collapsed stone hut and a souterrain. 6½ m. NNW., in Knockane, are two wedge-tombs only 12 ft apart.

4¼ m. SW. (1 m. SSW. of Manch bridge) are the ruins of the 1585 O Hurley castle of Ballynacarriga (Nat. Mon.). This castle has a good sheila-na-gig in the external wall, high up, but quite visible. The window embrasures of the top floor (locked) have interesting carvings of *c.* 1585.

1½ m. W. is Fort Robert, formerly Connorville, birthplace of Fergus O Connor (1794–1855), leader of the Chartist Movement in England. Earlier in his career, he had joined O Connell's Repeal Movement, but later tried, without success, to oust O Connell from the leadership of the Movement.

BALLINGARRY, Co. Limerick (Map 6, H9), is a small village on the Croom (8 m.)–Newcastle West (9 m.) road, 5½ m. SE. of Rathkeale. The Lacy castle commanding the hill-pass was repaired as a dwelling in 1821, and in 1827 served as a barracks during the 'Rockite' land troubles.

To the E. rises Knockfeerina (Cnoc Fírinne; 948 ft), one of the celebrated Otherworld seats in Munster (seat of the god, Donn Fírinne) which formerly had its annual Lughnasa assembly. The cairn (Buachaill Bréige) on the summit, removed by Ordnance Survey sappers, has been replaced. On the N. slope is the Giants Grave, alias Fawha's Grave, a roofless wedge-tomb.

BALLINROBE, Co. Mayo (Map 7, G7), is a small market town where the Galway (31 m.)–Castlebar (18 m.) road crosses the Robe, 4 m. E. of Lough Mask.

The parish church has nine windows by Harry Clarke, all 1926: *SS Fursey and Fechin; Colman and Brendan; Gormgall and Kieran; Enda and Jarlath; Assumption* and *Coronation of B.V.M.; Presentation in the Temple* and *Immaculate Conception; Ecce Homo* and *Magdalen in the Garden; Baptism of Christ* and *Ascension; SS Patrick, Brigid, Columcille.*

On the N. edge of the town, close to the Claremorris road, are remains of the church of an Augustinian friary founded about 1313, probably by one of the de Burgos. It was in the friary that Émonn Albanach de Burgo seized his rival cousin Émonn na Féasóige on Low Sunday, 1338, and had him drowned in Lough Mask. This foul stroke marked an important stage in the Gaelicization of the vast de Burgo lordships.

4 m. NE. is Hollymount. In the Catholic church is an *Ascension* window (1926) by Harry Clarke.

4½ m. SW., on Lough Mask, is Inishmaine. St Cormac founded a monastery there in the 7th c. In the 12th/13th c. the monks became Canons Regular of St Augustine. The monastery is represented today by the ruins of an interesting little Transitional church (Nat. Mon.) with details in the CONG style. The 'transepts' are 13th/14th (?) c. additions. NE. of the church is the remnant of a small 15th c. gatehouse. – Near the W. shore of Inishmaine are the ruins of a unique sweat-house: two crypt-like sweating chambers with high-pitched stone ceilings.

4 m. SW. are the ruins of Lough Mask Castle, a MacWilliam (Burke) fortress of 1480, re-edified in 1618 by Sir Thomas Burke, last MacWilliam Íochtair. Nearby Lough Mask House was the residence of Captain Charles Boycott (1832–97), Lord Erne's agent. Because of his treatment of the tenants he was ostracized (1880) by tenants, workers, and tradesmen; the English vocabulary thus acquired a new word, 'boycott'. – 1½ m. E. in Carn, is great, ruined Eochy's Cairn (Nat. Mon.).

BALLINSKELLIGS, Co. Kerry (Map 5, B6), a village and quiet little resort on the W. side of Ballinskelligs Bay 10 m. SSW. of Cahersiveen and 8 m. NW. of Waterville, is the market centre of one of the last pockets of Irish speech in Co. Kerry.

On Ballinskelligs Point are remains of a MacCarthy castle. By the shore to the S. are the sea-eroded remains (13th c. and later) of Ballinskelligs 'Abbey' (Nat. Mon.), a priory of Canons

Ballynacarriga Castle, Co. Cork.

Regular of St Augustine, to which the monks of the Great Skellig are said to have removed.

2½ m. N., in the ancient burial ground of Killurly, is a prostrate ogham stone.

2½ m. NE., in Meelagulleen, is a ruined wedge-tomb.

2 m. SW., on the slope of Bolus, are the remains of Killerelig, alias Kildreelig, an interesting little anchoritic monastery. They comprise a diminutive ringfort-type enclosure with remains of a Gallarus-type (*see p. 61–2*) oratory, two clocháns, two rectangular structures, a cross-pillar, a souterrain, etc., and, outside the entrance, the remnant of a tiny dry-masonry oratory with a cross-pillar inside.

3 m. NW. is the picturesque mountain-saddle of Coom, affording fine views of the Skelligs and other islands, etc. 1 m. S. (by road) of the saddle, in Leabaleaha, is a 'boulder burial' with outlying monolith. 700 yds E., in Coom, is an excavated wedge-tomb.

4½ m. NW., in Rathkieran, the ruins of Killemlagh Church (Nat. Mon.) mark the site of an ancient monastery founded by St Fíonán Lobhar, after whom nearby St Finan's Bay is named. The church was Romanesque, but the W. door has been destroyed. 150 yds S., in the field called Keelmalomvorny, is the Pagan's Grave, called after one Maol-Mhórna, who is said to have tried to procure the assassination of St Fíonán. – 1¼ m. NE. of Killemlagh, commanding a fine view of the Skelligs, is the ancient anchoritic site of Killabuonia. On the uppermost of three terraces are remains of a diminutive oratory of the Gallarus (*see pp. 61–2*) type, a cross-pillar, and some graves. The Priest's Grave, SW. of the church, is a ruined shrine-shaped tomb; it has a circular opening in the W. gable. Another grave is marked by a small stone cross. On the middle terrace there survive two clocháns, in addition to traces of two rectangular structures. To the NNW., close to the top terrace, are remains of another clochán. On the lowest terrace are St Buonia's Well and Cross; in the next field to the S. are remains of a double clochán. Pilgrims resort to the well and the Priest's Grave. – 4 m. NE. of Killabuonia, in Killoluaig, is a neglected early eremitical site; there are remains of a shrine-shaped tomb, a broken cross, and a pillarstone, etc.

6 m. NW., in Ballynabloun Demesne, are the remains of Temple Cashel, a tiny oratory of Gallarus type. 4 m. NW. of Temple Cashel, on Doon Point in Reencaheragh townland, is a fortified promontory with a medieval or later gatehouse ('Reencaheragh Castle') and other additions.

BALLINTOBER, Co. Mayo (Map 7, G6), lies just ¾ m. E. of the Ballinrobe (7 m.)–Castlebar (11 m.) road. There are the remains of a small abbey founded beside the site of an early monastery in 1216, by Cathal Crovdearg O Conor, King of Connacht, for Canons Regular of St Augustine, and dedicated to the Holy Trinity. The nave of the church was rebuilt, following a fire, in 1265. In 1653 the church was unroofed by the Cromwellians. The ruined church continued to be used for public Mass throughout Penal times, and after unsatisfactory attempts in 1846 and 1889 (George C. Ashlin), the church was finally restored in 1966 (P. LeClerc), with Stations of the Cross by Imogen Stuart (1972), stained glass (*SS Patrick, Brigid* and *Colmcille*) by Gabriel Loire, and a wooden statue of *The Virgin and Child* by Oisín Kelly. The original church was an aisleless, cruciform building with low tower over the crossing, and with the E. part laid out on the Cistercian plan, i.e. with E. chapels in the transepts. The delicate Late Romanesque–Early Gothic details of windows, capitals, etc., are characteristic of a group or school of masons active in Connacht around the turn of the 12th/13th c. In the sacristy may be seen the battered remains of the elaborate Renaissance tomb of Tiobód na Long (Theobald of the Ships) Burke (d. 1629), son of Gráinne Ní Mháille, who was created Viscount Mayo in 1627. The claustral buildings (Nat. Mon.) include a chapter-house doorway in the Cong style. Excavations in 1963 uncovered remains of two or three successive cloister ambulatories, now partially re-assembled. Through the generosity of the Church of Ireland, the 15th c. W. door, taken to Hollymount in the last century, has been returned to the abbey. The surrounds of the abbey have recently been disfigured by the erection of natural stone formations.

7 m. SE., near the NE. corner of Lough Carra, are the ruins of Burriscarra church and 'abbey' (Nat. Mons.). The latter was founded by the Stauntons, alias MacEvillys, for Carmelites in 1298 and was abandoned in 1323. At the invitation of the MacEvillys it was taken over by Austin friars in 1430. The remains are largely early-14th c.; the nave aisle is an addition. 1 m. SW., by Lough Carra, are the tower and bawn of Castlecarra (Nat. Mon.), a MacEvilly castle.

9 m. SE., overlooking Lough Carra, are the ruins of Moore Hall, Georgian home of the Moore family, whose best known members were: John Moore (d. 1799), President of the Republic of Connaught on the occasion of the French invasion of 1798; George Henry Moore (1811–70), M.P. for Mayo, 1847–57, 1868–70, one of the leaders of the Tenant-Right Movement; and George Moore (1852–1933), novelist. Lough Carra has been well described in the opening pages of George Moore's *The Lake*; local places and persons figure in his celebrated trilogy, *Ave, Salve, Vale*. When he died his remains were cremated, inurned in a 'Food Vessel', and buried by the author and surgeon Oliver St John Gogarty (*see pp. 156 and 274*) in ¼ ton of cement under a cairn on Castle Island at the N. end of the lough.

BALLINTOBER, alias **TOBERBRIDE**, Co. Roscommon (Map 7, K6), a village on the Roscommon (12 m.)–Castlerea (6 m.) road, takes its name from a holy well dedicated to St Brigid. NW. of the village are the ruins of a great keepless castle of about A.D. 1300, with twin-towered gatehouse and polygonal corner towers. From early in the 14th c. until 1657 it was in the possession of the O Conors. In 1579, after the battle of the Curlieus, it was attacked by Red Hugh O Donnell, who breached the wall with Spanish guns and forced Hugh O Conor Don to recant his allegiance to the English crown. It was there the Catholic nobility and gentry of Connacht met in 1641 to consider participation in the Eleven Years' War. In 1642 a Parliamentarian force under Lord Ranelagh and Sir Charles Coote I defeated the Irish assembled at Ballintober, but failed to take the castle. At the Cromwellian transplantation the castle was assigned to Lord Kilmallock, but in 1677 it was restored to O Conor Don.

BALLINTOGHER, Co. Sligo (Map 7, K2), is a hamlet on the Collooney (6 m.)–Manorhamilton (12 m.) road.

The Catholic church (1931) is by Vincent Kelly. The

Protestant parish church dates from 1715. One of a pair of Georgian houses served as the Court House. 2 m. NW. are remains of the medieval church of Killery. In the churchyard is the 'Straining Thread', reputed to cure sprains. 2½ m. N., in Lough Gill, is Yeats's 'Lake Isle of Innisfree'.

2 m. WSW., in Carricknagat, are two megalithic tombs (Nat. Mons.). 1½ m. WNW. of these is Doonamurray, a univallate, stone-faced ringfort; O Donnell occupied it in 1516. ¾ m. N. of this fort, to the S. of Lough Dargan, is a fragment of Castle Dargan, a castle built early in the 15th c. by Conor Mac Donagh on the site of a cliff-top ringfort, perhaps the setting for Yeats's *Purgatory*.

½ m. W. is Drumcondra tower house, strategically placed S. of the Slish Wood gap.

1 m. NNW. is Cashelore, alias Castleore (Caiseal óir), alias Bawnboy Fort (Nat. Mon.), an oval, stone ringfort; 400 yds SE. are the remains of a court-tomb. 1½ m. W., in Carrownagh, is another; 800 yds further W., in Arnasbrack, is a third.

BALLINTOY, Co. Antrim (Map 1, I2), is a small village on the Ballycastle (7 m.)–Bushmills (8 m.) coast road.

1½ m. ENE. is Carrickarade (Carrickarede), an offshore islet linked to the mainland by a famous rope footbridge, erected each summer by local fishermen.

1¼ m. SW., in Magheraboy, is the Druid Stone, a passage-tomb set in a small round cairn.

3 m. W. of Ballintoy, on the Bushmills road, is the entrance to White Park Bay (Nat. Trust), a lovely, 1 m. long beach backed by dunes. 1 m. NW. of the entrance, and 300 yds W. of Portbraddan, the remains of St Lasair's Church and an ancient cross-slab mark the site of an early monastery.

BALLINTRA, Co. Donegal (Map 8, D7), is a village on the Ballyshannon (7 m.)–Donegal (7 m.) road.

¾ m. S., in Ballymagrorty, is Racoon (Ráth Chuinghe), where St Patrick is said to have founded a church. The site is represented by a flat, rectangular mound. Bishop Assicus, 'St Patrick's goldsmith', whom the saint had placed in charge of a religious community at Elphin, Co. Roscommon, fled to a hermitage on Slieve League (*see p. 93*). Discovered after seven years and induced to return to his post, he died on the way back at Racoon, where a vulgar 1956 monument has been intruded into the mound to mark his grave. Also in Ballymagrorty was the church where the Mac Robhartaighs kept the Cathach (*see p. 148*), whose hereditary custodians they were.

2½ m. SW. (1 m. W. of Ballymagrorty school-house) is Lurgan Carn: a neolithic (?) ring enclosure with a court-tomb gallery.

1 m. SW. (via the Rossnowlagh road), in Ballymagrorty Scotch, is Giants Grave, a ruined wedge-tomb.

BALLITORE, Co. Kildare (Map 3, H6), is a decayed village to the W. of the Kilcullen (9 m.)–Castledermot (8 m.) road. It originated as a Quaker settlement. Abraham Shackleton (1697–1771), a Yorkshire Quaker, founded a school here in 1726, of which the most illustrious pupil (1741–4) was Edmund Burke. The old Quaker meeting-house has now been restored to act as a library and museum.

2 m. S., on the Carlow road, is Timolin, site of an early monastery founded by St Mo-Ling (*see p. 277*). In the Protestant church is the mid-13th c. effigy of an armoured knight supposed to be Robert fitz Richard, Lord of Norragh and ancestor of the de Valle (Wall) family. – ½ m. further S. is Moone, site of a 6th c. Columban monastery of which the most important relic is St Columcille's Cross, an unusually slender granite High Cross (9th c.) found buried in the ground in 1835 and pieced together and re-erected, the base and head in 1850, the shaft in 1893. The subjects include: E. face: *The Fall, Sacrifice of Isaac, Daniel in the Lions' Den*; S. side: *The Children in the Fiery Furnace, Flight into Egypt, Multiplication of the Loaves and Fishes*; W. face: *Crucifixion, Twelve Apostles*; N. side: *SS Anthony and Paul Break Bread in the Desert, Temptation of St Anthony*. There is also a fragment of a Franciscan friary founded in 1258 by Sir Gerald Fitzmaurice, in which fragments of a second cross are at present mounted in cement. Not far off is the 15th c. tower of Moone Castle.

1 m. W. is the celebrated hill of Mullaghmast (563 ft). There, on New Year's Day 1577, the chiefs of Laoighis and Uí Fáilghe were treacherously massacred by the English and their O Dempsey allies. Garret Óg, 11th ('Wizard') Earl of Kildare, is supposed to sleep in the Rath, emerging every seventh year to ride around The Curragh (*see also p. 99*). Daniel O Connell held a famous 'Monster Meeting' in the adjacent 'Meeting Field' on 1 October 1843.

BALLYBAY, Co. Monaghan (Map 2, F5), is a small market town on the Castleblayney (8 m.)–Newbliss (11 m.) road. Coarse fishing may be had in local lakes.

4 m. NE., in Lennan, are the remains of a portal-tomb with scribings on one upright.

BALLYBOFEY, Co. Donegal (Map 8, F5), is a small market town on the Donegal (18 m.)–Letterkenny (14 m.) road.

Isaac Butt (1813–79), founder of the Irish Home Rule movement, is buried in the Protestant graveyard. He was born in Glebe House, 7½ m. NW. in Glenfinn.

The road SW. to Donegal passes through Barnesmore Gap (499 ft) between Croaghconnallagh (1,724 ft) and Barnesmore (1,491 ft). 5½ m. SW. via this road, on the S. slope of Croaghanierin and about 100 ft over Lough Mourne, is the large stone ringfort called Cashelnavean (Stone fort of the Fiana). S. of the road, at the NE. end of Lough Mourne, is the Giant's Bed, a chamber-tomb.

BALLYBOGHILL, Co. Dublin (Map 3, K2), is a hamlet on the Dublin (13 m.)–The Naul (12 m.) road. There are some remains of the medieval parish church.

2 m. ESE. is Grace Dieu, site of one of the most famous nunneries (Augustinian) of the English Pale. At the Dissolution, the English colony in Ireland pleaded in vain for the convent on the grounds that there 'the womenkind of the most part of the whole Englishry of this land be brought up in virtue, learning, and in the English tongue and behaviour'. The nuns retired to Portrane (*see pp. 129–30*), and the convent and its possessions were granted to the Barnewalls, who dismantled the buildings in

1565 to provide materials for Turvey House, Donabate (which was demolished in 1987). Traces of a cloister court and a few gravestones, etc., are all that survive.

BALLYBUNNION, Co. Kerry (Map 6, C8), is a popular little seaside resort with a fine beach at the mouth of the Shannon, 9 m. NW. of Listowel. There are caves (visited by Tennyson in 1842) in the sea cliffs.

SW. of the village, in the enclosure of a promontory fort, are the remains of Ballybunnion Castle.

NW. of the village, on the S. side of lovely little Doon Cove, is a large promontory fort with remains of later Pookeenee Castle inside the fosse.

4 m. SSE., in Rattoo House demesne, are a 92 ft Round Tower (roof restored) and also the remains of a small church (Nat. Mons.), relics of an early monastery. Near the demesne gate can be found remains of Rattoo 'Abbey', founded *c.* 1200 as the Hospital of St John the Baptist (Augustinian Canons Regular Hospitaller).

BALLYCASTLE, Co. Antrim (Map 1, I3), a market town and popular seaside resort 27 m. N. of Ballymena, stands at the junction of Glentaise and Glenshesk to the N. of Knocklayd (1,695 ft) and its great prehistoric cairn, Carn-na-truagh. The town takes its name from a castle built by Sir Randall MacDonnell, 2nd Earl of Antrim. By the shore is the cottage from which Marconi transmitted his first wireless message (to Rathlin), 1905.

1 m. E. are the ruins of Bunamargy Friary (in State care). A Franciscan Tertiary friary founded by Rory MacQuillan about 1500, it was burned down in 1584, when the MacDonnells attacked English troops garrisoned there. The remains include a gate-house and fragments of the claustral buildings, as well as an aisleless preaching church, the S. transept of which has been converted into a MacDonnell mausoleum (1621–66). Among those buried here are Somhairle Buidhe (Sorley Boye) MacDonnell himself (d. 1590), his son, the 1st Earl of Antrim (d. 1636), and Randall, 2nd Earl (d. 1682). The latter's tomb has inscriptions in Irish (very rare), Latin, and English. There is an interesting MacNaghten tomb of 1630 in the S. wall of the church, while near the E. end is the grave of Francis Stewart, Catholic Bishop of Down and Connor (d. 1749). A small, crude cross at the W. end of the church is said to mark the grave of Julia MacQuillan, the 'Black Nun'.

3 m. W., offshore, on Kenbane, are the remains of a castle (in State care; very dangerous approach) built in 1547 by the chief of the MacDonnells, Colla Dubh MacDonnell, who died in 1558.

5½ m. NE. is Benmore, alias Fair Head (636 ft), where coal was mined in the 18th and 19th c. Below Fair Head is Carraig Uisneach, rocks which legend links with the mythological tale of Deirdre and the Sons of Uisneach. ½ m. S. of the head is Lough na Cranagh, with an oval crannóg which has a dry-masonry revetment. About ½ m. W. is Doonmore, a motte-and-bailey carved out of a basalt outcrop; traces of stone defences survive.

2 m. SE., in Churchfield, is Culfeightrin 'Old Church', a fragment with a fine 15th c. window. In the graveyard are two pillarstones.

BALLYCASTLE, Co. Mayo (Map 7, F1), is a village and little resort at the foot of Ballinglen, 9 m. W. of Killala and 30 m. E. of Belmullet.

¾ m. WNW., in Ballyglass townland, is a court-tomb with a large elliptical court entered from the side and having a segmented gallery at each end. The foundations of a Neolithic timber house (almost 40 × 20 ft) were found under its W. end. 250 yds S. are the remains of a court-tomb with oval court and façade.

5 m. NNE. is Downpatrick Head (126 ft). Here are the ruins of St Patrick's Church, a holy well, and stations to which pilgrims used to resort on Garland Sunday (last Sunday in July). Here, too, is Pollnashantinny, a puffing hole with subterranean channel to the sea. Just off the head is spectacular Doonbristy, an isolated cliff rock on which there are two medieval houses.

2½ m. NE. are the ruins of Kilbride church.

3¾ m. ESE., in Barnhill Upper, is a court cairn.

1 m. SE., in Rathoonagh, are remnants of a court-tomb (200 ft). ½ m. SE. of this are remains of another.

6 m. SSE., in Ballybeg, is the Cloghabracka, a court-tomb with oval court and curved façade.

2 m. NW., in Doonfeeny Upper, are two old graveyards separated by a bohereen. In one are remains of a church, in the other traces of a circular enclosure in which stands a slender, 18 ft pillarstone with an elaborate pattern of two crosses low down on the W. face.

4 m. NW., on the NE. spur of Maumakeogh, in Behy, is The Roomeens (500 ft), a transeptal court-tomb with horseshoe-shaped court. The peat which covered the court has been replaced. The grave goods included Western Neolithic pottery. This tomb stands in an extensive pre-bog field system dating to Neolithic times. The cutaway bogs have exposed the stone walls of these fields over an area of 4 sq. m.

10 m. NW. is Belderg. In Belderg townland, a Neolithic and Bronze Age farm has been excavated. Evidence of ploughing and ridge cultivation was found beside a Bronze Age round house with a diameter of 30 ft.

BALLYCLARE, Co. Antrim (Map 1, K6), is a small town half-way between Larne (11 m.) and Antrim (11 m.).

2½ m. WSW., in Holestone, is the *holestone*, a pillarstone with an artificial hole, through which a troth was traditionally pledged.

BALLYCONNEELY, Co. Galway (Map 7, B9), is a hamlet on the isthmus between Ballyconneely Bay and Mannin Bay, 9 m. NW. of Roundstone and 6 m. SSW. of Clifden.

½ m. N. is Mannin Bay with its beautiful beaches, including Coral Strand.

2 m. SW. are remains of the small, late church of Bunowen (St Flannan's). The derelict 'castle' nearby was commenced in 1838 by Richard Geoghegan, descendant of a Cromwellian transplantee from Co. Westmeath.

Off the SW. tip of the peninsula are Doonawaul islet (with remnants of clocháns, etc.) and, 1 m. further SW., Chapel Island (with St Caillín's Well and remains of little St Caillín's Church). To the W. of the latter, on Ilaunamid, is Slyne Head lighthouse.

BALLYCONNELL, Co. Cavan (Map 2, C4), is a Border village at the foot of Slieve Rushen (1,279 ft), on the road from Belturbet (7 m.) to Swanlinbar (11 m.).

The Protestant church dates from the early-17th c.; the tower was added in 1814. A Romanesque door or window head (from Toomregon Round Tower?; *below*) stands outside the church. In the churchyard are remains of two diamond-shaped redoubts, relics of fortifications of the Williamite war. The Catholic church (1969–70) by Hubert Duffy has slab glass windows by Helen Moloney and an etched inscription by George Campbell.

4 m. SE., in Ballyhugh, overlooking Lough Dungummin, is a promontory fort with rock-cut ditch and remains of a stone rampart.

2½ m. S., in Mullynagolman and not far from Togher Lough, traces of a church and Round Tower mark the site of the early monastery of Toomregon, celebrated in Irish literary legend. According to that legend Cenn Faelad *Sapiens* (d. 679), grandson of Baetán, King of Tara, and cousin of King Oswiu of Northumbria (who came to Ireland to study), was severely wounded at the battle of Mag Roth (*see p. 248*) in 637, so that his 'brain of forgetting' was cut out. He was brought to Toomregon to be healed by Abbot Briccéne, a famous surgeon. At Toomregon 'there were three schools, a school of Latin learning, a school of Irish law, and a school of Irish poetry. And everything Cenn Faelad would hear of the recitations of the three schools by day he would have it by heart at night. And he fitted a pattern of poetry to these matters, and wrote them on slates and tablets, and set them in a vellum book'. Prof. Eóin Mac Néill interpreted this legend as reflecting the first reduction of traditional Irish law to writing, but other scholars do not agree.

3 m. SW., in Killycluggin, is a stone circle; the shattered remnants of a phallic stone ornamented with incised Iron Age Celtic patterns, which lay outside it, is now in the National Museum in Dublin. In Kilnavert, the adjacent townland to the SW., are two small stone circles, a wedge-tomb and two pillarstones. Magh Sléacht, celebrated in Irish literary legend as the seat of a fictitious high idol of Ireland (a pillarstone inside a stone circle, to which the name Crom Crúaich was attached) overthrown by St Patrick, is generally supposed to have been the plain round about Kilnavert and Killycluggin.

BALLYCOTTON, Co. Cork (Map 4, D9), a fishing village and small resort on Ballycotton Bay, 7 m. SE. of Cloyne and 8 m. S. of Castlemartyr, is a noted centre for deep-sea angling. A plaque commemorates the daring lifeboat rescue of the crew of the Daunt Rock lightship, 11–14 February 1936.

2 m. NNW., on the Cloyne road, is Shanagarry House. The out-offices incorporate fragments of a courtyard house built by Admiral Sir William Penn, who had been granted the castle and manor of Macroom by Cromwell. In 1667 Penn sent his son, William (of Pennsylvania), to Ireland to administer his estates. William resided at Shanagarry. It was on the occasion of a visit to Cork that he became a Quaker. Descendants of Admiral Penn held the Shanagarry estate until 1903.

BALLYCROY, Co. Mayo (Map 7, D3), is a hamlet on the Mallaranny (9 m.)–Bangor Erris (12 m.) road.

2 m. SSW., in Kildun, is a mound (Nat. Mon.) with two pillarstones. One pillarstone has a ringed cross on the W. face. Local legend makes the mound the grave of Donn, son of Míl.

4 m. NW. are the remains of Doona Castle, said to have been another of Gráinne Ní Mháille's castles (*see p. 104*).

BALLYFARNAN, Co. Roscommon (Map 7, L3), is a village on the Sligo (19 m.)–Drumshanbo (10 m.) road.

2½ m. SE., on the N. shore of Lough Meelagh, are the ruins of the church of Kilronan of the Duignans, erected in 1339 by Fearghal Muimhneach Duignan, and dedicated to St Lasair, who, with her father, St Rónán, is said to have founded the first church there (6th/7th c.). The Late Romanesque S. door of the ruin derives from a 12th/13th c. church. The *Annals of Connacht*, an important chronicle of the period A.D. 900–1563, used by the Four Masters, was compiled in the school of the Duignans, erenachs or hereditary lay proprietors of the church, and historiographers to the Mac Dermots. The celebrated songwriter and harpist, Turlough O Carolan (1670–1738), was buried in the N. side of the church. He had died at Alderford, the home of Mac Dermot Roe, just outside Ballyfarnan. An enormous concourse, including ten harpers, attended his four-day wake, which gave rise to still-told tales. Among O Carolan's compositions was the melody to which *The Star-Spangled Banner* is sung.

BALLYFERRITER, Co. Kerry (Map 5, B3), is a village and summer resort near Smerwick Harbour, 8½ m. NW. of Dingle and 3½ m. NE. of Dunquin. In the old school-house there is a Heritage Centre, displaying a number of local antiquities.

1½ m. N. is the beautiful strand of Smerwick Harbour (formerly the Haven of Ardcanny).

2½ m. N. is Smerwick village. 500 yds SE. are the remains of Dún an Óir (Nat. Mon.), constructed by a party of James Fitzmaurice's Italians and Spaniards who landed in the bay, 12 September 1580. English land and sea forces under Lord Deputy Grey and Admiral Winter attacked the fort, 7 November. After three days' bombardment the fort capitulated. The officers were spared, but some 600 common soldiers and 17 Irish men and women were butchered in cold blood. Prior to the surrender the Italian commander had delivered up Fr Laurence Moore, Oliver Plunkett, and an English Catholic, William Wollick. These, refusing to acknowledge the religious supremacy of Elizabeth I, were savagely tortured and mutilated before being hanged. A stone sculpture by Cliodna Cussen was erected (1980) near the entrance to the fort to commemorate those who died in the massacre. The remains of the fort include an eroded mainland outwork with two bastions, as well as an inner rock-fort cut off by a rock-cut trench.

1¾ m. ENE., in Reask, the remains of two clocháns, a cross-inscribed stone, an early cross-slab, two early cross-pillars (one with elaborate, incised cross-pattern), and an ancient burial ground mark the site of an early anchoritic monastery. Excavations in 1972–5 revealed burials and structures dating from the 5th c. onwards. The stone-walled enclosure, roughly oval in shape, was found to be divided by a wall into two parts, each containing clochāns (some double). A stone oratory (preceded by a wooden structure) in the S. part proved to be later than a lintel-grave cemetery with a small slab-shrine nearby. Traces of early

Gallarus oratory on the Dingle peninsula, Co. Kerry.

ironworking were also found in the enclosure. The burial area was ultimately converted into a *ceallúnuch*, or children's burial ground.

1 m. SE., in Ballineanig Church Quarter, are the ruins of Ballywiheen church (Nat. Mon.); there are two early cross-slabs there (one broken).

2¼ m. E., in Lateevemore, is the ancient church site of Templenacloonagh. In it stand the shell of a tiny church or oratory and two early cross-pillars. 1¾ m. (by road) NNE., is the celebrated church of Gallarus (date unknown), a corbel-roofed, dry-masonry structure (Nat. Mon.); an early cross-pillar (Nat. Mon.) is inscribed COLUM MAC DINET. ¾ m. NW. are the ruins of Gallarus Castle (Nat. Mon.), a Fitzgerald castle 1 m. E. of the castle, in Caherdorgan South, is a stone ringfort with ruined stone huts in the interior; to the E., NE., and SE. is the Saints' Road. 400 yds NE., in Caherdorgan North, is a stone ringfort with five ruined clocháns (Nat. Mon.). 400 yds N. of the latter is the Chancellor's House (Nat. Mon.). Some 350 yds NE. of the Chancellor's House the road passes between the Cow Stone (W.) and the Thief Stone (E.), two pillarstones. A short distance N. is Kilmalkedar village. There are: 15th c. St Brendan's House; St Brendan's Oratory; Kilmalkedar Church (Romanesque); the Alphabet Stone (an ogham stone); a stone cross; the Keelers (a stone); and a sun-dial (all Nat. Mons.); also St Brendan's Well. The 'oratory' was a structure of the Gallarus type. The Romanesque church (some details reminiscent of Cormac's Chapel, Cashel) had a corbelled barrel-vault roof; the chancel is a Transitional enlargement of the Romanesque original. The whole Gallarus–Caherdorgan–Kilmalkedar area is embarrassingly rich in antiquities.

2 m. NW., on the NW. side of sandy Ferriter's Cove, Ballyoughter South, are the fragmentary remains of Ferriter's Castle. (The best known of the Ferriters was the gallant poet-scholar, Piaras Feritéir, last Kerry commander to submit to the Cromwellians. His safe-conduct was dishonoured, and he was hanged on Martyrs' Hill, Killarney, 1653.) On the shore of Ferriter's Cove, excavations have revealed the presence of shell middens of the Mesolithic period (4th millennium B.C.).

BALLYGAWLEY, Co. Tyrone (Map 2, E2), is a village on the Omagh (12 m.)–Dungannon (10 m.) road.

1½ m. NE. is Martray House and lake, where George Vesey Stewart, founder of the Stewart settlements at Katikati in New Zealand, was born. 2 m. further E., turning S. off the main road at Dergina, is the ancestral home of President Ulysses S. Grant's mother, Hannah Simpson. The house is now a District Council Museum. Close by (1½ m. E.) is Killeeshil Church, one of the oldest original churches still in regular use in Northern Ireland.

3½ m. W., in Ballinasaggart townland, is Errigal Keeroge church, built in 1832, probably on the site of the Franciscan friary founded there by Conn O Neill in 1489. 1 m. W. of the church, in Gort townland, is the ancient graveyard of Old Errigal, with the remains of St Kieran's church (Hist. Mon.), as well as a primitive stone cross. Near the entrance to the graveyard is St Kieran's Well.

2 m. NW., at Greenhill, is the shell of the former Ballygawley Park, built in 1820 by Sir John Stewart. 1 m. SW. of it is Sess Kilgreen passage-tomb, with two decorated stones similar to those at Knockmany (*see p. 51*). In the next field is a stone with similar designs. In Glencull, the next townland to the W., is a wrecked cairn where one of the stones has 15 cup marks.

BALLYHAISE, Co. Cavan (Map 2, D5), on the Cavan (4 m.)–Clones (17 m.) road, is a village which has a good 18th c. Market House.

Ballyhaise House (now an agricultural school) is by Richard Cassels (*c.* 1750).

4 m. N. is Redhills village. Killoughter Protestant church has a three-light window (*The Sower*) by Catherine O Brien (1954).

$5\frac{1}{2}$ m. NE., in Magherintemple, the site of a medieval parish church is marked by a hill-top graveyard at the centre of a very large oval earthwork. Until the 16th c., this was the site of a fair.

BALLYHAUNIS, Co. Mayo (Map 7, I6), is a small market town on the Claremorris (11 m.)–Castlereagh (11 m.) road.

At the E. end of the town is an Augustinian priory which incorporates fragments of the church of an Augustinian friary dedicated to the Blessed Virgin Mary. The friary was founded, about 1430, by the Jordan Duff MacCostellos (alias Nangles). In the Convent of Mercy chapel are five single-light windows (1924–5) by Michael Healy: *The Good Shepherd, St Brigid, St Patrick, St Ita, St Columcille.*

9 m. N., on the N. shore of Urlaur Lough, are the ruins of Urlaur 'Abbey' (Nat. Mon.), a Dominican friary dedicated to St Thomas and founded in 1430 by the MacCostellos.

2 m. WNW., on a commanding site in Island townland, is a tumulus with an ogham stone ('Braghlaghboy Ogham Stone').

$5\frac{1}{2}$ m. NW. the ancient churchyard of Aghamore marks the site of an early monastery. In the next field is a rude 17th c. cross with an incised design and traces of an inscription.

BALLYHEIGE, Co. Kerry (Map 6, B9), is a quiet little resort on the Tralee (11 m.)–Ballybunnion (16 m.) coast road.

Derelict Ballyheige Castle, NW. of the village, was built for the Crosbies of Ardfert to the design of Sir Richard Morrison (1767–1849). It was burned down by Republicans in 1922.

$3\frac{1}{2}$ m. W., at the foot of Trisk Mountain (701 ft) in Glenderry, are: the defaced remains of St Macadaw's Church; a cupped pillarstone with incised, red-painted cross; a charmed stone ball; and St Macadaw's Well.

BALLYJAMESDUFF, Co. Cavan (Map 2, E7), a market town between Virginia (6 m.) and Cavan (10 m.), is the subject of Percy French's ever-popular ballad 'Come back, Paddy Reilly, to Ballyjamesduff'.

$5\frac{1}{2}$ m. SW., near Mountnugent, on an islet off the shore of Lough Sheelin, are the remains of Crover castle, built by Thomas, son of Mahon O Reilly, in the late-14th c.

BALLYLIFFIN, Co. Donegal (Map 1, D2), is a small resort 6 m. NW. of Carndonagh and $\frac{1}{2}$ m. S. of 2 m. Pollan Strand.

$2\frac{3}{4}$ m. N., at the NW. corner of Doagh Isle peninsula, are remains of the O Doherty castle of Carrickabraghy: a 16th (?) c. square tower with an added circular tower and fragments of a 16th/17th c. bawn.

$3\frac{1}{2}$ m. ENE., in Magheranaul, is a wedge-tomb with a holed portal slab. $1\frac{1}{4}$ m. NW., in Carrowreagh, alias Craignacally, is the Altar, a boulder covered with prehistoric scribings.

BALLYLONGFORD, Co. Kerry (Map 6, D8), is a village at the head of Ballylongford Bay, Shannon estuary, 5 m. WSW. of Tarbert and 8 m. N. of Listowel.

1 m. N., on the E. shore of the inlet, are the ruins (Nat. Mon.) of Lislaughtin 'Abbey', a friary founded in 1477 by O Conor Kerry for Franciscans of the Strict Observance. The long church has a short, aisled, S. transept and noteworthy sedilia. A fine processional crucifix (Ballylongford Cross) in the National Museum probably belonged to this friary.

2 m. NNW., in the channel between the mainland and Carrig Island, are the remains (Nat. Mon.) of Carrigafoyle Castle (O Conor Kerry). The fine 86 ft tower stood at the centre of a bawn which enclosed a dock for boats. There were outworks on the mainland. In March 1580, the castle was held by the Italian engineer Captain Julian, with 50 Irish and 16 Spaniards, for the Earl of Desmond against an English force under Sir William Pelham, who stormed it after two days. Pelham hanged all the survivors and sent the Earl of Desmond's plate to the Queen. The castle also figured in the Tyrone (1600) and Cromwellian (1649) wars; it was finally wrecked by the Cromwellians.–On Carrig Island are remains of Carrig 'Abbey', Friars Well, and a fine early-19th c. battery (Corran Point).

BALLYMAHON, Co. Longford (Map 3, C2), is a village where the Mullingar (19 m.)–Lanesborough ($12\frac{3}{4}$ m.) road crosses the River Inny.

Oliver Goldsmith (1728–74), essayist, poet and playwright, was born near Pallas about 1 m. N. of the road to Abbeyshrule, and Ballymahon itself was probably his last home in Ireland. There is a memorial window to him in Forgney church, $2\frac{1}{2}$ m. SE. of Ballymahon. The area chiefly associated with Goldsmith is AUBURN.

4 m. NE. of Ballymahon is the hamlet of Abbeyshrule. SE., on the E. bank of the Inny, are remains of the Cistercian abbey (Flumen Dei) from which it takes its name (Irish, Mainistear na Sruthra). The abbey was founded *c.* 1200 by O Farrel and was colonized from Mellifont. The sadly neglected remains include the choir and part of the nave of an aisleless 12th–13th c. church (Transitional details) with later modifications. In the graveyard NNE. of the abbey is the broken shaft of a small, early cross with a five-strand plait and other patterns. This is the only early cross in the county.

3 m. W. is Gorteen, native place of Leo (John Keagan Casey, 1846–70), author of 'The Rising of the Moon', 'Máire my Girl', and other ballads.

8 m. NW. are the remains of Abbeyderg Augustinian abbey (13th c.).

BALLYMENA, Co. Antrim (Map 1, I6), is a manufacturing and commercial town in mid-Antrim on the Belfast (28 m.)–Coleraine (27 m.)–Ballycastle (27 m.) road. It is a predominantly Presbyterian town, founded for Lowland Scottish settlers in the 17th c. by Willian Adair from Kinhilt. The prosperity of the town dates from the introduction of the linen industry, *c.* 1730. The finest recent building, County Hall (1967, Burman and Goodall), is outside the town, on Galgorm Rd. 'Arguably the best major modern building in Ulster', it won an R.I.B.A. award in 1971. On a ridge in the S. suburbs is Harryville Motte (in State care), a 40 ft high motte with a rectangular bailey on the E. It is one of the finest surviving Anglo-Norman earthworks in Ulster.

$3\frac{1}{2}$ m. SE., in Ballymarlagh, is a Neolithic court-tomb with four chambers. 5 m. SE. is Connor, site of an early monastery founded by Bishop Oengus Mac Nisse (d. 514), which has given its name to the diocese; marked now by fragments of a High Cross and two closed souterrains, one of which has ogham stones in its roofing. In 1315 Edward Bruce routed Richard III de Burgo, 'Red' Earl of Ulster, at Connor. In 1453 the diocese was united with that of Down.

$1\frac{1}{2}$ m. WSW. of Ballymena is Galgorm Castle, a Plantation castle and bawn built by Sir Faithful Fortescue in 1618–19; it was renovated in 1832. Beyond the demesne is Gracehill, a Moravian settlement with central square, founded in 1746.

3 m. NW., in Cullybackey, is the house in which Chester Alan Arthur (1830–86), 21st President of the U.S.A., was born.

BALLYMOE, Co. Galway (Map 7, K7), is a small village on the Dunmore (15 m.)–Castlerea (5 m.) road, 13 m. NW. of Roscommon.

4 m. SE. are the ruins of Glinsk Castle (Nat. Mon.), a fine late-17th c. fortified house attributed to Sir Ulick Burke, a prominent Jacobite. 1 m. W., in the ruined church of Ballynakill, is a good early-16th c. effigy of a mailed knight, originally from a Burke tomb.

BALLYMONEY, Co. Antrim (Map 1, H4), is an agricultural and market town on the Ballymena (19 m.)–Coleraine (8 m.) road.

3 m. NNE., in Conagher (Conacher), off the road to Dervock, is the family home of William McKinley, 25th President of the U.S.A.

$6\frac{1}{2}$ m. SSE. and $1\frac{3}{4}$ m. SE. of Finvoy, 650 ft up on the Long Mountain, Craigs, is the Broadstone, a three-chamber court tomb (in State care).

7 m. SE. is Dunloy. In Ballymacaldrack, $\frac{3}{4}$ m. SSE. of the village, under the E. slope of the Long Mountain, is Dooey's Cairn, an unusual oval court-tomb. Behind the single chamber was a boulder-lined (cremation?) trench, in the floor of which were three pits.

BALLYMORE, Co. Westmeath (Map 3, C2), is a village on the Mullingar (16 m.)–Athlone (15 m.) road. The principal de Lacy (later de Verdon) seignorial manor in W. Meath was there, and some remains of the castle still survive.

S. of the village is a remnant of Plary convent (dedicated to the Virgin Mary), founded in 1218 by the de Lacys for Cistercian nuns. About $\frac{1}{2}$ m. away was an Augustinian priory whose church was for a short time made cathedral of the diocese of Meath by Henry VIII.

$4\frac{1}{2}$ m. E. is Killare, where the remains of a church, to the S. of the crossroads, mark the site of Cell Fháir, one of the principal monasteries of Bishop St Áed mac Bric, a prince of the Uí Néill (*see pp. 93 and 297*). A *suí liag*, or master physician, he was highly reputed for his power of healing. In time, popular tradition invested him with some of the attributes of the ancient sun-god Áed.

5 m. E. is the Hill of Ushnagh (Uisneach). From the summit (602 ft) 20 of the 32 counties of Ireland are visible in clear weather. As the accepted centre of Ireland, the hill was a place of sanctity in pagan times, and seems to have been the seat of a fire cult with a great May Day (Bealtaine) festival. St Patrick is said to have founded a church on the hill. In 984 Brian Boru occupied the hill as a challenge to the King of Tara, Melaghlin II. In 1414 Sir John Stanley, the English king's Lieutenant in Ireland and an enemy of the Gaelic poets, plundered Niall Ó Huiginn (O Higgins), a member of Ireland's foremost family of hereditary poets, at Uisneach. Whereupon Niall made satires on him 'and he lived only five weeks after them'. To avenge Stanley's death his successor, John Talbot, 'Scourge of France', despoiled many of the poets of Ireland, including Díarmait O Daly of Meath. On the Hill of Ushnagh are ancient remains, of which the following are a selection. In Kellybrook Townland on the SW. slope, to the N. of the Ballymore–Mullingar road, is the Cat Stone, a large erratic at the centre of a low earthen ring 62 ft in diameter. This has been identified with the Aill na Míreann (Rock of the Divisions) of Irish literary legend, called Umbilicus Hiberniae by Giraldus Cambrensis. At the summit is St Patrick's Bed, a rectangular platform of stones despoiled by the Ordnance Survey sappers when setting up their trigonometrical station on the hill-top. In Togherstown Townland is a bivallate ringfort with secondary radial walls subdividing the area between the ramparts. In Rathnew Townland, on the SE. eminence of the hill, are the remains of a bivallate, conjoint ringfort of dry masonry; the line of an ancient roadway approaching the site from the S. may be traced as far as the Ballymore–Mullingar road. Inadequate excavations (1925–8) revealed that this site had had a complex functional and structural history: beneath the E. part of the fort were traces of a circular ritual (?) enclosure represented by ditches, pits, post-holes (and two burials?).

$1\frac{1}{2}$ m. SE. is Clare Hill (433 ft), probably the Cláthra where Medbh's army is described as camping in *Táin Bó Cualnge*. On the summit are remains of a strong castle set on a large raised platform.

$3\frac{1}{2}$ m. WSW. is Bryanmore Hill, the setting of Bruiden Da Choca, one of the five mythological festive halls of early Irish literature; on the hill are the remains of a ringfort.

BALLYMORE EUSTACE, Co. Kildare (Map 3, I5), is a Liffeyside village on the E. Naas (7 m.)–Baltinglass (15 m.) road, $1\frac{1}{2}$ m. W. of the great Liffey Valley reservoir. The village takes its name from the Anglo-Norman FitzEustaces who, 1373–*c.* 1524, were hereditary constables of the Archbishop of Dublin's manor there.

In the Protestant church is an early-16th c. armoured FitzEustace tomb effigy from New Abbey, Old Kilcullen.

In the old churchyard are a granite High Cross (the 1689 inscription is, of course, an addition), a smaller granite cross, and remains of an ancient church.

1½ m. S., on a hill-top in Broadleas Common, are the Piper's Stones, a large stone circle. ¼ m. NW., in Longstone townland, is the Long Stone, a prostrate pillarstone (13½ ft) of granite.

2 m. W., on the N. bank of the Liffey in Coghlanstown, are the remains of St James's Church, a granite cross base and a fragment of a 17th c. FitzEustace commemorative cross. ½ m. E. of the graveyard is a small roadside granite cross.

BALLYMOTE, Co. Sligo (Map 7, K3), is a town on the Ballaghaderreen (16 m.)–Sligo (15 m.) road. It takes its name from an early-13th c. Anglo-Norman motte (Rathdoony) 1¼ m. to the W.

At the N. end of the village are the remains of the 'Abbey', a small Franciscan Third Order friary, founded in 1442. At the W. end of the village are the ruins (Nat. Mon.) of the remarkable castle built *c.* 1300 by Richard de Burgo, 'Red' Earl of Ulster. This was a square, keepless fortress with twin-towered gatehouse, massive drum towers at the angles, and lesser D-towers in the curtain walls. By 1338 it had fallen to the O Conors and by 1380 to the Mac Donaghs, who held it for two centuries, though in 1567 it was still claimed by O Conor Sligo. The celebrated literary codex, *The Book of Ballymote*, was compiled about 1400 by Duignans and others for Tomaltach Óg Mac Donagh, Lord of Corann, partly in the castle. From 1584 until 1690 the castle changed hands many times between the Irish and the English. The great Red Hugh O Donnell made it his Connacht headquarters in 1598, and it was there he assembled his forces en route to Kinsale in 1601. The fortifications were dismantled and the moat filled up after the Williamites forced the castle to surrender in 1690.

4 m. SE. is Keshcorran (1,182 ft). On the summit is a great cairn, and a large enclosure, probably a hill-fort. On the W. face of the mountain are 17 small caves in which were found the remains of animals such as reindeer, Irish elk, cave bear and arctic lemming, as well as traces of ancient human occupation. Keshcorran figures in the literary legends of Cormac mac Airt

Ballynahinch Castle Hotel, Ballynahinch, Co. Galway.

and of Díarmait and Gráinne. (One cave in the W. escarpment is Umhaigh Chormaic mhac Airt, 'Cormac mac Art's Cave', for there the she-wolf reared him. ¾ m. N. of this, in Cross, is Tobar Chormaic, 'Cormac's Well', where Cormac's mother delayed his birth, as witness a stone with the imprint of the infant's head.) The greatest of Co. Sligo's Lughnasa celebrations was held on Garland Sunday in front of the caves of the W. escarpment; it survives in attenuated form.

In 971 the battle of Keshcorran took place between Vikings and a Connacht army. The latter was defeated, and the dead were brought for burial to the ancient monastery of Toomour (1 m. SE. of Kesh village). In the churchyard, on the altar, are four early cross-slabs.

4½ m. SW., in Rinnardogue, are remains of Cloonameehan, alias Bunnamaddan, 'Abbey', a Dominican friary founded in 1488 by Eóghan Mac Donagh.

4 m. NW., near Temple House, are some remains of a preceptory of the Knights Templars, and the base of a cross. When the Templars were suppressed (1312) the place became a dependency of St John's Hospital at Rinndown (*see p. 231*). The castle was destroyed by Aedh O Conor of Connacht in 1271, but was later rebuilt.

BALLYNAHINCH, Co. Down (Map 2, K2), is a small town and agricultural centre on the Dromore (10 m.)–Downpatrick (11 m.) road. S. of the town is Montalto House, formerly residence of the earls of Moira.

Ballynahinch figured in the 1798 insurrection, when the heights around Montalto were held by the United Irishmen under Henry Monro against General Nugent. The insurgents were driven to Slieve Croob, 6 m. SW. (*below*), Monro himself being captured and subsequently executed at LISBURN.

5½ m. SE. is Loughinisland. On a causewayed island on the W. shore of the lake, ruins of three churches (Hist. Mons.) mark an ancient monastic site. Of these, the Middle Church is probably 13th c., the North Church 15th c., while the South Church has the date 1636 and the initials PMC (Phelim Mac Cartan) on the elaborately carved door. 150 yds NE. of the lake is Annadorn Dolmen (Hist. Mon.), a collapsed portal-tomb.

The Twelve Cairns (little heaps of stone made from the spoil of a large prehistoric cairn) at the summit of Slive Croob (1,755 ft) were until the 1950s a place of Lughnasa celebrations (singing, dancing, etc.) on Blaeberry Sunday, alias Lammas Sunday (first Sunday of August/last Sunday of July).

BALLYNAHINCH, Co. Galway (Map 7, D8), 7 m. ESE. of Clifden and 42 m. NW. of Galway (via Oughterard; 51 m. via Casla and Screeb), takes its name from a small castle-crowned island (a crannóg?) in Ballynahinch Lake.

Ballynahinch Castle Hotel, a much altered 18th c. house superbly sited over the Owenmore, was the home of the Martin family, the best-known member of which was Richard (Humanity Dick) Martin (1754–1834), M.P., friend of the Prince Regent, and one of the promoters of the R.S.P.C.A. The vast Martin estates – largely mountain and moor – made him one of the greatest landlords in the West, and it was he who built the greater part of the house, which figures in Thackeray's *An Irish Sketch Book* and Maria Edgeworth's *Letters*. The property passed from the Martins as a consequence of the Great Famine. (Charles Lever's *The Martins of Cro Martin* is based on the story of the family.) It was acquired in 1926 by the Jam Sahib of Nawanagar – Ranjit Sinjhi, the cricketer; in 1945 it was converted into an hotel.

Before falling to the Martins, the Ballynahinch estate had belonged to the O Flahertys and, before them, to the O Keelys. Donal O Flaherty, first husband of Gráinne Ní Mháille ('Granuaile', *see p. 104*) built the small castle in the lake.

3 m. S., on the W. bank of the Owenmore, are remains of Toombeola 'Abbey', late-16th c. church of a Dominican friary, dedicated to St Patrick, which was founded in 1427.

BALLYPOREEN, Co. Tipperary (Map 4, C5), is a village on the Clogheen (5 m.)–Mitchelstown (8 m.) road. The parish church has a Michael Healy window, *St Patrick* (1916). In the centre of the village is the President Reagan Visitor Centre, commemorating the visit of the President of the United States of America on 3 June 1984.

2½ m. N. are the celebrated 'Mitchelstown Caves'. (Their misleading modern name is due to the fact that Coolagarranroe was part of the estate of the Kingstons of Mitchelstown.) The caves comprise two groups, Uaimh na Caorach Glaise, alias Desmond's Cave, and New Cave. Desmond's Cave (rope or ladder necessary) is so called because the Sugán Earl of Desmond sought refuge there, only to be betrayed by the White Knight (*see p. 225*) in 1601; the E. chamber is the largest cave-chamber in the British Isles. The New Cave (guide available), discovered in 1833, comprises 1½ m. of passages and chambers with splendid stalagmite and stalactite formations.

4 m. NE. is Burncourt Castle (Nat. Mon.), a great embattled house built in 1641 by Sir Richard Everard of Ballyboy, Clogheen. Sir Richard was a member of the Supreme Council of the Confederation of Kilkenny, and was one of those hanged by Ireton when Limerick capitulated in 1651; his great house had been captured and burned by Cromwell the year before.

2 m. W. is Templetenny churchyard, traditionally said to be the burial place of the ancestors of the American President Ronald Reagan.

BALLYRAGGET, Co. Kilkenny (Map 3, E8), is a village at the intersection of the Abbeyleix (10 m.)–Kilkenny (11 m.) and Castlecomer (6 m.)–Freshford (5 m.) roads. It takes its name from the Anglo-Norman le Raggeds, who had lands here in the 13th c. The tower (still roofed) and fossed bawn of a 15th/16th c. Butler castle still survive in good condition. In the late-16th c. the castle was the chief seat of the Butlers, Viscounts Mountgarret. Richard, 3rd Viscount, was President of the Supreme Council of the Confederation of Kilkenny. A branch of the Mountgarret Butlers resided in the castle until 1788. James Butler (1742–91), Archbishop of Cashel and author of the well-known *Butler's Catechism*, was a son of James Butler (d. 1746/7) of Ballyragget.

1 m. N., overlooking the Nore, in Moat (Moat Park), is Tullabarry motte-and-bailey.

2½ m. E., in Toormore, is Corrandhu Hill, where Eóghan O More of Laois seized 'Black' Thomas Butler, Earl of Ormond and Lieut.-Gen. of Elizabeth I's forces, 10 April 1600.

Aillwee Cave, Ballyvaghan, Co. Clare.

3½ m. SSE. is Foulksrath Castle, now a youth hostel. The de la Frenes were succeeded there by the Purcells in the 15th c. In Shanganny, next townland to the E., are remains of Coolcraheen church (St Nicholas's) and fragments of a 1629 Purcell tomb which include a *Virgin and Child* panel. 1 m. S. of Foulksrath is Swifte's Heath, a 17th–18th c. house acquired by Dean Swift's cousin, Godwin, *c.* 1720.

3 m. SSW. the ruined Protestant church of Rathbeagh incorporates fragments of medieval St Catherine's Church. On the brink of the Nore is Rathbeagh, an oval 'henge' or platform-type ringfort with rampart outside the fosse. This is thought to be the Ráith Bhethaigh named as the burial place of legendary Éremón, son of Míl.

BALLYSADARE, alias **BALLISODARE,** Co. Sligo (Map 7, K2), is a village prettily situated at the head of Ballysadare Bay, on the Collooney (2 m.)–Sligo (5 m.) road. It takes its name from the falls and rapids (Eas Dara) on the Owenmore. Close by are *The Sally Gordens* of Yeats' fame.

700 yds N. of the bridge, on the W. bank of the river, are the remains of a monastery founded in the 7th c. by St Féichín of FORE (*see also pp. 105 and 115*). There are ruins of three small buildings including a pre-Romanesque church with a Romanesque doorway in the S. wall. In the 12th/13th c. the community adopted the Rule of the Canons Regular of St Augustine, and built a new priory some 300 yds to the W., where part of a 13th c. church ('The Abbey') survives, although now surrounded by rubble from a quarry.

2¼ m. N. are the remains of the parish church of Kilmacowen; nearby are Tobar Phádraic holy well and a stone with the 'imprint of the Saint's knee'. There is a simple cross-slab there.

BALLYSHANNON, formerly **BELASHANNY,** Co. Donegal (Map 8, D8), is a seaport and market town at the head of the Erne estuary, on the Sligo (27 m.)–Donegal (14 m.) road. The falls at the river-mouth were called Assaroe (Eas Ruaidh) after the god Áed Rúad, whose seat was nearby Síd Áeda, now Mullaghnashee (*below*). The river-crossing has always been of strategic importance, and has figured prominently in history. (It was there, for example, that the celebrated Red Hugh O Donnell threw back an English force led by Sir Conyers Clifford in 1597.) In the Middle Ages the O Donnells made themselves masters of the crossing, and held it until the final collapse of the Gaelic North. The area was thereafter 'planted', and Ballyshannon received a charter of incorporation in 1611.

William Allingham (1824–89) was a native of Ballyshannon (birthplace in Mall marked by tablet). His best-known poem is probably 'Adieu to Belashanny and the winding banks of Erne'. He is buried in St Anne's churchyard on Mullaghnashee.

¾ m. NW., in Abbey Island by the estuary, are remains of the Cistercian abbey of Assaroe founded by Flahertach O Muldory, King of Tír Chonaill, and colonized from BOYLE in 1178. The

English occupied the abbey on the occasion of their 1597 attack on Ballyshannon. Miscellaneous fragments of 12th c. and later dates are to be seen in the graveyard, graveyard wall, and adjacent farm buildings.

3¼ m. NW. are the remains of Kilbarron Castle, where Michael O Clery, chief of the Four Masters, was born about 1580. ¾ m. SE. of the castle, in Kilbarron, is Giants Grave, a wedge-tomb.

5 m. N. is Rossnowlagh, with very fine Belalt Strand (2 m.). In Coolbeg, ½ m. SSW. of the strand, is a ruined court-tomb. A small collection of local antiquities, bygones, etc., is housed in Rossnowlagh Franciscan friary.

BALLYVAGHAN, Co. Clare (Map 6, F3), is a village and port on the S. shore of Galway Bay, 31 m. S. of Galway and 10 m. N. of Lisdoonvarna. It is a convenient centre for exploring the fascinating Burren country, whose karsts are so well known to geologist, botanist, and antiquarian.

2 m. N. is Aillwee Cave, with caverns, stalactites and subterranean rivers, accessible year-round with guided tours. The entrance building (A. Wejchert) houses a restaurant and craft-shop.

1½ m. NE., in Bishopsquarter, are the ruins of Drumcreehy Church, a nave-and-chancel structure with a Transitional E. window and Perpendicular N. door.

2½ m. SSW., on the W. side of the Corrofin road in Ballyallaban, is Cahermore, a stone ringfort with remains of houses, medieval gateway, etc. 1½ m. SE., on the SW. slope of Ballyallaban Hill, in Berneens, is a wedge-tomb. Three others are visible ½ m. S., in Gleninsheen. 2 m. S. of the Gleninsheen tombs, to the E. of the road in Poulnabrone, is a fine portal dolmen. Excavations in 1986 unearthed the bones of 14 adults and six children, as well as pieces of pottery and stone artefacts, which suggested a date of around 2500 B.C. ¾ m. S. of this, in Caherconnell, is the stone ringfort from which the townland takes its name.

1 m. SSW. of Caherconnell crossroads, in Poulawack, is a cemetery cairn (Nat. Mon.) excavated by Harvard archaeologists in 1934: Food Vessel, Urn, and other burials. 1¼ m. SSE. of the cairn, in Poulacarran, are the ruins of St Cronan's Church, a parish church of *c.* 1500 marking an early monastic site. 1¾ m. SSE. of St Cronan's Church, in Deerpark, is Cromlech, a wedge-tomb.

1½ m. SW., in Newtown, is an unusual castle tower: circular, rising from a pyramidal base.

3½ m. SW., in Derrynavahagh, is one of the best wedge-tombs in Burren.

3½ m. SW., at the foot of Corkscrew Hill, are the ruins of Craggan Castle (O Loughlin).

4 m. SW., the road to Lisdoonvarna climbs Corkscrew Hill, which affords delightful views N. to Galway Bay. 2 m. S. of the

The small fishing port of Baltimore, Co. Cork.

Corkscrew is Cahermacnaghten (Nat. Mon.), a stone ringfort castellated in the later Middle Ages. As late as the 17th c. the O Davorens had a school of Irish jurisprudence there, at which An Dubhaltach Óg Mac Fhirbhisigh (*see p. 205*) received part of his training.

BALLYWALTER, Co. Down (Map 1, H8), is a village on the E. coast of the Ards peninsula 11 m. SE. of Bangor.

¾ m. NNW. are the fragmentary ruins of Templefinn, a medieval parish church. At the E. gable are three Anglo-Norman grave slabs.

3 m. S., in Talbotstown, is a conspicuous motte.

1½ m. NW., in the grounds of Dunover House, is an imposing motte.

BALTIMORE, Co. Cork (Map 5, G9), 7 m. SW. of Skibbereen, is a small fishing port. It is a good sea-angling and sailing (Glenans) centre and the port for Sherkin Island (*see below*) and CLEAR ISLAND.

In 1631 it was raided by Algerine pirates, who carried off some 200 of the inhabitants. The event is commemorated in Thomas Davis's ballad, *The Sack of Baltimore*. Overlooking the harbour are the remains of the O Driscoll castle of Dunashad.

To the SW. is Sherkin Island. At the E. end of the island are the ruins (Nat. Mon.) of Farranacouth 'Abbey', a small friary founded 1460/70 by either Finghín or Dermot O Driscoll for Franciscans of the Strict Observance. The sacristy and bell-tower are 16th c. additions, as are also, perhaps, the E. chapels of the S. transept.

4 m. NE. are Creagh gardens, open in summer.

2½ m. ENE., in Ballymacrown, is Kill Burial Ground; there is a rude, ring-headed cross there.

BALTINGLASS, Co. Wicklow (Map 3, I7), is a small market town on the W. side of the Wicklow massif, where the River Slaney and the Dublin (37 m.)–Tullow (11 m.) road run between Tinoran Hill (1,023 ft) and Baltinglass Hill (1,256 ft).

While the place figures in early legend and tradition by reason of its ancient highway (Bealach Conglais–Baltinglass), its history really commences with Dermot Mac Murrough's foundation (*c.* 1148) of the Cistercian abbey of Vallis Salutis, whose ruins (Nat. Mon.) lie some 400 yds N. of Main St. John Stratford (Earl of Aldborough, 1777) enlarged and improved the town.

Baltinglass Abbey was a daughter foundation of MELLIFONT ABBEY, and itself sent out colonies to Maune (*see p. 122*), Jerpoint (*see p. 291*), ABBEYLEIX, and MONASTEREVAN. The remains comprise fragments of the church and traces of the cloister. The alternately square and cylindrical nave piers stand in a screen-wall which shuts off the aisles. The ornamental details are of modified Irish Romanesque type. The narrow tower at the crossing was a later medieval insertion; some of the medieval floor tiles have been cemented into the interior walls. In more recent times the presbytery (chancel), crossing, and E. end of the nave were walled off to serve as the Protestant parish church.

4 m. NNE., to the W. of the Little Slaney, is the village of Stratford-on-Slaney, laid out (*c.* 1783) and built for Edward Stratford, 2nd Earl of Aldborough, who provided houses and bleach greens for a cotton manufactory, built a church and a chapel, and encourage settlers. From 1785/6 to *c.* 1850 cotton and linen printing were carried on in the mills to the SE. of the village. The 19th c. Catholic church has been tastefully renovated, with interesting Stations, by Christopher Ryan.

5¾ m. NE., in Castleruddery Lower, are a large stone circle and a motte (Nat. Mons.). The circle is enclosed by an earthen bank, and the entrance is flanked by two white quartz portal stones.

1¼ m. ENE., on Baltinglass Hill (1,256 ft), is Rathcoran, a great hill-fort whose twin banks and fosse follow the 1,181–1,187 ft contour. Near the summit of the hill, commanding a broad prospect, are remains of a chambered cairn which covered two passage graves and three other tombs; six stones bear spiral and other signs.

6 m. ENE. (via Tuckmill and Kill crossroads), on the summit of Brusselstown Hill (1,328 ft), is Brusselstown Ring, a contour hill-fort. On the SE. slope of the hill, to the S. of the road, are remains of Castlequarter Church and Castle.

5¼ m. ESE. in Talbotstown Upper are remains of Talbotstown Fort, a quadrangular, moated house site which perhaps marks the *caput* of the medieval barony of Talbotstown. – 1¾ m. N., in Colvinstown Upper, are the remains of Kilranelagh Church, one of the oldest Christian sites in SW. Wicklow. In the churchyard are the Gates of Glory, two orthostats with intervening sill. Coffins for burial were formerly carried between the uprights. – 1½ m. E. of Kilranelagh, in Boleycarrigeen, is Crossoona Rath (Nat. Mon.); in the rampart is an ogham stone. Nearby are the Griddle Stones, an embanked stone circle with 11 complete stones and the stump of a 12th. 2 m. S. is Humewood Castle, an 1845 Scottish Baronial-cum-Norman house, where Michael Dwyer, the 1798 hero, surrendered to Col. Hume in 1803.

BANAGHER, Co. Offaly (Map 3, B5), is a village on the E. bank of the Shannon, 7 m. NW. of Birr and 17 m. SE. of Ballinasloe.

Anthony Trollope (1815–82) was stationed there as Post Office surveyor in 1841, and it was there he wrote his first two novels, both with Irish settings, viz. *The Kellys and the O'Kellys* (1848) and *The Mac Dermot of Ballycloran* (1843–7). The Rev. A.B. Nicholls, Rector of Birr, who married Charlotte Brontë in 1854, died there in 1906.

The ruined church and its shamefully kept graveyard mark the site of an early monastery. The shaft of a High Cross from the monastery is in the National Museum. The Catholic church (1972) is by Robinson, Keefe and Devane, with a statue of *The Madonna* by Imogen Stuart. On the Shannon's banks are a fine early-19th c. fortified bridgehead, batteries, etc.

BANBRIDGE, Co. Down (Map 2, I2), is a market and linen town beside the River Bann, on the main Newry (14 m.)–Belfast (24 m.) road. It is built along a curious main street sunk into a cutting.

Opposite the Protestant church is a statue of Captain Francis Crozier (1796–1848), a native of the town, who was second-in-command to Sir John Franklin on his last voyage in search of the North-West Passage.

4 m. SE., Emdale, Ballyskeagh, is where the Rev. Patrick Brontë (né Prunty), father of Emily, Anne and Charlotte Brontë, was born in 1771.

BANDON, Co. Cork (Map 5, K6), properly Bandonbridge, is a small market town on the Cork (19 m.)–Bantry (38 m.) road.

The town was founded by Richard Boyle, 'Great' Earl of Cork (*see pp. 237 and 307*), who acquired vast Munster estates – often by dubious means – in 1608, after the expropriation of the Mac Carthys, O Mahonys, O Driscolls, Desmond Geraldines, and other ancient stocks. He planted his ill-gotten lands with English Protestants and proceeded to exploit the mineral and timber resources on a large scale.

Some fragments remain of the town wall (dismantled in 1688). One of its gates is alleged to have borne the inscription:

> Turk, Jew, or Atheist
> May enter here;
> But not a Papist.

To which a local wit added:

> Who wrote it, wrote it well;
> For the same is written on the Gates of Hell.

5 m. NE., in Clashanimud, is Cashel Fort, a bivallate hill-fort (Nat. Mon.).

4 m. E., at the junction of the Bandon and the Brinny, are the remains of Downdaniel Castle, a 15th c. stronghold of Barry Óg. It was purchased in 1612 by the East India Company, which founded a settlement there for smelting iron ore.

BANGOR, Co. Down (Map 1, L7), is a prosperous light-manufacturing town and seaside resort on the S. shore of Belfast Lough, 13 m. E. of Belfast.

Near the E. end of Ballyholme Bay is the entrance to a Nat. Trust coastal strip with a fine walk round Ballymacormac Point to Groomsport (1½ m.), where Schomberg, the Williamite general, landed in 1689.

Bangor has a long and illustrious history. It was there that St Comgall, the master of St Columbanus of Luxeuil and Bobbio, and the close friend and collaborator of St Columcille, founded (*c.* 555/9) the abbey which, until the Vikings came, was one of the glories of Ireland, 'a place truly sacred, the nursery of saints' (St Bernard of Clairvaux).

Many of the great saints and scholars of the 6th c. were trained at Bangor. *The Voyage of Bran*, one of the oldest, most famous, and most beautiful of Irish poems, was probably shaped in the monastery.

Repeated Viking attacks led to the decay of the abbey. In 1124 the great reformer, St Malachy (*see p. 46*), succeeded to the abbacy and set about reviving the monastery. His introduction of Continental architecture aroused local ire ('We are Irish, not Gauls. What is this frivolity?'). About 1127 the place was ravaged by the King of the Northern Uí Néill, and abbot and monks fled to Munster (*see p. 304*). In 1137 Malachy resigned the primacy, to which he had been called in 1129, and, setting up a new diocese for the little kingdom of Ulster, fixed his see at the abbey of Bangor, to which he introduced Arroasian Canons Regular of St Augustine. He died at Bangor in 1148. John de Courcy, Anglo-Norman 'Prince of Ulster', transferred the see to DOWNPATRICK 29 years later.

Nothing remains of the buildings of the early monastery, and the only relics are a handsome bronze bell and a small 12th c. altar cross now in the Heritage Museum at Bangor Castle (the Town Hall, Castle Park; an early sun-dial on the terrace nearby; a fragmentary cross-shaft in Clandeboye chapel, and the *Antiphonary of Bangor*, a small service-book now in the Ambrosian Library, Milan, whither it was brought from Bobbio.

Bangor Abbey Church, W. of Castle Park, incorporates the tower which stood between nave-and-chancel of the Arroasian church. In the church are medieval fragments; also 17th–18th c. memorials, including a Hamilton–Mordaunt memorial by the Dutch sculptor Peter Scheemakers (1691–1769).

Near the harbour, adjoining the Tourist Information Centre, is Bangor Castle (Nat. Mon.), a small 1637 Scottish-style tower built by Lord Clandeboye as a customs house.

3 m. SW. is Clandeboye, the fine (private) house and demesne of Lady and the late Marquess of Dufferin and Ava, descendant of Sir James Hamilton, 1st Viscount Clandeboye. Helen's Tower (admission by permit from the Agent) was built by the 1st Marquess (d. 1902) to house a famous library, now dispersed; it is named after his mother, Helen, Lady Dufferin, the poetess.

BANTRY, Co. Cork (Map 5, G7), is a market town near the head of magnificent Bantry Bay, 20 m. W. of Dunmanway, 10 m. SSE. of Glengarriff, and 31 m. SW. of Macroom.

Bantry Bay, formerly a station of the British Atlantic fleet, was twice entered by French fleets: in 1689 to aid James II, and in December 1796, to aid a Republican insurrection. The great 1796 fleet was dispersed by storm and only 16 vessels made the bay (Wolfe Tone was on board the *Indomptable*); they returned to France without putting their troops ashore.

T. M. Healy (1885–1931), leader of the Irish Party at Westminster and first Governor-General of the Irish Free State, was a native of Bantry. The Tim Healy Pass (*see p. 36*) was so named in his memory.

On the façade of the Catholic parish church are two statues by Séamus Murphy (1907–75). The statue of *St Brendan* (1966) in the town square is by Imogen and Ian Stuart.

Immediately SW. of the town, in a beautifully sited demesne, is Bantry House (open to the public), home of the Shelswell-White family. The good Georgian house (brick) was built for Richard White, 1st Earl of Bantry. Its eclectic treasures of European paintings and *objets d'art* include tapestries said to have been made for Marie-Antoinette.

2 m. N., to the SW. of Ballylickey bridge, are the ruins of Reenadisert Court. 3¼ m. NE. of the bridge is Kealkil cross-roads: ¼ m. N., at the crossing of the Owvane, are the ruins of Carriganass Castle, a 15th/16th c. stronghold of O Sullivan of Bear (*see p. 101*). In Kealkil townland are two pillarstones and a small stone circle of W. Cork type.

8½ m. SSW., in Dunbeacon, ¼ m. W. of the by-road crossing the shoulder of Mount Corin, is an 11-stone circle, with an inclined central monolith. In a field on the E. side of the road, in Coolcoulaghta, is a very fine pair of re-erected pillarstones.

1 m. SW., to the S. of the road in Kilnaruane, is an early cross-pillar (Nat. Mon.), with *SS Paul and Anthony* and a boat thought to represent an early Irish canvas-covered currach.

9 m. SW. (via Carrigboy and Durrus) is Dromnea Well: 400 yds ESE. are pillarstones; 440 yds SSW. is the site of O Daly's Bardic School. 4½ m. SW., in Caherurlagh, is Ballyroon holed stone (Nat. Mon.).

1¾ m. W. is Whiddy Island, used as an oil-terminal. There are three 19th c. redoubts there, relics of the British naval station. At the S. end of the island are the remains of Kilmore church. At the N. end are situated the ruins of Reenabanny Castle (O Sullivan Mór).

BARRINGTONSBRIDGE, Co. Limerick (Map 4, B2), is a village 7 m. E. of Limerick.

¾ m. E. are the ruins (Nat. Mon.) of the small Romanesque church of Clonkeen, sole relic of a monastery founded in the 6th/7th c. by St Mo-Díomóg. 2½ m. SE., in Abington, is the site of the Cistercian abbey of Owney, founded by Theobald fitz Walter, ancestor of the Butlers, colonized from Furness, Lancs., *c.* 1206, and destroyed in 1647 by Parliamentarians.

4½ m. ENE. are St Columba's Abbey and school (Benedictine), Glenstal. The nucleus of the abbey is the great Norman-style 'castle' (incomplete) designed (1839 and later) by William Bardwell for Sir Matthew Barrington (1788–1861). It has many eclectic features, including a copy of the Romanesque doorway in Killaloe Cathedral; the figures flanking the principal door represent Henry II and Eleanor of Aquitaine. The 1956 abbey church (Sebastian Braun O.S.B.) has four three-light windows by Patrick Pye: *St Patrick on Croagh Patrick* (1960); *The Calling of St Peter, SS Peter and Paul, St Paul Meets the Romans* (1961); *Marriage Feast of Cana, The Women of Apocalypse XII, The Heavenly Jerusalem* (1964); *The Banquet on Mount Sion, The Cloud Descends on the Tent of the Ark, The Holy City* (1964); also a three-light window by Patrick Pollen, *SS Malachy of Armagh, Bernard, Columcille* (1959) and three memorial windows by Margaret Becker, *St Jarlath* (1971), *Michael the Archangel* (1972) and *St Martin* (1980). Painted interior (German-inspired), choir, organ case (incorporating reredos from the abandoned Catholic church in Dunamaggan, Co. Kilkenny) by Jeremy Williams. In the crypt (also by Jeremy Williams) is an icon or Byzantine chapel, with mainly Russian icons and stained glass by James Scanlon.

BECTIVE, Co. Meath (Map 2, G9), is a hamlet on the E. side of the Boyne, 6 m. S. of Navan and 7 m. NE. of Trim.

¼ m. WNW., on the W. bank of the river, are the ruins of Bective Abbey (Nat. Mon.). The first daughter house of MELLIFONT, it was founded in 1146 by Murchadh O Melaghlin, King of Midhe, and was dedicated to the Blessed Virgin Mary. In the late-12th or early-13th c. the abbey was entirely rebuilt. In 1195 Hugh de Lacy's headless trunk was re-interred at the abbey, his head going to St Thomas's Abbey, Dublin. A dispute arose between the two monasteries, nominally for possession of the complete remains, essentially for certain lands which went with them. In 1205 the Pope had to appoint a conclave of prelates and 'other discreet and venerable persons' to decide the issue. Of the original O Melaghlin abbey nothing at all survives. Of the 12th/13th c. buildings there remain the chapter-house with central column (the kitchen of the post-Dissolution house), part of the W. range, and fragments of the aisled cruciform church. In the 15th c. the church was shortened on the W., the aisles removed, new S. and W. ranges erected inside the lines of the old cloister, and a smaller cloister built. The S. and W. alleys of this latest cloister survive; the arcades have good and interesting details (*see also* Johnstown church, *p. 255*). After the Dissolution, the buildings were converted into a fortified

Bective Abbey, Co. Meath.

mansion (the great hall of the mansion was an adaptation of the monks' refectory; the tower was raised over part of the S. cloister range). Mary Lavin, author of *Tales from Bective Bridge*, *The House in Clew Street*, etc., has a house nearby.

BELCOO, Co. Fermanagh (Map 2, A3), is a Border village on the Enniskillen (14 m.)–Manorhamilton (14 m.) road. It is situated on the isthmus between Upper and Lower Loughs Macnean, in beautiful country (*see p. 78*).

¼ m. N. is Drumcoo Standing Stone, known locally as Crom Cruaich.

1¼ m. E. are Templenaffrin Church ruins, with a crudely carved head in W. gable.

2 m. SE. is Cushrush Island, around the shores of which have been found Mesolithic flint tools, marking the earliest evidence for man in this area.

1 m. NW. is Holywell village. There can be seen: Templerushin alias Holywell Medieval Church; three penitential stations (one a bullaun in graveyard) still visited between Garland Sunday (the last Sunday of July) and 15 August; St Patrick's holy well, described in Camden's *Britannia* as the best cold bath in Ireland and as being resorted to for the cure of paralytic and nervous complaints; and a small stone cross standing on the roadside near its original site as a market cross. – 1½ m. WNW. is Kilrooskagh portal-tomb with a large fallen capstone.

BELFAST (Map 1, K8), is 101 m. NNE. of Dublin and 74 m. ESE. of Derry. Capital of Northern Ireland since the partitioning of the country in 1921, it is Ireland's greatest seaport and commercial and manufacturing centre (shipbuilding, aero-engineering, textiles, etc.). As well as containing the headquarters of the Presbyterian Church in Ireland, it is the seat of two cathedrals and of an established university, while the main campus of a second, more recent, university is on its outskirts in Jordanstown.

Though basically a typical 19th c. industrial city, now struggling to cope with the decline of its staple heavy industries, Belfast has the advantage of being beautifully situated where the River Lagan, on which it stands, flows into Belfast Lough between the Castlereagh hills (600 ft) and the more striking Cave Hill and other heights (up to 1,600 ft).

The name of Belfast – the Irish *Beal Feirsde*, meaning 'mouth of the sandspit', where from earliest times the Lagan could be crossed – first appears in late-15th c. references to a castle of the Clannaboy O Neills commanding the ford. The city owes its origin to Sir Arthur Chichester, sometime commander of the English garrison at CARRICKFERGUS and Lord Deputy of Ireland for most of James I's reign. In 1603 Chichester secured for himself a grant of the Clannaboy Castle, which he rebuilt, and a large estate in SE. Antrim. By 1611 there were the beginnings of a small town, and two years later Belfast was incorporated as a parliamentary borough. By the mid-17th c. it had overtaken Carrickfergus as the main port of the area; by 1750 it had about 8,500 inhabitants, a figure that had risen to 20,000 by 1800. The great growth of Belfast, however, and its establishment as a major manufacturing city and port, took place during the 19th c. Till 1830 the linen industry was largely a rural and domestic one; thereafter, the production of first yarn and then cloth became concentrated in steam-powered mills. 'Linenopolis', as Belfast was sometimes called, became a place of smoking factory chimneys. Improvements in the harbour led to an enormous increase in trade and to the growth of shipbuilding. By the end of the century, Belfast had overtaken Dublin in population and had far outstripped the capital in the wealth of its manufactures.

In the later 18th c. Belfast was the centre of a liberal and democratic reform movement among Ulster Protestants, notably among the Presbyterians. It was strongly influenced by the American and French Revolutions and by Paine's *Rights of Man* (1791). Excluded from political power by the Anglican ascendancy, many Presbyterians felt aggrieved and inclined to make common cause with Catholics. Some, however – such as Dr William Drennan (1754–1820), poet (he coined the phrase 'emerald isle'), and first president of the United Irishmen – were not prepared to go so far as armed revolution, unlike Henry Joy McCracken (1767–98), who led the Antrim rebels in 1798 and was hanged for it, or Samuel Neilson (1761–1803; *see also p. 156*), proprietor and editor of the *Northern Star*. Men such as these and Thomas Russell (librarian of the Linen Hall Library, who brought his friend Wolfe Tone to the town in 1791) made Belfast the cradle of the United Irishmen and of Irish republicanism.

In the years after the defeat of the 1798 rebellion and the passing of the Act of Union, Belfast Presbyterians expressed their liberal feelings through social and educational projects (such as the Academical Institution, of which Dr Drennan was a founder) rather than political action. Later, a number of developments – the evangelical movement in the Protestant churches, the achievement of Catholic Emancipation, the rise of the Orange Order, and a significant rise in the proportion of Catholics in the town's increasing population – combined to lessen Protestant differences and to magnify their common fear of Catholics. Sectarian rioting became a regular feature of Belfast life in the latter part of the 19th c., and the city (it achieved this status in 1893) became the centre of Unionist resistance to Home Rule. Sectarian violence has never entirely died out in Belfast, and has manifested new life in the troubles of recent years, but the visitor to Belfast will find a warm welcome from citizens of every creed.

The focal centre of the city is Castle Junction, where Donegal Pl., Royal Ave., Castle St and Castle Pl. meet in the heart of the shopping quarter. Most of the distances given below are reckoned from there.

Castle Junction preserves the memory of the Chichester castle commanding the river crossing. At the end of the 18th c., ships still sailed up to the quays at the foot of High St. Henry Joy McCracken was hanged from the Market House, High St, 17 July 1798.

At the E. end of High St is St George's Church, 19th c. successor of the 'English Church', Belfast's first Protestant parish church. The fine portico was taken from Lord Bristol's palace at Ballyscullion, Co. Londonderry (*see p. 76*). The church, which was named after George III, was erected (1813–16) to the design of John Bowden, but the interior is a wholesale remodelling to the design of W.J. Barre. Nearby, at the junction of Victoria St and Queen's Sq., is the Albert Memorial (1867–9), a Gothic Revival clock tower also probably by Barre, who introduced the Gothic Revival to Ulster; the statue is by S.F. Lynn. To the E. is the fine Classical Custom

House (1857) by Sir Charles Lanyon (1813–89), an English-born engineer who spent his working life in Ireland and who, in his day, had a near monopoly of Belfast's architectural business (from 1860 to 1872 in partnership with W.H. Lynn); the vigorous stone carving is by Thomas Fitzpatrick: tympanum, *Britannia with Mercury and Neptune*; entrance figures, *Industry, Commerce, Manufacture, Peace*. $\frac{1}{4}$ m. N. of the Custom House, in Corporation Sq., is the Sinclair Seamen's Church (1857) by Lanyon. It has a 'maritime interior in the Moby Dick style'.

N. of Castle Junction, on the E. side of Royal Ave., is Rosemary St, with the charming First Presbyterian Church, a mellow brick ellipse of 1783 (by a local builder-architect, Roger Mulholland; chancel an addition, façade completely reconstructed in 1833). Features of the interior are: ceiling, galleries, curved passages, and box pews. To the E., in Waring St, are the Commercial Buildings (1820), which have a finely composed elevation. The Belfast Bank (1845), by Lanyon, was modelled on Barry's Travellers' Club in London; the interior was remodelled in 1895 by W.H. Lynn.

$\frac{1}{4}$ m. N. of Castle Junction, Royal Ave. joins York St, Donegall St and Clifton St. SE. of the intersection is St Anne's Cathedral, the disappointing joint extra cathedral of the Protestant dioceses of Connor and Down-and-Dromore (1898 with later additions). The baptistery is by W.H. Lynn, its mosaics by Gertrude Stein, the angel heads of the font by Rosamund Praeger. Lord Carson (1854–1935), Dublin-born leader of the opposition to Home Rule, is buried in the cathedral.

In Upper Donegall St is St Patrick's Church. In a side chapel is a mural painting by Sir John Lavery (1856–1941), who was born in nearby North Queen St.

In North Queen St is Clifton House. Clifton House (1771–4), alias the Belfast Charitable Institute, is a home for the aged and infirm. It was erected on the edge of the town by the Belfast Charitable Society as a hospital and poorhouse. Dr William Drennan, first President of the United Irishmen, was a member of the Committee. The building, Belfast's most important Georgian monument, is an attractive, if amateurish, essay. In its original form it enclosed three sides of an open square, and had open arcades to the wings. The Black Hole was for the incarceration of 'sturdy vagrants and beggars'.

200 yds S. of Castle Junction is Donegall Sq. On the N. side are the Linen Hall Library, founded in 1788 by the Belfast Society for Promoting Knowledge; the Robinson and Cleaver building (1887); and the former Water Office (1869) by W.H. Lynn. The City Hall in the middle of the square (1902–6, by Sir Brumwell Thomas) occupies the site of the 1783 White Linen Hall. It is an ostentatious Renaissance-style building around a central courtyard, the very symbol of the Edwardian city's wealth and self-confidence. Inside, there is a fine bronze statue of the young Earl of Belfast (d. 1853) by P. McDowell, R.A., and in the foyer his striking life-size group, in white marble, of the dying earl mourned by his mother. Among the monuments in the grounds are statues of Queen Victoria and Sir Edward Harland, both by T. Brock, R.A., and memorials to the

The Ulster Museum, Belfast.

Bunratty Castle, Co. Clare (see page 84).

first Marquis of Dufferin (Brumwell Thomas and F. Pomeroy) and to the victims of the *Titanic* (Brock). The Methodist Church (1850, by Isaac Farrell of Dublin) on the E. side of the square, has a good Classical portico in stucco. Around the corner is May St Presbyterian Church, an 1829 Classical building by W. Smith. To the S., in Albert St, is the Tudor-Gothick St Malachy's Church (1844; Thomas Jackson) with exuberant plasterwork.

At the SW. corner of Donegall Sq. is Bedford St. The Ulster Hall, the city's largest public hall, was commenced to the designs of W.J. Barre in 1860.

From the NW. corner of Donegall Sq., Wellington Pl. leads to College Sq. East and Fisherwick Pl. Across Great Victoria St at the corner of Glengall St, is the Grand Opera House, Frank Matcham's theatre of 1895, beautifully restored (1980) by Robert McKinstry. Almost opposite is the Crown Liquor Saloon (Nat. Trust), an 1890s gin palace with intoxicating interior decoration. In College Sq., uncouthly obscured by the City of Belfast College of Technology, is the Royal Belfast Academical Institution (familiarly known as 'Inst'), founded in 1807 by the Presbyterians. The austere brick buildings (1810) are by Sir John Soane, whose original design was for a grandiose two-court building of stone. Nearby in College Sq. North, are a few good terrace houses of *c.* 1825–40, including the Old Museum (1831, by William Duff and Thomas Jackson). Founded by the Belfast Natural History (and Philosophical) Society, the Old Museum was the first museum in Ireland built as such. Its chaste architecture derives directly from Athenian Stewart and Revett. Nearby Regency Christ Church (1833) is by William Farrell; the fantastic three-decker pulpit (1878) is by William Batt.

A short distance W. of Castle Junction is Chapel Lane. St Mary's Church is the successor (1868, by John O Neill) of Belfast's first (1783) Catholic 'chapel' or 'Mass-house', to whose erection both Presbyterians and Church of Ireland Protestants had contributed.

½ m. NW. of Castle Junction, the Townsend St Presbyterian Church (1878, by Young and Mackenzie) has a two-light window by Wilhelmina Geddes: *Faith*, *Hope*, *Charity* (1913).

½ m. W. of Castle Junction, in Derby St, is St Peter's Church (completed 1866), grimy, twin-spired, Gothic-Revival pro-cathedral of the Catholic diocese of Down and Connor. This is the heart of the Falls Rd Catholic quarter (denominational segregation of the working-class population has long been a feature of Belfast social conditions). ½ m. SW. of St Peter's on Falls Rd, is St Mary's Dominican Convent; the chapel has a single-light window (1948) by Evie Hone, *Our Lady of Mercy and Dominican Saints*. St Paul's Church, Falls Road, was renovated in 1971 (architect, Laurence McConville; sanctuary, stonework by Ray Carroll; fine window by Patrick Pye).

1 m. SSW. of Castle Junction is the Queen's University of Belfast, founded in 1845 as one of the three Queen's Colleges (*see pp. 120 and 189*) for the university education of those not belonging to the Church of Ireland and raised to independent university rank in 1908. The original 'Redbrick Tudor' buildings (1849), in University Rd, are by Lanyon. The Catholic chaplaincy Oratory (1972), Elmwood Ave., is by Laurence McConville; altar, screen and tapestry by Ray Carroll. Adjoining are the Botanic Gardens (38 acres) and the Ulster Museum.

The latter (1929, by J.C. Wynne, in 'Official Classical' style faced by Portland stone) was greatly enlarged and extended in concrete 1965–71 to designs by F. Pym. The museum houses an art gallery (good modern collection; Turner, Lawrence, Lavery, Yeats) as well as departments of antiquities (important early Irish and Spanish Armada material), natural history (fossil dinosaur), local history and technology. Between Stranmillis Rd and Malone Rd are the David Keir Buildings (1958) with a Redwing figure by F.E. McWilliam in the central court.

1 m. W. along Malone Rd, St John's Church (1894, by H. Seaver) has one window by Wilhelmina Geddes (*The Leaves of the Trees Were for the Healing of the Nations*, 1920) and three by Evie Hone (*St Brigid*, 1948; *Rose Window*, 1947–8; and *St Columba*, 1940).

½ m. E. of Castle Junction, Queen's Bridge and Queen Elizabeth Bridge link the heart of the city with Newtownards Rd and the E. suburbs. ¾ m. NNE. of the bridges is Queen's Island with its famous shipyards (Harland and Wolff), whose huge cranes dominate the view seawards. St Mark's Church, Dundela, in Holywood Rd (1878) is by the English architect William Butterfield; it has a three-light window (1932) by Michael Healy: *SS Luke*, *James*, *Mark*. 2¼ m. E. of Queen's Bridge, Sandown Rd joins the S. side of Newtownards Rd. Near the S. end of Sandown Rd, close to Knock burial ground, is a Norman motte.

3½ m. E. of Queen's Bridge, fronting Newtownards Rd in 300 acres of parkland, is Stormont, until 1974 seat of the Parliament and Government of the six counties of Northern Ireland. A ¾ m. processional way climbs from Newtownards Rd to Parliament House. This massive 'Official Classical' essay (1921–32), by Sir Arnold Thornby of Liverpool, was the gift of the British government and was opened by King George V. The statue of Lord Carson in front is by L.S. Merrifield.

3 m. E. of the Stormont entrance gate, in Greengraves townland, is a very fine portal-tomb (The Kempe Stones).

The City Hall, Belfast.

2½ m. S. of Castle Junction, via Ormeau Rd (passing Ormeau Park, a former demesne of the Chichester family) is Knockbreda Church (1747), sole survivor of the three Irish churches designed by Richard Cassels (the others were in Sligo and Castlebar): short cruciform with apsidal chancel and transepts. The exterior has been spoilt by ugly belfry louvres and the cementing of wall faces. The austere, typically Protestant interior remains attractive, despite the 19th c. windows.

2½ m. SW., in Ballynahatty, is the Giant's Ring (in State care), a 7-acre ritual enclosure bounded by a 15 ft bank; off-centre is a chambered tomb. 2 m. S., at Drumbo, the stump of a Round Tower marks the site of a monastery founded by St Mo-Chumma.

3 m. SW. of Castle Junction, via the Lisburn Rd, at Balmoral, are the King's Hall and the show grounds of the Royal Ulster Agricultural Society. It was there that the 'Covenant' against Home Rule was signed, 9 April 1912. 1¾ m. further is Dunmurry, where the First Presbyterian (Unitarian) Church (1779) is a good example of an 'Ulster barn church'.

2½ m. N. of Castle Junction, via Antrim Rd, in the grounds of Fortwilliam School, is a fine, if small, 17th c. earthen fort with star-shaped bastions. Overlooking Antrim Rd on the slope of Cave Hill (Ben Malighan, 1,182 ft), the grounds of Belfast Castle (1867), Hazelwood, and Bellevue combine to form Belfast's largest (290 acres) municipal park and pleasure gardens. The city's Zoological Gardens are at Bellevue. St Clement's Retreat House Chapel (1970), Antrim Road, is by Carr and McCormick; furnishings by Ray Carroll, and stained glass by Helen Moloney. The interesting stained glass panels (1980) in the Church of the Resurrection, Cave Hill Rd, are by Patrick Pye. The ascent of Cave Hill, as far as Mac Art's Fort, is well worth the climb. This strongly entrenched univallate ringfort on the very edge of the cliff was where Wolfe Tone and his Belfast friends vowed to subvert English authority over Ireland in 1794.

BELLAGHY, Co. Londonderry (Map 1, H6), is a village on the Randalstown (10 m.)–Maghera (6 m.) road. There are the remains of a Plantation bawn (Vintners' Company).

1½ m. E., in the grounds of Ballyscullion House, are the remains of a palace (by Michael Shanahan) built for the Earl Bishop (*see p. 114*), and destroyed before 1813. The portico has been incorporated in St George's Church, Belfast.

2 m. SE., on Church Island peninsula in Lough Beg, are a font and the remains of a medieval church associated with St Tida; the tower and spire were added for decoration in 1788 by the Earl Bishop.

BELLANAGARE, Co. Roscommon (Map 7, K5), is a village on the Rathcroghan (4 m.)–Frenchpark (2½ m.) road.

1½ m. N. is uninhabited Hermitage House, sometime seat of O Conor Don (representative of the ancient dynasts of RATHCROGHAN) and home of the celebrated Charles (Cathal) O Conor of Bellanagare (1710–90), Irish scholar and antiquary.

½ m. ESE., in Drummin, is a ring-work with an ogham stone at the rampart.

BELLAVARY, Co. Mayo (Map 7, G5), is a village situated on the Castlebar (6 m.)–Foxford (7 m.) road.

2¼ m. NE. is Strade, birthplace of Michael Davitt (1864–1906), Fenian and leader of the struggle for land and other social reforms, in whose honour a National Memorial Centre has been built. Close by are the ruins of a friary founded by Jordan de Exeter for Franciscans, but transferred to the Dominicans in 1252/3 by Jordan's son, Stephen. In the church are remains of a fine, figured, high altar with a *Pietà* flanked by donors, and a beautiful 15th/16th c. tomb, with flamboyant tracery and figures of Christ (displaying the Five Wounds) and saints. In the vaulted sacristy are some medieval gravestones.

BELLEEK, Co. Fermanagh (Map 8, E8), is a Border village on the River Erne some 4 m. below Lower Lough Erne, and on the Ballyshannon (5 m.)–Enniskillen (24 m.) road.

Belleek is renowned for its lustre-finish porcelain. The Pottery was founded in 1857 by Sir John Caldwell Bloomfield using clay from Castle Caldwell (*see below*). The Pottery is open to the public. The falls at Belleek have been harnessed to serve the Erne hydro-electric scheme (*see p. 67*).

6 m. NE. is Castle Caldwell. The original castle, now in ruins, was built in 1612 by the Blennerhassets. In 1662 it passed to the Caldwells. A stone fiddle at the castle gate inscribed:

> On firm land only exercise your skill
> That you may play and safely drink your fill

commemorates a fiddler of theirs who fell from a pleasure boat in 1770. Within the grounds (open to the public all year) are the ruins of a Protestant church built in 1641 by Sir Francis Blennerhasset and adapted as a private chapel by the Caldwells.

BELMULLET, Co. Mayo (Map 7, C2), is a small decayed seaport at the neck of the Mullet, 39 m. W. of Ballina and 48 m. NW. of Castlebar.

6¾ m. N., on offshore Illandavick islet, is Erris Head.

6 m. SE. of Belmullet, on the N. side of the Castlebar road in Glencastle, alias Glencashel, is Dún Domhnaill, a rock fort closing the Gates of Erris, with fine views to the NW.

2 m. S., in Binghamstown, is a church by Mary O Carroll, with tabernacle by Imogen Stuart. 11 m. S., by the seashore, 600 yds E. of Termon, is Kilbeg. There is an early cross-slab there.

14 m. SSW., at Fallmore, the SW. tip of the Mullet, are the ruins of St Derivla's Church (Nat. Mon.), St Derivla's Bed (or Grave), and early cross-pillars. The church is a small, primitive structure with a simple, Romanesque W. door on whose N. jamb is some much-weathered, interlaced ornament, while the arch is bordered within and without by incised lines. St Derivla's Bed, NE. of the church, is a small enclosure with an early cross-slab. – 2¾ m. offshore, SW. of Fallmore, is the small island of Duvillaun More (accessible only in very calm weather) abandoned nearly 90 years ago. There are remains of a small, early anchoritic settlement, including a small circular subdivided enclosure. In the E. sub-enclosure are remains of a small corbel-roofed oratory. Immediately to the S. of this is the Tomb of the Saint, at the head of which stands a slab with a remarkable, primitive, yet stylized, *Crucifixion* on the W. face and a ringed Maltese cross on the E. face. 4 m. offshore, NW. of Fallmore, is Inishkea North, with remains (Nat. Mon.) of an early anchoritic settlement. SW. of the deserted modern village are the ruins of St

Columcille's Church, a tiny, dry-masonry structure with lintelled doorway. E. of the deserted village are three dunes (Baileys), on which were corbel-roofed huts of slabs and dry masonry. Associated with those on the central dune, Bailey Mór, are nine early cross-slabs, cross-pillars, and cross fragments. The most interesting has a remarkable, primitive *Crucifixion* incised on it. On the circular platform SE. of Bailey Beag is yet another cross-slab. Some cross-slabs have been removed from the island to the National Museum in Dublin. On Inishkea South are: to the S. of the harbour, a broken cross-slab with an elaborate spiral and fret pattern; to the N. of the harbour, two concentric circles of small stones with a cross-pillar at the centre.

5½ m. SW., by the sea, 2 m. W. of Binghamstown, are the remains of Cross 'Abbey', a small medieval church. 1½ m. offshore is Inishglora with remains (Nat. Mon.) of a settlement founded by St Brendan the Navigator (d. 577). These comprise: traces of a monastic cashel; St Brendan's Cell; St Brendan's Chapel; Templenafear Monastery; fragmentary Templenaman Nunnery; St Brendan's Well; several early cross-slabs and pillars; and seven pilgrims' 'stations', five of them in the W. half of the island.

4½ m. WNW., in the sand dunes, less than 1 m. E. of the ruins of Bingham Lodge, is the ancient Kilmore, a small circular enclosure divided by a N.–S. cross-wall, with a large pillarstone and a cross-slab. A local tale has it that 'people in Kilmore churchyard are buried standing'.

5½ m. NW. are the last remnants of Doonamo (Nat. Mon.), a cliff-top fort with slight traces of *chevaux-de-frise*.

BELTURBET, Co. Cavan (Map 2, C5), is a market town on the River Erne between Cavan (10 m.) and Enniskillen (30 m.).

4 m. SSW. is Drumlane, site of a 6th c. monastery founded by St Mogue, founder of the celebrated monastery of FERNS (*see also p. 226*). In the Middle Ages Augustinian Canons were introduced from Kells. The remains (Nat. Mon.) comprise the lower part of a fine 12th c. Round Tower and ruins of a long, aisleless church. The church was burned down in 1246 and repaired at various dates between then and the 18th c. Attached to the N. wall is a medieval grave-slab with interlacings, etc.

BENBURB, Co. Tyrone (Map 2, G2), is a village on the River Blackwater, 8 m. S. of Dungannon and 10 m. NW. of Armagh, where Owen Roe O Neill won a great victory over General Munroe in 1646.

The Protestant church in the village dates from 1618, and is said to incorporate fragments from the early monastic site at Clonfeacle nearby.

Near the village was the castle of Seaán O Neill, which was burned in 1566. It was probably on the site of the present castle (Hist. Mon.), built in 1611 by Sir Richard Wingfield (who also built the church). The castle, which is dramatically sited on a cliff above the Blackwater, was sacked in 1641 and dismantled soon after 1646. The remains today are those of a quadrangular bawn with rectangular towers at the NE. and NW. angles, and a small circular tower at the SE. corner.

1¾ m. N. is situated Sessiamagaroll Fort, a large ringfort which has an oval motte on its W. side.

2 m. SW., in the ancient graveyard of Eglish (Co. Armagh), are the heads of two High Crosses, with solid recessed rings and a central boss.

½ m. W. is Drumflugh where, in 1597, the great Hugh O Neill defeated Lord Deputy Brough. Close by is Knocknacloy Castle, once the residence of Turlogh O Neill.

4½ m. NW. is Cadian sweat-house.

BERAGH, Co. Tyrone (Map 1, E8), is a small village 8 m. from Omagh on the road to Carrickmore and Pomeroy.

2½ m. E. is Sixmilecross, a village with a wide street, and a good rath to its NE. The district is associated with the Tyrone poet, Rev. W.E. Marshall, born in the area and minister of Sixmilecross Presbyterian church from 1916 until 1928.

1½ m. NW. is Clougherny Protestant parish church, built in 1746 on the site of an older church burned in the Williamite wars. The Glebe House of the church was built in 1778 by Rev. John Lowry.

3½ m. W. is the graveyard and ruin of Donaghanie Old Church, of which little now remains.

BIRR, Co. Offaly (Map 3, B6), is an old market and former garrison town on the Camcor River just above its confluence with the Little Brosna. It is an important road junction at the intersection of the road from Nenagh (24 m.) to Tullamore (23 m.) and the road from Roscrea (12 m.) to Athlone (28 m.).

The early monastery founded there by St Brendan of Birr produced the Gospels of Mc Regol, named after the Abbot at the turn of the 8th/9th c. and now to be seen in the Bodleian Library at Oxford. In the 16th c., the O Carrolls of Ely had one of their principal castles here. In 1620, after the death of Sir Charles O Carroll, this was granted to Sir Laurence Parsons, a kinsman of the Great Earl of Cork. It was he who established the town's first markets and ordinances (preserved in the castle's archives), and who also built most of the structure of the present castle.

The castle was twice besieged in the 17th c., and one of the flanking towers still shows the scars of the artillery of Patrick Sarsfield, Earl of Lucan, who tried unsuccessfully to take it after the Battle of the Boyne. The present Gothic aspect of the front was given to the castle in the 19th c., when the saloon was also added to the West flanker.

The castle still remains the seat of the Parsons family, whose present head, the 7th Earl of Rosse, represents the 14th generation to live there. As a family home, it is only open to the public for special events.

The surrounding demesne is, however, open every day of the year. This comprises interesting gardens with a particularly fine collection of trees and shrubs, all set in a landscaped park with lake, rivers and waterfalls. At its centre is the case of the Great Telescope, built by the 3rd Earl of Rosse (1800–67) in the 1840s and the largest in the world until 1917. The original lens is now in the Science Museum in London. The castle's stable block also now contains an exhibition gallery, with changing displays each summer. The town's 18th c. layout owes much to its close association with the Parsons family, who originally commissioned a statue of the Duke of Cumberland to go on top of the bare doric column now standing in the centre of the square. Possibly the town's finest building is the Ionic temple built in memory of John Clere Parsons in 1828 and now known as John's

Birr Castle, Co. Offaly.

Hall. In front of this, in the centre of John's Mall or Place, is a statue of the 3rd Earl of Rosse by John Henry Foley.

6 m. SE., near Clareen, is Seir Kieran (Saighir Ciaráin), site of an important monastery founded by St Ciarán (Old Ciarán, to distinguish him from his more celebrated namesake of Clonmacnois), patron of the ancient kingdom of Ossory. The place may previously have been a pagan sanctuary; a perpetual fire is said to have burned there. Until supplanted by AGHABOE, Saighir was the chief monastery of Ossory and the burial place of its kings. About 1200 the monastery was reorganized as a house of Canons Regular of St Augustine. The 25-acre site of Ciarán's monastery is marked by earthworks, church ruins, early gravestones (one inscribed OR[ŌIT] DO CHERBALL–'A prayer for Cerball'), part of a small, plain, stone cross, and the sculptured base of a High Cross (Nat. Mons.). The subjects on the latter include *The Fall* and a battle scene. The Protestant parish church incorporates ancient fragments. – About ½ m. S. of Clareen crossroads are St Ciarán's Bush and Stone.

BLACKLION, Co. Cavan (Map 2, A3), is a small village between Upper and Lower Lough Macnean, on the Belcoo (½ m.)–Dowra (12 m.) road.

4 m. S., in Moneygashel, are remains of three cashels or stone ringforts. Inside the S. cashel is a beehive-shaped stone sweat house. (The countryside between Blacklion and Dowra has a number of sweat-houses of different kinds, the majority of which fell into disuse about 70 or 80 years ago.)

6¼ m. S. (1¼ m. SE. of the central fort in Moneygashel), on the S. slope of Tiltinbane, is the White Cairn, the ruins of a court-tomb. About 1 m. to the SW. is Log na Sionna, the source of the Shannon.

1½ m. W., on the S. shore of Upper Lough Macnean, is the promontory of Killinagh. There are St Brigid's Stone and two smaller erratics; all three have cursing stones resting in bullauns or other depressions on their upper surfaces. According to tradition, the pillarstone, sometimes called Crom Cruaich, which stands in Drumcoo, Co. Fermanagh (*see p. 72*), originally stood in Killinagh beside St Brigid's Stone. Nearby are remains of a church (12th c.?), said to belong to a monastery founded by SS Brigid and Laighse.

BLACKWATERTOWN, or **PORT MÓR**, Co. Armagh (Map 2, G1), is a village 2½ m. S. of Charlemont and 1¾ m. E. of Benburb. O Neill's siege of the fort there in 1598 culminated in the defeat of an English relieving army under Sir Henry Bagenal at the Battle of the Yellow Ford.

BLANCHARDSTOWN, Co. Dublin (Map 3, J3), is a village on the Dublin (6 m.)–Navan (24 m.) road.

2¼ m. W. is Clonsilla Protestant church: Evie Hone window (*St Fiacre*, 1937).

1½ m. E. is Dunsink Observatory, from 1782 to 1921 the observatory of Trinity College, Dublin, and since 1947 the School of Astronomical Physics of the Dublin Institute for Advanced Studies. The buildings still retain something of their quiet, 18th c. charm. The greatest name connected with the Observatory is that of Sir William Rowan Hamilton (1805–65), who published his celebrated *Lectures on Quaternions* in 1835.

BLARNEY, Co. Cork (Map 4, A8), is a woollen-manufacturing village on the N. bank of the beautiful Shournagh River, 5 m. NW. of Cork. The Muskerry Hunt has its headquarters there.

SW. of the village is fine Blarney Castle demesne whose 18th c. delights are sung in Richard Millikin's *The Groves of Blarney*. In 1446 Cormac Láidir Mac Carthy (*see p. 54*) built the great castle (open to the public) whose 85 ft keep still stands on a rock over the Croomaun. Beneath it are two caves, one of them partly artificial. Just below the battlements is the famous Blarney Stone,

A stone that whoever kisses
O, he never misses to grow eloquent.

Father Prout

The origin of the ridiculous, and relatively modern, custom of kissing the stone is unknown. – The Mac Carthys contrived to retain their hold on Blarney until the Cromwellian confiscation, when the place was granted to Lord Broghill, son of Richard Boyle (*see p. 237 and p. 307*). At the Restoration the Mac Carthys recovered possession, only to lose it for ever at the Williamite revolution, when Donnchadh Mac Carthy, 3rd Earl of Clancarty, followed James II into exile (*see p. 121*). Blarney was then acquired by the Jefferyes family, from which it passed by marriage to the Colthursts, who built the nearby 19th c. mansion (also open to the public). Not far from the castle is Rock Close, a beautiful dell with trees and a circle of great stones – a piece of 18th c. landscape gardening.

For centuries the Mac Carthys of Blarney maintained a bardic school. With the downfall of the Gaelic order it withered away. The last official head of the school was Tadhg Ó Duinnín (d. 1726), who was driven to take up farming for a living. He later became a priest (*see p. 131*). After him the school was unofficially continued, first by Diarmuid mac Sheáin Bhuí Mac Carthy in the Blarney neighbourhood, then by Liam an Dúna Mac Cairteáin (1668–1717) at Whitechurch (*see p. 121*).

2 m. N., in Waterloo, is a Round Tower of 1836, with imitation Romanesque doorway.

3¾ m. WSW., in Cloghroe, are traces of a Mac Carthy castle built inside a ringfort.

3½ m. W. are the ruins of Cloghphillip, a Barrett castle transferred by deed to the Mac Carthys of Muskerry in 1488.

BLASKET ISLANDS, THE, Co. Kerry (Map 5, A3), lie off Dunmore Head at the SW. tip of the Dingle Peninsula.

Two Armada ships, the *Santa Maria de la Rosa* and the *San Juan de Ragusa,* sank in the Sound, 10 September 1588.

Prior to its depopulation in 1953, the Great Blasket was a noted resort of folklorists and students of the Irish language, and an interesting account of island life, as seen through sympathetic English eyes, is available in *Western Island* by Robin Flower, the distinguished English Celticist who, like Professor Kenneth Jackson of Edinburgh, made an important collection of the folklore of the islands. Flower also translated into English Tomás Ó Criomhthainn's remarkable autobiography, *The Islandman,* a classic piece of Irish writing. Other island autobiographies are Maurice O Sullivan's *Twenty Years Agrowing* (English translation by George Thomson), and Peig Sayer's *Peig* (translated by Bryan McMahon).

Inishtooskert is an uninhabited sheep-pasture, with remains (Nat. Mons.) of a small church dedicated to St Brendan the Navigator, three stone crosses, and four clocháns (and traces of others).

On Inishvickillane the ruins of a small church (St Brendan's Oratory) and of several clocháns, mark the site of an early anchoritic settlement (Nat. Mon.). An ogham stone which stood in front of the church is now in Trinity College, Dublin. The only house on the island was built as a holiday home by the Taoiseach (Prime Minister), Charles J. Haughey.

BLESSINGTON, Co. Wicklow (Map 3, I5), called Burgage until 1683, is a village on the Dublin (18 m.)–Baltinglass (19 m.) road.

The manor of Blessington was created in 1669 by Charles II for Michael Boyle, Archbishop of Dublin, who laid out the one-street village and built the Protestant parish church (*c.* 1682; memorial to Boyle by William Kidwell, the Dublin statuary, who died in 1736). In 1778 the manor devolved on Lord Hillsborough, later 1st Marquess of Downshire (*see p. 203*). The Catholic church in the village is by A. and D. Wejchert (1982). In the churchyard is St Mark's Cross (Nat. Mon.; formerly known as St Baoithín's Cross), a 14 ft granite cross, and another

The Stairway, Blarney Castle, Co. Cork.

ring-headed cross from an early monastic site (which is now submerged) in Burgage More.

Adjoining the village on the E. is the great lake of the Liffey hydro-electric works. It was formed by flooding the valleys of the King's River and the Liffey. Baltiboys nearby was the birthplace of Dame Ninette de Valois (1898–1988).

2¾ m. ENE., in Threecastles, is the 14th c. keep (Nat. Mon.) of a castle.

6 m. ENE., on the summit of Seefin (2,043 ft), is a round cairn (Nat. Mon.) covering a cruciform passage-grave which has six sub-chambers or recesses; two of the passage uprights have lozenge patterns.

3 m. SSW. is Russborough House (Sir Alfred Beit), one of Ireland's notable Palladian country houses (open to the public). It was designed by Richard Cassels and Francis Bindon of Clooney, Co. Clare, for Joseph Leeson (1st Earl of Milltown), a wealthy Dublin brewer. The interior includes some splendid apartments with riotous stucco. In 1988, Sir Alfred donated many of his superb paintings to the National Gallery of Ireland, but others are still displayed at Russborough.

5 m. SW. the Hollywood road crosses the Liffey at Poll an Phúca, where the river, having forced its way through a narrow gorge, plunges 150 ft in three stages. At the foot of the middle fall is the Púca's pool which has given its name to the picturesque cataract. (The Púca was a malicious sprite.) ¾ m. SE., in Ballysize Lower, is an ancient granite cross.

BORRIS, Co. Carlow (Map 4, J2), is an attractive Georgian village on the Carlow (16 m.)–New Ross (14 m.) road.

Borris House, to the W. of the village, is the seat of the Mac Murrough Kavanagh family, descendants of the Mac Murrough Kavanagh kings of Leinster. A remarkable 19th c. member of the family was Arthur Mac Murrough Kavanagh (1831–89), who, though born with only rudimentary limbs, learned to ride and to shoot, was a world traveller, and a Member of Parliament.

4 m. NE., at Killoughternane are the remains of the 12th c. White Chapel (Nat. Mon.), with *antae*.

BORRIS-IN-OSSORY, Co. Laois (Map 3, D7), is a village on the Mountrath (9 m.)–Roscrea (8 m.) road. It was of considerable strategic importance in the Middle Ages and was a major coaching centre in the pre-railway period. The Catholic church (1969) is by Shesgreen, Keaney and Partners, with an unusual Crucifix by Gary Trimble.

2 m. NW. is Clonfertmulloe, site of the principal monastery of Mo-Lúa (544–609). A disciple of St Comgall of Bangor, he was credited with the founding of 100 monasteries. The only ancient remains at Clonfertmulloe are a wall-fragment, St Mo-Lúa's Grave (marked by a rough stone at either end), an early gravestone nearby, St Mo-Lúa's Trough (a few hundred yds away), and St Mo-Lúa's Stone (now at Ballaghmore Catholic church). St Mo-Lúa's Bell is now in the British Museum.

BORRISOKANE, Co. Tipperary (Map 3, A7), is a market village on the Nenagh (11 m.)–Portumna (9 m.) road.

6 m. E. is Knockshigowna, celebrated in folklore as the Otherworld seat of Úna, 'fairy queen' guardian of the O Carrolls of Éile. The hill (699 ft) was a place of Lughnasa celebrations on Garland, alias Fraughan (*fraochán,* bilberry), Sunday.

6 m. SE. is Cloghjordan village, birthplace of Thomas Mac Donagh (1878–1916), poet and one of the signatories of the Proclamation of the Irish Republic, 1916. The Church of SS Michael and John has a five-light window *The Ascension with Five Irish Saints and St Michael and St James* by Harry Clarke (1924) and a two-light window (*Blessed Virgin, St Joseph*) by Evie Hone (1953).

6¾ m. WSW., via Newchapel, are the ruins of Kilbarron 'Abbey', a plain, Romanesque, nave-and-chancel church with traces of a later W. tower; in the nave is a late cross-slab. – Kilbarron Castle was an O Kennedy stronghold.

BORRISOLEIGH, Co. Tipperary (Map 4, D1), is a village at the E. end of the pass between the Devil's Bit and Slievefelim ranges. There are remains of a Burke castle.

1½ m. NW., in Glenkeen, are remains of a two-period church

Russborough House, Co. Wicklow.

Boyle Abbey, Co. Roscommon.

in which is an early-17th c. monument by Patrick Kerin to one Walter Burke; W. of the church is Glenkeen Well. Church and well probably mark the site of Kilcuilawn (Cill Chuileáin), founded in the 7th c. by St Cuileán. Bearnán Cuileáin (now in the British Museum), an ancient bell of bronzed iron encased in fragments of a 12th c. reliquary, is said to have been found 'some centuries ago' in a hollow tree at Kilcuilawn holy well.

BOYLE, Co. Roscommon (Map 7, L4), is a market town where the Carrick-on-Shannon (10 m.)–Sligo (26 m.) road crosses the River Boyle by a good, though rustic, Palladian bridge. In the Catholic church is a *Madonna and Child* by Cliodna Cussen.

On the N. side of the town are the fine ruins (Nat. Mon.) of the 12th–13th c. Cistercian abbey named Mainister na Búaille after the river. (The town took its name, properly Abbey Boyle, from the monastery.) A daughter house of Mellifont, its monks settled there in 1161, and later provided bishops to many Connacht dioceses. The most famous religious poet of medieval Ireland, Donnchadh Mór O Daly (d. 1244), who is thought by some to have been abbot of the monastery, lies buried there.

The abbey figured prominently in local history down to the Dissolution. In 1659 the buildings were occupied by Cromwellians, who did much damage to them.

The remains of the abbey, though fragmentary in places, are among the most beautiful and best preserved in Ireland. They comprise gatehouse with 17th c. porter's lodge (restored), cloister, kitchen, cellars beneath the refectory, sacristy, and noble church. The church (consecrated 1218) is of various dates, and is a most interesting example of the transition from Romanesque to Gothic in Ireland. The barrel-vaulted chancel (the lancet windows are early-13th c. replacements), the transepts (each with two barrel-vaulted chapels), and the crossing (the tower was increased in height in the 15th c.) date from the 12th c. Work on the nave commenced only after an interval. The whole S. arcade is Western Transitional, though the three W. bays are an extension of *c.* 1205–18. The whole N. arcade has blunt-pointed arches, though here, too, the five E. bays are earlier than the three W. The carvings of the arcade capitals – men, beasts, foliage – repay study; all belong to the latest phase of the building.

2½ m. NE. the Boyle flows into lovely Lough Key. Castle Island was for centuries a seat of Mac Dermot of Moylurg. There, in 1541, Tadhg Mac Dermot feasted the literati of Ireland. There, too, and at Mac Dermot's house at Cloonybrien in the parish of Ardcarn, the well-known *Annals of Loch Cé* were abstracted from the *Book of the Duignans.* On Trinity Island are the ruins of Trinity 'Abbey', a Premonstratensian priory founded in 1215 by Maoilín O Mulconry, member of the principal family of historiographers in Connacht. There the so-called *Annals of Boyle* were compiled. The grave of Sir Conyers Clifford is still pointed out. W.B. Yeats once had a project for a community on the island. On the S. shore of the lake is the beautiful demesne (now a public park) of Rockingham. A concrete tower unworthily takes the place of Rockingham House, burned down in 1957.

4 m. E., on the site of an early monastery, is the Protestant parish church of Ardcarn: 1935 window, *SS. Patrick, Brigid, Barry*, by Evie Hone.

1 m. W. is Asselyn (Eas Uí Fhloinn, O Flynn's waterfall), where there are remains of a medieval church, said to have been founded by St Columcille. – 1 m. further W., to the N. of the Sligo railway, is the fine portal-tomb of Drumanone.

Killruddery, Bray, Co. Wicklow.

BOYNE VALLEY (Map 2, H–I–J8), is an area stretching from the mouth of the River Boyne at Drogheda to an area upstream of Trim. In this *Guide*, the area is covered under the following entries: BECTIVE, DROGHEDA, MELLIFONT ABBEY, MONASTERBOICE, NAVAN, NEWGRANGE, SLANE and TRIM.

BRAY, Co. Wicklow (Map 3, L5), a popular seaside resort on the Dublin (13 m.)–Wicklow (19 m.) road, is one of the most beautifully situated towns in these islands. It is also a convenient base for exploring some of the more celebrated beauty spots of Co. Wicklow, e.g. Powerscourt (*see p. 177*), the Glen of the Downs (*below*), the Devil's Glen (*see p. 48*), GLENDALOUGH, and Avoca valley (*see pp. 46 and 280*).

The town is essentially the creation of the 19th c. railway entrepreneur William Dargan, and itself has nothing to offer the tourist interested in history or antiquities, though there is a small museum of local bygones in the Heritage Centre, located on the upper floor of the Town Hall.

Christ Church (Protestant) is by the English architect William Slater. The Catholic church of St Fergal, Ballywaltrim (1981), at the SW. end of the town, is by Eamonn Murphy (1981), with good Stations of the Cross by Yann Goulet, and *The Crucifixion*, with Christ writhing in contortion, by the Austrian artist Josef Zenzmaier, is a gift of the Archbishop of Salzburg.

At the S. end of the 1 m. long Esplanade, Bray Head (791 ft) rises steeply from the sea. In a housing estate on the N. side are the ruins of Ráithín a' Chluig church (Nat. Mon.), a small structure of *c.* 1200.

¾ m. S., in the grounds of Oldcourt House (private), is a tower (restored) of Oldcourt Castle. Close to a stream in the grounds is the base of a stone cross with traces of panelled figures.

1 m. S., in the valley between Bray Head and the Little Sugar Loaf (1,120 ft), is Killruddery, seat of the Earl of Meath. The 'Elizabethan' mansion was built in 1820 to the design of Sir Richard Morrison (1767–1849) and his son, William Vitruvius (1794–1838). House and gardens are open to the public in summer.

1¼ m. SW., at the foot of the Rocky Valley, is the hamlet of Kilmacanoge, with remains of the church which gives the place its name. This is the best point from which to climb the Great Sugar Loaf (1,659 ft), a steep but simple quartz cone.

2 m. W. (via Little Bray), in the valley of the Bray river, are the remains of Ballyman church, rebuilt in the 12th/13th c.

3½ m. NW. is Carrickgolligan (912 ft). The walk hither via Little Bray, Old Connaught, and Ballyman, offers delightful views. The chimney on the summit was connected by a 1 m. long flue with Ballycorus lead works.

BRIDESWELL, Co. Roscommon (Map 3, A3), on the Athlone (7½ m.)–Mount Bellew Bridge (17 m.) road, takes its name (Tobar Brighde) from a well formerly reputed for its cures and for a great *pátrún* which commenced on Garland Friday (last Friday of July). The waters from the well flow through a bath house (roofless) erected in 1625 by Sir Randall Mac Donnell, 1st Earl of Antrim; his wife was cured of barrenness at the well.

2 m. WNW., in Cam(ma), the remains of a simple, early church with Transitional window marks the site of one of the seven principal monasteries of Uí Maine. 2½ m. W. is Díseart churchyard, with remnants of a small Transitional church (with 15th/16th c. windows), etc. S. of the churchyard a 1639 cross commemorates Phelim O Conor and his wife, Sara.

BRIDGETOWN, Co. Wexford (Map 4, K5), is a village on the Rosslare (8 m.)–Duncormick (5 m.) road.

The country there, between Wexford Harbour and Bannow Bay (the baronies of Forth and Bargy), was among the earliest in Ireland to be colonized by the Anglo-Normans. The colonists, strongly fortified in their numerous castles, intermarried only with their own kind. So this area was neither reconquered nor assimilated by resurgent Gaelic Ireland in the 14th and 15th c. Indeed, until quite modern times, the inhabitants retained their own distinctive dialect, the most ancient English speech in Ireland. Moreover, though they rejected the Reformation, they remained stubbornly loyal to the English Crown, and many lost their estates to the Cromwellians in the 1650s. In 1798 the exasperated peasantry, though so largely of ancient English stock, took a conspicuous part in the insurrection.

3 m. NE. are the remains of Mayglass Church, burned down in 1798. A tablet commemorates the unfortunate Beauchamp Bagenal Harvey of Bargy Castle (*see below*), Protestant landlord and local leader of the United Irishmen and of the insurgent Catholic peasantry in 1798. After the collapse of the rising he fled to the SALTEE ISLANDS, but was tracked down and brought to Wexford, where his head was mounted on the Sessions House and his body thrown into the river. His remains were afterwards buried at Mayglass.

4 m. ESE. is much modified Bargy Castle (still occupied), built by the Rosseters.

BROUGHSHANE, Co. Antrim (Map 1, J5), is 4 m. E. of Ballymena, on the road to Carnlough (13½ m.).

3 m. ENE., in Magheramully, are the remains of Skerry Church and 'St Patrick's Footmark' (a hollow in a stone, the legendary toe-mark of a visiting angel). The church is popularly believed to occupy the site of the home of Miliuc, to whom, according to legend, St Patrick was sold as a boy slave; the E. end served as a mausoleum of the Clannaboy O Neills from the 15th to the 18th c.

5 m. ESE. is Slemish Mountain (Sliabh Mis, 1,437 ft), where the boy Patrick is supposed to have herded swine.

BRUFF, Co. Limerick (Map 6, I9), is a village on the Limerick (15½ m.)–Killmallock (5 m.) road.

3 m. E. (½ m. N. of the Hospital road) is Kilballyowen House, an 18th c. O Grady residence.

1 m. S. is the ruined Kildare Fitzgerald, later Foxe, castle of Ballygrennan, a complete bawn with 16th c. tower and remains of 17th c. houses.

3 m. NW., over an area of some 500 acres in Caherguillamore, are remains of a medieval settlement (fields, roads, house-sites). Excavation showed 14th–16th c. houses to be similar to the local farmhouses surviving to the present day.

BRUREE, Co. Limerick (Map 6, I9), is a village on the Ballingarry (9 m.)–Kilmallock (4 m.) road, which crosses the Maigue there by a good six-arch bridge. It is a well-known hunting centre. At the W. end of the village is a restored mill, and a small museum devoted to Eamon de Valera (1882–1975), President of Ireland, and local bygones. On the W. side of the river, in Ballynoe, are remains of Bruree Castle, Upper.

1 m. N. is the cottage where de Valera spent his youth.

½ m. NW. is the unusual Bruree Castle, Lower. Its ringfort-like lower bawn had three turrets; as well as the main tower, there is also a lofty gate-tower; a third tower was levelled early in the 19th c.

BUNCLODY, Co. Wexford (Map 4, L2), is a village on the Enniscorthy (12 m.)–Tullow (12 m.) road. It is charmingly situated.

By the streams of Bunclody where all pleasures do meet

that is where the little Clody joins the Slaney at the foot of the Blackstairs Mountains (Mt Leinster, 2,610 ft; Black Rock Mountain, 1,975 ft).

Bunclody was attacked in 1798 by a body of insurgents led by Father Kearns, in an unsuccessful effort to break out of Co. Wexford.

1 m. S., in the graveyard at Kilmyshall, are remains of a church with a simple, Romanesque W. door.

BUNCRANA, Co. Donegal (Map 1, C3), is a small port and holiday resort on the E. shore of Lough Swilly, 14 m. NW. of Derry and 19 m. S. of Ballyliffin.

½ m. NW. is the 14th/15th c. tower (rebuilt in 1605 by Hugh O Doherty, modified later in c.) of a castle of the O Dohertys, lords of Inishowen. The castle was burned by the English on the occasion of Sir Cahir O Doherty's rebellion (1608), and thereafter was granted to Sir Arthur Chichester (*see p. 72*), who leased it to Henry Vaughan. The Vaughans lived in it till 1718, when Sir John Vaughan built the adjacent house of materials quarried from the castle bawn, etc.

4¼ m. S. is Fahan (Fahan Mura), a pretty little resort where St Mura, patron of the O Neills, was first recorded abbot (early 7th c.) of a Columban (?) monastery here. From the time of the early monastery there survive a cross-slab (built into the road wall near the entrance to the graveyard) and St Mura's Cross (Nat. Mon.), a magnificent work of early Irish art variously dated to between the 7th and the 10th c. The latter is a flat stele 7 ft high, with an arm projecting slightly on either side. On the W. face is a superb cross, of broad interlaced ribbons, flanked by two standing figures of ecclesiastics on whose robes there are inscriptions which have hitherto defied satisfactory decipherment. On the E. face is a ribbon cross of different design with two birds above it. On the N. edge is inscribed a Greek rendering of the version of the *Gloria Patri* approved by the

Cross-decorated slab at Fahan, Co. Donegal.

Council of Toledo in 633: 'Glory *and honour* to the Father and the Son and the Holy Ghost.' Other important relics and surviving art treasures which once belonged to the monastery are St Mura's enshrined bell (Wallace Collection, London) and St Mura's enshrined *bachall,* or staff (National Museum, Dublin). There is a window (*St Elizabeth of Hungary*) by Evie Hone (1948) in Fahan Protestant Church. – 2½ m. S. is Inch, formerly a large island in Lough Swilly, now joined to the mainland as a result of drainage works. In Castlequarter, on the S. tip of the island, are the ruins of a strongly sited castle said to have been built about 1430 by Neachtan O Donnell for his father-in-law, O Doherty. In 1454 Rúairí O Donnell tried to burn alive in the castle his rival, Donal O Donnell.

2¾ m. NNW., in Desertegney, is the interesting Star of the Sea Church (1964) by Liam McCormick, with stained glass by Helen Moloney (eight windows) and Margaret Becker (*Our Lady, St Brigid, St Patrick*), exterior mosaic by Imogen Stuart, and furnishings by Ray Carroll. 2 m. further NW. is Fort Dunree, an early-19th c. fortification, open as a military museum.

BUNDORAN, Co. Donegal (Map 8, D8), is a seaside and golfing resort on the Ballyshannon (4 m.)–Sligo (21 m.) road.

At the S. end of Tullan Strand are the Fairy Bridge, the Pigeon Hole, and the Wishing Chair, rock-formations curiously eroded by the sea.

1 m. W., on the sea coast, are remains of Magheracar passage-tomb, excavated in 1986 and, 1,000 yds E. of this, a wedge-tomb.

1½ m. W. is the River Drowes. Near Bundrowes (Foot of the Drowes), in the refugee Franciscan community of DONEGAL, the *Annals of* the *Four Masters* were compiled (1630–6).

BUNMAHON, Co. Waterford (Map 4, G6), is a fishing village, 10 m. WSW. of Tramore and 5 m. E. of Stradbally. There are many old copper mines in the area.

2½ m. NNW. is Ballylaneen churchyard, burial place of Tadhg Gaelach Ó Súilleabháin (1715–95). His Latin epitaph was composed by his friend and fellow-poet Donnchadh Rúa Mac Conmara.

BUNRATTY, Co. Clare (Map 6, H7), is noteworthy for the keep of a great O Brien castle (Nat. Mon.) commanding the crossing of the little Ratty River, 8 m. NW. of Limerick and 6 m. SE. of Newmarket-on-Fergus. Following on the Anglo-Norman invasion of the O Brien kingdom of Limerick, alias Thomond, Robert de Muscegros built (*c.* 1250) a castle there whose motte may be seen to the N. of the O Brien castle. In 1277 Sir Thomas de Clare built the first stone castle at the river-crossing, and a small town grew up about it. The existing structure was erected *c.* 1460 (by one of the Mac Namaras?). In the early part of the following c. it was in the possession of the O Briens, later Earls of Thomond, who remained its owners until 1712. In 1642, and again in 1645, Brian, 6th Earl of Thomond, handed the castle over to the Parliamentarians. In the latter year the English commander was Admiral William Penn, father of William Penn of Pennsylvania (*see p. 61*). The large, massive, rectangular keep of three storeys has four complex angle turrets, those on the N. and S. sides being linked by broad arches. The original entrance, in the N. face, leads into a vaulted hall, into the S. wall of which has been inserted a sheila-na-gig. Beneath the hall is a vaulted cellar, above it a once splendid upper hall with traces of elaborate 16th c. stucco. In the SE. turret is a chapel with rich stucco ceiling. In its heyday the castle and its gardens were remarkable for their beauty, winning the praise of Rinuccini, the Papal Nuncio, in 1646: 'In Italy there is nothing like the palace and grounds of the Lord Thomond, nothing like its ponds and park with its three thousand head of deer.'

In 1954 the ruined keep was purchased by Viscount Gort and admirably restored (with subventions by Lord Gort and Bórd Fáilte) by the Office of Public Works. Excavations revealed remains of the curtain wall which originally enclosed the castle, as well as some of the garden paving. Only the reconstruction of the roofs and battlements is conjectural. It was, however, suggested by contemporary work elsewhere in Ireland. The castle, which houses the late Lord Gort's collection of medieval furniture, paintings, tapestries, and glass, is managed by a Trust, and is the scene of nightly medieval banquets. Nearby, the Shannon Airport Development Company created a Folk Park, with traditionally furnished cottages of types found within a 50 m. radius. It has also re-created a typical but phoney Irish 19th c. village street, and an 8th c. horizontal mill.

BUSHMILLS, Co. Antrim (Map 1, H3), is a small town on the Ballycastle (12 m.)–Portrush (6 m.) coast road, 12 m. N. of Ballymoney. The Old Bushmills distillery was first licensed to produce whiskey in 1608. The Catholic Church at Billy, just outside off the road to Ballymoney, has three one-light windows by Michael Healy (*Resurrection,* 1925; *Virgin Mary,* 1929; *Ecce Homo,* 1935).

2½ m. WNW., on the road to Portrush, is Dunluce Castle (in State care), romantically situated on a high sea-tunnelled rock and occupying the site of an earlier settlement. In the early-16th c. it was a MacQuillan (de Mandeville) fortress, but the MacQuillans were ousted by the MacDonnells, who occupied it (apart from brief intervals when it was in the hands of Seeán O Neill and the English) until the mid-17th c. In 1639 part of the domestic quarters (along with some domestics) fell into the sea; the rest fell into decay later in the c. The extensive remains are of different periods. The Scottish-style gatehouse appears to date from *c.* 1600. The S. curtain, SE. tower and NE. tower might be 13th/14th c. In the upper court are the ruins of an early-17th c. house. Between it and the S. curtain are remains of a 16th c. loggia. On the mainland are the remains of a large 17th c. courtyard house ascribed to the Duchess of Buckingham, wife of the 2nd Earl of Antrim.

2½ m. N. is the Giant's Causeway (Nat. Trust), a remarkable geological phenomenon. Enormous quantities of basalt have cooled into thousands of polygonal columns (with three to nine sides). These present many curious and spectacular formations, to which Victorian visitors gave fanciful (and silly) names: the Giant's Chair, the Giant's Organ, the Fan, and so on. The Causeway (together with 10 m. of cliff walks with wonderful views) is open to the public. A Visitor Centre houses Nat. Trust facilities, interpretive displays and a café.

4½ m. NE., on a flat, steep-sided rock, are the scanty remains of Dunseverick Castle, probably on the site of the early capital of the kingdom of Dal Riada.

In the 16th c. it was held by a branch of the O Cahans (O Kanes), apparently under the MacQuillans. It was destroyed by Cromwellian forces, the last O Cahan of Dunseverick being executed in 1653. The remains seem to belong to a 16th c. gatehouse.

BUTTEVANT, Co. Cork (Map 5, K2), is a small market town beside the Awbeg River, on the Cork-Limerick road 8 m. N. of Mallow and 8 m. S. of Charleville (Ráthluirc).

The town was founded by the Anglo-Norman (de) Barrys, getting its name from *botavant,* the Norman-French word for a defensive outwork. Its Irish name was Cill na Mullach, the *mullach* of which, though not the name of the river, suggested the '*gentle Mulla*' of Edmund Spenser's *Colin Clout's Come Home Againe* (written in the Ballyhoura Mts; *see p. 131*):

> Mulla, the daughter of old Mole so hight
> The nymph which of that water course hath charge,
> That springing out of Mole, doth run down right
> To Buttevant, where spreading forth at large
> It giveth name unto that cittie
> Which Kilnemullah cleped is of old.

The earliest recorded steeplechase took place at Buttevant in 1752, the course being from the church to the steeple of St Leger Church (4½ m.).

The principal relic of medieval Buttevant is the ruined church (Nat. Mon.) of the Franciscan friary of St Thomas, founded in

Giant's Causeway, Co. Antrim.

1251 by David Óg Barry. It comprises choir, nave, and S. transept with a single E. chapel. The original 13th c. work has sandstone details; the 15th c. additions are in limestone. Unusual features are the crypt and sub-crypt beneath the chancel. The adjacent Catholic parish church is a Gothic structure (1831–7) by Charles Cotterel of Cork. The belfry incorporates Killeens Castle, part of a medieval tower attributed to the Earls of Desmond. At the S. end of the town are remains of one of the towers, etc., of Lombard's Castle, called after the Lombards who figure in the 16th c. affairs of the town. On a riverside rock S. of the town are the tower and bawn of the medieval castle of the Barrys.

1 m. S. are the remnants of Ballybeg 'Abbey' (Nat. Mon.), a priory of Augustinian Canons Regular, dedicated to St Thomas. It was founded in 1237 by Robert de Barry. Apart from the late, castle-like tower, the church is 13th c. (the W. end late-13th). ESE. is the priory dovecot.

4 m. SW. are remains of the ancient church of Kilmaclenine, called after St Colmán mac Lénéne of CLOYNE. Nearby are the ruins of Kilmaclenine Castle, a 1640 house of the Barrys.

C

CABINTEELY, Co. Dublin (Map 3, K4), is a suburban village on the Dublin (8 m.)–Bray (7 m.) road.

1¼ m. SSW. is Tully, site of an early-6th (?) c. foundation of one of the several SS Brigid. The remains (Nat. Mon.) comprise the ruined, Transitional chancel of a church whose earlier nave has almost disappeared, two stone crosses, and two early gravestones. The NW. cross, by the roadside, is a plain High Cross; the (13th c.?) W. cross (in the field to the S.) has the figure of an ecclesiastic on the E. face and on the W. face a human mask. In the chancel are two gravestones of uncertain date, bearing circular and herring-bone decoration (for related examples, *see pp. 62, 177 and 239*).

1 m. SW., is Brenanstown portal-tomb (Nat. Mon.), with its large granite capstone.

CAHERDANIEL, Co. Kerry (Map 5, C6), is a hamlet near the N. side of the entrance to Kenmare Bay on the Kenmare (18½ m.)–Waterville (8¾ m.) road. It takes its name from a fine, small, stone ringfort ½ m. to the W., on the slope of Tullig Mt (1,640 ft). There is beautiful scenery thereabouts.

2 m. ENE., on the slope of Coad Mt (1,093 ft), are the ruins of Kilcrohane (St Criomthann's Church), which gives its name to the parish; ½ m. NNW., at Carrigcrohane, are St Crohane's Hermitage and Tobercrohane; nearby are old copper mines.

3 m. NE. is Staigue Fort (Nat. Mon.), a fine, univallate, stone ringfort with an elaborate system of stairways leading to the terraces of its 13 ft thick rampart (in which are two small chambers).

1½ m. SW. is Darrynane Abbey (Nat. Mon.), ancestral home (*see right*) of Daniel O Connell (1775–1847). It houses many interesting – if hideously Victorian – relics of the Great Liberator. On the seashore is an ogham stone. Offshore, in Darrynane Bay, is Abbey Island which may be reached on foot at low tide. There are remains of a monastery – the real Darrynane Abbey – founded by St Fíonán Cam.

3½ m. W., in Coumatloukane, near the summit of Coumakista Pass (683 ft), with beautiful views, is an excavated wedge-tomb.

CAHER ISLAND, Co. Mayo (Map 7, C6), lies 5 m. SW. of Roonah Quay (*see p. 241*).

The island is said to have been the last station on the pilgrimage to Croagh Patrick (*see p. 305*). In a hollow to the W. of the landing place at Portatemple are remains of a small, early eremitical monastery. Fragments remain of a cashel, or enclosing wall of dry-built masonry. At the E. side of the enclosure, in front of a chamber in the cashel, are the ruins of Templepatrick, a diminutive oratory of dry masonry renovated in the 14th/15th c. E. of the oratory is Labapatrick, a grave covered by an early carved slab and having a carved headstone. In and about the enclosure are many stone slabs and platforms (*leachtaí*) which served as pilgrimage stations. 200 yds to the SE. are Caherpatrick, a small enclosure, and Bohernaneeve, an ancient track.

CAHERSIVEEN, Co. Kerry (Map 5, C5), is a small market town beside the Valencia River, at the foot of Bentee (1,245 ft). It is 10 m. N. of Waterville and 7 m. SW. of Glenbeigh.

1 m. ENE., on the Killorglin road, are the ruins of Carhan House, birthplace of Daniel O Connell, the Liberator (*see left*).

¾ m. N. is the ancient anchoritic site, Killobarnaun, with remains of a small, Gallarus-type (*see p. 62*) oratory. 1¾ m. W. are the ruins of the 15th c. Mac Carthy Mór Castle of Ballycarbery. ¾ m. N. of the castle, in Kimego West, is Cahergal (Nat. Mon.), a Staigue-type (*see left*) ringfort with ruined clochan and rectangular house. ¼ m. NW. of Cahergal is the stone ringfort, Leacanabuaile (Nat. Mon.), which has remains of four dry-stone huts, and two chambers in the terraced rampart. Excavation has dated it to the 9th–10th c. 300 yds N. of Leacanabuaile is Cathair na gCat, a large, stone ringfort.

7 m. NE., on a commanding site with splendid prospects, in Caherlehillan, is a small ancient graveyard with two early cross-pillars, one with the outline of a bird incised above the cross, etc.

4 m. ENE., in Ballynahow Beg, is a stone with Bronze Age scribings.

2 m. S., on Bentee, in Letter, is Ceallúrach (400 ft), a small, ancient, ringfort-type anchoritic site with an ogham stone in the rampart. 1½ m. ESE. are the remnants of Killoe, another anchoritic site. Some 600 yds S. of the road, in Killogrone, is the ancient anchoritic site which gives the townland its name: a sub-rectangular enclosure with remains of clocháns and small rectangular structures; near the centre is a cross-inscribed ogham stone (upside down).

6¼ m. S. (via Aghnagar bridge, 3 m. S. of Letter Ceallúrach, *above*), in Aghatubrid, is the ancient anchoritic site, Kilpeacan: a subrectangular enclosure with remains of rectangular structures and a tall, cross-inscribed, ogham stone. 1½ m. E., to the S. of the road, in Cloghanecarhan, are the remains of an ancient, ringfort-type, anchoritic settlement with remains of buildings, souterrains, and a cross-slab; in the E. entrance is an ogham stone.

10 m. WSW. is Portmagee, a small resort; there is a ferry to Skellig Michael. To the NW. is Illaunloughan, an islet with remains of an ancient anchoritic settlement: tiny oratory, clochán, souterrain, shrine-shaped tomb.

CAHIR, Co. Tipperary (Map 4, D4), is a small market town charmingly situated at the E. foot of the Galty Mt, where the main Dublin (126 m.)–Cork (50 m.) and Limerick (40 m.)–Waterford (43 m.) roads cross the Suir, 11 m. S. of Cashel and 17 m. NE. of Mitchelstown. Adjoining the town on the SW. is the beautiful demesne of Cahir Park (open to the public); a noteworthy feature is the charming *cottage orné*, recently restored.

On a rock-island in the Suir is an impressive 15th–16th c. (and earlier) Butler castle, the largest castle of its period in Ireland (Nat. Mon.; entrance fee; guided tour). Though somewhat incorrectly restored (1840), it gives a good idea of the greater feudal castles of Ireland. The towered curtain encloses two wards or courts, a great hall, and a massive square keep. In Elizabeth I's reign the castle was 'the bulwark for Munster, and a safe retreat for all the agents of Spain and Rome'. Elizabeth's Lord Lieutenant, Robert Devereux, Earl of Essex, attacked it in May 1599. His artillery was too much for the garrison, which fled after a siege of two or three days. In 1647 the castle surrendered after an even briefer defence to Murrough 'the Burner' O Brien, Parliamentarian Lord President of Munster. In 1650 it surrendered to Cromwell without firing a shot. The Butlers of Caher, like other junior branches of their house (*see p. 89*), inclined towards the Gaelic way of life. Unlike the Earls of Ormond, they contrived to remain Catholics, and at the same time to retain, or recover, their titles and estates.

In Church Rd, at the E. side of the town, are some remains of the medieval parish church. The Gothick Protestant church, at the N. end of the town, was built 1817–20 to the designs of the celebrated Regency architect John Nash.

½ m. N., on the W. side of the Suir, are the interesting choir and tower of Cahir 'Abbey', a priory of Canons Regular of St Augustine which was founded about 1220 by Geoffrey de Camville.

3½ m. N., on the E. side of the Suir, in Knockgraffon (Nat. Mon.), a very fine motte-and-bailey marks the site of a castle erected in 1192 – probably by Philip of Worcester – during the progress of an Anglo-Norman 'drive' against Donal Mór O Brien's kingdom of Limerick. To the N. of the motte are remains of a medieval nave-and-chancel church, further N. the ruins of a 16th c. Butler castle. The church is said to have been that in which Seathrún Céitinn (*see* Tubbrid, *below*) delivered the sermon which infuriated the English Lord President of Munster.

3½ m. NNE. are the ruins of Outeragh Church and Castle. Seathrún Céitinn was parish priest of Outeragh in 1610.

5 m. SSW., at Tubbrid, are the ruins of a mortuary chapel, burial place of the vicar, Father Eóghan Ó Dubhthaigh (1550), and of Seathrún Céitinn (Geoffrey Keating; *c.* 1570–1650), who erected it in 1644. Ó Dubhthaigh was the author of a metrical satire on the notorious Miler Mac Grath (*see p. 77*). Keating, poet, historian, and religious writer, is celebrated as the master of classical Modern Irish prose. He was born in Burgess, 1 m. W. of Tubbrid. In middle life he was parish priest of Outeragh (*above*), and later of Tullaghorton. A sermon against vice in high places enraged the Earl of Thomond, and the priest-scholar had to seek safety in flight.

4 m. SW. is Ballylooby. The Catholic church has two windows by Harry Clarke *Beheading of John the Baptist* and *Vision of Bernadette at Lourdes* (both 1925), and *The Holy Family* (1925) by Hubert McGoldrick.

4½ m. WNW., at the foot of the Galty Mt in Toureen, is the ancient monastic site of Peakaun, named after the celebrated anchorite Béagán (Beccanus). The remains (Nat. Mons.) include a small church with a simple W. door and Romanesque E. and S. windows (insertions), four stone crosses, some 30 early gravestones (mostly fragmentary), a holy well, and two bullauns. The great E. cross (shaft only *in situ*) was composite in character (of the same crutched form as St Patrick's Cross, Cashel), and formed part of an elaborate construction; it bears a long inscription in Irish and rudimentary incised ornament. The best-preserved gravestones are inscribed CUMMENE-LADCEN, SOADBAR, DOMNIC, SOERLECH, FLAND, DONGUS.

CALEDON, Co. Tyrone (Map 2, F3), is a small and picturesque village on the River Blackwater on the road between Aughnacloy (8 m.) and Armagh (7 m.). Originally an O Neill estate, later owned by the Earls of Cork and Orrery, it came into the possession of the Cork and Orrery Alexanders, who were created Earls of Caledon at the Union in 1800. It was the 2nd Earl who did most to develop the attractive stone-built village. The most interesting stone building on the street is the Court House (*c.* 1822), probably by William Murray.

Toureen Peakaun, Co. Tipperary.

Caledon House, Co. Tyrone.

St John's Protestant Church dates from 1768, and has a fine spire added by John Nash in 1808. At the other end of the village there was once a huge five-storey flax mill, later used for making woollens and Caledon 'tweeds', which sadly is no more. The same is now the fate of the Caledon monument, an elegant Doric column surmounted by Thomas Kirk's statue of the 2nd Earl.

1 m. S. of the village is Caledon House, built by the 1st Earl and one of the finest Georgian residences in Ireland. The core dates from 1779, and is the work of Thomas Cooley. John Nash then added a colonnade in 1812. The interiors have good Adam plasterwork, and the oval drawing-room has a frieze of gilded dolphins above the doors. The park, which was laid out by the 5th Lord Orrery around 1740, has a herd of red deer and an unusual bone-house folly of 1747. The head and shaft of two separate High Crosses brought here from Glenarb, 3 m. N., are also to be seen in the grounds. Two more crosses from Glenarb are now at TYNAN, Co. Armagh.

CALLAN, Co. Kilkenny (Map 4, G3), is a market town where the Kilkenny (10 m.)–Clonmel (22 m.) road crosses the little Owenree River.

At the Anglo-Norman invasion William the Marshal established a manor at Callan and founded the town (1217). In 1391 the manor was sold to James Butler, 3rd Earl of Ormond.

In the town are the ruins of the 15th c. parish church and of the 'Abbey', a friary of Augustinian Observants. The former, dedicated to the Assumption of the Blessed Virgin Mary, is a very interesting, aisled, nave-and-chancel edifice with square W. tower (13th c.?; upper part 17th?). The chancel was until recently adapted for use as the Protestant parish church, but the nave and aisles (Nat. Mon.) have long been roofless. In the chancel are preserved a large medieval font and fragments of several 16th c. tombs. In the nave are fragments of 15th–17th c. monuments.

The friary was founded about 1462 by Émonn mac Risderd Butler of Pottlerath (*below*) and was colonized from Connacht. The buildings were erected (1467–70) by Émonn's son, James (father of Sir Piaras Rúa Butler, Earl of Ossory and Ormond). In 1462 the friary was affiliated to Santa Maria del Popolo, Rome. The conventual buildings have long since disappeared, but substantial remains of the church survive in the middle of a pitch and putt course! In the chancel are fine sedilia.

In Main St is a Peter Grant statue of Edmund Ignatius Rice.

NW. of the town, in West Court demesne, are the great motte (Nat. Mon.) – a modified hillock – and traces of the bailey of William the Marshal's castle of Callan. 1 m. NW., in West Court North, is the farmhouse in which was born Edmund Ignatius Rice (1762–1844), founder of the Irish Christian Brothers and Presentation Brothers. It is now preserved as a Museum, with small chapel nearby; all the stained glass is by Helen Moloney. Other furnishings are of lesser quality.

4½ m. SW. is Killamery, where St Gobán Fionn (alias Mo-Ghobóg) founded a monastery in the 6th c. Among the relics of the monastery are a fine 8th/9th c. High Cross (Nat. Mon.) and an early gravestone. Most of the carving on the cross consists of interlaces, frets, and other abstract ornament. The weathered figure subjects include: N. arm: apparently scenes from the life of St John the Baptist; W. face: *Hunting Scene; Procession with Chariot*. S. arm: *Noah's Ark*. The W. side of the base is said to bear the inscription: OR[ÕIT] DO MAELSECHNAILL ('A prayer for Mael-Sechnaill'). Nearby to the S. is the early gravestone. It has the (repeated) inscription: OR[ŌIT] AR ANMAINN AEDAIN – OR[ŌIT] AR ANMIN AEDAEN ('A prayer for the soul of Aedán').

6 m. SW. is Mullinahone, home of Charles Joseph Kickham (1828–92), Young Irelander, Fenian, and novelist (*Knocknagow*, etc). His epitaph, in the local graveyard, is by the celebrated Fenian John O Leary.

1 m. N. of Killaloe, in Ballykeefe Bog, is preserved the 14th c. effigy of a woman, said to have come from Ballykeefe Castle nearby.

6 m. NNW. is Kilmanagh, site of an early monastery founded by St Nadál, master of St Seanán of Inis Chathaigh (*see p. 226*). The only relic there is Tobar Nadán, St Nadán's (Nadál's) Well. A medieval wooden figure of St Nadán, preserved at Kilmanagh till about 1875, is now in St Kieran's College, Kilkenny. – 1 m.

SW. is Pottlerath (Ráth an Photaire, potter's ringfort). Near Pottlerath House was the castle of Émonn mac Risderd Butler (d. 1464). Émonn was a noted patron of Irish literature, and in his castle Seán Buidhe O Clery wrote (*c.* 1454) the celebrated Bodleian manuscript Laud Misc. 610 (*Saltair Émuinn mhic Risderd*), which was one of two manuscripts given to the Earl of Desmond in ransom for Émonn after the battle of PILTOWN, 1462. Near the site of Émonn's castle are the ruins of Teampall na Rátha, a small nave-and-chancel church and an apparently post-medieval dovecot.

CAMPILE, Co. Wexford (Map 4, J5), is a village on the New Ross (8 m.)–Ramsgrange (3 m.) road situated to the E. of the River Barrow.

4 m. SSW. are the twin fishing villages of Arthurstown and Ballyhack, on the E. shore of Waterford Harbour. At Ballyhack there is a ferryboat service to Passage East on the opposite side of the estuary. Ballyhack Castle originated as a preceptory of the Knights Templar, subject to the preceptory at Kilcloghan. It was wrecked by Cromwell and his troops in 1649. The chapel recalls that at FERNS. Pottery imported from France, Spain, Portugal, Holland and England was found deposited in a garderobe in the castle.

1 m. WSW. is Dunbrody Abbey (Nat. Mon.), the finest medieval ruin in Co. Wexford. The abbey was built by the English Cistercians of St Mary's Abbey, Dublin, at that time a dependency of Buildwas (Shropshire), to which Hervey de Montmorency (*see* Great Island, *below*) – Strongbow's uncle and seneschal – had granted lands thereabouts 1178. It was transferred to St Mary's Abbey in 1182. The remains comprise cruciform church with five-bay, aisled nave, six transept chapels, and low central tower; also a cloister garth with some remains of the sacristy, six-bay, groin-vaulted chapter-house, and undercroft of the dormitory, etc., on the E. side; of a possible lavabo on the S. side, and of the refectory on the S. side. The work is, in the main, early-13th c., but the tower is a 15th c. insertion; the living-rooms over the S. transept chapels are additions of about the same period. The architectural details, in the austere Cistercian tradition, are good, but the foundations of the church and the construction in general are poor. (In places the walls were bonded merely with tough clay.) And so the church had to be buttressed at an early stage of its history.

3 m. WNW., at the N. end of Great Island (formerly Hervey's Island, after Hervey de Montmorency, who had the *caput* of his barony on the island), which is no longer insulated and which now has a large electricity generating station, are the remains of the large circular earthwork of Kilmokea. Surviving only in isolated sectors, they consist of two banks of earth and stones with intervening ditch. The enclosure is some 1,000 ft in diameter from N. to S., and 900 ft from E. to W. In the SW. quadrant are the graveyard and site of the ancient church of Kilmokea with a small stone cross and a cross-base; in the NW. and on the N. periphery are remains of a circular annexe with internal structures. The whole possibly represents a fortified Anglo-Norman village of the 13th–14th c., something otherwise unknown among Irish monuments. To the E. is a large rectangular earthwork (254 ft); this is probably the site of a medieval manor-house.

CAPPOQUIN, Co. Waterford (Map 4, E6), is a small market town on the Dungarvan (11 m.)–Lismore (4 m.) road, set in beautifully wooded country where the Glenshelan River joins the Blackwater at the foot of the Knockmealdown Mts.

3 m. NW. is Mount Melleray Cistercian abbey, founded in 1832 in what was then a barren wilderness by Irish monks expelled from France in 1822. The new abbey church (built of the stones of George Richard Pain's 'castle' for Lord Kingston at Mitchelstown) is a disappointing essay in the Gothic manner. The abbey guest-house dispenses hospitality gratis, but offerings from the guests never come amiss. At the abbey are five ogham stones from the ancient cemetery of Kilgrovan.

2½ m. SSE. is Affane, scene of a celebrated battle, 1 February 1565, between the Earls of Ormond and Desmond. Affane House occupies the site of Affane Castle, birthplace of Valentine Greatraks (1629–83), 'The Stroaker', who cured scrofula and other diseases by stroking with his hands and by hypnotism and faith-healing; Charles II of England was among his patients.

5 m. SSW., to the W. of the Blackwater, are the ruins of Okyle church (14th/15th c.).

CARLINGFORD, Co. Louth (Map 2, J5), is a small resort and seaport charmingly situated on the Newry (12 m.)–Greenore (3 m.) road, at the foot of Slieve Foye (splendid views) which rises 1,935 ft above the S. shore of Carlingford Lough.

In the Middle Ages an English town grew up there under the shadow of the castle, first built in the 12th c. by Hugh de Lacy. King John stayed at the castle for three days on his way to attack de Lacy at Carrickfergus. Later on the place came to be an important border fortress of the English Pale. In 1689 the place was fired by Berwick's retreating Jacobites; Schomberg subsequently used it as a hospital station.

The only considerable fortification surviving today is the shattered King John's Castle (Nat. Mon.), strikingly sited on a rock commanding the landing-place. The D-shaped plan is unusual, while the gateway (on the W. side) is noteworthy as having been designed to admit only a single horseman at a time. Only the W. wall, SW. tower, and the remains of the gatehouse belong to the earliest phase (late-12th or early-13th c.). The E. part, originally three storeys high with the courtyard doorway on the first floor, dates from 1262.

The Mint (Nat. Mon.), situated just off the Square, is a fortified town house of the 15th/16th c. It is said to occupy the site of a mint erected in 1467. It has curious window-carvings ('revived' pre-Norman motifs, etc.).

Taafe's Castle, opposite the station, is a fortified 16th c. town house. The Taafes were a leading family of the Pale (*see p. 43*).

The Tholsel, originally one of the town gates, is so called because it served for a time as the meeting place of the Sovereign and 12 Burgesses of Carlingford. In the 18th c. it also served as the town gaol.

The tower of the Protestant church was originally one of the towers of the town wall, other portions of which also survive.

Mountain View, in Dundalk St, behind the Protestant church, was the birthplace of Thomas D'Arcy Magee (1825–68), poet and Canadian statesman.

To the S. of the Protestant church are the ruins of a Dominican friary founded in 1305 by Richard de Burgo (?) and rebuilt in the 16th c.

3 m. SE. is Greenore, a beautifully situated small seaside resort and decayed port.

¾ m. S., in Roosky, is the 'Priory', where considerable traces of a medieval monastery can be recognized; the church had a trabeate doorway. ¾ m. SW., in Commons, is a townland dual-court cairn (550 ft); in neighbouring Irish Grange is another court-tomb.

4 m. S., near the coast, is Ballug Castle, a 15th c. stronghold of the Bagnalls. 1 m. SE., in Templetown, are the remains of Kilwirra (Cill Mhuire, St Mary's Church). 5½ m. W., at Rockmarshall House, is a court-tomb (Nat. Mon.) with a long gallery.

5 m. N., in Cooley, is Omeath, a small resort near the head of beautiful Carlingford Lough. The Omeath district was the last area in Leinster where Irish survived as a living language. (The Cooley peninsula preserves the name of the Cúailnge of early Irish literature and history.)

CARLOW, Co. Carlow (Map 3, G8), pleasantly sited on the E. bank of the Barrow, 12 m. S. of Athy and 9 m. N. of Bagenalstown, is capital of its county, cathedral town of the Catholic diocese of Kildare and Leighlin, an important road and marketing centre, and a manufacturing town of some consequence.

Its strategic position made Carlow an important Anglo-Norman and English stronghold in the Middle Ages. About 1180 Hugh de Lacy built a (motte-and-bailey?) castle to command the river crossing. This first castle was succeeded by a strong stone fortress (*below*), built (probably by William the Marshal) between 1207 and 1213 at the confluence of the Burren and Barrow. Carlow then passed, through William's daughter, Maud, to Roger le Bigod, Earl of Norfolk. Subsequently the castle fell to the Crown and was granted to the Howards who held it until the reign of Henry VIII, though after 1327 much of the modern County Carlow was recovered by the Irish of Leinster. The town was walled in 1361 by Lionel, Duke of Clarence, son of Edward III and his Lieutenant in Ireland.

The once great castle is now represented by only a fragment (Nat. Mon.) of the keep, or innermost citadel. This was of that peculiarly Norman-Irish type, viz. a rectangle with drum towers at the angles.

The Court House (1830) is a typical Classical building by William Vitruvius Morrison (1794–1838).

In the Town Hall is a museum concentrating on 19th c. life in the county, and local celebrities.

The Cathedral of the Assumption of the Blessed Virgin Mary (1828–33) is a Gothick essay by Thomas A. Cobden, who took over from Joseph Lynch in 1829. It contains a fine monument (1839) by John Hogan to Bishop James Doyle (1786–1834) who, as J.K.L. (James, Kildare and Leighlin), was a prominent champion of Catholic emancipation. Behind the cathedral is St Patrick's Diocesan Seminary. Its chapel was refurbished (1978) by Richard Hurley, with furnishings by Roy Carroll and Benedict Tutty. Housed in the same building is the Irish Institute for Pastoral Liturgy which has inspired many interesting modern church furnishings in Co. Carlow and elsewhere throughout the country. Its own stark white chapel is a 19th c. room transformed (1980) by Richard Hurley, with crucifix by Benedict Tutty and tabernacle by Peter Donovan.

The Protestant parish church (St Mary's) is partly 18th c., partly early-19th c. Gothick.

2 m. NE. is Oak Park, a good early-19th c. house with Ionic portico; now an agricultural research centre.

2 m. E., in Kernanstown, in the demesne of Browne's Hill House, is the Mount Browne Dolmen, a very fine portal-tomb whose capstone, the largest in Ireland, weighs over 100 tons.

2½ m. ESE. is Bennekerry. The Catholic church was refurbished (1978) by Kenneth O Brien, with sanctuary stonework by Michael Biggs, bronze and enamel by Patrick McElroy, and batik Stations of the Cross by Bernadette Madden – one of the country's more successful conversions after the Second Vatican Council.

3 m. SE. is Tinryland. The Catholic church has a *Baptism* window by A.E. Child (*c.* 1935), sanctuary windows by Helen Moloney, metalwork by Seán Adamson and stoneware Stations by Christopher Ryan.

3 m. WNW., at the foot of Slieve Margy, is Killeshin, Co. Laois. St Comghán founded a monastery there before the close of the 5th c. The church was destroyed in 1041, the monastery burned in 1077. The lofty Round Tower was wantonly demolished in 1703, and all that now survive are the W. gable and fragments of the N. and S. nave walls of a Romanesque church, together with fragments of a 15th c. chancel (Nat. Mons.). The richly carved Romanesque W. doorway (four orders) is particularly fine; there are traces of a mutilated inscription on the jambs and imposts.

1 m. NNW., near the W. bank of the Barrow, are the remains of Sleaty (Sléibhte) church (partly 12th c.) and two plain early crosses (Nat. Mons.). The earliest church there is said to have been founded by Bishop Fíacc Finn, a convert of St Patrick's. Muirchú's celebrated 7th c. *Life of St Patrick*, the basis of all subsequent Patrician biography, was written 'at the dictation' of Bishop Áed of Sleaty (d. 700).

CARNA, Co. Galway (Map 6, C1), is a small village and quiet holiday and fishing resort on Ard Bay, Connemara, 36 m. W. of Galway and 22 m. SE. of Clifden.

3½ m. WSW. is An Más (Mace), convenient starting point for the crossing (1½ m.) to Crúanacára (Cruach Mhac Dhara), alias St Mac Dara's Island, one of the most venerated holy places of the West. (Local boats dipped their sails three times when passing it.) Pilgrimages take place there on 16 July (regatta afterwards) and 25 September. St (Síonnach) Mac Dara founded an eremitical monastery here. The remains (Nat. Mons.) comprise the ruins of a small stone-roofed church (restored 1976) of unusual interest (timber, elbow-cruck construction translated into stone), its carved gable-finial (replaced by a stiff modern version), the saint's *leaba*, a holy well, and three pilgrimage 'Stations' with early crosses, cross-slabs, etc.

CARNDONAGH, Co. Donegal (Map 1, D2), is a market and manufacturing village situated on the Derry (20 m.)–Malin (3 m.) road.

The Catholic parish church (1945) is an Italianate-Romanesque structure by Ralph Byrne (*see pp. 102 and 252*). The statues and such details as columna and capitals are good, but the Stations of the Cross are bad.

St Mary's Church, Callan, Co. Kilkenny (see page 88).

The Rock of Cashel, Co. Tipperary *(see page 96).*

$\frac{1}{3}$ m. W. is Donagh, site of an early bishopric, possibly Patrician. The church was presumably monastic originally, but it later became a parish church of the diocese of Derry. From the early period there survive four remarkable monuments: St Patrick's Cross with its two flanking stelae (Nat. Mons.), by the roadside E. of the Protestant church, and a tall cross-pillar in the graveyard. Some would date St Patrick's Cross to the 7th c., and regard it therefore as one of the most important monuments of early Christian art in the British Isles. Others see it as a provincial product of the 9th/10th c. At the top of the E. face is a cross of two broad, interlaced ribbons, with birds beneath the arms; in the middle is a grotesque *Crucifixion*; at the foot are three figures (*The Three Women Coming to the Tomb?*). The W. face is covered by an interlacing of broad ribbons. The S. side bears the outlines of four figures, one above the other. The stelae have human figures, spirals, etc., carved in the same shallow manner. The graveyard cross-pillar has on the E. face a *Crucifixion* above an interlaced cross, which stands on a fret-pattern base; on the W. face a 'marigold' cross, with fret-pattern shaft flanked by two ecclesiastics. The Protestant church has medieval fragments, including a (12th c. ?) carved door-lintel.

$3\frac{1}{2}$ m. E., in Carrowmore, two stone crosses and a rock with a bullaun and an incised cross mark an ancient church site; the W. face of the East Cross bears the figure of Christ in glory.

CARNEW, Co. Wicklow (Map 4, L1), is a village on the Gorey (9 m.)–Tullow ($13\frac{1}{2}$ m.) road. The 17th c. O Toole castle, modernized and incorporated in the Rectory, was a British garrison post in 1798. It was captured by the Insurgents, who fired the village. Thirty-six of them were afterwards executed at the castle, where there is now a monument to them.

CARRAN, Co. Clare (Map 6, G4), is 10 m. S. of Corcomroe Abbey and 11 m. N. of Corrofin, near the edge of a large *polje* in the limestone. The surrounding country is rich in megalithic, early historic, and medieval remains. To the W. lie some of the finest of the Burren karsts.

1 m. NE., in Termon, are the ruins of Templecronan (Nat. Mon.), a small 12th c. church: trabeate W. door ornamented with Romanesque animal masks; angle mouldings; carved heads in the W., N., and S. walls; in the N. wall a Late Gothic door. SE. of the church is St Cronan's Bed (Nat. Mon.), a gabled, stone tomb. NE. of the church (next field) is a second tomb.

1 m. S., is Castletown. $1\frac{1}{2}$ m. due E., in Cappaghkennedy, is a well-preserved wedge-tomb. 1 m. SSW. of Castletown, on a roadside rock-pinnacle in Tullycommon, is Cashlaungarr (Nat. Mon.), a stone ringfort. $\frac{1}{2}$ m. ENE. is Cathercommaun, a trivallate cliff-fort of *c.* A.D. 800 or earlier (Nat. Mon.). Traces of 12 stone huts, including a guard-house and sentry post, survive. A souterrain in the largest hut led to an escape down the cliff face.

CARRICK, Co. Donegal (Map 8, B6), is a small village on the Killybegs (11 m.)–Glencolumbkille (6 m.) road.

2 m. S., on the W. shore of the estuary, is the little village of Teelin, a convenient place from which to climb Slieve League (1,972 ft), where the climber is rewarded with a prospect of the stupendous cliffs of Slieve League rising nearly 2,000 ft from the Atlantic. (Climbers are advised to be cautious and, if necessary, to take a guide.) The summit itself affords one of the most remarkable panoramas in Europe. Nearby the remains of St Aed mac Bric's Oratory and holy wells mark the site of a hermitage associated with SS Assicus (*see p. 59*) and Aed mac Bric (*see pp. 64, 193 and 297*).

CARRICKFERGUS, Co. Antrim (Map 1, L7), is a port (marina), resort, and market town on the Belfast (11 m.)–Larne (14 m.) coast road. The population of this historic place has increased in recent years by overspill from Belfast.

Carrickfergus Castle (in State care) is believed to have been begun by John de Courcy around 1180. In 1210 it was taken from his successor Hugh de Lacy by King John after a nine-day siege. In 1315–16 it held out for over a year against Edward Bruce. In 1384 it was destroyed by Niall Mór O Neill of Tír Eóghain. In 1690 the castle was taken from the Jacobites by Schomberg, and on 14 June in that year William of Orange landed beneath its walls at the spot now marked by a commemorative stone. In 1760 the French naval commander Thurot took the castle and town after a gallant defence. On 24 April 1778, the first action in European waters by an American ship took place offshore, when Paul Jones, in the *Ranger*, defeated the British *Drake*. In the 18th c. the castle served as a prison. Among those confined there in 1796 were the United Irishmen Luke Teeling and William Orr. The castle comprises three 12th to mid-13th c. wards. The entrance is between massive, D-shaped (originally circular) towers, reduced in height at a Tudor-period adaptation for artillery. In the outer ward are Tudor gun platforms, that on the left having storerooms beneath. The curtain between outer and middle wards survives only in fragmentary form. At the S. end of the middle ward is a water gate. The curtain of the inner ward (entrance modern) marks the limits of the first stone castle, the nucleus of the fortress; the lower part dates from the 1180s. In the NW. corner of this ward is the great, four-storey, Norman keep, with its entrance (as normally) at first-floor level. The ground floor has two barrel-vaulted chambers, one with a well shaft. On the second floor is the Great Hall (restored); the arch is 16th c. The original Great Hall seemingly stood against the E. curtain of the inner ward. The keep houses a small museum display.

The Town Hall, High St, retains the charming, 1779 façade of the County Court House.

St Nicholas's Protestant Church was commenced in 1185. It owes its aisleless, cruciform shape to a rebuilding for Protestant use in 1614, but had previously had both N. and S. aisles, the latter double. In the truncated nave are to be seen fragments of the original arcades. The N. transept (Donegall Chapel) was rebuilt in 1614 by Sir Arthur Chichester, the ground floor as a mausoleum, the upper storey as a family pew (Jacobean woodwork); at the N. end is an elaborate Renaissance memorial with effigies of Sir Arthur (d. 1625), his wife, infant son, and brother, Sir John Chichester (d. 1597); the *St John the Beloved* window (1929) is by Ethel Rhind, the *St Andrew* window (1929) by Catherine O Brien. The chancel is 14th/15th c. The three-light *Good Shepherd, Good Samaritan, Prodigal Son* window is by C. O Brien (1911); the three-light *SS Columba, Patrick, Aidan*, is by A.E. Child (1912); *Christ and the Knight* is by Lady Glenavy (1918). The tower dates from 1778.

The Catholic church in Minorca Place (1981) is by Liam McCormick. Much of the 17th c. town wall survives, including the North (or Spittal) Gate and N. corner bastion.

On the outskirts of the town, on the road to Larne at Bonneybefore, is a thatched cottage (reconstructed), the ancestral home of Andrew Jackson (1767–1845), 7th President of the U.S.A.

It was in Carrickfergus that the poet Louis MacNeice (1907–63) spent his 'saddened black dreams' childhood.

3 m. NE., in Ballyhill (Bellahill), is Dalway's Bawn (in State care), probably built in 1609 by John Dallowaye. This is the best preserved of Ulster's Plantation 'bawn and flanker towers'. The rectangular bawn has circular towers at three angles. The ring over the gateway is said to have served as a gallows.

2 m. ENE. is Kilroot, where Dean Swift held his first living (1694–6).

CARRICKMACROSS, Co. Monaghan (Map 2, G6), is a market town on the Ardee (12 m.)–Monaghan (26 m.) road, famous for the hand-made lace industry established in 1820. The steepled Protestant church dates from 1779.

The Catholic church has ten two-light windows by Harry Clarke (1925): *St Oliver Plunkett; St Rita; St Laurence O Toole; St Dabhac* (sic); *Death of Our Lady; Entombment of Christ; St Kieran; Death of St Joseph; Death of St Patrick; St Dymphna.*

3½ m. N., in Donaghmoyne, is Mannan Castle (Nat. Mon.), a great hill-top motte-and-bailey constructed, *c.* 1193, by Peter Pipard, brother and heir of Gilbert Pipard (*see p. 42*). In 1244 Sir Ralph Pipard encased it with stone.

CARRICKMORE, Co. Tyrone (Map 1, E8), is a village on the Pomeroy (7 m.)–Omagh (10 m.) road. The place grew up around the remnants of a monastery thought to have been founded by St Columba. St Columcille's well, chair and bed nearby give credence to the early monastic claims.

2½ m. NE. is Creggandeveskey court-tomb (Hist. Mon.), on the W. side of Lough Mallon. This impressive tomb, with a three-chambered cairn, was excavated in 1979 and 1982, when it was discovered that some of the roof corbels were still intact. Finds included pottery and flint implements.

½ m. SW. is Relicknaman, the Women's Cemetery (Hist. Mon.) where, it is said, some women sinners were buried. Local superstition holds that no woman will enter the place.

2 m. NW., in Clare, are The White Stones, a court-tomb. 2½ m. further NW. is Lough Macrory and Loughmacrory House, a Regency lodge close to which are a court-tomb and a wedge-grave. ½ m. W. of Loughmacrory House and ¼ m. ENE. of Lough Dorpin, in Altdrumman, is a small portal-tomb.

2 m. NNW. is Aghnagreggan court-tomb.

CARRICK-ON-SHANNON, Co. Leitrim (Map 7, M4), the small county town of Co. Leitrim, is situated by the River Shannon, on the Longford (23 m.)–Drumshanbo (9 m.) road. The town was incorporated by James I and acquired a reputation for its strong Protestantism. It is a good coarse-angling centre, and has a fine marina for inland-waterway cruisers.

2 m. SE. is the village of Jamestown, called after James I. In 1650 the Catholic hierarchy met in a friary there to try and devise means of saving the Catholic cause from the victorious Cromwellians. Sir Charles Coote I founded the town in 1622 to command the Shannon crossing. In 1645 it was captured by a royalist force under Lord Carlingford; in 1689 by the Enniskillen Williamites (subsequently driven off to Sligo by Sarsfield). Of the 17th c. town fortifications only the lower part of one gateway survives.

CARRICK-ON-SUIR, Co. Tipperary (Map 4, B4), is a beautifully sited market town on the Suir, 15 m. NW. of Waterford, 24 m. NE. of Dungarvan, 13 m. E. of Clonmel, and 16 m. S. of Callan.

The town was the creation of the Butlers, Earls of Carrick and Ormond, who acquired the property in the 14th c. By the river, at the E. end of Castle St, are the unusually interesting remains of the latest castle (Nat. Mon.). The first Butler castle there was erected in 1309; but the oldest part of the existing buildings – two towers, etc., on the S. side – was built by Émonn mac Risderd Butler (*see p. 88*), a famous warrior and a noted patron of Irish letters. It has been claimed that Anne Boleyn, mother of Elizabeth I of England, was born in the castle; she was a granddaughter of Thomas, 7th Earl of Ormond (d. 1555). To Émonn mac Risderd's castle the 10th Earl of Ormond (Black Tom, d. 1614) added the good Elizabethan manor house (entrance fee) which forms the N. side of the castle court; the Long Gallery, recently repaired and partly restored, is the sole surviving Irish example of its period.

On the S. side of the river is the suburb of Carrickbeg (Abbeyside). St Molleran's parish church (1827) incorporates the tower and part of the N. wall of the church of St Michael's Franciscan friary, founded 1336/47 by James, 1st Earl of Ormond; John Clyn, the annalist, was the first Guardian; in 1447 the friary was re-founded by Émonn mac Risderd.

4½ m. NNE., in Ahenny, is the ancient monastic site, Kilclispeen (St Crispin's Church). The remains there include two splendid 8th/9th c. High Crosses (Nat. Mons.) and the base of a third. The crosses are decorated with carved bosses, interlaces, spirals, frets, and other abstract motifs. The bases have figured panels. The panels of the S. cross are very weathered; they include figurations of horsemen and of *Daniel in the Lions' Den.* Those on the N. Cross are in better condition. The subjects include: W. face: *The Raised Christ* with six apostles; N. face: a chariot procession; E. face: *The Creation of the Birds and the Beasts* or *Adam Naming the Animals*; S. face: procession with a headless corpse (Goliath?). The missing cross, 'the most beautiful of the three', is said to have been stolen (*c.* 1800) and lost in a shipwreck off Passage East. – 1 m. SE. is the ancient monastic site, Kilkieran. The remains (Nat. Mons.) include three stone crosses – two of them High Crosses of Ahenny type – and one other carved cross. Fragments of a fourth cross are currently displayed at Jerpoint Abbey (*see p. 291*). The W. Cross is covered on all faces with interlaces, frets, spirals, etc. On the E. face of the base is a procession of horsemen. The E. Cross is not decorated. In 1858 these two crosses, then prostrate and broken, were 'restored . . . by a blind mechanic'. The tall, slender, N. Cross bears some faint traces of superficial ornament.

3½ m. SE. are the fragmentary remains of Mothel 'Abbey' (Nat. Mon.), a priory of Canons Regular of St Augustine which succeeded an early monastery founded by St Broccán (Brogan).

Butler castle, Carrick-on-Suir, Co. Tipperary.

In the church is a tomb-chest of *c.* 1500; its figure sculpture includes *The Virgin and Child; St Michael; St Peter; St Paul; St Francis* and a *Crucifixion*. At the entrance to a farmyard S. of the 'abbey' is Cloch na Coimirce (Stone of Protection), an early cross-pillar.

6½ m. NW., on the slope of Slievenamon, is Kilcash. The remains of a small church (in dangerous condition) with battered, Romanesque S. doorway, and incorporating the gable of an earlier structure, mark the site of an ancient monastic foundation which had associations with St Colmán úa hEirc. The haunting, early-18th c. song *Cill Chais* (English rendering by 'Frank O Connor'), mourns the death of Margaret Butler, Viscountess Iveagh ('Lady Veagh'), who lies buried in the tomb of Archbishop Butler (1673–1757) in the churchyard. To the E. are the ruins of Kilcash Castle.

CARRIGAHOLT, Co. Clare (Map 6, C7), is a seaside village at the mouth of the Shannon, 8½ m. SSW. of Kilkee. In 1588 seven Armada ships sheltered for four days off Carrigaholt.

SE., by the pier, are the turreted bawn and tower (Nat. Mon.) of a Mac Mahon castle taken after a four-day siege in 1599 by the renegade 4th Earl of Thomond, who hanged the defenders (in breach of the surrender terms) and gave the place to his brother Donal. The latter's grandson, another Donal, was the celebrated 3rd Viscount Clare, who raised Clare's Dragoons and two regiments of infantry for James II. The 6th Viscount Clare (d. 1761) became a Marshal of France and fought against England at Dettingen (1743) and Fontenoy (1745).

1 m. NE. are the ruins of Kilcrony, a small oratory.

3½ m. ENE. is Doonaha, birthplace of the noted scholar Eoghan Ó Comhraidhe (Eugene O Curry, 1796–1862).

1½ m. S., in Kilcredaun, are remains of two small churches. The larger, Kilcredaun proper, has a Romanesque E. window and remnants of a plain Romanesque W. door (*c.* 1200). The smaller, ruder, church, Teampall an Áird, is on a ridge to the S.; to the E. is a 19th c. coastal battery.

3 m. W. is Cross. ½ m. W. are the ruins of Killballyowen parish church. – 5 m. W., via Kilbaha, is Moneen Church. In a side chapel is preserved the '(Little) Ark', relic of the worst days of landlordism. The only place where the local tyrant was powerless in law to prevent the celebration of Mass was on the foreshore between high and low water. In 1852, Fr. Michael Meehan devised the movable 'Ark' so as to provide the celebrant with shelter from wind and rain. The minor road SW. from Moneen leads (3 m.) to Loop (properly *Leap*) Head, which takes its name (Irish *Ceann Léime*) from Léim Chon Chulainn ('Cú Chulainn's Leap'), the chasm sundering Dermot and Grania's Rock from the mainland.

CARRIGALINE, Co. Cork (Map 5, M6), is a village on the Cork (8 m.)–Crosshaven (5 m.) road, at the head of the Owenboy estuary. There is a noted pottery there. The South Union Hunt has its headquarters at the village.

In the estuary below the village is Drake's Pool, where Sir Francis Drake is reputed to have taken shelter from pursuing Spaniards in 1587.

¾ m. ENE., on the N. side of the estuary, are remains of Carrigaline Castle, a Cogan stronghold which passed to the Desmond Geraldines. This was the birthplace of James Fitzmaurice (killed in 1579), leader of the great Munster revolt against Elizabeth I.

3 m. ENE., at Castle Warren to the SW. of Ring(askiddy) village, are remains of Barnahely Castle (de Cogans). 1¼ m. further ENE. is an early-19th c. redoubt, part of the defences of Cork Harbour.

2 m. WNW., on a steep rock over the Owenboy, is 17th c. Ballea Castle, one of the few Co. Cork castles still occupied.

CARRIGART, alias Carrickart, Co. Donegal (Map 8, F2), is a village resort on the coast road from Milford (10 m.) to Creeslough (8 m.). It lies at the neck of beautiful Rosguill, the peninsula between Milford Bay and Sheephaven.

3 m. N., by the roadside at Clontallagh post office, is part of a small crude cross. A bohereen leads to Mevagh Old Church on Mulroy Bay: fragmentary remains of a small Transitional (?) church and a tall ancient stone cross. On the hill SW. of the churchyard, in Mevagh townland, is a large series of rock scribings.

CARRIGTOHILL, Co. Cork (Map 4, C8), is a village on the Cork (10 m.)–Middleton (6 m.) road. There are remains of a medieval church.

½ m. SE. are the ruins of Barryscourt, alias Claidhe Dubh Castle, rebuilt in 1585; the chapel is interesting.

1 m. SW., in Cork Harbour (road causeways), is Foaty, alias Fota, Island. Fota House, built in 1820 by Sir Richard Morrison for the Smith-Barry family, once Earls of Barrymore, is a fine Regency house now owned by University College, Cork. In 1983, it was exquisitely re-decorated by John O Connell, with 18th/19th c. Irish furniture and fittings, and Richard Wood's Irish landscape paintings (1750–1870), the most comprehensive of its kind in the country. In the extensive demesne is the internationally famous Arboretum (tropical and other trees and plants), begun in the 1820s, but currently threatened by the prospect of a major tourist development on the Estate.

CASHEL, Co. Tipperary (Map 4, E3), is a small market town at the junction of roads from Thurles (13 m.), Urlingford (20 m.), Fethard (10 m.), Clonmel (15 m.), Cahir (11 m.), and Tipperary (12 m.). In medieval times the ecclesiastical capital of Munster, it is noted for the variety of its historic monuments.

Secular and ecclesiastical history combine to make Cashel one of the most celebrated places in Munster. In the 4th/5th c., Eóghanacht dynasts led by Conall Corc conquered the rich countryside and set up a fortress on St Patrick's Rock, which dominates the town from the N. Previous contact with the Roman Empire is reflected in the Latin name, *caiseal*, cashel (= *castellum*), of their fortress; no other Irish royal seat had a Latin name. The Eóghanacht quickly spread to other fertile regions of Munster, and until 944 their principal ruler was unchallenged Over-King of Munster. Kings of the heretofore obscure Dál Chais (*see p. 219*), viz. Mahon and his brother, Brian Boru, led their forces to Cashel in 963 and crushed the Norse at Solohead (*see p. 293*) in 976. Two years later, Brian made himself undisputed King of Cashel. Though his descendants (the O Briens of Thomond) dominated all Munster until 1119, and North Munster (Thomond) until the Anglo-Norman conquest, their capital naturally remained by the Shannon. In 1101, the year he had made good his claim to the high-kingship, Muirchertach O Brien handed over the Rock to be the see of the projected archbishopric of Munster.

In 1111, the archdiocese of Cashel was formally constituted, and Malchus Úa hAinmire, Bishop of Waterford, became its first ruler. (The Catholic archdiocese still exists, but since Penal times has had its see at THURLES; the Protestant archbishopric was abolished in 1839, and the diocese is today united to those of Waterford and Lismore.) In 1169, Cormac Mac Carthy's cathedral proving too small, Donal Mór O Brien, King of Thomond, commenced the building of a new cathedral. It can scarcely have been completed when the most momentous event in the history of Cashel took place. This was the meeting, in the winter of 1171–2, of a national synod summoned by Henry II of England, which rounded off a century of ecclesiastical reform by hopefully acknowledging the English King's claim to the lordship of Ireland.

In the following century Donal O Brien's cathedral was swept away to make room for the church whose ruins still dominate the Rock. The builders were three successive archbishops: Máirín O Brien (1224–37), David, son of Ceallach Ó Gilla Phátraic (1239–52), and David Mac Cearbhaill (1255–89). In 1495 this church was set on fire by Gearóid Mór Fitzgerald, Great Earl of Kildare, because, as he explained to Henry VII of England, he 'thought the archbishop was inside'. It was fired a second time, 13 September 1647, when the infamous renegade Murrough (Murchadh) 'the Burner' O Brien, Earl of Inchiquin, attacked Cashel with a Parliamentarian force, butchered all and sundry, and profaned its sacred treasures. Thereafter the buildings remained derelict until 1686, when the cathedral was repaired for Protestant use. In 1729 it was again re-edified, only to be abandoned once more in 1749. In 1874 the ruins were handed over to the State, to be preserved as a national monument.

Access to St Patrick's Rock (200 ft) is gained through the gateway. Adjoining this is the Hall of the Vicars Choral (15th c., with some 17th c. features). This has recently been restored by the Office of Public Works (D.N. Johnson). The ground floor now houses the original sandstone St Patrick's Cross (*see below*), a 13th/14th c. knight's effigy from St John's Church in Friar St, and a tomb-front with knights (*c.* 1271?) from Athassel (*see p. 194*). The upper floor has been furnished to suggest how it may have looked in the 16th or 17th c.

Between this and the S. porch of the cathedral is a modern concrete replica of St Patrick's Cross (original now in the Hall of the Vicars Choral, *see above*). It is of a rare, crutched design, as at Peakaun. On the W. face of the shaft is a *Crucifixion*; on the E. face the figure of a bishop. On the E. face of the pedestal is an Urnes-style interlacement, enmeshing ribbon-beasts and birds, which enables us to date the cross to about 1150; the N. face has a Romanesque lion which is ringed by pellets and concentric circles.

In the angle between the S. transept and the choir of the 13th c. cathedral. is Cormac's Chapel, properly Cormac's Cathedral. Built by Cormac Mac Carthy, King of Desmond, it was begun in 1127 and consecrated in 1134. This richly decorated little Romanesque church is one of the gems of 12th c. Irish art, and its details repay close inspection. Its solid construction and superb double roof of stone preserved it from the worst effects of the disasters which wrecked the adjoining Gothic cathedral. It is cruciform in plan; but this is due to the unequal square towers which flank the junction of nave and chancel. (The S. tower has lost its original pyramidal roof and acquired a parapet.) The exterior wall faces are decorated with blind arcading, varied capitals and corbels, etc. The entrance is now through a doorway of three richly decorated orders in the S. wall; but originally this doorway was subordinate to the great gabled N. porch of six orders, which is obstructed by the 13th c. cathedral. Both doorways have carved tympana, features very rare in Irish Romanesque; that of the S. door has a grotesque beast with trefoil tail, that of the N. door a centaur shooting with bow and arrow at a great trefoil-tailed lion which has struck down two smaller beasts. Despite the gaping holes hacked through the S. wall a century or so ago by Archdeacon Cotton, the interior is today dark and gloomy. This is partly the result of the blocking up of two of the three windows in the W. gable and of the shading of the third by the later cathedral, partly the result of the loss of the polychrome painting which covered roofs and walls (the frescoes in the chancel have recently been conserved). The nave is roofed by a ribbed barrel vault, the chancel by a groined sexpartite vault. The side walls are arcaded in two storeys. The arcading was filled with painted figure subjects, diaper patterns, etc., while capitals, columns, mouldings, and the like, were picked out in colours. The principal feature of the interior is the grand chancel arch of four orders, still retaining some of its original polychrome enrichment. The chancel, which is dimly lit by a small window in each side wall, is closed by a shallow, rectangular, altar recess. The latter was lit by a curious slanting ope in each side wall. A doorway of three orders gives access to the four-storey N. tower; the upper storeys were presumably reached by ladders; an external doorway in the E. wall has been closed up. The smaller S. tower, a belfry, contains the stairs leading to the crofts under the outer roof of stone; these may have been divided into two storeys by a timber floor. At the W. end of the nave (not *in situ*), is a great stone tomb-chest with a superb carving of the Urnes combat theme. Originally polychrome, the tomb is contemporary with the church.

The Round Tower (92 ft), at the NE. angle of the N. transept of the 13th c. cathedral, is doubtless somewhat earlier than Cormac's church, for the decoration of the Romanesque doorway consists simply of a low, flat architrave.

The 13th c. cathedral occupies the site of Donal Mór O Brien's cathedral of 1169. It is an aisleless, cruciform building with disproportionately long choir, excessively short nave, two E. chapels in each transept, and a great tower over the crossing. W. of the crossing was a rood screen (note responds). The nave had N. and S. porch arches half-way along its projected length; but only the S. porch was completed, for, early in the 15th c., Archbishop O Hedian built a massive castle on the site of the W. end of the nave; he provided the castle with a Great Hall by inserting a floor over the nave. About the middle of the 14th c. the central tower was raised in height and the church walls were crowned with battlements.

In nave, transepts, and choir are the remains of altars, tombs, and other monuments, including the following: N. Transept: figures of apostles and saints (*Michael, John the Baptist* and *Thomas à Becket*), etc., from a Hacket-Butler tomb; figures of apostles, etc., from a 15th c. tomb; Choir: S. side: tomb of the notorious renegade and pluralist Miler Mac Grath (d. *c.* 1622), for whom it was made in 1621 by Patrick Kerin. Mac Grath was consecrated bishop of Down and Connor by the Pope in 1567. Two years later he conformed to the Protestant state church and was rewarded by Elizabeth I with the bishopric of his native Clogher in 1570, and this without incurring papal censure, which was not passed on him until 1580. In 1571 he had himself promoted to the Protestant archbishopric of Cashel, to which he contrived to add the bishoprics of LISMORE and Waterford in 1581. In 1608 he exchanged Lismore and Waterford for Killala and Achonry. In addition to his bishoprics he accumulated no fewer than 77 other benefices.

½ m. W. of the Rock, off the Mount Judkin road, are the ruins (Nat. Mon.) of Hore Abbey, last daughter of Mellifont. It was founded in 1272 for the Cistercians on the site of an earlier priory-hospital of the Irish Benedictines from Regensburg. The remains, typically Cistercian (save that the claustral buildings were N. of the church), comprise fragments of the E. cloister range – including chapter-house and sacristy – as well as the ruins of a cruciform church with aisled nave, and with two chapels in each transept. The central tower and the screens shutting off the aisles and choir, etc. from the nave are 15th c.

Off the N. side of Main St is Cashel Palace Hotel, formerly palace of the Protestant archbishops. This charming brick house was built by Sir Edward Lovett Pearce, architect of the Dublin Parliament House, for Archbishop Bolton (1730–44).

On the S. side of Main St is Quirke's Castle, a 15th c. tower.

In Moor Lane, off the E. end of Main St (N. side), are the ruins (Nat. Mon.) of the fine church of the Dominican friary founded by Archbishop David Ó Gilla Phátraic (1243). Destroyed by fire, it was restored by Archbishop Cantwell *c.* 1480.

In John St is the Protestant cathedral and parochial church of St John the Baptist (1750–83; spire, 1812), a good, small, Classical building. The nearby Diocesan Library, re-edified 1965, and renamed the GPA-Bolton Library after its sensitive restoration in 1986, is noteworthy for its collection of rare printings, including Caxton. Built into the churchyard wall is a fine series of medieval tomb effigies from the old cathedral and some of the town churches; among them is the 14th c. effigy of an armoured knight said to be the cover of the tomb-chest now in the porch of the Catholic church; also the effigies of three ladies of the same period.

3¼ m. ESE. is Knickeenagow, Mocklershill, birthplace of Charles Kickham, Fenian and novelist, 1828–82 (*see p. 188*).

4¼ m. S. is Rockwell College, a boarding school for boys conducted by the Holy Ghost Fathers. The school has three Evie Hone decorative windows (1941).

5 m. NNE. is Longfield House, *c.* 1760 (not open to public). It was the home of Charles Bianconi (1786–1875), whose cabs provided the first nationwide public transport in Ireland.

CASTLEBAR, Co. Mayo (Map 7, G5), the county town of Mayo and a market town with some small-scale industries is at the junction of roads from Westport (11 m. SW.), Claremorris (18 m. SE.), Foxford (15 m. NE.), Newport, (11½ m. WNW.), Bangor Erris (37½ m. NW.), and Ballina (20 m. NNE.).

The town was founded at the beginning of the 17th c. (incorporated 1613) by John Bingham, ancestor of the Earls of Lucan. On 27 August 1798, Gen. Humbert (*see p. 219*) advanced on Castlebar with 700 French troops and 1,000 untrained peasants. The British, who held the town, broke at the fourth assault, leaving their stores, guns, and 1,200 prisoners in Humbert's hands. From the precipitate flight of the British cavalry to Hollymount and Tuam, the event has ever since been known as the 'Castlebar Races'.

In the Mall is a former chapel whose foundation stone was laid by John Wesley in 1785. Michael Davitt founded the epoch-making Land League in the Imperial Hotel, 16 August 1879.

3 m. NE., at Turlough on the Foxford road, a Round Tower and the ruins of a 17th c. church mark the site of an early monastery (traditionally Patrician).

CASTLEBELLINGHAM, Co. Louth (Map 2, I6), is a village on the Drogheda (14 m.)–Dundalk (8 m.) road. It takes its name from the Bellinghams, who displaced the long-established Gernons in Cromwellian times.

The castellated gateway at the S. end of the villge is the entrance to Castle Bellingham, an early-18th c. mansion with castellated additions (now a hotel), on the site of a castle burned by Jacobite troops in 1689.

In the churchyard is buried Dr Thomas Guither, the 17th c. physician who introduced frogs into Ireland.

1¼ m. S. is the Greenmount (Nat. Mon.), a much-mutilated motte and bailey.

2½ m. SE. is the fishing village of Annagassan. The monastery of Linn Duachaill, founded by St Colmán, son of Lúachán (d. 699), is believed to have stood in Linns townland. Caemhán, the last recorded abbot, was slain in 842 by the Vikings, who had a fortress there 840–927. Near the mouth of the river is a promontory fort.

2¾ m. W., in Mansfieldstown, are remains (Nat. Mon.) of a late-17th c. church incorporating fragments (15th c. E. window, etc.) of a pre-Reformation church.

CASTLEBLAYNEY, Co. Monaghan (Map 2, G4), is a 'Border' market town beside pretty Lough Muckno, on the Dundalk (18 m.)–Monaghan (15 m.) road. It takes its name from Sir Edward Blayney, who built a castle there and was Governor of the county under James I.

CASTLECOMER, Co. Kilkenny (Map 3, F8), is a small market town where the Athy (14 m.)–Kilkenny (12 m.) road crosses the pretty valley of the little Dinin Rua.

The town takes its name from a castle erected at the Anglo-Norman invasion (probably by William the Marshal) on the E. side of the town. The invaders' first (motte) castle was destroyed by the O Brennans in 1200, but was soon replaced. Despite the castle, the O Brennans retained their hold there until 1635, when their lands were awarded to Sir Christopher Wandsford. The new proprietor planted English colonists, exploited the local anthracite mines, introduced hay-making to the district, and laid out 'an elegant town exactly on the model of a famous one in Italy, viz. Alsinore'. The buildings he erected included a castle on Colliery Hill and a Protestant church. The Protestant church has a three-light memorial window (1920) by Michael Healy.

CASTLECONNELL village, Co. Limerick (Map 6, I7), is an angling resort – it gave its name to the two-piece, spliced, salmon rod – and decayed spa beside the Shannon, 8 m. NE. of Limerick and 7 m. SSW. of Killaloe. On a rock over the river are remains of a Burke castle destroyed by the Williamite general, Ginckel, in 1691. Before the Burkes, the Ó Conaings were lords of the place; whence the name Castleconnell (Ó Conaing's castle).

In the 18th c. its medicinal well made Castleconnell a popular resort of Limerick folk. Relics of that era are to be seen in the many attractive old villas of the neighbourhood.

On Cloon Island are remains of a church; built into the W. wall are two early gravestones.

CASTLEDERG, Co. Tyrone (Map 1, C7), is a small market town where the Strabane (12 m.)–Kesh (15 m.) road crosses the River Derg. There are remains (Hist. Mon.) of a large bawn built by Sir John Davies around 1610. The Catholic Church of St Eugene (1980) is by Liam McCormick. The appliqué dossal hanging was designed by Helen Moloney and woven by Jane Almqvrist; there are also two windows by Helen Moloney.

1 m. NNE., in Churchtown, is Todd's Den (300 ft), a small wedge-tomb (Hist. Mon.). 300 yds SSW. is a ruined portal-tomb (Hist. Mon.)

1 m. E. is Drumahey, where the church has a *St Francis* window by Helen Moloney (1983).

6 m. SW. is Killeter court-tomb.

CASTLEDERMOT, Co. Kildare (Map 3, H7), on the Kilcullen (17 m.)–Carlow (7 m.) road, was once a walled town, but is now a mere village.

St Díarmaid (d. 823), had a hermitage (Dísert Díarmada) here, which became the nucleus of an important early monastery (*see p. 298*). Of the latter there survive (Church Lane) a 66 ft high Round Tower with medieval battlemented parapet (Nat. Mon.), two 9th/10th c. High Crosses (Nat. Mons.), the Romanesque W. doorway (innermost order missing; Nat. Mon.) of a church, a 'hogback' stone possibly related to those known from Viking Northumbria, and The Swearing Stone, an early, granite cross-slab with a circular perforation at the centre of the cross. The subjects carved on the High Crosses include *SS Paul and Anthony, The Apostles, The Crucifixion, The Fall, The Sacrifice of Isaac,* and *Daniel in the Lions' Den.* At the Norman conquest Walter de Riddlesford built a motte-and-bailey castle at Castledermot (1181). About 1295 the town was enclosed by walls, of which fragments survive, notably between Barrack St and Main St. At the E. end of Abbey St are the ruins of a fine, Franciscan, friary church (Nat. Mon.) with 13th c. nave-and-chancel, preaching church enlarged in the 14th c. by extending the choir and adding a short N. nave aisle and an elaborate, aisled N. transept with three E. chapels. The Protestant church has a window by Catherine O Brien (*The Sower*, 1925–6). At the N. end of the village is St John's Tower, alias The Pigeons' Tower (Nat. Mon.), sole remnant of St John the Baptist's Hospital (Augustinian Cruciferi) built in the 13th c. by Walter de Riddlesford.

3½ m. N. are remains of Belan House and its demesne ornaments. The house was built in 1743 for the 1st Lord Aldborough by Richard Cassels and Francis Bindon. The house was dismantled from 1821 onwards, and only an ornamental temple, two of three obelisks, and the original stables survive.

3 m. NW. is Kilkea Castle, 1849 'restoration' (an extra storey added all around, etc.) of an already much altered Fitzgerald castle wrecked in 1798. Near the castle are the ruins of Kilkea, a small, simple, manorial church with later chancel and sacristy, containing many Fitzgerald memorials. Close to the River Greese is the motte of a castle erected in 1180 for Walter de Riddlesford, Strongbow's grantee of the manor (which passed in the 13th c. to Maurice Fitzgerald, 3rd Baron O ffaly).

CASTLEGREGORY, Co. Kerry (Map 5, D2), is a small village and quiet seaside resort, 1 m. N. of the Tralee (15 m.)–Dingle (23 m.) road through Connor Pass.

The village takes its name from a castle built by Gregory Hoare in the 16th c., of which not a trace remains.

4 m. N., on the E. side of little Scraggan Bay, is the ruined church of Kilshannig, with a tall early cross-pillar (chi-rho, etc.). 2½ m. WSW. is the little village of Fahamore, point of departure for the Maharee Islands. The largest of these, Ilauntannig, takes its name (Oiléan tSeanaigh) from St Seanach, 'brother' of St Seanán of Scattery Island (*see p. 226*), who founded an anchoritic monastery there in the 6th/7th c. The remains of the monastery (Nat. Mon.) are enclosed by a massive dry-masonry cashel and include a tiny church (also a fragment of a second), three clochâns, three *leachtaí* or burial monuments, and a rude stone cross.

10 m. W., in the W. of two ancient graveyards on the slope of Brandon Mountain, in Faha townland, are a cross-slab and a cross-inscribed boulder.

CASTLEISLAND, Co. Kerry (Map 5, G2), is a small market town where the Limerick (47 m.)–Killarney (14¾ m.) road crosses the little Shanowen. There are remains of a Desmond castle, successor of one built in 1220 by the English Justiciar, Geoffrey de Marisco.

CASTLEKNOCK, Co. Dublin (Map 3, J3), is a village on the Dublin (6 m.)–Navan (24 m.) road, at the edge of the Phoenix Park. To the SW., in the grounds of Castleknock College (founded 1834 to become the ecclesiastical seminary of the archdiocese, now a well-known boarding school for boys conducted by the Vincentian Fathers), are remains of the castle from which the village takes its name. These consist of a ditched and ramparted oval motte, at one end of which is a secondary mound with remains of an octagonal keep. The first castle was constructed by the Norman Hugh Tyrel, but the High-King Rory O Conor used it as a base in his unsuccessful bid to oust the invaders from Dublin in 1171.

North Cross, Castledermot.

The Protestant church has a three-light window (*SS Luke, George, Hubert*) by Harry Clarke (1928).

¼ m. NE. of the centre of the village, the Catholic church of Our Lady Mother of the Church (1982–3) by Campbell, Conroy, Hickey has good stone and steel furnishings, a woven *Crucifixion* by Imogen Stuart, and two windows (*Virgin and Child* and *St Anthony of Padua*) by Margaret Becker. *The Joyful and Sorrowful Mysteries of the Rosary* was woven by Cathy Mac Aleavey.

CASTLEMAINE, Co. Kerry (Map 5, F3), is a small market town where the Tralee (10 m.)–Killorglin (6¼ m.) road crosses the Maine. It takes its name from a Desmond castle. Various families and notabilities have taken titles from the place, among them the notorious Roger Palmer, Viscount Castlemaine (1634–1705) and husband of the Duchess of Cleveland (1641–1709).

2¼ m. SW., in the NW. corner of the demesne of Kilcolman Abbey, is the ruined nave-and-chancel church of Killaha 'Abbey', properly the priory De Bello Loco. Dedicated to Our Lady, this house of Canons Regular of St Augustine was founded in 1215/16 by the Anglo-Norman Justiciar, Geoffrey de Marisco. Restored and enlarged in 1445, it survived the Dissolution until 1576; the reticulated E. window is very late.

Clonalis House, Castlerea.

CASTLEMARTYR, Co. Cork (Map 4, D8), is a small market town on the Middleton (6 m.)–Youghal (11 m.) road. In the demesne on the W. side of the village are Castlemartyr House (now a Carmelite priory) and the ruins of the castle of the Earl of Desmond's seneschal for the barony of Imokilly (*see p. 113*). In 1581, the Earl of Desmond being then in revolt against Elizabeth I, it was attacked by the Earl of Ormond, who hanged the seneschal's mother in sight of the walls. At the Desmond confiscation the castle and estate were granted to Sir Walter Ralegh (*see p. 308*), who sold them to Richard Boyle. Boyle restored and improved the buildings. At the Cromwellian victory it passed to his son, Roger, Lord Broghil, later Earl of Orrery (1621–79), who repaired and enlarged it. The remains comprise a 15th c. bawn (with angle towers) and keep (incorporated in the curtain), and 17th c. domestic quarters, etc.

3½ m. NE., on the Little Dissour River, is Killeagh village. – 1½ m. S., in Castle Richard, is ruined, 15th c. Inchicrenagh Castle (alias Castle Richard). The Fitzgeralds who lived there were hereditary keepers of the Imokilly Amulet, which was used to cure hydrophobia and murrain in cattle.

3 m. ESE. is Ightermurragh Castle, an embattled house built in 1641 by Edmund Supple and his wife 'whom love binds one'.

4¼ m. SE. are the ruins of Kilcredan Protestant church, built in 1636 by Sir Robert Tynte of Ballycrenane Castle, and callously unroofed by the church authorities in the 19th c., thereby exposing and wrecking two fine Renaissance monuments, one of them the tomb of Sir Robert Tynte himself; one of the 'weepers' was an effigy of Sir Robert's second wife, Elizabeth Boyle, widow of Edmund Spenser.

CASTLEPOLLARD, Co. Westmeath (Map 2, D8), is a market village on the Mullingar (16 m.)–Granard (16 m.) road.

4½ m. S., overlooking Lough Derravaragh, is Knockeyon (710 ft). Half-way up the steep slope over the lake are St Eyen's (Ion's) ruined chapel and holy well, formerly a place of pilgrimage on the first Sunday of harvest, *i.e.* a Lughnasa station.

7 m. S. is Taughmon (Teach Munnu, *see p. 287*), called after a 6th c. monastery founded by St Munnu (alias Finnu, alias Fintán). The ruins (Nat. Mon.) are those of a 15th c. semi-fortified manorial church dedicated to St Patrick. It was a rectangular, stone-roofed building with battlemented walls and castle-like W. tower (the latter an addition). In it is the tomb of Sir Christopher Nugent of Moyrath and Farrow (d. 1619).

1½ m. NW. is Tullynally (from *c.* 1730 to 1961 called Pakenham Hall), until 1961 seat of the Earls of Longford, now home of Mr Thomas Pakenham, a well-known author, and son of the Labour Peer, Lord Longford. Lord Longford's father, the late Earl of Longford was a well-known Dublin figure: poet, playwright, and theatrical manager. The nucleus of the house was a 17th c. stronghouse. About 1740, and again in 1780, this was enlarged and Georgianized. Between 1801 and 1806 it was castellated and embellished in the Gothick manner by Francis Johnston. James Shiel designed the octagonal dining room, and a Gothick gate lodge. In 1839 Sir Richard Morrison added the office and stable court and a new ceiling in the Great Hall.

CASTLEREA[GH] Co. Roscommon (Map 7, K6), is a market town on the Roscommon (19 m.)–Claremorris (24 m.) road.

Castlerea was the birthplace of Sir William Wilde (1815–76), noted antiquary and oculist, husband of Lady Wilde (Speranza), and father of Oscar Wilde. His father, Dr Thomas Wilde, was a physician in practice there.

2 m. SE., near the railway, in Emlagh, are the base and shaft of a High Cross (Nat. Mon.) with interlaced and other ornament.

2½ m. NW. is Clonalis House, former seat of O Conor Don, representative of the once proud dynasty of the O Conors of Connacht, which gave two high-kings to Ireland in the 12th c. The dull late-19th c. house (open to the public) preserves many interesting historic items associated with the family.

CASTLETOWN BEARHAVEN, Co. Cork (Map 5, D7), is a small port and seaside resort on the N. side of Bantry Bay, 9 m. WSW. of Ardrigole and 15 m. SW. of Lauragh, Co. Kerry. Bear Island, to the S. and SE., shelters deep Bear Haven, formerly a fortified anchorage of the British Atlantic fleet.

6 m. N., overlooking Ballycrovane Bay in Faunkill and the Woods townland, is a 17½ ft ogham stone (Nat. Mon.).

1 m. SSW. is a fragment of the 15th c. O Sullivan Beare castle of Dunboy. It was heroically defended against an English force under Sir George Carew in 1602 by an Irish-Spanish garrison commanded by Richard Mac Geoghegan. The assailants forced their way into the cellar just as Mac Geoghegan was about to blow up the castle. The few survivors were butchered.

15 m. SSW. is Dursey Island, birthplace (1590) of Don Philip O Sullivan, author of *Historiae Catholicae Iberniae Compendium* (Lisbon, 1621). Access by cable car during most daylight hours. 11 m. W. is Allihies. Its 19th c. copper mines figure in Daphne du Maurier's *Hungry Hill.*

CASTLETOWN GEOGHEGAN, Co. Westmeath (Map 3, D2) is a village on the Ballymahon (14 m.)–Kilbeggan (5 m.) road, to the SW. of Lough Ennell. There is a large Anglo-Norman motte-and-bailey there, but the place takes its name from a castle of the Mac Eochagáins who held lands there until Cromwellian times, and after whom the country round about is often called Mageoghegan's Country.

4 m. NW. is Carn (Carn Fhiachach), where Fiachu, son of Niall Nine Hostager and King of Meath, had his residence. One of his sons, so the story goes, slew some of St Patrick's company at Uisneach, and the outraged saint's curse excluded his descendants from the succession. An alternative version of the tale recounts that Patrick visited Fiachu at Carn, but Fiachu refused to accept his teaching.

CASTLETOWNROCHE, Co. Cork (Map 5, L3), is a village where the Fermoy (9 m.)–Mallow (8 m.) road crosses the little Awbeg. Castle Widenham demesne has superb gardens. The house incorporates the remains of the Roche castle from which the village takes its name. The castle was attacked by Sir Walter Ralegh in the course of the Elizabethan wars.

The Protestant church, with curious windows in the steeple, dates from 1825. Caves in the river valley thereabouts have yielded traces of prehistoric fauna.

2 m. N., W. of the Awbeg, is Annes Grove with its wonderful gardens (open to the public), noted for their combination of limestone-loving and hating plants in close proximity.

4 m. SE., on a lovely reach of the Blackwater, is Ballyholly village. The Roche castle there, wrecked in the 1641–52 war, was restored as a residence by Lady Listowel in 1862.

1¾ m. S., close to the beautiful junction of the Awbeg and Blackwater, are the remains of Bridgetown (Ballindroghid) 'Abbey', a 13th c. Augustinian (Congregation of St Victor) priory. The remains include a church with long, Augustinian choir and fragments of the cloister and claustral buildings.

3 m. SW., on the N. bank of the Blackwater, is Monanimmy Castle (private), associated with the Knights of St John. Edmund Burke (1729–97), who spent his early childhood with his maternal grandmother in Ballyduff, got his earliest schooling at a 'hedge-school' held in the castle ruins. There he learned 'all that the village schoolmaster could teach'.

3 m. W., in Ballygriffin, is a centre opened in 1984 as a monument to Nano Nagle (1718–74), the founder of the Presentation Sisters, who was born there.

CASTLETOWNSHEND, Co. Cork (Map 5, H8), is a village on the W. side of beautiful Castlehaven, 5 m. SE. of Skibbereen and 14 m. SW. of Glandore.

ENE. of the village, overlooking the landing place, in private property, are the ruins of 'Bryans' Fort', a small star fort erected by the English planter Col. Richard Townshend *c.* 1650. It was attacked by Jacobites in November 1689 and taken in 1690, only to be recovered shortly afterwards by the local Williamites.

At the SW. end of the village is Drishane House, life-long home of Edith Oenone Somerville (1858–1949), joint author with 'Martin Ross' of *Some Experiences of an Irish R.M., The Real Charlotte,* etc. Both now rest to the E. of the Protestant church of St Barrahane in the town. In the church are three stained glass windows by Harry Clarke: *The Nativity* (1918), *St Luke* (1926) and *St Louis IX and St Martin of Tours Cutting His Cloak* (1920). In the church are interesting memorials of the town's major families – Somervilles, Townshends, etc. The floor mosaic in front of the altar was designed by Edith Somerville.

¾ m. NW., on Knockdrum, is The Fort (420 ft, Nat. Mon.), a fine stone ringfort (restored). It has a guard-chamber in the rampart, remains of a central square clochán, and three souterrains. An early cross-pillar has been set up inside the entrance. Outside is a stone with 39 cup marks. 300 yds NNW., in Gurrane, are the Three Fingers, an alignment of pillarstones.

1 m. S., in Glenbarrahane, are Toberbarrahane, remains of St Barrahane's Church, and the ruins of the O Driscoll castle which gives to Castle Haven its name. On 1 December 1601, six Spanish ships arrived in the haven with some 700 troops, food, stores, and five guns, for the expeditionary force at KINSALE. They succeeded in repelling the English admiral Sir Richard Leveson, and retained Castle Haven as a base, but had to capitulate after Kinsale.

CASTLEWELLAN, Co. Down (Map 2, K3), is a town on the Downpatrick (11 m.)–Newry (19 m.) road. The principal feature is the former demesne of the Annesleys of Newry, which is now the Castlewellan Forest Park and National Arboretum.

3 m. SE. are the remains of Maghera Church (13th c. ?) and a Round Tower (Hist. Mons.), on the site of a monastery founded in the 6th c. by St Domangard (*see p. 256*).

2½ m. SW., in Drumena, are a stone ringfort (500 ft) and a souterrain (Hist. Mons.).

7½ m. NNW., on the S. slope of Cratlieve, is Legananny Dolmen (850 ft, Hist. Mon.), a noteworthy portal-tomb. In the ancient churchyard 1¾ m. ESE. is an early cross-pillar.

CAVAN, Co. Cavan (Map 2, D6), is the county town of Cavan and the cathedral town of the Catholic diocese of Kilmore. It lies on the main Dublin (71 m.)–Enniskillen (42 m.) road. The town grew up around a Franciscan friary founded about 1300 by Giolla Íosa Rúa O Reilly, Lord of East Breany. Nothing now remains of the friary, nor indeed of any other antiquity in the town, which was destroyed in 1690 after the defeat of Berwick's Jacobite force by the Enniskillen men under Gen. Wolsey.

St Patrick's Cathedral (1942) is a disappointing sham-Renaissance structure by Ralph Byrne; it has sculptures by Albert Power.

The Protestant parish church (1810) and the Court House (*c.* 1828) are by John Bowden.

3½ m. SW., on the road to Crossdoney, is Kilmore (Cell Mór, the 'great church' founded by St Feidhlimidh), which gives its name to the diocese. There is St Fethlimidh's Cathedral (Protestant). The cathedral is a modern Gothic edifice, but incorporates a fine, Late-Romanesque doorway from the early monastery (afterwards Premonstratensian) on Trinity Island, 3 m. W. in Lough Oughter. (The stones of the doorway have not all been correctly reset.) In the churchyard is the tomb of the Englishman William Bedell, Protestant bishop of Kilmore from 1629 to 1642, compiler of an Irish grammar, and (in collaboration with Murtagh King, James Nangle, and Denis Sheridan) first translator of the Old Testament into Irish; he was buried with full honours by the Confederate Catholics. Nearby is a motte-and-bailey dismantled by Cathal O Reilly in 1226. – 4 m. further SW., in Cornafean, is The Pighouse Collection, a private museum with folk and other items, assembled by Mrs Phyllis Faris.

6 m. NW., on an island in Lough Oughter, are the ruins (recently conserved) of Cloghoughter Castle (Nat. Mon.). The two lower storeys of this round castle were probably built by the Normans *c.* 1220–4, and the upper part was added *c.* 1610–20. In 1641–2 Bishop Bedell was imprisoned there by the Confederate Catholics, whose great general, Eóghan Rúa O Neill, died there in 1649, a grievous loss to the Irish cause. Besieged by the Cromwellians in 1653, the garrison surrendered on good terms.

CELBRIDGE, Co. Kildare (Map 3, I3), is a Liffeyside village on the Leixlip (4 m.)–Clane (9 m.) road. It takes its name from a monastery founded by St Mo-Chúa of Clondalkin, whose well, Tobar Mo-Chúa, is near the mill.

Oakley (Park), now St Raphael's, was built (by the architect of Castletown?) *c.* 1724 for Arthur Price, who, when Vicar of Celbridge, proposed to Swift's 'Vanessa', when Bishop of Meath began Ardbraccan House (*see p. 255*), and when Archbishop of Cashel wrecked the cathedral there. Oakley became the home of the Napier family to which belonged: Emily, Duchess of Leinster and mother of Lord Edward Fitzgerald of 1789 fame; Caroline, Lady Holland and mother of Charles James Fox; and Gen. Sir William Napier (1785–1860), military historian. 300 yds W. of the house are the ruins of the Protestant parish church destroyed in 1798. The Conolly mausoleum has a splendid monument (by Thomas Carter; d. 1756) to William Conolly (1662–1729) of Castletown (*see below*); the effigies are of Conolly and his wife, Catherine Conyngham; the wrought iron is noteworthy.

Celbridge Abbey was built by Dr Marley, Bishop of Clonfert. Later it was the home of Esther Vanhomrigh (1690–1723), Swift's 'Vanessa'. A seat beneath the rocks by the river is alleged to have been the lovers' favourite retreat.

1 m. NNE. is Castletown, built about 1722 for William Conolly, Speaker of the Irish House of Commons, 1715–29 (open to the public). Until 1966 the home of Conolly's descendants, and reputedly the largest private house in Ireland, Castletown is an accomplished Early Georgian mansion, perhaps the most important, architecturally, of its period. The general scheme of block, colonnades and wings, as well as the front elevation, were probably designed around 1719 by the Florentine architect Alessandro Galilei, but the design of the entrance hall, and the colonnade and wings, seems to be the work of the youthful Edward Lovett Pearce, architect of the Dublin Parliament House. The stucco for the stairway, by the Franchini brothers, dates from *c.* 1760. 1¾ m. NW. of the house (2½ m. NNW. of the village) is Conolly's Folly, a large, obelisk-crowned triumphal arch erected in 1740 (to the design of Richard Cassels?) by William Conolly's widow.

3 m. S., to the E. of the Liffey, in Lyons Demesne (since 1962 seat of the Faculty of Agriculture of University College, Dublin), is Lyons Hill (Liamhuin), one of the early royal seats and public assembly places of the kingdom of Leinster. Lyons House is a large stone mansion with colonnaded wings. The central block was built in 1797 by Oliver Grace for Michael Aylmer, the wings added in 1810 by Valentine Lawless, 2nd Lord Cloncurry (1773–1853). The interior has some good stucco ceilings; also charming tempera mural paintings. Lord Cloncurry was a member of the United Irishmen and an active opponent of the Union. For tactical reasons he opposed O Connell's campaign for Catholic Emancipation and refused to join his Repeal movement. He was a generous landlord and lover of the arts. (John Hogan's admirable *Hibernia and Cloncurry* is a reminder of his patronage of that neglected sculptor.) The Hon. Emily Lawless (1845–1913), poet and author, lived in Lyons House. 1 m. WSW., on the other side of the Grand Canal, is St Anne's Church Ardclough, by Paul O Daly, with furnishings by Christopher and Elizabeth Ryan.

2 m. SSW., in Ardrass Lower, is St Patrick's Chapel, a stone-roofed, 15th c. chapel (restored).

CHAPELIZOD, Co. Dublin (Map 3, K3), is a suburban Liffeyside village on the Dublin (3 m.)–Lucan (10 m.) road. The Protestant parish church has a late medieval tower.

Edward Tingham, 17th c. statuary, lived at Chapelizod.

Alfred Harmsworth (1865–1922), first Lord Northcliffe, celebrated British press lord and propagandist, was born in Chapelizod.

1 m. NW., on the S. side of the river, is Palmerston House (now incorporated in the Stewart Institution for Imbecile Children). This great mansion was erected by John Hely

Hutchinson, Prime Serjeant-at-Law, who later became Provost of Trinity College, Dublin; he purchased the property in 1763.

CHARLEMONT, Co. Armagh (Map 2, G2), is a village on the Blackwater River on the Armagh (7 m.)–Dungannon (5½ m.) road. Commanding the river crossing are the remains (Hist. Mon.) of a fort erected during Mountjoy's 1602 campaign against Hugh O Neill. The first Governor was Captain Toby Caulfeild and the main star fort was completed by 1624 with the massive outer earthworks added in 1673 to give the finest example of a 17th c. artillery fortification in Ulster. The surviving gateway, with the Caulfeild arms, was probably erected in the late-18th c. Held by the Jacobites in 1689–90, it surrendered to Schomberg's Williamites in the latter year, and remained an English garrison until 1858. When the Caulfeilds were raised to the peerage, they took their title from Charlemont, the most distinguished bearer of which was the Volunteer Earl, a patriot and patron of the arts (*see p. 160*).

On the opposite side of the Blackwater, in Co. Tyrone, is Moy, a village laid out after the plan of Marengo in Lombardy for the Volunteer Earl, once famous for monthly horse fairs.

5 m. E., is Ardress House (Nat. Trust), a 17th c. farmhouse charmingly remodelled by George Ensor, the Dublin architect, who came to live in it about 1770. It has lovely stucco by Michael Stapleton of Dublin, including *Cupid Bound* (based on a Bartolozzi print after a painting by Angelica Kauffmann). The stucco has been restored in accordance with Stapleton's designs.

4 m. E., is The Argory (Nat. Trust), with a neo-classical 1820 house designed by the Williamson Brothers for Walter MacGeough Bond and presented to the Trust in 1979 by W.A.N. MacGeough Bond, Esq. The house is lit by its own acetylene gas plant and features a cabinet barrel organ by Bishop of London on the first floor landing.

CLANE, Co. Kildare (Map 3, I4), is a Liffey-side village on the Kilcock (10 m.)–Naas (7 m.) road.

SE. of the village are remains of a Franciscan friary founded in 1258 by Sir Gerald fitz Maurice Fitzgerald, 4th baron O ffaly (d. 1287), whose mutilated effigy is still there; to the S., overlooking the Liffey, is a de Hereford motte.

2 m. NE. is beautifully situated Clongowes Wood College (1814), the well-known Jesuit boarding school. The nucleus of the school buildings is Castle Browne, a much altered (1718 and 1788) FitzEustace castle which was a border fort of the English Pale. Forfeited for participation in the Catholic Confederation (*see p. 26*), it was purchased in 1667 by the Brownes, who intermarried with the Wogans. In 1813 Gen. Michael Wogan-Browne, A.D.C. to the King of Saxony, sold the castle to the Society of Jesus. The chapel, an uninspired Gothic edifice, has Stations of the Cross by Seán Keating and a series of beautiful windows by Michael Healy (1873–1941) and Evie Hone (1894–1955). The Healy windows began with a remarkable three-light *St Joseph* in the choir (1916), continued with his two-light *St Patrick and St Brigid* (1920), and ended with the first three of a *Seven Dolours* series of two-light windows in the nave (1936–41): *Prophecy of Simeon, Flight into Egypt*, and *Search for the Holy Child*. Healy's work was cut short by death, and ended with the base and top of the fourth window, *Christ Meets His Mother*, which was completed by Evie Hone. Evie Hone continued the series with *The Crucifixion* and *The Taking Down from the Cross* (1941). Her design for the last window of the series, *The Entombment of Christ*, exists only as a cartoon. In a chapel off the sacristy are two other Hone windows: a circular *Head of Christ Crucified* (1949) and a two-light *SS Ignatius and Francis Xavier* (1955). The great artist died before she had quite completed the latter. In a dark corridor near the chapel is hung Evie Hone's *The Taking Down from the Cross*. In the school museum is The Prosperous Crozier, a 10th c. bachall-shrine found in a bog in Prosperous. N. and S. of the college are sectors

Castletown House, Celbridge, Co. Kildare.

of the Pale. To the N. of the main gate is Mainham, where there is an old churchyard with the ruins of a church and the 1743 mausoleum (note inscription over entrance; the Rev. John Daniel was the Protestant rector) of the Wogan-Brownes. Nearby is a motte, relic of the castle of the first Anglo-Norman proprietor, John de Hereford. 2½ m. NE. of Mainham Church is the gatehouse (Nat. Mon.) of Rathcoffey Castle, chief seat of the Wogans. To a branch of the family which lived at Richardstown belonged the celebrated Jacobite soldier Sir Charles Wogan (1698–1752?), who rescued the Princess Clementine Sobieska from Innsbruck and escorted her to Bologna to marry the Old Pretender. In the 19th c. the castle was purchased by Archibald Hamilton Rowan, member of the United Irishmen, who demolished it to make room for a new residence.

1 m. S. is Blackhall House, birthplace of the Rev. Charles Wolfe (1791–1823), poet ('The Burial of Sir John Moore'). The family was related to the Wolfes of Castlewarden, after whom Wolfe Tone was named.

CLARA, Co. Offaly (Map 3, D4), is a market town and manufacturing centre where the Moate (4 m.)–Tullamore (15 m.) road crosses the Brosna River. It originated as a Quaker settlement. The Protestant parish church dates from 1770.

3 m. SE. is Ballycumber. The Protestant church has a window (*Music and Literature*, 1929) by Harry Clarke.

5 m. W., beyond Ballycumber, is Boher Catholic church. There is preserved the large, portable, tomb-shaped shrine or reliquary made in the 12th c. to contain the bones of St Manchán of Lemanaghan (*see p. 179*). This reliquary is one of the most important products of the post-Viking Irish revival. It appears to have been made in the same atelier (Clonmacnois?) as the superb, contemporary Cross of Cong, now in the National Museum. The 12th c. bronze figurines formed no part of the original shrine.

CLARECASTLE, Co. Clare (Map 6, G6), formerly Clare, a village where the Ennis (3 m.)–Limerick (19 m.) road crosses the estuary of the Fergus, takes its name from a castle (incorporated in the derelict military barracks) commanding the river-crossing.

The Catholic church has a window by Michael Healy: *Veronica's Towel, Christ Meets His Mother, Ecce Homo* (1927).

1 m. N. are the ruins (Nat. Mon.) of Clare 'Abbey', a priory of Canons Regular of St Augustine, dedicated to SS Peter and Paul, which was founded in 1189 by Donal Mór O Brien, King of Limerick. The remains are largely 15th c., but include some late-12th or early-13th c. work. At the Dissolution the monastery was granted to Donnchadh O Brien, Baron of Ibracken, on condition he gave up the name of O Brien and undertook to use English manners, language, dress, etc.

1½ m. SE. is Carnelly House, a good early-18th c. Stamer house (noteworthy saloon).

CLAREGALWAY, Co. Galway (Map 6, G1), is a hamlet where the Galway (6 m.)–Tuam (14 m.) road crosses the Claregalway River. The crossing is dominated by the massive tower of a 15th c. Clanrickard Burke castle. W. of the castle are the ruins (Nat. Mon.) of a fine Franciscan friary founded by John de Cogan *c.* 1240/50. The slender bell-tower, N. transept, and E. window are 15th c. There are some interesting 18th c. tombstones with occupational symbols (ploughs, etc.). The modern church of St James (1975) is by Robinson, Keefe and Devane.

5 m. NNE., W. of the Tuam road, in Caheravoley, is Cregboyne Fort (Nat. Mon.), a 17th c. bawn with two angle turrets.

6 m. NE. (1 m. E. of the Tuam road) are the remains of the tower and square bawn of Anbally Castle (Burkes). The castle was erected on a built platform.

CLARE ISLAND, Co. Mayo (Map 7, C5), is a mountainous island (Croaghmore, alias Knockmore, 1,520 ft) at the mouth of Clew Bay. It is most conveniently reached from Roonah Quay. Overlooking the harbour is the defaced Grania Wael's Castle (Nat. Mon.), a 15th/16th c. O Malley castle tower modernized in 1831 to serve as a coastguard station. Popular legend names it after Gráinne Ni Mháille, Grace O Malley, though she never held it. Gráinne (*c.* 1530–1600) was the daughter of Dubh-Dara O Malley, lord of Upper Umhall. Her freebooting exploits on land and sea have passed – with the inevitable romantic exaggerations – into legend. She married, first, Donal O Flaherty, lord of Ballynahinch, and, second, Richard an Iarainn Burke, lord of Carra and Burrishoole. In 1574 she beat off an English seaborne expedition against Carraig an Chabhlaigh Castle (*see p. 258*). In 1577 she was captured by the Earl of Desmond and imprisoned in Limerick and Dublin. In 1580 she helped the English against her rebel husband. After his death, in 1583, she took up her residence at Carraig an Chabhlaigh. In 1586 she was arrested for complicity in the Burkes' rebellion. Seven years later she appeared before Elizabeth I to petition for maintenance and a licence to harry the Queen's enemies with fire and sword. The well-known story about Gráinne and the heir of Howth, Co. Dublin (*see pp. 204–5*), is apocryphal. The earliest version is told of Richard O Cuairsci Burke (d. 1479).

1½ m. WSW. are the remains of Clare 'Abbey' (Nat. Mon.). The ruins are those of a small, late-15th c. nave-and-chancel church with two-storey N. annexe; over the chancel is a dwelling tower. Noteworthy is the sadly decayed, 15th and 17th c. painting on the founder's tomb, E. wall, and chancel vault.

CLAREMORRIS, Co. Mayo (Map 7, H6), is a small market town and railway junction on the Ballyhaunis (11 m.)–Castlebar (16 m.) road.

7 m. NE., on the Kilkelly road, is Knock (Cnoc Mhuire), a place of pilgrimage ever since the apparitions claimed to have been seen at the gable of the church, 21 August 1879. Just over 100 years later, on 30 September 1979, Pope John Paul II visited the shrine. The outsize, barn-like Basilica of Our Lady Queen of Ireland (1979), by Louis and Brian Brennan, and Daithí Hanly, has statues of *The Sacred Heart* (Eamon Hogan), *St Joseph* (Imogen Stuart), *Our Lady of Knock* (Domhnall Ó Murchadha), *St John the Evangelist* (Nuala Creagh) and *St Columbanus* (Henry Flanagan, O.P.). Two of the Stations of the Cross are by Nell and Patrick Pollen, the tabernacle is by Patrick McElroy, and the large tapestry by Ray Carroll. Associated with the shrine is a small Folk Museum.

CLARINBRIDGE, Co. Galway (Map 6, H2), is a small village on the Galway (10 m.)–Gort (14 m.) road. The locality is noted for its oysters and scallops.

Adjoining the village on the SE. is the demesne of Kilcornan House. The house, now a school and training centre for the handicapped, incorporates the tower of a 15th/16th c. castle. Beside the avenue is a small, simple, 12th/13th c. church (restored).

2 m. NW., beside the Galway road, is Caheradrine(en), an early ecclesiastical site enclosed by remains of a strong cashel.

CLASHMORE, Co. Waterford (Map 4, E7), is a village where the Cappoquin (12 m.)–Ardmore (7 m.) road crosses the little Creagagh River.

The roofless Protestant church occupies the site of a monastery founded by St Mo-Chúa, disciple of Cárthach of Lismore.

CLAUDY, Co. Londonderry (Map 1, E5), is a village off the main Dungiven (11 m.)–Derry (10 m.) road. It is at the centre of an area exceptionally rich in archaeological remains, of which only a few can be noted.

4¼ m. NNE., on top of a hill at Ballygroll, is a remarkable complex (Hist. Mon.) of prehistoric remains including: a court-tomb with cup-marked capstone; several wedge-tombs; two stone circles and various other features.

5 m. NE. (¾ m. SSW. of Loughermore bridge), on Ballyholly Hill, is a complex of stone circles and other prehistoric (?) remains.

4½ m. SE., beside Park village, is the Tireighter wedge-tomb.

2½ m. NW. at Crossalt, on the main road, are the ruins of Brackfield Plantation Bawn built by the Skinners' Company (Hist. Mon.).

CLEAR ISLAND, Co. Cork (Map 5, FG9), lies 6 m. SW. of Baltimore, from which it may be reached by mail-carrying motor-boat (enquire locally for sailing times). Fastnet Rock, 4 m. SW., is the most southerly point in Ireland, and the location of a lighthouse completed in 1904, which replaced that on the S. of Clear Island.

The population is still Irish-speaking and preserves many traditional customs.

The rocky island, 3 m. by 1½ m., has been almost cut in two by the inlets, Ineer, or South Harbour, and Trawkieran, or North Harbour.

Trawkieran (Tráigh Chiaráin) is called after St Ciarán of Seir Kieran (*see p. 78*), who was a native of the island. Near the NW. corner of the inlet are the remains of Teampall Chiaráin and Gallán Chiaráin, an early cross-pillar (Nat. Mons.); 'rounds' are made at the pillar on the vigils of 15 March (St Kieran's day) and 25 March. Nearby is Tobar Chiaráin, a hollow in the shingle where water is procured for blessing the islanders' homes and sick. Teampall Chiaráin was a simple, medieval church with a small, two-light E. window and plain S. door.

The following mileages are reckoned from Trawkieran:

¾ m. ENE., in Lissnamona, at the early church site called An Cillíneach, is an early cross-pillar. Nearby, close to the church, is a small museum (open in summer).

1 m. SSE., in Glen West, overlooking South Harbour, is Gallán na mBánóg, an alignment of low stones; also on the hill is a pillarstone. A stone slab decorated in the passage-tomb style with spiral and serpentiform devices (now in Cork Public Museum) is said to have been found there.

½ m. W., in Ballyieragh North, on a broken-away promontory are remains of the O Driscoll castle of Dún an Óir.

CLEGGAN, Co. Galway (Map 7, B8), is a hamlet with a small fishing harbour on Cleggan Bay, 7 m. NW. of Clifden and 7 m. W. of Letterfrack.

3 m. E., in Clooncree, fragments of a small ornamented (17th? c.) cross and St Ceannanach's Stone mark the spot where, says legend, the decapitated martyr placed his head while resting before returning to Aran. His blood left its mark on the stone.

6 m. SW. is Omey Island, which may be reached on foot at low tide. In the sandhills near the N. shore the ruins of Templefeheen, a small interesting medieval church, preserve the memory of a monastery founded by St Féichín of CONG, and of Ardoileán (*see below*).

7 m. W. is Ardoileán, alias High Island, where St Féichín had another eremitical settlement. The remains (Nat. Mons.) include a diminutive church, two clocháns and several early cross-slabs. Near the highest point of the island there is an early cross-slab.

6 m. NW. is Inishbofin, a pleasant place for a simple holiday. When he was defeated at the Synod of Whitby in 664, Bishop Colman of Lindisfarne withdrew from the English mission. He came with his adherents – who included 30 English monks – to Inishbofin and set up a monastery. Disputes having arisen between the English and Irish brethren, he founded a new monastery for the English monks at Mayo (*see p. 53*) and ruled both houses until his death (674/6). The Inishbofin monastery disappears from history after 900. In the 16th c. the celebrated Gráinne Ni Mháille (*see p. 104*) is said to have fortified the island for her fleet. At the harbour entrance is Cromwell's Barrack, embodying Bosco's Castle. Bosco is said to have been a pirate – Dane or Spaniard – allied with Gráinne Ni Mháille. The sadly defaced Barrack was a 24-gun star fort erected about 1652–7. 1 m. NE. is the site of St Colmán's monastery, with a featureless church and a bullaun.

CLIFDEN, Co. Galway (Map 7, C8), 'capital of Connemara', is a small market town and fishing port beautifully sited at the head of the N. arm of Clifden Bay, 50 m. NW. of Galway (via Oughterard) and 21 m. SW. of Leenaun. It was founded about 1812 by John Darcy of Killtullagh, whose derelict 'castle' (1815) is 1½ m. W. It is a noted angling centre and a convenient base for exploring some of the loveliest regions of the W. The Connemara Pony Show, held at Clifden in mid-August, is worth visiting. Clifden Marconi Wireless Station, destroyed during the last Anglo-Irish war, was the first transatlantic wireless-telegraph station in Europe.

5 m. SSW. (1 m. NE. of Ballyconneely) is Derrygimlagh bog, where John Alcock and Arthur Whitten Brown crash-landed at the end of the first W.–E. flight across the Atlantic, 15 June 1919. A cairn has been erected at the edge of the bog close to the landing-place, and a monument (1959) at a viewing place on high ground 1½ m. away.

5 m. SW., by the N. shore of Loughnakilla, on Errislannan (Iorrus Fhlannáin, Flannan's peninsula), are Kilflannan – a ruined medieval church – Tobar Fhlannáin, and St Flannan's Bed; they are dedicated to St Flannán of Killaloe.

CLIFFONEY, Co. Sligo (Map 8, C8), is a village on the Bundoran (8 m.)–Sligo (13 m.) road. It was formerly part of an estate belonging to Viscount Palmerston (1784–1865), British statesman and Prime Minister, some of whose property, including Classiebawn Castle 2½ m. to the NNW., descended to the late Countess Mountbatten. Lord Palmerston carried out many improvements on the estate, including the construction of the harbour at Mullaghmore, a little resort overlooking Bunduff Strand 2½ m. N. of Cliffoney, where boats may be hired for the crossing to INISHMURRAY. It was in the harbour of Mullaghmore that Lord Louis Mountbatten of Burma was assassinated in 1979. In Bunduff is a well-preserved court-tomb.

1 m. NE., slightly to the E. of the Bundoran road and the hamlet of Creevykeel, is Creevykeel court-tomb, one of the finest full court-tombs in the country. An entrance passage through the E. end of the wedge-shaped cairn leads to a subrectangular ritual court, off whose W. end opens a two-chamber gallery grave. To the W. of the latter were two other tombs, opening off the N. and S. sides of the cairn respectively. The cairn was excavated in 1935 by the Harvard archaeological expedition. Four cremated burials were discovered, as well as Western Neolithic pottery, polished stone axes, flints, etc.

CLOGHAN, Co. Offaly (Map 3, B5), is a village on the Banagher (6 m.)–Clara (15 m.) road.

2 m. NW., on the road to Shannonbridge, are the well-preserved tower (modernized) and 17th c. bawn of Clononey Castle. It was occupied down to the 19th c. In the bawn is a noteworthy slab commemorating two members of the Bullen (Boleyn) family exiled to Ireland after the execution of Anne Boleyn by Henry VIII.

CLOGHEEN, Co. Tipperary (Map 4, D5), is a village on the Clonmel (14 m.)–Mitchelstown (13 m.) road, at the N. foot of the Knockmealdown mountains. The road S. to LISMORE climbs Sugarloaf Hill by the well-known V-road, a series of hairpin bends affording superb panoramas of mountain and plain.

The Catholic parish church (1862–4), is by J.J. McCarthy.

2 m. E., on the N. side of the River Tar at Castle Grace, are remains of a de Bermingham (?) castle of *c.* 1250; rectangular, with angle towers (three round, one square).

1 m. W. are the remnants of Shanrahan Church and Castle. In the churchyard is buried Father Nicholas Sheehy, who was hanged at Clonmel, 15 March 1766, after a trial on trumped-up charges brought against him (in gross breach of faith) by the bigoted gentry of S. Tipperary.

CLOGHER, Co. Tyrone (Map 2, E2), which gives its name to the diocese, is a small town on the Enniskillen (23 m.)–Dungannon (20 m.) road, in the centre of the pleasantly wooded Clogher Valley, once served by a narrow-gauge railway.

St Macartan, according to legend St Patrick's 'strong man' or bodyguard, is honoured as the first Bishop of Clogher, which appears to have been the seat of a pagan oracle before he fixed his seat there. Subsequently, an important monastery grew up on the spot, but of this the only surviving relics are fragments of High Crosses of the 9th/10th c., assembled to the W. of the Cathedral, and a sundial with fish-decoration now in the Cathedral porch. The present St Macartan's Cathedral, built in 1744, is a small classical edifice, thought to have been the work of James Martin, the builder of Baronscourt (*see p. 261*). It was restored by Sir Albert Richardson in 1956. The building has some fine stained glass, notably *The Good Shepherd* (1908) by A.E. Child and *Christ Enthroned* (1918) by Catherine A. O Brien, as well as an interesting collection of portraits of former bishops in the porch.

Just off the main street is the Convent of Mercy, formerly the bishop's palace, an imposing plain classical block begun in 1799 by Bishop John Porter and completed by his successors, Beresford and Tottenham. In the bishop's demesne stands the great hill-fort known as Rathmore (excavated in the 1970s), which was the seat of the Kings of Oriel in the time of St Patrick. The earthworks comprise a hill-fort, a substantial ringfort and a barrow. The excavations suggested links with Roman Britain.

The Catholic Church (1979) is by Liam McCormick, and a substantial market-house erected in 1780 by Bishop John Garnett is now an Orange Hall.

3 m. SW. is Fardross House, formerly the seat of the Gledstanes. The demesne contains many unusual trees and a small forest park. Just above Fardross, on the summit of Ballyscally, is Brackenridge's Monument, a three-tier tower erected as a mausoleum by George C. Brackenridge of Ashfield Park (1 m. E. of Fardross).

CLONAKILTY, Co. Cork (Map 5, J7), is a small market town on the Bandon (13 m.)–Skibbereen (19 m.) road. The town was founded in 1614 by Richard Boyle, afterwards 'Great' Earl of Cork (*see p. 70*). The West Cork Regional Museum is housed in the former Methodist National School.

1½ m. N. is the ancient church site of Templebryan, a large enclosure with remains of a primitive church, a souterrain, a well (Tobernakilla), and an 11 ft pillarstone; low down on the W. face of the stone is a cross *pattée*; on the adjoining angle is a faint ogham inscription.

1½ m. S. (via causeway) is Inchdoney, an island across the mouth of the bay. On the S. side of the island projects the Virgin Mary's Rock whose legend is the theme of Jeremiah Callanan's ballad.

4¼ m. WSW., at Sam's Cross[roads], is a memorial, by Seamus Murphy, to Michael Collins (1890–1922), the great guerrilla organizer against the British, who was born in nearby Woodfield. It was unveiled, Easter 1965, by Gen. Tom Barry, who fought against Collins in the tragic Civil War of 1922–3.

CLONASLEE, Co. Laois (Map 3, D5), is a village on the fine Mountmellick (11 m.)–Birr (17 m.) road.

2½ m. W. are the ruins of Castle Cuffe, built in the 17th c. by Sir Charles Coote.

CLONDALKIN, Co. Dublin (Map 3, J4), once a walled town of the English Pale, is now a rapidly growing, unattractive, industrial suburb, to the N. of the Dublin (6¼ m.)–Naas (14¾ m.) dual carriageway.

The main road of the village cuts through the site of a monastery founded in the 7th c. by Bishop St Mo-Chúa. For a time in the late-8th c. the abbacy seems to have been confined to the founder's kin, the Lugaedón sept. The 'translation' of St Mo-Chúa's relics took place in 789. In 833 the monastery was pillaged by the Vikings, who made a settlement nearby. They were defeated, and their fortress burned, by the king of Laois in 867. After the Anglo-Norman conquest the church was annexed to the deanery of St Patrick's Cathedral, Dublin. Of the monastery there survive the Round Tower (Nat. Mon.), climbable to the top and, in the Protestant churchyard, a large granite cross (Nat. Mon.), a small granite cross, and a rude granite basin.

SE. of the Protestant church is Clondalkin Castle (Tully's Castle, Nat. Mon.), a small, 16th c. tower with 17th (?) c. lean-to.

1½ m. S., on the Tallaght road, is the Georgian house, Belgard Castle (now the headquarters of Cement-Roadstone Holdings). It incorporates a fragment of a castle of the Talbots (*see pp. 243–4*) which was an important border fortress of the English Pale.

1 m. SW. is Baldonnell (renamed Casement) military aerodrome. It was from this aerodrome that the German fliers Kohl and von Huenfeld, with the Irish airman James Fitzmaurice, took off on the first successful E.–W. Atlantic flight, 1932.

CLONEGALL, Co. Carlow (Map 4, K1), is an attractive village where the Tullow (7 m.)–Enniscorthy (14 m.) road crosses the little River Derry.

Beside the village is the demesne of Huntington Castle (Durdin-Robertson), a fortified house of the 17th c. which has been considerably modernized.

CLONES, Co. Monaghan (Map 2, D4), is a market and Border town on the Dundalk (41 m.)–Enniskillen (24 m.) road.

The history of Clones commences with a monastery founded by St Tighearnach, who died there 549/50. There survive: in Abbey St, a fragment of a small 12th c. church; in the ancient graveyard nearby, an imperfect Round Tower and St Tighearnach's Grave, the latter a 12th (?) c., church-shaped tomb; in the Diamond (market-place), a High Cross (Nat. Mon.) made up of the head and shaft of separate 9th/10th (?) c. crosses. The weathered figurations on the cross include: South Face: *Fall of Adam and Eve, Sacrifice of Abraham, Daniel in the Den of Lions*; *Crucifixion*; North Face: *Adoration of the Magi, Miracle of Cana, Multiplication of the Loaves and Fishes.*

W. of the Diamond is a conspicuous motte-and-bailey (Clones Fort).

2 m. E. is Annakilly, birthplace of James Connolly (1870–1916), Irish Labour leader and patriot, who commanded the Republican insurgents of Dublin in 1916 and was executed by the British.

CLONFERT, Co. Galway (Map 6, L2), is a townland 1 m. N. of the Ballinasloe (12 m.)–Banagher (5 m.) road and 5 m. NE. of Eyrecourt. In 558/64 St Brendan the Navigator, whose legend

Clonmacnois, Co. Offaly.

made its own contribution to medieval literature and to the story of Atlantic discovery, founded a monastery there. At the 12th c. reformation it was transformed into a priory (St Mary's *de Porto Puro*) of Augustinian Canons Regular. The same reformation saw Clonfert become the see of the newly founded diocese to which it has given its name. The skeleton of the small cathedral ascribed to Conor Maenmoy O Kelly, King of Uí Maine, 1140–80, survives substantially; its superb W. doorway is one of the glories of Irish Romanesque. In its original form, the cathedral was a single-chamber church with *antae* at each gable. The chancel is an early-13th c. addition. In the 15th c. the friary-type bell-tower (the incorrect parapet is a modern 'restoration') and the transepts (N. transept now missing) were added, the Transitional (presumably) chancel arch was replaced by the existing Gothic arch, Gothic windows were inserted in the chancel walls, and the inner (limestone) order was inserted in the Romanesque doorway. The cathedral was wrecked in the 16th c. and its interior much modified in the meantime. In the nave is an interesting 13th c. font; affixed to the adjacent wall is an early stone slab inscribed BECGÁN. Two Jacobean wood-panels attached to the inner wall of the tower came from the 17th c. bishop's palace. In the roofless S. transept is another early gravestone. (The Catholic cathedral is now at LOUGHREA. The Church of Ireland diocese is united with that of KILLALOE.)

CLONMACNOIS, Co. Offaly (Map 6, L1), site of one of Ireland's foremost early monasteries, lies on the E. bank of the Shannon, 4 m. N. of SHANNONBRIDGE, 13 m. (9 m. by boat) S. of ATHLONE, and 14 m. SW. of MOATE. The ideal approach is by boat from Athlone. The remains (comprising eight churches, two Round Towers, three High Crosses, over 400 early memorial slabs and two holy wells, Nat. Mons.) are of exceptional interest to the student of early Irish art and architecture.

As an ecclesiastical centre Clonmacnois (Cluain moccu Nóis, meadow of the race of Nós) had only one rival, Armagh. As a centre of Irish art and literature it had none. Many Kings of Tara and Kings of Connacht were buried there.

The monastery was founded by St Cíarán, Son of the Wright and disciple of St Finnian of Clonard, who came down-river from Inis Ainghin (Hare Island, *see p. 240*) with eight companions on 25 January 545. Seven months later (9 September), Cíarán died. From shortly after his death, his grave became a great centre of pilgrimage for people from all over Ireland. The most famous foreign pilgrim was Pope John Paul II who visited the site in September 1979. Because Clonmacnois was at the crossing of the main N.-S. traffic artery, namely the Shannon, it maintained links with, and drew its abbots and community from, many parts of the country, though it had a special relationship with Connacht, the province which adjoins it on the opposite side of the river.

The significance of Clonmacnois for the development of early Irish vernacular literature and historical records is made clear by the surviving products of its scriptorium: *Lebor na hUidre* (*Book of the Dun Cow*), the Bodleian Library manuscripts, Rawlinson B.502 – these are the two oldest of the great Irish literary codices – *Chronicon Scotorum*, the *Annals of Clonmacnois*, and the *Annals of Tigernach*. Its importance as a centre and repository of early Irish art is indicated by the nature and quality of the works which have come down to us, though these can represent but a fraction of the output of its workshops: the High Crosses, the unparalleled series of early memorial slabs, St Kieran's Crozier, the Crozier of the Abbots of Clonmacnois, the Cross of Cong (Nat. Museum), and St Manchán's Shrine (*see p. 108*).

Clonmacnois had more than its share of misfortunes. It was ravaged by fire 13 times between 722 and 1205, and plundered by the Vikings eight times between 832 and 1163. In 844 the notorious Thorgestr (Turgesius) burned down the monastery, and his wife, Aud (Ota), gave oracles from the principal altar. Irish enemies assailed it no less than 27 times between 832 and 1163, English foes six times between 1178 and 1204. It was finally reduced to complete ruin by the English garrison of Athlone in 1552, when 'not a bell, large or small, or an image, or an altar, or a book, or a gem, or even glass in a window, was left which was not carried away'.

In 1955 the Church of Ireland presented the site to the State, which up to then had owned only the masonry of the ruins. Since then the treatment and maintenance of the monuments has signally improved, and many of the modern tombstones laid flat. A tragic blunder has, however, been committed in allowing the cemetery to be extended without an investigation, and new graves are constantly being dug through archaeological deposits.

In its heyday Clonmacnois was more than just a monastery. It was rather a monastic city (in 1179 no fewer than 105 houses were burned down), with workshops, and dwellings of workers and armed retainers as well as of the monks, and some 12 or 13 small churches and oratories, of which fragments of eight survive today. In addition, the group as a whole exemplifies the incoherent character of early Irish monasteries – with their multiplication of scattered, small-scale, simple churches – which contrasts so markedly with the Continental coherent monasteries dominated by a single, complex, great church.

The tour of Clonmacnois may conveniently commence with the new Interpretative Centre, where many of the memorial slabs and some of the cross-fragments are displayed. The visit to the old monastic site itself should perhaps begin with the South Cross, a 9th/10th c. High Cross, for the most part covered with panels of interlacing vine-scrolls and other ornaments, but having a *Crucifixion* on the W. face of the shaft.

Immediately NE. is a small early church called Temple Dowling because of re-edification in 1689 by Edmund Dowling of Clondalare as a family chantry or mausoleum. Built on to the E. end is a later Gothic church, Temple Hurpain.

NE. of these two churches is Temple Melaghlin, alias Temple Rí, a late-12th c., rectangular structure. The E. window is a Western Transitional, two-light window with plain mouldings. In the S. wall are an Early Gothic lancet and a Late Gothic doorway.

N. of Temple Melaghlin is diminutive Temple Kieran. The fragmentary masonry is a patchwork of different dates, but includes remains of three *antae*. This is traditionally the burial place of St Cíarán, and devotees still collect the sacred earth in the NE. corner. In the late-17th c. the local peasantry kept 'St Cíarán's Hand' here as a sacred relic. The 11th c. 'Crozier of the Abbots of Clonmacnois', now in the National Museum, is said to have been found here early in the last c. along with a chalice and other objects. Against the E. wall stands a 13th c. gravestone.

NW. of Temple Kieran are the foundations of Temple Kelly, thought to be the church erected in 1167 by Conor O Kelly and the Uí Maine. Near the SW. corner is a bullaun.

SW. of Temple Kelly is the Cathedral, which may partially incorporate the 'great stone church' built early in the 10th c. by Flann Sinna, King of Tara, and abbot Colmán. The remains are those of a rectangular church with *antae* at each gable and an early-13th c. sacristy on the S. side. In the W. gable are fragments of a fine Romanesque doorway inserted in the late 12th c. and reconstructed in the 15th. There are remnants of an unusual Gothic chancel inserted into the E. end about 1460. It consisted of three low, groin-vaulted aisles or chapels. Turloch Mór O Conor (d. 1156), King of Connacht and High-King, was buried to the S. of the high-altar; his son Rúairí (d. 1198), last of the High-Kings, was buried to the N. of the altar. By the N. wall of the nave are two weathered, 13th c. gravestones. At the NW. corner is an interesting Perpendicular doorway with figures of SS Patrick, Francis, and Dominic above; the inscription reads:

Clonfert Cathedral (see page 107).

Near Maam Cross, Connemara, Co. Galway *(see page 116)*.

DOM[INU]S ODO DECANUS . . . ME FIERI FECIT ('The Lord Aodh [Úa Máel-Eóin] Dean [of Clonmacnois] had me made'). A Gothic door in the S. wall leads to the stone-vaulted sacristy, in which are stored miscellaneous carved fragments.

W. of the cathedral is Cros na Screaptra, The Cross of the Scriptures. A partly defaced inscription at the base of the shaft has been variously interpreted to suggest a date for the cross in the 9th or 10th c. The subjects figured include: Base: *Horsemen, Charioteers*; Shaft: W. face: *Soldiers Guarding the Tomb of Christ, the Mocking, Soldiers Casting Lots, Crucifixion;* E. face: *The Last Judgement*, scenes from the life of Joseph (?) and *Christ Hands the Keys to Peter and the Gospels to Paul.*

NE. of Cros na Screaptra is the shaft of the N. Cross; a seated figure with crossed legs and antler head-dress is discernible.

W. of the N. Cross is O Rourke's Tower, an imperfect Round Tower some 62 ft high which has been attributed to Fergal O Rourke, King of Breany, who was killed in 964, but it was probably not completed until 1120/4. The top was struck off by lightning in 1135.

NE. of the belfry is 12th c. Temple Conor. It was in ruins in 1735, but has been restored to serve as the Protestant parish church. The W. door and the smallest of the S. windows are old.

At the N. edge of the cemetery is fragmentary Teampall Finghin, a small nave-and-chancel church of unusual interest. The fragments of the nave include the remains of a Romanesque S. door and W. window. The handsome chancel arch is rather mutilated; the innermost order is an insertion. In the stone-roofed chancel, a doorway gives access to a fine, small Round Tower which is an integral part of the church.

A paved way (1070?) leads, via a gate in the E. wall of the cemetery, towards the fragmentary remains of the secluded Nuns' Church, a beautiful, small, nave-and-chancel Romanesque church built by Dervorgilla, wife of Tiernan O Rourke of Breany (*see p. 246*). It was completed in 1167. The W. doorway and fine chancel arch (on which is an exhibitionist) were re-erected in 1865. Unfortunately, the restorers swept away most of the ancient cashel which had surrounded the church. To the N., the Pilgrims Road marks an ancient highway to the monastery.

W. of the cemetery, on a motte beside the Shannon, are the shattered remains of a strong castle with gatehouse on the NW. and keep on the N. This is possibly the castle erected in 1220 by the English Justiciar, John Gray.

¼ m. W. of the cemetery, beside the Shannonbridge road, is St Ciarán's Well. There is a crude late Crucifixion slab there.

3 m. E., near Clonfinlough Church, is the Clonfinlough Stone (Nat. Mon.), a large boulder covered with prehistoric scribings.

CLONMANY, Co. Donegal (Map 1, C2), is a beautifully sited village 1¾ m. SSW. of BALLYLIFFIN.

1¼ m. N., at an ancient church site in Binnion, is a stone cross.

1¼ m. S., is Clonmany Glebe where, in the Middle Ages, the O Morrisons were hereditary keepers of the Miasach, a book shrine now in the National Museum in Dublin.

2 m. SSW. is Raghtinmore, where – says a local tale – Fionn mac Cumhaill dispensed his laws.

5 m. SW., between Mamore Hill (1,381 ft) and Croaghcarragh (Urris Hills, 1,379 ft), is the steep, difficult pass of Mamore, noted for its splendid views.

CLONMEL, Co. Tipperary (Map 4, F4), county town of the South Riding of Tipperary, is an important market town and small-scale manufacturing centre (cider, computers, pharmaceuticals etc.) in the beautiful Suir valley (noted for its scenery), 13 m. W. of Carrick-on-Suir, 22 m. N. of Dungarvan, 11 m. E. of Cahir, and 15 m. SE. of Cashel.

At the Norman conquest the de Burgos acquired a manor at Clonmel, and Richard (d. 1243) probably founded the town. In 1338, it was purchased by the Earl of Desmond, whose family subsequently feuded over it with the Earls of Ormond until overthrown in 1583. Clonmel remained loyal to the English Crown throughout the Middle Ages, but was ultimately driven to seek safety in the national camp and, in December 1641, admitted a Confederate Catholic garrison. The Supreme Council of the Confederation (*see pp. 214–5*) assembled there in June 1647. On 27 April 1650, Cromwell appeared before the town, which was garrisoned by the gallant, able Hugh Dubh O Neill with 1,250 ill-supplied Ulster troops. Having inflicted heavy losses on the Cromwellians, they escaped by night. Next day the townsfolk capitulated on a guarantee of life and estate, but the capitulation marked the ruin of the ancient burgher families, and for the next 200 years Clonmel was controlled by a new oligarchy.

Clonmel produced several notable Catholic leaders and scholars in the 16th and 17th c. Thomas White, S.J. (d. 1622) founded the Irish College in Salamanca (closed 1951); his brother Stephen (1574–1650), also S.J., was a noted historian who taught at German universities and collaborated with the Protestant Primate Ussher, and Colgan, among others, in exploiting the rich mine of Irish ecclesiastical literature on the Continent. Geoffrey Baron (1607–51) took a very prominent part in the affairs of the Catholic confederation and was hanged by Ireton when Limerick capitulated in 1651. His brother Bartholomew, better known as Father Bonaventure Baron (1610–96), was famous as orator, philosopher, theologian, historian and Latin poet.

Laurence Sterne (1713–68), author of *A Sentimental Journey*, was born in Clonmel, his mother's native place. George Borrow (1803–81) attended school in the town during the few months his father was stationed there (1815).

Father Abram Ryan, army chaplain and songwriter of the Confederate States (*The Sword of Robert Lee, Re-united, Erin's Flag*), was the son of Matt and Mary Ryan of Clonmel.

The Court House, Nelson St, is by Sir Richard Morrison (1803). It was the scene of the state trial of William Smith O Brien, Thomas Francis Meagher, Terence Bellew Mac Manus, and Patrick O Donohue, after the abortive Young Ireland insurrection of 1848. In Parnell St is the Tipperary (S.R.) County Museum, showing the history of the county, and works of art. Hearn's Hotel nearby was once the headquarters of Bianconi's coach system, established in 1815.

In Sarsfield St is the Mainguard, built in 1674 as the seat of the courts of the Palatinate of Ormond, whose coat of arms, together with those of the municipality, still adorn it. James II was received by the Corporation there, 21 March 1689. After the extinction of the Palatinate jurisdiction in 1715, the building served as Tholsel and seat of the royal assizes, and the infamous trial of Father Nicholas Sheehy (*see p. 106*) took place there in 1766.

At the Town Hall are preserved the civic regalia and municipal muniments: they may be inspected (apply to Town Clerk).

The Franciscan church, by W.G. Doolin (1884–6), incorporates the 15th c. tower and 13th c. N. choir wall of the church of a friary founded in 1269. The friary was converted into a citadel after the Cromwellian conquest. In the church may be seen the tomb (*c.* 1533) of the Butlers of CAHIR. The latter has effigies of an armoured knight and his lady; the basin of a font which came from medieval St Mary's (*below*) is in the yard beside the church.

Mary St takes its name from the medieval parish church of the Assumption of the Blessed Virgin Mary, otherwise 'Our Ladye of Clonmell' (13th c., rebuilt in 15th). St Mary's parish church (Protestant), erected in 1857 to the design of Welland, occupies the site, and incorporates interesting 15th c. fragments (fine E. window – with stained glass of *Christ* and *Four Evangelists* (1931–3) by C. O Brien; chancel arch, basement of tower, vestry, aisle walls, W. window, W. window of porch). Some 16th and 17th c. tombstones of burgher families are preserved in the church. The N. and W. sides of the churchyard are bounded by portions of the medieval town wall, including the NW. angle tower and two flankers.

West Gate (1831), which closes the W. end of O Connell St, occupies the site of the medieval town gate whose name it bears. Nearby is the Grammar School attended by George Borrow, and described in *Lavengro*. It is now the Engineering section of the County Council.

The present parish church of the Assumption (St Mary's), Irishtown, is a Classical building of 1837–50; steeple and portico 1875–90. It has a good stucco ceiling; the expensive high altar (1867) was designed by the English architect George Goldie. In the church may be seen the monument (1615) of John fitz Geoffrey White, first Mayor of Clonmel; it came from the old Franciscan church. The new pulpit and baptismal font (1983) are by Michael Biggs.

4½ m. N., in Lisronagh, is the site of an Anglo-Norman manor, with remains of a castle and burgh. In the neighbourhood are several ringforts and other earthworks.

5 m. E., on the S. side of the Suir, is Gurteen (-le-Poer) with its beautiful demesne and woods.

5½ m. E., on the N. side of the Suir, is Kilsheelan. There are ruins of a nave-and-chancel church with Romanesque-Transitional N. doorway (mutilated) and a plain Romanesque chancel arch; both added in the 12th/13th c. A motte (now complete with Marian grotto) marks the site of a castle erected by William de Burgo (?) at the Anglo-Norman conquest.

4¾ m. SW., in Glebe (Co. Waterford), are the remains of Kilronan, a 12th (?) c. church with 14th and 15th c. features; it appears to have had a double roof of stone in the Irish manner.

2¼ m. WSW., in Marlfield, the Protestant church of Inishlounaght marks the site and incorporates some fragments (Transitional door-head of three orders, E. window, tomb fragments, etc.) of the Cistercian abbey De Surio, founded before 1148 by Melaghlin O Phelan of the Déise and colonized from Monasternenagh (*see p. 123*) in 1151; it was re-endowed by Donal Mór O Brien of Thomond in 1187. The abbeys of Fermoy, CORCOMROE, and Glanragh were daughters of Inishlounaght. The celebrated *Life* of St Malachy of Armagh by St Bernard of Clairvaux was written at the instance of 'his dear friend', Abbot Comgán of Inishlounaght.

2¼ m. W., romantically sited in Patrickswell, are the ruins of a 17th c. church, a stone cross, and St Patrick's Well. The church incorporates Romanesque and other fragments of an older structure. In it are the remains of the altar tomb of Nicholas White of Clonmel (d. 1622). The tomb was erected in 1623 in a chantry chapel attached to the SW. corner of old St Mary's, Clonmel, and removed there in 1805. The figure subjects include *Crucifixion, Resurrection,* and *Virgin and Child.*

3 m. NW., in Giantsgrave, is the Giant's Broad Stone, a 9 ft pillarstone with crosses on two faces.

4¾ m. NNW., in Donaghmore, Domhnach Mór Maighe Feimhin, the site of an early monastery founded by St Forannán is marked by the ruins (Nat. Mon.) of St Forannán's Church, a small, 12th c., nave-and-chancel structure with the mutilated remnants of a fine Romanesque W. doorway and of a Romanesque chancel arch.

CLONTARF/DOLLYMOUNT, Co. Dublin (Map 3, K3), is a seaside suburb on the Dublin (2 m.)–Howth (7 m.) road. In 550 a church was founded there by St Comgall of Bangor; nothing is known of its history. Clontarf is celebrated as the place of Brian Boru's great victory over Leinster and Norse Dublin, Good Friday, 1014. The Church of St John the Baptist (Protestant) has a Catherine O Brien window, *Our Lord with Children* (1950). Clontarf Castle (19th c., now a hotel) stands on the site of a medieval commandery of the Knights Templar (later of the Knights Hospitaller of St John of Jerusalem). St Anne's was the residence of Lord Ardilaun; the demesne (Dublin Corporation) has a fine rose garden. The 'Bull Wall', a breakwater running out to the North Bull, is a popular bathing place. The North Bull is a large island of sand heaped up by the tides; it is a Bird Sanctuary and popular bathing place. (For Clontarf Presbyterian Church, *see p. 156.*)

CLOUGH, Co. Antrim (Map 1, I4), is a village on the road from Ballymena (7 m.) to Ballycastle (16½ m.). On a high basalt outcrop are some remains of a castle of various dates. The original castle was apparently constructed by the de Mandevilles (MacQuillans), who were eventually ousted by the MacDonnells. In 1641 the castle was besieged by the insurgent Irish. It was finally destroyed by Cromwellians.

CLOYNE, Co. Cork (Map 4, C9), is a village on the Middleton (6 m.)–Ballycotton (7 m.) road.

The celebrated St Colmán mac Lénéne (d. 604), who had been a professional poet before becoming a monk, founded his principal monastery at Cloyne (*see p. 86*). He is the earliest known Irish poet making use of Latin rhymes. At the 12th c. reformation it was made the see of the newly organized diocese of Cloyne. The Catholic cathedral has been in COBH since the passing of Penal times. The Protestant diocese has long been united with those of Cork and Ross.

Bishop John O Brien (d. 1768), was the author of the first Irish-English dictionary (published in Paris in 1768), as well as of works pirated by the notorious Gen. Vallancey. The celebrated philosopher, George Berkeley, was Protestant Bishop 1734–53. Dean Swift's 'Vanessa' had bequeathed her entire estate to Berkeley and Robert Marshall of Clonmel near Cobh. Berkeley decided to use the money 'for converting the savage

Americans to Christianity' by founding St Paul's College, Bermuda (1725).

Of the ancient monastery the only relics are the 100 ft Round Tower and a remnant of the Fire House. The tower was struck by lightning in 1748/9 and the conical roof wrecked; the 'restorers' reduced the height of the tower and added the battlements. On the opposite side of the street is much altered St Colman's Cathedral (Protestant), a cruciform church of *c.* 1270–80 with aisled nave of five bays and with a sacristy (chapter-house) projecting from the N. side of the choir. 17th c. repairs, 18th c. 'improvements', and 19th c. 'restoration' have altered the building in the meantime. In the N. aisle is the monument of Bishop John Brinkley (1826–35), celebrated astronomer, by the noted Tallow sculptor John Hogan. In the long roofless N. transept (Fitzgerald Aisle), is the monument of George Berkeley (by Bruce Joy, 1890); also the 1611 tomb of the Fitzgeralds, seneschals of Imokilly (*see* Rostellan *below, and p. 100*); only fragments of the Fitzgerald effigies remain. In the choir is a window (*c.* 1953?) by Patrick Pye: *Christ in Gethsemane* and *St Colmán* as bard, and as young and old man. In the NE. corner of the churchyard are the scant remains of the Fire House (*see pp. 206 and 212*), of which nothing is known; it seems to have been an early church or oratory.

3 m. WSW. is Rostellan Castle, formerly seat of the Marquess of Thomond. The first castle here was built at the Anglo-Norman invasion by Robert de Marisco. Later the Fitzgeralds, seneschals of Imokilly, had a castle there. By the seashore (below high-water mark), is a re-erected megalithic chamber.

Aghada (4 m. W.) and Whitegate (6 m. SW.) were pleasant little resorts before the building of an electricity generating station and an oil refinery respectively. Near Whitegate is the Trabolgan Holiday Centre.

COACHFORD, Co. Cork (Map 5, K5), is a village and angling resort on the beautiful Cork (15 m.)–Macroom (9 m.) road. The mountains to the NW., N., and NE., are particularly rich in ancient remains.

7 m. NNE. is Donaghmore, where St Laichtín (d. 622; *see p. 185*) founded a monastery. The early-12th c. Shrine of St Laichtín's Arm, now in the National Museum, belonged to this monastery. 1½ m. SE., in Garryadeen, is Tobar Laichtín, St Laichtín's Well.

3 m. NNW. of Donaghmore, in Gowlane North, is a recumbent-stone circle with an entrance passage.

3 m. S., in Roovesmore, is a large ringfort excavated by General Pitt-Rivers; three ogham stones, now in the British Museum, came from the souterrain.

3¾ m. WSW., on the Lee, is Carrigadrohid. On a rock beside the bridge are the ruins of a late Mac Carthy castle. In 1650 the castle was attacked by Cromwellians commanded by Roger Boyle, Lord Broghill, who hanged Boetius Mac Egan, Bishop of Ross, in sight of the walls for refusing to exhort the garrison to surrender. In the end Boyle took the castle by a ruse. The entrance from the bridge is supposed to have been constructed by order of Cromwell himself. – 1¾ m. SW. of the bridge, in Bawnatemple, is an early monastic site; a cross-decorated stone from there is preserved in Canvee National School.

4¼ m. NW. via Peak, in Coolineagh, is the ruined ancient church of Aghabulloge, founded by St Ólann, teacher of St Finn Bárr of Cork. 22 yds SE. of the church ruin is an ogham pillarstone crowned by St Ólann's Cap, a lump of quartzite. In 1831 the Caipín consisted of two superimposed stones. People swore by it and also used it to cure female complaints, headaches, etc. The phallic character of the monument caused the local priest to remove the Caipín, but it was promptly replaced by the existing one. 150 yds N. is St Ólann's Stone, a boulder with the 'imprint of the Saint's feet'. Some 440 yds NNE. of the church is St Ólann's Well, covered by a clochán. Close by to the S. is an ogham stone set up here in 1851. It had been discovered in the foundations of Mullenroe, an old mill on the site of an erased ringfort a short distance to the N. of the well. Pilgrims make their 'rounds' at the Caipín, Stone, and Well, on St Ólann's Day (5 September) and at other times. 2 m. NW. of St Ólann's Well is Sheskinny crossroads. The following mileages are reckoned from this crossroads.

2 m. N., in Knocknagoun, is a wedge-tomb. 1 m. E., in Rylane, is a stone circle; two fields E. is a large pillarstone; 1 m. E. of the circle, in Kilcullen South, is a cillín, or ancient cemetery, with two pillarstones (one of which has an ogham inscription). – ¾ m. SW., in Knockrour, is Kill, an ancient church site with two pillarstones (one with an ogham inscription) flanking the entrance. – ½ m. W. (by road), in Oughtihery, is a stone circle.

COALISLAND, Co. Tyrone (Map 1, G8), is a small town once renowned for its brick industry and its coalfield. It stands on the road between Dungannon (4 m.) and Stewartstown (4 m.), and is the terminus of the former Tyrone Canal. 2 m. NE., on the road to Newmills, there is a stone aqueduct which carried the canal over the River Torrent. The Catholic Church (1980) is by Liam McCormick, with stone sanctuary furnishings by Michael Biggs and Stations by Elizabeth Ryan.

COBH, Co. Cork (Map 4, B9), from 1849 to 1922 called Queenstown, is a port and yachting centre beautifully sited on the S. side of Great Island, 14 m. SE. of Cork. It is noted for its mild climate.

During the French and American wars of the 18th c., British Atlantic convoys assembled in Cork Harbour, which remained a British naval station until 1937; it was the principal base of American naval forces in European waters during the First World War. The ship *Sirius*, first steamer to cross the Atlantic, sailed from Passage West nearby, 4 April 1838.

Cobh is the cathedral town of the Catholic diocese of Cloyne, St Colman's Cathedral (1868–1949) dominating the harbour. This is a large Gothic-Revival church by Edward Welby Pugin and George C. Ashlin; the interior is good of its kind; the carillon (42 bells) is the largest in the British Isles.

On the Quay – a good promenade – is an incomplete *Lusitania* memorial by Jerome Conor, the cost of which was subscribed in the United States. In the former Scots' church nearby, there is a small museum of local antiquities.

¾ m. N. is the ruined church of Clonmel. The Rev. Charles Wolfe (1791–1823), author of 'The Burial of Sir John Moore', and John Tobin (1769–1804), the dramatist, are buried there; so are many of the *Lusitania* victims. – 2 m. N is the 15/16th c. tower of Belvelly Castle and early-19th c. martello towers.

1 m. S. is Spike Island, with a large 19th c. fort and former British base. From 1847 to 1885 the island was the principal penal depot in Ireland, the convicts being employed on the fortifications, dockyards, and other harbour works. Previously political prisoners (among them the celebrated John Mitchell) and other convicts had been detained in hulks anchored off the island pending transportation to Botany Bay and other penal settlements.

COLERAINE, Co. Londonderry (Map 1, G3), is a market and administrative centre on the River Bann, and on the Ballycastle (19 m.)–Limavady (14 m.) road. Its ancient origins can be traced to a monastery, dedicated to St Patrick, and the arrival of Normans in the area in the 12th c. The town proper dates from 1613 when the former O Cahan lands were granted to the London Companies (collectively now known as the Honourable Irish Society) as part of the Londonderry Plantation. The original Plantation street plan is preserved in the modern town. St Patrick's Parish Church dates from 1614 but has many later additions. The modern headquarter campus of the University of Ulster is 1 m. N.

1¼ m. SSE. is the Mount Sandel complex (Hist. Mon.), including the location of an important, excavated mesolithic campsite, and an earthen mound overlooking the river, which probably dates from the Norman period.

3 m. SSE., in Camus graveyard at Macosquin village, is a remnant of a High Cross and a bullaun stone, all that survive of a monastery associated with St Comgall of Bangor.

6½ m. S. at Crevolea is the 'Grey Stone', a chambered grave with a massive basalt capstone, estimated to weigh nearly 40 tons. 3½ m. WSW., at Dunalis, is a three-chambered souterrain. One roofstone has an ogham inscription. 6½ m. NW. is the small resort of Castlerock (two Michael Healy windows in the Protestant church). The National Trust maintain the Hezlett thatched cottage at Liffock crossroads, which dates from 1691. Nearby is the Lions Gate of Downhill Castle built about 1780 for Frederick Augustus Hervey (1730–1803), the Earl of Bristol and Bishop of Derry. The house is now in ruins but parts of the estate gardens and outbuildings survive, including the domed rotunda (built 1783–5) known as the Mussenden Temple. This building, on a cliff edge with extensive views, is also owned by the National Trust. Opposite the castle are the remains of Dunbo medieval church, abandoned in 1691. 2½ m. further W., beneath Benevenagh Mountain, is the magnificent Magilligan Strand. An 1812 martello tower (Hist. Mon.) is located at Magilligan Point; along with a similar structure on the opposite shore, it protected the entrance to Lough Foyle. The station for the N. end of the original 1828 Ordnance Survey base line is located nearby in Ballymulholland Townland.

COLLON, Co. Louth (Map 2, H7), is a village on the Slane (6 m.)–Ardee (7 m.) road. The Protestant church (1813) is an attempt at copying King's College Chapel in Cambridge.

Adjoining the village, in the demesne of Mount Oriel (built for John Foster, 1740–1829, Speaker of the Dublin House of Commons), is the Cistercian Abbey of New Mellifont (1938); the lands belonged to medieval MELLIFONT ABBEY.

8 m. W., beyond Slieve Beagh, in Lobinstown, is the early monastic site, Killary. There are remains of two High Crosses and of a church (Nat. Mons.). The West Cross figurations include *The Fall, Noah's Ark, The Baptism of Christ, The Adoration of the Magi.* 3 m. SSW., in Knock, alias Lisknock, is an early monastic site: ring enclosure with portion of a small, early, decorated cross.

COLLOONEY, Co. Sligo (Map 7, K2), is a town pleasantly sited 7 m. S. of Sligo.

Collooney Gap was of major strategic importance in former times, and a strong castle to command it was built at Collooney in the Middle Ages, of which nothing of note remains. On 5 September 1798, a mixed force of militia and dragoons under Col. Vereker attempted to hold the Gap against Humbert's tiny French force marching from CASTLEBAR, but was thrown back on Sligo with the loss of its guns. A late-19th c. rustic monument near the former Midland Great Western railway station commemorates the gallantry of Humbert's Irish aide, Capt. Bartholomew Teeling.

The Church of the Assumption (*c.* 1813) is a Gothic-Revival essay by Sir John Benson (a native of Collooney), who also (1837) enlarged and remodelled the 1720 Protestant church (Cooper memorial by Gibson, executed in Florence).

3 m. NE., SW. of the summit of Slieve Daeane (903 ft), is Cailleach Bhéarra's House, a passage-tomb.

2¼ m. SW., beside the Owenmore, is lovely Annaghmore demesne with many rare shrubs and trees. O Haras, one of the ancient noble stocks of the region, have lived there since the Middle Ages; Cormac O Hara of Annaghmore was a patron of the celebrated poet Tadhg Dall Ó Huiginn (1550–91).

COMBER, Co. Down (Map 1, L8), is a small linen town on the Belfast (9 m.)–Downpatrick (18 m.) road, to the W. of Strangford Lough.

7 m. SE., via Ringneill, is Mahee Island (causeway to mainland). W. of the golf course are remains (Hist. Mon.) of Nendrum Abbey, which was founded in the 5th c. by St Mo-Chaoi (after whom the island is called), and which disappears from history after 974. In 1178 Malachy, Bishop of Down, joined with John de Courcy in introducing English Benedictines. The remains include three concentric enclosing ramparts of dry masonry, a church (12th c.), the stump of a Round Tower, the ruins of huts and houses, the monks' cemetery, early grave-slabs, a reconstructed sundial, etc. These comprise one of the best surviving examples of the layout of a primitive Irish monastery. Nendrum Castle (Nat. Mon.) was probably built in the 15th c.; it was altered in 1570.

7 m. SE., via Ardmillan, is Sketrick Island (causeway to mainland). There are remains (Hist. Mon.) of the tower and bawn (with subterranean, corbel-vaulted well) of a Mac Quillan castle seized by Clannaboy O Neills, but restored to Mac Quillan by Henry O Neill of Tyrone, 1470.

CONG, Co. Mayo (Map 7, G8), is a village in a beautiful setting near the NE. corner of Lough Corrib, 9 m. SSW. of Ballinrobe, 23 m. NW. of Tuam, and 28 m. N. of Galway. Adjoining the village on the S. and SW. is the beautiful demesne of Ashford

Downhill Strand and Mussenden Temple, Co. Londonderry.

Castle. Now a hotel, the magnificent mock castle was built by F.J. Fuller for Sir Arthur Edward Guinness, member of the famous Dublin brewing family. Loughs Mask and Corrib are connected and fed by rivers which often flow underground. Sir William Wilde mistakenly associated many of the prehistoric monuments in the area with the first Battle of Magh Tuireadh, well known in early Irish mythology. The real Magh Tuireadh is in Co. Sligo (*see p. 224*).

Cong is known in Irish history as the site of a monastery founded by St Féichín of FORE in the 6th c., and rebuilt as an abbey of Augustinian Canons Regular by King Turloch Mór O Conor early in the 12th c. Turloch's son, Rory, last High-King of Ireland, retired to the monastery in 1183 and died there in 1198; he was buried at CLONMACNOIS.

Of the ancient monastery of Cong the only relic – apart from the superb Cross of Cong in the National Museum – is Leac na bPoll, a five-basin bullaun behind a cottage at the SE. end of the village. The Augustinian monastery is represented by the base of a medieval cross in the village street, and by beautiful fragments of an early-13th c. abbey (Nat. Mon.) to the SW. of the village. The cross-base is inscribed OR[ŌIT] DO NICHOL AGUS DO GILLIBERD O DUBTHAICH RAB I NABAIDDEACHT CUNGA ('A prayer for Nicholas and Gilbert O Duffy who were abbots of Cong'); the inscribed shaft is modern.

Cong Abbey: of the abbey church only the chancel survives; of the conventual buildings only part of the E. range and a tiny fragment of the cloister arcade. The beautiful N. door in the chancel was put together in 1860 with stones said to have been taken from a doorway further W. in the N. wall. (The top of the central light of the E. window is also a 19th c. restoration.) The outstanding features of the ruins are the three exquisite doorways of the E. range, the central one opening into the chapter-house. The delicate, Romanesque–Early Gothic details of these doorways are among the finest products of Irish medieval stone carving. They are typical of a school or lodge of masons active in the West at the opening of the 13th c. Some of the stones, however, are the work of Peter Foy, a local stone-carver employed by Sir Benjamin Lee Guinness, 1860. Foy was also responsible for most of the cloister arcade, of which the only original parts are the first arch and its coupled columns, at the N. end. To the S. of the abbey is a detached ruin of the 16th c.; beside it is the church of St Mary (1973) by Curley and Dowley; it is completely out of keeping with the adjoining abbey, and windows from the Harry Clarke studios have been reset at awkward angles.

1 m. NNW. are the ruins (Nat. Mon.) of the 15th c., MacDonnel castle of Aghalahard. The MacDonnells were galloglas in the service of MacWilliam (Burke) Íochtair.

1¼ m. NE., in Glebe and Tonaleeaun townlands, are four adjacent stone circles (Nat. Mons.) of different kinds. – 2 m. NE. of the stone circles, at the junction of the Cong–Ballinrobe and Headford–Cross–Ballinrobe roads, is The Neale. In the derelict demesne of Neale House, to the NE. of The Neale village, is a curious 18th c. stepped pyramid.

2 m. E., ½ m. S. of the road, is Moytura House, built by Sir William Wilde in 1865. To the N. of the road is the great passage-tomb-type cairn (Nat. Mon.) of Ballymacgibbon North.

4¾ m. SW. is the little island of Inchagoill, one of the beauty-spots of Lough Corrib. There are (Nat. Mons.) the ancient St Patrick's Church, a cross-pillar inscribed LIE LUGUAEDON MACCI MENUEH ('the stone of Luguaedon, son of Menb'), Templenaneeve, an early cross-slab, a cross-pillar and three bullauns. St Patrick's Church was a nave-and-chancel structure; the Luguaedon stone is near the trabeate W. door; the inscription is the oldest surviving Irish inscription in Latin characters. Templenaneeve is a Romanesque nave-and-chancel church with a notable W. doorway. This is not only much weathered, but was incorrectly reassembled in 1860. The early cross-slab has been built into the S. wall.

5½ m. WNW., on the shore of Lough Mask in Cappaghnagappul, are remains of Ballindonagh Castle. Offshore is Oileán Rúa, alias Red Island, sometime seat of a branch of the O Flahertys.

3 m. NW., by Lough Mask, are remains of the unusual little Castle of Ballykine.

CONNEMARA, Co. Galway – in older Irish Conmhaicne Mara – is, properly speaking, more or less identical with the barony of Ballynahinch. In more recent times, however, the name is often taken to include parts of the barony of Moycullen (IarChonnacht) and of the half barony of Ross ('Joyce's Country') as well, and it is in this convenient, if inaccurate, sense that it is used in this *Guide*.

The landscape is dominated by two fine mountain groups, the Twelve Bens (Beanna Beóla) and the Maumturk range, whose peaks reward the climber with superb panoramas of lake, moorland, and sea.

As might be expected of so barren a countryside, antiquities are relatively few, but include some monuments of real interest.

The population is, for the most part, concentrated round the periphery of the moors and mountains. It is particularly dense along the low shores W. from Galway to Bertraghboy Bay, where the harvest of the sea (fish and seaweed) makes a vital contribution to the economy of the crofters and farmers of an ungrateful land. This concentration has helped to save the Irish language, and so this coastal fringe includes one of the largest of the few surviving regions of Irish speech. With the ancient language goes something of the ancient way of life, and the traditional story-telling and singing of the S. Connemara coast are famous in folklore circles, just as its homespun tweeds enjoy high repute among discriminating judges. Much has been done by local effort to improve the strain of the versatile and sought-after Connemara pony.

COOKSTOWN, Co. Tyrone (Map 1, G7), is a market town 10 m. W. of Lough Neagh on the Dungannon (10 m.)–Maghera (16 m.) road.

The town was founded in 1609 by Allan Cook, and its distinctive 1¼ m. Main St was laid out by a successor, William Stewart of Killymoon (*see below*) *c.* 1750. The Gothic-style Catholic Church of 1860 is by J.J. McCarthy. The Convent of Mercy has a noteworthy modern chapel (1965) by Lawrence McConville. The bronze figure of Christ and the evangelist symbols are by Patrick McElroy, the Stations of the Cross by Benedict Tutty, and the stained glass windows *Mary* and *The Passion* are by Patrick Pye. The altar was the first executed by Michael Biggs.

SE of the town is Killymoon Castle, formerly the home of the Stewarts, later of the Moutrays, and now a golf club. The house is essentially the work of John Nash, who enlarged and remodelled a house of the Earls of Tyrone for Col. William Stewart around 1803, at a cost of £80,000. It was Nash's first great Irish house and, to all intents and purposes, his showpiece.

2 m. NNE. is Lissan Rectory, another Nash house, built in 1807 for the Rev. John Staples. Not far distant is Lissan House, by Davis Ducart, the seat of the Staples family.

6 m. E is Coagh village on the Ballinderry River. Its square dates from 1728, when it was named in honour of the House of Hanover. Noteworthy is the Presbyterian church with its box pews and half-hipped roof. Just across the river, in Co. Londonderry, is Cloghtogle portal-dolmen.

13 m. E. (via Coagh), at Arboe point on the W. shore of Lough Neagh, are the ruins of Arboe Abbey and High Cross (Hist. Mons.). The Abbey is a small ruin N. of the graveyard. It and the High Cross, probably 9th c., together mark the site of a monastery founded in the 6th c. by St Colmán. The scenes on the E. face of the cross include: *Adam and Eve, Sacrifice of Isaac, Daniel in the Lions' Den, Three Children in the Fiery Furnace,* and *The Last Judgement*. On the W. face are: *Adoration of the Magi, Marriage Feast of Cana, Multiplication of the Loaves and Fishes, Christ's Entry into Jerusalem* and *The Crucifixion*. On the N. side are: *Baptism of Christ, (?) Christ before the Doctors, Slaughter of*

the Innocents and *Annunciation to the Shepherds*; the scenes on the S. side are: *Cain and Abel, David and the Lion, David Slays Goliath* and *SS Paul and Anthony Breaking Bread in the Desert.*

3 m. S., at Aghacolumb, is Arboe Protestant parish church, erected in 1713 by Stewart Blacker and W. Latham. Parts of this church, including the E. window, are said to have come from Arboe.

2½ m. SSE. is Tullaghoge (Hist. Mon.), where each new O Neill chieftain was inaugurated by the O Hagans, who occupied the ringfort. The stone inauguration chair was broken up by Lord Deputy Mountjoy as he advanced against the O Neills in 1602.

2½ m. SW are the ruins of Derryloran Old Church (Hist. Mon.), built *c.* 1622, but incorporating stones from a much earlier building.

A good B class road to the WNW. up the Ballinderry valley leads to the heart of the S. Sperrin moors, with their remarkable wealth of prehistoric remains. In Tulnacross, close to Dunnamore bridge (7 m. from Cookstown) is a pair of pillarstones. – ¼ m. W. of Dunnamore Catholic church, is Dunnamore wedge-tomb (500 ft). Just beyond Black Rock, in Beaghmore, the road cuts through a remarkable series of prehistoric monuments which have recently been exposed by turfcutting. They include the Bronze Age stone circles at Beaghmore, alignments, avenues, pillarstones, cairns etc. (Hist. Mons.). The circles sometimes occur in pairs with tangential alignments and associated cairns.

2 m. W. is Drum Manor Forest Park, the former demesne of the Earls of Castlestewart. Of the house only the façade and bell tower remain. The demesne has two lakes, a heronry and a butterfly garden. About ½ m. further W. is Wellbrook Beetling Mill (Nat. Trust – open May–September), where the firm of John Gunning and Son bleached and beetled linen from 1851. The building dates from 1765, and was still in operation in 1965 when it was handed over to the National Trust with its machinery intact.

6 m. NW. is Ballynagilly, where excavations in 1966–9 uncovered the foundations of a Stone Age house with upright planks forming the walls, as well as extensive Beaker remains. 2 m. NNE is attractive Lough Fea.

COOLANEY, Co. Sligo (Map 7, J2), is a village on the Owenboy, 5½ m. W. of Collooney and 10 m. NE. of Tobercurry.

3 m. SSW., to the SE. of Killoran Lough, are the remains of Killoran Church.

2½ m. W., to the S. of the road in Gortakeeran, is the Giants Grave, a fine wedge-tomb. In Cabragh, which adjoins Gortakeeran on the W., are two further wedge-tombs.

COOTEHILL, Co. Cavan (Map 2, E5), is a market town on the S. road from Cavan (16 m.) to Monaghan (14 m.). It takes its name from the Cootes, English Planters, whose notoriously brutal ancestor, Sir Charles Coote, acquired confiscated O Reilly lands there in the 17th c. Just N. of the town is Bellamont Forest, a Palladian villa in brick attributed to Sir Edward Lovett Pearce (d. 1733) and built most probably in 1728 for Thomas E. Coote, who was a lawyer. From Bellamont the Cootes took the title Earls of Bellamont. After a lapse of 80 years, possession of the house is now once more in the hands of the Coote family.

Cootehill was the birthplace of the distinguished Austrian Field-Marshal, Thomas Brady (1752–1827).

3 m. NE., in Dartry demesne (in Co. Monaghan), is a derelict 1770 monument by Joseph Wilton (1722–1803) to Lady Anne Dawson (1733–69).

3 m. SE., just N. of the Shercock road, near Drumgoon, is Cohaw Giants Grave, a dual-court tomb with five chambers.

3½ m. SW. is Tullyvin, a Plantation village, which still retains its 17th c. layout and circular green.

CORCOMROE ABBEY, Co. Clare (Map 6, G3), is a ruined Cistercian abbey (Nat. Mon.) on the S. side of Abbey Hill, 5 m. W. of Kinvara and 6 m. E. of Ballyvaghan. The abbey (de Petra Fertili) was founded in 1180 by Donal Mór O Brien, King of Limerick, and was colonized from Inishlounaght (*see p. 112*) *c.* 1195. A shortlived daughter house was established at Kilshane, Ballingarry, in 1198.

The remains include a church (*c.* 1210–25) with interesting Transitional features, fragments of the claustral buildings, infirmary-guesthouse (to the S.), and gatehouse (to the W.). The church was a cruciform building with aisled nave (N. aisle never built?) and a single E. chapel in each transept. In the 15th c. parts of the nave arcade were blocked up, a stone screen supporting a skimpy, friary-type tower was inserted between choir and nave (lay-brothers' choir), and an altar tomb and sedilia were inserted in the N. wall of the presbytery (chancel). The tomb, traditionally that of King Conor na Siudaine O Brien (d. 1267/8), but probably of *c.* 1300, has a crude royal effigy. In the wall above it is a slab with 13th c. abbatial figure. Traces of polychrome painting can be discerned here and there on the plasterwork of the church.

2½ m. SE. of the abbey, is Oughtmama, site of an early monastery associated with St Colmán (mac Duach?). The largest of three churches (Nat. Mons.) has a pre-Romanesque nave and a plain Romanesque chancel. In it are a carved stoup and defaced early gravestones.

3½ m. N. is New Quay. ¾ m. W. is Mount Vernon Lodge, seaside resort of the Gregorys of Coole (*see p. 196*), where Lady Gregory was visited by her literary friends, including W.B. Yeats and George Bernard Shaw. Yeats set his verse play *The Dreaming of the Bones* in the hills about Corcomroe Abbey. Shaw, impressed by the naked limestone of Burren – his 'region of stone-capped hills and granite fields' – set Part IV, Act 1, of *Back to Methuselah* at 'Burrin Pier', i.e. New Quay.

CORK, Co. Cork (Map 5, L5), third largest city in Ireland, is charmingly situated at the mouth of the beautiful Lee valley. It is an important seaport and a commercial and manufacturing centre of note. It is also the cathedral city of the Catholic diocese of Cork and of the united Protestant diocese of Cork, Cloyne, and Ross.

The history of Cork commences in the 6th/7th c. with the foundation of a monastery by St Finnbárr (d. 630; *see pp. 112–3*), on the hill slope SW. of the present city. St Fin Barre's Cathedral may be on the site, as the stump of a Round Tower survived until the foundations were laid and there are Romanesque fragments preserved in the chapter-house. The monastery came in time to be the head of an important confederation of South

Munster monastic churches. The Augustinian monastery at Gill Abbey (built *c.* 1134) was the setting for the 12th c. satire, *Aisling Meic Conglinne, The Vision of Mac Conglinne.* Like so many Irish monasteries of the time, it suffered from the raids of the Vikings (820, 838, 845, 863), and again from the Norse pirate-traders who erected a shortlived fortress on one of the islands in the marsh (*corcach*) by the river in 846. In 917 these dangerous intruders returned and founded a settlement. This Norse (Ostman) settlement, like others, was gradually absorbed into the Gaelic polity, though continuing to be ruled by its own mórmáer or jarl. Cork became the capital of the Mac Carthy *Regnum Corcagiense,* or Kingdom of South Munster in the 12th c. At the Anglo-Norman invasion King Dermot Mac Carthy submitted to Henry II of England (1172), but failed thereby to save his kingdom, for it was attacked the following year by Raymond le Gros (*see p. 237*), and in 1177 was granted by Henry to Robert Fitzstephen and Milo de Cogan. The grant reserved to the English Crown the city of Cork and the surrounding 'cantred of the Ostmen'. Cork city, though garrisoned with Anglo-Normans as early as November 1177, was left in King Dermot Mac Carthy's hands until his death in 1185, when the town was declared a dependency of the English Crown. The principal dates in the later history of the city are:

1188	Charter from Prince John of England in his capacity of 'Lord of Ireland'.
1195	Besieged and recaptured by the Mac Carthys.
1199	Grant of the liberties of Bristol.
1214	Franciscan friary (North Mall).
1229	Dominican friary (St Marie's of the Isle).
1241	Charter from Henry III.
1284	New city walls.
*c.*1300	Augustinian friary.
1378	City burned by the Irish.
1495	Arrival of Perkin Warbeck, Yorkist pretender to English throne.
1642	English Lord President of Munster is besieged in the city by insurgent Irish.
1644	Murrough 'the Burner' O Brien captures the city for the Parliamentarians, and expels the Irish inhabitants.
1649	Captured by Cromwell; Irish once more expelled.
1690	Besieged and captured for William of Orange by John Churchill, later Duke of Marlborough.
1691	Patrick Sarsfield and the Jacobite army sail away to France.
1845	Queen's College, now University College.
1920	Assassination of Lord Mayor, Thomas Mac Curtain, by British forces. Death of Mac Curtain's successor, Terence Mac Swiney, after 74 days of hunger strike in Brixton prison. Patrick St, City Hall, Public Library, and other buildings, are burned down by British forces.
1922	British garrison evacuates the city. Anti-treaty Republican forces occupy it, but withdraw when Free State troops land at Passage West.
1938	British naval defences in Cork Harbour handed over to the Irish government.

In the 18th and early-19th c. Cork silverware and glass enjoyed a high reputation. About the middle of the 19th c. crochet-work and lacemaking began to flourish in the city as cottage crafts. Representative examples of all four crafts may be seen in the Public Museum, Fitzgerald Park.

The roll of Cork artists and writers is short, but the city can claim more painters of quality than any other in Ireland.

Painters

James Barry (1741–1806), a pupil of West's.

Robert Fagan (1745–1816).

Nathaniel Grogan (d. 1807), a pupil of the Cork painter John Butts.

Samuel Forde (1805–28), a painter who did much work for the architect George Richard Pain.

Daniel Maclise (1806–70), historical painter.

William McGrath (1838–1918), Member of the New York Academy.

Sculptors

Thomas Kirk (1777–1845), son of a Scotsman and father of Joseph Robinson Kirk (1821–94), also a sculptor.

John Hogan (1800–1858), the noted Classical sculptor, who was brought up in Cork.

Seamus Murphy (1907–75); though born in Mallow, he worked largely in Cork.

Architects

Sir Thomas Deane I (1792–1871) and his brother, Kearns Deane.

Sir Thomas Deane II (1828–99).

Benjamin Woodward (1815–61), who seems to have been responsible for much of the best work attributed to his partner, Sir Thomas Deane I.

Writers

Richard Millikin (1767–1815), poet.

William Maginn (1793–1842), author of *Homeric Ballads,* etc.

Thomas Crofton Croker (1798–1854), antiquary and folklorist.

Francis Mahony, 'Father Prout' (1804–66), humorous poet.

Daniel Corkery (1878–1964), author of *The Threshold of Quiet,* etc.

Seán O Faoláin (b. 1900), novelist and biographer.

Michael O Donovan ('Frank O'Connor'; 1903–66), poet, playwright, novelist (*The Saint and Mary Kate,* etc.), and master-craftsman of the short story.

Scarcely a fragment is left of medieval Cork – nothing at all of the 16th and 17th c. town. While the 18th c. town had its quota of charming private houses, some of which survive in decay, there were very few buildings of any architectural pretensions prior to the advent of the brothers James and George Richard Pain, about the year 1818, though there is a fine Queen Anne-style house of *c.* 1740 at 11 Emmet Place (restored 1985). They had been pupils of John Nash and had been sent over to Ireland to superintend the erection of some of Nash's country houses (*see p. 196*). James (1779–1877) soon removed to Limerick, but George Richard remained in Cork. Later, the Gothic Revival contributed one or two noteworthy buildings. In the following list of the more notable buildings, etc., the three major, natural, divisions of the city are covered in the order: North City: the city N. of the North Channel of the River Lee; Central City: the older, central part of the city between the main branches of the river; South City: the city S. of the South Channel of the Lee.

St Fin Barr's Cathedral, Cork.

NORTH CITY

Our tour commences at Griffith Bridge (head of North Main St).

½ m. W., at Sunday's Well, is St Vincent's Church, a large Gothic-Revival work (1851–6) by Sir John Benson; the presbytery was added by Goldie. St Vincent's Orphanage, Wellington Rd, is also by Goldie; the chapel is by Samuel Hynes.

400 yds E., on Pope's Quay, is St Mary's Church (Dominican), a Classical building (1832–9), by Kearns Deane. On the Lady Altar is displayed the worn ivory figurine of *Our Lady of Graces*. Flemish work of the 14th c.

¼ m. N. of St Mary's, Pope's Quay, is St Anne's Church, Shandon, a Protestant parish church erected 1722–6. It is famous for its chiming bells. Also in Shandon are the Butter Exchange and Fírkin Crane building, refurbished (1987–8) as a craft centre and home of the Irish National Ballet.

150 yds N. of St Anne's, in Roman St, is St Mary and St Anne's Cathedral, popularly known as the North Chapel. The building was commenced in 1808, but after a fire in 1820, the interior was remodelled in 1828 by George Richard Pain (further remodelling 1965). The tower, etc., date from 1862–7. The 27 figures of apostles and saints, and the bas-relief *Last Supper*, are by John Hogan. The Bishop Murphy mural monument (1857) is one of Hogan's last works. The bust (1818) of Bishop Moylan is by Belfast-born Turnerelli.

½ m. N. of St Mary's is the Church of the Assumption, Blackpool. It was designed by the well-known Cork sculptor Séamus Murphy, who also carved the statues.

¾m. E. of St Mary's, in Old Youghal Road, is Collins Barracks. The chapel has a three-light window (*St Michael, Christ in Glory, St Patrick*) by Evie Hone (1939).

¾ m. S. of the barracks and close to the junction of Lower Glanmire Rd and Mac Curtain St, is St Patrick's Church (1836), a Classical edifice by George Richard Pain. In the baptistery is a small stained glass panel (*The Baptism of Christ*) by Hubert McGoldrick.

CENTRAL CITY

Patrick St, principal shopping street of the city, curves from Grand Parade in the W. to St Patrick's Bridge in the N. At the N. end of the street is a dull statue of Father Theobald Mathew (1790–1861), apostle of Temperance, by John Henry Foley.

500 yds E. of St Patrick's Bridge, at the junction of the North and South Channels, is the Custom House – now the Harbour Board office – a good Classical essay (1814–18) by William Hargrave.

300 yds W. of St Patrick's Bridge, in Cornmarket St, is the Old Market. The lower portion of the façade is 'Cork's only example of the Grand Style of the early 18th century'. Nearby,

at the junction of Lavitt's Quay and Emmet Pl., is the Opera House (1963–5), by Michael Scott and Associates.

In Emmet Pl. is the Crawford Municipal School of Art and Art Gallery. The collections include: casts from antique sculptures in Rome, prepared under the supervision of Canova and presented by Pius VII to the Prince Regent, who gave them to Cork in 1818; through these John Hogan made his first acquaintance with Classical sculpture; 13 casts from Hogan's works; and paintings by recent and contemporary Irish artists, including a collection presented by Sir John Lavery.

300 yds SW. of the Art School, off Paul St, is St Paul's Protestant Church, a Classical edifice of 1723 with a good interior; it is now a factory. Nearby, in a narrow lane linking Paul St and Patrick St, is SS Peter and Paul's Church, an excellent Gothic Revival building by Edward Welby Pugin. The tower and spire were never completed. The high altar was designed by Pugin's pupil, George C. Ashlin of Dublin.

500 yds NW. of SS Peter and Paul's, on the W. side of North Main St, is St Peter's Protestant Church (1783–8). Some memorials from its predecessors survive, including a Deane memorial of 1710 in the N. porch.

300 yds W., at the W. end of Peter's St, is the Mercy Hospital, which incorporates the Mayoralty House built in 1767–73 to the design of Davis Ducart. It has some good stucco ceilings by Patrick Osborn. The County Hall, on Carrigrohane Rd, with 17 storeys the tallest building in the country, is by P.L. MacSweeny. Looking up at it is the wonderful statue of *The Workers* by Oisín Kelly (1970).

¼ m. SE. of the Hospital, in Washington St, is the Court House erected in 1835 to the design of the brothers Pain.

SE. of the Court House, on the E. side of South Main St, is the Protestant Church of the Holy Trinity, alias Christ Church, and now the Cork Archives Institute. It occupies the site of a medieval parish church, burial place of the leading families of the town, and probably scene of Edmund Spenser's marriage to Elizabeth Boyle (*see p. 308*). The church was erected, about 1720, to the design of Coltsman. In 1825 the interior was remodelled and the W. front erected by George Richard Pain. The relics of old Christ Church include the interesting cadaver tombstone of Mayor Thomas Ronan (d. 1554) and his wife, Johanna Tyrry (d. 1569).

In Grand Parade is Bishop Lucey Park, where part of the old city walls are enhanced by *The Onion Seller* by Seamus Murphy and a fountain by John Behan.

300 yds SE. of Christ Church, at the S. end of Grand Parade, is South Mall, financial centre of the city. The Cork and County Club is by George Richard Pain. The Cork Savings Bank (1841–2), at the corner of Parnell Place, is by the brothers Kearns and (Sir) Thomas Deane.

To the S. of South Mall, on Father Mathew Quay (Charlotte Quay), is the Capuchin Church of the Holy Trinity (1825), an interesting Gothick essay (1825) by George Richard Pain for Father Theobald Mathew.

SOUTH CITY

¼ m. SW. of Holy Trinity Church, off Abbey St, is St Nicholas's Protestant Church (1850). The Tracton monument is by John Bacon, R.A. sculptor of the Pitt memorial in Westminster Abbey and of the Dr Johnson and Howard memorials in St Paul's Cathedral, London. A short way E. is the tower of Red Abbey, sole relic of the monasteries of medieval Cork. Red Abbey was an Augustinian priory founded *c.* 1300.

Nearby, in Dunbar St, is St Finbar's, South, alias the South Chapel, a Georgian church of 1766 (transepts later), 'restored' in the 1960s. The altar-piece is a later, less successful, version of John Hogan's *Dead Christ* (*see p. 152*). The *Crucifixion* is by the Fermoy painter John O Keeffe (*c.* 1797–1838).

1¼ m. SE. of St Nicholas's Church, at Turner's Cross, is the Church of Christ the King, an essay in a modern idiom by Barry Byrne of Chicago; the great doorway figure, *Christ the King,* was designed by the American sculptor John Storrs; the *opus sectile Crucifixion* (1936) is by Hubert McGoldrick (1897–1967).

Some 300 yds W. of St Nicholas's Church, in Fort St (off Barrack St), is Elizabeth Fort. The first fort there was built in the reign of Elizabeth I. The curtain wall of the 17th c. fort survives.

A short distance W. of the fort is St Fin Barre's Protestant Cathedral (1867–79) in the French Gothic style, by William Burges of London.

½ m. SW. of the cathedral, in Lough Rd, is the Church of the Immaculate Conception (alias St Finbar's, West), a Romanesque piece (1881) by George C. Ashlin.

½ m. W. of St Fin Barre's Cathedral, in Fernhurst Ave., is the Honan chapel (1915), by James F. Mc Mullen. The interior and its appointments repay examination. The Tabernacle has good enamels by Oswald P. Reeves. The antependium and other embroideries are by the Dun Emer Guild, Dublin. There are good *opus sectile* Stations of the Cross. Eleven of the windows are by Harry Clarke, and others are by Sarah Purser, Catherine O Brien, Ethel Rhind and A.E. Child. The window subjects are as follows: Chancel: E. window, *Our Lord* (Purser), N. window, *St John* (Purser), S. windows, *Our Lady* (Clarke), *St Joseph* (Clarke); Nave: S. wall (commencing at E. end), *St Ita* (Clarke), *St Colman* (Purser), *St Brendan* (Clarke), *St Gobnet* (Clarke), *St Flannan* (O Brien), *St Cárthach* (Rhind); W. wall, *SS Brigid, Patrick,* and *Colmcille* (Clarke; the *St Patrick* is one of the artist's best windows in Ireland); N. Wall (commencing at the W. end), *St Munchin* (O Brien), *St Fachtna* (Child), *St Ailbhe* (Purser), *St Déaglán* (Clarke), *St Albert* (Clarke), *St Finbar* (Clarke). The pavement illustrates the Canticle of the Three Children in the Fiery Furnace. The statue of St Finnbárr in the gable of the W. doorway is by Oliver Sheppard. The altar, sedilia, ambo and wedding seats are by Imogen Stuart (1985).

Adjoining the Honan chapel is University College (main entrance in Western Road), the most successful example of 19th c. university architecture in the country. The college was founded in 1845 as one of the hotly disputed Queen's Colleges. It is now a constituent college of the National University of Ireland. The original buildings, unfortunately never completed, are by the firm of Sir Thomas Deane I. The quality of the design suggests the hand of Deane's gifted partner, Benjamin Woodward (*see p. 146*). The W. wing was rebuilt after destruction by fire in 1862. The Science Laboratories are additions by Arthur Hill. Recent expansion has spread the college over the site of the former County Gaol, but the excellent Classical gaol gate (1818), by James and George Richard Pain, has been happily preserved. The college has a fine library (the Boole library, 1983) and an important collection of ogham stones.

A short distance N. of the college is Fitzgerald Park. The

Public Museum has collections illustrating the story of Cork and Munster from prehistoric times. In the grounds are modern Irish sculptures by Seamus Murphy, John Burke, Oisín Kelly, Marshal Hudson, Edward Delaney and Joseph Higgins.

Places and monuments within easy reach of the city

2¼ m. N. is Glennamought Bridge. ¾ m. N. of the bridge are the remains of Kilcully Church. 2¼ m. NW. of the church, in Ballinvarrig, are standing stones (The Long Stone). 1½ m. further N. is Whitechurch, celebrated for its early-18th c. Court of Poetry – successor of the ancient bardic school of BLARNEY. The Court was initiated by Liam an Dúna Mac Cairteáin (1688–1717), and continued by Liam Rúa Mac Coitir (1680–1738) and Seán na Raithíneach O Murchadha (1700–62).

7 m. N. is the village of Carrignavar. There are remains of the castle of the Mac Carthys of Muskerry near their later residence (now the Sacred Heart Missionary College). In the village is a 1962 memorial to the Bardic School of Blarney, of which the Mac Carthys were patrons.

4½ m. NE. is Riverstown House. In the wing built in 1745 by Jemmet Brown, Protestant Bishop of Cloyne, is the dining-room with a splendid figured ceiling and eight bas-relief wall-panels of Classical subjects, all the work of Paul and Philip Franchini; reconditioned by the Irish Georgian Society, 1965, and now open to the public at certain times of the year.

3½ m. E., on the S. side of the Lee estuary, is Blackrock Castle, built in 1830 to the design of James and George Richard Pain. Dundanion Castle, Blackrock Rd, sometime home of Sir Thomas Deane, architect, preserves the name of the castle from which William Penn set out for America in 1669.

5½ m. SE., in Rochestown Capuchin church, are four Michael Healy windows (1906): *St Kevin, St Columcille, St Enda, St Finnbar.*

3 m. W., on the Macroom road, is Carrigrohane bridge. 1 m. WNW. are the remains of Carrigrohane church. Nearby, incorporated in a modern residence, are the remains of Carrigrohane Castle. Great Hugh O Neill lodged at the castle in the course of his 1599 Munster campaign.

CORROFIN, Co. Clare (Map 6, G5), is a small market village on the Kilfenora (8 m.)–Ennis (8 m.) road, SE. of the picturesque Lake Inchiquin, on the edge of which are the ruins of two O Brien castles.

Timoleague Abbey, Co. Cork (see page 122).

Sir Frederick Burton (1816–1900), painter and Director of the National Gallery, London, was born at Corrofin House. In the former Protestant church (*c.* 1820) is the Clare Heritage Centre, a thriving local museum and genealogical research station for the whole county.

2¼ m. NNW. is Killinaboy. Remains of a church, with 11th (?) and 12th c. and later work, and a Round Tower, mark an early monastic site named after St Inghean Bhaoth (*see also p. 213*); in the W. gable is a reset double-armed cross and over the S. door is a perfect sheila-na-gig. W. of the church, beside the Fergus, is De Clare's House, a bawn with ivied turret. – 1 m. NW. of the church is Rooghaun road junction. ¾ m. (via steep hill) NNE. of the junction and 300 yds W. of the road, in Parknabinnia, is a wedge-tomb, one of a number in the area.

COURTMACSHERRY, Co. Cork (Map 5, K7), is an attractive fishing village and little seaside resort on the Argideen estuary near the NW. corner of Courtmacsherry Bay. It is 11 m. S. of Bandon, 9 m. E. of Clonakilty and 19 m. SW. of Kinsale.

1¼ m. W., by the seashore in Abbeymahon are remains of a castle. Nearby are featureless fragments of the Cistercian abbey De Fonte Vivo, alias Maune.

3 m. WNW., at the mouth of the Argideen, is the village of Timoleague. It takes its name, Tigh Mo-Laga, from an early monastic foundation of St Mo-Laga's (*see p. 247*). Attractively sited by the sea are the ruins (Nat. Mon.) of a large Franciscan friary founded in 1312 by Donal Glas Mac Carthy. Dispersed by the Reformation, the friars returned in 1604 and repaired the friary, making many alterations to the buildings. In 1642 the friary was burned, 'with all the towne', by an English force led by Lord Forbes. The remains comprise church and claustral buildings. As befits a house of the Strict Observance, the architectural details are severely plain. The lofty, arcaded recesses of the choir are unusual. The bell-tower is an addition by Edmund de Courcy, Franciscan Bishop of Ross (d. 1518). Only a fragment of the cloister remains, but the claustral buildings are relatively well preserved. The parish church (a Romanesque essay by the Limerick brothers, M. and S. Hennessy) has one of Harry Clarke's last windows (three-light, 1929–30): *Holy Family* and *Flight into Egypt; Coronation of the Virgin, Assumption,* and *Christ Meets His Mother; Miracle of Cana* and *Death of St Joseph.* Near the N. end of the town are the compact Castle Gardens (with some rare and exotic shrubs and trees – open to the public), built around a mansion on the site of a demolished 13th c. castle. The nearby Protestant church has the interior covered in mosaics (*c.* 1870–1926). – 5½ m. E., in Kilbrittain, was one of the principal castles of Mac Carthy Riabhach, built in 1596.

CRAIGAVON, Co. Armagh (Map 2, I2). In 1965 an area of approx. 100 sq m., including the Boroughs of Portadown and Lurgan and the Rural Districts of Lurgan and Moira, was designated as the site for a new city.

CRAUGHWELL, Co. Galway (Map 6, H2), is a small village on the Galway (16 m.)–Loughrea (7 m.) road. Nearby are the Galway Blazers' kennels.

1¾ m. E. is St Cleran's, home of the late John Huston, film director. The good early-19th c. house (re-edified by Michael Scott) was the birthplace of Australian explorer Robert O Hara Burke (1820–61). There are remains of a castle and of a manorial church (on an early site?).

3¾ m. SE., in Toorclogher, is a wedge-tomb.

5 m. SW., in the neglected graveyard of Killora, is the neglected grave of Antoine Ó Reachtabhra, 'Blind Raftery' (1784–1834), whose songs are still popular.

CREESLOUGH, Co. Donegal (Map 8, F2), is a village on the Letterkenny (16 m.)–Dunfanaghy (6 m.) road, near the head of Sheephaven. In a commanding position at the NW. end of the town is Liam McCormick's striking Church of St Michael (1971), with stained glass by Helen Moloney, who also did the altar tapestry with Veronica Rowe; metalwork by John Behan. The lettering with workmens' names is by Ruth Brandt.

½ m. E. are a picturesque bridge and waterfall on the Duntally River.

2 m. NE., enclosed by the sea and a rock-cut fosse, are the bawn and keep (Nat. Mon.) of Castle Doe, Caisleán na dTúath. Modernized *c.* 1800 and occupied until *c.* 1900, this was originally the stronghold of Mac Sweeney na Doe, Mac Sweeny of the Túatha. The celebrated Red Hugh O Donnell was fostered there. Sir Cahir O Doherty set up his headquarters at the castle in 1608 before attacking the English fortress at Derry. It was at the castle that Eoghan Rúa O Neill landed from Flanders in 1642 to take his place in the great Ulster effort to undo the Plantation. In 1650 the castle fell to the Cromwellian commander, Coote. At the Williamite rebellion it was seized for James II by the Mac Sweenys. A late-medieval Mac Sweeny tombstone, attached to the wall inside the entrance, resembles the Mac Sweeny tombstone at KILLYBEGS.

4 m. NNE. are the very beautiful peninsula and demesne of Ards, much of it now forming the beautifully wooded Ards Forest Park (admission fee for vehicles).

Creeslough is a convenient place for climbing Muckish, 4 m. SW., and for visiting the fine scenery in the vicinity.

CROOKHAVEN, Co. Cork (Map 5, E9), is a delightful inlet 8¾ m. SW. of Skull. Its safe anchorage is a favourite resort of yachtsmen. The haven has given its name to a fishing village and quiet little resort, part of which lies on the N., part on the S. shore. There is a beautiful sandy beach at Barley Cove, 1¾ m. W.

CROOKSTOWN, Co. Cork (Map 5, J5), is a village on the S. road from Cork (18 m.) to Macroom (9 m.). There are several Mac Swiney and other castles in the area; also numerous megalithic monuments.

1¼ m. NE., on Carraig an Dúna, are the ruins of Dundrinane Castle. At the Norman invasion the de Cogans built a castle there. The place was later recovered by the Mac Carthys of Muskerry. In the late-16th and early-17th c. the castle was held for Mac Carthy by Mac Swiney galloglas.

4 m. SE., in Garranes, is Lisnacaheragh (Nat. Mon.), a large, trivallate ringfort. It has been claimed that this fort is the birthplace of St Finnbárr of Cork. Excavation showed that metal-

Castle Doe, Co. Donegal.

workers and allied craftsmen had been very active in the fort during the period round about A.D. 500. (St Finbar's father was a craftsman in metal). The interior had contained a number of timber-post houses.

CROOM, Co. Limerick (Map 6, H8), is a small market town where the Limerick (12 m.)–Charleville (12 m.) road crosses the Maigue. About 1197/1200 Hamo de Valognes granted a manor there to Gerald fitz Maurice. It was this manor, which remained with his descendants, the Kildare Fitzgeralds, until Silken Thomas's rebellion in 1534, that suggested the celebrated Fitzgerald motto and war-cry, 'Crom Abu'. All that survives of the castle is a fragment of a 15th/16th c. tower. The town itself was walled in 1310.

The poet Seán Ó Tuama an ghrinn (1706–75), in his palmy days, kept a hostelry at Mungret Gate, near the Fair Green. On the death of Seán Clárach Mac Domhnaill, 1754, he summoned the local poets to a Court of Poetry which continued to meet at intervals. Aindrias Mac Craith and Father Liam Inglis were among the active members of the Court. Ó Tuama is buried in Croom churchyard, Mac Craith at Kilmallock.

2½ m. E., to the S. of Monaster, are remains of Monasternenagh, the Cistercian Abbey of Magium, founded in 1148 by Turloch O Brien, King of Thomond, in thanksgiving for his victory over the Norse at Rathmore (*below*), and colonized from Mellifont. The abbey was the parent of the abbeys of Inishlounaght (*see p. 112*), ABBEYDORNEY, Holy Cross (*see p. 293*), and Monasterore (*see p. 246*). In 1209 the abbey of Abbeyfeale was annexed to it as a cell. In 1227 it was itself affiliated to Margam in Glamorganshire. The fragmentary remains (Nat. Mon.), which date largely from the later 12th c., have some interesting Late Romanesque and Transitional features. The cruciform church (*c.* 1185–1205) had an aisled nave, a barrel-vaulted chancel, and three E. chapels in each transept. Only the E. half of the nave was arcaded. The church was altered in the 15th c. Only fragments survive of the claustral buildings. Nearby, on the Camoge, are remains of the abbey mill and bridge. Two battles took place at An Aonach, the fair which gave its name to the abbey, the first on 19 July 1370, when King Brian of Thomond routed his deposed uncle, Turloch, and Gearoid *file*, 3rd Earl of Desmond. In the second battle, on 3 April 1580, Sir Nicholas Malby, Elizabethan Governor of Connacht, routed Sir John of Desmond and Papal Legate Saunders. On both occasions, the defeated sought refuge in the abbey, but were slaughtered when its sanctuary was violated.

4 m. E. is Rathmore, scene of Turloch O Brien's victory over the Norse, 1148. There are remains of a late-15th c. Desmond castle here. It was held by Irish and Spanish troops in 1579–80, but fell to Malby after the battle of Monasternenagh.

2 m. NW., in Carrigeen, an imperfect Round Tower (65½ ft, Romanesque doorway) and a ruined church (Nat. Mons.),

formerly enclosed by a square cashel, mark the site of Dísert Oéngusso, Aonghus's Hermitage, called after Oéngus céle Dé (*see p. 249, 285 and 287*).

CROSSHAVEN, Co. Cork (Map 5, M6), a popular small resort on a little sheltered cove at the mouth of the beautiful Owenboy estuary, 13 m. SE. of Cork, is a noted yachting centre (Royal Cork Yacht Club).

1¼ m. NE., on Rams Head, at the mouth of Cork Harbour, is Camden Fort, one of the 19th c. fortifications of Cork Harbour.

CROSSMAGLEN, Co. Armagh (Map 2, H5), is a village 13 m. NW. of Dundalk.

2 m. N., in Annaghmare, is the Black Castle (Nat. Mon.). Excavated in 1963–4, it is a wedge-shaped cairn with a court-tomb at the broad end and two lateral chambers situated near the narrow end.

4 m. NE., in Dorsey and Tullynavall, is The Dorsey (Nat. Mon.), a 300 acre enclosure bounded by an earthen rampart set between two ditches, and where it crossed boggy ground the rampart was carried on piles. The Dorsey was traditionally constructed to guard the highway to the North, and the wood used for its construction dates to around 100 B.C.

CROSSMOLINA, Co. Mayo (Map 7, G3), is a small market town where the Ballina (8 m.)–Belmullet (39 m.) road crosses the River Deal.

¾ m. N. are remains of Abbeytown 'Abbey', thought to have been founded in the 10th c.

3 m. SE., on Castle Island, Lough Conn, are remains of an O Conor castle.

6¼ m. SE., near the N. tip of a peninsula in Lough Conn, is little Errew Abbey (Nat. Mon.): remains of a house of Augustinian Canons, successor of an early monastery founded by St Tighearnán. Nearby Templenagalliaghdoo (Nat. Mon.) is a fragment of a nunnery.

3¾ m. W., close to a farmhouse 100 yds S. of the Bangor Erris road, in Carrowkilleen, is a remarkable long cairn containing a dual-court cairn and a single-court example.

CRUMLIN, Co. Antrim (Map 1, J8), is a village on the road from Lisburn (12 m.) to Antrim (9 m.).

¾ m. ENE. are the ruins of Crumlin Church, with eight remarkable sedilia at the E. end.

CRUSHEEN, Co. Clare (Map 6, H4), is a village on the Gort (11 m.)–Ennis (9 m.) road.

½ m. SW., in Caheraphuca, is Giant's Grave (Nat. Mon.), a wedge-tomb.

¾ m. S is Inchicronan, a lake peninsula. At the neck of the peninsula are remains of a 15th c. O Brien castle. ¾m. SSW. of the castle are the ruins (Nat. Mon.) of an Augustinian priory founded *c.* 1400 on a site whose history goes back to St Crónán of Tuamgraney (*see p. 278*). There are remains of a Transitional, nave-and-chancel church of *c.* 1200, with later additions. In 1615 the church was adapted for Protestant parochial use by Donogh O Brien, Earl of Thomond.

CULDAFF, Co. Donegal (Map 1, E2), is a village on the main road from Moville (9 m.) to Carndonagh (6 m.). In the Culdaff River is St Bodan's Boat, a stone on which the saint crossed over from Scotland, as witness the marks of his fingers.

1¾ m. NNE., beyond Bunnagee pier, is Doonowen, a double promontory cut off from the mainland by a wall of dry masonry.

2 m. S., in Clonca, are the ruins of a church mainly of the Plantation period; but the lintel of the W. doorway belongs to an earlier church (12th c.). On the lintel are traces of carving. Inside the church is the 16th c. gravestone of Magnus Mac Orristin; the symbols include sword, hurley or shinty stick, and ball; the inscriptions read FERGUS MAK ALLAN DO RINI IN CLACH SA ('Fergus Mac Allan made this stone') and MAGNUS MEC ORRISTIN IAE (?) FOTRL SEO ('Magnus Mac Orristin . . .'). In the outer face of the W. wall is a fragment of a gravestone with an Irish inscription. In the field to the W. of the church is the 12 ft shaft of St Buadan's (Bodan's) Cross, an elaborately carved High Cross (Nat. Mon.). The figured panels include *Miracle of the Loaves and Fishes* (top of E. face). In the next field to the W. lies the head of a second High Cross. St Buadan's Bell is preserved in the parochial house at Culdaff.

CUSHENDALL, Co. Antrim (Map 1, J4), is a quiet little resort, delightfully situated at the N. end of the famous Antrim Coast Road. It takes its name from the little Dall River. It is 23 m. NW. of Larne, 15 m. SE. of Ballycastle, and 20 m. NNE. of Ballymena.

1 m. NE. are the ruins of Layd Church (in State care), a burial place of the MacDonnells; the vaulted tower is a 15th c. addition. The 1832 Protestant church has a Michael Healy window, *The Light of the World* (1917).

1½ m. S., at the foot of Glenariff, is Red Bay, overlooked by the scant remains of a MacDonnell castle which was finally destroyed by Cromwellians in 1652. The beautiful so-called Fairy Glen (Forest Park) is in the upper valley, and has woods, streams and waterfalls. Lurigethan, the inland promontory overlooking Glenariff, is crowned by a huge promontory fort, whose four earthern ramparts run ¼ m. from cliff to cliff.

2 m. WNW. (via lane from the Ballymoney road), 450 ft up in Lubatavish on the slope of Tievebulliagh (1,346 ft), is a Neolithic 'axe factory', whose products have been found as far away as SE. England.

CUSHENDUN, Co. Antrim (Map 1, J3), is an attractive small summer resort charmingly sited by the little River Dun, 4½ m. N. of Cushendall and 12 m. SE. of Ballycastle.

Most of the village – in style a pastiche of a Cornish fishing village – was built for Ronald MacNeill, Lord Cushendun (1861–1934) by Clough Williams Ellis. Village, green and beach belong to the National Trust.

Near the N. end of the beach is Rockport Lodge, once home of Moira O Neill (d. 1951), author of *Songs of the Glens of Antrim*. A neighbouring monument commemorates Sir Roger Casement (1864–1916) and other local patriots.

The steep, winding road N. to Torr Head (7 m.) is narrow for cars and hard on cyclists but offers splendid views, and the Mull of Kintyre (13 m.) and Ailsa Craig in Scotland are constantly visible. 1½ m. SW., on the summit (1,253 ft) of the mountain of the same name, is Carnanmore, alias Carnlea, a passage-tomb wih typical passage-tomb art on a stone in the corbelled roof of the chamber.

D

DAINGEAN, Co. Offaly (Map 3, F4), formerly Philipstown, is a village on the Tullamore (12 m.)–Edenderry (11 m.) road. It takes its name (*daingean*, fortress) from the medieval island fortress of O Conor Faly. When the region was Planted under Mary Tudor the capital of the newly constituted King's County was set up there and named Philipstown after Mary's husband, Philip II of Spain. The place never prospered.

5 m. N. Croghan Hill (769 ft) rises above the Bog of Allen. On the hill – referred to in Spenser's *Faerie Queene* – are a prehistoric chambered cairn, several holy wells, the ruins of two churches, and the remains of O Conor Faly's Castle, alias Croghan Castle.

DALKEY, Co. Dublin (Map 3, L4), is a coastal suburb and resort between Dalkey Sound and Dalkey Hill, 8 m. SE. of Dublin city. From Sorrento Park (to the SE., crowned by Niall O Neill's sculpture *Thus Daedalus Flew*, 1986) and Dalkey Hill views may be had of some of the loveliest stretches of the Irish coast. The earliest surviving antiquities are the medieval ruined church (Nat. Mon.) and an early gravestone in the churchyard in Main St. In the Middle Ages Dalkey was an important landing place for cross-channel passenger traffic, and three fortified houses of the 15th–16th c. still survive. Of these, one is incorporated in the Town Hall. Another, Archbold's Castle (Nat. Mon.), stands on the opposite side of the street. The third, Bullock Castle, overlooks Bullock Harbour about 1 m. N. beside the main Dún Laoghaire road.

George Bernard Shaw lived in Torca Cottage on Dalkey Hill from 1866 to 1874. He has paid his own tribute to the inspiring beauty of his boyhood home.

300 yds offshore to the SE. (boats obtainable at Coliemore Harbour) is Dalkey Island, from which the suburb takes its name (Norse for Thorn Island). The island, which was inhabited already in the 4th millennium B.C., has on it the ruins of St Begnet's Church (Nat. Mon.), a small early structure with massively lintelled W. doorway, bold *antae* at either gable, and living quarters over the W. end. In front of the door is a rock with a ringed cross carved in relief. The E. end of the church was altered by the builders of the nearby martello tower and battery, who set up their living quarters in it. The many goats formerly on the island are commemorated in a statue *Goats* by Katy Goodhue (1986), which stands in Dillon's Park on the mainland, looking out at the island.

The beautiful coast road S. of Dalkey (Vico Road) skirts Dalkey Hill and then Killiney Hill which, in large part, is now preserved as a public park (Victoria Park). The Protestant church (Holy Trinity) in Killiney has a Harry Clarke window *Angel of Hope and Peace* (1919). About ¼ m. W. of Killiney strand are the ruins (Nat. Mon.) of an early nave-and-chancel church with later N. aisle. It takes its name (Cill Inghean Léinín) from the saintly daughters of Léinín (*see p. 112*). On the soffit of the trabeate W. doorway a Greek cross is carved in relief. On Killiney Hill Rd is Pearse McKenna's delightful church of St Stephen (1982), with superbly finished wooden altar and tabernacle, terracotta *Virgin and Child*, Stations of the Cross and font by Imogen Stuart, stained glass by Helen Moloney (large panel) and Margaret Becker (*St Joseph*), and metal furnishings by Niall O Neill. ¾ m. to the SSW., and close to the Ballybrack–Shankill road, is Ballybrack (Shanganagh) Dolmen, a portal-tomb. 1 m. W. of Killiney, in Wyattville, Ballybrack, is Richard Hurley's Church of the Apostles (1982), with fine Stations of the Cross by Benedict Tutty, the *Virgin and Child* in wood by Cliodna Cussen, and furnishings by Niall O Neill.

DELGANY, Co. Wicklow (Map 3, L5), is a prettily situated village on the Bray (6 m.)–Wicklow (12 m.) road, 1½ m. SW. of Greystones.

In the Protestant parish church is the splendid 1790 monument of David Digges La Touche of Bellvue (*below*). It is the work of the Dublin sculptor John Hickey (1756–95): figures of La Touche, his wife, and sons, David, John, Peter; repaired by Harrison, 1895.

A fragment of a church, St Crispin's Cell, and the shaft of a granite High Cross (Nat. Mons.) with unsatisfactorily deciphered inscription mark the site of a 6th/7th c. foundation attributed to St Chuaróg, royal Welsh disciple of St Kevin.

W. and NW. of the village is Delgany State Forest, formerly Bellvue Demesne, where David Digges La Touche (d. 1785) had a house.

¾ m. N. are remains of the Archbold castle of Kindelestown (Nat. Mon.).

3 m. SE. is the quiet little resort of Kilcoole with remains (Nat. Mon.) of St Mary's Church of *c.* 1200.

1 m. W. is the Glen of the Downs, a wooded defile on the Dublin–Wicklow road.

DELVIN, Co. Westmeath (Map 3, G1), is a village on the Castlepollard (12 m.)–Athboy (9 m.) road.

The scrub-covered motte near the S. end of the village is a relic of the castle built in 1181 by Hugh de Lacy for his brother-in-law, Gilbert de Nangle (de Angulo), to whom he granted the barony of Delvin. (From Gilbert descends the Nugent family, one of whose most notable members was Francis Nugent, 'one of the four most learned men in Europe', who founded the Irish province of the Capuchin order in the 17th c.) Close to the motte are the ruins of a 13th c. keep of the distinctive Norman-Irish variety found at CARLOW and a few other places.

1¾ m. NW. is Ballinvalley, birthplace of Brinsley Mac Namara (1890–1963), the playwright, whose novel, *The Valley of the Squinting Windows*, and 'Heffernan' plays are set in this area.

DERRY, Co. Londonderry (Map 1, D5), officially Londonderry, is the second largest city in N. Ireland. It is located on the River Foyle a short distance above Lough Foyle. It is a manufacturing and service centre.

Although possibly a ritual place in Iron Age times, the history proper of Derry begins with the foundation of a monastery in the 6th c. (traditionally by St Columcille/Columba) in Calgach's oakwood (Doire Calgaich). Derry remained small until the 12th c. when, under the patronage of the local Mac Lochlainn dynasty, it replaced KELLS (Co. Meath) as the metropolis of the Columban monasteries and developed into a relatively large settlement which, however, declined in importance during the later Middle Ages. After repeated attempts during the 16th c., Derry was finally captured by English forces under Sir Henry Docwra in 1600, thus securing a strategic routeway to the interior of Gaelic Ulster. A small trading town grew up around the garrison, but this was destroyed in 1608 by Sir Cahir O Doherty in the course of a shortlived rebellion. In 1613 James I granted a charter to the London Companies (the 'Irish Society') to found a new city as part of the wider Plantation scheme. The renamed and walled City of Londonderry was laid out in accordance with Renaissance town-planning ideas, and seems to have influenced some later town plans in America. The city was populated by Protestant settlers from Britain. In 1648 and 1649 the town was held by Parliamentarians under Sir Charles Coote against Royalist besiegers; and was relieved by Eoghan Rua O Neill with a Catholic army. George Farquhar, dramatist, was born there in 1678. The most important event in the history of the city was the epic siege of 1688–9, when the citizens refused to admit a Jacobite garrison (and later King James II himself), and held out for the Williamite cause. The city was unsuccessfully blockaded from 18 December 1688 to 28 July 1689 by Irish and French Jacobite forces (which were actually outnumbered by the defenders). Boom Hall, beside the magnificent new Foyle Bridge, recalls the site of a boom built across the river by the besiegers to prevent relief ships getting to the city. The city was an important embarkation point for emigrants to America in the 18th and 19th c., but its major growth was associated with its successful shirt industry from 1850 onwards.

The kernel of the modern city is the small Plantation town encompassed by the walls (Hist. Mon.) completed in 1618. The whole circuit, with two watch towers, survives, although the external 30 ft wide ditch has been covered over and three of the original bastions have gone. Within the walls the original Plantation layout has largely survived: a central square (the Diamond) at the intersection of four main streets leading from the four gates (the 17th c. gates have been replaced, and three more recent gates cut through). Twelve cannon are displayed on the N. and W. ramparts, and others can be seen in different parts of the city. The Bishop's Gate at the S. end of the city is a triumphal arch built to commemorate the centenary of the siege in 1789. It is decorated with carvings by Edward Smyth, noted for his work on Dublin's Custom House and Four Courts (*see pp. 142 and 154*). The head facing SW. represents the River Foyle and that to the NE. the River Boyne.

On the highest ground within the walls is St Columb's Protestant Cathedral, built 1628–33, the first Protestant cathedral to be erected in these islands after the Reformation. It has had several alterations and additions during its history, of which the most recent is the chapter house (1910), which now functions as a small museum. The philosopher George Berkeley was Dean (1724–33). Nearby, in Bishop St, is the Court House (1813–17) by John Bowden; the portico is modelled on the Erechtheum; the coat of arms above the pediment and the statues of Justice and Peace on the wings are by Edward Smyth. The Freemasons' Hall facing the Court House is the former Bishop's Palace. The house, gardens and nearby St Augustine's Church occupy the site of the ancient Columban monastery and medieval Augustinian abbey known as the Black Church. SW. of Bishop's Gate is St Columba's 'Long Tower' Catholic Church (begun in 1784 but added to on several occasions). The adjoining precincts occupy the site of the Round (Long) Tower, and 12th c. Tempull Mór or Great Church medieval cathedral, which gave its name to the parish.

Inside the walls from the Gate, Bishop St leads N. to the 1914–18 War Memorial in the Diamond. Nearby in Society St is the Apprentice Boys' Memorial Hall which also houses a small museum. Shipquay St, which drops steeply towards the river, includes a number of 18th c. Georgian houses. Between Shipquay Gate and the river is the Tudoresque Gothic Guildhall (City Hall) begun in 1887, and twice restored following damage (1908 and 1972). It has a large collection of stained glass depicting the history of the city, and also houses the civic archives. Opposite the Guildhall, within the walls at Magazine Gate, is the new O Doherty Tower interpretative centre.

½ m. WNW., on a hill separated from the walled city by the Bogside, is St Eugene's Catholic Cathedral (1873). It is dedicated to the patron (properly St Eoghan) of Ardstraw. The church of St Mary's in the Creggan (1959) is by Corr and McCormick. ½ m. N. along the Northlands Road is Magee College, now a campus of the University of Ulster. The original Gothic buildings date from 1865. Nearby is Old Foyle College (1814) by John Bowden, now an arts centre. The statue of Sir John Lawrence, Governor General of India (1864–9), by Sir Joseph Edgar Boehm, which formerly stood there, was brought to the new school 1 m. N. at Springtown. In the garden of Belmont House 2 m. N. is a medieval tomb-effigy of an armoured knight. 1 m. N. at Steelstown is Our Lady of Lourdes Church (1976, Liam McCormick and Partners) with furnishings by Helen Moloney, Patrick McElroy (bronze and enamel), Oisín Kelly, and Sister Aloysius (Stations). Nearby at Ballyarnett, on the N. edge of the city, *Wind Sculpture* by Eilish O Connell and an interpretive centre mark the landing place in May 1932 of Amelia Earhart, the first woman to fly solo across the Atlantic.

The Foyle Valley Railway Centre, beside the unusual two-deck Craigavon Bridge near the city centre, is a museum dedicated to the city's interesting railway (particularly narrow gauge) history.

In St Columb's Park in the Waterside suburb on the E. side of the Foyle are the remains of St Brecan's pre-Plantation Church. A bronze statue by F. E. McWilliams, *Princess Macha*, stands near the entrance to Altnagelvin Hospital. The new Free Presbyterian church at Lisnagelvin is an interesting example of modern ecclesiastical architecture.

DINGLE, Co. Kerry (Map 5, C3), is a small market town and fishing port on the S. side of the Corcaguiney peninsula ('Dingle Peninsula') 30 m. WSW. of Tralee. The W. end of the peninsula

Slea Head on the Dingle Peninsula, Co. Kerry.

Donegal Castle, Co, Donegal (see page 130).

has an extraordinary wealth of prehistoric and early historic remains. There is a Heritage Centre in the town.

In the Protestant churchyard is a Desmond tomb of 1504. St Mary's Catholic Church in Green St was refurbished (1967) by Robinson, Keefe and Devane, with furnishings by Enda King and Imogen Stuart (Madonna group, 1980). At the upper end of Main St is a boulder with cup marks, etc.

The secondary road to Tralee, via Stradbally and CASTLEGREGORY, climbs 6 m. NE. to Connor Pass (1,300 ft), providing splendid views of Dingle Bay and Iveragh.

2¼ m. N., in the Commons of Dingle, are several clochāns. (The whole W. slope of Ballysitteragh is littered with clochāns and other ancient remains, *see* Ballyheabought, *below*.)

2 m. E., in Ballineetig, is Gallán Mór, a pillarstone (Nat. Mon.).

4½ m. E. is Lispole village. In Churchfield, NW. of the bridge, is St Martin's Church (Nat. Mon.), an early church with architraved trabeate W. door; it stands in a large, oval earthwork.– 2 m. S., in Aghacarrible, is a ringfort with L-shaped souterrain; in the latter are three ogham stones and an early cross-slab. There are many ringforts, clochāns and pillarstones in the area.

2 m. SE., in the ancient, oval graveyard of Ballintaggart, are nine ogham stones (Nat. Mons.). 1¼ m. E., in Emlagh East, are a ringfort and Cloch an tSagairt, a cross-inscribed ogham stone (Nat. Mons.). The stone, on Trabeg strand, was the first ogham stone to be noticed by an antiquarian (Edward Lhuyd).

1¼ m. W., in Milltown (beyond the village), are two prostrate stones, one having cup-and-circle and other prehistoric scribings. W. of these are remains of a chamber tomb. To the N. are the Gates of Glory, a pair of pillarstones, and there are other single examples in nearby fields.

2½ m. SW., on the W. side of Dingle Harbour, is Burnham, formerly home of the de Moleyns family (Lords Ventry). Now Coláiste Ide, it has three ogham stones and a cross-inscribed slab beside the driveway.

3½ m. WNW., in Ballymorereagh, ruined Teampall Geal (alias St Manchan's Oratory; Nat. Mon.), St Manchan's Grave (with an early cross-slab), two small cross-inscribed stones, Tobar Mancháin, and a partly defaced ogham stone (with two incised crosses and an inscription in half uncials), mark the site of an early anchoritic establishment. The half-uncial inscription, FECT QUENILOC SON, is thought to be an 18th c. forgery.

2½ m. NW. is Kilfountain, St Fiontán's Church, or Cell (Nat. Mon.). In the disused burial ground are the foundations of a small church, remains of clochāns, a bullaun, and an early cross-pillar with *chi-rho* and inscriptions in both ogham (EQODDT) and half-uncials (S[AN]C[T]I FINTEN).

2 m. NNW., in Ballyheabought, are remains of a great, bivallate ringfort; the inner rampart is stone-faced and terraced; in the enclosure are remains of clochāns.

4 m. NNW., at the ancient burial ground of Reenconnell, is a stone cross (Nat. Mon.).

4¾ m. NNW. is Ballinloghig. A splendid mountain walk, with magnificent views, may be made E. and NE. to the knife-ridge between the cirques of Brandon Peak, to the summit (2,764 ft), and thence NNW. above the tremendous cirques of Brandon Hill. ¾ m. WSW., at the ancient burial ground of Curraulу, is an early cross-pillar (broken).

5½ m. NNW. is Ballybrack. In the townland is a clochān with a covered chamber (Nat. Mon.). The Saints' Road from Curraulу (*above*), still used by pilgrims (29 June) and marked by Stations of the Cross, climbs NE. from Ballybrack 'village' to the summit of Brandon Mountain (3,127 ft), second highest mountain in Ireland. Just below the summit are St Brendan's Well, remains of St Brendan's Oratory (Nat. Mon.), and ruins of several penitential stations (Nat. Mons.), enclosed by traces of a cashel. These mark the site of an early anchoritic settlement associated with the celebrated St Brendan the Navigator, 484–577 (*see p. 107*). The aluminium cross on the oratory has been made from spars of a German bomber which crashed on the mountain during the Second World War. A walk N. and NNW. along the mountain ridge leads the pilgrim-tourist to Brandon Monument (Nat. Mon.) in Arraglen in the saddle with Masatiompán (2,509 ft). This is a prostrate ogham stone with incised Maltese crosses (one with chi-rho); the ogham inscription reads: 'The priest Ronann son of Comogann'.

7 m. NNW., in Ballynavenooragh, are stone forts with clochāns.

The Guildhall, Derry City.

DONABATE, Co. Dublin (Map 3, K2), is a village and holiday resort to the E. of the Dublin (11½ m.)–Balbriggan (7½ m.) road. The parish church has a two-light window by Harry Clarke: *Suffer Little Children to Come unto Me* (1926). The Protestant church (1758) has gallery stucco (by Robert West?).

1 m. NE. is Portrane, a small seaside resort with remains of a 15th c. church and castle. The former has a small, square W.

tower. Portraine House was the home of Swift's Stella; there is now a psychiatric hospital in the demesne, close to the excellent beach. The Round Tower to the E. of the hospital is modern.

1 m. SW. are remains of Kilcrea Castle.

1¼ m. WSW., in the demesne of Newbridge House, are the ruins of Lanestown Castle. Newbridge House was enlarged (by Richard Cassels?), 1736–43, for Charles Cobbe, Protestant Archbishop of Dublin. Cobbe's son made additions which include a drawing-room with fine ceiling by Robert West. John Wesley stayed at Newbridge House in 1767. The house is now open to the public, and in the ownership of the same Dublin County Council which ordered the 1987 demolition of Newbridge's older neighbour, Turvey, a house with origins going back to 1565.

DONAGHADEE, Co. Down (Map 1, M7), is a small port and quiet resort, 4¾ m. ESE. of Bangor (7 m. by coast road).

The harbour (1821–37), prior to 1865 a packet station on the short route to Scotland, together with its handsome lighthouse (lantern altered), is the work of Sir John Rennie, who was assisted by his son, John, and by David Logan of Eddystone Lighthouse fame.

Overlooking the harbour is The Moat, a motte crowned by a 19th c. folly.

The Protestant parish church was built in 1636 for Hugh, Viscount Montgomery, but it has been greatly altered.

3 m. S. (1 m. W. of Millside), in Ballycopeland, is a carefully restored 18th c. tower-windmill (Hist. Mon.).

DONAGHPATRICK, Co. Meath (Map 2, G8), is on the N. side of the Blackwater between Navan (6 m.) and Kells (6 m.). It takes its name from the 'great church' (*domnach*), 60 ft long, which St Patrick built on a site given to him by Conall Cremthainne, son of Niall Nine Hostager. The site is marked by the graveyard (originally circular) of St Patrick's Church (Protestant, 1886), which incorporates the 15th c. residential tower (a human mask high up in the N. face; windows and parapet modern) of the medieval parish church. A plain polygonal font, a plain cross (?) shaft, and one gable of an early tomb (?) of Slane type have been grouped together NE. of the church.

1½ m. W. of Donaghpatrick church, in Teltown, is Ráth Dubh ('Black Ring Fort'; Nat. Mon.). In Teltown (Old Irish *Tailtiu* 'the well formed'), the celebrated Aonach Tailteann – (pre-Gaelic?) Lughnasa festival and principal public assembly and fair of the Uí Néill confederation – was held each year at the beginning of August. The place was a prehistoric cemetery, and games in honour of the dead were a primary purpose of the gathering. To preside at the aonach was a prerogative of the King of Tara. The assembly was in abeyance for most of the 10th and 11th c. It was revived in 1120 by Turloch O Conor of Connacht, aspirant to the high-kingship, and again (for the last time) in 1168, after the landing of the first Anglo-Normans, by his son, Rory. A memory of the ancient aonach survived in the tradition of Teltown Marriages, chance espousals for a year and a day. On the expiry of that term, a couple desiring to separate should come to the centre of Ráth Dubh, there stand back to back, one facing N., the other facing S., and walk away from one another out of the fort.

1 m. NNW., in Oristown, is St Catherine's Church (1970) by Fehily Associates with sanctuary cross by Richard Enda King.

DONARD, Co. Wicklow (Map 3, I6), is a village 1 m. E. of the Baltinglass (7½ m.)–Ballymore Eustace (10 m.) road. It has been claimed that Bishop Palladius, St Patrick's predecessor, founded a church there for his disciple, St Sylvester. In the garden of the former Civic Guard station is preserved an ogham stone which originally stood close to an uninscribed stone on Old Mills farm, Whitestone, 3 m. SW.

½ m. N., at Box Bridge, is a stone with 19 bullauns. On the adjacent eminence are two ruined mounds (Nat. Mons.).

2 m. N., in Kilbaylet Upper, is the King's Stone with the 'print of St Kevin's foot'; the saint once stepped from the top of Slieve Gad (*see p. 203*) on to the stone, and thence to Mullica, the next ridge to the W.

A fine walk of 4 m. SE. leads to the remains of fortified Leitrim Barracks in the Glen of Imaal. Michael Dwyer, celebrated 1798 leader, was born in the glen in 1771, and it was one of his retreats when 'on the run', hence the erection of Leitrim Barracks. In a plantation ⅓ m. NE. of the barracks is Knickeen Long Stone, a pillarstone with an ogham inscription. In Derrynamuck (5½ m. SE. of Donard in the SE. corner of the glen) is Michael Dwyer's Cottage (Nat. Mon.). In 1799 Dwyer and his companions were trapped there by British troops. Samuel MacAllister gave his life by drawing their fire so as to enable Dwyer and the rest to escape. The NE. slopes of the Glen of Imail are used as an artillery range (caution!).

DONEGAL, Co. Donegal (Map 8, E7), which gives its name to the county, is a market town and small seaport where the road from Ballyshannon (14 m.) to Ballybofey (17 m.) crosses the River Eske at the NE. corner of Donegal Bay.

The place was occupied in Viking times (Dún nan Gall, Fort of the Foreigners) and, in the later Middle Ages, it became the chief seat of the O Donnells, Kings of Tír Chonaill. After the 'Flight of the Earls' in 1607, the town was planted by Sir Basil Brooke, to whom it owes its Plantation layout (including the Diamond, or market-place).

The ruins of Donegal Castle (Nat. Mon.), near the Diamond, include the great square tower of the castle erected by Red Hugh II O Donnell in 1505 and altered by Sir Basil Brooke, who inserted the 17th c. features and added the fine Jacobean fortified house in 1610. The banqueting hall has a splendid Jacobean fireplace. Near the pier is a large anchor thought to have belonged to the French frigate *Romaine*, which accompanied General Humbert's expedition, but cut her cable and left for France on hearing of his surrender.

¼ m. S. are the remnants (Nat. Mon.) of Donegal 'Abbey', a Franciscan friary founded by Red Hugh I O Donnell and his mother, Nuala O Conor, in 1474, who are buried there. In 1591 the English seized the friary and fortified it, but were expelled in 1592 by Great Red Hugh O Donnell. In 1601 the English seized it once more, and it was attacked a second time by Red Hugh. On this occasion the English magazine blew up and wrecked the buildings. In 1607 the friary was granted to Sir Basil Brooke. The fragments include parts of the church and of the cloister arcade, etc. After the English conquest of Tír Chonaill the

Franciscan community of Donegal remained in being for many years, moving about from one place of refuge to another. In the convent, then settled at Bundrowes, the Four Masters, Michael and Peregrine O Clery, Peregrine Duignan and Fearfeasa O Mulconry, compiled their celebrated *Annals* between the years 1630 and 1636.

There are two recent memorials to the Four Masters in the town, an obelisk in the diamond and disappointing St Patrick's Church (1931–5) by Ralph Byrne (refurbished by Wilfrid Cantwell in 1979).

5 m. NE., in a beautiful setting at the foot of the Bluestack Mountains is Lough Eske. On an island at the S. end of the lake are the keep and bawn of an O Donnell castle which figured in the 16th c. wars.

1 m. S., on the Eske estuary, are remnants of Magherabeg 'Abbey', a small, 15th c., Franciscan Tertiary friary.

DONERAILE, Co. Cork (Map 5, L2), is a village on the Buttevant (3 m.)–Mitchelstown (14 m.) road, beside the Awbeg.

The town was part of Edmund Spenser's estate (*see* Kilcolman Castle, *below*). His son sold it to Warham St Leger, English Lord President of Munster and ancestor of Viscount Doneraile, in 1627. The estate is now a Forest Park; in it stands Doneraile Court, a fine brick house erected in 1725 to the design of Rothery. It was there that Mary Barry, wife of the 1st Viscount Doneraile (later Mrs Aldworth), hid herself in a clock to spy on a meeting of Freemasons. Discovered, she was admitted to membership for secrecy's sake, so becoming the first woman Mason.

Tadhg Ó Duinnín, last hereditary poet to the Mac Carthys and last official head of the Blarney bardic school, died parish priest of Doneraile in 1726.

Canon Sheehan, author of *Luke Delmege, My New Curate*, and other novels, was parish priest of Doneraile from 1895 to 1913. His memorial is a statue (1925, by Francis Doyle-Jones) in front of his church.

1¼ m. E., by the Awbeg, are the remains of Creagh Castle.

4½ m. E., on the S. bank of the Awbeg, are the ruins of Wallstown church and castle.

3½ m. SE. are the ruins of Castle Kevin (Roches).

3¼ m. NNW. are the remains of Kilcolman Castle, now a wildfowl refuge, which can only be entered by permission. A Desmond stronghold, it was granted, together with 3,028 acres of land, to Edmund Spenser after the Desmond Rebellion. Spenser had come to Ireland in 1580 as secretary to Lord Deputy Grey of Wilton. In 1587 he took up residence at Kilcolman, where he was visited by Sir Walter Ralegh in 1589. After settling there he became Clerk to the English Council of Munster. His barbarous views on the treatment of the Irish provoked his ostracism by Maurice, Viscount Roche of Fermoy, who proclaimed that 'none of his people should have trade or commerce with Mr Spenser'. At Kilcolman Spenser wrote *View of the Present State of Ireland*, the first three books of the *Faerie Queene, Colin Clout's Come Home Againe*, the lovely *Amoretti* sonnets, and *Epithalamion*, the last two for Elizabeth Boyle of Kilcoran (*see p. 308*), whom he married in 1594. Apart from a visit to London in 1590–1, Spenser resided continuously at Kilcolman from 1587 until the insurgent Irish burned the castle in October 1598. The following year the poet died in London.

DOOLIN, Co. Clare (Map 6, E4), is a fishing village 5 m. SW. of Lisdoonvarna, and a haunt of traditional musicians.

1 m. NE. are the ruins of Killilagh parish church (*c. 1500*).

The road S. to Liscannor (7 m.) passes Doonagore Castle, an unusual, circular tower (restored) inside a small bawn.

DOWNPATRICK, Co. Down (Map 2, L3), from which the diocese and county of Down take their name, is a cathedral and market town near the SW. corner of Strangford Lough, 21 m. S. of Belfast and 32 m. NE. of Newry.

Inhabited since prehistoric times, the former Dún-dá-leth-glas, or simply An Dún, acquired the name Dún Pádraig, 'Patrick's Dún', at the time of the 'discovery' (*below*) of the relics of SS Patrick, Columcille, and Brigid.

About 1 February 1177, John de Courcy took the place, then the seat of Rory Mac Donlevy, King of Ulster (i.e. Co. Down), by surprise, and established his principal castle there. In 1260, Brian O Neill, King of Tír Eóghain, who had been acknowledged King of Ireland by Connacht and Thomond, marched against the northern citadel of the foreigners. In the desperate Battle of Down which followed, Brian himself and eight Connacht lords and 15 of the principal Ó Catháins (*see p. 232*) perished.

The most important feature of Downpatrick is the Protestant cathedral. According to legend, St Patrick founded a church inside Ráth Celtchair, a hill-fort, part of whose rampart is traceable SW. of the cathedral. There certainly was an early monastery there, which was revitalized when St Malachy introduced the Canons Regular of St Augustine in 1137. Six years after seizing Down, de Courcy grasped the opportunity offered by the 'discovery' of the relics of SS Patrick, Brigid, and Columcille to transfer the see of the diocese from Bangor to his capital. He replaced the Irish Augustinians by English Benedictines from Chester, and changed the dedication of their church from the Holy Trinity to St Patrick. In 1184 the Benedictines began to build a new cathedral, which – if ever completed – was already ruined by the mid-16th c. Between 1790 and 1826 Charles Lilly of Dublin drastically 'restored' the E. end of the cathedral to serve as second cathedral of the Protestant diocese of Down and Dromore (*see pp. 134, 203 and 237*). In the course of the 'restoration' all traces of the early and medieval monasteries were swept away, the Round Tower serving as a quarry for the 1826 tower of the cathedral.

Lilly's Holy Trinity Cathedral (dedication restored 1609) represents merely the aisled choir and chancel of the Benedictine cathedral. Of the medieval fragments incorporated in the fabric, the most interesting are the capitals and responds of the arcades. Relics of the pre-Norman age are two fragments set into the E. wall of the Chapter Room (S. 'transept'): a small wheel cross with defaced figure of an abbot (or bishop) bearing bachall and book(?); and a fragment of a smaller figured cross. The nearby font basin was probably a cross base. The choir stalls and pews are good 18th/19th c. work.

Outside the E. end of the cathedral is a 9th/10th c. High Cross which formerly stood at the centre of the town. The fragments were re-erected there in 1897; the weathered figurations include a *Crucifixion*. S. of the cathedral a monolith inscribed PATRIC marks the alleged grave of St Patrick. This is a bogus antiquity commissioned (1900) by Francis J. Biggar. Patrick died at Saul

Downpatrick Cathedral, Co. Down.

(*below*), and knowledge of his burial place had been lost by the 9th c. E. of the cathedral is the attractive Southwell School (Bluecoat School), 1733. Opposite is the old gaol which now houses the 'Down Museum', whose 'St Patrick's Heritage Centre' contains two of four cross-slabs removed from Saul.

The Protestant Parish Church, Church Ave., dates from 1560; much altered; tower 18th c. In the churchyard is buried Thomas Russell of the United Irishmen ('The man from God knows where'; *see p. 72*). He was hanged in Downpatrick for complicity in Emmet's Rebellion (1803).

1½ m. N. (via English St) is what may be a motte-and-bailey (Nat. Mon.), relic of John de Courcy's castle.

2 m. NE. is Saul (Sabhal Pádraic, 'Patrick's Barn'), legendarily the place of Patrick's first church, a barn (close to his landing place) given him by Díchú, the local lord. Later there was an important monastery (Augustinian after 1130) on the site, which is occupied today by St Patrick's Churchyard (300 yds W. of village), with cross-pillars, a medieval gravestone and two ancient, stone-roofed mortuary houses, one of them appropriated as a mausoleum. In the 1933 Protestant church is part of an interesting early gravestone; the 13th c. font-basin is from Burnchurch (*see p. 209*); the *St Patrick* window (1933) is by Catherine O Brien. The statue of St Patrick by Francis Doyle-Jones, on the hill overlooking Strangford Lough, commemorates the supposed 15th centenary (1932) of Patrick's landing.

1¾ m. E., in Struel, are St Patrick's Wells (Nat. Mons.) and the ruins of an 18th c. church. There are four wells, fed from a common source: one for drinking, one for eyes, the others for bathing body and limbs. – 1 m. E., beside the road, is Ballyalton Druidical Ring (Nat. Mon.): an elliptical court-tomb. 1 m. S., on the Killough road, is St Colmcille's Church (1972).

3 m. S., in Ballynoe (¼ m. – by sunken lane – from the former railway station), is Ballynoe Stone Circle (Nat. Mon.) – 1½ m. W. of Ballynoe village is Castleskreen (Nat. Mon.), a 13th c. motte inside a univallate ringfort. ½ m. W. is a later Castleskreen (Nat. Mon.): motte with fragments of a stone castle. In Erenagh, the townland adjoining Castleskreen townland on the N., was the site of Carrick Abbey, founded in 1127 for monks of the reformed Benedictines of Savigny (Normandy), which is the earliest recorded abbey of a Continental order in Ireland, predating MELLIFONT ABBEY by 15 years. About 1180 de Courcy gave the monks a new home at the ancient monastery of Inch.

1 m. SW., in Demesne townland, is Magnus's Grave, a low, tree-grown mound alleged to mark the grave of Magnus Barefoot, King of Norway, who was slain (1103) on a foray into Ulster when on his way home from a visit to High-King Muirchertach O Brien at Kincora (*see p. 220*).

2½ m. NW., on the left bank of the Quoile, in Inch (Inis Cumscraigh), are the beautifully sited remains (Nat. Mon.) of St Mary's Abbey De Insula. About 1180 de Courcy established the homeless monks of Carrick (*above*) there. Then, the place (site of an early monastery) belonged to the Cistercians of Combe Abbey in England. Little more than the E. end of the abbey church survives, but the foundations of the whole complex have been uncovered. The E. wall of the chancel has three Transitional lancets (*c.* 1200). The transepts each had two E. chapels (*see p. 201*). In the 15th c. the nave was abandoned, and the choir enclosed by walls which cut off the transepts as well.

DOWRA, Co. Cavan (Map 7, M2), is a Shannon-side village on the Drumshanbo (10 m.)–Belcoo (10 m.) road, about 2 m. N. of mountain-ringed Lough Allen. Between the E. bank of the river and the foot of Slievenakilla (1,787 ft) a 3 m. stretch of the Worm Ditch, or Black Pig's Race, an ancient frontier earthwork, runs S. and SW. from the village to the head of the lake. It is generally supposed to mark a prehistoric or protohistoric frontier of Ulaid (Ulster). For further stretches *see pp. 190 and 198*.

6 m. WSW., on a small hill N. of Lough Allen, in Kilnagarns Lower, is a ruinous court-tomb; excavation yielded neolithic shards and flints. Close by are remains of a wedge-tomb which yielded a Beaker shard.

DRAPERSTOWN, Co. Londonderry (Map 1, G6), locally known as the Cross of Ballynascreen, is a village at the SE. edge of the Sperrin Mountains (near the head of Glenconkeine), on the road from Derry (28 m.) to Cookstown (16 m.) in an archaeologically rich area. It was given its official name in 1818 and built about 1830 by the proprietors, the Drapers Company of London.

4 m. SW. is Ballynascreen, which takes its name from the ancient church-site, Scrín Cholaim Chille (Colmcille's Shrine).

5 m. SSW., in Ballybriest, is Carnanbane (Hist. Mon.), the damaged remains of a dual court-tomb, excavated in 1937. There are many other prehistoric remains in the vicinity.

2½ m. WNW. in Drumderg is a wedge-tomb known as 'Dergmore's Grave'.

DRIMOLEAGUE, Co. Cork (Map 5, H7), formerly Dromdaleague, is a village on the Dunmanway (18 m.)–Bantry (12 m.) road, 8 m. N. of Skibbereen. The Church of All Saints (1956, by Frank Murphy) is one of the first churches to have been built in a modern idiom in Ireland after the Second World War. A fresco on the E. wall is by Schröder.

3 m. NW., near Leitry bridge, are the ruins of Castle Donovan (15th/16th c.).

DRIPSEY, Co. Cork (Map 5, K5), is a woollen-manufacturing village to the E. of the River Dripsey, on the picturesque Cork (13 m.)–Macroom (12 m.) road to Killarney (41 m.).

1½ m. NNW., in the demesne of Dripsey Castle, are the ruins of the moated rock castle of Carrignamuck, built in the 15th c. by Cormac Láidir Mac Carthy (*see pp. 54 and 133*).

DROGHEDA, Co. Louth (Map 2, I8), is a historic town on the Dublin (30 m.)–Dundalk (21 m.) road. In recent years it has become an important manufacturing centre and seaport.

The Anglo-Norman invaders were quick to appreciate the strategic significance of the town, and Hugh de Lacy built a motte castle and a bridge across the Boyne before the close of the 12th c. Until 1412 there were two municipalities there, one on either side of the river. Both were walled in the 13th c.

During the Middle Ages Drogheda was one of the most important English towns in Ireland. In 1395 Richard II received the submissions of Niall Óg O Neill, Prince of the Irish of Ulster, and other Gaelic rulers in the Dominican friary, where he held his court. Several parliaments met there in the later Middle Ages, the most notable being those of 1465, which passed an Act setting up a university at Drogheda; of 1467–8, which attainted and beheaded Thomas, 7th Earl of Desmond; and of 1494, which enacted the notorious Poynings' Law extending to Ireland 'all statutes concerning the public weal, made within the realm of England'.

In 1649 Sir Arthur Aston held it for King Charles with a garrison of 3,000 men, mostly English, against Cromwell. On 10 September Cromwell stormed the town, which fell at the third assault. Some 2,000 of the defenders, including Aston, were butchered by express command of Cromwell, and many of the survivors transported to Barbados.

In West St is Peter's Church (Oliver Plunkett Memorial Church), Gothic-Revival successor to a church by Francis Johnston. At the W. door is a small, 15th c. font (figures of angels, symbols of the Passion). On a side altar is displayed the embalmed head of St Oliver Plunkett (1629–81), Archbishop of Armagh, who was hanged, drawn, and quartered at Tyburn.

In Old Abbey Lane (off the W. end of West St) are some remains of the church of the Hospital of St Mary d'Urso, founded *c.* 1206 by Ursus de Swemele.

Near the N. edge of the town, in Upper Magdalene St, is 14th c. Magdalene Steeple, central bell-tower of the church of the Dominican friary of St Mary Magdalene, founded in 1224 by Lucas de Netterville, Archbishop of Armagh.

A short distance SE., in William St, is Protestant St Peter's Church, (1749–52, tower and spire added by Francis Johnston, 1792) second successor of the church in whose steeple 100 men held out against Cromwell until he burned it about their ears. In the porch, as well as medieval fragments, is an early gravestone inscribed TNUDACH COCMAN F; it was removed from Marley churchyard. In the church is a medieval font with *Baptism of Christ* and *The Twelve Apostles*. The churchyard has some interesting tombstones, including a double-cadaver stone (early 16th c.). Isaac Goldsmith (d. 1769), uncle of Oliver, and John Van Homrigh (d. 1785), father of Swift's 'Vanessa', are buried there.

Not far away, to the SE., at the junction of Palace St and St Lawrence St, is 'St Lawrence's Gate', a splendid 13th c. barbican (two lofty, battlemented, circular towers linked by a loop-holed curtain) which stood on the outer edge of the moat in front of the vanished gate whose name it bears.

The town S. of the river is dominated by Mill Mount (Barrack St), motte of the Norman castle built in the 12th c. to command the bridge; the bailey is covered by the military barracks. It now houses the Museum of the Old Drogheda Society. SE., in Mary St, is St Mary's Church, on the site of the church of a Carmelite friary founded in the 13th/14th c. Fragments from the friary were built into the graveyard wall, etc. Nearby is a section of the medieval town wall.

E. of the town is the Boyne Viaduct (1854), by Sir John McNeill, noted Scottish engineer.

3¾ m. N. (via the Annagassan road), in Ballymakenny, is an original and graceful Protestant church designed by Francis Johnston for Primate Robinson (*see p. 173*) and completed in 1793, when he was also building Rokeby Hall nearby as the Primate's residence. It was Johnston's first essay in the Gothick manner. The primate's arms are carved over the door. The interior retains its pristine character, for the clear windows and high pews have all survived. The glebe house is also by Johnston.

2 m. ENE. is Beaulieu House (Mr Waddington). From the Anglo-Norman invasion until the Cromwellian conquest Beaulieu, alias Bewley, was the property and seat of the illustrious Plunkett family, from which have sprung the noble houses of Louth, Fingal, and Dunsany, and to which belonged St Oliver Plunkett. The Cromwellian regime granted the property to Sir Henry Tichborne, afterwards 1st Baron Ferrard of Beaulieu (line extinct), from whom it passed to the Montgomerys. Beaulieu House is a beautiful stone mansion doubtfully attributed to Sir Christopher Wren; it was built for Tichborne about 1660–6. At the nearby Protestant church are a medieval coffin slab with floriated cross and a typical 15th c. cadaver tombstone. They are said to have been found in the river.

5 m. E., on the S. side of the Boyne estuary, is Mornington (properly Mariners' Town). The Maiden Tower originated as an Elizabethan shipping beacon.

4 m. SE. is the seaside resort of Laytown. The Catholic church (1979) is by Liam McCormick, with Stations of the Cross by Nell Pollen and tabernacle by David King.

4 m. SE., in the grounds of Pilltown House, is an ogham stone from Painestown.

4 m. W., on the N. side of the Boyne in Co. Louth, is Townley Hall, a large, rather gaunt, Georgian-style mansion by Francis Johnston. It is now the School of Philosophy and Economic Science. ½ m. SW. of the house are remains of a mound with a devolved passage grave. It had been erected on top of a Neolithic habitation site. At the E. side of the demesne is King William's Glen. On the day of the Battle of the Boyne (1 July 1690), the Williamite right flank rested there, and the left flank in a similar ravine 1 m. to the E., the centre and artillery being drawn up on the high ground in between. William's main force crossed the river at Oldbridge, while 15,000 of his men crossed upstream at Rosnaree and SLANE, and cut off the communications of the Jacobite army drawn up in front of Donore Hill. Outflanked, outnumbered, and outgunned, the Jacobites had to retreat, but their rearguards put up a spirited resistance.

DROMAHAIRE, Co. Leitrim (Map 7, L2), is a pleasantly sited village on the Sligo (12 m.)–Drumshanbo (21 m.) road.

Dromahaire was the chief seat of the Ó Ruairc (O Rourke) kings of Bréifne, who played a conspicuous rôle in pre-Norman Ireland. It was later the seat of their descendants, the O Rourke lords of West Breany. It is from Dromahaire that Dervorgilla (founder of the Nuns' Church at CLONMACNOIS and benefactress of MELLIFONT ABBEY) is alleged to have eloped from her husband, Tigernán Ó Ruairc, King of Bréifne. The banishment (1167) of her paramour, Díarmait Mac Murrough, King of Leinster, provided Henry II of England with the wished-for pretext to undertake the conquest of Ireland.

½ m. W., on the left bank of the Bonet, are the ruins of Creevelea 'Abbey' (Nat. Mon.), a Franciscan friary founded in 1508 – and thus the last of the pre-Reformation Irish friaries – by Margaret O Brien, wife of Eóghan O Rourke. Accidentally burned down in 1536, its restoration was undertaken by Brian O Rourke. After banishment early in the 17th c., the friars returned on two different occasions to re-occupy the buildings. The well-preserved remains are those of a typical Irish friary, but the details (including carvings of St Francis on the pillars of the cloister arcade) are often curious and degenerate rather than beautiful. The tower, which is coeval with the church, has been much modified since the Dissolution.

1 m. E., adjoining the fragmentary remains of O Rourke's Castle on the left bank of the Bonet, is Old Hall, which incorporates portions of a castle and bawn built in 1626 by Sir Edward Villiers, brother of the Duke of Buckingham and grantee of escheated O Rourke lands.

2½ m. E., in Mullaghmore, is a court-tomb.

4 m. NW. in Kilmore, on the NE. shore of Lough Gill, is Parkes Castle (Nat. Mon.), a Plantation castle with large bawn defended by a gatehouse and two flanking towers. It figured prominently in the war of 1641–52. It has been conserved by the Office of Public Works, whose excavations in 1972–3 showed the existence of an earlier tower house on the site.

DROMISKIN, Co. Louth (Map 2, I6), is a hamlet 1 m. W. of the Dundalk (7 m.)–Castlebellingham (1¾ m.) road.

St Patrick founded a church here, which was later succeeded by a monastery whose most celebrated abbot, St Rónán (d. 664), is associated with the story of Suibne Geilt and the battle of Mag Roth. The monastery was occupied by Vikings for some years in the late-10th c. The only certain relic of it is the stump of a Round Tower (Nat. Mon.), the roof of which is modern. The head of a figured High Cross (Nat. Mon.), which stands on a modern shaft, is said to have come from Baltray. The E. gable of a small 13th c. church marks the position of the monastic church.

3½ m. W. is modernized Darver Castle, a 16th c. square keep with corner turrets. 1 m. N., adjoining a modern house, is the well-preserved tower of Killincoole Castle.

1 m. NW. is the tower of Milltown castle.

DROMORE, Co. Down (Map 2, J2), is a cathedral and market town where the Banbridge (8 m.)–Hillsborough (5 m.) road (main Dublin–Belfast road) crosses the Lagan. It gives its name to the diocese of Dromore, the Catholic cathedral of which is at Newry. The Protestant diocese is united with that of Down.

The Protestant Cathedral of Christ the Redeemer and its churchyard occupy the site of a monastery, founded *c.* 600 by St

Parkes Castle, Kilmore, Co. Leitrim.

Colmán. The nucleus of the cathedral dates from Bishop Thomas Percy's transformation (1808) of the church built by Jeremy Taylor soon after 1661 to take the place of medieval St Colmán's Cathedral, burned down in 1641. Taylor was administrator of Dromore, as well as Bishop of Down and Connor. The only ancient relic in the cathedral is an early gravestone ('St Colmán's Pillow'). Bishop Percy, 1729–1811 (*see pp. 57 and 235*), rebuilder of the cathedral and author of the celebrated *Reliques of Ancient English Poetry*, is buried in the transept of the cathedral.

By the Lagan bridge is a 9th/10th c. High Cross of granite (Hist. Mon.), which had been demolished during the religious upheaval of the 17th c., and was put together again and set up in its present position in 1887. The base, the lower part of the shaft, and most of the head are original.

In Mount St, beside the Lagan, is the Mount, alias the English Mound (Hist. Mon.), perhaps the best-preserved motte-and-bailey in Northern Ireland.

DROMORE, Co. Tyrone (Map 1, C9), is a village on the Omagh (10 m.)–Enniskillen (12 m.) road. Tradition has it that St Patrick founded the first nunnery in Ireland there. The ruins of Dromore Old Church, WSW. of the village, date from 1694. St Davogs Catholic Church (1987), with its impressive 90 ft campanile, is by E.M. Corr of Derry. The unusual statue of Our Lady Mother of the Church is by Imogen Stuart; the stone and metal furnishings are by Michael Biggs, and the foundation stone was carved by Tom Glendon.

The village of Dromore is the birthplace of the novelist Benedict Kiely (b. 1919).

4 m. SSW., in Castlemervyn Demesne, are the ruins of Trillick Castle, which was built by Lord Castlehaven around 1630.

DROMORE WEST, Co. Sligo (Map 7, I2), is a village charmingly situated where the Sligo (22 m.)–Ballina (18 m.) road crosses the little Dunneill River. ½ m. E. of the village are the ruins of the medieval parish church of Kilmacshalgan; the church was re-edified for Protestant use in 1616, and abandoned in 1812.

2¼ m. S., near the W. bank of the Dunneill River in Belville, is a court-tomb gallery.

5 m. SW., in Tawnatruffaun, close to the confluence of the Easky and Fiddengarrode, is the Giant's Griddle, a portal-tomb.

Berechtuine slab and upright, Tullylease, Co. Cork.

$1\frac{1}{2}$ m. WSW., close to the Owenykeevan in Caltragh, but reached from the main Ballina road at Cullee, are the Great Griddle of the Fiana and the Small Griddle of the Fiana, a court-tomb and a wedge-tomb.

$1\frac{1}{2}$ m. NW. ($\frac{1}{2}$ m. N. of Ballymeen), are the bed and well of St Farannán, a contemporary of Columcille and Mo-Laise of Inishmurray, who was celebrated for his austerities. Known as Alternan, the place was for centuries a centre of pilgrimage where man and beast were cured. Alternan figures in the 12th c. tale *Buile Shuibhne*.

DRUMCLIFF, Co. Sligo (Map 7, K1), is a hamlet where the Sligo ($4\frac{1}{2}$ m.)–Bundoran (18 m.) road crosses the Cowney or Drumcliff River.

SE. of the Cowney bridge the main road cuts through the site of a monastery (partially excavated) which was founded, tradition asserts, by Columcille himself. Of the monastery there survive (Nat. Mons.) the stump of a Round Tower (on the W. side of the road) and, in the Catholic graveyard, the shaft of a tall, plain, stone cross, as well as a figured High Cross (9th c.?) The sculptures of the latter include subjects from the Old and New Testaments (*The Fall of Adam and Eve, David Decapitates Goliath, Daniel in the Lions' Den, The Crucifixion*, etc.). Two fragments of another cross are now in the National Museum in Dublin.

In the Protestant churchyard is the grave of the poet William Butler Yeats (1865–1939), at his own request buried there (where his grandfather had been vicar, 1811–46), in the heart of a countryside he knew and loved so well and of which he sang in some of his loveliest lyrics. He died at Roquebrune in the south of France, but his remains were brought home by naval vessel in 1948. The epitaph is his own composition.

2 m. NE. rise the precipitous slopes of flat-topped Ben Bulben (1,750 ft) and Slievemore (1,527 ft), whose flora include *Arenaria ciliata* and *Saxifraga nivalis*. It was on the slope of Ben Bulben that Díarmait Ó Duibhne, lover of Gráinne, was supposed to have met his tragic fate at the hands of the vengeful Fionn Mac Cumhail.

4 m. E., is Glencar, which lies between Slievemore and Truskmore to the N. and Crockauns to the S. In the valley are a small lake and the cascades of Sruth-i-naghaidh-an-áird – which fling themselves over the cliffs of Tormore in three wind-tossed leaps – and (1 m. further E.) Corglass.

DRUMCOLLIHER, Co. Limerick (Map 5, I1), is a village on the Newcastle (9 m.)–Mallow (17 m.) road.

3 m. SW., at Tullylease, Co. Cork, are remains (Nat. Mon.) of an early monastery and its Augustinian successor. The monastery was founded by the 7th c. Anglo-Saxon saint, Berechert. The remains comprise: Berechert's Well and House; a bullaun; a nave-and-chancel church with 12th and 15th–16th c. work; and a number of early gravestones. Fragments of gravestones removed to the National Museum in Dublin are represented by cement casts.

The most important gravestone has an excellently incised cross and other patterns and bears the inscription: QUICUMQUAE HUNG TITULU[M] LEGERIT ORAT PRO BERECHTUINE ('Whoever reads this should pray for B.'). The cross resembles closely that on a well-known page of the early-8th c. *Book of Lindisfarne*, but it is not known if the stone commemorates the founder or a namesake who died in 839. St Berechert's name is still popular in the area in the form of Benjamin.

4 m. WSW. via Broadford, in Lacka Lower, are the remains (Nat. Mon.) of Killaliathan, alias Killagholehane, a church of various dates.

DRUMQUIN, Co. Tyrone (Map 1, C8), is a small village on the road between Castlederg (8 m.) and Dromore (9 m.). It was built by Sir John Davies *c.* 1617.

$1\frac{1}{2}$ m. W. are the ruins of Lackagh Church, with a holy well nearby.

$5\frac{1}{2}$ m. W., further along the same road and close to Lough Bradan Forest, is Ally court-tomb.

$1\frac{1}{2}$ m. NW., in Kirlisk, are the remains of Castle Curlews, a Plantation castle erected by Sir John Davies. 3 m. NW., in Killoan, is the Head Stone (Hist. Mon.), the base of a stone cross. One side of the Head Stone is decorated with four panels of rude spirals.

DRUMSHANBO, Co. Leitrim (Map 7, M3), is a village at the S. end of Lough Allen, 11 m. N. of Carrick-on-Shannon.

5½ m. NNE., in Cleighran More, is Cromlech, a court-tomb.

6 m. NW., on either side of the Arigna valley, Co. Roscommon, are coal-pits where small-scale mining is carried on. They supply, among other things, a small power station.

DRUMSNA, Co. Leitrim (Map 7, M4), is a village where the Longford (17 m.)–Carrick-on-Shannon (3 m.) road crosses the Shannon. The Dún, a remarkable, and possibly prehistoric, earthwork, ½ m. long, cuts off the great loop in the Shannon between Drumsna and Jamestown. The main work consists of a great ditch and bank and had only one entrance.

DUBLIN, Co. Dublin (Map 3, K3), at the mouth of the River Liffey, is the capital of Ireland and the seat of government of the Republic. It is a cathedral and university city and, after Belfast, the second largest port and manufacturing centre in the island. Sited at the head of a lovely bay, where the fertile Central Lowland meets the sea by the foot of the Dublin–Wicklow mountain massif, it lies within easy reach of many delightful beauty spots, excellent beaches, and lonely mountain moors. From the point of view of architecture and layout it is one of Europe's beautiful capitals. As befits a city with a distinguished tradition in letters, the sciences, and the arts, it has good libraries, theatres, museums, and art galleries. Few cities of its size offer so many and so varied opportunities for outdoor enjoyment: golf-courses, race-courses, sailing, bathing, fishing, hunting, and sporting clubs of every kind.

HISTORY

Though human settlement on and about the site of the city goes back to remote prehistoric times, and there were several churches and monasteries in the area in the early historic period, the story of Dublin as a city does not begin until A.D. 841, when Norse Vikings constructed a defended shipstead by the Black Pool (Duibhlinn, Norse Dyfflin, whence English Dublin) below a hurdled ford (*áth cliath*, whence the Gaelic name of the town, Baile Átha Cliath) which carried an ancient highway across the Liffey. In 852/3 the settlement was reinforced by fresh Norse arrivals led by Olaf the White, who constructed a small fortified town on the steep ridge where Christchurch and Dublin Castle now stand. Within a century the town overlooking the Liffey had become the capital of a little Norse pirate and trading kingdom (Dyfflinarskiri, Dublinshire) which never reached westwards further than Leixlip and Clondalkin, but which at its maximum extended northwards to include most of the modern Co. Dublin and stretched southwards as a narrow coastal fringe as far as Wicklow or Arklow. Until 1042 Dublinshire was ruled, with few interruptions, by descendants of Ivarr (Olaf's successor), who made it their base for piratical, commercial, and dynastic enterprises in the Scottish islands, Man and northern England. (In 873 there began a long-drawn-out, intermittent struggle between Dublin and York, whose Danish rulers belonged to the same family as Dublin's.) The last Irish effort to expel the Norse from Dublin ended in the disastrous 'Battle of Dublin' fought at Cell Mo-Shámhóg (Islandbridge) by the Liffey, where Niall Black-knee, King of Tara, was slain, A.D. 919. Thereafter Dublin assumed more and more the character of a useful trading centre, became more and more susceptible to Gaelicization, and gradually found an accepted place in the Gaelic polity. On Good Friday 1014 in the celebrated Battle of Clontarf, the Norse of Dublin, allied with Leinster and strongly reinforced from overseas, were destroyed by Brian Boru. Norse Dublinshire lived on, however, under its half-Irish, half-Danish ruler, Sigtryggr Silkbeard (who reigned until 1036), and it was probably only after Clontarf that it entered on its most prosperous phase (Sigtryggr was the first ruler in Ireland to issue a coinage, which was modelled on that of Æthelræd II of England). It was now, too, that the inhabitants finally abandoned heathenism, and that Sigtryggr founded Dublin's first cathedral, Christchurch (probably after a pilgrimage to Rome in 1028). The first bishop, Dunan, was an Irishman, but Sigtryggr sent him for consecration to England.

By this date the little walled town had, doubtless, attained to the size and form it was to keep until the 14th c.: about 700 yds from E. to W. (i.e. from Cork Hill to Cornmarket) and less than 300 yds from N. to S. (i.e. from about the line of Cook St and West Essex St to that of Little Ship St and the S. side of Dublin Castle). Excavations carried out in the 1960s and 1970s have revealed the richness of the archaeological remains in the town, with well-preserved timber and wattle houses, and a town wall (*see also p. 166*).

After Sigtryggr's death his dynasty died out, and the power and status of Dublin's Scandinavian rulers declined as the town came under the domination of Leinster and Munster kings in turn. At the opening of the 12th c. the immediate rulers of Dublin were the new Norse dynasts, who ranked merely as earls and who remained subject to one or other of the Irish over-kingdoms until the coming of the Anglo-Normans. In 1166 Dublin acknowledged the high-kingship of Rory O Conor of Connacht, and joined with him the following year in driving Dermot Mac Murrough overseas. When Dermot had secured the help of Anglo-Norman adventurers, Dublin was one of the first places against which he turned, and on 21 September 1170 he and his hirelings seized the town by treachery. On Dermot's death, his Anglo-Norman lieutenant and son-in-law, Richard Strongbow, set himself up as heir to Leinster (including Dublin) in defiance of Irish law, and was strong enough to impose his claim on both Norse Dublin and the Irish High-King. A year later Henry II of England gathered a great army to prevent Strongbow from setting up an independent kingdom in Ireland. One of his first steps was to force Strongbow to surrender Dublinshire and the maritime towns of Leinster to the English Crown. From that date until 1922 Dublin was to remain the citadel and key base of England's fluctuating power in Ireland. Henry spent the winter of 1171–2 in the town, where he received the formal submission of several trusting Irish princes. Before his departure he granted the town to 'his men of Bristol', with the free customs and liberties of their native city. About the same time the surviving Norse, by now fairly thoroughly Gaelicized, removed themselves (or were removed) to Oxmantown, N. of the Liffey where, by the 14th c., they had ceased to be a distinct element in the population.

Apart from a 1312 extension N. to the river, the walled town of Dublin hardly grew at all during the Middle Ages. Within the walls the principal buildings were the castle, Christchurch, and the parish churches, and outside them lay St Patrick's Cathedral, and a number of abbeys, friaries and hospitals.

The Reformation, the wars of the 17th c., and neglect dealt hardly with Dublin's medieval heritage. At the close of the Cromwellian period the town wall, with its eight gates and nine towers, was in poor repair; the castle was 'the worst in Christendom'; the cathedrals and parish churches were ruinous; the abbeys and friaries were gone. The population, too, had decayed, city and suburbs between them mustering no more than 9,000 souls. The next 140 years were to witness a remarkable transformation. By 1800 the population was climbing to 200,000, and the city had spread in all directions; notably to the NE. and SE., where a splendidly planned series of noble squares and thoroughfares provided the worthy setting for superb public buildings and magnificent private houses embellished by the skill of stucco workers, stone-carvers, wood-carvers, painters, glassmakers, silversmiths, and other craftsmen. These spectacular developments were the outward expression of the sense of security of the new Protestant ascendancy, supplanters of the ancient Catholic aristocracy, Gaelic and Old English, destroyed by the conquests of the 17th c. Their culmination coincided with the assertion of that ascendancy's legislative independence of England. When that independence was sold in 1800 for cash, titles, and the prospect of enduring ascendancy, Dublin's brief glory dimmed and a long, slow decline set in.

When the Union caused the great landowners to abandon Dublin, and brought about the decay of Irish industry and commerce, the lot of the masses went from bad to worse. Then came the famines and land clearances of the 19th c. Ever-renewed hordes of the homeless and penniless crowded into Dublin, where one splendid street after another degenerated into slum. Only in our own time, and as a result of social and political revolutions, has the process of decay been stopped, the wheel turned back. In the interval Dublin had lost much of her treasure. Nonetheless enough of greatness survives to make the city even yet a capital of uncommon beauty.

By far the largest part of Dublin's 18th c. building was devoted to secular purposes, for the State Church had money only for its prelates, and the law confined the Catholic Church to humble back-lane retreats. Dublin's 60 or 70 Catholic churches are all buildings of the 19th and 20th c. At first the Classical tradition still prevailed, and gave the city several churches of merit. In due course the Gothic Revival killed that tradition, but itself gave Dublin a couple of good churches. Since then the standard of ecclesiastical architecture in the capital has fallen, though a few noteworthy exceptions were built in the city's suburbs after the Second Vatican Council.

The tale of 19th and 20th c. secular building (and street planning) follows a more or less parallel course, good work continuing to be done until as late as the 1860s or 1870s. Unfortunately, most of Dublin's recent suburban development, municipal or private, does little credit to the city's taste. It may be that the worst is now over, at least in the industrial and commercial spheres, where occasional buildings like the Central Bus Station, Dublin Airport, the new library in Trinity College, the headquarters of the country's two major banks and some of the suburban factories, raise hopes of a future not unworthy of the past. If these hopes are to be realized, the Dublin craftsmen will need to resume their discarded skills.

Outstanding dates in Dublin's history

837	Norse arrive with fleet of 60 ships at the Liffey and make a settlement by the river.
841	Norse found a harbour-fort.
852/3	Foundation of fortified Norse town.
871	Ivarr the Boneless founds Dublin's Danish dynasty.
919	Battle of Dublin; Niall Glúndubh, King of Tara, routed and slain by Norse.
921	Sigtryggr of Dublin becomes ruler of York also.
937	Dublin burned by Donnchad Donn, King of Tara. Norse power begins to decline.
1014	Battle of Clontarf.
c. 1030	Dunan first Bishop of Dublin; foundation of first Christchurch.
1052–72	Dermot I of Leinster master of Dublin.
1072–1114	Dublin a dependency of the O Brien kings of Munster.
1096	Bishop Samuel O Hanly founds St Michan's Church to the N. of the Liffey.
1147	St Mary's Abbey, hitherto Savignian, becomes Cistercian.
1152	Dublin becomes one of Ireland's four archbishoprics.
1161/2	St Lorcán O Toole becomes archbishop.
1163	Dermot Mac Murrough of Leinster founds All Hallows and St Mary de Hogge.
1170	Dermot Mac Murrough recovers Dublin with help of Strongbow's Anglo-Normans.
1171	High-King Rory O Conor fails to expel Normans; last Norse earl slain.
1171/2	Henry II of England appropriates Dublin and grants town to Bristol men.
1173	Rebuilding of Christchurch commences.
1213	St Patrick's collegiate church becomes Dublin's second cathedral.
1213–28	Castle built.
1229	Henry III grants a new charter and the right to elect a mayor.
1312	City walls extended to river.
1317	Edward and Robert Bruce march on Dublin; the citizens set fire to the suburbs.
1348	The Black Death; 14 000 die in Dublin between August and Christmas.
1394–5	Richard II winters in Dublin and knights O Neill, O Brien, O Conor, and Mac Murrough in Christchurch, 25 March 1395.
1487	Lambert Simnel crowned as Edward VI of England in Christchurch.
1534	Silken Thomas Fitzgerald rebels, seizes city, but fails to capture castle.
1536	Anglo-Irish parliament acknowledges Henry VIII of England as King of Ireland and Head of the Church of Ireland.
1591	Foundation of Trinity College.
1641	An Irish plot to seize both the city and the castle ends in failure.
1647	Royalist Ormonde surrenders Dublin to Parliamentarians to prevent it falling into Confederate Catholic hands.

1649 Battle of Rathmines: Parliamentarians defeat Ormonde's attempt to recover the city. Landing of Cromwell.
1662. Ormonde returns as representative of Charles II; beginnings of modern Dublin.
1665 The Mayor of Dublin becomes Lord Mayor.
1667 Royal College of Physicians founded.
1680–1701 Royal Hospital, Kilmainham.
1689 The Patriot Parliament summoned by James II: 'the last legislative assembly of the older Irish race up to 1922, and the last in which the Roman Catholic faith was represented'.
1690 Dublin falls to William of Orange.
1714 The North Wall commenced; beginnings of the modern port of Dublin.
c. 1720 Luke Gardiner commences development of the Henrietta St–Gardiner St area as a fashionable quarter.
1729 New Parliament House begun.
1745 Leinster House begun.
c. 1750 Development of Merrion Square region begun.
1751–7 Rotunda Hospital.
1752–9 Parliament Square, Trinity College.
1757 Wide Streets Commissioners set up.
1774 Royal Exchange (later the City Hall).
1781–91 Custom House.
1782–3 England acknowledges independence of the Dublin Parliament.
1785 Royal Irish Academy founded.
1786–1800 The Four Courts built.
1800 Union of Ireland and Great Britain.
1802 Parliament House converted into Bank of Ireland.
1803 Robert Emmet's rebellion.
1814–18 General Post Office.
1815 Dublin's first post-Reformation Catholic church: St Michael's and St John's, on the Blind Quay.
1816 St Mary's 'Metropolitan Catholic Chapel', alias the Pro-Cathedral, Marlborough St.
1834 The Dublin and Kingstown Railway opened.
1840 Reform of Dublin Corporation, with consequent election (1841) of Daniel O Connell as first Catholic Lord Mayor.
1851 Catholic University of Ireland founded; John Henry Newman, Rector, 1853–8.
1865 International Exhibition, Earlsfort Terrace.
1881 Catholic University transformed into University College.
1908 National University of Ireland founded; University College granted a charter as a constituent college.
1913 Eight-month lock-out commences in August. Labour Movement founds the Citizen Army; Irish Republican Brotherhood and Eoin Mac Neill found the Irish Volunteers.
1916 Easter Week Rising of the Irish Volunteers and Citizen Army. Proclamation of the Irish Republic. General Post Office, together with Lower O Connell St and neighbouring streets, destroyed; Four Courts damaged by shell-fire.
1919 First Dáil Éireann meets in Mansion House.
1919–21 Armed struggle for independence; Dublin becomes the scene of almost constant guerrilla activities, during which the Custom House, among other buildings, is destroyed (1921).
1922 Dáil Éireann ratifies Anglo-Irish Treaty of 6 December 1921, setting up Irish Free State. British garrison withdraws. Civil War. Four Courts and Upper O Connell St destroyed.
1988 Dublin celebrates a (bogus) millennium, but brightens up the city in the process.

EMINENT DUBLINERS

The roll of illustrious Dubliners includes the names of:

Letters

Richard Stanyhurst (1547–1618), historian and Catholic theologian.

Sir James Ware (1594–1666), historian and antiquary.

Jonathan Swift (1667–1745), patriot, pamphleteer, satirist (*Gulliver's Travels*, etc.).

Sir Richard Steele (1672–1729), essayist, dramatist, and founder of the London *Tatler*.

Edmund Burke (1729–97), orator and political philosopher, champion of American liberties.

Edmund Malone (1741–1812), Shakespearean scholar.

Richard Brinsley Sheridan (1751–1816), actor and dramatist (*The School for Scandal, The Rivals, The Duenna*, etc.).

Thomas Moore (1779–1852), poet and adapter of traditional Irish airs (*Lallah Rookh, Moore's Melodies*).

Charles Robert Maturin (1782–1824), whose 'novels of terror' won the regard of Baudelaire and Balzac.

Samuel Lover (1797–1868), poet and novelist (*Handy Andy, Rory O Moore*, etc.).

Charles James Lever (1806–72), novelist (*Harry Lorrequer, Charles O Malley*).

Joseph Sheridan Le Fanu (1814–73), novelist (*The House by the Churchyard, In a Glass Darkly*, etc.).

William E.H. Lecky (1838–1903), historian.

Oscar Wilde (1854–1900), poet, wit, dramatist (*The Importance of Being Earnest, The Ballad of Reading Gaol, The Picture of Dorian Grey*, etc.).

John Millington Synge (1871–1909), dramatist (*The Playboy of the Western World, Deirdre of the Sorrows*, etc.).

George Bernard Shaw (1856–1950), wit, dramatist, Nobel Prize winner.

William Butler Yeats (1865–1939), poet, dramatist, Nobel Prize winner.

James Joyce (1882–1941), poet and writer (*Dubliners, A Portrait of the Artist as a Young Man, Ulysses, Finnegan's Wake*, etc.).

James Stephens (1882–1950), poet, author (*The Crock of Gold*).

Seán O Casey (1884–1964), dramatist (*The Plough and the Stars, Juno and the Paycock*, etc.).

Samuel Beckett (b. 1906), dramatist (*Waiting for Godot*, etc.).

Brendan Behan (1923–64), author and dramatist (*Borstal Boy*, etc.).

Tererce de Vere White (b. 1912), novelist.

Thomas Kinsella (b. 1928), poet.

Music

John Field (1782–1837), pianist and composer whose nocturnes inspired Chopin; he taught Glinka, founder of the Russian school.

Michael William Balfe (1808–70), conductor and composer of operas (*The Bohemian Girl, Il Talismano*).

Sir Charles Villiers Stanford (1852–1924), composer of opera, songs, chamber music and symphonies.

Painting

Edward Luttrell (1650–1710), painter and one of the earliest mezzotint engravers.

Nathaniel Hone I (1718–84), portrait painter and a founder member of the Royal Academy, London.

George Barret (1732–84), landscape painter and a founder member of the Royal Academy.

Robert Carver (1750–91), landscape painter.

Sir Martin Archer Shee (1769–1850), portrait painter.

William Sadler (1782–1839), landscape painter.

James Arthur O Connor (1791–1841), landscape painter.

Nathaniel Hone II (1831–1917), landscape and seascape painter, member of the celebrated Barbizon Group, and founder of the modern school of Irish painting.

Patrick Vincent Duffy (1836–1909), landscape painter.

John Butler Yeats (1839–1922), portrait painter; father of Jack Yeats and William Butler Yeats.

Walter Frederick Osborne (1859–1903), painter of field and street life.

Sir William Orpen (1870–1931), portrait painter.

Jack Butler Yeats (1871–1957), brother of W.B. Yeats.

Francis Bacon (b. 1909), expressionist.

Louis Le Brocquy (b. 1916), portrait heads, illustrator.

Patrick Collins (b. 1909), abstract painter.

Patrick Scott (b. 1921), abstract painter.

Edward McGuire (1932–87), portrait painter.

Robert Ballagh (b. 1943), realist painter.

Sculpture

Thomas Kirk (1777–1845).

John Henry Foley (1818–74).

Oisín Kelly (1916–1981).

Stained Glass

Michael Healy (1873–1941).

Harry Clarke (1889–1931).

Evie Hone (1894–1955), latest representative of the remarkable Hone dynasty of artists, and perhaps greatest of the trio whose work has spread the fame of Dublin glass.

Patrick Pollen (b. 1928).

Medicine

Abraham Colles (1773–1843), remembered for 'Colles's Law', 'Colles's Fracture', and 'Colles's Fuchsia'.

Sir Philip Crampton (1777–1858), surgeon. Co-author with Robert Graves of the bedside teaching which made the Dublin medical schools famous.

Robert Graves (1796–1853), who introduced bedside teaching into medical education. His *Clinical Lectures* was an international textbook.

Francis Rynd (1801–61), inventor of the hypodermic syringe.

Sir Dominic Corrigan (1802–80), specialist in diseases of the aorta; gave his name to 'Corrigan's Disease', 'Corrigan's Pulse'; inventor of 'Corrigan's Button'.

William Stokes (1804–78), author of *Diseases of the Chest* and *Diseases of the Heart and Aorta*. Also remembered for 'Stokes-Adams's Syndrome' and 'Cheyne-Stokes's Respiration'.

Sir William Wilde (1815–76), noted ophthalmologist, otologist, and archaeologist; father of Oscar Wilde. In medicine remembered for 'Wilde's Incision' and 'Wilde's Cord'.

Science

Sir William Rowan Hamilton (1805–65), discoverer of quaternions, whose work foreshadowed the quantum theory and recent discoveries in nuclear physics.

George Salmon (1819–1904), mathematician.

Sir Robert Stawell Ball (1840–1913), astronomer and mathematician.

George Francis Fitzgerald (1851–1901), mathematician.

E.T.S. Walton (b. 1903), Nobel Prize winner (1951) physicist; one of the first to split the atom.

STREET GUIDE

The streets and suburbs close to the city, and principal buildings, are listed below in alphabetical order.

Arran Quay, laid out *c.* 1680, lies between Inns Quay and Ellis Quay. Edmund Burke (1729–97) was born at No. 12.

St Paul's Church (1835–42) is a good building erected, with very slender resources, to the design of Patrick Byrne (1783–1864). The classical portico, surmounted by bell-tower and cupola, is a feature of Dublin's riverside architecture. The wall-painting behind the high altar was a good copy of Rubens's *Conversion of St Paul* until some 'itinerant dauber was permitted to introduce an incongruous figure into the centre'. Recently a vulgar, concrete 'Lourdes Grotto' has been heaped against one of the outer walls of the church.

Aughrim St runs from Manor St (continuation of Stoneybatter) to the N. Circular Rd. In the mortuary chapel of the Church of the Holy Family is a *Resurrection* window by Hubert McGoldrick.

Aungier St leads from South Great George's St to Redmond's Hill. No. 12 occupies the site of the house where Thomas Moore (1779–1852) was born. In the Calced Carmelite Priory Church (by George Papworth) the only feature of note is the 15th c. wooden statue of *Our Lady of Dublin*. Said to have come from St Mary's Abbey, this fine statue is displayed in a vulgar and utterly incongruous setting.

Back Lane runs from Cornmarket to Nicholas St. The Tailors' Hall (1704–8, by Robert Mills?), restored in 1971, is the sole survivor of Dublin's guild halls, and now serves as the headquarters of Au Taisce, the National Trust for Ireland. In 1792 the hall was the meeting place of the 'Back Lane Parliament', i.e. the Catholic Committee (*see p. 28*), whose secretary at the time was the Protestant 'father' of Irish republicanism, Wolfe Tone. The simple interior has a good wooden screen and staircase.

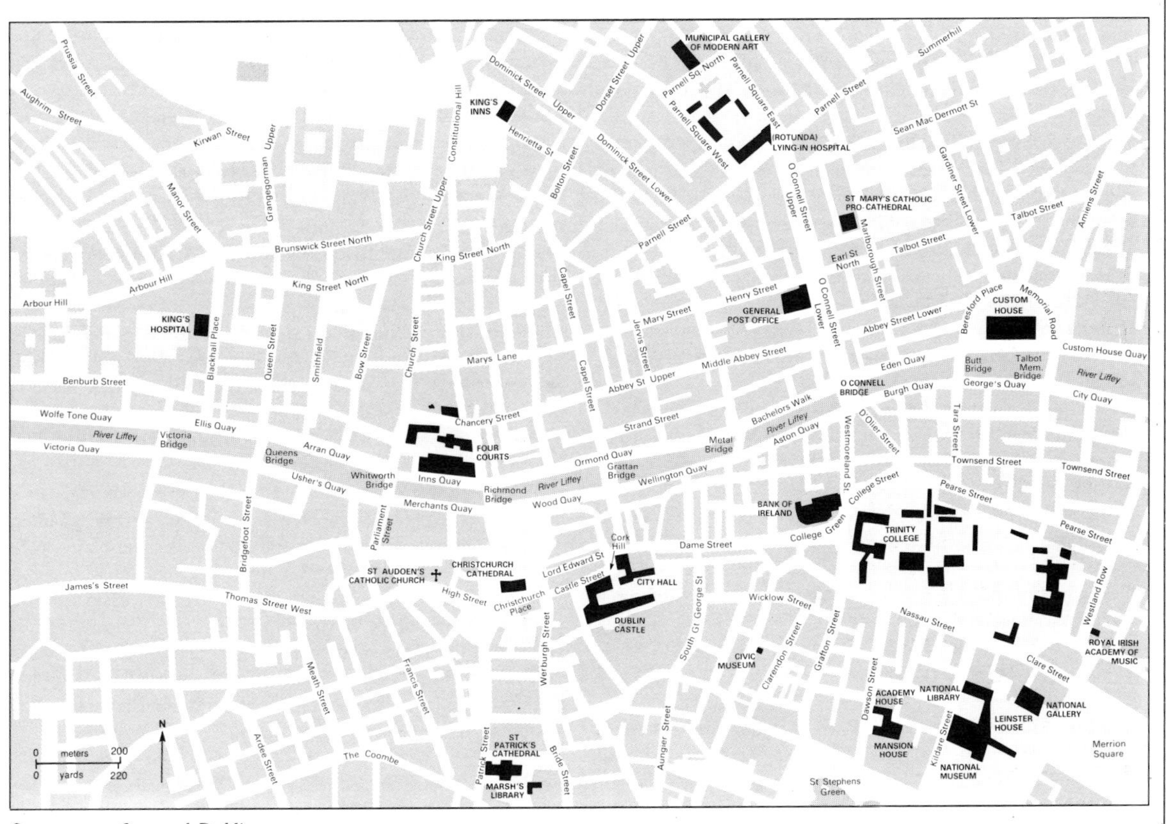

Street map of central Dublin.

Baggot St, Lower (1791), the ancient Baggotrath Lane, alias Gallows Lane, leads from Merrion Row to Upper Baggot St and Mespil Rd. Pleasant walks along the Grand Canal may be had from Baggot St Bridge. It takes its name from the Baggots, remains of whose castle of Baggotrath stood at the corner of Herbert St until the 19th c. The street is now dominated by the dark Bank of Ireland headquarters (1968–79) by Ronald Tallon. One of Europe's most rigorous examples in the style of Mies van der Rohe, the bank's three major blocks cluster round a slightly cramped forecourt, with a sculpture by Michael Bulfin. The bank houses a notable collection of modern Irish art. No. 67 Lower Baggot St was the home of Thomas Davis (1814–45), Young Ireland leader; No. 128 the home of the patriot brothers, John and Henry Sheares, executed in 1798. The Bórd Fáilte offices (1962), at the bridge, are by Michael Scott and Associates.

Ballsbridge, Dublin's diplomatic quarter and one of the city's finest suburbs, takes its name from the bridge spanning the Dodder on the Dublin–Merrion road. Formerly the township of Pembroke, the district is notable for its excellently planned streets and terraces of good houses. These date, for the most part, from *c.* 1830 to 1860, but retain the spacious dignity of the preceding age. The finest are probably Ailesbury Rd, Lansdowne Rd, Mespil Rd, Morehampton Rd, Pembroke Rd, Wellington Rd, and Upper Baggot St. On the W. side of the main Merrion road are the show-grounds and the headquarters of the Royal Dublin Society, though economic necessity may soon force it to move to a more rural location. The Society was founded in 1731 to promote the application of practical economics. Its first home was in Mecklenburgh St. In 1756 it moved to Shaw's Court; in 1766 to Grafton St; in 1815 to Leinster House, Kildare St (*see p. 155*). Its more important activities today include the publication of Scientific Proceedings, a world-famous Horse Show (August), a Spring Show (agricultural and industrial, May), and a winter series of chamber music recitals. On the opposite side of the street is the headquarters of Allied Irish Banks (1975–9), by Andrew Devane, consisting of eight interlinked building masses, brilliantly offset by Alexandra Wejchert's abstract steel structure *Freedom*. Like its competitor in Baggot St (*see above*), the building houses a noteworthy collection of modern Irish art.

In Lansdowne Rd is the headquarters stadium of the Irish Rugby Football Union, venue for international and other major matches.

The American Embassy (1963–4), at the junction of Pembroke Rd, and Clyde Rd, is by the American architect John McL. Johansen.

St Bartholomew's Church, Clyde Rd, has Catherine O Brien windows *St Patrick* (1925), *St George* (1926), *St Margaret of Scotland* (1938) and *Emmaus* (1941).

In Shrewsbury Rd is the Chester Beatty Library and Gallery of Oriental Art: a collection of Islamic, Far Eastern and Western manuscripts, bindings, prints and artefacts.

When Sir Alfred Chester Beatty, the American mining

millionaire died in 1968, he left this priceless collection to the Irish people. It is housed in two galleries – one opened in 1953, and the other enlarged and extended in 1973. The exhibitions change on a regular basis, and reflect the richness of some 40 years of collecting by Chester Beatty.

The Library has a major collection of Biblical papyri, containing some of the oldest-known witnesses to the New Testament and the Septuagint. There are also Egyptian and Coptic papyri as well as Mesopotamian day tablets.

The Islamic material consists of manuscripts and miniatures from Persia, India, Turkey and the Arab World. There is an important collection of Qur'ans from all over the Islamic world, and some 3,000 manuscripts covering the full range of secular and religious literature.

From Japan there is a comprehensive collection of woodblock prints together with fine scrolls and albums, while from China there is a collection of jade books, rhinoceros horn cups and snuff-bottles.

The Library has a small, but important collection of Western manuscripts. They include a *Rosarium* illustrated by Simon Bening and several fine 15th c. *Books of Hours*. There is a collection of prints by major European artists, including a substantial collection of Albrecht Dürer's work. There is also a collection of early-printed and fine colour-plate books.

There is no entrance charge.

Beresford Pl., at the junction of Eden Quay, Lower Abbey St, Gardiner St, Store St, and Custom House Quay, was laid out as a quadrant of matching houses to provide a setting for the Custom House. The achievement was successfully undone by the 1889 'Loop Line' overhead railway. The place is now dominated by the 1962–4 Liberty Hall, which was the first of the city-centre breaches in Dublin's Georgian skyline.

The magnificent Custom House (1781–91) is by James Gandon, London-born son of a Huguenot father and a Welsh mother, and pupil of Sir William Chambers. Gandon's masterpieces, the Custom House and Four Courts, remain even yet – time, war, and patriotism notwithstanding – the glories of Dublin's architecture. The Custom House was virtually burned out in 1921 when the I.R.A. set it on fire to disable the British civil administration, destroying valuable documents in the process. After the establishment of the Irish Free State it was reconstructed by the Office of Public Works, which radically altered the interior plan and made several significant changes in the exterior. Much more recently (1986–8), it undertook another major reconstruction of upper parts of the building, and successfully replaced stonework which had cracked. The black-faced clock is a reversion to the original design, though not of exactly the same size.

The sculptures of the Custom House are, for the most part, of remarkable quality. Until the great fire the pediment of the S. portico was crowned by allegorical statues of *Neptune, Mercury, Plenty*, and *Industry*, the two former by Agostino Carlini, the two latter by Edward Smyth. (Their loss, too, contributes to the weakening of the 'visual abutment' of the dome.) Smyth also did the colossal statue of *Commerce* which crowns the dome; the heads about the base of the dome; the allegorical sculpture (designed by Carlini) in the tympanum of the S. front (*Union of Britain and Ireland* – seated on a marine chariot drawn by seahorses, with Neptune banishing Famine and Despair); the admirable keystones (symbolizing the Atlantic Ocean and the thirteen principal rivers of Ireland) of the lower storey (on these he was assisted by Benjamin Schrowder from Winchelsea); the superb Arms of the Kingdom of Ireland on the end pavilions; and the ox-head frieze on the N. front. The mediocre statues of the N. front are by Joseph Banks of London; they represent the Quarters of the Globe. The Dublin Brigade memorial at the W. front is by the Breton sculptor Yann Renard-Goulet.

The nearby Bus Station, by Michael Scott and Associates (1953), is the first landmark in post-war architecture in Dublin.

Blackhall Pl. extends from Stoneybatter to Hendrick St. On the W. side is beautiful King's Hospital, alias the Bluecoat School, now the headquarters of the Incorporated Law Society, the governing body of the solicitors' profession in Ireland. It was built (1773 onwards) to the design of Thomas Ivory (1720–86), one of the best Irish architects of his day. When Parliament failed to vote the funds necessary for the completion of Ivory's designs, he resigned (1780). The ornamental carving is by Simon Vierpyl (who was in charge of the stonework); the plasterwork by Charles Thorp, Sen. The building was 'completed' by John Wilson. In 1894 the unfinished central tower was taken down, and the stunted cupola erected in its stead. The chapel (1777) is very good; the *Resurrection* window (1936) is by Evie Hone.

Blackhall Pl. and Blackhall St (down which King's Hospital faces) were laid out by Ivory on the site of Oxmanstown Green, a Viking settlement north of the Liffey.

Bridge St runs from Cornmarket to Whitworth (alias Father Matthew) Bridge. No. 9 was the house of Oliver Bond (1762–98), United Irishman. The Brazen Head Hotel, Dublin's oldest tavern (founded 1688), was a meeting place of the United Irishmen.

Castle St parallels Lord Edward St from Cork Hill to Christchurch Pl. Sir James Ware (1594–1666), noted Anglo-Irish antiquary, lived and died in Castle St. An Dubhaltach Mac Firbhisigh, last of an illustrious line of hereditary Gaelic scholars (*see p. 205*), worked for a time in his house. Castle St was the birthplace of Thomas Doggett (d. 1721), the actor who became joint manager of Drury Lane Theatre, London, and initiated the annual 'coat and badge' race of the Thames Watermen. At the E. end of the street are the Municipal Buildings, originally Newcomen's Bank. The oldest part, by Thomas Ivory, contains an elliptical room with fine painted ceiling. In 1856–8 the building was doubled in size by duplication of the E. elevation. The porched entrance was added at the same time. On the opposite side of the street are the fragments of the La Touche House of the early 1750s; a lovely stucco ceiling which graced the principal room has been re-erected in the Bank of Ireland (*see p. 147*). A dingy passage through Bristol Buildings is the present entrance to St Werburgh's Church, Werburgh St (open weekdays, 10 a.m.–4 p.m.). In its day one of the most attractive of Dublin's Protestant churches, this unfortunate building was erected in 1715, to the design of Thomas Burgh. Burned in 1754 and restored by John Smith (*c.* 1759), its spire and tower added in 1767 were taken down (1810 and 1836) at the instance of fearful Dublin Castle authorities. The interior was restored in the early 1960s. As the parish church of the castle, St Werburgh's served as Chapel Royal down to 1790. Hence the

Christ Church Cathedral, Dublin.

Lord Lieutenant's pew in the gallery, with Royal Arms inserted by Smith in 1767 when adding the upper, school-children's, gallery and the organ case. The curious, but attractive, wooden pulpit was carved by Richard Stewart to the designs of Francis Johnston. In the porch is preserved a 16th c. Fitzgerald tomb with effigies of an armoured knight and his lady and niched figures of the *Twelve Apostles*, etc. In the church vaults are buried Sir James Ware and Lord Edward Fitzgerald (*see p. 29*); in the churchyard, Lord Edward's captor, Town Major Sirr.

Christchurch Pl., formerly Skinners Row, at the intersection of Lord Edward St., High St, Nicholas St and Winetavern St, was the heart of the Norse and medieval cities. It is dominated by Christchurch Cathedral, cathedral church of the Protestant archdiocese of Dublin and Glendalough. The first cathedral (aisled) here was built about 1038 by Sigtryggr Silkbeard, king of Norse Dublin, but, about 1172, shortly after the Anglo-Norman conquest of the city, it was swept away and the crypt, choir, and transepts of a new, greater, church begun, in accordance with an agreement between the archbishop, St Laurence O Toole (1162–80) and Strongbow, Robert FitzStephen, and Raymond le Gros. An aisled five-bay nave was begun about 1212, and lengthened westwards by an additional bay about 1234. About the same period a new priory for the cathedral canons was erected on the S. side of the church, of which the walls of the chapter-house are still visible. In the second half of the 14th c. the choir was extended E. so as almost to equal the nave in length. At the same time the Chapel of Great St Mary, on the N. side of the choir, was rebuilt. In 1539 the Augustinian priory, founded by Laurence O Toole, was dissolved and replaced by a secular Dean and Chapter. On Easter Sunday, 1551, the English Protestant liturgy was read for the first time. In 1562 the nave vaulting collapsed, bringing down the S. wall, which was only crudely replaced. Neglect and decay during the 17th and 18th c. had reduced the church to a dangerous condition by 1829, when it had to be closed for repairs and alterations. These included the transference of the Norman door from the W. wall of the N. transept to its present position in the S. transept. Finally, between 1871 and 1878, the entire church was savagely 'restored' by George Edmund Street, one of the best English Gothic Revivalists, at the expense of Henry Roe, a wealthy Dublin distiller. Street swept away the great 14th c. choir and built a new E. arm on the plan of the 12th c. crypt. He also built the present Chapter House, rebuilt the tower and S. nave arcade, refaced most of the exterior, removed the N. porch, and added the flying buttresses and the baptistry. Street also built the adjacent Synod Hall (incorporating the bell-tower of St Michael and all Angels) and linked it to the cathedral by the attractive covered footbridge spanning the roadway of St Michael's Hill. The great complex is, therefore, as it stands today, in large part a Gothic-Revival work. It has, none the less, real architectural merit, which can no longer be fully appreciated since the building of the Civic Offices to the N.

As the principal church of the old English colony in Ireland, intimately associated with the viceregal court and the civic life of Dublin, Christchurch was the scene of many stirring events. Down to the 16th c. it was there that the Lord Deputies took the oath of office. It was there, too, that Lambert Simnel was crowned Edward VI of England, 24 May 1487, his crown a golden circlet from the statue of the Blessed Virgin Mary in St Mary's Abbey (*see p. 140*). In 1608 the semi-ruined priory buildings were turned into law-courts. In 1695 the first Four Courts were erected by Sir William Robinson, probably on the remains of the early 17th c. structure. These structures were all swept away in 1821 to open up the S. side of the Cathedral to view for the first time. During the 1980s, the Cathedral has been admirably conserved, and provided with a new organ.

Of the surviving medieval portions of the cathedral, the most remarkable is the groin-vaulted crypt, the only one of its age (12th/13th c.) in these islands to extend under an entire church. Here are many medieval mouldings, gravestones, etc.; likewise statues (1684), by William de Keyser, of Charles II and James II, which adorned the Tholsel, pulled down in 1806. (These are the oldest secular statues in Dublin.) The most interesting features of the cathedral itself are the late-12th to early-13th century Transitional transepts (which retain their original choir-aisle arches and chapels), the W. arches of the choir, and the arcade capitals and upper parts of the N. nave wall. (For all its originality of detail, the nave was very much a West English building, the work of imported masons and carvers.) The monuments include: W. Wall of Nave: Sir Samuel Auchmuty (d. 1822) by Thomas Kirk, R.H.A.; S. Nave Arcade: the tomb effigies of a FitzOsbert knight (*c.* 1260–1320) and a demi-figure, perhaps a visceral monument commemorating the burial of Strongbow's bowels in Dublin; Chapel of St Laud, where hangs the iron casket containing the heart of St Laurence, brought home *with solemn* rejoicing in 1180; on the floor nearby is the medieval effigy of a crowned lady found under the floor of the 13th c. chapter-house ruins; St Laurence Chapel: a slab with an effigy of Archbishop Comyn; note the stained glass window of *The Virgin and Child with St Luke* by Patrick Pollen (1966) in memory of Catherine O Brien. S. Transept: very fine monument of Robert, 19th Earl of Kildare (1674–1743), by Henry Cheere (1703–81); a Renaissance mural monument with kneeling effigies of Francis Agard of Newcastle, Co. Wicklow, and his daughter, Lady Cecilie Harrington; SE. apsidal chapel: a medieval effigy; S. Porch: a 1751–6 Prior monument by John Van Nost, Jr.

Church St leads from Inns Quay to North King St. St Michan's Protestant Church was built in 1685–6, but drastically restored in 1828. There is a 13th c. episcopal effigy in the chancel. Handel is said to have used the Renatus Harris organ during his Dublin visit. The church has a window *Our Lord Quelling the Tempest* by Catherine O Brien (1909). The 17th c. vaults happen to be constructed of magnesium limestone, which absorbs moisture. The resultant dryness of the atmosphere tends to 'mummify' corpses buried there. Viewing them is one of Dublin's macabre entertainments for tourists.

College Green, at the junction of Westmoreland St, Dame St, and Grafton St, is the last relic of the wide Hoggen Green which lay outside the E. wall of the medieval town.

On the E. side is Trinity College – 'The College of the Holy and Undivided Trinity near Dublin' – founded in 1592 by Elizabeth I, at the insistance of the Protestant establishment, so as to reduce the numbers seeking higher education in France, Italy, and Spain, 'whereby they have been infected by popery'. The college occupies the site of the Augustinian priory of All Hallows, founded by Dermot Mac Murrough of Leinster.

Until the 1960s, Trinity remained essentially Protestant and English in spirit, but the majority of its 7,000 students are now Irish Catholics. The roll of famous Trinity men includes the names of William Congreve (1670–1729, English-born of English parents), George Farquhar (1678–1707, Derry-born of English parents), Oscar Wilde (1854–1900), John Millington Synge (1871–1909), and Samuel Beckett (b. 1906), dramatists; Jonathan Swift (1667–1745, Dublin-born of English parents), satirist, patriot, and political pamphleteer; Theobald Wolfe Tone (1763–98), Henry Grattan (1746–1820), Robert Emmet (1778–1803), Thomas Davis (1814–45), John Mitchel (1815–75), James Clarke Luby (1821–1901), and Isaac Butt (1813–79), patriots; George Berkeley (1685–1753), philosopher; Oliver Goldsmith (1728–74), poet; Edmund Burke (1729–97), orator and political philosopher; Sir William Rowan Hamilton (1805–65), mathematician; George Francis Fitzgerald (1851–1901) and Ernest Thomas Sinton Walton (Nobel Prize winner), physicists; John Joly (1857–1933), geologist and inventor; Lord Clare (1749–1802), one of the architects of the Union; Lord Carson (1854–1935), leader of the Protestant, Unionist resistance to Home Rule.

The college buildings were reconstructed on a grand scale in the 18th c., and extended in the 19th, so that practically nothing survives of earlier date than 1700.

The Palladian façade, College Green, is attributed to Theodore Jacobsen. The statues of Edmund Burke and Oliver Goldsmith, like the statue of Henry Grattan (1874) at the centre of College Green, are by John Henry Foley (1808–74).

The W. square (1752–9) is called Parliament Sq. because the Dublin parliament defrayed most of the cost. Its wings terminate in externally identical buildings by Sir William Chambers. That on the S. side (begun 1777) is the Theatre (examination hall), that on the N. (begun 1787) the Chapel. The Theatre has one of the best interiors in the college, with stucco by Michael Stapleton (d. 1801). It contains an organ case built in Dublin by Lancelot Pease in 1684; also a fine monument to Provost Baldwin, carved in Rome about 1771–82 by Christopher Hewetson of Kilkenny (1739?–98). The gilt oak chandelier is from the House of Commons on the north side of College Green. The Chapel has good stucco (by Michael Stapleton) and woodwork; also dreadful 19th c. stained glass. The 17th c. plate survives. NE. of the Chapel is the Dining Hall (Richard Cassels, 1745–9), shortly afterwards rebuilt by other hands and sensitively restored after a fire in 1984. In it are displayed portraits of George III as Prince of Wales (by Hudson), Adam Loftus, first Provost of the college, Henry Grattan, and members of the college who attained to high office under the British regime. Adjoining the W. side of the Dining Hall is the exciting three-storey wooden Atrium by de Blacam and Meagher (1986), an excellent example of the modern woodworker's craft.

The belfry (1853) is alleged to mark the position of the crossing of the medieval priory church of All Hallows. Flanking it are statues of William Hartpole Lecky (1838–1903; historian), by Sir William G. John, and of Provost George Salmon (1819–1904; Protestant theologian), by John Hughes (1911). Behind the latter is *Reclining Connected Forms* by Henry Moore (1969).

Georgian doorway, Upper Fitzwilliam St, Dublin.

Dublin's Mansion House, Dawson St (see page 148).

On the E. side of Library Sq. are the Rubrics, a range of brick apartments dating from 1700. On the S. side is the great Library (1712–32) by Thomas Burgh. The ground floor, designed as an open loggia to insulate the library above from the marshy ground below, was unfortunately glazed in 1892 to provide increased storage space. The roof-line, too, has been altered; it was originally masked by the parapet balustrade. The W. pavilion has rococo plaster by Edward Semple; the staircase (1750) is by Cassels. The splendid Long Room on the first floor was altered in 1857 by Benjamin Woodward, who added the bookcases in the gallery and replaced the flat ceiling with a barrel vault. The busts which adorn the room include *Swift* by Roubilliac, *Dr Patrick Delany* by Van Nost, *Thomas Parnell* and *Dr Clements* by Edward Smyth.

The Library houses Ireland's greatest collection of books, manuscripts, and historical papers. The more remarkable treasures include:

Codex Primus Usserianus, a mutilated 7th c. Irish gospel book ('Old Latin' text).

The *Book of Durrow*, an important 7th c. illuminated gospel book from the Columban monastery of Durrow, Co. Offaly (*see p. 297*).

The *Book of Kells*, most famous of insular illuminated gospel books, dating from the late-8th or early-9th c. It was for long the chief treasure of the Columban monastery of KELLS, Co. Meath, though some think it may have been written and painted in the celebrated Columban monastery of Iona, in Scotland.

The *Book of Dímma*, an 8th or 9th c. illuminated gospel book from the ancient monastery of ROSCREA. Its silver-plated bronze case was made *c.* 1150 for Tadg O Carroll of Éile.

The *Book of Mulling*, a 7th c. illuminated gospel book (9th c. additions) from the monastery of ST MULLINS, Co. Carlow.

The *Garland of Howth*, an 8th–9th c. illuminated gospel book from Ireland's Eye, HOWTH.

The *Book of Armagh*, a 9th c. gospel book which contains the only surviving early Irish copy of the complete New Testament. It also has an important collection of Patrician documents, including a copy of the saint's famous *Confessio*, perhaps transcribed from the original draft.

The so-called *Book of Leinster*, an important Irish literary codex compiled in the monastery of Terryglass (*see p. 266*) some time between 1151 and 1224, and long preserved in the monastery of Núachongbháil, Co. Laois (*see p. 285*).

Also worthy of notice is the Library's fine, medieval, Irish harp ('Brian Boru's Harp').

To the S. of Burgh's Library is Fellows' Square (with *Cactus* by Alexander Calder, 1967), on the other side of which is the Arts block by Paul G. Koralek (1978); this includes the Douglas Hyde Gallery. Between Burgh's Library and the Museum Buildings (*below*) is the new library (1964–6), also by Koralek. In front of the entrance is *Sphere and Sphere*, a sculpture by Arnaldo Pomodoro (1987).

E. of the Rubrics is New Sq., bounded on the N. and E. by mechanical 1843 essays in the 18th c. manner. At the NW.

corner is the Printing House, a little Doric temple built in 1734 by Richard Cassels for John Stearne, Bishop of Clogher, who left his collections of books and manuscripts to the college. On the S. side are the interesting Museum Buildings (1853–5), by Benjamin Woodward (1815–61) of the firm of (Sir Thomas) Deane and Woodward (architects also of the Kildare Street Club on the opposite side of College Park). This, 'the finest secular building the Gothic Revival ever produced', houses the engineering and geological departments. The delightful carvings are the work of the brothers John and James Shea. The interior has been recently remodelled, but the excellent domed entrance-and-staircase hall survives. Ruskin was so pleased with this building that he commissioned Woodward and his stonecarvers for the Oxford Museum.

S. of Parliament Sq. and facing the N. end of Grafton St is the Provost's House (1759), the only one of Dublin's great Georgian houses still serving its original purpose. The designer of the house is unknown, but the façade is an adaptation of that by Lord Burlington for General Vade's house in London (now demolished).

On the N. side of College Green is the Bank of Ireland, a post-Union transformation of the beautiful Parliament House built between 1729 and 1739 to the design of Sir Edward Lovett Pearce (1699?–1733) and enlarged between 1785 and 1794 by James Gandon and Robert Parke. Of Pearce's work the most important survivals are the superb Ionic 'piazza' and projecting gallery-pavilions facing College Green, the House of Lords, and the corridor surrounding the altered House of Commons. The only external sculpture here in Parliament's time was the royal arms of the central pediment (by John Houghton, who also carved the capitals of the colonnade). Between 1785 and 1789, the building was extended eastwards by James Gandon, who erected the E. front, with its magnificent Corinthian portico, and joined it to Pearce's work by an austere, niched, quadrant screen devoid of columns or balustrade. Gandon's great portico, designed as a new, major entrance to the House of Lords, opens on to a vestibule, which in turn gives on to a delightfully chaste little rotunda, and thence on to a corridor skirting the N. side of the House of Lords. Edward Smyth carved the now eroded statues of *Minerva* (*Wisdom*), *Justice*, and *Liberty* over the portico. Before Gandon's work was completed, the Commons' accommodation was extended westwards to Foster Place. This task, carried out between 1787 and 1794, was entrusted to Robert Parke, who balanced Gandon's work by a new W. front (with Ionic portico), which he linked to Pearce's front by an open quadrant 'piazza' of balustraded, free-standing columns set in advance of a niched screen.

Pearce's House of Commons was a noble, octagonal, domed chamber. In 1792 it was destroyed by fire, and replaced by an inferior, circular chamber designed by Vincent Waldré. The last session of Parliament held in College Green ended 2 August 1800, and in 1802 the British Government sold the buildings to the Bank of Ireland. Francis Johnston (1761–1829) was chosen to make the transformation into a bank. Johnston blocked up the windows and central doorway of Pearce's 'piazza' and added the statues of *Commerce, Hibernia*, and *Fidelity* to the portico. (These were designed by Flaxman, but carved by Edward Smyth and his son, John.) He replaced the Commons' and Lords' entrance halls by the present W. and E. halls; the stucco, which blends with that of Pearce's corridors, is by Charles Thorp. Johnston replaced Waldré's House of Commons by the Bank Board Room, Governor's Office, and Accountant General's Office. (The stucco of the Board Room ceiling is by Thorp.) Externally, Johnston's most significant alterations were to the quadrant screens: he abolished Parke's 'piazza' by bringing the screen forward and re-erecting it between the columns, and replaced Gandon's screen by the existing balustraded-and-niched screen with engaged columns. He also added the monumental guardhouse gateways in Foster Place.

Since Johnston's time the only significant addition to the building has been the great gateway (1860) in Westmoreland St. The principal showpiece of the building today is Pearce's House of Lords. It contains a magnificent Dublin glass chandelier (1,233 pieces) of 1788 and two tapestries (1733) by Robert Baillie, probably to the design of Johann van der Hagen; also the original mantelpiece (1748/9), a fine example of Dublin work of its period, and the House of Commons Mace (London-made, 1765). In the Directors' Luncheon Room is a very fine rococo ceiling of the early 1750s from La Touche's House in Castle St. The subject is *Venus Wounded by Love*, the artist unknown.

The College Green memorial (1966) to Thomas Davis, Young Ireland leader, is by Edward Delaney.

The entire College Green block between Foster Pl. and Anglesea St was formerly filled by Richard Johnston's first (1790) Dublin building, Daly's Club, founded in 1750 by Patrick Daly, and closed down in 1823. Johnston's clubhouse, 'the most superb gambling house in the world', consisted of a lofty, pilastered, central block with plain, slightly lower, side wings. The central block survives in a mutilated form.

Constitution Hill leads from Church St to Dominick St. On the E. side are the King's Inns (*see p. 153*). Just off the Hill is Broadstone Station (1841–50), an unusually fine example of early railway architecture by John Skipton Mulvany (now a bus depot).

Cork Hill is the short street linking Castle St with the junction of Dame St and Parliament St. It takes its name from the Earl of Cork's house, which stood beside Lucas's Coffee House on the site of the present City Hall.

The City Hall (1769–79) was erected as the Royal Exchange by Thomas Cooley (1740–84; of London?), whose design was chosen in open competition with the architects of Great Britain and Ireland. (The rest of Cooley's life was spent in Dublin.) The principal feature of his Exchange was a noble, domed and colonnaded rotunda, designed as the meeting place of Dublin's merchants. The ponderous balustrade in front of the entrance steps is an 1814 replacement of the original iron railings. All the ornamental carving in the building was done by Simon Vierpyl. The statues displayed in the rotunda include: an excellent baroque *Charles Lucas* by Edward Smyth; *Henry Grattan*, by Sir Francis Chantrey; *Daniel O Connell, Thomas Davis* and *Thomas Drummond* by John Hogan. In the Muniment Room are stored municipal archives going back to the 12th c., and also the civic regalia. These include the Lord Mayor's great gold S-collar presented by William III and a great sword, probably the gift of Henry IV.

Just beside the City Hall is a park (established 1987), with statues thought to represent three of the Dublin guilds, and formerly part of the façade of the Royal University of Ireland in

Earlsfort Terrace (*see p. 150*). The park includes the birthplace of Dr Barnardo, who did so much to care for children.

Besides Cork House and Lucas's Coffee House, old Cork Hill was also the site of the Eagle Tavern, meeting place of the notorious Hell Fire Club founded in 1735 by the first Earl of Rosse and others. One of the members set fire to their place of carousal so as to savour the sensations of the damned!

Behind the City Hall is Dublin Castle (*see p. 149*).

Crow St, between Dame St and Temple Bar, was famous in its day for the Theatre Royal of which 'Buck' Whaley (*see p. 165*) was a patentee. Among the stars who appeared on the theatre's boards was Peg Woffington.

Dame St, Dublin's principal commercial and insurance street, runs from College Green to Cork Hill. The street was widened in 1785–6 by the Commissioners for Making Wide and Convenient Streets, the enlightened planning authority (1757–1840) to which Dublin owes so much. The best building in the street today is Edward Parke's Commercial Buildings (1796–9; windows mutilated), re-erected at right angles to the street when the Central Bank built its new headquarters (by Sam Stephenson) in 1976–7. The Bank had to be reduced by one storey when it was discovered that it had exceeded its permitted height; even now it ruins the skyline, particularly when the Bank of Ireland is viewed from College St. The Munster and Leinster Bank, at the corner of Palace St, is by Sir Thomas Deane; enlarged some years ago. There are also fine Victorian bank and other buildings in the same street. At the junction with South Great George's St is *The Chair* (1988), a sculpture by Carolyn Mulholland.

Dawson St (*c.* 1705) links Nassau St and St Stephen's Green, N. In its heyday it was a fashionable residential street. The Mansion House (1705), official residence of the Lord Mayor since 1715, is a good Queen Anne house of brick, spoiled by stucco, balustrade (replacing figure-subject panels), windows and other Victoriana. There are some good portraits there, including the 1st Duke of Northumberland (1742–86), by Reynolds. The Round Room was run up in 1821 by John Semple (architect of the 'Black Church', Mary Pl.) for a ball and banquet in honour of George IV, and has served ever since as a public hall. It was there that the first Dáil Éireann assembled on 21 January 1919, to adopt Ireland's Declaration of Independence and ratify the proclamation of the Irish Republic by the insurgents of 1916.

No. 19, Academy House, originally Northland House, was built in 1770 for the Knox family of Dungannon, probably by John Ensor, architect of the Rotunda, Parnell Sq. (*see p. 160*). The interior contains some notable plasterwork. In 1852 the house was acquired by the Royal Irish Academy. Founded in 1783 and granted a royal charter in 1785, the Academy is Ireland's foremost learned society, still recruiting its membership from the whole island. Its *Transactions, Proceedings*, and other publications include notable contributions to Science and Mathematics as well as to 'Polite Literature and Antiquities'. Its magnificent collection of Irish antiquities now forms the nucleus of the National Museum's collection, but the Academy's library, with a remarkable collection of Irish manuscripts, still remains in Academy House. The more important treasures include: the *Cathach*, 6th or 7th c. manuscript of the Psalter, possibly written by St Columcille (*see p. 59*); *Lebor na hUidre*, Book of the Dun Cow, an 11th–12th c. literary codex compiled at CLONMACNOIS; the *Stowe Missal*, an 8th–9th c. Mass-book which belonged to the monastery of LORRHA; the *Leabhar Breac*, Speckled Book, an early-15th c. liturgical codex (*see p. 172*); the *Book of Ballymote* (*see p. 65*), *Leabhar Úa Maine*, and the *Book of Lecan* (*see p. 205*), 14th–15th c. literary codices; and a holograph text of the *Annals of the Four Masters* (1632–6).

St Ann's Church (Protestant), despite its 1868 'Romanesque' façade by Sir Thomas Deane, remains essentially the 1720–1 church of unusual quality by Isaac Wills. The Elizabeth Phibbs memorial (S. gallery) is by Edward Smyth, of Custom House and Four Courts fame. The *Charity* (1913), *St Christopher* (1916), and *Michael* (1918) windows are by Wilhelmina Geddes, one of the first of the Dublin stained glass artists; she worked in London for many years.

D'Olier St (*c.* 1800) leads from O Connell Bridge to the junction of College St and Pearse St, where the grassed area is said to occupy the site of the Steyne, or Long Stone, a Norse pillarstone which survived until *c.* 1700, and where Cliodna Cussen's 1986 memorial to it (with stone heads) now stands. No. 9 was the residence of novelist Samuel Lover (1797–1868).

Dominick St, Lower and Upper (1755 onwards), leads from Parnell St to Constitution Hill. In the early 1960s it lost most of its 18th c. houses. The first house here was No. 20, Lower Dominick St (five doors S. of the church), built for himself by Robert West, a master-builder and brilliant stuccoer. It is now St Saviour's Orphanage, but the interior is still one of the sights of Dublin. St Saviour's Dominican Priory and Church (1858) are by J.J. Mc Carthy. The church has a *Dead Christ* by John Hogan (completed by his son, John Valentine Hogan, d. 1920). *The Path of the Lamb* was painted by Patrick Pye (1965); the stained glass window of St Dominick is by Margaret Becker (1986). Arthur Griffith (1872–1922), founder of Sinn Féin and President of the Provisional Government of the Irish Free State, was born in Dominick St. Joseph Sheridan Le Fanu (1814–73), novelist, lived at No. 45 Lower Dominick St.

Donnybrook is a residential suburb on the main Dublin ($2\frac{1}{2}$ m.)–Bray ($10\frac{1}{2}$ m.) road. The old village was the scene of a famous fair founded in 1204. Having become notorious for disorder, it was suppressed in 1855. The Sacred Heart Church has a two-light window (*SS Patrick, Ethne, Fedelm*) by Michael Healy (1914–15) and *SS Rita and Bernard* by Harry Clarke (1924). In the grounds of Montrose, Stillorgan Rd, are the studios of Radio Telefís Éireann (Irish Television), by Michael Scott and Associates. Nearby is the 300-acre site of University College (*see p. 150*), with 10,600 students the largest university in the country. The Physics, Chemistry, and Bio-chemistry buildings (1962–4) are by Downes and Meehan. The Arts (1968–9) and Sports (1980) buildings are by A. Wejchert; the restaurant is by Robin Walker and the Library by Basil Spence (1972). At the SE. angle of the University College grounds, Foster Ave. joins Stillorgan Rd. St Thomas's Church has a porch window, *St George* (1941), by Evie Hone. On the opposite side of Stillorgan Rd is the entrance to St Helen's (1750), one of the first country houses erected on the Fitzwilliam estate. It is now one of the provincial headquarters of the Irish Christian Brothers.

Dorset St, connecting Bolton St (Municipal College of Technology) with Drumcondra Rd, follows the ancient highway to the North. Richard Brinsley Sheridan was born at No. 12 Upper Dorset St. The Bank of Ireland occupies the site of the house where Seán O Casey, playwright, was born (1884).

Drimnagh is an unprepossessing new suburb on the Dublin–Crumlin–Clondalkin road. Drimnagh Castle, now a house of the Irish Christian Brothers, was a stronghold of the Barnewalls, with whom it remained until 1606. It was conserved in 1988.

Drumcondra is a 19th–20th c. suburb on the main Belfast road beyond the Royal Canal. St John the Baptist Church (Protestant; 1743) contains a splendid monument to Marmaduke Coghill (1673–1738) by Scheemakers, teacher of Simon Vierpyl. The life-size figures represent Coghill (robed as Chancellor of the Irish Exchequer), Religion and Minerva. In the churchyard are buried Thomas Furlong (d. 1827), one of the principal translators employed by James Hardiman for his *Irish Minstrelsy*, and, in one grave, Francis Grose (1731–91), antiquarian and artist, and James Gandon (1742–1824).

The nearby Missionary College of All Hallows (Gothic Revival building by J. J. McCarthy) incorporates Drumcondra House, erected about 1720 by Sir Edward Lovett Pearce (architect of the Parliament House) for Marmaduke Coghill, and perhaps the best-preserved early Georgian mansion in Dublin. The S. front is severe, the (later?) E. front highly ornamented. There are some good, early-Georgian interiors. In the grounds is a charming, 18th c. temple (a fake ruin), associated with the name of Alessandro Galilei (*see p. 102*). The college chapel has a rose window (*Assumption* and symbols) by Evie Hone, 1953.

St Patrick's Training College incorporates Belvedere House, a late-17th c. house with 18th–19th c. additions. The drawing-room is a fine, mid-18th c. apartment. The new chapel, students' lodgings, etc. (1963 onwards), are by Devane of Robinson, Keefe and Devane. In the chapel, the *Last Supper* panel is by Nell Murphy; the beautiful slab-glass windows by Gabrielle Loire, and two smaller windows by Patrick Pye; the tabernacle and cross by Benedict Tutty O.S.B. and the slightly disappointing Stations of the Cross by Christopher Ryan.

Dublin Castle is situated at the rear of the City Hall. It may be entered from Palace St (off the W. end of Dame St) or by way of the principal gate, at the junction of Cork Hill and Castle St. It was built sometime after 1204, and until 1922 it was the citadel of English authority in Ireland, the offical residence of Lords Deputy and Lords Lieutenant, the seat of State Councils and, from time to time, of Parliament and the Law Courts. Very few English kings ever stayed in it; Richard II (probably) in 1384, 1394, and 1399; James II and William III (perhaps) in 1690; George V in 1911. Notable prisoners incarcerated in it include Donal Mac Murrough, King of Leinster (1327–30); Dermot O Hurley, Archbishop of Cashel (1584); Red Hugh II O Donnell and Art O Neill (1587–91); Richard Nugent, Lord Delvin (1607); Peter Talbot, Catholic Archbishop of Dublin (1678); Ernie O Malley, Dick McKee, Peader Clancy, and other guerrillas (1920). The castle was never called on to withstand a major siege or assault. In 1534 it was unsuccessfully besieged by Silken Thomas Fitzgerald. The plan of Rory O More and Conor Maguire to seize it, 23 October 1641, was betrayed. A project to seize it by *coup de main* in 1916 was abandoned, when, as it happened, it was manned only by a corporal's guard.

The history of the structure is one of recurring decay, disaster, and reconstruction, culminating in the wholesale rebuilding carried out between 1680 and the 1780s, which gave it in all essentials the form it has today, although few indications of the medieval structure survive. The Upper Castle Yard coincides, more or less, with the layout of the medieval fortress. At the NW., NE., and SE. angles stood great drum towers. At the SW. angle the castle impinged on the town wall, and there the tower was rectangular. A little to the E. of this is a fourth drum tower, known as the Bermingham Tower. Midway between it and the SE. angle was a smaller, projecting tower. The twin-towered gateway stood at the centre of the N. curtain, between the present main gate and the Bedford Tower. Of the towers only the SE. tower (Record Tower) and fragments of the Bermingham Tower, of the NE. tower (uncovered 1961) and NW. tower (*see below*), and of the small S. curtain tower now survive. The SE. tower was 'restored' by Francis Johnston; the others are hidden by 18th–19th c. work.

The complacent, intimate, 18th c. Castle is Dublin's last great building in brick. George Ensor and Joseph Jarratt appear to have had a hand in it. In its original form the main entrance to the state and viceregal apartments was an open, pillared hall, and the ground floor of the S. range was an open arcade. Hall and arcade were, unfortunately, blocked up in the 19th c. In the same century the high roof with dormer windows was removed, so as to permit the addition of the attic storey all around the yard, so spoiling the elevations.

Since 1961 the early-18th c. E. range and part of the S. range have been demolished and were rebuilt with further modifications. Excavations in 1986–7 uncovered the original moat and the base of the Corke tower at the NW. angle of the Castle. Both will be visible from the new conference and exhibition centre being constructed at the W. end of the castle, into which the W. and NW. portions of the 18th c. buildings will be incorporated. It is also planned to open a Visitor Centre near the entrance to the Castle from Castle St.

The best architectural feature of the Upper Yard is the elevation of the N. side: two great, triumphal-arch gateways flanking the Office of Arms with its pillared Musicians' Gallery and charming Bedford Tower. The lead statues (*Justice* and *Fortitude*) crowning the gateways are the work of Van Nost (restored 1986–8).

The State Apartments in the S. range (guided tours) are approached from the main entrance by the Grand Staircase. A lobby to the left of the landing leads to St Patrick's Hall (1783), which was the State Ballroom and (after the disestablishment of the Church of Ireland, 1869) the place of investiture of the Knights of St Patrick. It is now the place of inauguration of the Presidents of the Republic. (It was there that President John Fitzgerald Kennedy of the United States received the Freedom of Dublin and honorary doctorates of the National University and of Dublin University, 1963.) The paintings at either end of the ceiling depict St Patrick lighting his first Paschal Fire and Henry II receiving the submission of the Irish kings. The centre-piece is an allegory of George III (with Liberty and Justice). All are the work of Vincent Waldré, who rebuilt the House of Commons in College Green. On the walls are displayed the banners and armorial achievements of the Knights of St Patrick. A curving passage leads to the circular Supper Room in the Bermingham Tower; a doorway in the N. wall leads to the panelled State Drawing Room, alias the Picture Gallery, and the ornate Presence Chamber, or Throne Room. (The central part of the Drawing Room was originally the State Dining Room.) The oval painted panels in the Presence Chamber are by an unknown (Venetian?) painter. The 18th c. Presence Chamber, in the E. wing, a finer apartment than Johnston's, was turned into a drawing room *en suite* in the 19th c. and was restored after a fire in 1941. The Apollo Room from Tracton House (St Stephen's Green) and the *Hibernia* and *Arts and Sciences* ceilings from Mespil House (Mespil Rd) have been re-erected in this wing.

An archway (widened, 1962) in the middle of the E. range leads to the Lower Castle Yard. Here is the great Record Tower (now the State Paper Office), refaced and re-battlemented by Francis Johnston (1811–19). At its foot is the Chapel Royal (1807–14), an interesting example of Johnston's work in the Gothick manner. All the exterior carvings are by Edward Smyth and his son, John, who also did all the interior stucco, apart from George Stapleton's ceiling. The woodcarving is by Richard Stewart. (His pulpit is now in St Werburgh's, *see p. 142*.) The coats of arms along the galleries and in the gallery windows are those of the successive representatives of the English Crown. The E. window contains some old Continental glass depicting scenes from the Passion. In 1943 the chapel was re-consecrated as a Catholic church dedicated to the Most Holy Trinity.

Duke St connects Grafton St with Dawson St. The Smoking Room (remodelled) on the first floor of the Bailey Restaurant was the meeting place of Parnell and his closest associates, and later of Arthur Griffith and his friends (including James Montgomery, noted wit, and Oliver St John Gogarty, surgeon and poet). On the first floor is preserved the doorway of No. 7 Eccles St (*see right*), associated with James Joyce's *Ulysses*. Davy Byrne's public house, on the opposite side of the street, had associations with James Joyce and other writers. The character of the place has been completely altered.

Earlsfort Terrace links Adelaide Rd with the junction of Lower Leeson St and St Stephen's Green. On the W. side is the old University College building, before the College moved to Belfield near Donnybrook (*see p. 148*), though part of the building is still retained by the College. The Earlsfort Terrace buildings occupy the site and part of the buildings erected for the Great Exhibition of 1865, and extended in 1888 to provide examination halls for the non-teaching Royal University of Ireland (1882–1909). The old examination hall has been totally transformed and now functions as the National Concert Hall. Only a fraction of Rudolph M. Butler's projected college buildings were erected (1914–19). The college has been a constituent college of the National University of Ireland since 1909, but traces its origin to the Catholic University of 1851 (*see p. 165*). It played a leading part in creating the new Ireland, and the roll of its members includes such names as those of Eóin MacNeill (1867–1945), historian, founder of the Gaelic League, founder of the Irish Volunteers, Minister of Education in the first Irish Free State Government; Douglas Hyde (1866–1949), co-founder of the Gaelic League, Professor of Modern Irish, and President of Ireland; Thomas MacDonagh (1878–1916), poet, Lecturer in English Literature, a founder of Edward Martyn's Irish Theatre (1914), and Commandant of the Dublin Brigade in the 1916 Rising; Kevin O Higgins (1892–1927), Minister for Justice in the first Irish Free State Cabinet; Patrick McGilligan, Minister for Industry and Commerce in the first Irish Free State Cabinet; Osborn J. Bergin (1873–1950), eminent Celtic scholar; Hugh Ryan (1873–1931), chemist; Arthur Conway (1875–1950), mathematical physicist; and E.J. Conway, biochemist, a pioneer of the micro-diffusion technique and inventor of the Conway Unit. The historic Dáil Éireann Treaty Debate (14 December 1921–10 January 1922) took place in the Council Chamber, above the present entrance.

Eccles St (*c.* 1750–*c.* 1820) connects Dorset St with Berkeley Rd. As planned, it was to have had an elliptical circus at the W. end. No. 7 (now demolished) was the home of James Joyce's *Ulysses* character, Bloom. The doorway is now preserved in the Bailey restaurant in Duke St (*see left*). No. 64 was the home of the celebrated architect Francis Johnston (1761–1829). Johnston doubled the width of the house by adding the portion (later increased in height) adorned with plaques emblematic of the arts. The house was afterwards occupied by Isaac Butt (1813–79), founder of the Parliamentary Home Rule Party. His parties in Johnston's Octagon Room were famous, and the bailiffs were frequent callers. At the W. end of the street is the Mater Misericordiae Hospital (1860).

Ely Pl. is a cul-de-sac continuing the line of Merrion St to the S. of Merrion Row. It contains several fine late-18th c. houses, some with good ironwork, and admirable interiors. No. 8, Ely House, was built by Michael Stapleton in 1770 for the extravagant Henry Loftus, later Earl of Ely (*see p. 270*); now the headquarters of the Knights of Columbanus, it has some particularly fine stucco and other decorations. Palatial No. 6 also has an excellent Stapleton interior; it was the home of execrated 'Black Jack' Fitzgibbon, Earl of Clare (1749–1802), whose promotion of the Union so aroused the fury of the Dublin mob. No. 4 was the town house of John Philpot Curran (1750–1817), famous forensic orator and father of Robert Emmet's sweetheart; later it was the residence of George Moore (1852–1933). A small plot on the opposite side of the street was once Moore's garden. House and garden (and Ely House too) figure prominently in his great Dublin trilogy, *Ave, Salve atque Vale*. The garden plot is now occupied by the Gallagher Gallery of the Royal Hibernian Academy of Art (1988), designed by Raymond McGrath and named after the builder Matt Gallagher. No. 5, another Stapleton house, was the home of Chief Justice Kendal Bushe (1767–1843). No. 15 is also a Stapleton house.

Essex Quay extends from Wellington Quay to Wood Quay. William Mossop (1751–1804), the celebrated medallist, whose designs were from the hand of Edward Smyth, lived here in 1784. St Michael's and St John's Church (1815; Thomas Betagh monument by Turnerelli), by J. Taylor occupies the site of the celebrated Smock Alley Theatre (1662–1815). Among the famous names associated with the theatre are those of George Farquhar (1678–1707, author of *The Beaux' Stratagem*), Thomas Doggett (d. 1721; *see p. 142*), Peg Woffington (1716–60), Charles Macklin (1697–1797), and Henry Mossop (1729–74), father of William Mossop.

Detail from the Custom House, Dublin, see page 142.

Fishamble St runs from Christchurch Pl. to the junction of Essex and Wood Quays. Henry Grattan and James Clarence Mangan were born there. Kennan's Ironworks incorporates the entrance of the Charitable Musical Society's Music Hall, erected to the design of Richard Cassels in 1741. Handel conducted the first performance of *Messiah* there, 13 April 1742, a fact commemorated by an unfortunately sited plaque by Michael Biggs. Handel also conducted *Acis and Galatea* there. In 1748 his *Judas Maccabaeus* was given its first performance there.

Fitzwilliam Sq., between Pembroke St and Fitzwilliam St, is the smallest, latest (1820), and perhaps best preserved of Dublin's Georgian squares. Like Fitzwilliam St and Fitzwilliam Pl., it is now for the most part given over to the consulting rooms of physicians and surgeons: No. 2 was the town house of William Dargan (1799–1867; *see p. 157*).

Fitzwilliam St, Lower and Upper, extends from Merrion Sq. to Fitzwilliam Pl. Until the 1965 demolition of the block between Baggot St and Upper Mount St, it combined with Merrion Sq. E. (begun *c.* 1780), Fitzwilliam Sq. E., and Fitzwilliam Pl (*c.* 1830–40) to provide Dublin's longest Georgian street. The vista is closed at the S. end by a distant glimpse of the Dublin mountains; at the N. end (since 1934) by the pseudo-Georgian National Maternity Hospital. No. 28 Fitzwilliam Pl. is that Dublin rarity, a Gothic-Revival dwelling.

Francis St leads from Cornmarket to the Coombe and Dean St, which has become a centre of the antique trade. The Church of St Nicholas of Myra (1829; portico and tower, 1860) is by John Leeson. The cost of the church was largely defrayed by the parish priest, Fr Flanagan, an amateur sculptor, some of whose work may be seen there. Fr Flanagan also commissioned the fine plaster *Pietà*, by John Hogan, which fills the reredos of the high altar. Hogan also did the two kneeling angels which flank the altar. Their wings are said to have been added later.

Gardiner St (Lower, Middle, and Upper) leads down from Lower Dorset St to Beresford Pl. It was laid out about 1787. In its heyday this was one of the very finest of Dublin's Georgian residential streets, with a magnificent, $\frac{3}{4}$ m., downhill vista closed by the Custom House, a vista long since ruined by the infamous 'Loop Line' railway. By 1900, the street was largely badly decayed tenements. The Labour Exchange at the S. end of the street was originally Trinity Church (Protestant), by Frederick Darley, 1838. At the N. end is the Jesuit church of St Francis Xavier (1829–32), by John B. Keane; behind the altar is a fine triptych of *c.* 1535 by the Master of Güstrow. The houses opposite (1810) may be by Francis Johnston.

Glasnevin is a suburb beyond the Royal Canal, to the W. of Drumcondra. St Mo-Bhí (d. 545) founded a monastery on the banks of the Tolka, of which no trace survives. His disciples include SS Comgall of Bangor and Columcille of Derry and Iona.

The Botanic Gardens (founded 1795 by the Royal Dublin Society and taken over by the State in 1878) are particularly beautiful. Some of the conservatories are by Frederick Darley, but the most noteworthy is that by Richard Turner, who also designed conservatories in Belfast and in London's Kew Gardens. Of particular interest are the cycads, orchids, herbaceous borders, and conifers. The nearby Bon Secours Nursing Home occupies the site of Delville, residence of Swift's celebrated friends, Dr and Mrs Delaney. Prospect Cemetery, Finglas Rd, Dublin's principal burial ground, dates from 1831. There are buried: Daniel O Connell (1775–1847), the Liberator; John Philpot Curran (1750–1817); Barry Sullivan, celebrated actor (1821–91); Charles Stewart Parnell (1846–91); O Donovan Rossa (1831–1915); Sir Roger Casement (1864–1916); Arthur Griffith (1872–1922); Michael Collins (1890–1922), and Eamon de Valera (1882–1975). The disappointing Catholic church of Our Lady of the Seven Dolours by Vincent Gallagher (1972) has a rood cross, tabernacle and three bronze reliefs by Patrick Pollen. The pyramidal Meteorological Office (not open to the public) is by Liam McCormick.

Grafton St, linking College Green and St Stephen's Green, originated as a country lane. It became a residential street in the 18th c. but has long since succumbed to increasingly vulgar commercialization. Percy Bysshe Shelley lodged at No. 17 in 1812. No. 60 was the birthplace of Samuel Lover (1797–1868), novelist. No. 78, Bewley's Café, one of the great meeting-places in Dublin, has decorative windows by Harry Clarke. No. 79 occupies the site of Whyte's Academy, whose pupils included Richard Brinsley Sheridan, Thomas Moore, and Robert Emmet, as well as the future Duke of Wellington. About the middle of the W. side is Johnston's Court, giving convenient access to Powerscourt House and St Teresa's Church (Discalced Carmelites) where, under the high altar, is a *Dead Christ* in marble by John Hogan (1829).

Granby Row links Parnell Sq. with Dorset St. The Wax Museum is an awful, pale reflection of Mme Tussaud's.

Grand Canal St leads from Fenian St to Shelbourne Rd. The former Sir Patrick Dun's Hospital (closed in 1987) is named after its founder, a Scottish doctor (1642–1713), who was a pioneer of Dublin medicine. The uninspired building (1799–1808) is by Richard Morrison. Restoration of the building for its new owner (the Institute of Clinical Pharmacology) has brought to light some of the original ceilings of high quality.

Grand Parade, on the S. bank of the Grand Canal, leads W. from Leeson St Bridge to Charlemont St Bridge. In the foyer of the new office-warehouse of Carroll Group Distributors Ltd is a noteworthy Aubusson tapestry designed by the contemporary Irish painter Louis le Brocquy: *Legend of St Brendan the Navigator*.

Grangegorman Rd leads from Brunswick St to the N. Circular Rd. The great complex of Grangegorman Mental Hospital includes the former Richmond General Penitentiary (1812) and the former Richmond Lunatic Asylum (1814–17), typical examples of Francis Johnston's institutional architecture. The Protestant church in Grangegorman has a window *Ruth and Naomi* by Catherine O Brien (1914).

Great Charles St (*c.* 1800) leads from the SE. corner of Mountjoy Sq. to Richmond Pl. No. 12 was the house of George Petrie (1789–1866), antiquary, painter, and collector of Irish folk-music.

Great Denmark St, begun as Gardiner's Row (about 1775–80), leads from Frederick St and Parnell Sq. to Gardiner's Pl. and Mountjoy Sq. Belvedere House was built around 1776 by Michael Stapleton, 'the Dublin Adam', for William Rochfort, 2nd Earl of Belvedere. Splendidly sited at the head of superb North Great George's St, it is still one of Dublin's finest mansions. The interior is lavishly decorated with excellent Stapleton stucco. The principal apartments are the Venus Room, Apollo Room and Diana Room. Since 1841 the house has been part of a Jesuit school (Belvedere College). James Joyce went to school there (1893–8), and the school figures in his *A Portrait of the Artist as a Young Man*.

Green St leads from North King St to Boot Lane. The Central Criminal Court sits in the dull court-house (1792–7) by Whitmore Davis. The court-house was the place of trial of the brothers Sheares (1798); Robert Emmet (1803); John Mitchel, Charles Gavan Duffy, and William Smith O Brien (1848); and the Fenian leaders of 1867. Lord Edward Fitzgerald died of wounds in the prison, 1798, and the 1848 Young Irelanders were incarcerated there while awaiting trial.

Harcourt St (1778) leads from the SW. corner of St Stephen's Green to the S. Circular Rd. This once fashionable residential street is now given over almost entirely to hotels and commerce. Thanks to its pleasant curve and the scale of its houses, it is still one of the best of Dublin's great Georgian streets, the efforts of insurance companies and other philistines notwithstanding. No. 4 was the birthplace of Edward Carson (Lord Carson, 1854–1935), organizer of Orange resistance to Home Rule. No. 6 was in its time St Mary's House of the Catholic University (Newman resided there with some of the students). No. 9 is a Michael Stapleton house. No. 14 was the home of Sir Jonah Barrington, rascally patriot and author of *Historic Anecdotes and Secret Memoirs of the Union*. No. 17 was the central block of Clonmell House, built (by Stapleton?) about 1777–8 for 'Copperfaced Jack' Scott, Earl of Clonmell, who amassed a fortune by swindling Catholics out of lands held in trust. The house has lost its low side wings, but still retains some good ceilings and other features. In 1830 it was divided into two parts, the larger of which served as Sir Hugh Lane's Municipal Gallery of Modern Art from 1908 until 1932, when it moved to Parnell Square (*see p. 160*). At the S. end of the street is Harcourt St Station (1859), an exceptionally good piece of early railway architecture, by George Wilkinson.

Hardwicke Pl., at the intersection of Temple St and Hardwicke St, is the setting for Francis Johnston's Great St George's Church (1802–13), perhaps the finest of Dublin's later Protestant churches. The 200 ft spire is a highly individual adaptation of the spire of Gibbs's St Martin-in-the-Fields, London, but the interior is wholly Johnston. Galleries on three sides are cantilevered on an inner wall. The chancel is at the middle of a long side. The very wide, flat ceiling was a fine constructional feat. The Johnstonian decorations – woodcarving and the rest – are by Richard Stewart and others. The memorials include some by Edward Smyth's son, John; Sir Charles Metzler Giesecke, F.R.S. (1761–1833); and Ephraim Mc Donnell (d. 1835). The *Faith, Hope,* and *Charity* keystones under the portico are by Edward Smyth.

Harold's Cross, once a rural village with some pleasant houses, is now a built-up suburb to the S. of the Grand Canal, between Rathmines and Kimmage. Mount Jerome Cemetery includes Dublin's largest Protestant burial ground, in which are buried Thomas Davis (1814–45), Young Ireland leader; Thomas Kirk (1777–1845), sculptor; George Petrie (1789–1866), antiquary, painter, and collector of Irish folk-music; and Edmund Dowden (1843–1913), poet and literary critic. No. 142 Harold's Cross Road, a small, late-Victorian house, was for many years the home of John Butler Yeats (1839–1922), painter and father of the gifted brothers William Butler Yeats, the poet, and Jack Butler Yeats, the painter.

Hatch St (1810 onwards) leads from Lower Leeson St to Harcourt St. University Hall is a Jesuit hall of residence for university students. The chapel has five single-light symbolical windows by Evie Hone (1947).

Henrietta St (*c.* 1720 onwards) leads from Bolton St to the entrance of the King's Inns. It was the earliest of N. Dublin's great 18th c. residential streets, and remained the most fashionable until the Union. Thereafter it declined. No. 3 was the Earl of Kingston's house; No. 4 the Earl of Thomond's; No. 5 (now 5 and 6) the Rt Hon. John Ponsonby's. Nos. 8, 9, 10 are now a convent of the Sisters of Charity of St Vincent de Paul. Nos. 9 and 10 were built in 1730, the latter (Mountjoy House) for Luke Gardiner, Lord Mountjoy, the bank-landlord who laid out this and so many other great N. Dublin streets. Frederick Darley's bleak King's Inns Library (1827) occupies the site of the three earliest houses in the street. The King's Inns (1795–1817), at the head of the street, is the Irish Inns of Court, headquarters of the governing body (The Benchers of the Honorable Society of the King's Inns) of the Irish Bar. In 1795 James Gandon was commissioned to design the buildings. Associated with him in

The Custom House (see page 142).

the work was his pupil and partner, Henry Aaron Baker. A curved, triumphal arch (royal arms by Edward Smyth) gives access to a narrow court set at an angle to the axis of the street. On the N. side of the court is the Benchers' Dining Hall; on the S., the Prerogative Court (now the Registry of Deeds). At the W. end a second triumphal arch pierces the central block to give access to the principal front, facing Constitution Hill. There are the ceremonial entrances to the Dining Hall and Prerogative Court. The Caryatids and Persae flanking these (*Security* and *Law* guarding the Prerogative Court; *Ceres* and a *Bacchante* guarding the Dining Hall) are by Edward Smyth. Smyth also did the rather unsuccessful bas-reliefs of the upper storey (*Prudence, Justice and Wisdom at a Blazing Altar; Restoration of the Society of the King's Inns*, 1607; *Ceres and Companions Offering the Fruits of the Earth*). In 1808, annoyed by ignorant interference, Gandon resigned his commission, and handed over all his drawings for the completion of the work to Baker. The building was not completed until 1816–17, when Francis Johnston finished the Prerogative Court and built the cupola and its colonnade in accordance with the Gandon-Baker design. Since then a wing has been added to each side of the W. front, which unfortunately throws it out of scale. However, the Dining Hall, with Edward Smyth's stucco figures of *Justice, Prudence, Fortitude,* and *Temperance,* remains pretty much as Gandon left it, making this the least abused and altered of all the great architect's works.

Herbert St (about 1830) leads from Lower Baggot St to Mount St Crescent. Sir Charles Villiers Stanford (1852–1924), composer, was born and grew up in No. 2.

Heuston (formerly **Kingsbridge**) **Station,** beside the Liffey at the junction of Victoria Quay and Steevens' Lane, was erected 1845–61 as terminus of the Cork and Limerick railways. It is a good 'Renaissance palazzo' by Sancton Woods.

High St, between Christchurch Pl. and Cornmarket, was the principal street of medieval Dublin, and here stood two of the Norse town's parish churches. St Michael's Church is represented by the bell tower incorporated in the Synod Hall, Christchurch Pl. (*see above*), St Columcille's by its medieval successor, St Audoen's. The tower of St Audoen's (probably 1670; restored 1826 and later) has the three oldest (1423) bells in Ireland. In the porch are: a pre-Norman gravestone; the double-effigy mensa of a tomb-cenotaph commemorating Roland FitzEustace (Lord Portlester; d. 1496) and his wife, Margaret Jennico (d. 1482; *see also p. 211*); a very weathered 14th c. tomb effigy; a good, medieval tomb slab callously used as a paving stone; and some medieval floor-tiles (set in the window ledges). The nave, tastelessly re-pointed, serves as the Protestant parish church: the Transitional doorway dates from 1190; the four W. bays of the blocked-up arcade are late-13th c., the fifth bay later; the font is medieval; in the N. wall are two Renaissance monuments with kneeling effigies. The 14th c. chancel and the S. nave aisle, together with its E. chapel are roofless ruins (Nat. Mon.). Close to the N. side of the church is a fragment of the medieval town wall, including St Audoen's Arch (1240; upper part 19th c.), sole survivor of the town gates (it gave access to a Liffey strand). Here some of Dublin's medieval guilds at one time held their Halls.

St Audoen's Catholic Church, High St, one of the last of Dublin's Classical churches, was erected 1841–7, to the design of Patrick Byrne. The inferior portico (1898) is by Ashlin and W. H. Byrne. The basement is currently used for Irish Life's 'Viking Adventure', a reconstruction of life in Viking Dublin 1,000 years ago.

Inns Quay lies between Upper Ormond Quay and Arran Quay. The name recalls the fact that the site of the medieval Dominican friary here was occupied by the King's Inns from 1541 to 1775. The erection of the Public Record Offices on the W. end of the site began in 1776, architect Thomas Cooley. Cooley's plans were for a quadrangle entered through an open screen on the S. side. Cooley died in 1784, when only the S. and W. sides had been completed. The following year it was decided to transfer the Four Courts from St Michael's Hill (*see p. 143*) to Inns Quay, and to integrate the necessary building with Cooley's work. The task was entrusted to James Gandon, who thus gave Dublin his second masterpiece. Now mutilated, it is the seat of both the Supreme Court and the High Court of the Republic.

Gandon's Four Courts (1786–1802) were controlled by the cramped site and the existing Cooley work. The architect was also constantly hampered by lack of funds and by carping criticism. He reduced the size of Cooley's quadrangle, modified the W. and N. ranges, substituted the great, domed, central block for Cooley's E. range, and replaced the S. side by a longer, more monumental screen with a triumphal-arch centre-piece. The new quadrangle thus obtained he duplicated on the E. side of the central block.

The dominant feature of the building is the great, domed, central mass. (Gandon proposed to have the portico project out over the footpath.) The excellent statues (1792) on the pediment are by Edward Smyth; *Moses* flanked by *Justice* and *Mercy,* with *Wisdom* and *Authority* seated on the corners; the *Moses* is a masterpiece of architectural sculpture. Behind the portico a curved porch gave access to an apsidal vestibule opening on to the admirable rotunda beneath the double dome. From this the four courts (King's Bench, Chancery, Exchequer, and Common Pleas) radiated towards the corners of the enclosing square; a fifth court, the Rolls Court, lay on the main N.–S. axis. The four axial entrances to the rotunda and the four open entrances to the courts were flanked by pairs of great Corinthian columns standing in depth.

In the 19th and 20th c. inferior structures (Law Library, Public Record Office, Land Registry, etc.) were crowded in behind Gandon's building. The Four Courts were severely damaged by explosives during the Civil War (1922). The double dome and the interior of the central block were destroyed; the W. wings and part of the arcaded screen were badly damaged. The Law Library, too, and the Public Record Office, with its irreplaceable archives, were completely destroyed.

In the work of reconstruction (completed 1932) by the Office of Public Works the open arcades of Gandon's quadrangles were blocked up, and the site of the Rolls Court and most of the rest of the interior were replanned on new lines.

The Law Library is the focal centre of the Irish legal profession. Irish barristers, unlike their English counterparts, do not have chambers. Instead, they wait for business in the Library, and the loud calling of their names when solicitors arrive with briefs is a local phenomenon.

James's St, leading from Thomas St to Mount Brown and Kilmainham, was the start of the ancient highway to the West. The site of St James's Gate is incorporated in the world-famous Guinness Brewery, successor of Rainford's Brewery purchased by Arthur Guinness in 1759. The vast complex includes some pleasant late-18th and early-19th c. features, as well as imposing examples of 19th–20th c. industrial architecture. There is also a Guinness Museum. The former hop store of the brewery has been re-modelled to function as a modern art gallery. St James's Church is an example of Patrick Byrne's Gothic and has a decent interior (now a lighting emporium!). No. 174 was the birthplace of William Thomas Cosgrave, Arthur Griffith's successor as President of the Executive Council of the Irish Free State (1922–32). In Bow Lane, which runs from the junction of James's St and Steevens Lane to Kilmainham Lane, is St Patrick's Hospital, better known as Swift's Hospital. It was founded by Dean Swift:

He gave the little wealth he had
To build a house for fools and mad;
To show by one satiric touch,
No nation wanted it so much.

The attractive building was erected 1749–57 to the design of George Semple, and enlarged in 1778 by Thomas Cooley, who added the low side wings and extended the rear wings. (The windows and one of Cooley's wings have since been spoiled.) The hospital, an up-to-date psychiatric centre, has an interesting collection of Swiftiana and other 18th c. relics.

Jones's Rd connects the N. Circular Rd with Clonliffe Rd. Croke Park, headquarters stadium of the Gaelic Athletic Association and venue each Aug.–Sept. of the final matches for the All-Ireland Hurling and Gaelic Football championships, is situaled there. Hurling is Ireland's only native outdoor game.

Kildare St (1745 onwards) runs from St Stephen's Green N. to Leinster St.

At the NE. corner, overlooking College Park, is the Kildare Street Club, a distinguished, Venetian-style, brick palazzo (1860–1) by Thomas Deane I and Benjamin Woodward. Its interior was barbarously gutted in 1971, when the Club sold the N. half of its premises to the Phoenix Assurance Company, now occupied by the Alliance Française. The S. half is now the Genealogical Museum. The Club amalgamated in 1976 with the former University Club, to form the Kildare Street and University Club at No. 17 St Stephens Green (*see p. 162*). The noteworthy stonecarving is the work of John and James O Shea and Charles W. Harrison; it was Harrison who carved the engaging monkeys, birds, and other beasts. Nos. 4 (refronted) and 5 were built in 1748 by Edward Nicholson. No. 6, the Royal College of Physicians of Ireland, is a decadent effort (1860–4) in the Classical manner by William G. Murray; re-fronted 1966. It occupies the site of the first Kildare Street Club (destroyed by fire, 1860). The College was founded by the Duke of Ormond in 1667. The statues of Sir Dominic Corrigan (1802–80), Sir Henry Marsh (1790–1860), and William Stokes (1804–78) are by John Henry Foley.

Facing Molesworth St is Leinster House, present seat of Parliament (Dáil Éireann). It is flanked on the N. by the National Library, on the S. by the National Museum.

Leinster House (*see also p. 246*), by Richard Cassels, was begun for the Earl of Kildare in 1745. Having two formal fronts, and a central corridor on the long axis, it is a country rather than a town house. This is hardly to be wondered at, as it was built on the SE. edge of the city, with open country to the E. The entrance hall and principal rooms are noble apartments. They were redecorated towards the end of the 18th c., James Wyatt participating in the work. The house has been claimed as the prototype for the White House, Washington, U.S.A., built on a suggestively similar plan by Carlow-born James Hoban (1762–1832). The house was sold in 1815 to the Royal Dublin Society, whose additions included an octagonal lecture theatre on the S. side. In 1922 it was purchased by the first Irish Free State Government to serve as a parliament house. The Senate meets in the 18th c. saloon, Dáil Éireann in the remodelled lecture theatre. The public is admitted to the debates of both Houses. (Admission tickets may be obtained from deputies or senators, or from the Superintendent.) The principal apartments may be seen only when Parliament is not sitting. (Applications should be made to the Superintendent.) On Leinster Lawn, at the E. front of Leinster House, is a memorial by Raymond McGrath and F. du Berry to the founders of the Irish State, Arthur Griffith, Michael Collins, and Kevin O Higgins; the bronze portrait medallions are by Laurence Campbell.

As the headquarters of the Royal Dublin Society, Leinster House became the focus of some of the Society's most important activities and institutions. From these developed the National College of Art, the National Library, and the National Museum.

The National Library and National Museum are matching buildings (1885–90) of pedestrian design by Sir Thomas Deane II; the elevations have been significantly altered by the removal of corroded statuary and the replacement of corroded details in Mount Charles stone by plainer work in limestone and granite. The Library has important collections of books, manuscripts, prints, drawings and historical archives (including the Ormond Archives from Kilkenny Castle and collections of designs by 18th–19th c. architects and stucco decorators). A valuable new feature is the collection of microfilm copies of Irish manuscripts and documents in foreign archives and libraries.

The National Museum houses overcrowded collections of various kinds, some of them of outstanding importance and worldwide fame. The Irish Antiquities, Irish Military History, Ethnographical, Art and Industrial, and Botanical collections are housed in the Kildare St building; the main Natural History collections in Merrion St. The Kildare St building is currently undergoing major structural repairs, and it would be premature to predict when it will be fully open to the public again, and which parts of the collection will then be put on display. During the alterations, those parts of the Museum open to the public comprise a room devoted to President de Valera, and the Treasury Room. The Treasury Room (entrance fee) houses the nation's most treasured possessions from the prehistoric period up to the Middle Ages. Particularly noteworthy are:

Bronze Age: The splendid series of gold lunulae, torques, gorgets, fibulae, etc.; the bronze buckets and cauldrons, and the bronze, leather, and wooden shields.

Iron Age: The magnificent gold collar with Celtic repoussé ornament from Broighter, Co. Derry, the repoussé bronze dishes, the Petrie 'Crown', and the bronze horse trappings.

Early Historic Period: Such masterpieces as the Moylough

Belt Reliquary (8th c.); 'Tara' Brooch (8th c.) and other splendid penannular brooches; Ardagh Chalice (8th c.); the Derrynaflan hoard of religious vessels, discovered in 1981; Shrine of St Patrick's Bell (12th c.); Cross of Cong (12th c.); and the series of 10th–12th c. enshrined staffs, including the Lismore Crozier (12th c.).

An extension of the Museum's display of antiquities is at Nos 7–9 Merrion Row (*see p. 157*). It is expected that, in due course, a part of the Museum's collections will be housed in the vast development planned along the Liffey banks in the area to the E. of the Custom House.

On the W. side of the street is the Department of Industry and Commerce (1939–42) by J.R. Boyd Barrett. The stone carvings are by Gabriel Hayes.

Kilmainham is an urban district at the W. end of the S. Circular Rd, between James's St and Inchicore. The Royal Hospital for old and disabled soldiers (entrance from Military Rd) was erected between 1680 and 1687 to the design of Sir William Robinson, Surveyor-General of Ireland, but the fine tower and spire (136 ft) were only built – 'as it was first intended' – in 1701. The hospital was laid out on a courtyard-and-piazza plan with open, ground-floor loggia on three sides and on parts of the fourth. The doorways at the centre of each range have excellent tympana of carved wood. Over the main door are the arms of the 1st Duke of Ormonde, in whose Lord Lieutenancy the building was erected. In the N. range are, from W. to E., the Master's Lodging, the Great Hall with grand portico and tower, and the Chapel. In front of the chapel door is a pair of beautiful wrought-iron gates (cypher of Queen Anne). The chapel ceiling is a papier-mâché facsimile (1902) of the excellent stucco original. The very fine woodcarving at the corners of the sanctuary is the work of James Tabary, a Huguenot craftsman. The canopied pew in the gallery was that of the Master, who was always the Commander-in-Chief in Ireland. The former Deputy Adjutant-General's house, at the E. end of the terrace, dates from 1800. The former Adjutant-General's Office (1808) is by Francis Johnston. The Hospital survived the establishment of the Irish Free State by only five years. Subsequently the buildings served as headquarters of the Civic Guard. In 1949 they were vacated as unsafe, but were admirably restored by the Office of Public Works under the direction of John Costello in 1980–4, at a cost of around £20 million, to serve as a National Centre for Culture and the Arts (guided tours). It houses the fine collection of 16th–20th c. prints of German, Flemish, Dutch and British works, presented by Mrs Claire Madden in memory of her daughter, Étain, and her son-in-law, Dr Friedrich Arnholz. The Hospital is also due to house a Museum of Modern Art, based on 50 paintings generously donated to the nation by Sir Sydney Nolan, the Australian artist of Irish ancestry, and on the collection of Gordon Lambert and others. The castle-like gate-tower on the S. Circular Rd is also by Johnston; it originally stood on the Liffey quay at Bloody Bridge. Nearby, on the N. side of the avenue, is an ancient graveyard with a weathered High Cross (Nat. Mon.), sole relic of the old monastery of Cell Maighnenn.

At the junction of the S. Circular Rd and Inchicore Rd is Kilmainham Courthouse, said to be by George Papworth. Derelict Kilmainham Gaol (1800, architect unknown), now restored as a memorial, figured prominently in 18th–20th c. history. Among the patriots held there at one time or another were: Henry Joy Mac Cracken (1797); Sam Neilson (1798); Robert Emmet (1803); Thomas Russell (1803); William Smith O Brien, whose son was baptized in the prison chapel (1848); John O Leary, Fenian (1865); Charles Stewart Parnell (1881); 26 Invincibles (1883); Patrick Pearse and other 1916 men. A short distance W., in Colbert Road, is the entrance to Island-bridge Park of Remembrance, memorial to the Irishmen who fell in the First World War. It was designed by Sir Edwin Lutyens. When clearing the site excavators found several Viking graves.

Lincoln Place, formerly Park St, leads from Leinster St to Westland Row. Sir William Wilde had an eye hospital here. Fanning's public house (now Lincoln's Inn) figures in Oliver St John Gogarty's *As I Was Going Down Sackville Street.* Lower Abbey St runs from Lower O Connell St to Beresford Pl. In the forecourt of the large Irish Life Centre (by Andrew Devane) is a fountain with *Chariot of Fire* (1978), the last large-scale sculpture by Oisín Kelly (1916–81).

Marino, a new suburb to the W. of the Howth road beyond Fairview, preserves the name of Marino House, seaside retreat of the 'Volunteer Earl' of Charlemont (*see p. 160*). In the grounds of the former O Brien Institute, Malahide Rd, is the delightful Casino (Nat. Mon.) designed in the late 1750s for Charlemont's garden by Sir William Chambers and erected 1762 by Simon Vierpyl, sculptor and builder, whom Charlemont had brought from Rome in 1750. Vierpyl worked from models and instructions supplied from London. Edward Smyth (1749–1812), great architectural sculptor and stuccoer, was at that time an apprentice of Vierpyl's, and may have had a hand in the decorations. In the basement are kitchen, scullery, pantry, butler's pantry, wine cellar, servants' hall, and ale cellar. On the principal floor are vestibule, saloon, study, and a bedroom. The upper floor has bedrooms and dressing closets. Though for many years callously abandoned to neglect and decay, this architectural gem has recently been carefully restored, though landscaping around it has been partially left as a wasteland. The parapet offers a delightful view.

No. 3 Marino Terrace was the home of William Carleton (1794–1869), novelist and folklorist. No. 8 Inverness Rd was the home of James Joyce in 1890.

Clontarf Presbyterian Church (1889–90), at the corner of Howth Rd and Fairview, is by Sir Thomas Drew. It has an unusual Harry Clarke window, *Resurrection and Deposition* (1914–18 War Memorial).

Marlborough St (*c.* 1740–60) runs from Eden Quay to Parnell St. Near the S. end is the Abbey Theatre, founded in 1904 by Lady Gregory and W.B. Yeats (with the financial assistance of Miss Annie Elizabeth Fredericka Horniman of Manchester). The dramatists and players who made the theatre world-famous include Yeats, John Millington Synge, Seán O Casey, Máire O Neill, Sara Allgood, Barry Fitzgerald (William Shields), Maureen Delaney, F.J. McCormick (Peter C. Judge), Eileen Crowe, Siobhán McKenna, and Cyril Cusack. In 1951 the theatre was destroyed by fire, with the loss of many precious relics. The new theatre, by Michael Scott and Associates, opened in 1966.

Just N. of the Earl St-Talbot St intersection is Tyrone House, built in 1740 by Richard Cassels for Marcus Beresford, Viscount (later Earl of) Tyrone. The house, which has some good ceilings and a fine staircase, is today the secretariat of the Department of Education. In 1835 the Board of Education defaced the house by substituting the building-blocks porch, etc., for Cassels' elegant doorway and by removing the Venetian window which formed the centrepiece above it. The white marble *Deposition of Christ* is by the Italian sculptor Luppi. It was the Italian Government's thank-offering for Irish post-war relief.

On the opposite side of the street is St Mary's Catholic Pro-Cathedral (1815), by the amateur architect, John Sweetman, whose only work it is. Prior to the introduction of the dome and a new window system, the interior revealed the inspiration of Chalgrin's St Philippe du Roule, Paris (1769–94). Extensions of the aisles have spoiled the interior vistas and proportions. The high altar, by Belfast-born, Dublin-taught Peter Turnerelli (1774–1839), was starkly reduced (1987); above it is a good stucco *Ascension*. The monuments in the church include statues (1855 and 1882) of Archbishop Murray (1768–1852) and Cardinal Cullen (1803–78) by Sir Thomas Farrell. The Pro-Cathedral's Palestrina Choir was endowed by Edward Martyn of Tullira, Co. Galway (*see p. 45*). The celebrated tenor John, Count McCormack (1884–1945) was for a time a member.

Mary's Abbey, linking the intersection of Upper Abbey St and Capel St with the junction of Boot Lane and Arran St, preserves the name of the Cistercian abbey of St Mary. It was affiliated to Savigny in Normandy (*see p. 132*). The only portions of the abbey surviving today are the chapter-house (Nat. Mon.) and adjacent slype of *c.* 1190. (They form the basement of a warehouse in Meeting-house Lane.) In the Middle Ages the abbey was frequently used as a meeting-place of the English Council, and it was in the chapter-house that Silken Thomas Fitzgerald dramatically threw off his allegiance to Henry VIII in 1534, by flinging down his Lord Deputy's Sword of State in the presence of the Council.

Mary Pl. joins Dorset St with Mountjoy St. Here is St Mary's Chapel-of-Ease (1830), by John Semple; it is now owned by Dublin Corporation. Best known as the 'Black Church', this classic example of Semple's highly individual Gothick (*see also pp. 162 and 172*) is remarkable for its parabolic, corbelled vault. (In effect the building has neither walls nor ceiling, but is, structurally speaking, all vault.) The W. gallery is a timber-and-plaster simulation of stonework.

Mary St (*c.* 1675) continues the line of Henry St to Capel St. Shabby St Mary's Church (1700) is the oldest unaltered Protestant church in Dublin, and the first to be built with galleries. In it Theobald Wolfe Tone (born nearby in Wolfe Tone St), the 'Volunteer Earl' of Charlemont and Seán O Casey were baptized, and John Wesley preached his first sermon in Ireland. Archibald Hamilton Rowan, United Irishman, is buried in the churchyard. The impending alteration of the church into a shop imperils the future of the building and its interesting original furnishings.

Merchant's Quay lies between Wood Quay and Usher's Quay. St Francis's Church (1834) was by James Bolger, but the design was never completed. The mural paintings are by Muriel Brandt. (The popular name of the church, 'Adam and Eve's', recalls the fact that its Penal-times predecessor was hidden away in nearby Cook St behind a tavern with the sign *Adam and Eve*.) The gilt bronze *Our Lady* (1955), on the Winetavern St corner of the convent, is by Gabriel Hayes.

Merrion Row runs from the NE. corner of Stephens Green to the joining of Merrion St and Ely Place. Nos. 7–9 are an extension of the National Museum, usually displaying temporary exhibitions. Nearby is a Huguenot cemetery opened in 1693.

Merrion Sq., second largest of Dublin's great squares, lies to the NE. of St Stephen's Green. It was laid out in 1762 by John Ensor for the Fitzwilliam Estate, but was not completed until the end of the century. The great brick houses preserve their Georgian elevations in varying degree, and combine to offer splendid vistas, particularly along the E. and N. sides. Many of them have excellent stucco interiors. The Rutland Memorial (1791), on the W. side of the park, is by Francis Sandys; it has lost its fountain and most of its Coade stone ornaments, but was sympathetically restored in 1975. Statues within the park include *Eire*, in bronze, by Jerome Connor (1876–1943), *Tribute Head* by Elizabeth Frink, and *Henry Grattan* (1746–1820) by Peter Grant.

Many of the great names in modern Dublin history are associated with Merrion Sq.: No. 1, Sir William and Lady Wilde ('Speranza' of *The Nation*) and their son Oscar; No. 5, Sir William Stokes, physician; No. 14, Sir Philip Crampton (1777–1858), surgeon; No. 42, Sir Jonah Barrington (1760–1834), diarist; No. 58, Daniel O Connell (1775–1847); No. 70, now the Arts Council's headquarters, Joseph Sheridan Le Fanu (1814–73); No. 82, William Butler Yeats (1865–1939).

No. 8 is the Royal Institute of the Architects of Ireland; No. 49, the offices of the National University; No. 63, the Royal Society of Antiquaries of Ireland; No. 84, Plunkett House, the headquarters of the Irish Agricultural Organization Society. Plunkett House preserves the memory of Sir Horace Plunkett (1854–1932), founder of the Irish co-operative movement. The poet-painter George William Russell (AE.; 1867–1935) worked there for many years as editor of the *Irish Homestead* (merged with the *Irish Statesman* in 1923); he is commemorated by a bronze bust in the square.

On the W. side of the square is Leinster Lawn, garden of Leinster House, Kildare St (*see p. 155*). It is flanked on the N. by Sir Charles Lanyon's National Gallery, 1859–60 (extensions, including the long Leinster Lawn façade, by Sir Thomas Deane II, 1884, and to the N., 1968). Deane's work is repeated on the S. side of the lawn by the National History Division of the National Museum.

The National Gallery was erected by subscriptions to a testimonial to William Dargan (1799–1867), railway entrepreneur and 'arch improver of his time', whose statue (by Thomas Farrell, R.H.A.) stands on the lawn. George Bernard Shaw, whose favourite statue (by Troubetskoy) also stands nearby, left a third of his estate to the Gallery. The collections of over 6,000 paintings, of which about 700 are on view, is of very high quality and includes a number of celebrated works. The excellence is largely due to Sir Hugh Lane (*see p. 160*).

The General Post Office, O Connell St.

In 1950 the National Gallery received a large and important gift of pictures from Sir Alfred Chester Beatty, which includes a representative collection of works of the Barbizon Group. Its collections were further extended by Sir Alfred and Lady Beit's most generous donation (1987) of superb works by Velazquez, Murillo, Frans Hals and Gainsborough, among others. The remainder of their paintings are housed in Russborough House (*see p. 80*).

The Hugh Lane Municipal Gallery of Modern Art in Parnell Square (*see p. 160*) and the projected Gallery of Modern Art in the Royal Hospital, Kilmainham (*see p. 156*), display the main body of 20th c. art in the nation's capital, so that – with few exceptions – the material on exhibition in the National Gallery comprises European masters of earlier centuries. Indeed, the Gallery's holdings give a high-quality overview of the major schools of European painting, and other than those mentioned above, the major artists represented are:
Austrian: Huber and Seisenegger.
British: Gainsborough, Hogarth, Hoppner, Kneller, Lawrence, Lely, Reynolds, Stubbs and Wheatley, as well as an interesting collection of watercolours by Constable and Turner, among other masters.
Dutch: Avercamp, Bol, Claesz, Cuyp, Van Goyen, Hobbema, de Hooch, Maes, Rembrandt, van Ruysdael, Steen, Stomer, Ter Borch and Weenix.
Flemish: Bosch, Bouts, Brueghel the Younger, David, van Dyck, Jordaens, Rubens, Snyders, Teniers, van der Weyden (school of) and Ysenbrandt.
French: Chardin, Clouet, Daubigny, Delacroix, Géricault, Lorraine, Monet, Morisot, Nicolas, Perronneau and Poussin.
Irish: Ashford, Barret, Chinnery, Hone (Elder and Younger), Kavanagh, Lawless, Leech, Mulready, Orpen, R. O Conor, J.A. O Connor, Osborne, T. and T.S. Roberts, Slaughter and John and Jack B. Yeats.
Italian: *Bologna*: Crespi; *Brescia*: Moroni; *Ferrara*: Mazzolino and Tura; *Florence*: Fra Angelico, Fra Bartolomeo, del Biondo and Michelangelo; *Genoa:* Castiglione, Magnasco and Strozzi; *Milan*: da Solario; *Padua*: Mantegna; *Parma*: Correggio; *Rome*: Feti, Panini and Penni; *Siena*: da Bartolo and di Paolo; *Tuscany*: Gentileschi and Uccello; *Umbria*: Perugino; *Venice*: Bassano, Bellini, Bellotto, Canaletto, Guardi, Lotto, Piazzetta, del Piombo, Tiepolo, Tintoretto and Titian.
Spanish: Goya, El Greco, Gris, Ribera and Zurbaran.
In addition, the Gallery has an interesting collection of icons from the Allen collection, and an alleged Romanesque fresco from the church of St Pierre de Campublic, near Arles.

The small collection of 20th c. art includes a recent bequest by the late Máire Sweeney (otherwise Máire Mac Neill, author of the famous book on *The Festival of Lughnasa*), including works by Picasso, Miró and Gris.

Merrion St, Upper, leads from Merrion Sq. West to Merrion Row. The great building (1911–15) on the W. side (by Sir Aston Webb and Sir Thomas Deane II) was built to house the College of Science and government offices. Many of the houses on the E. side of the street have been vacated by the Land Commission; their future is unknown. Among them is No. 24, Mornington House, where the future Duke of Wellington was born in 1769.

Mespil Rd, beside the tree-lined Grand Canal from Leeson St Bridge to Baggot St Bridge, acquired its name from Mespil House, a country house built near Leeson St Bridge in 1751 by Dr Barry. (The house, which had three of Dublin's very finest ceilings, has been replaced by blocks of flats. The *Jupiter and the Elements* ceiling has been re-erected in Árus an Uachtaráin, Phoenix Park; the *Hibernia* and the *Arts and Sciences* ceilings in Dublin Castle.) In its last days Mespil House was the home of Sarah Purser (d. 1943), painter, stained-glass artist and patron of the arts, to whom the Irish art revival owes so much. Her weekly 'At Homes' were assemblies of the artistic and intellectual talent of Dublin, assemblies she dominated by her personality and acid tongue.

Milltown: *see under* **Sandford Rd,** *below.*

Molesworth St (1727 onwards) leads from the middle of Dawson St to the middle of Kildare St. It contains some of Dublin's earliest 18th c. houses. No. 15 is of the 'Dutch Billy' type normally associated with the weaving or other trades. No. 20 (1730), by Ralph Spring, has a particularly beautiful doorway.

Mount St Lower (about 1820) continues the line of Merrion Sq., North, SE. to Northumberland Rd. John Millington Synge died at No. 130 in 1909. Ugly office blocks now occupy much of the street.

Mount St Upper (about 1820) continues the line of Merrion Sq., South, to Mount St Crescent. The vista along the street and square is very fine, closed on the W. by Leinster House, on the E. by St Stephen's Church. This admirably sited building is the last (1824) of Dublin's neo-Grec Protestant churches. It was designed by John Bowden and completed by John Welland. The portico is modelled on the Erechtheum, the clocktower belfry on the Tower of the Winds and the Monument of Lysicrates in Athens. The *Christ Among the Doctors* window is by Lady Glenavy (1907). E. of the church is Huband Bridge (1791), one of the most attractive of Dublin's unaltered canal bridges.

Mountjoy Square (1792–1808) was laid out for Luke Gardiner, Lord Mountjoy. It is now badly decayed, especially on the S. and W. Nos 7, 8, and 39–44 were fine houses by Michael Stapleton; they have very good interiors. The original intention was to have St George's Church (*see p. 153*) at the centre of the square.

North Circular Rd runs from the Phoenix Park to Portland Row. At the junction with Cabra Rd is St Peter's Church (Vincentian), a large, Gothic-Revival essay by George Goldie of London. In the S. aisle is a three-light *Sacred Heart* window (1919) by Harry Clarke. The door light and four two-light windows of the adjacent Mortuary Chapel are also by Clarke (1921): Symbols of the Passion, etc. Nearby is Dalymount Park, Dublin's principal soccer stadium.

North Great George's St (*c.* 1775 onwards) runs downhill from Great Denmark St to Parnell St. It is one of the finest of Dublin's 18th c. streets, but its splendid vista S. has now been ruined by modern buildings. No. 2 was the Dublin residence of John Dillon (1851–1927), son of the Young Ireland leader John Blake Dillon and himself leader of the Irish Nationalist Party at Westminster. No. 20 was the home of Sir Samuel Ferguson (1810-86), poet and antiquary. Nos. 34 and 35 (Kenmare House) are by Michael Stapleton. No. 38, by Charles Thorp, Sen., was the home of Sir John Pentland Mahaffy (1839–1918), Provost of Trinity College and noted 'character'. No. 45 was the home of Charles Thorp, Sen., builder and stuccoer. In recent years, great efforts have been made by private owners to restore some of the houses.

O Connell St has been in turn Drogheda St and Sackville St. Once the home and haunt of fashion, it is today a vulgar commercial thoroughfare 'resplendent with cinemas and ice-cream parlours' (Maurice Craig). In the late 1740s banker Luke Gardiner replanned the then narrow N. half as an 'elongated residential square', with tree-planted Gardiner's Mall forming a fashionable promenade down the middle. From 1784 onwards the Wide Streets Commissioners laid out the S. half on the same great scale (and with ground floor shops), so spoiling Gardiner's concept. In the 19th c., the thoroughfare was gradually invaded by commercial interests. Nevertheless, it still retained something of its 18th c. dignity until the bombardments of 1916 and 1922. The only noteworthy feature today is the Classical façade of the General Post Office, all that survives of Francis Johnston's work (1814–18); the statues over the portico, *Fidelity, Hibernia,* and *Mercury,* are by John Smyth, eldest son of Edward Smyth (*see pp. 142 and 154*). The Post Office was the headquarters of the 1916 insurgents, who there proclaimed the Irish Republic. (commemorated by the fine Michael Biggs plaque of *c.* 1964 in the wall under the portico). Destroyed in the fighting, it was rebuilt in 1929 by uninspired architects of the Office of Public Works. In the public office is a 1916 memorial, *Death of Cuchulainn* by Oliver Sheppard.

In the C.I.E. Passenger Bureau (No. 59 Lower O Connell St) may be seen a bronze figure of *St Christopher* by Patrick McElroy.

The centre of the street is lined by statues, mostly of indifferent quality. They are (from N. to S.):

Charles Stewart Parnell (1846–91), Home Rule leader, by the Dublin-born American sculptor, Augustus St Gaudens (1911).

A Millennium fountain (1988) by Seán Mulcahy and Eamonn O Doherty.

Father Theobald Matthew (1790–1861), Temperance reformer, 'by Miss Redmond'.

Jim Larkin (1876–1942), labour leader, by Oisín Kelly (1979).

Sir John Gray (1816–75), proprietor of *The Freeman's Journal,* by Sir Thomas Farrell.

William Smith O Brien (1803–64), Young Ireland leader, by Sir John Farrell.

Daniel O Connell (1775–1847) by John Henry Foley. The base, with *Éire Casting off Her Fetters,* and the winged figures of

Patriotism, Fidelity, Eloquence, and *Courage* are by Thomas Brock, who completed the monument in 1882, eight years after Foley's death.

O Connell Bridge, originally Carlisle Bridge, was built in 1791 to the design of James Gandon. In 1880 it was rebuilt to its present width, the slopes flattened, and Edward Smyth's sculptured keystones removed to a warehouse façade on Sir John Rogerson's Quay, where they may still be seen.

Palmerston Park. At No. 20 is the Museum of Childhood, with an exhibition of dolls and toys.

Parliament St runs from Grattan (formerly Essex) Bridge to Cork Hill. It was the first (1762) street opened by the Wide Streets Commissioners. James Clarence Mangan (1803–49), gifted lyric poet, lived at No. 3.

Parnell Square, originally Rutland Square, is the second earliest of Dublin's great Georgian squares. It was begun about the middle of the 18th c. By 1792 the residents included 12 members of the Irish House of Lords, 12 members of the Commons, and two Protestant bishops. It is now largely given over to offices and institutions of various kinds.

On the N. side, Palace Row, is mutilated Charlemont House, since 1932 the Municipal Gallery of Modern Art, renamed the Hugh Lane Municipal Gallery of Modern Art, after its principal benefactor (*see below*). In its day one of the finest of Dublin's mansions, it was built (1761–3) by Sir William Chambers for James Caulfeild, Earl of CHARLEMONT, Commander-in-Chief of the Irish Volunteers who helped secure the independence of the Dublin legislature. The chaste façade has been marred by the 1933 doorway. Little survives of the 18th c. interior except the oval staircase and rooms on the upper floors.

The nucleus of the collection of paintings in the Municipal Gallery was due to the talent and generosity of Sir Hugh Lane. Lane was drowned in the *Lusitania*, shortly after making a codicil to his will, leaving the famous 'Lane Pictures' to Dublin. The codicil was unwitnessed, and therefore invalid. A battle went on between the British and the Irish – individuals, public bodies, and State authorities – until 1959, when an agreement was reached that the collection would be divided into two parts to be shown alternately in Dublin and London in five-year cycles, starting in 1960. By this arrangement half of the collection is always to be seen in Dublin. The 39 pictures of the Impressionist period include works by Boudin, Corot, Courbet, Daubigny, Daumier, Degas, Forain, Jongkind, Manet, Monet, Morisot, Pissarro, Renoir, Rousseau, and Vuillard.

Besides the pictures mentioned there are many important works by 19th and 20th c. masters, including Chinnery, Constable, Fantin-Latour, Géricault, Harpignies, Ingres, Augustus John, Gwen John, Mancini, Millet, John Nash, Roderick O Conor, Segantini, Sargent, Wilson Steer, Turner, and Whistler.

The Irish school is represented by John Butler Yeats, Sir William Orpen, Walter Osborne, Evie Hone, Nathaniel Hone, Jack B. Yeats, Louis Le Brocquy, Patrick Scott, Patrick Collins, Norah Mc Guinness, George Campbell, Gerald Dillon, Derek Hill, Patrick Hennessy, Edward McGuire, Brian and Cecil King, Robert Ballagh, Michael Farrell and Theo Mc Nab.

Contemporary European painting is represented by the following painters: Albers, Ashur, Bonnard, Lhote, Lhurcat, Picasso, Piper, Rouault, Souter, Utrillo and Vlaminck.

The stained-glass collection includes work by Evie Hone and Harry Clarke. The latter's *Eve of St Agnes* window (1924) is particularly noteworthy.

The small sculpture collection includes works by Degas, Epstein, Henry Moore, Rodin, Jerome Connor, and Andrew O Connor.

'Findlater's Church' (Presbyterian; by Andrew Heiton of Perth), at the NE. corner of the square, figures in Joyce's *Ulysses*.

The 1916–22 Garden of Remembrance (1966) was designed by Dáithí P. Hanly. The oval pool has a symbolic sculpture, *The Children of Lir* (1966) by Oisín Kelly.

The E. side of the square (and its southerly prolongation, Cavendish Row) contains some of the most palatial of Dublin's Georgian houses, the exteriors too often mutilated. No. 11 was the town house of the Earl of Ormond. No. 9, erected 1756/7 by Frederick Darley and John Ensor for Dr Bartholomew Mosse, has fine stucco. No. 6 was the house of Richard Kirwan (1733–1812), noted Co. Galway scientist. No. 5 was the birthplace of James Joyce's 'Buck Mulligan' (Oliver St John Gogarty). No. 4 was the town house of the Earl of Wicklow. (For the W. side of Cavendish Row *see* Rotunda Hospital, *below*.)

On the S. side of the square, but facing Parnell St, is the (Rotunda) Lying-in Hospital, celebrated in the annals of obstetrics. Designed for the philanthropist Dr Bartholomew Mosse, by Richard Cassels, it was erected after Cassels' death by his assistant, John Ensor. Typical of Cassels is the combination of central block and curved flanking colonnades with end pavilions. (While never one of Dublin's best buildings, the hospital has been altogether spoiled by horrid 19th–20th c. additions on the W. side.) The staircase has fine stucco by William Lee. But the glory of the hospital is the exotic, almost baroque, chapel designed and executed by Barthélemy Cramillion, a little-known French stucco worker. The gardens (now largely built over) at the rear of the hospital were laid out by Mosse as a revenue-raising pleasure ground for the world of fashion. At the E. end of the hospital is the Rotunda after which it is now named. The Rotunda was erected in 1764 as an assembly room, to the designs of John Ensor, and improved by James Gandon in 1786, when the frieze and Coade stone plaques by Edward Smyth were added. In the course of its chequered history this fine hall witnessed many memorable events: the first public appearances of John Field and of Michael O Kelly, Mozart's friend; a concert by Franz Liszt; Newman's University Discourses; and the 1783 Volunteer Convention. About 1910 the building was savagely adapted for use as a cinema; it has since been subjected to further abuse. Adjoining it on the NE., i.e. on the W. side of Cavendish Row, are the New Assembly Rooms (1784–6). The plan was by Frederick Trench, the elevations by Richard Johnston, elder brother of Francis. The Supper Room has been for many years the well-known Dublin Gate Theatre. In general, the 20th c. treatment of these attractive buildings has been on a par with that of the Hospital, the Rotunda, and the Gardens. In 1961 and again in 1987 the Pillar Room was redecorated; it is now used as a lecture hall for medical students and, occasionally, as a concert-hall.

Patrick St connects the junction of New St, Upper Kevin St, and Dean St, with Nicholas St, and so with Christchurch Pl. Here, in the valley of the little River Poddle (now covered over), was one of the early suburbs outside the walled town, a suburb with its own pre-Norman parish church. From the Middle Ages until 1860 much of the district was the Archbishop's Liberty. On the S. side of St Patrick's Park, provided by the first Earl of Iveagh, is St Patrick's Cathedral, the largest church (300 ft long) ever built in Ireland. It occupies the site of the pre-Norman parish church of St Patrick. In 1191 the church was rebuilt as a collegiate church by Archbishop Comyn. Comyn's successor, Henry de Londres, having quarrelled with the dean and chapter of Christchurch, advanced St Patrick's to cathedral status in 1213. The rivalry between the new and the old cathedrals was ended in 1300 by a papal decree recognizing the precedence of Christchurch. At the Reformation Christchurch wholly ousted its rival, and St Patrick's was reduced to the status of a parish church; but the short-lived Catholic restoration under Philip and Mary gave it back its cathedral status.

In 1320 Archbishop Alexander de Bykenore instituted the University of Dublin at St Patrick's, but it languished from the start for lack of endowment, and finally petered out sometime after 1494. The Cathedral retained its diocesan status until the disestablishment of the Church of Ireland in 1869, when it was set apart as 'national cathedral' of that Church. Jonathan Swift was Dean of the cathedral, 1713–45.

The cruciform church has aisled nave (eight-bay), transepts, and choir (four-bay), and a four-bay, square-ended, eastern Lady Chapel recalling that of Salisbury. It is thought that the westernmost bay of the S. aisle, now the baptistry, is a relic of Comyn's collegiate church; but the rest of the building derives from the 13th–14th c. cathedral. The Lady Chapel was built in 1270. Around 1362, Archbishop Minot built the great NW. tower (147 ft), curiously out of alignment with the church. In 1544 the piers and vaulting of the nave collapsed; at the rebuilding the piers were replaced by granite shafts. In 1749–50 the 100 ft granite spire (architect, George Semple) was added to Minot's tower. (Swift had prevented the erection of a brick one in 1714.) In the 17th, 18th, and early-19th c. the fabric suffered severely from neglect and abuse, necessitating a general restoration of the cathedral, undertaken in 1864–9 (architect, Sir Thomas Drew) at the expense of Sir Benjamin Lee Guinness. Drew found it necessary to rebuild much of the structure from the ground up. Most of the exterior facing is his work, as are the piers of the nave arcade, and all the vaulting (stone only over the choir). The N. and S. porches, the W. door and window, and the nave buttresses are new features. In 1901 the organ chamber was added by Drew, Lord Iveagh defraying the cost.

The usual entrance is by the S. porch. Nearby is a statue of Sir Benjamin Lee Guinness by John Henry Foley (1818–74).

The Choir is the best preserved part of the medieval fabric. It served as the chapel of the now moribund Order of St Patrick, which was instituted in 1783 by George III. The knights' banners hang above the stalls. After the disestablishment of the Church of Ireland the installation ceremony was transferred to Dublin Castle.

The principal monuments, etc., of the cathedral are:

South aisle: at the foot of the second pier are the graves of Jonathan Swift (1667–1745) and his 'Stella' (Esther Johnson, 1681–1728). The nearby door of the robing-room is flanked by Swift's monument to 'Stella' and Patrick Cunningham's bust (1775) of Swift, the latter the gift of Swift's publisher. The immortal epitaph above the door was composed by Swift himself. On the N. side of the aisle is the old chapter-house door with a hole cut through it, which recalls an armed quarrel in 1492 between the Earls of Kildare and Ormond. The latter took refuge in the chapter-house. When the quarrel was patched up the hole was cut in the door so that Ormond might safely shake hands with Kildare.

South transept: 'Statue' of 'St Patrick', consisting of a 17th c. (?) head attached to the body of a 13th c. effigy. In the SW. corner is the tomb of Swift's servant, McGee. The adjacent monument to Lady Doneraile is by Simon Vierpyl.

South choir aisle: in the wall are interesting brasses in memory of Dean Sutton (d. 1528), Dean Fyche (d. 1537), Sir Edward Fitton (d. 1579), and Sir Henry Wallop (d. 1608); the Fyche brass has silver inlay. In a small recess is the tomb effigy of an unidentified archbishop.

St Stephen's Chapel: by the S. wall is the tomb of Archbishop Tregury (d.1471).

North choir aisle: here are the mutilated effigy of an archbishop, and the tablet with which Swift marked the grave of the Duke of Schomberg (1615–90), William III's general, who fell at the Boyne.

North transept: in the NW. corner may be seen Swift's simple wooden pulpit.

North aisle: the monuments here include the Renaissance monument of Archbishop Thomas Jones (d. 1619), with effigies of the prelate and his son, Lord Ranelagh; a statue (intended for O Connell St) of the Marquess of Buckingham by Edward Smyth (1788); a bust of John Philpot Curran (1750–1817); and Lady Morgan's memorial to Turloch O Carolan (1670–1738), celebrated harpist and writer of Gaelic songs. In the NW. corner may be seen a pre-Norman cross-inscribed stone found at St Patrick's Well, close to Minot's tower.

Nave: built against the westernmost bay of the S. arcade is a monument (by Edward Tingham of Chapelizod) which was originally erected in the choir by Richard Boyle, 'Great' Earl of Cork (1566–1643), to the memory of his wife. Its removal in 1633 by Lord Deputy Strafford to its present, more appropriate, position fomented a feud which contributed to Strafford's downfall and execution in 1641.

SE. of the cathedral, in St Patrick's Close (cut through the Deanery grounds at the 1864–9 restoration), is Marsh's Library, oldest public library in Ireland. It was founded by Archbishop Narcissus Marsh, and the building was begun about 1701 by Sir William Robinson. The exterior was refaced and altered in details at the Guinness restoration, but Robinson's altogether charming interior happily survives. The library has an interesting collection of manuscripts and early printed books.

Adjoining the library on the SE. (entrance Upper Kevin St) is a police station which incorporates fragments (vault, window, etc.) of the medieval archiepiscopal palace of St Sepulchre and its 16th and 17th c. successors.

St Patrick's Deanery (entrance now from Upper Kevin St) is the 1781 successor of Swift's Deanery. It has a fine staircase hall, some wood-carving by John Houghton, and a few relics of Swift.

In St Patrick's Park, to the N. of the cathedral, is a sculpture *Bell Sound* (1988) by Vivienne Roche (b. 1953).

Pembroke St, Upper and Lower (*c.* 1820), connects Lower Baggot St with Lower Leeson St. Between Nos 25 and 26 Upper Pembroke St (now demolished) was An Túr Gloine, the Tower of Glass, co-operative studio for ecclesiastical art founded in 1903 by Sarah Purser (d. 1943), who contributed so signally to the creation of the Dublin school of stained glass. Besides Sarah Purser herself, Wilhelmina Geddes, Michael Healy (1873–1941), Catherine O Brien (d. 1963), Evie Hone (1894–1955) and Patrick Pollen were all members of the studio for greater or lesser periods.

Phoenix Park, The, on the NW. side of the city (principal city entrances from Parkgate St, the N. Circular Rd and Conyngham Rd, Islandbridge), covers 1,752 acres, and is one of the largest and most magnificent city parks in Europe. In 1662 lands were acquired for the purpose of creating a royal deer park of over 2,000 acres around The Phoenix, a viceregal Country Residence, but the acreage was reduced in 1679. In the Lord Lieutenancy of the Earl of Chesterfield (1744–7) the park received the essentials of its existing layout.

Just inside the Main Gate (Parkgate St) are the beautiful People's Gardens. To the E. is the Department of Defence, designed as the Royal Military Infirmary by James Gandon, but erected (1787 onwards) by W. Gibson, who designed the cupola. Beyond the People's Gardens are the Zoological Gardens (1830), noted for the breeding of lions.

On the S. side of the main road are hundreds of acres of playing fields for hurling, football, cricket, etc. Here, too, is the colossal Wellington Testimonial (205 ft) by Sir Robert Smirke (1817 onwards). The bronze *Emancipation* panel designed by John Hogan was executed by his Italian friend, Benzoni, from Hogan's model. Further W., to the N. of the main road, is the Polo Ground.

Close to the main road-junction of the park is the beautiful Phoenix Column, erected by Lord Chesterfield in 1747. Nearby is Áras an Uachtaráin, residence of the President of the Republic. The house originated as a small park ranger's lodge *c.* 1751–2. In 1782 it was purchased for the Lord Lieutenant's use, and later enlarged to make it his chief official residence. Michael Stapleton did work there in 1787. The Doric porch of the N. front was added in 1808. In 1815–16 Francis Johnston added the Ionic portico of the S. front; also dining and other rooms. In 1840 the formal garden was laid out by the celebrated Decimus Burton. The E. and W. wings of the garden front were added, seemingly, for Queen Victoria's 1849 visit; the W. wing was reconstructed 1946–7, the E. wing 1954–7. In 1952 the lovely *Jupiter and the Elements* ceiling from Mespil House (*see p. 159*) was erected in the President's Reception Room. The house also has good 18th c. mantelpieces from Mountjoy Sq. On 6 May 1882, Lord Frederick Cavendish, newly arrived Chief Secretary for Ireland, and T.H. Burke, the Under-Secretary, were stabbed to death in sight of the house. These Phoenix Park Murders did much to embitter Anglo-Irish relations.

SW. of Áras an Uachtaráin is the residence of the United States Ambassador (originally the Chief Secretary's Lodge). This is an 18th c. house enlarged in 1775 and subsequently modified; it has stucco by Michael Stapleton.

On the S. side of the park, sited on the steep terrace of the Liffey, is St Mary's Chest Hospital, built in 1766 as the Royal Hibernian Military School. The chapel is by Thomas Cooley (1771). The main building was enlarged by Francis Johnston (1808–13); it has recently been mutilated. To the N. is a tall steel cross erected to commemorate the spot where Pope John Paul II addressed a crowd of about one million people in 1979.

Rathfarnham: *see p. 270.*

Rathmines is a 19th c. suburb to the S. of the Grand Canal. In 1649 the Parliamentarian garrison of Dublin decisively routed Ormonde's besieging Royalist army here.

Portobello Barracks chapel (most convenient entrance from Rathmines Rd) has a three-light window (*Good Shepherd, St Patrick, St Joseph*) by Evie Hone (1937).

The Church of Our Lady of Refuge (1850), Rathmines Rd, was by Patrick Byrne. The Protestant parish church, Belgrave Rd, is by John Semple (1833). It has an early (1909) Michael Healy four-light window (*SS Philip, Peter, Paul, Andrew*).

St Andrew St leads off Suffolk St. St Andrew's Protestant Church, a good Gothic-Revival essay by Lanyon, Lynn, and Lanyon, is the successor of one (1793–1807) by John Hartwell, completed by Francis Johnston, which had over the entrance a statue of St Andrew by the great Edward Smyth. The gentlemen of Daly's Club, College Green, used this for pistol practice. Badly corroded, it stands in the churchyard.

St Stephen's Green, earliest and largest of Dublin's great squares, was originally a common outside the town wall. In 1664–5 the periphery was laid out in building plots and the central part enclosed. The following year the enclosed green was levelled to serve as a military exercise ground. In the course of the 18th c. the older houses about the Green were replaced by lordly mansions which still survive. Many of these came through mortgages into the hands of the La Touche family of bankers.

North Side: No. 8, now the United Services Club, and No. 9, now the Stephen's Green Club, date from 1754 and 1756 respectively. Both have suffered from refronting, but contain good 18th c. stucco. No. 16, now offices, was built (1776) for Gustavus Hume of Castle Hume, Co. Fermanagh. It was later the palace of the Protestant Archbishop of Dublin. The stucco is by Michael Stapleton. No. 17 (1776–8), from 1850 the Dublin University Club (and since 1976 the Kildare St and University Club), was originally Milltown House (Leeson family); it too has fine ceilings and other stucco by Michael Stapleton. The Shelbourne Hotel occupies the site of Kerry House, alias Shelburne House. Among the many famous guests of the Shelbourne Hotel were Amanda McKittrick Ross, Thackeray (it figures in his *Irish Sketch Book*), and George Moore (it figures in *A Drama in Muslin*). Nos 32 (Shelbourne Rooms), 33, and 34 date from 1770 and contain much good plasterwork by Michael Stapleton; two floors have been added to No. 32.

East Side: The Bank of Ireland office at the corner of Merrion Row occupies the site of Tracton House whose splendid Apollo room has been re-erected in Dublin Castle. Outside the bank is the arched sculpture *Trace* (1988) by Grace Weir (b. 1962). Nos 52 and 53 are a Michael Stapleton pair of 1771. The former, now the office of the Ombudsman, has stucco by Stapleton. No. 56 was built by the brothers West in 1760 for Usher St George, later Lord Hume.

South Side: Iveagh House, now the Department of Foreign

Grand Canal, Dublin.

O Connell Bridge and O Connell St, Dublin (see pages 159 and 160).

Affairs, incorporates Nos 80 and 81. (No. 80 was built in 1730 by Richard Cassels for Bishop Clayton of Killala.) Some of the 18th c. interior work has survived. Benjamin Lee Guiuness was his own architect when he re-modelled the house for himself and his family in the 1860s. Nos 82–87 formed the main buildings of the Catholic University (the Medical School was in Cecilia St, St Mary's House at No. 6 Harcourt St); with the exception of No. 87, they now form part of University College (*see p. 150*). No. 84 was rebuilt in 1878 as the Aula Maxima of the then University College. No. 85, Clanwilliam House, was built about 1740 by Richard Cassels; the beautiful saloon has a splendid coved ceiling with stucco figure-subjects and arabesques by the Franchini brothers. No. 86, Newman House, is one of the finest of Dublin's great houses. It was built, 1760–5, probably by Robert West (*see p. 148*), for Richard Chapell ('Burn Chapel') Whaley, execrated priest-hunter and father of the notorious rake, 'Buck' Whaley. The interior has notable stucco, probably by West. The lead lion on the portico is by John Van Nost, Jr. Tradition ascribes the scale of Whaley's house to a vulgar desire to outdo No. 85. In 1853 both houses were purchased by Cardinal Cullen and thrown together to form the headquarters and St Patrick's House of the Catholic University of Ireland, which opened its doors the following year with John Henry Newman as first Rector (1853–8; it was in preparation for this that Newman had delivered his celebrated *Discourses on the Scope and Nature of University Education* at the Rotunda, Parnell Sq., 1852). After Newman, the most distinguished names connected with the University were probably: Eugene O Curry (1796–1862), whom Newman appointed Professor of Archaeology and Irish History, thereby founding University College's fine tradition in Celtic Studies; John Hungerford Pollen (1820–1902), member of the Oxford Movement, Professor of Fine Arts; Denis Florence McCarthy (1817–82), poet and translator of Calderón, Professor of English Literature; and George Sigerson (1838–1925), physician, scientist, poet, and historian, Lecturer in Botany. The Faculties of Arts and Science were transformed into University College in 1881, and the following year the college was entrusted to the Jesuits. This Jesuit college, seated in Nos 84–6, was the University College where Gerard Manley Hopkins (1844–89) was professor, and Patrick H. Pearse (1879–1916), Eamon de Valera (1882–1975), Thomas M. Kettle (1880–1916), and James Joyce (1882–1941) were students. (In the students' magazine, *St Stephen's*, Joyce's first writing appeared; references in the magazine to 'the Hatter' are to Joyce.) In 1909 the college was reunited with the medical school and transformed into a college of the new, undenominational, National University of Ireland. In due course the lecture halls and library were transferred to Earlsfort Terrace (*see p. 150*). Adjoining No. 86 is the neo-Byzantine University Church (1855–6) by John Hungerford Pollen. It was erected by Newman as chapel and place of ceremonial assembly of the Catholic University, but now serves parochial purposes. In the nave is a bust of Newman by Farrell.

West Side: The Unitarian Church has windows by Ethel Rhind (two-light *Good Samaritan*, 1937) and A.E. Child (five-light *Discovery, Truth, Inspiration, Love, Work*, 1918). Nos 119 and 120 were formally designed as a pair in 1761; the elevation is said to be after Cassels. The Royal College of Surgeons at the corner of York St was built in 1806 to the design of Edward Parke. In 1827 it was extended N., and recentred, by William Murray, losing in the process. Interiors by both architects survive. The statues of *Aesculapius, Minerva* and *Hygieia* are by John Smyth, son of Edward Smyth. In 1916 the college was the headquarters of a contingent of the Citizen Army under the command of Michael Mallin and the Countess Markievicz (Constance Gore-Booth). Nos 124–5 (now demolished) were the home of Dr Robert Emmet, whose patriot sons, Robert and Thomas, were born there. On the opposite side of the road is a statue of Robert Emmet (1916) by Jerome Connor.

St Stephen's Green Park owes its beauty to the munificence of Sir Arthur Guinness (Lord Ardilaun), at whose expense it was laid out in 1880. The triumphal arch at the NW. corner is a Boer War memorial to the Dublin Fusiliers. Close by is a memorial, by Séamus Murphy, to Jeremiah O Donovan Rossa (1831–1915), the Fenian leader. Other monuments in the park are: a statue of Lord Ardilaun by John Henry Foley; a *Three Fates* fountain by Josef Wackerle, gift of the German people in thanksgiving for Ireland's share in relieving distress after the Second World War; excellent busts of James Clarence Mangan (1803–49), poet, by Oliver Sheppard; Thomas M. Kettle (1880–1916), patriot and orator, by Francis Doyle; the Countess Markievicz (*see p. 268*), by Séamus Murphy; and memorials to W.B. Yeats by Henry Moore, and James Joyce by Marjorie Fitzgibbon. At the NE. corner are *The Famine* and *Wolfe Tone* (1907) by Edward Delarney (b. 1933).

Sandford Rd leads from Ranelagh to the junction of Eglinton Rd and Milltown Rd. The Protestant church has a 1927 Harry Clarke window (*SS Peter and Paul*). Milltown Park is a Jesuit house of studies and retreats. In one of the chapels are four Evie Hone windows (symbols of the Evangelists, 1953). Nearby Gonzaga College, a Jesuit school, has an interesting 1959 chapel, triangular on plan, by Andrew J. Devane with fine stained glass (1967 and 1980) by Frances Biggs. Milltown Protestant church has a three-light War Memorial window (*Sacrifice, Victory, Peace*) by A.E. Child (1920).

Sandymount is a seaside suburb to the E. of Ballsbridge (*see pp. 141–2*), with many attractive, early-19th c. villas. The Methodist church has windows by A.E. Child (*St Paul,* 1922), Ethel Rhind (*Dorcas Seated,* 1933) and Evie Hone (heraldic window, 1943; *Rock of Ages,* 1945). W.B. Yeats (1865–1939) was born at No. 2, Georgeville, Sandymount Ave; he is commemorated by a bust in Sandymount Green by Albert Power.

Seán MacDermott St, originally Gloucester St, joins Cathal Brugha St to the intersection of Amiens St, Portland Row, and North Strand.

At the E. end of the street is gaunt and much mutilated Aldborough House (1792–8), latest of Dublin's great Georgian mansions (now Bord Telecom). It was built by Edward Stratford, 2nd Earl of Aldborough, on the then edge of the city – whence RUS IN URBE on the portico.

Shrewsbury Rd: *see under* **Ballsbridge.**

South Wall, The (1708–62), is the longer of the two great 18th c. works designed (by Capt. Bligh of the *Bounty*) to improve the navigation of the Liffey. It stretches from Butt Bridge to the Poolbeg Lighthouse (1762), a distance of more than 4 m. The construction of the wall also made possible the reclamation of the slobands on which so much of SE. Dublin now stands. On the Wall, to the E. of Ringsend, is the Pigeon House, where the E.S.B. coal-fired power station occupies the Pigeon House Fort, named after an innkeeper named Pigeon, whose hostelry, on the site of the fort, was frequented by packet-boat passengers.

Steevens Lane, which runs from the junction of Bow Lane and James's St to Kingsbridge, takes its name from Dr Richard Steevens (d. 1710), son of a Cromwellian immigrant. Steevens left his large estate in trust for his sister Grizel (1654–1747), better known as Madam Steevens, and for the founding of a general hospital after her death. Madam Steevens decided to found the hospital in her own lifetime. Plans were drawn up by Thomas Burgh as early as 1713, but the building was not begun until about 1720, and was not opened until 1733. Government cutbacks forced it to close in 1987, and the future of the buildings is in doubt. The hospital's valuable library, bequeathed by Edward Worth (d. 1733), one of the early trustees, has been given to Trinity College. Dean Swift was one of the early trustees of the hospital, and when he died the hospital gave the site for nearby Swift's Hospital (*see p. 155*).

Suffolk St: *see* **St Andrew St.**

Synge St leads from Grantham St to Lennox St across Harrington St (South Circular Rd). George Bernard Shaw was born in No. 33 (then No. 3) in 1856.

Terenure (formerly Roundtown), a village on the Harold's Cross–Rathfarnham road, has been engulfed by 19th–20th c. suburbs. St Joseph's Church has one of Harry Clarke's best windows, *The Adoration of the Cross* (three light, 1920). The Holy Ghost Missionary College, Whitehall Rd E., has a *St Columcille* window (chapel) by Hubert McGoldrick (1940).

Thomas St, linking Cornmarket with James's St, takes its name from the abbey of St Thomas the Martyr (founded in 1177 by Henry II for Augustinian Canons of St Victor), which stood to the S. of the present St Catherine's Church. At the E. end of the street is the great Gothic-Revival Church of SS Augustine and John (1860–72), by Edward Welby Pugin and George C. Ashlin (timber vault). It has a very fine four-light window (*St Augustine*, 1934) by Michael Healy, set up opposite the position for which it was designed and obscured by a wire screen; it is best viewed by bright morning light. No. 152 Thomas St is the successor of the house in which Lord Edward Fitzgerald was arrested, 18 May 1798. At the W. end of the street is St Catherine's Church (1760–69) by John Smyth. The façade is a good composition and the decaying galleried interior (good chancel) is interesting. Robert Emmet was executed in front of the church in 1803.

Usher's Quay lies between Merchant's Quay and Usher's Island. No. 15, the home of his aunts, was the setting of James Joyce's short story *The Dead*. Queen's Bridge (1764–8), oldest and most beautiful of Dublin's bridges, is attributed to Gen. Vallancey, army engineer and antiquary.

Werburgh St runs from the junction of Castle St, Lord Edward St, and Christchurch Pl., to Bride St. (For St Werburgh's Church *see p. 142*.) Dublin's first theatre was opened in Werburgh St in 1636 by John Ogilby, Master of the Revels. The same year saw the production of the first Anglo-Irish play, James Shirley's *Saint Patrick for Ireland*.

Westland Row connects Pearse St with Lincoln Pl. Oscar Wilde (1854–1900) was born in No. 21. The Royal Irish Academy of Music (founded 1856) occupies the old town-house of Lord Conyngham; the façade was freed of a plaster blanketing in 1963; the interior has good ceilings and wall plaques and noteworthy door cases. St Andrew's Catholic Church (1832–7), by James Bolger, is one of the largest of Dublin's post-Emancipation, neo-Grec, churches. It has an excellent small *Transfiguration* group by John Hogan (1800–1858; completed by his son, John Valentine Hogan). Hogan also carved the lovely Elizabeth Farrell monument. Above the altar is a wooden *Crucifix* by Oisín Kelly.

Westmoreland St (together with the adjoining D Olier St) was laid out about 1800 by the Wide Streets Commissioners as a street of shops with uniform, pilastered ground floors (?by James Gandon). The statue (1857) of Thomas Moore (1779–1852), at the junction with College St, is by Christopher Moore.

William St connects St Andrew St with Johnston's Pl. (junction of Lower Mercer St and South King St).

Powerscourt House (1771–4) was built for Viscount Powerscourt by Robert Mack. In 1807 it was sold to the Commissioners of Stamp Duties, who filled the sides of the courtyard with brick buildings, now forming Dublin's most elegant shopping arcade. The house is one of the most imposing of Dublin's private palaces (ground floor windows spoilt). The overwhelming façade, with its coarse details, is a contrast to the delicately decorated interior. Hall and staircase are by James McCullagh (carving by Ignatius McDonagh); the reception rooms by Michael Stapleton.

No. 58, the Civic Museum, was built (1765–71) for the Society of Artists, the octagonal room being for the Society's exhibitions. From 1791 to 1852 this room served as Municipal Council Chamber, whence the former name, City Assembly House. (In 1799 the Irish Bar met there and voted against the proposed Union of Ireland with Britain.) It was later the Court of Conscience, presided over by the Lord Mayor until 1924. From 1920 to 1922 the outlawed Supreme Court of the Irish Republic held its sessions here. The collection of Dublin relics is in the custody of the Old Dublin Society.

Wood Quay, linking Essex Quay with the N. end of Winetavern St, gets its name from the wooden quays which increasingly encroached on the shores of the Liffey from *c.* 1200. Adjoining them are the two towers of the Dublin Corporation's Civic Offices (1985, by Sam Stephenson; entrance from Fishamble St) which the City Fathers, against the wishes of 20 000 citizens who marched in protest in 1978, insisted on erecting on the site of a part of the old Viking city excavated by the National Museum in 1972–8. These excavations unearthed the foundations of wood and wattle houses built on top of one another for generations after the 10th c., and which showed evidence of retaining the same property boundaries over a number of centuries. They also revealed the cramped and unhygienic conditions in which Dubliners of the time lived. A small proportion of the finds from the excavations are on display in the National Museum.

DULEEK, Co. Meath (Map 2, I9), now bypassed by the Drogheda (5 m.)–Ashbourne (11 m.)–Dublin (23 m.) road, is a place with a long history. It takes its name from a *daimh liag*, house of stones, i.e. an early stone-built church. Its history begins about A.D. 450 with the setting up of a bishopric by St Patrick, who confided it to the care of St Cíanán (d. 24 November 489), but it apparently became monastic later. The place was sacked several times by the Norse between 830 and 1149, and was pillaged by the Anglo-Normans in 1171. The bodies of Brian Boru and his son lay in state there in April 1014, on their way to Armagh. In the 12th c., seemingly, the monastery was reconstituted as St Mary's Abbey of Canons Regular of St Augustine by one of the O Kellys of Brega.

Hugh de Lacy established a manor at Duleek and constructed a motte-castle. About 1180 he granted St Cíanán's Church (by then parochial), together with certain lands, to the Augustinian priory of Llanthony Secunda outside Gloucester, and the Llanthony canons built a grange, or farmhouse, as the headquarters of their estate.

The churchyard at the disused Protestant church occupies part of the site of the early monastery and its Irish Augustinian successor. The ruins of St Cíanán's Church are outside the churchyard to the NW.; St Cíanán's grave was at the N. side of the chancel. Inside the churchyard, to the N. of the modern church, stands the 9th c. (?) North Cross: the figure subjects include scenes from the early life of the Virgin (?) and a *Crucifixion*.

The remains (Nat. Mon.) of St Mary's Abbey are SW. of the modern church, viz. the S. aisle and arcade of a 15th c. church and a massive tower erected in the 16th c. at the W. end of the nave. This tower had been built against the Round Tower of the early monastery (as at LUSK), as is shown by the 'matrix' of the Round Tower in its N. face. Within the church ruins are some early cross-slabs, a Romanesque pilaster-capital and the base and head (with *Crucifixion*) of the South Cross (Nat. Mons.). In the aisle are some 16th–17th c. monuments, including the effigial tomb (defaced) of Dr James Cusack, Bishop of Meath (1679–88), with the 'first draft' on the underside, and the rich tomb of John, Lord Bellew, 'shot in the belly in Oughrim (*sic–see p. 52*) 1691'. The mensa-slab of the latter is supported by tomb-surrounds bearing the arms of Bellew, Plunkett, Preston, and St Lawrence, as well as figure carvings (*Crucifixion; SS Michael, Peter, Patrick, Thomas of Canterbury* (?), *Catherine of Alexandria*). The E. window of the aisle (arms of Sir John Bellew and Dame Ismay Nugent beneath it) is a 1587, post-Gothic replacement.

S. of the churchyard, in the village marketplace, is part of the shaft (Nat. Mon.) of a rudely figured wayside cross erected in 1601 by Jennet Dowdall in memory of herself and her husband, William Bathe (d. 1599) of Athcarne (*below*): Bathe–Dowdall arms and figures of SS Cíanán, Patrick, James, Thomas, James the Less, and Catherine of Alexandria, as well as an *Ecce Homo*. (For other Ienet Dowdall-William Bathe and Reask-Gaulstown crosses, *see below and pp. 42 and 281*.) Another cross erected by Thomassina Berford in 1635 was re-erected in 1981 at the outskirts of the town, beside the Drogheda road.

An inscription on the bridge (of St Mary Magdalen) over the old bed of the Nanny Water records that it was [re]built in 1587 by William and Genet Bathe of Athcarne.

3 m. N. is Donore, a village on the southern Navan (13 m.)–Drogheda (4 m.) road. At the Battle of the Boyne, 1 July 1690

The North Cross, Duleek.

(*see p. 134*), the Jacobite camp stretched along the slopes of Donore Hill (402 ft), and James II's command-post was near the ruined hill-top church. In Donore church are the remains of a Synnott altar-tomb.

1¾ m. S., beside the Dublin road in Lunderstown, and near the entrance gate to Annesbrook, is a second Ienet Dowdall-William Bathe wayside cross (1600). Annesbrook is a good small house with Ionic portico.

2¼ m. SW., by the roadside on the border of Reask and Gaulstown, is the White Cross (Nat. Mon.), erected by Cecilia Dowdall *c.* 1665; the figure carvings include a *Crucifixion* and *Virgin and Child*. About ½ m. SE. is Athcarne Castle, an Elizabethan stronghouse (with additions) built in 1590 by William Bathe.

1¾ m. W. of the White Cross, on the W. side of the Slane road and to the N. of Balrath crossroads, is the Aylmer Cross (Nat. Mon.), a late-medieval wayside cross 'beautified' in 1727 by Sir Andrew Aylmer and his lady, Catherine; on one face is a *Crucifixion*, on the other a *Pietà*.

Proleek dolmen, Ballymascanlon, Co. Louth.

DUNCANNON, Co. Wexford (Map 4, J5), is a pleasant little village and resort situated on the E. shoreline of Waterford Harbour.

On a rocky promontory W. of the village is Duncannon Fort which, in 1645, was taken by the Confederate Catholics after a two-month siege. It was successfully held by them against the Cromwellian general, Ireton, in 1649, but surrendered after the capitulation of Waterford. Thereafter the fort was rebuilt several times, and the latest works date from the last century. In 1690 the defeated James II took ship at Duncannon for Kinsale, en route for France, and shortly afterwards John Churchill, later 1st Duke of Marlborough, captured the fort. From Duncannon he advanced into S. Munster to take Cork and Kinsale for William of Orange, who himself sailed from Duncannon for England that same year.

DUNDALK, Co. Louth (Map 2, I5), county town of Louth, is a prosperous manufacturing town, seaport and market centre. It stands at the head of Dundalk Bay, on the main Dublin (52 m.)–Belfast (51 m.) road.

The town traces its origin to the grant by Prince John of the surrounding country to Bertram de Verdon in 1186. Under the protection of de Verdon's castle (*see* Castletown, *below*) a settlement sprang up which grew in time into a walled town, taking its English name from Dún Dealgan, a prehistoric fort in the neighbourhood, which early Irish literature treats as the home of the mythical hero Cú Chulainn. In the later Middle Ages the town was an important border-fortress of the English Pale and a base for English attacks on Ulster. As such it figures prominently in the various wars, and was burned many times, among others, by Edward Bruce, who was crowned King of Ireland in the presence of his allies on neighbouring Knocknamelan in 1316. The town walls were finally thrown down in 1724.

In the Market Sq. is the Court House (1813–18) by Edward Park (John Bowden supervising architect), its Doric portico modelled on the Temple of Theseus in Athens.

At the N. end of Clanbrassil St is the Protestant parish church of St Nicholas. It incorporates the remains of the 13th c. parish church, but the church was remodelled in 1707. Early in the 19th c. considerable alterations and additions were carried out by Francis Johnston. The E. window contains fragments of 16th and 17th c. Dutch stained glass. In addition to the interesting medieval monuments in the churchyard, there is a memorial erected in 1859 to Robert Burns, whose sister, Agnes Galt, is buried in the churchyard.

St Patrick's Church, Francis Pl., is a Gothic essay (1835–47) by Thomas John Duff of Newry. The high altar and reredos were designed by J.J. McCarthy. The side-altar sculptures, *Agony in the Garden* and *The Dead Christ* are by Sir Thomas Farrell (1827–1900).

Seatown 'Castle', at the corner of Castle St and Mill St, is actually the 15th c. tower of a Franciscan friary founded *c.* 1244 by John de Verdon. Admiral Sir F. Leopold M'Clintock, K.C.B., F.R.S. (1819–1907), Arctic explorer (*The Voyage of the 'Fox' in Arctic Seas*), was born at Kincora House, Seatown Pl.

Near the W. end of the town, in Ard Easmainn, is the oval church of the Holy Redeemer (1969) by F.M. Corr and Associates. The exterior Stations of the Cross in wire are by Imogen Stuart; the lettered bronze doors by Frank Morris, the dark but effective stained glass by Gabriel Loire, the font and altar by Michael Biggs, the sanctuary and stone furnishings by Ray Carroll, and the steel Calvary on the roof by Oisín Kelly.

4 m. N. is Faughart, supposed birthplace of St Brigid (*see p. 211*). There are remains of an old church on the site of a monastery attributed to her.

Near the W. corner of the church is the Grave of King Edward Bruce. Also in the churchyard are Tobar Bhríde and the rough base of a cross. WNW. of the churchyard is a fine Anglo-Norman motte erected on an earlier dwelling-site.

4–4½ m. N., to the W. of the Newry road, in Aghnaskeagh, are two prehistoric cairns (Nat. Mons.) and a ringfort. One of the cairns enclosed a roofless portal-tomb; the other, 50 yds to the S., contained four separate chamber-tombs of Neolithic age. 1¾ m. S. of the reservoir, in Proleek, are the Giant's Load (Nat. Mon.) – a fine portal-tomb – and a wedge-shaped gallery grave ('the grave of Para Buí Mór Mhac Seóidín, a Scottish giant who came here to challenge Finn mac Cool').

4 m. SE. is the small seaside resort of Blackrock. 3 m. W., on the road to Louth, are Heynestown motte and castle, the latter a tower with round angle turrets.

1 m. S. is the Carroll factory (Scott, Tallon, Walker), with a large Louis le Brocquy tapestry *The Hosting of the Táin* (1969), and the mobile sculpture *Sails* by Gerda Fromel.

1½ m. WNW., in Castletown, is Dealgain, a motte-and-bailey of Bertram de Verdon's castle, which in modern times has been identified with the Dún Dealgan of early Irish literature. Castlefolly, whose ruins crown the summit, was built in 1780 by a Capt. Byrne. NE. is Bellews Castle, built (1472–79) by Richard Bellew and modified in the 16th and 17th c.; it has beautifully crenellated parapets. Near it, on the site of an older church, are the ruins of a 15th–16th c. manorial church. 1¾ m. N. is Kilcurry Catholic church with two windows designed by Sarah Purser (1909): *Episodes from the Lives of SS Patrick,*

Columcille, Brigid (painted by Catherine O Brien), *Episodes from the Lives of SS Fainchea and Enda* (painted by H. Barden). The church was refurbished (1976) by Tyndall, Hogan and Hurley, with wall hanging by Helen Moloney, and bronze cross by Patrick McElroy.

3 m. NW., in the Catholic church, Bridgeacrin, is a single-light window (*Agony in the Garden, St Thomas, Judith*) by Michael Healy (1923).

4½ m. NW., affording beautiful views, is Castle Roche (Nat. Mon.), a strong rock-castle built early in the 13th c. by Rohesia Verdon. The remains include a fine, twin-towered gatehouse and a battlemented curtain, as well as fragments of a great hall and a keep (?). A window in the W. end was popularly known as Fuinneóg an Mhurdair, because Rohesia was said to have had the builder thrown from it. The larger rock surface E. of the castle seems also to have been enclosed by a wall.

DUNDRUM, Co. Down (Map 2, L3), is a village and small port on Dundrum Bay, 2½ m. S. of Clough and 4 m. NNE. of Newcastle. On a hill-top are the beautifully maintained remains (Nat. Mon.) of a great castle which was an important fortress of the abortive Norman Earldom of Ulster. The earliest castle, of motte-and-bailey type, was taken from de Lacy in 1210 by King John of England. The great donjon probably dates from 1230–40, the fragmentary gatehouse from *c.* 1300. Some time after 1333 the castle fell to the Magennises, who held it until 1601, and again from 1641 till 1652, when the Cromwellians slighted it.

The remains comprise three distinct parts: a 13th c., polygonal, upper ward with gatehouse, donjon and, in places, a great rock-cut ditch; a 15th c. lower ward; and remains of a 17th c. house of the Blundells, who owned the castle briefly from 1636 to 1641.

2½ m. N. is Clough Castle (Hist. Mon.), a fine motte-and-bailey with added stone tower, of which two storeys survive.

1½ m. SSW., 300 yds NW. of the 12-arched Slidderyford Bridge, is Wateresk Dolmen, a portal-tomb with massive capstone.

DUNDRUM, Co. Dublin (Map 3, K4), is a village and suburb on the Milltown (10 m.)–Enniskerry (9 m.) road. In St Nathi's Church (Protestant) may be seen Evie Hone's earliest (1933) work in stained glass, three small panels of the *Annunciation* and abstract subjects, also one by Ethel Rhind, *Psalm 18* (*c.* 1914) and five by Catherine O Brien: '*I am the Resurrection and the Life*' (1917), *Emmaus* (1919), *Jesus at the Sea of Tiberias* (1919), *After the Transfiguration* (1936), *Christ Blessing Little Children* (1947). The Catholic church has a three-light window (*Our Lady Queen of the Rosary with SS Catherine and Dominic*, 1919) by Michael Healy. There are ruins of a medieval castle in the grounds of Dundrum Castle. Roebuck Lodge, near Clonskeagh, was the home of Maud Gonne MacBride (1866–1953). A woman of remarkable beauty, she inspired some of Yeats's loveliest poems and devoted her life to the struggle for Irish freedom in all its phases. Her husband, Major John MacBride, was executed for his part in the 1916 Rising. Their son Seán (d. 1988) was awarded both the Nobel and Lenin Peace Prizes.

1 m. SE. is the round Church of the Ascension (1982) by McCormick, Tracey and Mullarkey, with metalwork by David King and Stations by Sally O Sullivan.

Castle Roche, Co. Louth.

1 m. SSW., on Ballinteer Ave., is the church of St John the Evangelist (1973) by Morris, McCullough and Associates, with beautiful stained glass by Patrick Pollen, beaten bronze Stations of the Cross by Cecil King, tabernacle by Patrick McElroy and stone altar by Ray Carroll.

DUNFANAGHY, Co. Donegal (Map 8, E2), is a village and holiday resort with an excellent, sandy beach on the W. shore of Sheep Haven, 28 m. NW. of Letterkenny and 8 m. NE. of Falcarragh. The coast thereabouts provides beautiful scenery and many excellent sandy beaches.

2½ m. NNW., in Cleggan, is Dermot and Grania's Bed, a ruined court-tomb.

DUNGANNON, Co. Tyrone (Map 1, G9), is an old market town which was once the county town and, in earlier days, the chief seat of the O Neills. It is 40 m. from Belfast, and is conveniently sited at the end of the M1 motorway.

The O Neills occupied the fort at Dungannon from the 13th c., and in 1489 founded a Franciscan friary there. It was there, in 1542, that Con O Neill submitted to the English and accepted the title of Earl of Tyrone from Henry VIII, while his illegitimate son Matthew was created Baron of Dungannon. In 1602, following the Irish defeat at KINSALE, the castle and town were burned to prevent them falling into English hands. At the Plantation, the place was granted to Sir Arthur Chichester, who rebuilt the castle and laid out the plan of the modern town. In 1692, it was sold to Thomas Knox, whose descendants, the Earls of Ranfurly, developed the town's markets and business. It was in the old Meeting House that the delegates of the Irish Volunteers met in 1782 to act as a pressure group seeking parliamentary independence and untramelled trade for Ireland.

Nothing survives now of the town's castles; the building at the head of the square, though called O Neill's Castle, was built in 1790 by Thomas Knox Hanyngton. St Anne's Protestant Church is probably Ulster's best example of the work of the eminent Victorian architect W.J. Barre. It was built in 1865, just two years before work was begun on the impressive Catholic Church of St Patrick, by J.J. McCarthy.

The Royal School (founded in 1628) dates from 1786, when Primate Robinson transferred it to the present site. Brigadier-General John Nicholson, of Indian Mutiny fame, went to school there, and Brock's statue of him was brought from Delhi in 1960. The Shiel's Institute (1867) is by Lanyon.

2 m. SW. is Castlecaulfield. St Michael's Protestant church, built in 1685 and enlarged in 1838, is an interesting structure with noteworthy S. and W. doorways. Parts of a medieval church at Donaghmore (*see below*) are incorporated in the window heads. The stained glass windows include *The Ascension* (1925) and *Suffer Little Children to Come unto Me* (1938), both by A.E. Child. The Rev. Charles Wolfe, author of *The Burial of Sir John Moore*, was rector there. S. of the village are the ruins of Castle Caulfield, erected between 1611 and 1619 by Sir Toby Caulfeild, the ancestor of the Earls of Charlemont. In 1642 it was burned by the O Donnellys, the pre-Plantation landowners, but re-occupied and repaired by the Caulfeilds. The remains are those of an U-shaped manor house in the Elizabethan style. 1½ m. from Castlecaulfield is Parkanaur Forest Park.

2½ m. NW. is Donaghmore. St Patrick founded a church there, and a monastery grew up on the site. All that remains of it today is the High Cross (Hist. Mon.) of the 9th/10th c. which, in reality, consists of parts of two separate crosses placed one on top of the other in 1776 at the top of the main street. The scenes on the W. face include *Adam and Eve*, *Cain and Abel*, *Sacrifice of Issaac* and *Daniel in the Lions' Den*. On the E. face are: *Annunciation to the Shepherds*, *Adoration of the Magi*, *Baptism of Christ* and, on the upper fragment, a *Crucifixion*. Just SW. of the village is Donaghmore Convent School. Originally the glebe house of the Rev. George Walker (of Denny fame), it was built in 1707, but was considerably re-modelled around the 1830s.

DUNGARVAN, Co. Waterford (Map 4, F7), administrative centre of Waterford county, is a market town and small seaport 27 m. SW. of Waterford, 11 m. ESE. of Cappoquin, and 18 m. NE. of Youghal. The Drum Hills region to the S. and SW. is the last area of Irish speech in E. Munster.

The town grew up in the shelter of an Anglo-Norman castle, of which substantial remains are incorporated in the ruins of the British military barracks destroyed in 1921. The castle surrendered to Cromwell in 1649, when it and the parish church were wrecked by the conqueror.

The Church of the Assumption is a renovation (*c.* 1890) by George Ashlin of a plain structure erected in 1828 to the design of George Richard Pain of Cork.

St Augustine's Church, Abbeyside, incorporates the tower of a small Augustinian friary founded *c.* 1290. A fragment of the choir also survives.

8 m. NNE. are remains of Kilrossanty Church.

9 m. NNE., via the Carrick-on-Suir road, in a moorland field near the ancient church site of Garranmillon, are two ogham stones.

6 m. NE., in Ballykeroge, are the ruins of a Walsh castle. Nearby is Cloch Labhrais, a boulder which was said to speak from time to time.

6 m. SSW., in the Déise Gaeltacht, is An Rinn, alias Ring. Nearby are good small beaches. 1 m. E. is the old fishing village of Ballynagaul, to the E. of which is Helvick Head (230 ft) commanding very fine views. 4 m. S. of Ring, near the coast in Ballynamona Lower, is Cailleach Bhéarra's House, one of the few court-tombs in Munster.

3 m. NW., at Ballymacmague crossroads, where the road bifurcates to Cappoquin and Clonmel, is a memorial to Master McGrath, the greyhound which won the Waterloo Cup in 1868, 1869, and 1871, and was defeated only once in 37 courses. 7 m. N. of Ballymacmague crossroads and 1½ m. E. of the Clonmel road, in Knockboy, are the ruins of St Seskinan's Church (15th c.); at least four ogham stones have been built into the fabric, and another lies inside the church.

6½ m. NW. are the limestone caves of Kilgreany, Ballynamintra, and Carrigmurrish. Prehistoric remains found in Kilgreany cave included two human skeletons of the 4th millennium B.C.

DUNGIVEN, Co. Derry (Map 1, F5), is a small town where the Maghera (14 m.)–Derry (21 m.) road crosses the head of attractive Glengiven (Roe Valley) 9½ m. S. of Limavady. To the

O Heney tomb, Banagher Old Church, Co. Londonderry.

S. rises the main Sperrin range (Mullaghaneany, 2,070 ft; Sawel 2,240 ft) with several pretty glens.

John Mitchel (1815–75) of Young Ireland fame was born nearby at Camnish, where his father was a Unitarian minister.

½ m. S., on a 200 ft cliff above the Roe, is Dungiven Priory (Hist. Mon.) on the site of an early Christian monastery associated with St Nechtan. An Augustinian Priory was founded there in the 12th c., associated with the O Cahans who built a castle there in the late medieval period. At the time of the Plantation the buildings (recently excavated) were remodelled as a house and bawn by Sir Edward Doddington. The nave is mid-12th c.; the stone-vaulted chancel 13th c. and the ornate tomb (traditionally of Cooey-na-nGall O Cahan, d. 1385) is 15th c., probably by a Western Scottish mason.

3 m. ESE., in Boviel, is Cloghnagalla wedge-tomb. 1 m. SW., in Cashel, is the early Christian period White Fort.

2 m. SSW. in Maghermore is Banagher Church (Hist. Mon.), situated on a prominent hill, said to have been founded by St Muiredach O Heney. The nave, which has a semi-circular-headed window and W. door (with sloping jambs, massive lintel and internal semi-circular arch) probably dates from the first half of the 12th c. The windows date the chancel to the early-13th c., but it was remodelled in the 15th c. SW. of the church is the saint's tomb (*see* Bovevagh *below* and *p. 232*), the source of Banagher sand which brings fortune to the O Heney family. Nearby are two simple crosses and a bullaun stone. At the graveyard gate are the foundations of a medieval priest's stone house.

3 m. NNW., on the site of an early monastery, is Bovevagh late medieval church (Hist. Mon.). W. of the church is the mortuary house or saint's grave similar to that at Banagher.

DUNGLOW, alias **DUNGLOE**, Co. Donegal (Map 8, C4), is a small fishing port and angling resort on the Lettermacaward (10 m.)–Burtonport (5 m.) road. The Catholic Church of St Crona (1980) is by Carr, Sweeney and O Farrell, with *Last Supper* batik by Bernadette Madden.

5 m. SW. is Maghery, where there is a good beach. On the peninsula to the N. are remains of the ancient church of Teampall Crone.

5½ m. NW., off Burtonport, is Rutland Island. In 1785 William Burton Conyngham tried to establish a port there, traces of which remain. He and his nephew, Earl (later Marquess) Conyngham developed Burtonport, which is now an important herring-fishing station.

7 m. NW. is Aran, alias Arranmore, Island (reached by motor-boat from Burtonport). On the W. side of the island are fine cliffs and interesting marine caves.

DUNIRY, Co. Galway (Map 6, K2), is a small village on the Loughrea (8 m.)–Portumna (7 m.) road. It takes its name from a fort, Dún Daighre. In the later Middle Ages a branch of the celebrated Mac Egan family of hereditary scholars, which had its home at the Mill of Duniry, possessed the celebrated *Leabhar Breac*, an early-15th c. codex of religious literature, and the 13th/14th c. Trinity College, Dublin, codex, H.2.152, the oldest surviving 'brehon law' manuscript.

1½ m. ESE. are the unusually well-preserved ruins of Pallas Castle (private), a Burke stronghold which remained in Nugent hands until recently. The remains comprise a large, unusually well-preserved bawn (gate house rebuilt), a 16th c. tower, fragments of a large 17th c. house, and an 18th c. malthouse. 3 m. E., in Kilcorban, are the ruins of St Corban's Church. A Dominican friary was founded here in 1466 and re-dedicated in 1987. In Loughrea Museum are several wooden figures which probably came from this friary.

DUNKINEELY, Co. Donegal (Map 8, C7), is a fishing village on the Donegal (12 m.)–Killybegs (5 m.) road.

1 m. SW. are the fragmentary remains of Killachtee Church (Transitional); in the graveyard is a fine, early cross-slab. ¾ m. S., on the shore of Mac Swyne's Bay, are remains of the 15th c. castle of Mac Swyne of Banagh.

2½ m. NW., and ½ m. N. of Bruckless village, is the Reilig, where 'stations' are held during the nine days following 23 June. The remains there include St Conall's Bed, a holy well, and early cross-slabs.

DUN LAOGHAIRE, Co. Dublin (Map 3, L3), 8 m. SE. of Dublin, with which it forms a single conurbation, is the terminus of the principal Ireland–England passenger shipping service (car ferry inaugurated 1965). Dun Laoghaire was joined to Dublin by rail as early as 1834. It is a major seaside resort and Dublin's largest dormitory suburb. Dun Laoghaire is the headquarters of Irish yachting (Royal Irish Yacht Club, National Yacht Club, Royal St George Yacht Club, and others) and the base of the Irish Lights Service, which maintains the lighthouses, lightships, etc., around the Irish coasts. The great harbour (1817–21), by Rennie, was a major work of 19th c. marine engineering. The East Pier is a popular promenade where band recitals are given during the summer. From 1821 to 1920 Dún Laoghaire was called Kingstown, in commemoration of George IV's departure from the harbour after his state visit to Dublin. A dull monument near the Mail Boat Pier records the royal occasion.

150 yds N. of the Town Hall is St Michael's Church, a 1973 replacement, by Pearse McKennà, of a predecessor burned in 1965. Only the tower of the old church remains. The lovely bronze doors, and the figure of *St Michael* above one of them, are by Imogen Stuart; the interesting stone altar, font, etc., are by Michael Biggs. The stained glass is by Patrick Pye, and other furnishings are by Richard King (tabernacle and cross) and Yvonne Jammet. The tapestries are by Eoin and Pat Butler.

300 yds E. of the Town Hall is the former Mariners' Church (1837), now appropriately the home of the National Maritime Museum. It is situated on Haigh Terrace, at the N. end of which is the American-Irish sculptor Andrew O Connor's (1874–1941) powerful triple-Crucifixion sculpture *Christ the King*. Designed as a memorial to the dead of the First World War, it was first shown in the Paris Salon in 1926, but it was only after years of languishing in a Dublin suburban garden that it was finally erected on this site in 1978.

1¼ m. E. of the Town Hall are Sandycove Baths and the 'Forty Foot' (men's bathing place). The martello tower figures in Joyce's *Ulysses* and is now a Joyce Museum.

1 m. SW. of the Town Hall, York Rd Presbyterian Church has three noteworthy Ethel M. Rhind two-light windows, these are: *Prudent Virgin* and *Faithful Servant* (1909), *The Kingdom of Heaven is Like unto a Net* (1922), *The Good Samaritan* and *The Lost Coin* (1925).

1 m. W. of the Town Hall is Monkstown Protestant Church, a highly individual, Gothick structure (*c.* 1830) by John Semple (*see p. 157*): noteworthy plaster vault; chancel memorial to Richard Browne (d. 1838) by Thomas Kirk. ½ m. S. is 15th c. Monkstown Castle (Nat. Mon.): small keep, gatehouse, and part of curtain.

2 m. W., on the Dublin road, is Blackrock. St John's Church was Patrick Byrne's first (1842) essay in the Gothic manner. In the new aisle is a three-light window (*Our Lady, St Brigid, St Patrick*) by Evie Hone, one of the artist's last works (1954–5). All Saints Church (Protestant) has two windows (1918) by Wilhelmina Geddes: *Michael*, *Raphael*. – 'Leoville', 23 Carysfort Ave., was the home (1892–3) of James Joyce and his parents. Further W., in Williamstown, is Blackrock College (1860, Holy Ghost Fathers), the well-known boys' school. Éamon de Valera was a pupil and, later, mathematics master there. The buildings (nucleus, Castledawson House) are devoid of merit, but have three armorial and decorative windows (1936–7) and a lunette (*Our Lady*, 1940), by Evie Hone. The school chapel has two pairs of single-light windows (1938) by Michael Healy: *Annunciation*, *Visitation*. The Senior House ('Castle') chapel has a three-light *Pentecost* (1940–1) by Evie Hone.–1¾ m. S. of St John's Church, on the Cabinteely road, is Deansgrange. In Kill Ave. is St Fintan's Church, alias Kill o the Grange (Nat. Mon.), a small pre-Romanesque church with chancel of *c.* 1200. N. of the church is a simple cross.

DUNLAVIN, Co. Wicklow (Map 3, I6), a village 11 m. N. of Baltinglass and 6½ m. SE. of Kilcullen, was founded by the Bulkeleys, 17th c. grantees. In 1702 it passed to the Worth Tyntes. The 'baroque' stone-domed Market House was erected by the first Worth-Tynte proprietor. It has been attractively restored (by Niall Montgomery) to serve as the local library.

2 m. NE., in two adjacent fields of Forristeen townland, are the Piper's Stones, two large granite boulders. The larger has a cross.

3 m. ENE., in 'Crushlow Churchyard' is Crehelp, a granite pillarstone with a sub-rectangular perforation. It is said locally to mark the grave of Norse 'Prince Harold'. Marriages used to be solemnized at it.

2 m. S., in Tornant Lower, is Tornant Moat, a platform ringfort with external bank. On a ridge to the SE. (beyond St Nicholas's Graveyard) is the remnant of a tumulus in which was found a stone with passage-grave scribings, now in the National Museum. At the E. end of the ridge, in Tornant Upper, are the remnants of a circle of great stones.

2½ m. SW., on the summit of Brewel Hill (Co. Kildare), are the Piper's Stones consisting of four large boulders; one of them (the Piper's Chair) is of white quartz.

3½ m. SW., in Colbinstown (Co. Kildare), is the ancient cemetery of Killeen Cormac, so called, it is said, after 'King Cormac of Munster'. According to local legend a dispute arose about the king's place of burial, so the corpse was placed on a car drawn by unguided oxen. These drew it to the neighbourhood of Killeen Cormac, whereupon a hound leaped from a neighbouring hill to a stone in the cemetery, leaving the imprint of a paw on the stone to indicate the position of the king's grave. The remains in the cemetery comprise: King Cormac's Grave, marked by a pair of pillarstones, one of which bears two lines and the 'imprint of the hound's paw'; seven other pillarstones – two with grooves; a cross-base; a unique slab with incised figure of Christ Crucifer (retouched in the last c.); and one complete and two fragmentary ogham stones. One bilingual ogham stone was taken to the National Museum.

DUNLEER, Co. Louth (Map 2, I7), is a village on the Drogheda (9 m.)–Dundalk (13 m.) road. There was an early monastery (Lann Léire) there, associated with St Brigid, who is said to have lost and regained her sight at the local holy well. The W. tower of the 19th c. Protestant church has Transitional fragments which, with three early gravestones in the adjacent hall, are the sole relics of Lann Léire.

2¾ m. SE. is Rokeby Hall (Mr L. Muldoon), designed by Francis Johnston for Archbishop Robinson (Lord Rokeby) of Armagh and completed in 1793–4.

1¼ m. S. is Athclare castle (16th c.), still inhabited. It has good Jacobean carvings.

2 m. NW., on the Ardee Rd, Dromin medieval church marks the site of a monastery founded by St Finnian of Movilla (*see p. 260*). Nearby is Móta Dhruim Fhinn, an Anglo-Norman motte.

DUNMANWAY, Co. Cork (Map 5, I7), is a small market town where the Bandon (18 m.)–Bantry (20 m.) road crosses the little Dirty River.

6¼ m. NW., on the N. side of the Bandon, is the unusual tower of Togher Castle, built probably by Tadhg an Fhórsa Mac Carthy of Gleann an Chroim, about 1590 (?). It was re-roofed and restored in the late-19th c. by a local priest.

DUNMORE, Co. Galway (Map 7, I7), is a market village on the Tuam (10 m.)–Ballyhaunis (11 m.) road. It takes its name from a great fort belonging to Turloch Mór O Conor, King of Connacht

Stained glass window by Evie Hone, Blackrock College, Co. Dublin.

and High-King (1106–56). At the Anglo-Norman conquest the manor was granted by de Burgo to one of the de Berminghams, whose descendants, becoming Gaelicized, changed their name to Mac Fheorais. The ruined 'abbey' (Nat. Mon.) was the church of a small Augustinian friary founded in 1425 by Walter Mór de Bermingham, Baron Athenry (d. 1428). It has a Perpendicular W. doorway with Bermingham arms above.

The country about Dunmore is very rich in ringforts of various kinds.

½ m. NW., beside the little Sinking River in Castlefarm, are the remains (Nat. Mon.) of the strong, 13th c., Bermingham castle of Dunmore, thought to occupy the site of King Turloch O Conor's fort. The first castle there was clearly of the motte kind.

7 m. SE. (6 m. SW. of Glenamaddy), in Park West, are remnants of Park Castle, for centuries the home of a branch of the Mac Egans (*see p. 172*), who were hereditary brehons to the O Conors of Connacht.

3½ m. W., in Addergoole, is the head of a 12th c. granite cross with an unfinished *Crucifixion*.

DUNMORE EAST, Co. Waterford (Map 4, I6), is a small resort and sea-fishing port at the W. side of the entrance to Waterford Harbour, 11 m. SE. of Waterford. The Protestant church has a window *The Pilgrimage of Life* by Catherine O Brien (1948). The harbour was constructed as a mail-packet terminus from 1814 onwards to the design of Nimmo. On the coast SW. to Brownstown Head (7 m.) are five promontory forts.

2 m. N., commanding a very fine view, is Carrick a Dhirra, alias Knockadirragh (430 ft). Near the summit at the S. end, in Harristown, is a V-passage-tomb set in a round cairn. The primary grave-goods included a stone axe-amulet. Secondary deposits included three Bronze Age urn burials.

DUNNAMANAGH, Co. Tyrone (Map 1, D6), is a village on the Strabane (8 m.)–Claudy, Co. Derry (8 m.) road. The principal buildings are the Church of Ireland parish church built in 1877, and the five-sided Catholic church (1968) by Patrick Haughey.

4½ m. ESE., in Loughash, is Cashelbane, a wedge-tomb (500 ft). 1 m. SW., near Loughash school, is Loughash Giant's Grave, a wedge-tomb. There are 12 cupmarks on the central jamb of the portal. Excavations yielded cremated burials, Beakers and Bronze Age relics.

2½ m. W., in Ballylaw, are the remains of White Fort, a stone ringfort.

3½ m. NNW., in Gortmellan, is the Grey Stone, a chambered round cairn.

DUNQUIN, Co. Kerry (Map 5, A3), 3½ m. SW. of Ballyferriter and 5 m. (8 m. via the coast and Slea Head) W. of Ventry, is well known to students of the Irish language. It is the 'port' for the crossing to the BLASKET ISLANDS.

½ m. E., in Baile an Bhiocáire, alias Vicars-town, is Tigh Mhóire, an ancient burial ground with an early cross-pillar and Uaigh an Spáinnigh, 'the grave of a Spanish nobleman lost off the Blaskets' in 1588.

1¼ m. SSW. a slight earthwork cuts off the 80 acre promontory fort of Doonmore. At the summit of the fort is Gallán an tSagairt, an ogham stone re-erected in 1839.

1¾ m. S. is Coumeenole 'village'. 400 yds E. is a small, perfect modern clochán. 180 yds S. is an ancient burial ground; there are two cross-slabs here. A short distance SE. is Púicín Mháire Ní Sháirséal, a ruined clochán largely below ground level. SSW. of this is Clochán O Lee, a complex of three clocháns with a 'yard'. On the summit of the hill are four clocháns (Nat. Mons.).

DUNSHAUGHLIN, Co. Meath (Map 3, I2), is a village on the Dublin (20 m.)–Navan (12 m.) road. It takes its name (Domhnach Seachnaill) from a church founded by Bishop Secundinus (Seachnall), who came to Ireland, probably from Gaul, with Auxilius and Iserninus *c.* 438/9, and who died in 447/8. To Secundinus has been attributed a celebrated hymn in honour of Patrick, *Ymnum sancti Patrici magister Scotorum*. Secundinus's church was on or near the site of the Protestant parish church, where the lintel (Nat. Mon.) of the W. door of a Romanesque church is preserved; on it is carved a primitive *Crucifixion*. A fragment of the nave arcade of a medieval church also survives.

The small Classical court-house is by Francis Johnston.

2 m. N. is Trevet, site of an early monastery. Sir Thomas Cusack, Lord Chancellor under Henry VIII and Mary Tudor, was buried there with his wife, Matilda D'Arcy, in a double-effigy tomb now at St Columcille's Church near SKREEN.

2 m. E. is Lagore, where a bog represents the silted-up lake, in which was a crannóg, seat of the Kings of Brega. It was excavated (1934–6) by the Harvard Archaeological Mission.

2½ m. NW., on the Kilmessan road, is Killeen Castle, until recently seat of the Plunketts, Earls of Fingal. The mansion was an 1801 remodelling by Francis Johnston of a medieval castle, but it was burned in 1981. Killeen Church, probably built by Sir Christopher Plunkett (d. 1445), has an aisleless nave and chancel with intervening rood-loft, and a priest's dwelling over the sacristy. In the church are remains of 15th c. Plunkett tombs, including effigies of a knight and lady, and a bishop.

1½ m. NW. of Killeen, on the Kilmessan road, is Dunsany Castle, seat of the Plunkett Barons Dunsany (private) in which are preserved some relics of St Oliver Plunkett. The late Lord Dunsany (1878–1960), friend and patron of Francis Ledwidge (*see p. 280*), was a poet and novelist of distinction. E. of the castle are the ruins of St Nicholas's Church, built about 1425/50 by Sir Christopher Plunkett in the style of Killeen Church. (The E. window is modern, the tracery copied from Killeen Church.) In the chancel are five sedilia, an interesting, 15th c. baptismal font, and a 15th c. double-effigy tomb. The carvings on the font include a *Crucifixion*, as well as figures of the Apostles. The tomb effigies are possibly those of Sir Christopher Plunkett (armoured) and his wife; the figure-carvings on the ends of the tomb include a *Scourging of Christ*. At the demesne gate is a 16th/17th c. roadside cross with a rude *Crucifixion*.

DURROW, Co. Laois (Map 3, E8), is a Noreside village at the intersection of the Abbeyleix (6 m.)–Urlingford (13 m.) and Borris-in-Ossory (14 m.)–Ballyragget (5 m.) roads.

Castle Durrow, now a convent, is a fine house overlooking the Nore. It was built in 1716 for the first Lord Castle-Durrow.

6½ m. SW., to the W. of Cullahill, is Aghmacart, formerly a seat of the Mac Gillapatricks (Fitzpatricks) of Ossory who founded an Augustinian priory there before 1168.

DYSERT O DEA, Co. Clare (Map 6, G5), formerly Díseart Tola, lies to the S. of the Corrofin (4 m.)–Ennis (22 m.) road.

A hermitage or anchoritic establishment (díse[a]rt = *desertum*) was founded there by St Tola (d. 737), a bishop of Clonard. There are remains (Nat. Mon.) of a nave-and-chancel Romanesque church with interesting door and window (incorrectly re-assembled). Close to the NW. angle are remains of a Round Tower. E. of the church is a fine, 12th c. High Cross (Nat. Mon.). On the E. face are a Crucifixus and the figure of a bishop. The base is made up from Romanesque fragments taken from the church. To the N. is O Dea's Castle, with a fine bawn. It is now a Museum and Archaeology Centre.

Nearby, in 1318, Muirchertach O Brien and his allies routed Richard de Clare (*see p. 84*) and put a halt to the Anglo-Norman conquest of Thomond.

1 m. NNW., in Rath, is Rathblamack, called after St Blathmac ('Blawfugh'), founder of a church about ½ m. to the SW., where are remains of a nave-and-chancel church of various dates (interesting Romanesque fragments with Urnes ornament, sheila-na-gig, etc.).

E

EASKY, Co. Sligo (Map 7, H1), is a village and small seaside resort on the coast road from Sligo (25 m.) to Ballina (17 m.).

¾ m. N., on the shore, is the ruined tower of the Mac Donnell castle of Roslee. The Mac Donnells were by origin Hebridean galloglas in the service of the O Dowds (*see p. 280*).

By the roadside to the E. of the village is Fionn Mac Cool's Fingerstone. Fionn, the story runs, tried to hurl the stone into the ocean, but it fell short. Enraged, he struck it with a second stone and split it.

¾ m. S., in Fortland, are the ruins of a court-tomb gallery.

EDENDERRY, Co. Offaly (Map 3, G4), is a market town on the Innfield, alias Enfield (12 m.) – Tullamore (22 m.) road at the edge of the Bog of Allen.

Immediately S. of the town are the remants of hill-top Blundell's Castle. The second Marquess of Downshire (1753–1801; *see p. 203*) married a Blundell, and so acquired the Edenderry property. The Downshires built most of the town, including the handsome, 1826 Corn Market-cum-Court House (later spoiled by the blocking up of the ground-floor loggia). Only the shell survived a fire. It has since been cheaply reconstructed as the Father Paul Murphy Memorial Hall.

Edenderry stands near the edge of the English Pale, and there are many border castles in the vicinity.

3 m. N., on Carrick Hill (387 ft), are the remains of the medieval Bermingham church and castle of Carrickoris. In 1305 Muirchertach O Conor, king of Uí Fáilghe, and 31 other leaders of the O Conors Faly were murdered after a banquet in the castle by 'the treacherous Baron', Sir Pierce Bermingham, and Jordan Cumin. The English king failed to punish the murderers, and the crime was one of the complaints cited by the Irish princes in their Remonstrance of 1317 to Pope John XXII. Pierce's son, John, defeated Edward Bruce at Faughart (*see p. 168*).

5 m. N., in Ballyboggan on the W. bank of the Boyne in Co. Meath, are the ruins of a large, plain, cruciform, 13th c. church, all that survives of the once wealthy English priory De Laude Dei, founded for Canons Regular of St Augustine by Jordan Cumin. In 1538 the Protestant reformers publicly burned the venerated crucifix belonging to the priory.

4 m. ENE. the road to Innfield (Enfield) crosses the shoulder of Carbury Hill (470 ft), where is a motte, probably constructed by the first Anglo-Norman proprietor, Meiler fitz Henry, who had been granted the district by Strongbow. In the 14th c., castle and district (thenceforth 'Bermingham's Country') were acquired by the Berminghams, but the castle came into Irish hands in the 15th c. In 1562 it was granted to the Cowleys (Colleys), later Wellesleys, ancestors of the celebrated Duke of Wellington, and it was they who built the Tudor – Jacobean stronghouse. SE. of the castle are scant remains of Teampall Do-Ath; Colley mausoleum in churchyard. On the SE. slope of the hill is the source of the Boyne. The Catholic Church in Carbury has two windows by Catherine O Brien: *The Annunciation* and *SS. Conleth and Brigid* (both 1904).

2 m. W. is Monasteroris, where Sir John Bermingham, Earl of Louth, founded a Franciscan friary in 1325. The remains there include a small parish church, a dovecot on a tumulus or motte, and the overgrown ruins of the friary. A modern cross commemorates Fr Mogue Kearns and Anthony Perry, who were hanged at Edenderry for their part in the 1798 Insurrection.

3½ m. NW. are remains of the strong Bermingham castle of Kinnafad, commanding a ford of the Boyne.

EDGEWORTHSTOWN, alias **MOSTRIM**, Co. Longford (Map 2, C8), is a market village on the Mullingar (17¾ m.) – Longford (8¼ m.) road. It takes its modern name from the Edgeworth family. Edgeworthstown House, now a nursing home, was built by much-married Richard Lovell Edgeworth (1744–1817), author and inventor and father of the celebrated novelist Maria Edgeworth (1767–1849). The Edgeworth family vault is at the Protestant church, where there is also a tablet to the memory of Richard Lovell Edgeworth.

3 m. N. is Firmount, once owned by Essex Edgeworth, Protestant Rector of Edgeworthstown and father of the Abbé Edgeworth de Firmont who attended Louis XVI on the scaffold.

6 m. N. is Ballinalee, native place of Gen. Seán Mac Eóin ('the Blacksmith of Ballinalee'), famous guerrilla leader in the struggle for Irish independence, later a general officer in the Irish army and a cabinet minister in three governments. Just S. of Ballinalee is Currygrane, birthplace of Sir Henry Wilson (1864–1922), Chief of the Imperial General Staff, who was assassinated in London for his part in the British effort to crush the Irish independence movement.

5 m. S., beside the Caldragh Stone in Caldragh, Killeen, is an early cross-slab.

3 m. SW. is Ardagh, which has given its name to the diocese. St Patrick is said to have founded a church there, over which he set St Mel as first bishop. It is represented today by the ruins of St Mel's 'Cathedral', a small, primitive, stone church in which St Mel is reputed to be buried. Excavations in the 1960s revealed remains of what was probably an earlier wooden church beneath it, as well as some early gravestones. The saint's enshrined bachall, or staff, is preserved in St Mel's Diocesan Museum, LONGFORD. Ardagh Hill (650 ft), formerly Slieve Golry, is Brí Léith, the setting of much of the charming tale of Midir, Étaín, and Eochu. Ardagh House, now a convent, is the house Goldsmith mistook for an inn, recalled in *She Stoops to Conquer*.

ELPHIN, Co. Roscommon (Map 7, L5), is now only a market village on the Roscommon (18 m.) – Boyle (16 m.) road, but it had an important place in the ecclesiastical history of Connacht and has given its name to a diocese. St Patrick established a bishopric there, over which he placed Bishop Assicus (*see p. 59*) and later, Bishop Betheus, the nephew of Assicus. To these Patrician bishops the modern diocese of Elphin ultimately traces its origin. The pre-Norman cathedral was burned by de Burgo's forces in 1235, and of Elphin's medieval churches and religious houses nothing remains. Sligo is now the cathedral town.

Oliver Goldsmith (1730–74) was educated at Elphin Diocesan School, as was later the distinguished oculist and antiquary Sir William Wilde. Dr Charles Dodgson, great-grandfather of Lewis Carroll, was Protestant Bishop of Elphin (1775–95).

EMO, Co. Laois (Map 3, F5–6), is a small village ½ m. S. of the Monasterevan (7 m.) – Port Laoise (6 m.) road.

In the Catholic church is a recumbent effigy of Alexandrina Octavia, Countess of Portarlington (d. 1874), by Sir Joseph Edgar Boehm.

½ m. E. is Emo Court, built 1790–6 for the Earl of Portarlington to the designs of James Gandon (1743–1823), best known as the architect of the Custom House in Dublin (*see p. 142*). The gardens (open on summer afternoons) are noted for their camelias, azaleas, rhododendrons and maples.

½ m. NE. is Coolbanagher Protestant church (1786), the only church known to have been built by Gandon. His N. and S. walls remain intact (except for the windows). The ceiling, however, is a later alteration, and the apse was added in 1870.

ENNIS, Co. Clare (Map 6, G6), on the Galway (42 m.)–Limerick (23 m.) road, is the capital of the county and the cathedral town of the Catholic diocese of Killaloe. The only modern building of note is the (1852) County Court House, which has a good, Ionic portico. In the grounds outside is a curious monument to Éamon de Valera (1882–1975), who represented the Clare constituency in the Daíl from 1917 until 1959, before he became President of Ireland.

Close to the bridge over the River Fergus are the ruins (Nat. Mon.) of a Franciscan friary founded about 1250 by one of the O Briens of Thomond. The magnificently tall five-light E. window, which held blue painted glass, dates from the restoration by Turlough Mór O Brien (1287–1306), while the vaulted sacristy dates from the early 14th c., and the transept, cloister, and tower (pinnacles modern) from the 15th. The church has interesting figure-carvings, notably a series of panels (*Christ's Passion and Death*, etc.) from a Mac Mahon tomb of *c.* 1470, and modelled on Nottingham alabasters; also a group of apostle figures, probably from a separate tomb originally.

The column at the centre of the town commemorates Daniel O Connell (1775–1847), who was M.P. for Clare 1828–31. Clare (the 'Banner County'), with Ennis as its capital, has been very much to the fore in 19th and 20th c. politics.

In the County Library is a collection of local antiquities, including a fine medieval font from Kilballyowen.

At the Limerick end of the town is the little Cathedral of SS Peter and Paul, commenced (1831) shortly after Catholic Emancipation, to the design of Dominic Madden (*see p. 296*), and consecrated in 1843; belfry 1871. The interior, an interesting example of 'carpenter's Gothick', was refurbished (1975) by Robinson, Keefe and Devane, with furnishings by Enda King.

William Mulready (1786–1863), the painter, was a native of Ennis, while Thomas Dermody (1775–1802), poet, author of *The Harp of Erin*, rake, and soldier, was the son of an Ennis school-master. Harriet Smithson (1800–54), the actress, was the adopted daughter of the Rev. Dr James Barrett, Rector of Ennis. (Her father was an actor-manager.) She was much admired by Gautier, and in 1833 she married Hector Berlioz, the composer, who described her as 'La Belle Smithson, dont tout Paris délirait'. She died of a stroke, and is buried at Montmartre.

4 m. SW., via the Kildysart road, in the grounds of Newhall House, are the ruins (Nat. Mon.) of Killone, an Augustinian nunnery dedicated to St John. The foundation is attributed to King Donal Mór O Brien. The church has interesting Transitional features of *c.* 1225. Under the E. end is a crypt (unusual). The claustral buildings are 15th c. Newhall House is a fine brick house built by Francis Bindon *c.* 1745 for Charles Mac Donnell of Kilkee. It was locally believed that the nearby lake turned red whenever a Mac Donnel was to die. This belief was explained by the legend of the slaying of a mermaid from the lake by the Newhall butler, who had found her robbing the cellar; her blood turned the lake red.

2 m. NW., off the road to Corrofin, in Drumcliff, are the remains (Nat. Mons.) of a Round Tower and an altered 12th/13th c. church. St Conall founded an early monastery there.

ENNISCORTHY, Co. Wexford (Map 4, L3), an important market town and distributing centre, picturesquely sited where the road from Ferns (7 m.) to Wexford (15 m.) crosses the Slaney at the head of the navigable tidal waters, is also the cathedral town of the Catholic diocese of Ferns.

The town grew up around the 13th c. castle built on a rock at the head of the tideway. The castle was repaired by Sir Henry Wallop in 1586, and Edmund Spenser had a lease of it for a time. It was attacked and captured by Cromwell in 1649. In 1798, during the occupation of the town by the insurgents, it served as a prison. It now houses the County Museum collection which includes interesting crosses, as well as an ogham stone found on the SALTEE ISLANDS. The remains are those of the peculiarly Norman-Irish type of rectangular keep with drum towers at the angles. The place of the SE. tower is taken by a turret.

St Aidan's Cathedral (1843–48), by Augustus Welby Pugin, is a Gothic Revival building with poor windows and furnishings.

The spire-crowned tower at the crossing was built largely of stones taken from the ruins of a Franciscan friary which formerly existed in the town.

In the Market Sq. is a 1798 memorial by Oliver Sheppard, with bronze figures of Fr John Murphy of Boleyvogue (*below*) and a Wexford pikeman. The insurgents stormed the town on 28 May 1798, and set up their principal encampment on Vinegar Hill (39 ft) to the E. There, on 21 June, a large force of them was almost completely surrounded by Generals Lake and Johnson with 20 000 troops. The ill-armed insurgents stood up to overwhelming fire for several hours, before making their escape through the last remaining gap in the enemy lines. The windmill (stump, Nat. Mon.) on the hill was the insurgent command-post.

3 m. NE. is Crane, where Corbett Wilson crash-landed after the first flight across the Irish Sea on 22 April 1912.

8 m. NE. is Boleyvogue. It was the burning by British soldiery of the Catholic chapel, Fr John Murphy's dwelling, and some 20 farmhouses, on the night of Saturday 26 May 1798, which precipitated the great Wexford insurrection.

7 m. E. is Oulart Hill (500 ft), where, on 27 May 1798, Fr John Murphy's small insurgent force defeated the British troops sent against them. Next day the insurgents went N. and took Camolin, where they found some arms. They then marched via Ferns to Scarawalsh bridge, where they recrossed the Slaney. On 28 May, their numbers swollen to 7,000, they stormed Enniscorthy, and their victory there caused the revolt to spread through the entire county.

ENNISKERRY, Co. Wicklow (Map 3, K5), is a village very beautifully situated in the Dargle valley, 12 m. S. of Dublin (via, Dundrum–Stepaside–The Scalp) and 3½ m. SW. of Bray. The Catholic church (about 1843), by Patrick Byrne, was one of the first Gothic Revival churches in Ireland. Adjoining the village on the SW. is magnificent Powerscourt Demesne, formerly the property of Viscount Powerscourt, now of Mr and Mrs Slazenger. It is noted for its exotic and other trees and offers a series of delightful walks and drives, including one of 4 m. up the Dargle to Powerscourt Waterfall (Deerpark townland), where the stream comes slipping down 398 ft. Superbly sited, Powerscourt House was built by Richard Cassels *c.* 1730, but was enlarged, and the garden front altered, in the 19th c. A disastrous fire in 1974 left the main part of the house in ruins. The beautiful terraces (1843–75) were designed by Daniel Robertson. The Japanese Garden dates from 1908. The Demesne and Gardens (entrance, Eagle Gate) are open to the public. The Waterfall (entrance, Waterfall Gate) is accessible all the year round. Driving from Eagle Gate through the demesne to the waterfall involves payment of both fees.

2 m. N., to the W. of the Dublin road, are the fragmentary remains of Killegar, a medieval nave-and-chancel church. There are two early gravestones and a fragment of a granite cross. Traces of a circular enclosing wall or bank survive.

1 m. E., to the W. of the Bray – Arklow road, near the house called St Valery, Fassaroe, is a granite cross (Nat. Mon.) with a rude *Crucifixion*. Nearby is a stone 'font'. Neither is *in situ*.

2 m. ESE., via the Bray road, are remains of Kilcroney Church (Nat. Mon.) with fine trabeate W. door.

½ m. SE. is 'The (Glen of the) Dargle' (Powerscourt Demesne, pedestrians only), where the little river tumbles its way through a deep, wooded defile. Lover's Leap, a great rock nearby, has engendered the inevitable tales of romantic doom.

1 m. SSW. Tinnehinch bridge crosses the Dargle at a lovely spot. 1 m. further SSW. is Charleville House, built *c.* 1810 for the 2nd Viscount Monck; the elevation echoes that of Lucan House (*see p. 241*). The demesne has some splendid trees.

4 m. W. of Enniskerry is Glencree. The Reformatory (now a Peace and Recreation Centre) was a barracks guarding the 1798 Military Road from Rathfarnham through the Wicklow Mts. Nearby is a small German cemetery. 1 m. S. of the Peace Centre, in deep basins under Kippure, are Lower and Upper Loughs Bray. Kippure, with RTE's television mast, is used as the main triangulation point by the Ordnance Survey.

ENNISKILLEN, Co. Fermanagh (Map 2, B3), on the Omagh (27 m.) – Sligo (40 m.) road, is the county town of Co. Fermanagh and a cathedral town of the Protestant diocese of CLOGHER.

Enniskillen's strategic situation in the difficult Erne valley early marked it out as a place of military importance, and in the later Middle Ages it was a key stronghold of the Maguires. When the English at last conquered the North, James I granted the place, together with considerable estates, to Capt. (later Sir) William Cole, and Enniskillen became an important stronghold of the Protestant settlers. It served them as a rallying point during the Irish uprising of 1641, and in 1689 rallied to the cause of William of Orange, in whose name the inhabitants repelled an attack (1690) by Tyrconnell, James II's Lord Lieutenant.

Fort Hill takes its name from the 1689 star fort in whose remains is set the column (excellent view and open to the public) to Gen. Sir Galbraith Lowry Cole (1772–1842), who became Governor of Cape Colony. Overlooking the W. bridges is the Redoubt, a military hospital of *c.* 1796 within an impressive square fort, built on the site of an earthen fort of 1688.

St Macartan's Cathedral, Church St, second cathedral of the Protestant diocese of Clogher, was built in 1840, but incorporates a 17th c. tower and N. porch. The font dates from 1666, and there are 17th c. monuments.

Enniskillen Castle (Hist. Mon.) next to the more recent of the two W. bridges is in the middle of early barracks buildings and was itself repaired and rebuilt as a barracks at the end of the 18th c. First built by the Maguires early in the 15th c., strategically situated to guard one of the passes into Gaelic Ulster, the castle figured prominently in the Elizabethan wars, being often attacked and defended, taken and retaken. Following on the Gaelic defeat, Maguire was finally dispossessed in 1607 and in 1612 command of the castle was given to Capt. William Cole. Cole rebuilt the castle and along its outer walls built the two distinctive turrets today inappropriately named the Watergate. The castle now houses Fermanagh County Museum and the Regimental Museum of the Royal Inniskilling Fusiliers. The fine theatre in the town (1987) is by Tom Mullarkey.

The Convent of Mercy has seven windows by Michael Healy (1905 and 1906): four windows of Irish saints, an *Annunciation*, a *St Benedict Joseph Labre*, and a *St Anthony*; also two windows by Sarah Purser: *St Michael* (1905), *St Elizabeth* (1906); and six by Lady Glenavy: *The Presentation* (1905, two windows), *St Margaret Mary* (1905), *Sacred Heart* (1905), *Immaculate Conception* (1906), *St Macartan* (1906). The stalls (1904) are the work of the woodcarver William Scott.

¾ m. NW. is beautifully situated Portora Royal School, a free school founded by James I in 1608. Oscar Wilde and Samuel Beckett went to school at Portora.

The colonnades and wings are 19th c. additions to the original 18th c. house. The War Memorial front gates (1945) incorporate Corinthian columns from Inishmore Hall, Upper Lough Erne. In the grounds are the remains of a Plantation castle built by William Cole.

1½ m. SE. is Castle Coole, seat of the Earl of Belmore, now the property of the Nat. Trust. Held to be the finest Classical mansion in Ireland, this noble house was built (1789–98) for the 1st Earl. The exterior is by Richard Johnston, elder brother of Francis, but James Wyatt, Jnr, who designed the interior, may have Grecianized Johnston's design. The house has excellent stucco by Joseph Rose, and carvings by David Sheehan and John Houghton. The joinery is excellent and the joiners made much of the furniture on the spot. Lough Coole has Ireland's only breeding colony of grey lag geese (introduced *c.* 1700).

5 m. SE. in Fyagh are the ruins of Derrybrusk Church – a medieval parish church with a fine E. window on the site of an Early Christian foundation by St Senach.

9 m. SE., in Upper Lough Erne, is Belleisle, formerly Seanadh, where, in the 15th c. Cathal MacManus Maguire compiled the celebrated *Annals of Ulster*.

3 m. S. are the ruins of Lisgoole 'Abbey'; from 1580, a Franciscan friary close to a Franciscan convent. Bro. Michael O Clery completed his redaction of the *Book of Invasions* on 20 December 1631 there.

Interior of Florence Court, Co. Fermanagh.

11 m. S. is Knockninny (St Ninnidh's hill 630 ft; cf. Inishmacsaint, *p. 239*). There are three court-tombs on the lower slopes (300–400 ft).

On the SW. slope, in Shehinny, is a natural cave (300–400 ft) inhabited and used as a burial place in prehistoric times. On the lower E. slope in Corratrasna are the ruins of a 17th c. Maguire Castle. Brian, son of Conor Modarra, Maguire lived there, and after the Williamite triumph, his castle became a rendezvous for impoverished Gaelic scholars and scribes. They were maintained in his house and employed to copy the principal historical manuscripts of Ireland.

19 m. S. is Aghalane Castle, a Plantation castle built by James Creighton in 1614–19.

11 m. SSW. are the ruins of Kinawley parish church on the site of an early abbey or church founded by St Náile (successor of St Rabharnóg), from whom the place takes its name. 3 m. W. of Kinawley, to the W. of the road to Swanlinbar and on the E. slope of Benaughlin, is Doohatty Glebe court-tomb (5,504 ft).

8½ m. SW. is Florence Court (Nat. Trust), magnificent seat of the Earls of Enniskillen (descendants of William Cole). The main block may have been built by John Cole M.P., Baron Mount Florence about 1764. The arcades and wings (by the Sardinian architect Davis Ducart?) were probably added by his son William (created Earl of Enniskillen in 1789). The excellent rococo plasterwork is of the Dublin school (by Robert West?). Badly damaged by fire in 1955, the house has been restored under the direction of Sir Albert Richardson.

4½ m. W. is the Marble Arch, where the Claddagh River emerges from a huge system of underground chambers and galleries. A visit to the caves there (open to the public) includes a boat journey across an underground lake amid flood-lit stalactites.

½ m. W. of the Claddagh bridge, in Carrigan, is St Lasair's 'Cell', a three-chamber souterrain in a mound. ¼ m. to the N. is Killesher Church named alter St Lasair; the remains here are those of a medieval church re-edified for Protestant use in the 17th c. Part of a High Cross from Killesher graveyard is now in Fermanagh County Museum.

8 m. W., near Boho, is a series of labyrinthine caves with a subterranean stream. 1 m. SW. of Boho crossroads is Coolarkan Cave, which has a large chamber and engulfs a surface stream. The moorland NW. of Boho has many swallow-holes and pot-holes, including Noon's Hole, the deepest in Ireland. A plain Gothic doorway (from a medieval church ¾ m. NW.) has been re-erected as the W. doorway of Boho Protestant church. In Toneel churchyard are the base, shaft, and a fragment of the head of a 9th/10th c. High Cross. The figure sculptures include *The Fall of Adam and Eve*, *Baptism of Christ*, etc. The cross derives from an early monastery which stood there. ⅓ m. W. of Toneel church are the Reyfad Stones, six large stones, five of which have 'cup-and-ring' marks. 3½ m. W. of the church, on the shore of Loughnacloyduff (2½ m. NE. of Black Bridge on the Belcoo–Garrison road), is Clogherbog 'inscribed' cave (900 ft), a partly artificial cave with inscribed crosses. – 1½ m. NW. of Boho crossroads is Aghanaglack 'Standing Stone, a plain cross-shaft. Nearby is Aghanaglack Cave, artificially modified. Further W., 1 m. N. of the 'Devil's S' on the Boho–Belcoo road (700 ft) is Aghanaglack 'Giants Grave' (Hist. Mon.) a dual court-tomb.

4 m. NW., by the lake, was Castle Hume, Richard Cassels' first (*c.* 1727) Irish house; he was brought to Ireland by Sir

Gustavus Hume to build it; only the dovecot and part of the stable block survive.

3 m. W. of Castle Hume in Castletown Monea is Monea Castle (Hist. Mon.), a Plantation castle with Scottish features. It was built (1618–19) by the Rev. Malcolm Hamilton, Rector of Devenish and in 1688 was the residence of Gustavus Hamilton, Governor of Enniskillen. In the mid-18th c. the castle was gutted by fire. In the Protestant parish church of Monea is a Wilhelmina Geddes window (1913) and a limestone window (*c.* 1500) from St Mary's Priory, Devenish (*see p. 239*). ¾ m. SW. of the church are the ruins of Tullykelter Castle, an English-style fortified house built (*c.* 1617) by James Somerville, a Planter from Cambusnethan, Ayrshire. 3¼ m. NW. of Monea Church are the ruins of Derrygonnelly Church, built in 1627 by Sir John Dunbar. 3 m. NW. of Derrygonnelly on the shore of Carrick Lough, are the ruins of Aghamore or Carrick Church built towards the end of the 15th c. by Gilbert O Flanagan and his wife Margaret Maguire. Nearby in Carrick Lough is a crannóg. 5 m. NW. of Derrygonnelly, in Lough Navar Forest Park, is Braade sweat-house. 3 m. N. of Derrygonnelly, on the W. shore of Lough Erne, are the ruins of Tully Castle (Hist. Mon.), a fortified house and bawn built by Sir John Hume from Berwickshire, between 1610 and 1619. It was destroyed by Capt. Rory Maguire on Christmas Day, 1641, when most of the garrison were slaughtered (*see p. 207*).

EYRECOURT, Co. Galway (Map 6, L2), is a village on the Killimor (7 m.)–Banagher, Co. Offaly (6 m.) road. It is called after the Eyres, one of whom, George Eyre, master of the Galway Blazers and M.P. at the end of the 18th c., has been immortalized as Charles Lever's 'Charles O Malley'.

3 m. NW. on the road to Belview, at Lawrencetown, is a fine gateway (urn of pediment missing) erected by Walter Lawrence (1729–96) to commemorate Grattan's Volunteers.

2½ m. E., in Lismore, are remains of one of the principal castles of the O Maddens. They include the tower and parts of the bawn of a 15th–16th c. castle, and a 17th c. house.

3 m. SE. is Meelick, a Shannonside hamlet. Nothing survives of the motte built there by William de Burgo in 1203, nor of the castle built by his son Richard in 1229, and destroyed by Felim O Conor in 1316. Close to the site of the castle is the parish church (tomb of Fergus Madden of Lismore, 1671), re-roofed church of a Franciscan friary founded in 1414 by an O Madden. Dispersed at the Reformation, the friars returned in 1630. John Colgan, celebrated historian, was Guardian in 1635. The friary lay derelict from the Cromwellian victory until 1686. The church was refurbished in 1986 by Ray Carroll.

F

FEAKLE, Co. Clare (Map 6, I5), lies in the remote heart of the hills of East Clare, on the N. road between Gort (15 m.) and Scarriff (6 m.).

The poet Brian Mac Giolla-Meidhre, alias Merriman (1757–1805), is buried in the old churchyard, but no monument marks his grave. His celebrated satire *Cúirt an Mheadhon Oidhche* (The Midnight Court) has been translated into English by the late Lord Longford, Arland Ussher, Frank O Connor, and Bowes Egan. Merriman was born at Clondegad, and was schoolmaster at Kilclenin near Feakle. He is commemorated by a plaque outside the graveyard, and his memory is honoured annually in the county by the holding of a Merriman Summer and Winter School.

FENIT, Co. Kerry (Map 5, E2), is a village 8 m. W. of Tralee, of which it is the outer port.

St Bréanainn moccu Altai, Brendan the Navigator (484–577, *see pp. 107* and *129*), was born in the vicinity.

5 m. N., on a rocky promontory near the NW. entrance to Barrow Harbour, is Round Castle.

FERBANE, Co. Offaly (Map 3, C4), is a village on the Clara (10 m.)–Cloghan (4 m.) road.

½ m. S., on the E. bank of the Brosna, is Gallen Priory (now a convent). It derives its name from Gallen of the Britons (Welsh), a monastery said to have been founded by St Canoc, or MoChonóg, in the 5th c., and which was situated between the house and the river. In the Middle Ages the monastery became an Augustinian priory. A short distance S. of the convent are the ruins of a 15th c. parish church (Nat. Mon.) where a remarkable early carved slab, as well as a number of cross-slabs recovered in excavations in 1934–5, are displayed.

6 m. N. are remnants of Doon Castle, an O Mooney stronghold with a sheila-na-gig.

5 m. NE., on the Ballycumber road, is Lemanaghan, where fragments of a Romanesque church and an early slab mark the site of a monastery founded by St Manchán (d. 665). N. of the church are traces of St Machán's House. E. of the church is St Manchán's Well, from which an ancient causeway leads to the 'abbey'. The latter is an enclosure with a diminutive pre-Romanesque oratory, traditionally the cell of St Manchán's mother, St Mella. Between well and 'abbey' is the stone where, legend asserts, mother and son met each day without conversing. St Manchán's shrine, a splendid, 12th c. tomb-shaped reliquary containing bones of the saint, is now preserved at Boher Church (*see p. 104*).

FERMOY, Co. Cork (Map 4, B6), is a market town and important road junction, 23 m. NE. of Cork, 10 m. S. of Mitchelstown, 16 m. W. of Lismore, and 18 m. E. of Mallow.

As a town, Fermoy is the creation of John Anderson, a Scots merchant settled in Cork, who purchased the Fermoy estate in 1791. He offered the British Government sites for large barracks, and built the town to meet the needs of the garrison. From 1797 to 1922 the town was one of the principal British military centres in Ireland, with training grounds at Kilworth Camp and Moore Park (*see* Kilworth, *below*).

In the Middle Ages the Cistercian Abbey of Castrum Dei (Mainistear Fhear Maighe) stood on the S. bank of the river, but no trace survives.

In the unusual Protestant church (1802) on the N. side of the river is a medieval stoup, or mortar, with grotesque masks; its history is unknown. The bridge across the Blackwater dates from 1689; it was widened by Anderson.

3¼ m. NE. is Kilworth. ¾ m. SW. of the village, above the Funshion River (trout), in the grounds of Moore Park, is Cloghleagh, one of a number of Condon castles in the area. 2 m. SE., to the N. of the Araglin, are the ruins of Ballyderown Castle. 3½ m. NW., in the Kilworth Mts, is Kilworth Camp.

4½ m. SE., in the grounds of Coole Abbey (by Davis Duckart?), the remains of two early churches with *antae* (Nat. Mons.) mark the site of an early monastery. The large church had a Gothic chancel and SW. porch added in the 13th c. St Patrick's tooth was said to be preserved there in the Middle Ages.

5 m. SSE. is the village of Castlelyons. St Nicholas's Protestant church (ruined), SW. of the village, was built in 1776 by Lord Barrymore within the nave of a medieval church whose E. window it incorporates. E. of the church are the Barrymore mausoleum, with wrought-ironwork of local make, and a monument (1753) to James Barry, Viscount Barry and Buttevant (1676–1747). The monument is by David Sheehan (d. 1756). On the E. side of the village are the remains (aisleless nave, tower, chancel, E. and W. cloister ranges; Nat. Mon.) of the Carmelite friary of the Virgin Mary, founded in 1307 by John de Barri; there are some medieval gravestones there (Nat. Mons.). At the S. end of the village are remains of Castle Lyons, a Tudor stronghouse with later additions, which was the chief seat of the Lords Barrymore until its destruction by fire in 1771. – 4½ m. SE. of Castlelyons are the ruins of the early church of Britway; NW. is St Brigid's Well.

2½ m. W., on the N. bank of the Blackwater, is Castle Hyde demesne (owned by a consortium). On a rock behind the house are remains of Castle Hyde (by Davis Ducart?), originally an O Mahony stronghold. The first Hydes there were Cromwellian Planters; a descendant, Douglas Hyde (1860–1949; *see p. 185*), was co-founder of the Gaelic League, Professor of Modern Irish in University College, Dublin, and President of Ireland (1938–45).

FERNS, Co. Wexford (Map 4, L2), now a quiet village on the Gorey (11 m.) – Enniscorthy (8 m.) road, gives its name to one of the principal dioceses of the ancient kingdom of Leinster, and was also for a time the royal seat of that kingdom. Its history commences with the foundation of a monastery by St M'Aodhóg (Mogue), alias Aidan (d. 626), whose relics were subsequently enshrined in a casket which, together with its satchel, is now preserved in the National Museum. Ferns survived repeated ravaging by the Norsemen, and at the 12th c. reformation became the see of a diocese corresponding to Hy Kinsella. The notorious Díarmait na nGall Mac Murrough fixed his residence nearby. He was a generous pattron of the Church and founded St Mary's Abbey for Canons Regular of St Augustine. It was burned down in 1154, but he rebuilt it in 1160, and died there in 1171. After Díarmait's death Ferns passed (by Anglo-Norman law) to his son-in-law, Strongbow, and subsequently to Strongbow's heirs, but was recovered by the Mac Murroughs in the 14th c. The see of the Catholic diocese is now at ENNISCORTHY. The Protestant diocese is united with those of Leighlin and Ossory.

The castle (Nat. Mon.), at the NW. end of the village, is thought to occupy the site of King Díarmait's residence. It is a rectangular keep with drum-towers at the angles; in the SE. tower is a chapel. Excavations in 1972–5 revealed a rock-cut fosse and remains of a drawbridge structure on the S. side, and another possible entrance on the E. side. The castle was presumably built (about 1226) by some member of the Earl Marshal's family (*see pp. 90* and *258*), but was for long the residence of the bishop. In the 14th c. it fell to the resurgent Mac Murrough Kings of Leinster, at which time it was probably abandoned.

Burned down in 1577, the early-13th c. cathedral is represented only by its chancel, shorn of its aisles and incorporated in little St Edan's [*sic*] Cathedral (Protestant, 1817). There is a 13th c. episcopal tombstone. The *St Patrick* window is by Catherine O Brien (1931). E. of the cathedral is a beautiful fragment of an early-13th c. church (Nat. Mon.). In the graveyard is a portion of the shaft (Nat. Mon.) of a High Cross, alleged to mark the grave of King Díarmait. Portions of three plain High Crosses stand in the churchyard. Outside the graveyard is St Mogue's Well; the 1847 well house has carved heads from Clone Church (2 m. S.).

S. of the cathedral is St Mary's Abbey (Nat. Mon.), which is usually assumed to have occupied the site of M'Aodhóg's monastery and is represented today merely by the vaulted sacristy, NW. bell-tower, and N. wall of a navel-and-chancel church. The most interesting feature is the ruined belfry, square on plan as far as the level of the church roof, where it turns into a Round Tower.

NE. of the cathedral, to the W. of the Road, are fragmentary remains of St Peter's Church (Nat. Mon.), a modest, nave-and-chancel structure with a Late Romanesque window in the S. wall of the chancel and two Gothic lancets in the E. gable, all three possibly taken from other churches.

2 m. S. are remains of Clone church, from which fragments were taken to Ferns.

FETHARD, Co. Tipperary (Map 4, F3), is a small, decayed market town where the Callan (14 m.) – Cashel (10 m.) road crosses the little Clashawley River 7 m. N. of Clonmel.

The town came into being in the 14th c., and in 1376 Edward III of England gave permission to the townsfolk to enclose it with walls. Fragments of the towered wall and of one of its four gates survive; likewise four 'castles', i.e. tower houses, and a number of houses with the armorial bearings of their builders. The Protestant parish church of the Holy Trinity incorporates some windows, the W. tower, etc., of the late-15th c. parish church. E. of the church is a castle, or tower house; S. of this are two others. At the E. end of the town are the ruins (refectory, dormitories, kitchen, etc.) of an Augustinian friary founded outside the walls, *c.* 1303–6, by Walter de Mulcote; built into a wall near the E. end of the church is a sheila-na-gig. Early in the 19th c. the friars returned to Fethard and re-edified the remains of their church.

¾ m. S. are the ruins of Templemartin, a small church.

4½ m. N. (3¼ m. S. of Killenaule), on the borders of Cooleagh and Grangebarry, is a crossroads. The neighbouring townlands are exceptionally rich in ringforts, earthworks of various kinds, and other ancient remains.

Glen of Aherlow, Co. Tipperary *(see page 186).*

Gowran Abbey, Co. Kilkenny (see pages 197–8).

$2\frac{1}{2}$ m. NNE. are the ruins of Slainstown Castle.

$\frac{1}{4}$ m. NE., on the Cashel road, is the Folk and Transport Museum, housing a collection of old vehicles and agricultural implements.

$2\frac{1}{2}$ m. NE. are the ruins of Knockkelly Castle, a 16th c. castle with large bawn and angle turrets.

3 m. SE., above the River Clashawley, are the remains of Kiltinan Castle (private). W. of the castle are the ruins of a medieval church which, from *c.* 1195 to the Dissolution, belonged to St Mary's Abbey, Osney, Oxfordshire; there is a sheila-na-gig in the church. N. of the castle and church is the site of an extensive medieval village.

5 m. SE. rises Slievenamon (2,368 ft), renowned in song and Fiana story; it is the Síd ar Femin of Irish mythology.

$1\frac{3}{4}$ m. W. is the 15th/16th c. tower of Barretstown Castle (Nat. Mon.).

$4\frac{3}{4}$ m. NW. is Knockbrit, birthplace of the authoress Marguerite Power (1789–1849), who became Countess of Blessington. She was a celebrated beauty and a friend of Lord Byron.

FETHARD, Co. Wexford (Map 4, J6), is a village on the E. coast of the Hook Peninsula.

$1\frac{1}{2}$ m. SSE. is rocky Baginbun Head. Some 30 acres of the main headland are cut off on the landward side by the remains of a great ditch flanked by ramparts, probably the fortifications constructed by Raymond le Gros, who landed there with the vanguard of Strongbow's army at the beginning of May, 1170. Their camp was attacked by a combined force of Waterford Norse and Déise and other Irish, some 3000 strong. The attackers were thrown back with great slaughter, and after their victory, the Anglo-Normans broke the limbs of their prisoners, among them 70 of the leading citizens of Waterford, and hurled them into the sea.

The country round about is rich in church and castle ruins. One of the best of the castles is that (Nat. Mon.) by the pier at Slade, 6 m. SW. of Fethard. The remains there comprise a gracefully tapered tower of perhaps the late 15th c. and, attached to it, a slightly later fortified house. The castle used to be the home of the Laffans. The annexes at the E. and W. ends are later additions.

$4\frac{1}{2}$ m. N. the house called Tintern Abbey stands inside the remains of the church of Tintern (Minor) Abbey, a daughter of Tintern Major in Monmouthshire (currently closed; viewable from the outside only). The abbey was founded in 1200 by William the Marshal, Earl of Pembroke, in fulfilment of a vow made when imperilled by a storm at sea. The remains (*c.* 1300) comprise nave (aisles gone), crossing with tower (upper part 15th c.), presbytery (inserted Tudor windows), and S. transept (pseudo-Gothic reconstruction) with three chapels. Some of the presbytery details derive from Tintern Major (1269–88). After the Dissolution the lay grantee built a residence inside the church, the traces of which are gradually being cleared.

FINGLAS, Co. Dublin (Map 3, K3), is a village and industrial suburb on the Dublin (4 m.) – Ashbourne (10 m.) road. It takes its name, Fionn-Ghlais, Fair Rill, from a holy well (chalybeate) formerly resorted to by sufferers from eye diseases. Dr Achmet Borumborad, *né* Patrick Lynch, the 18th c. quack, extracted an annual grant from the Dublin Parliament in order to provide the citizens with sea-water baths. He built a pump-room over the well, and Finglas had its brief day as a fashionable watering place.

A monastery was founded at Finglas *c.* 560 by St Cainneach (Canice). In the 8th and 9th c., as one of the 'Two Eyes of Ireland', it was intimately associated with TALLAGHT in the Céle Dé movement. In 780 Abbot St Dub-litir (d. 796) presided at the 'congress' of Tara. It declined as a result of Viking raids from nearby Dublin.

The ruins of the medieval parish church of St Canice, in Protestant use until 1843, are those of a nave-and-chancel building with later S. aisle and vaulted N. porch. In the SE. corner of the churchyard is a High Cross. It stood on the old abbey land of Finglas until Cromwellian times, when it was buried for safety. It was recovered, and set up in its present position, in 1816. William of Orange camped at Finglas 5 July 1690, after his victory at the Boyne.

$3\frac{1}{2}$ m. NNW. is Dunsoghly Castle (Nat. Mon.), a fine residential tower with traces of extensive outbuildings (and a courtyard?) on the N. and the ruins of a 16th c. chapel on the S. To the W., SW., S., and E. are remains of 17th c. hornworks with three bastions. The three-storey tower has rectangular corner turrets. A stairway in the NE. turret gives access to the upper floors and roof-walk. The original timbers were largely

Dunsoghly Castle, Co. Dublin.

replaced recently. The castle was built by Thomas Plunkett, Chief Justice of the King's Bench and a cadet of the Plunketts of Killeen (*see p. 174*), who purchased the property early in the 15th c. The chapel was erected in 1573 by Sir John Plunkett (d. 1582), Chief Justice of the Queen's Bench. A tablet over the doorway bears the symbols of the Passion and the initials of Plunkett and his third wife, Genet Sarsfield. Sir John also built a chapel at St Margaret's (*see below*), where he likewise enclosed St Margaret's Well to make a bath for pilgrims. During the 1641–53 war the castle served as an important English outpost.

1 m. ENE., near the Catholic church, is St Margaret's (originally St Brigid's) Well, 'a tepid medicinal spring which never freezes'. ¼ m. NE. of the well are the ruins of the medieval parish church of St Margaret. Attached to the church at the SE. are the ruins of the chapel built by Sir John Plunkett of Dunsoghly (d. 1582) for his place of burial. 3¼ m. NNW. is Kilsallaghan Church, where there is a Michael Healy window: *Christ the King* (1917). Nearby are the ruins of a medieval church and castle.

FINTONA, Co. Tyrone (Map 2, D1), is a small market town on the Omagh (9 m.) – Fivemiletown (8 m.) road. It had an unique horse-tram connecting Fintona Station to the Great Northern railway line at Fintona junction, 1 m. NW. The E. window in the ruined parish church at Castletown came from the old church at Donacavey (*see below*).

1½ m. N., at Donacavey, are the ruins of a medieval church, and the shaft of a stone cross (17th c.).

½ m. S. are the remains of Ecclesville House, with the date 1703 and the Eccles arms above the door.

FIVEMILETOWN, Co. Tyrone (Map 2, D2), is a small town, 6 m. from Clogher and 16 m. from Enniskillen, on the main Belfast road. It dates from *c.* 1736, when the small handsome parish church was built. The town was an important station on the former Clogher Valley railway (1887–1942), and the small museum in the main street has some relics of the railway days.

Just NE. of the town, in an attractive demesne, stands Blessingbourne, a large Elizabethan-style house designed by Pepys Cockerell for Hugh de F. Montgomery in 1874. The house has original William Morris wallpapers, and in the yard there is both a carriage museum and a fine collection of domestic utensils and family memorabilia. Both are open to the public by arrangement.

FORE, Co. Westmeath (Map 2, E8), is a village on the Kells (16 m.) – Castlepollard (2½ m.) road, which takes its name, Tobhar Féichín, St Féichín's Spring, probably from that 'wonder' which flows underground from Lough Lene and springs up in the valley beside the ancient church.

Fore was the site of an important early monastery, of a medieval Benedictine priory, and of a small walled town which was one of the fortresses of the English marches.

The early monastery was founded by St Féichín (*see also pp. 65, 105 and 115*). Féichín, noted even in childhood for his singular asceticism, was born 580/90 at Bile Féichín, probably in Co. Sligo, and he died of the yellow plague, 20 January 664/5. In his lifetime Fore is said to have had 300 monks. At the 12th c. reformation the monastery appears to have adopted the Rule of the Canons Regular of St Augustine. Of this ancient monastery only the church (9th/10th c.?) and some miscellaneous fragments remain. The ruins of the church (Nat. Mon.) stand in the W. graveyard. The original building was a simple rectangular structure with *antae* and high pitched gables. The most notable feature is the trabeate W. doorway with its massive (2½ tons), cross-inscribed lintel. The chancel is an addition of about 1200. The 15th c. E. window replaces a twin-lancet original; underneath it is a fragment of the altar table. In the chancel are also preserved two early gravestones, and a fragment of a stone cross, etc. In the nave is a medieval font. In the graveyard is a stone ring-cross (Nat. Mon.). Nearby are situated the remains of St Féichín's Mill and of the Anchorite's Cell, a 15th c. tower altered in the 17th c. and adapted as the Greville-Nugent mausoleum in the 19th.

The Benedictine priory of SS Taurin and Fechin was founded *c.* 1200 by one of the de Lacys. A motte with rectangular bailey on the slope of the Ben of Fore to the E. of the village probably represents the first de Lacy stronghold. The priory was a dependency of the abbey of St Taurin at Évreux in Normandy. It consequently suffered from the Anglo-French wars of the 14th c. After the Dissolution the priory was granted to Christopher Nugent, Baron of Delvin.

The remains of the priory (Nat. Mon.), the only certain Benedictine remains in Ireland, comprise those of the claustral buildings and of the church. The latter is an austere nave-and-chancel structure with castle-like W. and SE. towers which recall the priory's role of advanced fortress of the English Pale. It dates from 1200/1210, but the towers are 15th c. additions. The surviving claustral buildings are also 15th c. date, but incorporate 13th c. fragments on the ground floor. The fragments of the beautiful cloister arcade (re-erected 1912) exemplify a type peculiar to 15th c. Ireland. In the cloister are two 13th/14th c., Anglo-Norman tomb-stones. To the NE., on Knocknamonaster, are remains of the priory pigeon-house; to the NW, remains of a rectangular building and a gateway.

In the E. graveyard are the remains of the medieval church of St Mary. The 19th c. church in the same graveyard was renovated (1975) by Tyndall, Hogan, Hurley, with attractive furnishings in stone (by Michael Biggs) and bronzes and enamel (by Patrick McElroy).

Of the medieval town defences only the ruined N. and S. gateways survive. Fragments of the priory cloister have been built into the masonry, showing that the gateways have been repaired since the Dissolution.

In a grassy triangular area in the village are a plain stone cross and the socket of another. Within 2 m. of Fore are the remains of no less than 14 wayside crosses, most of them small and plain, and dating probably from around the 17th c.

FOXFORD, Co. Mayo (Map 7, H4), is a village on the main Castlebar (12 m.) – Ballina (10½ m.) road, 1¾ m. E. of Lough Cullin. Its woollen manufactures enjoy a high repute.

Admiral William Brown (1777–1857) and the poet Frederick Robert Higgins (1896–1941) were natives of Foxford. Admiral Brown, 'father' of the Argentine navy, is commemorated by a bronze bust by the Argentinian sculptor Vergottini (1957).

3¼ m. S., beyond Ballylahan Bridge, are the ruins of a keepless castle with twin-towered gatehouse. It was built by Jordan d'Exeter (ancestor of the Mac Jordans) late in the 13th c.

4¾ m. W. is Pontoon, one of the angling centres for Loughs Conn and Cullin.

FOYNES, Co. Limerick (Map 6, F8), is a Shannon estuary village and port on the Limerick (24 m.) – Tarbert (17 m.) road. For some years there was a transatlantic seaplane base there, but it was superseded by Shannon Airport, further up the estuary on the N. shore.

Sir Stephen de Vere (1812–1904), brother of Aubrey de Vere (*see p. 48*), is buried in Foynes churchyard. He and Charlotte O Brien (1845–1909), daughter of William Smith O Brien (*see p. 42*), were prominent social workers. They led the campaign against the notorious 'coffin ships' used to transport poverty-stricken emigrants to America.

On a hill overlooking the village is a cross to the memory of Edmond Spring-Rice (1814–65), member of a famous Liberal family (*see p. 234*).

FRENCHPARK, Co. Roscommon (Map 7, K5), is a hamlet on the Castlerea (9 m.) – Boyle (10 m.) road. Douglas Hyde (1860–1949; *see p. 180*), who was co-founder of the Gaelic League and first professor of Modern Irish in University College, Dublin, retired to Ratra House, which had been purchased for him by public subscription; but he was soon recalled by the unanimous agreement of all political parties to be first President of Ireland under the Constitution of 1937.

1 m. E., in Cloonshanville, a badly wrecked, small-towered church is all that remains of Holy Cross Dominican friary, founded in 1385 by Mac Dermot Gall. 400 yds SW. is a rough, stone cross having a raised circle on the W. face. In early times Cloonshanville was the site of a church associated with Bishop Comitius, disciple of St Patrick.

3½ m. SW. is Tibohine, which takes its name (Tigh Bhaoithín) from St Baithín Mór, great-grandson of Niall Nine-hostager, who founded a monastery there. An interpretative centre commemorating Douglas Hyde (*see above*) was opened there in 1988. The parish church, at Fairymount, has three Michael Healy windows (1908): *God the Father with SS. John the Baptist and Elizabeth; Ecce Homo and Mater Dolorosa; SS Peter and Anne with Lamb*; also *SS Jarlath and Brendan* (1910) – all of these recently mutilated by 'improvements'; also a Hubert McGoldrick window (*St Brigid*, 1922).

FRESHFORD, Co. Kilkenny (Map 4, G1), is a village on the Kilkenny (9 m.) – Urlingford (9 m.) road, 6 m. SW. of Ballyragget. Its name is a misinterpretation of Irish *achadh úr*, 'fresh (green) field'. The Protestant parish church (1730) incorporates the W. gable and fine, unusual, Late-Romanesque porch of a monastic church, successor of one founded by Bishop St Laichtín (Lachtán, d. 622), a disciple of St Comgall of Bangor (*see p. 113*). The porch has a small, shallow, figured frieze above the impost of each outer pilaster; on the return face of one jamb is a figured panel. The plain innermost arch and the S. jamb carry the inscriptions: OR[ŌIT] DO GILLA MO-CHOLMOC U CE[NN]CUCAIN DO RIGNE and OR[ĪT] DO NEIM INGIN CUIRC ACUS DO MATHGAMAIN U CHIARMEIC LASDERNAD IN TEMPUL SA ('A prayer for Gilla Mo-Cholmóc Ó Cenncucáin, who made [this]' and 'A prayer for Niam, daughter of Corc (Ó Cuire?), and for

Pontoon, Co. Mayo.

Mathgamain Ó Ciarmeic, for whom this church was made'). Nothing is known of the persons named. The small round window above the porch may be a restoration.

1¾ m. N., in Clontubrid, at the Saint's Well, may be seen the figured gable-finial of an ancient church.

3½ m. ESE., in Three Castles Demesne, are the ruins of the Church of Three Castles, a parish church with castellated residence at the W. end.

1½ m. SE., beside Wellbrook House, are the ruins of the small 13th/14th c. parish church of Clashacrow, with residential W. tower. To the NE. is a medieval dovecot.

5½ m. SSW. is Tullaroan, formerly also known as Courtstown, where a large castle of the Grace family stood until *c.* 1800. SE. of the village are the remains of a small medieval parish church dedicated to the Assumption of the Blessed Virgin Mary. To the original nave-and-chancel church Sir John Grace added, in 1543, a S. chapel, or transept, with richly decorated, Perpendicular doorway. In the ruins are several medieval gravestones. The neighbourhood is rich in ringforts and other earthworks.

1¾ m. SW. are the ruins of Ballylarkin 'Abbey' (Nat. Mon.), a small 13th c. parish church with good, later-14th c. sedilia. 2¼ m. SW., in Upper Tubbrid (-britain), are remains of a nave-and-chancel church and of a Grace castle.

3 m. NW., via the Fertagh road, are the remains of Balleen Church and hill-top castle. The latter was the principal seat of the Mountgarret Butlers in the early 17th c.; the latest part dates from 1640. It was dismantled by the Cromwellians in 1650.

G

GALBALLY, Co. Limerick (Map 4, B4), is a small village near the head of the beautiful Glen of Aherlow, 9 m. SW. of Tipperary, 5 m. S. of Emly, and 11 m. N. of Mitchelstown.

At the village are remains of a narrow, 15th c., parish church.

½ m. E., in Co. Tipperary, is the ruined church (Nat. Mon.) of Moor 'Abbey', a Franciscan Friary founded in 1471, only to be destroyed by fire the following year. During the Elizabethan wars the friary frequently served as a strong point; it was burned by English troops in 1569. The visible remains are those of a simple, friary-type church of 1470, with a Franciscan-type belfry of somewhat later date.

1 m. NE., in Corderry, is a wedge-tomb.

9 m. E., in Ardane on the S. side of the Glen of Aherlow, is St Berrahert's Kyle (Nat. Mon.), an oval enclosure with over 50 early cross-slabs, fragments of two early crosses (one figured), and a bullaun; to the E. is St Berechert's Well. This early church site is called after the 7th c. Anglo-Saxon saint, Berechert of Tullylease (*see p. 136*).

2 m. WSW., in Ballingarry, is Ballingarry Down, a platform ringfort with a fine view of Slievereagh and the Galtees. On the summit were remains of a rectangular medieval house, latest of a succession of houses, those at lower levels being of different type as well as of pre-12th c. date.

1½ m. W. is Duntryleague Hill (822 ft). W. of the summit is a fine passage-tomb. The summit of the hill is crowned by a cairn with a dry-stone wall kerb.

GALWAY, Co. Galway (Map 6, G2), is situated at the mouth of the short Galway River, near the NE. corner of Galway Bay, 132 m. W. of Dublin and 64 m. NW. of Limerick. It is the principal town of Connacht as well as of its county, and is a small seaport and a thriving industrial centre; it is also an important market centre, a university town and the cathedral town of the diocese to which it has given its name. Galway Races (on the Tuesday, Wednesday, and Thursday preceding the first Monday of August) are an all-Ireland occasion at which many Grand National winners have made their appearance.

John Lynch (*c.* 1599–1673), author of *Cambrensis Eversus*; Roderick O Flaherty (1629–1718; *see p. 285*); An Dubhaltach Óg Mac Fhirbhisigh (1585–1670; *see p. 205*); Richard Kirwan of Cregg (1733–1812), 'great chymist of Ireland'; John Wilson Croker (1780–1857), journalist and founder of London's Athenaeum Club; Joseph Patrick Haverty (1794–1864), painter; his brother, Martin Haverty (1809–87), essayist and historian, were all either natives of Galway or intimately associated with it.

The town, like its clear river, takes its name from the locality (Gaillimh) in which it is set. It originated with the permanent seizure (1232–43) of parts of the O Flaherty–O Halloran territories by Richard de Burgo and his fellow Anglo-Normans. De Burgo built a castle by the river in place of an O Flaherty stronghold. The town as such seems to have begun as a seignorial borough of the de Burgo manor of Loughrea (charter from Walter de Burgo, Earl of Ulster, who died in 1271) and had native Irish as well as 'English' burgesses. By an obscure process it attained the status of a royal borough (1396 letters patent from Roger Mortimer, Earl of March and Ulster, in his capacity as Lieutenant of Richard II of England). This helped to detach it from the local de Burgo – by now Mac William *Úachtair* – interest and to make it a firm bulwark of the English Crown in the West, and an island of English speech and culture. At the same time its isolation from the seat of English power, combined with its ever-increasing prosperity – based on security and the expansion of trade with France, Flanders, the Baltic, and Spain – fostered a spirit of independence. In effect, the town developed into a sort of tiny city-state, ruled by a merchant oligarchy (chief officer accorded the rank of mayor by 1484 letters patent). A disastrous fire in 1473 cleared the way for a well laid-out 16th–17th c. town of tower and courtyard houses (a 1651 picture-map may be seen at University College), many of which survived into the 18th and 19th c.

The ruling oligarchy of medieval Galway was drawn from a group of aristocratic merchant families, almost all of Anglo-Norman or English extraction. The most celebrated of these were the 14 'Tribes': Athy, Blake, Bodkin, Browne, Darcy, Deane, Font, French, Joyce, Kirwan, Lynch, Martin, Morris, and Skerret. Foremost of the Tribes were the Lynches, who supplied the town with 84 mayors between 1485 and 1654.

Some of these Tribes, we are told, had their hereditary traits: the Joyces were 'merry', the Blakes 'positive', and so on; not all the traits were complimentary. Traits common to all were the gift of making money, and unswerving loyalty to the English Crown and to the Catholic Church.

St Berechert's Kyle, in the Glen of Aherlow, Co. Tipperary.

Second only to the Burkes – if even to them – as traditional foes of the townsfolk were the despoiled O Flaherties, and a celebrated 1549 inscription over the West Gate read:

> This gate was erected to protect us
> from the ferocious O Flaherties Good Lord deliver us.

(In 1951 and 1964 a 'ferocious O Flaherty' was elected mayor of the town!)

In 1580, Mayor Dominick Lynch founded, near the quay, a Free School which developed into an important centre of Catholic culture and nationalist activity, drawing its pupils from far and near. It was suppressed by James I in 1615, but revived early in the following reign. Its most famous headmasters were Alexander Lynch – under whom the school is said to have had 1200 students! – and Dr John Lynch, author of *Cambrensis Eversus*. Both John Lynch and Roderick O Flaherty acquired their polished Latinity at the school. In 1627 the number of scholars flocking to Galway was so great that the Corporation ordered all 'forreigne beggars and poor schollers' to be whipped out of the town. The school disappeared amid the universal ruin which followed the Cromwellian victory in 1652.

Galway's loyalty to the English Crown survived all religious and other injustices until 1642. Only then, too late, did the townsfolk join their fate with that of the nation. The outcome was a nine-month land-and-sea blockade by the Cromwellian Sir Charles Coote II, which ended with the surrender of the town, 5 April 1652.

The Williamite rebellion was another disaster for Galway, one from which the town but slowly recovered. A century and a half later came the great Famine of 1846–7, which seemed to mark the end. In the present century, however, and notably since the re-establishment of the Irish state, the town has gradually recovered, and today the population is greater than it has ever been before.

The focal centre of the town is Eyre Sq., originally an open space in front of the main gate. The John Fitzgerald Kennedy Memorial Garden (1965–6) was designed by Wilfrid Cantwell and James Fehily. Centrepiece of the square is now the fountain, with Eamonn O Doherty's iron sculpture representing the sails of a Galway hooker (symbolizing the city's maritime tradition), erected in 1984 to commemorate the 500th anniversary of the city becoming a borough with mayoral status. The doorway (with oriel above) from a Browne mansion in Lower Abbeygate St stands forlorn on the W. side. Nearby is a 1936 memorial to Pádraic Ó Conaire (1882–1923), Galway-born Irish writer, by Albert Power, R.H.A. Opening off the NE. corner of the square is

Foster St: the chapel of the Magdalen Asylum has a window (*Sacred Heart*, *Blessed Virgin Mary*, *St Joseph*, *St Mary Magdalen*) by Evie Hone (1952).

From the head of the square the principal shopping street winds its way westwards to the river and William O Brien Bridge. In its short length it has four different names: Williamsgate, William's St, Shop St (formerly High Middle St), Mainguard St. Its continuation beyond the bridge, to the SW. in the direction of Salthill, is called Dominick St, Upper and Lower. Excavations to the W. of Eyre S. revealed foundations of towers from the 17th c. town walls.

At the junction of Shop St and Upper Abbeygate St (formerly Littlegate) is Lynch's Castle, now occupied by the Allied Irish Bank. This much-altered, early-16th c. tower-house (ruthlessly scoured in 1966) preserves some interesting features: arms of Henry VII of England, of the Lynch family (both in Shop St), and of the Kildare Fitzgeralds (Abbeygate St); also gargoyles, rare in Ireland. Nearby houses, and others further W. and S., preserve sorry fragments of the limestone houses for which 16th and 17th c. Galway was famous.

NE. of William O Brien Bridge, in Market St, is the Protestant parish church of St Nicholas of Myra. It preserves the shell of the medieval town parish church, which began as a dependency of the Cistercian abbey of Knockmoy (*see p. 34*). In 1484, Archbishop Donatus O Murray of Tuam, quondam vicar of the parish, secured a bull from Innocent VIII transforming the vicarage into a college (community) of priests elected by the mayor, bailiffs, and equals of the town, to serve the church; the Warden, or head of the college, was elected annually by the same municipal authorities. Resistance of the townsfolk delayed the introduction of the Reformation; but in 1568 the Mass was at last prohibited and the Protestant service was introduced into their church. Thereafter the townsfolk were burdened with a Protestant college (official) as well as a Catholic college (unofficial). At the time of the Confederation of Kilkenny the Catholics recovered possession of both the church and the college house. At that time, too, Galway became a centre of unprecedented Irish cultural activity, and we find An Dubhaltach Óg Mac Fhirbhisigh compiling part of his celebrated *Book of Genealogies* in the college house.

The Galway symbol in the Spanish Arch Museum.

The church occupies the site of an earlier chapel, fragmentary traces of which may be discerned in the chancel S. wall. At first it had no tower, and the nave aisles were low and narrow. The tower (smothered in cement in the early 1960s) seems to have been added about 1500; the pyramidal spire dates from 1683; the parapet is an 1883 restoration. Between 1486 and 1535 the S. aisle was enlarged to its present size by Dominick Dubh Lynch and his son, Stephen. In 1561 the S. transept was lengthened and galleried by Nicholas Lynch to provide for a family chantry; the S. window is 15th c. work from the older transept. Between 1538 and 1583 the N. aisle was enlarged to its present size as a French family chantry; the Blessed Sacrament Chapel (reroofed) dates from about 1538. The W. door of the nave is an insertion of the late 15th c.; it has been mutilated by the 17th/18th c. Gothick window above it. The S. porch apparently dates from the 15th c., but the doorway is a 16th c. insertion. The gargoyles of the S. aisle are closely akin to those of Lynch's Castle. Noteworthy features inside the church are: the fine, 15th c., Joyce wall-tomb in the S. transept; the 16th c. font; the 15th c. stoup; the 15th c. reader's desk (the 'Confessional') from some monastic or similar refectory, which has been stupidly erected at the entrance of the Blessed Sacrament Chapel; and the gravestones (set in the floor) with symbols of crafts and callings. The church and its monuments were savagely mutilated by the Cromwellians; they continue to suffer from 'restorers'.

At the NE. corner of the churchyard, in Market St, are fragments of two 16th/17th c. houses. 19th c. fantasy has inserted in one of them a tablet which declares that James Fitz Stephen Lynch, Mayor in 1493, executed his son 'on this spot'. It is doubtful if any Lynch ever executed his son; even if he did, there is no reason for selecting 'this spot' as the scene of horror.

Parallel to Shop St, on the S., is Middle St. The pro-cathedral of St Nicholas of Myra (1816, closed 1965) exemplifies Catholic church architecture towards the close of Penal times. The nearby Augustinian church exemplifies the change that had taken place by 1855. Taibhdhearc na Gaillimhe, 'The Galway Theatre', produces plays in the Irish language only. The foremost names connected with it are those of Mícheál Mac Liammóir, Hilton Edwards, Siobhán McKenna, and Walter Macken. A nearby lane houses the smaller, but equally famous, Druid Theatre.

At the SW. corner of the old town, by the river mouth and the site of the medieval quay, is the old Fish Market. On the N. side is a fragment of a 16th c. tower-house. On the S. side is a fragment of the town wall, with twin-arched gateway. To it and to an adjacent portion of the Fish Market modern fantasy has given the names Spanish Arch and Spanish Parade.

To the N. of Williamsgate, in Francis St, is the Franciscan church, an 1849, neo-Grec essay by James Cusack; the original altars are pleasantly rustic pieces. The church occupies a portion of the site of the friary, which was founded in 1296 by Sir William Liath de Burgh, just outside the town wall and which became the principal burial-place of the leading families of the town. To the rear of the portico may be seen fragments of 'Sir Peter French's tomb gilt with gold . . .', with 'weepers in the Gothic tradition', but the ornamental details reflect Renaissance influence. In a small enclosure on the S. side of the church (entrance through the friary) are fragments of a 17th c. *Holy Trinity* resembling those in the cathedral. These, and a few miscellaneous scraps, are all that have survived the Cromwellian fury of 1652.

N. of the Franciscan church is the skinny-columned Court House, a dull, neo-Grec piece (1812–15) by Sir Richard Morrison. The English royal arms which crowned the pediment (and further overweighted the portico) are preserved at University College.

Behind the Court House is the Upper Bridge, which affords one of Galway's popular sights: shoals of salmon ascending the crystal-clear river. The Cathedral of Our Lady Assumed into Heaven and St Nicholas (1957–65) occupies the site of the County Gaol of British days where generations of patriots were imprisoned; Wilfred Scawen Blunt was gaoled there in 1887 for championing the cause of Lord Clanricarde's oppressed tenants (*see p. 307*). The cathedral, by J.J. Robinson, is a sad disappointment. The plaques of the main (N.) doors (*Prodigal Son*, *Mary Magdalen*, *Woman of Samaria at the Well*, *Christ Calms the Storm*, *Christ Cures the Paralytic*, *Christ Cures the Blind Man*, *Christ and St Thomas*, *Conversion of St Paul*, *Martyrdom of St Stephen*) and the bronze *Virgin and Child* over the central door are by Imogen Stuart. The tympana sculptures (*Baptism*, *Marriage*, *Confirmation*) are by Murphy. The chief features of the spacious interior are the mosaics (*Crucifixion*, angels of the dome pendentives) and windows (*Temptation of Christ*, *Multiplication of the Loaves and Fishes*, *Transfiguration*, *Mission of the Apostles*; W. aisle) by Patrick Pollen and the rose windows (*Mysteries of the Rosary*) designed by George Campbell; Pollen also did the *St Joseph the Worker* mosaic for the shrine in the nave. The Stations of the Cross are by Gabriel Hayes. There are also windows by John Murphy (*Melchisedech*, *Isaac*, *Jacob*, *Joseph*; N. transept), Laurence Walsh (*Samuel Anoints David*, *David with Goliath's Head*, *King David*, *Judgement of Solomon*; W. transept), and Gillian Deeney (*Adoration of the Magi*, *Christ Teaches the Multitudes from the Ship*, *Thou Art Peter*, and *Christ Heals the Paralytic*; E. aisle). In the Chapel of St Nicholas three limestone panels (*God the Father*, *God the Son*, *Blessed Virgin*) from a *Coronation of the Virgin* group have been reassembled (*Holy Ghost* modern) as the altar reredos. Long preserved separately in the pro-cathedral, they are said to have come from medieval St Nicholas's and date from some 17th c. phase of Catholic recovery. The Mortuary Chapel has a Patrick H. Pearse-John Fitzgerald Kennedy memorial mosaic (*Resurrection* with portrait roundels) by Patrick Pollen.

SW. of the bridge is the Poor Clares' convent, Nuns Island. A 13th c. *Enthroned Madonna* and 17th c. figures of St Clare and the Infant Jesus are preserved there.

A short distance NW. of the cathedral is rapidly growing University College, founded in 1845 as one of the unacceptable Queen's Colleges, since 1908 a constituent college of the National University of Ireland. As befits a university so close to large areas of Irish speech, many of the courses are given through the medium of Irish as well as of English. The original building (1846–50), by Joseph B. Keane, is an interesting, Tudor-style period piece suggested by the Oxford-Cambridge type of college. The modern University buildings, including the Library and the Science and Arts blocks, are by Scott, Tallon, Walker. In the library may be seen the 1485–1818 municipal records and a large pictorial map of the town as it was in 1651. In front of the library is a sheet metal sculpture by Brian King, symbolizing the Celtic knot. In the grounds are preserved miscellaneous fragments from old houses in the town; also the English (Hanoverian) royal arms from the Court House, an amusing example of rustic architectural sculpture.

The Dominican Convent, Taylor's Hill, has an Italian Baroque (17th c.) statue of the Blessed Virgin Mary; also a 17th/18th c. (Penal-times) Irish copy of another continental statue of Our Lady.

The Claddagh, on the SW. side of the town, beyond the river, preserves no more than the name of the Irish-speaking fisher quarter. The once large fleet of púcáns and gleótógs has dwindled away; the great huddle of thatched cottages was replaced in 1937 by arrays of unsightly concrete houses; the distinctive Claddagh costume has disappeared; the King of the Claddagh no longer reigns; few of the inhabitants now speak the ancient tongue. The so-called Claddagh Ring, once hand-made by Galway goldsmiths, was the traditional wedding-ring of a wide area (including the Aran Islands, Connemara, Iar-Chonnacht, Joyce's Country, etc.) served by Galway; the oldest datable examples were made in 1784. The Dominican friary and church occupy part of the site of the friary founded in 1488 and razed *c.* 1651. In the church are windows by Michael Healy (*St Dominic Receiving the Rosary*; 1935) and Hubert McGoldrick (*St Dominic Leading Nuns to the Convent of San Sistò*; 1939); also a 17th c. Italian Baroque statue of the Blessed Virgin Mary. Nearby is a badly sited statue (by Kavanagh) of Fr Tom Burke (1830–83), noted preacher and controversialist, who was born in Galway.

The Jesuit church, Sea Rd, has a small Lady Chapel by Michael Scott; the feature is a lovely mosaic, *Our Lady of the Wayside*, designed by Louis Le Brocquy (1957).

Salthill, suburb to the SW., is a popular seaside resort. The tawdry Church of Christ the King has a *Crucifixion* in wood by Claire Sheridan, figures of the Sacred Heart and the Blessed Virgin by Oisín Kelly, and three altars by Michael Scott.

On the E. side of the Galway River:

1 m. N., beside the river, are the remnants of Terryland Castle, a 17th c. house of the Earls of Clanricarde.

2 m. N. is Menlo Castle.

1 m. NE., in Renmore, is the church of St Oliver Plunkett (1975) by Patrick Sheahan with stone sanctuary furnishings by Michael Biggs, and the Stations (1980) and two tapestries (1988) by Frances Biggs.

3 m. NE., via the Tuam or Monivea roads, in Ballybrit, is Galway racecourse.

11 m. NE., via the Headford road, is Cregg Castle, ancestral home of Richard Kirwan (1733–1812), eminent scientist and Fellow of the Royal Society. The Queen Anne house (much restored in 1949) incorporates the tower of a 15th/16th c. castle.

Eyre Square, Galway.

4 m. E., to the S. of the Oranmore road, is Roscam, site of an early monastery. The remains comprise ruined Round Tower, fragments of a medieval church (Nat. Mons.), two bullaun stones, and a massive, semi-circular cashel enclosing the site.

On the W. side of the Galway River:

On Seamus Quirke Rd is the Church of the Sacred Heart (1983, Simon J. Kelly and Partners), furnishings by Ray Carroll.

GARRISON, Co. Fermanagh (Map 8, E8), a village at the head of Lough Melvin, on the Belleek (5 m.)–Manorhamilton (10 m.) road, is a good angling and holiday centre. The Catholic church was built in the 1973 by J.J. Tracey of Liam McCormick and Partners, with furnishings by Ray Carroll.

4½ m. SE. is the site of Kilcoo Monastery founded by or dedicated to St Patrick. In the adjoining field to the E. is a cross-shaft and base. A cross-slab from Kilcoo with an Irish inscription OR (ŌIT) DO MAELCLUCHI ('a prayer for Máel-Cluchi') is now in Fermanagh County Museum. Nearby across the County River is a remarkable natural limestone bridge.

5 m. SE., in Kiltyclogher village (Co. Leitrim), is a statue (by Albert Power) of Seán Mac Dermot, the 1916 leader. 2 m. SE. and 1 m. W. of Upper Lough Macnean, on a hill-slope to the W. of the linear earthwork known as the Black Pig's Race (*see below*), is Corracloona (Co. Leitrim) wedge-tomb (Hist. Mon.); the portal slab has a 'kennel hole'. Cornacully (Co. Fermanagh) court-tomb is 2½ m. NE.

7 m. SE. (1 m. NE. of Tullyrossmearn post office) is Cornacully Giant's Grave, a ruined court-tomb.

3 m. S. is the N. end of a long sector of the Black Pig's Race (*see p. 133*), which extends along the W. side of the valley nearly the whole way to Upper Lough Macnean.

GARVAGH, Co. Derry (Map 1, G5), is a small town where the Coleraine (11 m.)–Maghera (10 m.) road crosses the Agivey River. It was laid out by the Canning family to whom the land was granted in the 17th c. These later became Lords Garvagh. George Canning (1770–1827), British Prime Minister, was born there, as was Denis O Hempsey (1695–1807), the harpist.

3 m. E. at Monedig is the Daff stone, a portal-tomb in a cairn. 3 m. S., in Ballydullaghan, is Cornaclery multiple cist-cairn. About 1 m. S. is Tamnyrankin court-tomb.

GEASHILL, Co. Offaly (Map 3, E5), is a neat village on the Tullamore (9 m.)–Portarlington (9 m.) road. A motte points to early Anglo-Norman occupation, but in the later Middle Ages the district was held by the O Dempseys, then by the Fitzgerald Lords O ffaly. Near the Protestant church are remains of the castle (originally O Dempsey) which was held in 1642 by Lettice Fitzgerald against two attacks by Confederate Catholics under her cousin, Lord Clanmaliere (O Dempsey).

GLANDORE, Co. Cork (Map 5, I8), is a fishing village and quiet, small resort beautifully situated on Glandore Harbour, 6 m. WSW. of Ross Carbery and 9 m. E. of Skibbereen.

W. of the village are remains of a medieval church. Nearby, incorporated in a modern residence, are remains of Glandore Castle. The Barrets first built a castle there in 1215, and it later belonged to the O Donovans.

1¾ m. E., in Drombeg, is a fine stone circle (Nat. Mon.). At the centre was a dedicatory burial in an urn; the large stone at the SW. has cup and other markings on the upper surface. To the W. is an ancient hut-site with an open-air cooking-place.

On the opposite side of Glandore Harbour (road bridge) is the little village of Union Hall. 650 yds NW. is Rock Cottage, where Swift wrote *Carberiae Rupes* in the summer of 1723. Union Hall is the main gateway to Myross, the promontory between Glandore Harbour and Castle Haven, 'one of the most secret places in Ireland' (Daniel Corkery). Here Seán Ó Coileáin (1754–1817), the roystering 'Silver Tongue of Munster' and author of the lovely Jacobite song, 'An buachaill bán', conducted a 'hedge school'. 1¾ m. SE. of Union Hall, close to the sea, in Carrigillihy, are the remains of a small, oval, stone 'ringfort', of the Early Bronze Age or later. It had enclosed a little oval house of dry masonry and timber posts (model in the Cork Public Museum, *see p. 118*).

3 m. SW. of Union Hall, by a beautiful byroad, is Castle Haven. ½ m. N. are the ruins of Raheen Castle.

1¾ m. NW. is the village of Leap, so called from its proximity to the wide ravine (the 'leap' proper) at the head of Glandore Harbour. 'Beyond the Leap, beyond the law' was an old saying.

GLANWORTH, Co. Cork (Map 5, M3), is a pleasant village on the Fermoy (6 m)–Kilmallock (18 m) road, beside the pretty little Funshion River. There are fragmentary remains of a 13th c. Roche castle. There are also ruins of the church of a Dominican friary founded by the Roches in 1475. At the S. end of the village are remains of the church, Teampall Lobhair.

2 m. NW., at Killeenemer, a small, early church (Nat. Mon.) with *antae* and trabeate, architraved, W. doorway, mark the site of an early monastery.

1¼ m. SE., in Labbacallee townland, is Labbacallee (Nat. Mon.), largest and finest of Irish wedge-tombs. Remains of at least five persons had been buried in the tomb with Neolithic/Early Bronze Age pottery, animal bones, etc. The primary burial, in the closed E. chamber, was that of a woman whose skull was deposited in the large, outer chamber.

1 m. SW., to the W. of the road, in Moneen, is a low cairn. This has had a four-phase history, stretching from the Neolithic, through the Early Bronze Age to both the Middle and Late Bronze Age.

GLENAMOY, Co. Mayo (Map 7, E2), is a hamlet and road junction on the Belderg (7½ m.)–Belmullet (12½ m.) road.

8 m. NNW. is Portacloy, a delightful little cliff-ringed cove with a small beach. ¾ m. NNW. is Doonvinalla, a great promontory fort (largely eroded). 1¼ m. offshore are the Stags of Broadhaven, four sheer rocks which reach up to 300 ft high. 1½ m. W. is Benwee Head (829 ft), with a stupendous cliff and magnificent views.

9 m. NW., in the sandhills, is the ancient churchyard of Kilgalligan, which includes a large cairn.

6 m. NW., SSW. of Ross Port, in Rosdoagh, is a ruined court-tomb (Nat. Mon.).

5 m. WNW., on the W. side of Sruwaddacon Bay, is the little village of Pollatomish. 2½ m. NW. is the cliff fort, Dooncarton.

GLENARM village, Co. Antrim (Map 1, K5), at the foot of the glen from which it takes its name, is on the Antrim Coast Road, 12 m. NW. of Larne and 14 m. SE. of Cushendall.

Glenarm was the birthplace of Eoin MacNeill (1867–1945), historian, Celtic scholar, founder of the Gaelic League, commander-in-chief of the Irish Volunteers (1914), and Minister of Education in the Irish Free State 1923–6; also of his brother, James MacNeill (1869–1938), first Irish High Commissioner in London and second Governor-General of the Irish Free State.

Glenarm Castle has been the seat of the MacDonnells, Earls of Antrim (*see p. 40*) since 1636; it was largely remodelled in the early-19th c. by William Vitruvius Morrison in neo-Tudor style.

GLENAVY, Co. Antrim (Map 1, J8), is a small village on the road from Lisburn (10 m.) to Antrim (11 m.).

5 m. W. (via Sandy Bay), in Lough Neagh, is Ram's Island (bird sanctuary), where a ruined Round Tower marks an early monastic site.

GLENBEIGH, Co. Kerry (Map 5, D4), is a small seaside resort and noted tourist, angling, and golfing centre on the Killorglin (8 m)–Cahirsiveen (17 m.) road. Close to the village are ruins of Winn's Folly (Winn Castle, alias Glenbeigh Towers), a castellated mansion erected in 1867 for the 4th Lord Headley of Aghadoe, a notorious landlord, who aspired to set up there as a feudal baron. The 5th Lord Headly turned Muslim and, having made the pilgrimage to Mecca, assumed the title 'Al Hadji'. The house was burned down in 1922.

3 m. NE., beyond the River Caragh, are the sandhills of Dooks. 2 m. E. of Caragh bridge is Lough Caragh, which fills the lower part of beautiful Glencar. 3 m. E. of Glencar is Lough Acoose, a convenient starting-point for the ascent of Macgillicuddy's Reeks (Carrauntuohil, 3414 ft, highest mountain in Ireland).

1½ m. W., at Ross Behy, are sandhills and an excellent, 2 m. beach.

The road SW. from Glenbeigh to Cahiriveen affords a spectacular view of the Dingle Peninsula and the Blasket Islands. Beside the old road over the brow of Drung Hill (5½ m. SW.) is Laghtfinnan Penitential Station, a cairn with an ogham stone, said to mark the grave of St Fíonán, patron of the parish.

GLENCOLUMBKILLE village, Co. Donegal (Map 8, A6), takes its name from its valley, set remotely amid splendid mountain and coastal scenery at the SW. corner of Co. Donegal, 7 m. NW. of Carrick and 16 m. WSW. of Ardara. Its inhospitable soil long made the district one of the poorest in Ireland, but a successful cooperative movement organized by the

Glencolumbkille, Co. Donegal.

curate, Fr MacDyer (d. 1987), made life better for everybody. The neighbourhood is rich in antiquarian remains.

The valley is called after the great saint of Derry and Iona. There was an early monastery – seemingly Columban – in the valley; the Mac Niallusaighs (Mac Eneilis) were hereditary coarbs. On Columcille's Day (9 June) a 3 m. *turas* (pilgrimage) brings the devout to 15 'stations' round and about the village. Most of the stations are marked by early cross-slabs and pillars (Nat. Mons.).

The first station is the remnant of a court-tomb (Nat. Mon.) in the W. wall of the ancient churchyard at the Protestant church; nearby is a souterrain. The second station is a very fine cross-pillar W. of the churchyard. The third station is Áit na nGlún ('place of the knees'), a cairn ¾ m. NW. in Garveross. ¼ m. N. of this, in Beefan, is the fourth station: a ring-enclosure with cairn and small cross-slab. NE. is the fifth station: a ring-enclosure (Nat. Mon.) with ruinous dry-masonry Columcille's Chapel and three cairns with cross-slabs; in the NE. corner of the chapel is Columcille's Bed. Outside the enclosure, on the E., is the sixth station: cross-inscribed Leac na mBonn ('stone of the footsoles'). Further N. is the seventh station, Columcille's Well. ¼ m. NW. is rocky Screig na nDeamhan where Columcille overcame the demons according to a local legend. ¼ m. SSE. of Columcille's Well is the eighth station, Garraidhe an Turais ('pilgrimage garden'), having three cairns, each with a cross-slab or fragment. The ninth station – a cairn – is ¾ m. SE., in Farranmacbride. The Farranmacbride cairn has a fine, perforate, cross-pillar called Clo'n Aoineach. ¼ m. NW. of it is Munnernamortee (Nat. Mon.), a large, much-disturbed, central-court-tomb. 400 yds SE. of Clo'n Aoineach, in Faugher, is the tenth station, a roadside cairn with cross-slab. The 11th station (a cairn) is a short distance E. The 12th station is across the road in Drumroe: cairn with very fine cross-pillar. Some 400 yds N. of the 11th station, in the roadway in Drum, is a cross-pillar; further up the slope, in Cloghan, is ruinous Cill an Spáinnigh ('the Spaniard's Church'); also in Cloghan are St Conall's Well and, not far away, a cross-slab; on the hill-top above Cill an Spáinnigh, in Drum, is another cross-slab; these were all stations of Turas Conaill ('St Conall's Pilgrimage'). The 13th station of Columcille's *turas* is in Gannew, near the police station: cairn with cross-pillar. ¼ m. SW. across the Murlin River (pilgrims cross by the stepping stones), in Cashel, is the 14th station: cairn with cross-pillar. The 15th, and last, station is at a broken cross-slab in the churchyard where the *turas* started.

¼ m. SW. of the churchyard, in Kilaned ('Fánad's Church'), are St Fánad's Well, a bullaun, St Fánad's Cell (remnant of a diminutive oratory), and St Conall's Well. Nearby is the Glencolumbkille Folk Village. 1 m. W. of these, near the shore in Doonalt, is a cross-slab with complex design.

3 m. SW. of Glencolumbkille village is Malin More village. ½ m. S. of the crossroads is a portal-tomb complex (Nat. Mon.).–½ m. ENE. of the crossroads is another; ¾ m. ESE. of this is a third. Less than ½ m. SSE. of this is Cloghanmore (Nat. Mon.), a full-court-tomb (largely reconstructed) with lozenge, curvilinear, and other devices on a jamb stone near the entrance. ½ m. further SE. is another court-tomb.

2 m. S. of Malin More village is Malin Beg village. To the SW. are remains of Teampall Caomháin, 'Caomhán's Church' (Nat. Mon.). There is another Teampall Camháin on Rathline O Birne, 2 m. W. of Ougue Port; nearby are penitential stations, crosses and a holy well. The island also has associations with St Áed mac Bric (*see pp. 64, 193 and 297*).

GLENDALOUGH, Co. Wicklow (Map 3, K6), 'Valley of the Two Lakes', famous for its beauty and its remarkable early monastic remains (Nat. Mons.), is a short, deeply incised valley 1 m. W. of Laragh. The visitor should call first at the Interpretative Centre (1987), with audio-visual presentation, model of the valley and a display of antiquities from the valley. These include some cross-inscribed stones, and the 12th c. Market Cross, with *Crucifixion* on one side of the head.

St Cóemgen (Kevin, d. 619?) established a hermitage after the completion of his monastic training at Kilnamanagh near Tallaght (*see also p. 203*).

Kevin's reputation for sanctity made the monastery a notable place of pilgrimage early on, and such it remained until the *pátrún* was suppressed by Cardinal Cullen of Dublin in 1862. It also soon became the burial-place of the local rulers and the most important ecclesiastical centre in the whole of Wicklow. Its early history is much like that of other early monastic centres, having suffered from fire. The greatest name in the history of the place, after St Kevin's, is that of St Lorcán O Toole, who was abbot from 1153 to 1162, when he became Archbishop of Dublin. In 1214 King John united the diocese to that of Dublin. In 1398 the monastic settlement was destroyed by the English of Dublin. It recovered, however, though with diminished resources. In 1450 the diocese was reconstituted, but it survived only until 1497. The monastery, on the other hand, endured until the 16th–17th c. English conquest of Wicklow. Thereafter the buildings gradually fell into decay. Their present condition is due to works of conservation and restoration carried out by the Office of Public Works since 1873.

What may be the earliest monastic sites are on the S. side of the Upper Lake, and two of them (Templenaskellig and St Kevin's Bed) can be approached only by boat. Together these may represent the original Dísert Caéimgin (Kevin's Hermitage).

Templenaskellig stands on a shelf above the lake. The remains of the church – a small, rectangular structure with round-headed, two-light E. window – are largely a Board of Works reconstruction. In the church are some early gravestones. To the E. is St Kevin's Bed, a small cave in the sheer rock 30 ft above the water. (The ascent calls for caution.) It seems to be artificial, at least in part. According to tradition St Kevin lived in it.

Near the SE. corner of the Upper Lake, and on the S. bank of the Poulanass River, is tiny Reefert Church. There, says tradition, was the burial-place of the local rulers. Church and cemetery were formerly enclosed by a dry-built cashel. (The existing enclosing walls and terraces are modern.) The church is a small, nave-and-chancel structure with trabeate W. doorway (re-assembled) and plain, Romanesque windows and chancel arch, the latter a reconstruction of the original stones. At the external angles of the nave are gable-brackets, or corbels, which took the verges of the roof. In the cemetery are a number of stone crosses and early gravestones. SW. of Reefert, high up on a cliff above the mouth of the Poulanass River, are remains of St Kevin's Cell, a beehive hut.

To the N. of the Poulanass River are the foundations of a small, rectangular structure (a church?). The two rude crosses in the W. wall may be post-monastic grave marks.

Further N. are the dilapidated remains of a small, stone circular enclosure. Nearby (to the SE., E., and NE.) are three stone crosses. Still further N., near the roadside and to the E. of the bridge over the Glenealo River, is a broken stone cross. Further E., at the car park, is a stone cross.

Immediately SW. of the Royal Hotel, on the S. side of the Glendasan River, is the old Gatehouse of the later monastic 'city'. (This is the only surviving example of an early Irish monastery gatehouse.) The passage from the gatehouse is flanked by ancient masonry, and its causeway paved with ancient paving. In the W. wall is set an early cross-slab.

SW. of the gatehouse is a fine Round Tower (103 ft). The roof has been reconstructed with the original stones.

In a square, raised enclosure 150 yds SW. of the tower is St Mary's Church, alias Our Lady's Church. It may have belonged to a convent of nuns situated outside the monastery. The Romanesque chancel and N. door are 12th c. additions. On the soffit of the fine, trabeate W. doorway is incised a saltire cross. The masonry suggests a rebuilding.

SE. of the Round Tower is SS Peter's and Paul's Cathedral, consisting of 10th c. (?) pre-Romanesque nave (48 × 30 ft) and 12th c. chancel and sacristy. The nave masonry indicates three phases of building and rebuilding. At the external angles of the nave are *antae*, or projections of the side walls, which carried the roof verges. The W. doorway is trabeate. In the N. wall are remains of an inserted, Late Romanesque doorway contemporary with the chancel arch. The latter is an 1875–9 reconstruction, largely with the original stones. Fixed to the inner face of the N. wall are early gravestones.

SW. of the cathedral is the monastic cemetery, at the centre of which stands the Priest's House, a curious, small, Late Romanesque building of *c.* 1170. The name is modern, and refers to its use as a burial-place for some of the local clergy. Originally it may have been a mortuary chapel, or have housed the shrine of St Kevin. The remains are largely a Board of Works reconstruction. The sculptured tympanum over the S. doorway was perfect in 1845. Petrie's drawing of that year shows a seated king or bishop flanked by two kneeling figures, that on the left bearing a crozier or a bachall, that on the right carrying a bell. In the external face of the E. wall is an unusual arched recess with fine Romanesque details.

St Kevin's Cross, to the E. of the cemetery, is a plain, granite monolith, 11 ft high.

SE. of the cemetery is the remarkable little St Kevin's Church. This is a steep-pitched, stone-roofed structure (22 ft

8 ins × 14 ft 7 ins) to which a stone-roofed chancel (disappeared) and sacristy were added. From the W. gable rises a small belfry of the standard, early Irish (Round Tower) kind. The W. doorway is trabeate, but there is a relieving arch above it. The door itself was hung on the outside. The nave was originally lit by only two tiny windows, one in the S., the other in the E., wall. Subsequently the latter was blocked up, the chancel arch opened in the E. wall, and the chancel (still standing in 1772) and sacristy added. The ruin served as the local Catholic church from 1810 to 1850.

St Kieran's Church, to the E. of St Kevin's Church, survives in fragmentary form. It is the smallest known nave-and-chancel church (nave 19 × 14½ ft, chancel 9 × 9 ft) in the country.

A path leading S. from the cemetery crosses the Glenealo River to the Deer Stone, a bullaun into which, says legend, a doe permitted herself to be milked when St Kevin had no cow. Less than 400 yds E. is St Kevin's Well. Less than 780 yds E. of the well, on the S. bank of the Glendasan River, is St Saviour's Priory. It is said to have been founded by St Lorcán O Toole in 1162 for Canons Regular of St Augustine. The remains are those of a small, Romanesque, nave-and-chancel church with a plain rectangular structure (the conventual building ?) on the N. side. The walls of the latter, the N. and S. walls of the nave, the chancel arch, and the E. window (not always correctly reassembled) have all been re-erected by the Board of Works.

At the road junction to the E. of the Royal Hotel is a slab with two crosses on the S. side. 180 yds further E. are the ruins of Trinity Church, a small, nave-and-chancel structure with a square annexe at the W. end. The latter was corbel-roofed in stone, and supported a 60 ft belfry of Round Tower type (*see* St Kevin's Church, *above*) which collapsed in a storm in 1818. The pre-belfry church was entered by the trabeate W. doorway, which is contemporary with the plain Romanesque chancel-arch and windows. The round-headed S. door is an insertion necessitated by the addition of the belfry.

GLENGARRIFF, Co. Cork (Map 5, F6), a craggy wooded glen of the Caha Mts, opening on to a delightful inlet of Bantry Bay, is one of the loveliest of the many lovely places in SW. Ireland. The village to which it gives its name is 17 m. S. of Kenmare, 10 m. NW. of Bantry, 20 m. ENE. of Castletown Bearhaven, and 35 m. WSW. of Macroom. The mild climate and sheltered location of the glen favour a luxuriant, Mediterranean flora (arbutus, fuchsia, etc.).

Offshore lies justly celebrated Garnish, alias Ilnacullin, with exquisite gardens (noted particularly for magnolias, camellias, rhododendrons, and rare conifers) laid out and planted (1910–13) by Harold Peto for John Allan Bryce, whose son, Rowland, bequeathed the island to the nation. It was there that George Bernard Shaw wrote *St Joan*.

GLENMALURE, Co. Wicklow (Map 3, J6–K7), is a wild, 8 m. valley 2¾ m. W. of Rathdrum. It may also be entered by the Military Road from LARAGH. From Arklow (via Avoca) and Aughrim the most direct approach is via Ballinaclash. The road up the valley is good as far as Barravore ford. Thereafter a track leads up to the divide (2,283 ft) between Glenmalure and the Glen of Imaal (*see p. 130*).

The remote situation of the valley made it a stronghold of the local resistance to English rule at various periods. In 1580 Fiach O Byrne routed Lord Deputy Grey de Wilton with heavy loss. It was to Fiach's house in Ballinacor – traditionally near Ballinacor House – that Red Hugh O Donnell of Tirconnell fled for shelter when he escaped from Dublin Castle in 1592. Betrayed to the English, Fiach was captured in a cave in the valley, and was beheaded, 8 May 1597. After the 1798 rising the valley was one of the refuges of Michael Dwyer and his followers. It was to suppress such obdurate resistance that the Military Road and its strong posts, including Drumgoff Barracks at the Avonbeg crossing, were constructed. (Dwyer destroyed Drumgoff Barracks, but they were rebuilt.)

GLENTIES, Co. Donegal (Map 8, D5), is a village at the SW. corner of the Donegal Highlands, on the Ardara (14 m.)–Ballybofey (22 m.) road. The striking church of St Conall (1974) by Liam McCormick, with its great sloping roof, blends into the landscape. The furnishings were made by Imogen Stuart (tabernacle, candlesticks and candelabra, handles and gangoyles), Michael Biggs (stone sanctuary furnishings), Ruth Brandt (lettering) and Nell Murphy (*St Patrick*, *St Conal* and *St Columkille*, and Stations). The vestments were designed by Joy McCormick.

5 m. NW., to the NW. of Gweebarra bridge and Lettermacaward, is the 2 m. sandy beach of Dooey. In the dunes is Cloch an Stucáin, a collapsed pillarstone making a settlement and burial place of the early centuries A.D.

GLIN, Co. Limerick (Map 6, E8), is a village on the Foynes (9 m.)–Tarbert (4 m.) road by the S. shore of the Shannon estuary. The glen to the S. (Glencorby), provides the title of the Fitzgeralds, Knights of Glin, whose home is at Glin Castle (about 1770; castellated in 19th c.; noteworthy outer and inner halls) to the W. of the village. The Knights of Glin descend from John, grandson of Thomas of Shanid (*see p. 278*), ancestor of the Geraldines of Munster; they have resided in or near Glin for some 700 years. A fragment of their old castle, destroyed in 1600, may be seen in the village.

GOLDEN, Co. Tipperary (Map 4, D3), is a Suirside village 4 m. WSW. of Cashel and 8 m. ENE. of Tipperary. There are remains of a round castle on a rock in the river.

1¼ m. S., on the W. bank of the Suir in Athassel, are the neglected, 4 acre ruins (Nat. Mon.) of St Edmund's Priory (Cannons Regular of St Augustine). This magnificent monastery is said to have been founded by William de Burgh (d. 1205) at the Norman invasion of the Kingdom of Limerick. Its wealth made it one of the most important Norman monasteries in Ireland, and the prior was a lord of parliament. A town which grew up about the priory was burned by adherents of the Earl of Desmond in 1319 and by Brian O Brien in 1330; no remains are visible. Much of the priory itself was destroyed in 1447. The entrance to the precincts is by a portcullis gateway and a gatehouse with porter's lodge. Long reaches of the enclosing wall survive on W., S., and E. The fine, four- or five-period church, on the N. side of the cloister garth, is basically Cistercian in

Athassel priory, Co. Tipperary.

plan: cruciform with aisled nave (six bays, arcades gone) and with chapels (two) in each transept; but the great NW. tower (foundations only) is an Augustinian feature. Choir, crossing, and transepts are early-13th c., the nave late-13th c. the nave late-13th c. Noteworthy details include: the arch or doorway (*c.* 1260) in the rood (?) screen ('rood-loft' blocked up) between nave and choir; the tomb effigy, of *c.* 1300, placed upright against the church wall; an early-14th c. incised slab with a man and a woman. A 13th c. tomb-front with five miniature figures of knights has been removed to the Hall of the Vicars Choral in CASHEL. After the 1447 disaster the nave was left roofless, and the central tower was replaced by a loftier one with living quarters. The cloister ambulatories are 14th/15th c. (post 1447?) work, but they include a fine refectory doorway of *c.* 1260 in the S. range.

2 m. W. are the ruins of Thomastown Castle, sometime seat of the Mathews, Earls of Llandaff. Fr Theobald Mathew (1790–1861), Capuchin apostle of Temperance, was born there; the memorial statue (1939) was unveiled by his great-nephew, Archbishop David Mathew, historian.

GOLDEN BALL, Co. Dublin (Map 3, K4), is a hamlet on the Dublin (8 m.)–Enniskerry (4 m.) road, 1¼ m. SW. of Carrickmines.

1½ m. SE. the Enniskerry road crosses The Scalp, a picturesque, boulder-strewn gorge carved by Ice Age meltwaters.

¾ m. SW., beyond Kiltiernan Lodge, are the remains (Nat. Mon.) of Cill Tighearnáin, an early monastery.

½ m. W., in Kiltiernan Demesne, is Giants Grave (Nat. Mon.), a magnificent portal dolmen with enormous, granite capstone (access over private ground not permitted). Finds there include neolithic sherds and flints.

½ m. N., in the grounds of Stepaside public golf course in Jamestown, is a curious medieval (?) cross which has a rude figure on one face.

GORESBRIDGE, Co. Kilkenny (Map 4, I2), a village on the Gowran (4 m.)–Borris (5 m.) road, is pleasantly situated beside the River Barrow.

2 m. S. are the ruins of Ballyellin (Co. Carlow) Castle.

1 m. W. are remains of Lord Galmoy's Castle.

GOREY, Co. Wexford (Map 4, M1), is a market town on the Arklow (12 m.)–Enniscorthy (19 m.) road, below the SE. slopes of the Wicklow Mts.

Like Enniscorthy, Wexford, and New Ross, Gorey figured prominently in the 1798 insurrection. To maintain their cause the insurgents had to break out into the surrounding counties. On 3 June, therefore, they stormed Gorey in an effort to reach the coast road to Dublin via Arklow, but did not know how to exploit their victory. Their camp was on Gorey Hill (418 ft), just SW. of the town.

The Loreto convent is by Augustus Welby Pugin, who may also have been architect of the adjacent church. The Protestant parish church has windows by Harry Clarke (*St Stephen*, 1922; *SS Luke and Martin of Tours*, 1923), and Catherine O Brien (*Angel*, 1910; *Christ and Peter on the Water*, 1957).

2¼ m. NE. is cairn-crowned Tara Hill (833 ft); nearby to the SE. is Ballymoney strand.

4 m. SE. is Courtown Harbour, a small seaside resort with a good 2 m. beach.

8 m. NNW., in Pallis, is a motte. A branch of the O Dalys, most celebrated of Irish bardic families, settled in Pallis. About

Thoor Ballylee, Co. Galway.

1600 Cearbhall O Daly persuaded Eleanor Kavanagh to elope with him by singing for her the lovely song she had inspired, 'Eibhlín' (Eileen Aroon), the oldest Irish harp tune whose original words survive.

GORT, Co. Galway (Map 6, H4), is a small, well-laid-out, market town on the Galway (23 m.)–Ennis (19 m.) road. The pleasant countryside is rich in prehistoric and historic remains and in literary associations. The town takes its names, Gort Inse Guaire, from Guaire Aidhne, celebrated 6th c. King of Connacht and patron of St Colman mac Duach. In the Middle Ages the O Shaughnessys had their principal stronghold there. In the 17th c. the confiscated O Shaughnessy lands were granted to the Verekers (later Viscounts Gort; *see* Louth Cutra Castle, *below*).

2 m. N. is the entrance to Coole Park (demolished), home of Augusta, Lady Gregory (1852–1932), who took an eminent part in the 19th–20th c. literary and dramatic revival. Coole Park was the resort of most of the leading writers of the revival; its woods and lake were sung by Yeats. The callous demolition of the house in 1941 came more swiftly than even Yeats's melancholy prophecy of 1927 can have envisaged:

Here, traveller, scholar, poet, take your stand
When all these rooms and passages are gone,
When nettles wave upon a shapeless mound
And saplings root among the broken stone.
And dedicate – eyes bent upon the ground,
Back turned upon the brightness of the sun
And all the sensuality of the shade –
A moment's memory to that laurelled head.

The sole relics of the great days are a lovely avenue of cedars and an immense copper beech tree, on which Lady Gregory's guests carved their initials. Many of these are now illegible, but *G*(eorge) *B*(ernard) *S*(haw), *S*(eán) *O C*(asey), *W*(illiam) *B*(utler) *Y*(eats), *J*(ack) *B*(utler) *Y*(eats), *V*(iolet) *M*(artin) – the 'Martin Ross' of 'Somerville and Ross' fame – *A.E.* (George Russell), and *K*(atherine) *T*(ynan) *H*(inkson) can still be read. Opposite the N. gate of Coole Park a side road to the SW. passes the shattered, but imposing, remains of Ballinamantain (alias Kiltartan) Castle, a 13th c. de Burgh castle with strong, towered bawn (Nat. Mon.).

5 m. NE. is the 16th c. tower of Ballylee Castle, the 'Thoor Ballylee' of Yeats's poems. The poet had it, and the adjoining cottages, repaired and made his home in them in the 1920s, and it was there that his volume of poems, *The Tower*, was written. His 'Meditations in Time of Civil War' (1923) describe the tower and the life about it. A tablet commemorates his sojourn:

I, the poet William Yeats,
With old mill boards and sea-green slates
And smithy work from the Gort forge,
Restored this tower for my wife George;
And may these characters remain
When all is ruin once again.

Yeats abandoned Ballylee in 1929, and all too soon everything was 'ruin once again'. The place was restored as a Yeats Museum for the centenary (1965) of the poet's birth. Ballylee was also the home of sweet Mary Hynes, the miller's daughter loved and sung by Blind Raftery (*see p. 122*).

6 m. NE. is Peterwell. In the church is a single-light window, *Our Lady of the Rosary*, by Evie Hone (1950).

3 m. SSE., on the W. side of the small, pretty lake after which it is called, is Lough Cutra Castle, built (1810) for the 1st Viscount Gort, by the brothers Pain of Cork to the design of John Nash. It bears a strong likeness to East Cowes Castle, Isle of Wight.

5 m. S. are the ruins of Ardamullivan Castle (Nat. Mon.), a 16th c. O Shaughnessy stronghold with interesting windows.

5 m. SSW., between Lough Aslaun and Lough Do, is the well-preserved 16th c. O Shaughnessy castle of Fiddaun (Nat. Mon.); the fine bawn is of unusual plan.

2 m. W. is St Colman's Church, Tirneevin; the single-light *The Sower Sowing His Seed* (1963) was designed by George Campbell, R.H.A., the painter.

3 m. NNW. is the 15th/16th c. tower of the O Hynes castle of Lydacan (Nat. Mon.).

GORTAHORK, Co. Donegal (Map 8, D3), is a village and resort at the head of Ballyness Bay, on the Dunfanaghy (10 m.)–Gweedore (9 m.) road, to the N. of the Errigal–Muckish range of mountains which provide some of Ireland's most magnificent panoramas. It is in the heart of the Donegal Gaeltacht.

1½ m. NE. is Falcarragh. The Catholic church of St Fionan was re-furbished (1981) by Wilfrid Cantwell, with metalwork and enamel furnishings by Patrick McElroy, and alter and ambo hangings by Helen Moloney (worked by Jane Almqvist). The slate Stations were designed by Michael Biggs, and cut by Tom Little. 1 m. NE., in the grounds of Ballyconnell House, is Cloch Cheannfaoladh (Ceannfaoladh's Stone), which gives its name to the village and parish of Cloghaneely. This is a large boulder with a red crystalline vein. The latter is explained as the petrified blood of Faoladh, whose head (*ceann*) was cut off there by Balor of the Baleful Eye, legendary giant of Tory Island. 2 m. NE., in Ray, the ruins of a medieval church and a great monolithic cross (Nat. Mons.) mark the early monastic site of Moyra. Legend asserts that the cross was hewn on Muckish by St Columcille himself. 1½ m. S. of Cloghaneely, in Ballintemple, is the ruined church of Tullaghobegly.

GORTIN, Co. Tyrone (Map 1, D7), is a village to 10 m. W. of Omagh on the road to Plum Bridge, where the Newtownstewart–Cookstown road forms a cross. Close to the village stand the ruins of Beltrim Castle, where a fine Georgian house dating from 1820 now exists.

2½ m. N., in Culvahullion the SE. slope of Slievebeg, are six stone circles and the remains of a chambered tomb.

2 m. S. is Gortin Glen Forest Park, which was opened in 1967. It has a pleasant 5 m. scenic drive (for cars) and walks and trails of various lengths, as well as a deer enclosure and a nature reserve at Boorin Wood (the remnants of an oak forest). Close to this site is a new History Park, at present under construction. The 35 acre site will feature full-size replicas of a whole range of prehistoric monuments, as well as an early Christian settlement and a 17th c. fortified house.

GORUMNA ISLAND, Co. Galway (Map 6, C–D2), lies to the S. of Lettermore Island (with which it is linked by a road bridge) on the E. side of Kilkieran Bay, some 30 m. W. of Galway. To the SW. lies Lettermullen Island, with which it is also linked by a road bridge.

5 m. SSW. of Lettermore bridge (1 m. SE. of Lettermullen bridge), in Maumeen, are the remains of a small, simple church with trabeate W. door.

GOWRAN, Co. Kilkenny (Map 4, I2), is a village at the intersection of the Kilkenny (9 m.)–Goresbridge (4 m.) and Leighlinbridge (9 m.)–Thomastown (8 m.) roads. In early and

The medieval church at Gowran, Co. Kilkenny.

medieval times the place was of strategic importance, as it commanded Bealach Gabhráin, ancient route through the bogs and forests of the Leinster–Ossory marches. At the Anglo-Norman invasion it fell to Strongbow, whose heir, William the Marshal, granted the manor to Theobald fitz Walter, ancestor of the Butlers. The manor remained Butler property until the 17th c., and the castle was the principal seat of the Butlers between the loss of NENAGH and the acquisition of Kilkenny (1391). The town was founded by Theobald fitz Walter.

The principal feature of the village is the medieval parish (collegiate) church of the Assumption of the Blessed Virgin Mary, burial place of the 1st and 3rd Earls of Ormond as well as of branches of the Butler family. In its original, late-13th c. form, the church consisted of an aisled nave and a long chancel. In the 14th c. a massive, square tower was inserted between nave and chancel; in the 17th, a Keally mortuary chapel was erected adjoining the W. end of the S. nave aisle. The site of the chancel is now occupied by a deconsecrated 19th c. Protestant church which incorporates the medieval tower. The nave and aisles (Nat. Mon.) are roofless and the S. arcade has gone, but many of the details are beautiful or otherwise interesting: foliage carving of Somersetshire type, early plate tracery, etc. The quatrefoil columns of the N. arcade recall St Canice's Cathedral, Kilkenny, as do windows in the aisles. The monuments include:

N. aisle: 14th c. effigy of a knight believed to be the 1st Earl of Ormond; 14th c. effigy of a lady believed to be the 1st Countess of Ormond; Renaissance cadaver monument (1646) of James Keally and his two wives, Ellen Nashe and Mary White.

Both wifves at once alive he could not have,
Both to inioy at once he made this grave.

Keally Chapel: Renaissance monument of Piers Keally and his wife, Alison Hackett.

Protestant church: a cross-inscribed ogham stone discovered in the foundations of the medieval chancel; a tombstone with effigy of Ralph 'Julianus' (d. 1252/3), parish priest: a tombstone with effigy of a lady (*c.* 1500); two 16th c. Butler tombs, one with effigies of two armoured knights, one with effigy of an armoured knight, both carved by the Ormond School.

Beside the town is the demesne of Gowran Castle, formerly seat of Lord Clifden. In the Pigeon Park is the tower of the Butler castle of Ballyshawnmore.

3 m. NE. is Paulstown, alias Polestown. There are remains of a castle belonging to a branch of the Butlers descended from Richard, a younger son of James, 3rd Earl of Ormond.

3 m. SW., in the old churchyard at Dungarvan, is a fragment from the 1581 tomb of Donal fitz Piers Archdekin, of Cloghala, and his wife, Catherine Blancheuld. It is signed by the maker, Walter Kerin. The carvings include miniature effigies of an armoured knight and his lady.

5 m. SW., at Tullaherin, is an early monastic site marked by a 73 ft, imperfect, Round Tower (Nat. Mon.) and the ruins of a nave-and-chancel church of various dates. Near the base of the tower is a fragment of an ogham stone.

GRAIGUENAMANAGH, Co. Kilkenny (Map 4, J3), a small market town on a beautiful reach of the Barrow, is at the junction of roads from Goresbridge (7 m.), Borris (8 m.), New Ross (11 m.), Insistioge (6 m.), and Thomastown (9 m.).

The town takes its name from the monks of the Cistercian abbey of Vallis Sancti Salvatoris, otherwise known as Duiske, founded about 1207 by William the Marshal (*see p. 258*), and colonized from Stanley in Wiltshire. Various parts of the church were re-roofed or restored in 1813 and again in 1886. The beautiful modern restoration of the church, under the supervision of Percy Le Clere, was completed in 1980, with a rose window and four others (*St Fiacre* and *St Moling*) by Patrick Pye. The plan of the abbey church (largest of Irish Cistercian churches), which was built about 1212–40, is identical with that of Strata Florida, Cardiganshire. It had an aisled nave of seven bays, three E. chapels in each transept, and a tower (square below, octagonal above) over the crossing. The chancel had a ribbed vault of three bays, and the chapels had barrel vaults. The transepts had an unusual clerestory of round, multi-cusped windows. A beautiful processional doorway opened from the S. aisle on to the cloister; it is now the entrance to the 1916 baptistery (access from S. transept). The Transitional features are strongly reminiscent of those at Kilkenny Cathedral, and may be the work of the same masons. Many of the carvings have been 'restored' by a modern hand (John O Leary). Some covered shafts in the floor allow inspection of the original medieval paving tiles, a few feet below the modern floor-level. The monumental remains include the effigy of a knight (*c.* 1310) armed in transverse banded mail. The fragmentary remains of the claustral buildings have to be sought out in backyards and gardens S. of the church. In the modern graveyard are two granite High Crosses. The North Cross is from an early monastic site in Ballyogan, 2 m. SSE. The figure subjects include: E. face: *Crucifixion*, *Fall*, *Sacrifice of Isaac*, *King David*; W. face: *Annunciation* and *Visitation*. The S. Cross is from the early monastic site, Aghailten near Ullard (*below*). It has a rude *Crucifixion* on each face and panels of interlacings.

3 m. NE. is Ullard, site of a monastery founded by St Fiachra, who died, A.D. 670, near Meaux, where his hermit's cell became the nucleus of the great abbey of Breuil. (As St Fiacre, he enjoyed high repute in medieval France.) The remains (Nat. Mons.) at Ullard include a 9th/10th c. High Cross (middle part modern) and a ruined church with altered Romanesque chancel arch and doorway. The figure subjects on the cross include: E. face: *Crucifixion*, King David with Harp, *Sacrifice of Isaac*.

2¼ m. SSE., in Ballyogan, are the remains of Galmoy Castle, called after the Butler Viscounts Galmoy.

GRANARD, Co. Longford (Map 2, C8), is a small market town on the Cavan (20 m.)–Athlone (30 m.) road, from which the Earl of Granard (*see p. 260*) takes his title. In 1798 a party of insurgents retreating from BALLINAMUCK was routed there, and most of those taken prisoner were slain.

There is a good motte-and-bailey (Nat. Mon.) there, constructed in 1199 by Richard de Tuit, who was enfeoffed in Granard by Hugh de Lacy. Close by is St Mary's Catholic church refurbished (1972) by Hogan, Tyndall and Hurley, which has furnishings by Benedict Tutty O.S.B., Ray Carroll and Yvonne Bergin.

1½ m. NE. the road to Bellanagh passes across a 3 m. sector of the Dúnchaladh, or the Black Pig's Dyke (*see also pp. 133, 190 and 269*), which blocked the gap between Loughs Kinale and Gowna.

Glendalough, Co. Wicklow: general view (top), and St Kevin's Church (see pages 193–4).

Kilkenny Castle: exterior (top) and interior (see page 215).

$2\frac{1}{2}$ m. SE., near Abbeylara, are remains of Laragh Cistercian Abbey, founded by Richard de Tuit (killed 1211) and colonized from St Mary's Abbey, Dublin, in 1214.

6 m. NW., in Aughnacliffe, is a tall portal-tomb.

GRANGE, Co. Sligo (Map 8, B9), is a village on the Sligo (9 m.)–Bundoran (14 m.) road, between the foot of Ben Bulben and Streedagh strand.

$2\frac{1}{4}$ m. W., by the seashore in Agharrow, the ruins of Staad 'Abbey' mark the site of a monastery founded by St Mo-Laisse (*see p. 206*).

The coast thereabouts saw the wreck of several ships of the Spanish Armada, whose fate is recalled by Carricknaspania (Carraig na Spáinneach, 'Rock of the Spaniards'). It was of this district that Sir Geoffrey Fenton reported to Lord Burleigh: 'I numbered in one strand less than five miles in length eleven hundred dead corpses'. Two of the wrecks have recently been located.

GREY ABBEY, Co. Down (Map 1, M8), a village of the Ards Peninsula to the E. of Strangford Lough, on the Newtownards (7 m.)–Portaferry (10 m.) road, takes its name from the small Cistercian abbey founded there in 1193, for monks from Holm Cultram in Cumberland, by Affrica, wife of John de Courcy and daughter (by his Irish wife) of Godred, King of Man. The abbey was dissolved *c.* 1541–3.

The beautifully conserved ruins (Nat. Mon.) are typically Cistercian in plan, and the earlier work typically Cistercian in the restrained use of ornament. The remains comprise those of an aisleless, cruciform church with two chapels in each transept, tower over the crossing, night stairs to church from dormitory, and fragments of the chapter-house, day-room, refectory (on S. side of cloister garth), etc. Most of the surviving work can be assigned to the end of the 12th c., but the rather elaborate W. doorway of the church is *c.* 1220, while the N. and S. windows of the chancel have Perpendicular tracery of the late 15th c. A recumbent tomb-effigy in the N. wall of the choir is thought to represent the foundress, while the mutilated figure of an armoured knight in a chapel of the N. transept is said to be the effigy of her husband. The church was re-roofed to serve as the local Protestant parish church in the 17th c. To this period of the church's re-use the bell-cote and small window of the W. gable can be assigned.

2 m. NW. is Mount Stewart House (Nat. Trust), an 18th c. Classical building which was formerly the seat of the Marquess of Londonderry, and childhood home of Lord Castlereagh, the

Mount Stewart House and Garden, Co. Down.

British Prime Minister who presided at the Congress of Vienna in 1815. The splendid 80 acre gardens are noted for their rare plans, shrubs and trees. ½ m. SW. is the 'Temple of the Winds', James Athenian Stuart's small but splendid banqueting hall of 1785.

GREYSTONES, Co. Wicklow (Map 3, L5), is a seaside resort on the Bray (5 m)–Wicklow (10 m.) road. The Catholic parish church has two single-light windows (*The Good Shepherd, Our Lady of the Rosary–Battle of Lepanto*) by Evie Hone (1948).

GURTEEN, Co. Sligo (Map 7, K4), is a village where the Boyle (9 m.)–Tobercurry (10 m.) road crosses that from Ballymote (8 m.) to Ballaghaderren (8 m.).

4 m. SW. is Carrowntemple, an early monastic enclosure. Six early slabs from here are in the National Museum in Dublin, and a further eight are in the custody of Sligo Country Council.

2 m. NW., in Knockmore, alias Mt Irvine, are the ruins of the Carmelite cell founded by the O Garas in 1320. Only one of the four early Christian slabs from there remain on the site.

2½ m. NW., in Knockgráinne, is a simple mounument to master-of-the-fiddle Michael Coleman (1892–1945), who was born near there. 2 m. further NW., in Kilturra, are Toberaraght (St Áthracht's Well), and a small cross-inscribed pillarstone.

GWEEDORE, Co. Donegal (Map 8, D3), is a hamlet on the Gortahork (8½ m.)–Dungloe (10¼ m.) road. The Catholic church (Teach Phobaill an Maighdeanna Muire) is by Carr, Sweeney and O Farrell (1973).

From Gweedore a fair road leads E. and SE. past Lough Nacung and Dunlewy Lough to the Dunlewy Gap (6 m.) between the Derryveagh Mts and the heights of Errigal (2,466 ft), Aghla More (1,916 ft), and Muckish (2,197 ft). Errigal is the highest mountain in Donegal. A beautiful cone with white quartzite facings, it rewards the climber (much loose scree) with one of the finest panoramas in Ireland.

¼ m. S. of Dunlewy is the ancient church site of Trian na Cille, where there is an early cross-slab.

H

HACKETSTOWN, Co. Carlow (Map 3, I8), is a village on the Baltinglass (9 m.)–Tinahely (7 m.) road, in the foothills of the Wicklow Mts. It was the scene of two battles in 1798.

3 m. S. is Clonmore, the ancient Cluain Mór M'Áedóc, where, in the 6th c., St M'Áedóc founded a monastery. The site of the monastery is divided by the roadway. In the graveyard S. of the road are the head and shaft of an unfigured High Cross; also early gravestones, etc. W. of the churchyard is St Mogue's Cross, another granite High Cross. 300 yds. WNW. are remains of a large, 13th c., English royal castle (keepless type).

HEADFORD, Co. Galway (Map 7, H8), is a market village and angling resort on the Galway (17 m.)–Ballinrobe (15 m.) road 4 m. E. of Lough Corrib. The country round about – which was the O Flaherty homeland prior to the Anglo-Norman invasion – is very rich in ancient remains, most notably ringforts of varying kinds.

2½ m. N., in Moyne, Co. Mayo, is an ancient oval church-site enclosed by a cashel; near the W. end of the church are two pillarstones between which coffins are carried. Not far away the ruins of Moyne Castle.

6½ m. ENE. are Castle Hacket demesne and Knockmaa. In the demesne are the bawn and tower of a Hacket – later Burke – castle. Knockmaa (552 ft), which dominates the countryside, is called after Meadhbh (Maeve), mythological 'Queen of Connacht', and is celebrated in oral tradition as the Otherworld seat of Finnbhearra, 'King of the Connacht Fairies'. Nearby is Finnbhearra's Castle, an 18th/19th c. folly.

4½ m. SE., at the ancient church-site of Kilcoona, is the stump of a Round Tower.

4 m. SW., on the lake shore, are remains of the late-13th c. Gaynard – later Burke – hall-type Castle of Cargin.

2 m. W., by the Annaghkeen road, are the ruins of Killursa, 'Church of Fursa' (Nat. Mon.), an ancient structure (trabeate W. doorway) enlarged in medieval times. The dedication implies that a monastery was founded there by St Fursa ('Fursey', 584–652), a disciple of St Brendan of CLONFERT (*see also pp. 39 and 129*), who himself founded a monastery at Rathmath, 4 m. to the W., near where St Fursa is said to have been born. Fursa afterwards settled for a time at Burgh Castle in Suffolk, and ultimately at Péronne in France, where his enshrined remains became the object of pilgrimage and whence his cult spread to the Low Countries and to Germany. The story of his visions of Hell and Heaven was celebrated in medieval Europe. (He has been called the 'precursor of Dante'.)

1½ m. NW. (½ m. N. of the Annaghkeen road) are the exceptionally well-preserved remains (Nat. Mon.) of Ross 'Abbey', a Franciscan Observantine friary founded by a Gaynard in 1498. The remains comprise church and conventual buildings. The church consists of chancel, central tower with rood-loft, nave with S. aisle and S. transept (double); the transept has three E. chapels; opening off the W. end of the aisle is a 17th c. Jennings chantry-chapel. The tiny cloister is exceptionally well preserved; there is a second court N. of the cloister garth. The conventual buildings give an excellent idea of the character and arrangements of a medieval Franciscan house. On the E. side of the N. court is the refectory, with reader's desk at the NE. window; overhead was the principal dormitory. At the NW. angle of the N. court is the kitchen with interesting fish-tank and fireplace; adjoining it on the N. is the mill, on the E. the bakery (with a second dormitory above).

HILLSBOROUGH, Co. Down (Map 2, J2), is a small linen town on the Dromore (4¾ m.)–Lisburn (4 m.) road. Like Hilltown, it takes its name from the descendants of Sir Moyses Hill, an English army officer who, at the Plantation, obtained confiscated Magennis lands, and who had married a sister of the redoubtable Somhairle Buidhe Mac Donnell, cousin and son-in-law of Great Hugh O Neill. About 1630 Peter Hill (son of Moyses) began the erection of a village and of a fort, and in the

1650s Peter's uncle and heir, Col. Arthur Hill, built an artillery fort in the pass 'for the incouragement of an English Plantation'. In 1660 the fort was made a royal garrison, with Hill and his heirs hereditary Constables. Two years later Hill obtained a charter for his new town (to be called Hillsborough), for which he built a Protestant church the same year. William of Orange stayed at the fort, 19–23 June 1690, en route to the Boyne, and there he granted the famous *Regium Donum*, or state stipend, to the clergy of the Presbyterian Church.

The most famous of the Hills was Wills Hill (1718–93), 1st Marquess of Downshire (*see p. 79*), sponsor of Goldsmith's *Deserted Village*, and George III's Secretary of State for the American Colonies. ('His character is conceit, wrongheadedness, obstinacy, and passion' – Benjamin Franklin.) The 2nd Marquess (1753–1801) was an advocate of religious toleration. His strenuous opposition to the Union cost him dear.

At the centre of the Market Sq. is the attractive Court and Market House (Nat. Mon.) commenced for Wills Hill, and completed for his son in 1797, by Robert Furze Brettingham (1750?–1806).

On the SW. side of the square is Hillsborough Castle, formerly Government House and seat of the erstwhile Governors of Northern Ireland. The splendid wrought-iron gates came (1936) from Richhill Castle, Co. Armagh; they may be the work of the Thornberry brothers from Falmouth, who had settled in Co. Armagh. The house was commenced for Wills Hill *c.* 1760, was enlarged for the 2nd Marquess of Downshire *c.* 1797 by Brettingham (who added most of the S. wing, portico excluded), and was further enlarged and modified at various subsequent dates. Here was signed the historic Anglo-Irish agreement of 1985, which provided for the voluntary consultation of the Irish Government by the British, and vice versa, in matters concerning Northern Ireland.

At the N. end of Main St, facing the gate of St Malachi's Church, is a statue (by W.H. Lynn) of the 4th Marquess of Downshire (1812–68).

St Malachi's Church (completed 1772) is an interesting, Gothick period piece with most of its original furnishings intact. Thought to incorporate much of the fabric of its 1662 predecessor, its interior furnishings were re-arranged by Sir Thomas Drew in 1898, and by Denis O'D. Hanna in 1951–65. Noteworthy features are: the 18th c. prayer desk, pulpit, and box pews; the E. window, by Francis Elgington of Bermingham to the design of Sir Joshua Reynolds (1723–92); the State Chair from the Chapel Royal, Dublin Castle (lent by the Dean and Chapter of Christ Church Dublin); the S. transept organ (from Hillsborough Castle) of 1795, by G.P. England; the nave monument (1774), by Nollekens, to Henry and Peter Leslie; and the W. gallery organ (1772), by John Snetzler (several times rebuilt). William Harty, father of Sir Hamilton Harty (1879–1941), composer and conductor, was organist to the church 1878–1918. Near the W. door is a birdbath memorial to Sir Hamilton.

The nearby Fort (Nat. Mon.) is Col. Arthur Hill's 17th c., star-shaped, artillery fort. A 1758 Gothick tower house occupies the site of the original gate-tower. A contemporary, Strawberry-Hill gazebo crowns the 1758 cart entrance. The lawn gates in front of the tower house are late 18th c., as are those at the Hillsborough Sq. entrance.

At the S. end of the town are the 1829 Shambles, now an art centre.

The 1848 hill-top column S. of the town commemorates the 3rd Marquess of Downshire (1788–1845).

HILLTOWN, Co. Down (Map 2, J4), is a village at the N. foot of the Mourne Mts, where the Newry (8 m.)–Newcastle (11 m.) and Rathfryland (3 m.)–Rostrevor (8 m.) roads meet.

2 m. NE., in Goward, is a portal-tomb with granite capstone of 50 tons.

1¾ m. ENE., also in Goward, is a court cairn (Hist. Mon.). There was found (1932) the first Neolithic pottery ever recovered from an Irish chamber-tomb.

1 m. ESE. is Ballymaghery motte-and-bailey (Hist. Mon.) with three concentric ditches.

HOLLYWOOD, Co. Wicklow (Map 3, I6), is a village E. of the Ballymore Eustace (12¾ m.)–Baltinglass (4 m.) road. Its name recalls a holy wood which figures in the *Life* of St Kevin of GLENDALOUGH, whose first hermitage was thereabouts. The hermitage is commemorated by St Kevin's Bed SSW. of the Protestant church, which has a 17th c. vaulted stone roof.

3½ m. SE. is Lockstown Upper road junction. The 'Hollywood Stone', a labyrinth boulder in the National Museum, came from an old roadway a short distance N. 5 m. ESE. of the junction are the remnants of Tampleteenawn, an ancient nave-and-chancel church. 2½ m. WNW. of the church, at Wooden Cross on the top (1,200 ft) of Togher ridge, is a roadside cross-inscribed boulder. 1 m. WSW. of this, beside an old road in Granabeg Upper, is an early cross-pillar. Boulder, cross-pillar, and the 'Hollywood Stone' were probably route markers on an ancient pilgrims' way (St Kevin's Road) from Hollywood to Tampleteenawn and so to Glendalough. 2½ m. SE. of Tampleteenawn is the summit of the Wicklow Gap (1,469 ft). In a corrie beneath Camaderry (2,296 ft), to the SE., is Lough Nahanagan (1,382 ft), the water of which is pumped up at night to an electricity generating station at the top of the hill. Between the lough and the modern road the overgrown course of granite-paved St Kevin's Road is visible (partially excavated in 1972, and now fenced in). In the valley to the E. are remains of abandoned lead workings.

From Hollywood two roads lead S. through Hollywood Glen (1½ m.), an Ice Age 'overflow valley' 3 m. long and 150 ft deep. At the head of the Glen, 1½ m. S. of Hollywood via the E. road (old road) to Donard, are remains of St Kevin's Church, Dunboyke, a primitive nave-and-chancel structure. ½ m. SW. of the church, close the the Baltinglass road in Athgreany, are the Piper's Stones (Nat. Mon.), a circle of 14 granite boulders with an outlier (the Piper). Legend has it that circle and outlier are a piper and dancers petrified for violating the Sabbath.

HOLYWOOD, Co. Down (Map 1, L8), cradle of Irish golf, is a holiday resort and dormitory suburb on the E. shore of Belfast Lough, 5½ m. NE. of Belfast and 6½ m. WSW. of Bangor.

St Laisrén founded a monastery there in the 7th c.

In High St is Ireland's only permanent maypole. In the same street is *Johnny the Jig*, bronze of a small boy playing an accordion; it is by Rosamund Praeger (1867–1954), 'who loved children and delighted in their ways'.

Near the junction of High St and Bangor Rd are the site of a former friary of the Franciscan tertiaries, and a Norman motte.

2 m. NE. is Cultra Manor, where the excellent 200 acre Ulster Folk and Transport Museum was inaugurated in 1964. A monument to the pioneering efforts of E. Estyn Evans, this was the first Folk Museum established in the British Isles. It displays re-erected buildings of various kinds from all over Ulster. A transport section has a variety of vehicles, old aircraft and a merchant schooner.

HORSELEAP, Co. Westmeath (Map 3, D3), is a hamlet on the Kilbeggan (5 m.)–Moate (6 m.) road.

½ m. N. are the remains of the motte-and-bailey castle of Ardnurcher, erected by Hugh de Lacy in 1192. The castle was burned by Felim O Conor of Connacht in 1234. A modern legend derives the name Horseleap from Hugh de Lacy's horse, on which he is said to have jumped across the fosse on to the motte when pursued by the Mageoghegans. The Protestant church at Ardnurcher has an A.E. Child window of 1917.

2 m. E. is the Mageoghegan castle of Donore. The Cromwellians took the castle in 1650 and put James Mageoghegan and 40 or 50 men, women, and children to the sword.

HOSPITAL, Co. Limerick (Map 4, B3), a village on the Limerick (17 m.)–Mitchelstown (16 m.) road, takes its name from the Ainy (*see* Knockainy, *below*) Preceptory of the Knights Hospitaller of St John of Jerusalem, founded before 1215 by the English Justiciar, Geoffrey de Marisco, then lord of the manor of Ainy (Anya). After Kilmainham, this was the most important house of the Hospitallers in Ireland. Remains of the 'Hospital Church' (Nat. Mon.) survive. In it are remnants of three interesting 13th/14th c. effigies, that of a single knight in high relief being particularly fine.

1½ m. NNW., in Ballynamona, is a stone circle.

3 m. NE., commanding a noble view, is Cromwell Hill (586 ft). There are a wedge-tomb, a hill-top tumulus, a stone and an earthen ringfort, and other remains, some of them associated with Finn mac Cumhall and his band of warriors, the Fianna. The S. spur of the hill was called Crom Dubh's Castle (Crom Dubh was an ancient harvest deity).

3 m. S. is Knocklong; S. of the village are remnants of a 16th c. O Hurley castle and a hillside carin. 2 m. SE. is Scarteen, headquarters of the well-known Scarteen Foxhounds, the original 'Black and Tans' whose name suggested the nickname of a notorious British force employed in Ireland 1920–1.

1½ m. W., at the SE. foot of Cnoc Aine, the 537 ft hill from which it takes its name, is Knockainy village. In Irish mythology Cnoc Áine is the Otherworld seat of the sun-goddess, Áine, whose name is associated with a cairn on the summit. Down to 1879 men used to bring flaming *cliara* (bunches of hay and straw on poles) to the summit, there make a *deiseal* circuit of Mullach an Triúir (three small ring-barrows), and then visit village fields, and herds to bring them good luck. Formerly also a great fair (Aonach Áine) was held there at the beginning of harvest.

HOWTH, Co. Dublin (Map 3, L3), is a fishing and yachting port and popular suburban resort on the N. side of Howth Head, 9½ m. NE. of Dublin. The name (Norse *höfuth*, head) is properly that of the great hilly promontory (Irish *Beann Eadair*, 563 ft), well known for its cliff and moorland scenery and walks, as well as for its prospects of the coast from the Mourne Mts in the NE. to the Wicklow Mts in the S.

Howth Harbour was built at the beginning of the 19th c. for the Holyhead–Dublin packet-boat service, but speedily silted up and was replaced by Dun Laoghaire. George IV landed there in 1821. On 26 July 1914, the harbour was the scene of the Howth Gun-running, when the Irish Volunteers, emulating the Ulster opponents of Home Rule (*see p. 230*), landed 900 rifles from Erskine Childers' yacht, *Asgard*.

Overlooking the harbour are the ruins (Nat. Mon.) of the collegiate parish church of the Blessed Virgin Mary ('St Mary's Abbey'). The first church on the site is said to have been erected by Sigtryggr (Sitric), King of Norse Dublin, as early as 1042. A parish church was certainly built there in 1235 (*see* Ireland's Eye, *below*). The twin-aisled remains, however, are for the most part those of a 14th c. building with 15th/16th c. modifications and additions. In the 15th c. the E. part of the S. aisle was remodelled by the St Lawrences (*see* Howth Castle, *below*) to serve as a family chantry. In it stand the tomb and effigies of Sir Christopher St Lawrence, 13th Baron of Howth (d. 1462), and his wife, Anna Plunket of Ratoath. The ends of the tomb are divided into panels with figures of *The Crucifixion*, *Angels with Censers*, *St Peter*, *St Catherine*, an abbess and an archbishop. S. of the church are the ruins of the 15th/16th c. college of the community of priests attached to the church.

A short distance W. of the harbour is the Protestant parish church, which has a two-light window (*St Peter; The Calling of St Andrew*) by Evie Hone (1943) and a three-light *Faith*, *Hope*, *and Charity* by Sarah Purser (1905). Nearby is the gateway to Howth Castle and Demesne. The great castle has been the seat of the St Lawrence family since the 16th c., but the first St Lawrence, Almeric I, had settled at Howth 400 years earlier, when he was granted the manor by Henry II. His motte-castle stood on the site of the martello tower at the head of the E. pier. The present castle dates from 1564. It was rebuilt in 1738, modernized and enlarged in the first half of the 19th c. to the designs of Sir Richard and William Vitruvius Morrison, and again in the 20th c., when the architect was Sir Edwin Lutyens. The 16th c. castle is represented by the keep (at the SW. corner of the existing complex) and by the disused NE. gate-tower. Legend associates the castle and the St Lawrences with the celebrated Gráinne Ni Mháille (*see pp. 104 and 258*). The sea-queen is said to have found the castle gate closed one day at dinner time. In revenge she carried off the young heir to Rockfleet, and released him only on the promise that Howth Castle would never again be closed against the hungry traveller. To this day a place is always set at the St Lawrence table in readiness for the unexpected guest. The demesne and gardens are justly renowned for their beauty, particularly when the rhododendrons and azaleas are in bloom. In the grounds of the Castle are a hotel, a municipal golf course, a Transport Museum and a portal-tomb known as Aedeen's Grave.

2 m. SSE. of the harbour is the Bailey lighthouse (1814), sited within a great (Iron Age?) promontory fort defended by ramparts and ditches.

1½ m. W. is Sutton cross-roads.–¼ m. ESE. is the fine modern Catholic parish church of St Fintan (1973) by A.D. Devane, with furnishings by Christopher Ryan and Enda King, while a further $\frac{1}{4}$ m. ESE. is its small, two-period, medieval predecessor.

$1\frac{1}{4}$ m. N. of Howth Harbour, on the island of Ireland's Eye, is Kilmacnessan (Church of Nessan's Sons), sole remnant of a monastery founded by three brothers in the 6th/7th c. Attacked in turn by Welsh, Viking and Irish, the church subsequently became parochial and was replaced in 1235 by the more convenient one at Howth. The excessively restored remains consist of a small nave-and-chancel structure which had a Round Tower rising from the chancel vault (as at St Kevin's Church and Trinity Church, GLENDALOUGH). The original W. gable and doorway were removed early in the 19th c. by the builders of a Catholic church in Howth. The only other relic of the ancient monastery is the *Garland of Howth*, an 8th–9th c. illuminated gospel-book now in Trinity College, Dublin.

Howth, Co. Dublin.

I

INCHIGEELAGH, Co. Cork (Map 5, I6), is a village, and a favourite resort for painters, on the N. shore of Lough Allua, a beautiful expansion of the Lee, 10 m. SW. of Macroom and 24 m. NE. of Bantry.

$1\frac{1}{2}$ m. E., on the S. side of the Lee, are the ruins of the O Leary castle of Carrignacurra (Castle Masters).

4 m. SSW., to the W. of the road in Lackabaun, is Mearogafin wedge-tomb. 2 m. SE., on the slope of Carrigarierk in Clogher, is another. $1\frac{1}{4}$ m. SE. of the latter, in Farranahineeny, is a five-stone alignment (Nat. Mon.).

$5\frac{1}{2}$ m. W. is Ballingeary, formerly a noted resort of students of Irish. $2\frac{1}{2}$ m. NW., in Bawnatemple, is a 19 ft 9 in. pillarstone, the tallest in Ireland. It fell and broke into two pieces on St Patrick's Day, 1985. $1\frac{1}{2}$ m. NW., to the N. of the Gougane Barra road in Keamcorravooly, is a wedge-tomb.

$2\frac{1}{4}$ m. WSW., to the N. of the Gougane Barra road in Gortafludig, is Tuama an Mhinistre, a wedge-tomb. $1\frac{1}{2}$ m. S., on Kealvaughmore hill, is an ogham stone. $2\frac{1}{2}$ m. S. (1 m. SW. of Kealvaughmore), in Derryvacorneen, is Bórd an Rí, a wedge-tomb. $3\frac{1}{4}$ m. SW. is the precipitous, romantic defile of Keamaneigh, where the Macroom–Bantry road pierces the Shehy Mts between Foilastookeen (1,693 ft) and Doughill Mt (1,553 ft).

$4\frac{1}{2}$ m. WSW. of Ballingeary ($1\frac{1}{4}$ m. NW. of Keamaneigh) is romantic Gougane Barra, where St Finbar of Cork had an island hermitage (pilgrimage, 25 September). Nearby is the source of the River Lee. The memorial church is by Samuel F. Hynes. The beautiful forest park was opened in 1966.

INISHCRONE, Co. Sligo (Map 7, H2), is a seaside resort with a good beach on the E. shore of Killala Bay, 10 m. N. of Ballina.

$2\frac{3}{4}$ m. N. is Lacken, alias Lecan (Leacán Mhic Fhirbhisigh). There are some remains of the castle erected in 1560 by the Mhic Fhirbhisigh (Ma Cribhsigh) family which supplied hereditary poets and historiographers to the O Dowds of Tireragh from the 14th to the 17th c. The head of the family conducted a school of historical lore at Lacken, and also filled a leading role at the inauguration of each O Dowd. Three celebrated codices were compiled by, or under the direction of, members of this family (two of them taking their names from the place): the *Great Book of Lecan* of *c.* 1416–18, in the Royal Irish Academy; the *Yellow Book of Lecan* of *c.* 1391, in Trinity College, Dublin, and *Book of the Genealogies of Ireland*, in University College, Dublin, compiled at various places and over many years by An Dubhaltach Óg Mac Fhirbhisigh (1585–1671), who was murdered at Doonflin, near Skreen, by the English planter Thomas Crofton.

$1\frac{3}{4}$ m. SSW., not far from the sea in Scurmore, is Cruckancornia, an enfossed tumulus on whose NE. side are seven pillarstones known as the Children of the Mermaid. One of the O Dowds possessed himself of a mermaid's mantle, and thereby changed her into a woman. They wed and had seven children. The wife recovered her mantle and was able to resume her true nature. She changed the children into the pillarstones and returned to the sea.

INISHMURRAY, Co. Sligo (Map 8, B8), a small island abandoned in 1948, lies 4 m. off the mainland. It is approached from Mullaghmore (*see p. 106*) or from Rosses Point (*see p. 283*).

The island (named after St Muireadhach of Killala?) is famous for its remains of the early monastic age. The monastery was founded by St Laisrén, alias Mo-Laisse, who seems to have been trained at Candida Casa in Galloway. Next to nothing is known of the history of the place, which vanishes from Irish records after a Viking raid of 807.

The monastery remains (Nat. Mon.) comprise a massive dry-stone rampart pierced by four openings, the main gateway facing NE. (The S. entrance is the creation of the Office of Public Works' 'restorers', 1880.) Beside the main entrance is a pilgrims' 'altar' with a cross-pillar from Teampall Mo-Laisse cemetery (*see below*). In the thickness of the rampart are several chambers. (The niches in the inner face are the creation of the 'restorers', who wantonly transferred several early gravestones to them.) Flights of steps give access to the parapet.

Inishmurray, Co. Sligo.

The pear-shaped enclosure is subdivided into three parts; the dividing walls have traces of chambers. One part was further subdivided *c.* 1880.

In the N. sub-enclosure is Tráthán an Charghais (the Lenten Praying Place), a sub-rectangular clochán.

In the largest sub-enclosure is Teach Mo-Laisse ('Mo-Laisse's House') a diminutive oratory with trabeate W. doorway and medieval stone roof (reconstructed). By the S. wall runs Leaba an Naoimh ('The Saint's Bed'), a stone bench. On the altar were fragments of inscribed stones, now in the National Museum in Dublin. Towards the centre of the sub-enclosure is Teampall Mo-Laisse, 'Mo-Laisse's Church', alias Teampall na bhFear, 'the Men's Church', seemingly the monastic church proper; in recent times only men were buried within the cashel. In the cemetery are a bullaun and eight early cross-slabs or gravestones, one of them inscribed OR[ŌIT] DO COINMURSCE ('A prayer for Cú-Mhursce'). S. of the church is a perforate cross-pillar. Beside this is a plain pillarstone. E. of the church is a platform of dry masonry.

SW. of the church, on the larger of two 'altars', are the celebrated Clocha Breaca ('Speckled Stones'). The Clocha Breaca (five of which are now in the National Museum in Dublin) have inscribed cross-patterns and other devices. They were originally used to bring down maledictions on one's enemies. Facing the S. entrance is Altóir Bheag ('Small Altar'), with a fine cross-pillar and several plain pebbles.

In the W. sub-enclosure are: Túr Uí Bhréanaill, the waking place of the Virgin, and Teach (alias Teampall) na Teine 'the Fire House', a small medieval building. The lintel of the Teach na Teine doorway is inscribed with a cross which is of much earlier date. A stone hearth in the floor is traditionally said to be the site of a perpetual fire.

Outside the cashel, on the N., is Teach an Aluis, 'the Sweat House', a rectangular, corbel-roofed bath house.

SE. of the monastery are Teampall Mhuire, 'St Mary's Church', alias Teampall na mBan, 'the Women's Church', and Reilig na mBan, 'the Women's Cemetery'. There is a bullaun here; also two early gravestones, one of them inscribed [ORŌIT AR]——AILADOCUS AR MAEL BR[IGTE?] Ó RÓRC OCUS AR ÉILEISE ('A prayer for . . . ailad and for Mael-Brigte (?) Ó Ruairc and for Éileise'). Nearby is a perforate cross-pillar venerated by women.

Spaced out round the shore of the island is a series of *leachtaí* ('memorials') and *tráthháin* ('praying stations'), usually having cross-slabs or cross-pillars at which pilgrims performed traditional exercises. These are as follows: Ula Mhuire ('St Mary's Station'), at the head of Clashymore Harbour; ¼ m. W. of the harbour: Tráthán (an) Rian (the place where the Holy Office was said), with remains of a clochán. A short distance N. is Poll na Sean-Tuinne, ('Cavern of the Strong Wave'); 600 yds NE. of this: Crois Mhór, a magnificently sited *leachta*; 600 yds E. of the third station: Tráthán Aodha, 'Aodh's Station'. Nearby are an altar and Leachta na Sagart, 'Memorial of the Priests', a few bleached stones. N. of Tráthán Aodha is Tobar na Cabhrach, 'Well of Assistance'. Attached to the corbel-roofed well-house is an open-air 'bath'. 300 yds E. is a nameless 'altar'; 500 yds SE. of this, at Rú, the E. point of the island: Leachta Phádraig, 'Patrick's Memorial', with a beautiful view of the mainland; ¼ m. WSW. of Rú: An Trínóid Mhór, 'The Great Trinity'; the cross-pillars here and at the next *leachta* are among the most interesting on the island; nearby, to the SW.: An Trínóid Bheag, 'The Little Trinity'; nearby, close to Teampall Mhuire: Tráthán Mhuire, 'St Mary's Station', with an early cross-pillar; W. of Teampall Mhuire: Leachta Cholaimchille, 'Columcille's Memorial'; the cross-slab here has three crosses on one face and a single cross on the other; SE. of the last: Cros an Teampall, 'Church Cross'; 150 yds W.: Reilig Odhráin, 'Odhrán's Cemetery'. There are two early crosses on the 'altar' there, and in the cemetery is a cross-pillar having five crosses on one face. The circuit of the island began with prayers in Teach Molaise, a circuit of the top of the cashel wall and then proceeding *deiseal* to Laghta Cholmcille, Roilig Odrain, Ula Mhuire, Trathán (an) Rian, Cros Mór, Tobar na Corach, Laghta Phádraig, Trionóid Mór Trionóid Beag, circuit of Relig na mBan, and in the cashel, Altóir Beag, Eastern Altar, Teampul na bhFear, Clocha Breacha and the circuit of Teach Molaise.

INISHTURK, Co. Mayo (Map 7, B6), is a beautiful, rarely visited island 8 m. SW. of Roonah Quay (*see p. 241*) and 10 m. NNW. of Cleggan. There is a lovely little harbour with a beach at Portadoon, on the S. coast.

INISTIOGE, Co. Kilkenny (Map 4, I3), is an attractive village in a beautiful setting where the Kilkenny (16 m.)–New Ross (10 m.) road crosses the Nore by an 18th c. ten-arch bridge.

About 1206–10 Thomas fitz Anthony, Anglo-Norman seneschal of Leinster, founded the Priory of SS Mary and Columba (Columcille) for Canons Regular of St Augustine. Around the priory a small town grew up. At the Dissolution the priory and its possessions were granted to the Butlers, and in 1778 they passed to the Tighes (*see below*).

In the tree-lined market square is a portion of a cross to the memory of David FitzGerald (d. 1621) of Brownsford (*see below*) and his wife, Johanna Morres.

The Protestant parish church occupies the site of the chancel of the medieval priory church, whose 15th c. central tower it incorporates. In the church is a three-light window *Valour, The Resurrection*, and *Charity* (1919) by Catherine O Brien. In its original form the church was a Transitional building with short, aisleless nave. The central tower, Lady Chapel, and N. transept with tower, were added at various dates. The Lady Chapel served as the Protestant church until 1824; in its ruins are two 16th c. tombstones. The N. tower ('Black Castle'), square below and octagonal above, was converted (1874) into a Tighe mausoleum. A separate mausoleum contains an effigy by Flaxman of Mrs Mary Tighe (1772–1810), daughter of the Rev. William Blatchford of Rosanna and author of *Psyche*. In the ruined nave is a tombstone with the early-14th c. effigy of one of the medieval priors. In the Protestant church is a 12th c. font from the medieval parish church of Kells; only one of the corners was carved originally.

On a rock over the river is the motte-and-bailey of a castle erected by Thomas fitz Anthony.

S. of the village, at the foot of Mt Alto (919 ft), is the demesne of Woodstock, now a State forest. Formerly the seat of the Tighes, Woodstock House, together with its splendid library, fell victim to the Civil War in 1922.

2½ m. SE., on the E. side of the Nore in Clo(o)namery, are remains of an ancient ecclesiastical foundation dedicated to St Bronndán (Broondawn): a 12th (?) c. nave-and-chancel church (Nat. Mon.), with cross in relief above the lintel, an early cross-pillar, a granite basin, and, W. of the churchyard, the foundations of two beehive huts.

3 m. SSE., on the W. side of the Nore, is the tower of the FitzGerald castle of Brownsford.

4½ m. S. are the remains of Mullennakill church. 1 m. NW., on Coolnahau Hill, is Tigh Mo-Ling, alias St Mo-Ling's Cave (*lit.* house), a rock-shelter where the saint is said to have lived before settling at ST MULLINS. ¾ m. SE. of the cave, in Mullennakill, are: Tobar Chrann Mo-Ling (Well of Mo-Ling's Tree); Crann Mo-Ling (Mo-Ling's Tree); the Altóir (a rough stone bench); and the Iomar (an ancient font from Mullennakill Church).

INNFIELD, alias **ENFIELD**, Co. Meath (Map 3, H3), is a village on the Dublin (27 m.)–Mullingar (24 m.) road. For some reason which was probably unknown even to itself, the old Midland Great Western Railway Company named its station there 'Enfield'.

1¾ m. E., in Cloncurry, Co. Kildare, are a tree-crowned motte and remains of a medieval church. In the churchyard is the grave of Teresa Brayton (1868–1943), author of the popular song 'The Old Bog Road'.

2½ m. S., in Dunfierth churchyard, Co. Kildare, built into a Hamilton vault, are fragments of the altar-tomb of Sir William Bermingham, 1st Baron Carbury (*see p. 175*), who died in 1548. They include the effigy of Sir William in 'white' armour.

IRVINESTOWN, Co. Fermanagh (Map 2, B2), is a small town on the Enniskillen (9½ m.)–Strabane (32 m.) road.

The old Church Tower at the head of Main St belonged to a Protestant parish church built by the rector Patrick Delany in 1734. 4½ m. SE. at the ancient church site of Kilskeery, Co. Tyrone, are many interesting 18th c. grave-slabs. ¾ m. S. is Castle Irvine, alias Necarne Castle, a Tudor Gothic house of 1833 by J.B. Keane, incorporating earlier parts and 17th c. towers.

4 m. W. in Castle Archdale Country Park is the fine stable block of the demolished Palladian house Castle Archdale built by Col. Mervyn Archdale in 1778. The estate was requisitioned by Coastal Command, R.A.F., in the Second World War and the stable buildings now house exhibitions and a Youth Hostel. In the demesne are remains of Old Castle Archdale (Hist. Mon.), a Plantation T-shaped house and bawn built in 1615 by John Archdale of Darsham, Suffolk, and destroyed in 1689.

3½ m. NNW., in Kiltierney Deerpark, is a passage-tomb surrounded by 22 small mounds. Also in the deerpark are remains of a Cistercian Grange attached to the Abbey of Assaroe (*see p. 67*).

4 m. NNW. at Ardvarny House is a stone cross head on a modern shaft.

2¾ m. N. is Keeran wedge-tomb.

ISLAND MAGEE, Co. Antrim (Map 1, L5–6), is a peninsula forming the S. and E. sides of Larne (2 m.) Lough.

The Gobbins Cliffs (240 ft) on the E. side of the peninsula, noted for the seabirds which breed there, are accessible by footpaths.

At the N. end of the peninsula, in the garden of a house in Ballylumford, ¾ m. SSW. of Brown's Bay (a good sandy cove) is the Druid's Altar, alias Ballylumford Dolmen (in State care), a single-chamber prehistoric tomb.

J

JULIANSTOWN, Co. Meath (Map 2, J8), is a village on the Drogheda (4 m.)–Balbriggan (6 m.) road. The Protestant church has a memorial window (1920) by Michael Healy. Facing it across the Ninny valley is the Catholic Church of St Mary (1981) by McCormick, Tracey and Mullarkey, with metalwork by David King.

2 m. E. is Laytown, where the Catholic Church of the Sacred Heart (1979) is also by the same architects. (Stations by Nell Murphy, and tabernacle by David King.)

1¾ m. SE., in Sarsfieldstown, to the E. of the Dublin – Drogheda road, are fragments of a cross of *c.* 1500, commemorating Sir Christopher Barnwall, 2nd Baron Trimleston, and his wife, Elizabeth Plunket. 200 yds W., in the garden of a private house at Keenoge, is a fragment of another cross: *Crucifixion, Pietà, St Laurence*, etc.

K

KANTURK, Co. Cork (Map 5, J3), is a small market town on the Mallow (13 m.)–Newmarket (6 m.) road, at the confluence of the Rivers Dalua and Allow. The rivers figure in Spenser's *Faerie Queene* *(see p. 131)*. The Gothic Revival parish church, convent, and schools (1860–5) are by John Hurley of Cork. There is a small Folk Museum on the W. outskirts of the town.

4 m. E. is Knocknanuss (448 ft), where, 13 November 1647, Murrough O Brien 'of the Burnings', Earl of Inchiquin and, at that stage of his career, Parliamentarian Lord President of Munster, destroyed Lord Taafe's Confederate Catholic army. Among the fallen was the gallant Alasdar Colkitto Mac Donnell, the comrade of Montrose.

5 m. ESE. are the ruins of Castle Magner. In 1649 Richard Magner went to Clonmel to pay court to the conquering Cromwell. Cromwell gave him a letter for Col. Phaire, governor of Cork. The letter contained instructions to execute the bearer. Magner, however, read the letter and passed it on to his enemy, the Cromwellian governor of Mallow, who, ignorant of the contents, conveyed it to Phaire, with the hoped-for result.

6 m. ESE. is Cecilstown village. ¾ m. SW. is Lohort Castle, incorporating the 15th c. tower of a Mac Donagh Mac Carthy stronghold. The castle was reduced with artillery in May 1650 by the Cromwellian Sir Hardress Waller. In 1750 the tower was repaired by the Earl of Egmont, and was continuously occupied thereafter. In 1876 it was refurbished once more.

1 m. S. are the ruins (Nat. Mon.) of Kanturk Castle, a large Mac Carthy fortified house of about 1609. The walls stop short at the corbels intended to bear the parapets; jealous English settlers complained to the Privy Council that the house was 'much too large for a subject', and the Council forbade its completion. The enraged Mac Carthy is said to have thrown away the glass tiles he had had made for the roof.

KELLS, Co. Kilkenny (Map 4, H3), is a village on the Kilkenny (8 m.)–Kilmaganny (7 m.) road, to the S. of the Owenree crossing.

About 1192 Strongbow's seneschal of Leinster, Geoffrey fitz Robert de Monte Marisco, erected a motte-and-bailey castle there and founded a town. He also founded (*c.* 1193) a priory (*see below*) for Canons Regular of St Augustine from Bodmin in Cornwall; this in place of an ancient monastery founded by St Ciarán of Seir. In 1252 the town was burned by William de Bermingham; in 1316 it fell to Edward Bruce. Early in the 14th c. the manor passed to Arnold le Poer. A sneer by the new proprietor at Maurice, 1st Earl of Desmond, for being an Irish poet, provoked a war in the course of which Kells was burned (1327) by Desmond's men and adherents (including de Berminghams). In 1346 the manor was granted to Walter de Bermingham. In the 16th c. it passed to the Mountgarret Butlers, who held it until the Cromwellian confiscations.

Adjoining the Catholic church are the Moat (motte of Geoffrey fitz Robert's castle) and remains of the heptagonal bawn of a stone castle. There are fragmentary remains of the medieval parish church: it served as a Protestant church until about 1850.

½ m. E. of the village are the impressive ruins (Nat. Mon.) of the 5 acre, fortified, Augustinian Priory of St Mary, founded by Geoffrey de Monte Marisco. They are enclosed by a wall and divided into two courts by a branch of the river and a high wall with central gateway. In the North Court are the ruins of the claustral buildings and cruciform church. The church, like that at Athassel (*see p. 194*) had a NW. bell tower and a NE. Lady Chapel. The nave had no S. aisle, while the N. transept had a W. aisle. In the 15th c. a low tower was inserted over the crossing. Traces of the medieval paving tiles were uncovered in recent excavations. In the N. transept is a slab of *c.* 1300 with two portrait heads in high relief. There are six dwelling-towers of 15th c. type: one (Pilib na mBonn's Castle, so called after an 18th–19th c. recluse cobbler whose life suggested Banim's *Peter of the Castle*) at the S. side of the chancel; one flanking the inner gateway, and four at the curtain of the South Court, alias

Kells, Co. Kilkenny.

the Burgess, which seems never to have had buildings of stone. The fortified outer gateway of the priory was in the E. curtain.

3½ m. NNW., at Burnchurch, are the ruins (Nat. Mon.) of the 15th–16th c. castle of the Fitzgeralds, barons of Burnchurch. Cromwell camped there in 1650. In the 18th c. the castle and estate passed to the Floods. The five-storey castle tower was occupied until 1817, and so is well preserved; it has an unusual number of passages and chambers in the walls.

3½ m. NE., in Annamult, are remains of the early church of Béal Bárr. Some 400 yds away are the ruins of the Friars' Castle and Friars' Barn and the site of the Friars' Chapel, relics of the grange of Annamult which belonged to the Cistercians of Duiske Abbey (see *p. 198*).

1½ m. S. is Kilree, site of an early Brigidine monastery which is represented today by an ancient church, a Round Tower belfry and a monolithic High Cross (Nat. Mons.). The ruined nave-and-chancel church has *antae* and a trabeate W. doorway; it was remodelled in the Middle Ages. The Round Tower (96 ft) has lost its top storey. The High Cross (8th/9th c.) is decorated with spirals, frets, and carved bosses, and also has figure subjects. These include: E. face, arms: *Hunting Scene and Procession of Horses*; W. face: *The Adoration of the Magi* (who approach with horses).

3½ m. SSW., in Dunnamaggan churchyard is an unusual medieval cross with a *Crucifixion* on the W. face and a niched figure on each of the four faces.

KELLS, Co. Meath (Map 2, F8), officially Ceanannus Mór, is a market town near the River Blackwater, on the Navan (11 m.)–Virginia (13 m.) road.

The name Kells is an English corruption of Anglo-Norman *Kenlis*, itself a corruption of Irish *Ceanannus*. The place is best known for its important Columban monastery which has left us such remarkable artistic treasures as the *Book of Kells* (now in Trinity College, Dublin), the Crozier of Kells (now in the British Museum), and the fine High Crosses described below. The date of the foundation of the monastery is unknown, but, in 804, Kells was given to Columcille the Musical. In 807, Iona having been thrice pillaged by the Vikings, Abbot Cellach transferred the headquarters of the league of Columban monasteries to Kells. But Kells itself was plundered by Norsemen that very year, and its church destroyed. The new church was not completed until 814. In the 12th c. the Rule of the Canons Regular of St Augustine was adopted. In March 1152, Kells was the meeting place of a national synod under the joint presidency of Cardinal Paparo, papal legate, and Christian, Bishop of Lismore (previously first abbot of Mellifont). The purpose of the synod was to crown the work of ecclesiastical reform by suppressing a number of petty bishoprics (including Kells itself) and instituting the four metropolitan provinces of Armagh, Cashel, Dublin, and Tuam. Little remains of the medieval town, which suffered much during the Middle Ages.

Of the Columban monastery there still survive, in whole or in part, five 9th/10th c. High Crosses, a Round Tower, St Columcille's House, and some other fragments.

The Market Cross stands at the centre of the town, where it was re-erected by the Sovereign of Kells in 1688. The figure subjects include: E. face: *Procession of Horsemen*; *Guards at the Tomb of Christ; Fall of Adam and Eve; Cain and Abel; Sacrifice of Isaac*; W. face: *The Crucifixion; Miracle of the Loaves and Fishes*, etc.

The remains of the other four crosses are in the graveyard of the Protestant parish church, which occupies the site of the Columban monastery. Inside the church is a 14th c. tombstone with effigies of a man and his wife and, above them, a *Crucifixion*. The E. Cross (on the S. side of the church) has the unusual interest of having remained unfinished, so that it reveals something of the method of fashioning these remarkable monuments; on the E. face are a *Crucifixion* and a panel of four figures. The N. Cross is represented merely by a small conical base with interlaced ornament. Of the W. Cross there survive the base and part of the panelled shaft. The subjects represented include: E.

face: *The Baptism of Christ, Marriage Feast of Cana*, etc.; W. face: *The Fall, Noah and the Ark*, etc. Nearby is the S. Cross, or Cross of Patrick and Columcille. On the E. face of the base is the almost illegible inscription, PATRICII ET COLUMBAE CRUX, to which it owes its name. The subjects include: E. face: *A Hunting Scene*; *The Fall*; *The Three Children in the Fiery Furnace*; *Daniel in the Lions' Den*, etc.; W. face: *A Procession of Horsemen with Dog and Chariot*; *The Crucifixion*; *The Last Judgement*. At the S. gate of the graveyard is the roofless Round Tower (90 ft, Nat. Mon.). N. of the church now stands detached the square bell-tower of a medieval church; the 15th c. windows are good; the spire was added in 1783 by Thomas Cooley, architect of the City Hall, Dublin; the battlements are more recent still. Set into the faces of the tower are miscellaneous fragments, including two gravestones from the early monastery.

NW. of the churchyard is St Columcille's House (Nat. Mon.), a stone-roofed structure thought to have been a church. The original (W.) doorway has been blocked up and the ground level lowered about 5 ft.

The simple court house is by Francis Johnston.

Robert Barker (1739–1806), portrait painter and inventor of the panorama, was a native of Kells.

1½ m. N. are the remains of Dulane Church, a pre-Romanesque structure with *antae* and a massive door lintel. – 4 m. N. is Moynalvey. In the grounds of the Catholic church are fragments of two late-16th c. crosses, one removed from Arodstown, the other from Kilmore.

2 m. ENE., on the ridge between the Moynalty River and the Blackwater, is Headfort House, ancestral seat of the Marquess of Headfort. The house, with its fine interior, now a school, was designed by Robert Adam.

1½ m. WNW., on the Hill of Lloyd is a tower (100 ft), with lighthouse-type lantern, erected (1791, to the design of Henry Aaron Baker) by Thomas Taylor, 1st Earl of Bective (b. 1724) in memory of his father, Sir Thomas Taylor. 2¼ m. WNW., between the railway and the road to the S. of the Blackwater, is Keim churchyard, Castlekeeran. There three High Crosses (Nat. Mons.) with some interlacing are disposed around the churchyard. The base of a fourth, an ogham stone and an early cross-slab have been assembled around a fragment of the church at the centre of the graveyard. The crosses were presumably boundary crosses of the monastery founded there by St Ciarán (d. 775), reputed author of a *Life* of St Patrick.

KENMARE, Co. Kerry (Map 5, F5), is a small market town and angling resort, charmingly sited where the Killarney (20 m.)–Glengarriff (17 m.) road crosses the head of the magnificent sea-inlet called Kenmare River.

The town was founded by Sir William Petty in 1670.

Near the bridge is Cromwell's Fort, a 17th c. castle. 600 yds SW., in Parknagullane (ground of The Shrubberies), Re-enagoppul, is a 'boulder burial' at the centre of a circle of 15 stones.

1½ m. E. is a Motor Museum. 7 m. E., in a beautiful setting, is Kilgarvan. In 1261 Finghin Mac Carthy halted the Anglo-Norman tide in Desmond at the famous battle of Callan near the junction of the Rivers Roughty and Slaheny. – 3 m. SSW., in Gurteen near Glanlough, is a stone circle, with internal 'boulder burial'.

1½ m. SE., in Kenmare Old, close to Sheen bridge, are a holy well and remains of a church dedicated to St Fíonán.

1½ m. W. is Dunkerron Castle, O Sullivan Mór's chief stronghold.

5 m. WSW. are the ruins of the MacCraith O Sullivan castle of Cappanacushy.

6¼ m. WSW. are the ruins of the O Mahony castle of Dromore.

KERRY, RING OF, is the name given to the superb 109 m. circuit of the Iveragh peninsula: KILLARNEY – Parknasilla – SNEEM – Darrynane – WATERVILLE – CAHERSIVEEN – GLENBEIGH – KILLORGLIN.

KESH, Co. Fermanagh (Map 1, B9), is a village on the Irvinestown (5½ m.)–Pettigoe (5½ m.) road.

3½ m. N. of Montiaghroe is a group of megalithic monuments not far from the church, including remains of alignments and stone circles. 1 m. further NE., in Drumskinny (Hist. Mon.) is a stone circle with tangent alignment and small cairn, which probably dates from the Bronze Age.

2 m. SW., on the shore of Lough Erne in Crevenish, are the ruins of a Plantation castle built before 1618 by Thomas Blennerhasset (*see p. 76*). In 1641 it was held by Deborah, Lady Blennerhasset, and her second husband, Capt. Rory Maguire, destroyer of Castle Archdale (*see p. 207*) and of Tully Castle (*see p. 179*). It was there that Sir William Cole of Enniskillen and other leading Planters were appraised of the imminent Irish rising.

4 m. NW. (1½ m. NE. of Clonelly bridge), in Formil, are remains of three stone circles (one with two converging alignments).

KILBEGGAN, Co. Westmeath (Map 3, D3), is a market village where the Kinnegad (19 m.)–Athlone (20 m.) road crosses the Brosna.

The village takes its name from a monastic church founded in the 7th (?) c. by St Béagán. In the centre of the village was Locke's Pot Still whiskey distillery, founded in 1757. Defunct since 1957, its original buildings still retain some of the 19th c. machinery. In the old grain loft is a private museum, and there is a café on the ground floor.

KILCOCK, Co. Kildare (Map 3, I3), is a village on the Maynooth (4 m.)–Kinnegad (20 m.) road.

4 m. W. is Newtown. The Catholic parish church of the Nativity (1974) by Tyndall, Hogan and Hurley, has stone sanctuary furnishings by Michael Biggs, batik Stations and *Resurrection* by Bernadette Madden, and metalwork by Patrick McElroy, as well as a terracotta *Mother and Child*, a suspended dove and a standing cross by Benedict Tutty.

KILCOLGAN, Co. Galway (Map 6, H2), is a hamlet on the Galway (11 m.)–Gort (11 m.) road, 2 m. S. of Clarinbridge. The countryside round about is very rich in ancient remains, especially ringforts of earth and stone. (The barony of Dunkellin, about 120 sq. m., has some 400 surviving forts.)

2 m. SE., in Kiltiernan East, is Kiltiernan (Nat. Mon.), an early monastic site. The circular enclosure of some 4 acres is surrounded by remains of a cashel, and is sub-divided by radiating and other walls. At the centre is the cemetery with the ruins of an early church (fine trabeate W. door); the chancel was an addition; no arch. To the W. are remains of a souterrain. In some of the sub-enclosures are remains of rectangular houses of dry masonry.

2 m. SW. (½ m. NW. of the Kinvara road), is Drumacoo, an early monastic site (Nat. Mon.). There are the remains of a small church, St Sorney's Well and St Sorney's Bed (ruined). The original church had a trabeate W. door. Early in the 13th c. it was lengthened and widened, Transitional lancets etc. were inserted at the E. end, and a new entrance was made in the S. wall. The beautiful S. door is one of the minor masterpieces of the Connacht Transitional style, and seems, like the E. windows, to be the work of the Boyle – Cong – Knockmoy – Corcomroe school of masons.

KILCONNELL, Co. Galway (Map 6, J1), is a village on the N., or Athenry, road from Ballinasloe (6 m.) to Galway (34 m.). It takes its name from an early monastery founded by St Conall, of which nothing remains. Beside the village are the fine ruins (Nat. Mon.) of the Franciscan friary founded *c.* 1414 by William Mór O Kelly of Uí Maine, which adopted the Observantine reform in 1464. The church is a typical friary church, with central tower, S. nave aisle, and aisled S. transept of *c.* 1450–75; the latter has three E. chapels. In the N. wall of the church are fine 15th/16th c. canopy tombs, with good tracery. That near the W. door has as 'weepers' SS John, Louis, Mary, James, and Denis. A portion of the monument of the celebrated Boetius Mac Egan, O.F.M., Bishop of Elphin (d. 1650), has been appropriated for the 1752 Dalton of Raara tomb in the transept. Only portions of the claustral buildings and the small cloister survive; they are crude and late.

At the W. end of the village is a Donnellan memorial cross of 1682 (Nat. Mon.).

KILCORMAC, alias **FRANKFORD**, Co. Offaly (Map 3, C5), is a village on the Birr (10 m.)–Tullamore (13 m.) road, at the foot of Slieve Bloom. A missal which belonged to a 15th c. Carmelite friary in the town is preserved in the library of Trinity College, Dublin. The parish church has a good, 16th c., wooden *Pietà*, reputed to have come from the pre-Reformation church of Ballyboy.

3 m. NW., in Lough Boora, excavations uncovered the earliest known traces of human activity in the Irish midlands, dating from about the 8th millennium B.C. The stonework discovered had seemingly belonged to a temporary habitation of a hunting-fishing community.

KILCULLEN, Co. Kildare (Map 3, H5), is a village where the Naas (8 m.)–Athy (18 m.) and Naas – Carlow (32 m.) roads cross the Liffey. The Church of the Sacred Heart and St Brigid (1869–75) is by J.J. McCarthy. The Protestant church has two 1920 windows by Ethel Rhind: *The Resurrection* and 'He Hath Delivered My Soul in Peace'.

1 m. E., beside the Liffey, New Abbey graveyard marks the site of a Franciscan Observantine friary founded in 1486 by Sir Roland Fitz Eustace of Harristown, 1st Baron Portlester. Fragments survive of the tomb of Sir Roland (d. 1496) and his wife, Margaret Jennico (*see p. 154*): mensa with effigies, panels with *Virgin and Child, St Michael, St Francis*, and the arms of Fitz Eustace and Dartas (?).

2 m. ENE. is Carnalway Church, where there is a Harry Clarke window: *St Hubert* (1922). In Harristown, next townland to the E., is a Long Stone of granite.

2 m. SSW. is Old Kilcullen, where St Patrick is said to have founded a bishopric over which he placed Bishop Mac Táil (d. 549). There was an early monastery there, of which there survive the base of a Round Tower, traces of a Romanesque nave-and-chancel church, and portions of three stone crosses (Nat. Mons.). The W. Cross has some panels of figure carving.

¾ m. NW. is Knockaulin (600 ft), crowned by a circular (20 acre) hillfort which is ringed by a massive earthen bank with internal ditch. Excavations in the 1960s and 1970s revealed a succession of round wooden structures of Iron Age date. Ancient embanked roadways lead up to it. The place has been identified with Dún Ailinne, an early seat of the Kings of Leinster.

4½ m. SSE., in Kilgowan, are a Long Stone of granite and the Piper's Stones.

1 m. NW. is Castlemartin (1730), a fine house belonging to Dr A.J.F. O Reilly. It occupies the site of a castle which was one of the chief seats of the Fitz Eustaces. Near the house is the manorial Church of the Virgin Mary, a small, simple, 15th c. structure with castle-like dwelling tower (restored by Percy Le Clerc in 1981); inside are the reconstructed fragments of a good 16th c. Fitz Eustace tomb with effigy and weepers.

KILDARE, Co. Kildare (Map 3, G5), is a small cathedral, garrison, and market town on the Newbridge (6 m.)–Monasterevin (8 m.) road.

While the town traces its origin to the Anglo-Normans, the place has a much more ancient and distinguished history. In the 5th/6th c. St Brigid, 'the prophetess of Christ, the Queen of the South, the Mary of the Gael', founded a monastery there which became the principal church of the Kingdom of Leinster. This was remarkable in Ireland for being a double monastery (i.e. one part for nuns and the other for monks) ruled by an abbess and an abbot-bishop. A 7th c. description of the church tells of an unusually large edifice having a screen, covered with paintings and hangings, cutting off the E. end. Another screen down the centre separated the nuns from the monks. To either side of the altar were the costly metal shrines of the first abbess, St Brigid, and of the first abbot-bishop, St Conlaed. The monastery may have been the successor of a pagan sanctuary, some of whose ritual it inherited. At any rate, a perpetual fire was kept burning there until the Dissolution. A 12th c. account describes the fire as burning in a circular-fenced enclosure, forbidden to men, where it was tended by 19 nuns. The abbey possessed an illuminated gospel-book whose beauty won the admiration of Giraldus Cambrensis. In 1111 the Synod of Ráth Breasail made Kildare the see of a new diocese. (The Catholic diocese is united with that of Leighlin; cathedral at Carlow since the close of Penal times. The Protestant diocese is united with Dublin and Glendalough.) By the 19th c. little more than the shell remained of the 13th c. Anglo-Norman cathedral. In 1875–96 the remnants were 'restored' by George Edmund Street, who was also responsible for the disastrous remodelling of Christchurch in Dublin. The interior contains a few medieval relics: the effigy of a bishop supposed to be John of Taunton (1233–58); a tomb mensa with effigy (Renaissance armour) of Sir Maurice Fitz-gerald of Lackagh (d. 1575), signed by the artist, Walter Brennagh (Breathnach = Walsh); some fragments of 15th/16th c. sculptures, including three small *Crucifixions* and an indulgenced *Ecce Homo*. In 1971, the magnificent effigy of Bishop Walter Wellesley (d. 1539) was brought from Great Connell (*see p. 256*) and placed in the S. Transept on 'weepers' from another tomb also brought from Great Connell, along with a 13th c. bishop's effigy. The modern features include a Harry Clarke window (*St Hubert*). SW. of the cathedral is the fine Round Tower (106 ft – open in summer, climbable to the top), which has a Romanesque porch originally crowned by a gabled pediment; the original conical roof was replaced by the battlemented parapet in modern times. S. of the tower are the remains of a tall granite High Cross; to the E. the remains of St Brigid's Fire House.

In the Market House at the centre of the town there is the incised effigy of a 13th c. lady from Castledillon, near Straffan, and other 16th and 17th c. stone fragments. Off the E. side of the Market Place is a 15th c. tower of Kildare Castle. For some years Lord Edward FitzGerald, Commander-in-Chief of the United Irishmen, and his wife, Pamela, had their home in adjacent Kildare Lodge. St Brigid's Catholic church was refurbished (1974) by Richard Hurley, with furnishings by Patrick Pye (window), Patrick McElroy (tabernacle), Bernadette Madden (abstract batik), Imogen Stuart (door) and Ray Carroll.

E. of the town is the entrance to Tully House, seat of the Irish National Stud, founded in 1916 by Lord Wavertree. There is an Irish Horse Museum in the grounds. The interesting gardens were laid out in 1906 by the celebrated Japanese gardener, Eito. They are open to the public.

1 m. SSE. of the Market Place, in Tully, is a fragment of a preceptory of the Knights Hospitaller, founded by the de Vescis.

8 m. NE. is the Hill of Allen (Allmhuin, 676 ft), famous in legend as the Otherworld seat of mythological Fionn mac Cumhail (Fionn son of Cumhal, Finn Mac Cool). The tower on the summit is a folly erected 1859–63 by Sir Gerald Aylmer of Donadea.

1¼ m. E. (via the Newbridge road) is the nearest point of The Curragh, the largest area of arable land in the country (5,000 acres). In the E. third is the Curragh Camp, an army training-centre with a Military Museum (open by appointment); St Brigid's Church is by G. McNicholl, T.J. Ryan and M.J. Curran, 1958–9. The *St Brigid* over the main door is by Oisín Kelly, the altar crucifix by Patrick Pye (a pupil of Kelly's), the Stations of the Cross by Imogen Stuart, the tabernacle and altar furnishings by Benedict Tutty of Glenstal Abbey. The Curragh is the headquarters of Irish horse racing, with several training stables nearby and a racecourse on the N. side. Scattered over the grasslands are a number of prehistoric ritual earthworks, ring-barrows, etc. 2 m. E. (to the W. of the Curragh Camp) is Gibbet Rath, where 350 United Irishmen were massacred in 1798 after laying down their arms, an event commemorated by an incongruous statue in the centre of Kildare town. ¾ m. E. of the Camp, on Racehorse Hill, are three barrows; at the foot of the hill is Donnelly's Hollow, where Dan Donnelly defeated the English champion, George Cooper, in a celebrated prize fight, 13 December 1815.

5 m. W., at Lackagh, are a motte and the ruins of a FitzGerald castle (*see* Kildare Cathedral) and of a medieval church.

6 m. NE. is Rathangan. The Church of the Assumption was refurbished (1977) by Richard Hurley, with stone altar and font by Michael Biggs, bronze and enamel work by Patrick McElroy, and batik Stations of the Cross by Bernadette Madden. McElroy and Madden, along with Benedict Tutty (Stations), did the furnishings at the same time for the chapel of the adjacent Convent of Mercy, also refurbished by Hurley.

KILDORRERY, Co. Cork (Map 5, L2), is a village on the Mitchelstown (7 m.)–Mallow (14 m.) road.

2¼ m. NNE., on the N. side of the Funshion in Aghacross, are St Molaga's Well and Church. A *pátrún* used to be held there on Easter Sunday, the devotional exercises being followed by athletic contests and dancing.

1½ m. W., to the NW. of Farahy village, is the site of Bowen's Court, former home (now demolished) of Elizabeth Bowen (1899–1973), the well-known novelist, who lies buried in Farahy churchyard nearby.

KILFENORA, Co. Clare (Map 6, F4), is a village in the heart of Co. Clare, on the Lisdoonvarna (5 m.)–Corrofin (8 m.) road. In the 12th c. the ancient church (Cill Fhionnabhrach) from which it takes its name was made the see of a little diocese now administered by the Bishop of Galway. (The Protestant diocese is united with those of Killaloe, Kilmacduagh, and Clonfert.) In the centre of the town is the Burren Display Centre, which gives a helpful interpretation of this fascinating limestone area.

Of little St Fachtnan's Cathedral there survive: the Transitional chancel (*c.* 1200) and the N. wing, both roofless (Nat. Mons.); incorporated in the ugly Protestant church, the W. gable and the five-bay Gothic arcades of the nave. Noteworthy are the E. window and the unique, sedilia-like, 15th c. tomb in the N. wall. In the graveyard are three stone crosses (Nat. Mons.) of the 12th c., one of which ('Doorty' Cross) has curious figure-carvings and Ringerike ornament. W. of the churchyard stands a very fine 12th c. High Cross (Nat. Mon.), with a *Crucifixion* on the E. face. Another Kilfenora High Cross is now in Killaloe Cathedral.

2 m. NE., in Ballykinvarga, is Caherballykinvarga, a ruinous bivallate stone ringfort with *chevaux-de-frise*, etc. 1¾ m. NNE., at Noughaval, Tobermogua (holy well) and the remains of a church and crosses mark an ancient monastic site. The ridge SE. of Noughaval Church has ruinous forts and chamber tombs. To the N. and E. are a number of wedge-tombs.

3½ m. ESE., on the road to Corrofin, are the interesting ruins of the O Brien castle of Leamaneh (Nat. Mon.). They comprise a residential tower of 1480 (at the E. end) and an early-17th c. fortified house. The surrounding bawn can still be traced; also some demesne walls. The ornamental gateway to the bawn was removed in the 19th c. to Dromoland (*see p. 258*), and a stone fireplace from the castle is now in the Old Ground Hotel in Rúa Mac Mahon, his wife. The story is apocryphal that when her husband's corpse was brought home, she told the bearers to take it away, as there was no place for a dead man in her house. To save her son's estate from sequestration, she then offered to marry any Cromwellian officer selected by Gen. Ludlow.

The surrounding country contains many O Brien and MacNamara castles, as well as stone forts and megalithic tombs. Crossinneenboy, a T-shaped stone (12th c.) with a human mask at each end of the transom, which formerly stood 1½ m. SE. of Leamaneh Castle, has been removed by the Office of Public Works to the Clare Heritage Centre in CORROFIN, and replaced by a stiff, modern copy.

KILFINNANE, Co. Limerick (Map 4, B4), is a village on the Kilmallock (6 m.)–Mitchelstown (12 m.) road, at the foot of the Ballyhoura Mts.

The principal feature of the village is the great trivallate mound; it may be an Anglo-Norman adaptation of a ringfort.

3 m. NE., on the W. end of Slieve Reagh (700–800 ft) in the townland of Cush, is an interesting series of ringforts and tumuli.

3½ m. NNE., in Balline, is the ancient church-site, Emlygrennan. St Mo-Lua's Well, 250 yds E., is perhaps the best-known holy well in the county.

1½ m. E. is Palatines Rock, said to have been the meeting-place of Palatines settled thereabouts in 1740 from the RATHKEALE area.

KILKEE, Co. Clare (Map 6, C7), a seaside resort since early Victorian days, is built along the ¾ m. sandy beach at the head of little horseshoe-shaped Moore Bay, 35 m. SW. of Ennis, 20 m. SSW. of Milltown Malbay, and 8 m. WNW. of Kilrush. Duggerna Rock at the W. side of the bay has several attractive rock pools (watch out for rising tides). Nearby is a puffing hole.

The parish church (1963) is by J. Thompson.

Gloomy Intrinsic Bay recalls the 1836 wreck of the *Intrinsic*.

2½ m. SW. is Foohagh Point (185 ft), with traces of Doonaunroe, a promontory fort. 2 m. SW. of the Point is Castle Point (151 ft) with remnants of a MacMahon – later MacSwiney (gallogla) – castle and of Doonlicka, a promontory fort.

4 m. NE. is Bealaha. 3 m. NW. overlooking Farrihy Bay, is Doonegall Point, with remains of the largest and strongest of Clare's promontory forts.

7 m. NE. is Doonbeg. An Armada ship (the (?) *San Esteban*) ran aground near the river-mouth. The local beaches are noted for their beautiful shells. By the bridge are remains of a 15th/16th c. MacMahon castle. (The MacMahons descended from Mahon O Brien, great-great-grandson of Brian Boru.) 2 m. N. is 2 m. Tráigh Bhán (White Strand) with its dunes.

KILKEEL, Co. Down (Map 2, K5), is a seaside resort and fishing port at the mouth of the Kilkeel River and at the foot of the Mourne Mts, 18 m. SE. of Newry and 13 m. S. of Newcastle. The Kilkeel River rises in the Silent Valley (6 m. N.), where it has been dammed to form great reservoirs, originally as a means of supplying water to the city of Belfast.

The 'Doorty' Cross, Kilfenora.

¼ m. NE. is the Crawtree Stone (Hist. Mon.), a portal-tomb.

4½ m. SW., on the shore of Carlingford Lough, are the 14th (?) c. great keep and fragmentary gatehouse and curtain of the English royal fortress of Green Castle (Hist. Mon.). The first castle (1261) may be represented by the artificial mound close to the ruins. The castle was entrusted to the de Burgo earls of Ulster. It was besieged and taken by the Irish in 1343, but was soon recovered. It later passed to the earls of Kildare, and was subsequently granted to the Bagnals. It seems to have been wrecked by Cromwellian artillery in 1652.

1 m. WNW., at Massfort, is Dunnaman Giants Grave (Nat. Mon.), a court-tomb gallery with four chambers.

2 m. WNW. is Ballyrogan, alias Mourne Park, the fine demesne and seat of the Earl of Kilmorey. In the demesne is Mourne Park court-tomb.

KILKENNY, Co. Kilkenny (Map 4, H2), capital of its county and cathedral town of the diocese of Ossory, is an important market centre where the Dublin (73 m.)–Clonmel (32 m.) road crosses the Nore, 24 m. SW. of Carlow, 30 m. N. of Waterford, and 21 m. SSW. of Abbeyleix. Though, in typical Irish fashion, it turns its back on its river, it is one of the most attractive, as it is one of the most interesting, of Ireland's inland towns.

The nucleus of the town was the monastery (Cill Chainnigh) founded by St Cainneach ('Canice') of AGHABOE. At the Anglo-Norman invasion most of the modern County Kilkenny fell to Strongbow, as pretended heir to the Kingdom of Leinster, and about 1172 he built a castle to command the crossing of the Nore. On his death Leinster passed, by English law, to his son-in-law, William the Marshal, who replaced Strongbow's castle by a stone fortress – where he had his chief seat – and incorporated the town (1207). In 1391 James Butler, 3rd Earl of Ormond, purchased the manor and castle of Kilkenny. Thereafter Kilkenny Castle was the principal seat of the Earls of Ormond, and Kilkenny town became the centre of an Anglo-Irish lordship which was never recovered by the Old Irish or their culture.

By reason of its strategic importance and of the power of its lords, the town played a conspicuous role in Anglo-Irish affairs throughout the Middle Ages, and was one of the principal meeting-places of Anglo-Irish parliaments. The parliament of 1366 enacted the notorious Statutes of Kilkenny, in an effort to stem the gaelicization of the Anglo-Norman colony in Ireland. (These enactments forbade the colonists, and the Irish living among them, to intermarry with the Irish; to use the Irish language, or Irish dress, or Irish surnames; to play hurling; or to admit Irish clerics and monks to cathedrals, benefices, or monasteries, in territories under Anglo-Norman control.) In the winter of 1348–9 the town was ravaged by the Black Death. In 1609 James I conferred on the town both the rank and dignity of a city. From 1642 until 1648 the city was the seat of the

St Canice's Cathedral, Kilkenny.

Supreme Council and the General Assembly of the Catholic Confederation ('Confederation of Kilkenny'). In the event, the choice of a capital in the heart of the Butler territory was to prove disastrous to the Catholic cause, for it exposed the Confederation unduly to the influence and machinations of the Marquess of Ormonde, Charles I's representative. In 1648 the town admitted Ormonde, who dissolved the Confederation and installed a royalist garrison under the command of Sir Walter Butler and Edward Walsh. On 22 March 1650, Cromwell laid siege to the place. Five days later, after the fourth assault, Butler and Walsh surrendered with military honours.

Father James Archer, S.J. (1550–1605), one of the most effective agents of the Counter-Reformation in Ireland, was a native of Kilkenny. Other celebrated citizens of Kilkenny were: John Banim (1798–1842), novelist and dramatist and co-author with his brother, Michael Banim (1797–1847), of the *O Hara Tales*; the biographer Francis Hackett (1883–1962) and the novelist Francis MacManus (1909–65), and Kitty Clive (1711–85), who acted with Colley Cibber at Drury Lane and also in David Garrick's company. Over her grave in Twickenham churchyard her friend, Horace Walpole, erected a memorial to her and wrote:

Ye smiles and jests, still hover round
This much consecrated ground.
Here lies the laughter-loving dame,
A matchless actress, Clive her name;
The comic muse with her retired,
And shed a tear when she expired.

The Castle, from 1391 until 1936 chief seat of the Butler earls, dukes, and marquesses of Ormonde, stands on an eminence over the Nore at the SE. corner of the old town. On 20 November 1645, it was the scene of the reception of the Papal Nuncio by the President and Supreme Council of the Catholic Confederation, which had set up its headquarters in the castle. William the Marshal's 13th c. fortress, which has imposed its form on all subsequent buildings on the site, was a trapezoid enclosure with a massive drum tower at each angle. It survived, substantially intact, until the 17th c. when it was Frenchified by the first Duke of Ormonde. Some rebuilding was undertaken towards the close of the 18th c., and large-scale restoration at various periods in the 19th c. The latest work included the great picture gallery designed by Benjamin Woodward of Cork. Three of the great angle towers and the main N. wall of the medieval castle survive, though in greatly altered form. The Classical gateway in the W. wall was one of the first duke's alterations (1684). All the rest of the structure is 18th–20th c. work. Guided tours are provided in the castle.

Facing the castle, on the opposite side of the Parade, are the Castle Stables, now the Kilkenny Design Workshops (silver, textiles, ceramics, wood-turning, etc.), remodelled by Niall Montgomery in 1961. The nearby offices of the Revenue Commissioners occupy the premises of the famous Kilkenny Private Theatre where Tom Moore played in 1808–10.

Among the few surviving fragments of the medieval town wall, Talbot's Tower may be seen behind the Vocational School in Lower New St.

Off the E. side of High St is St Mary's Lane with St Mary's Church (since 1963 a Protestant parish hall), which incorporates the ill-used nave (aisles gone), transepts, and part of the chancel of the 13th c. parish church of Blessed Mary. In the church is a 13th c. font found at St Kieran's Well near the Old Market. Church and churchyard contain some 30 medieval and early modern monuments. In the monument room (N. transept) are: Richard Rothe (1637); John (d. 1590) and Letitia Rothe (d. 1602). Churchyard: 14th c. tomb mensa with effigies of William and Margaret Goer; tomb mensa with effigy of Heleyn, wife of William de Armayl (now in the Shee burial place); Renaissance tombs of Sir Richard Shee (*c.* 1608; figures of apostles, etc.); Elias Shee (d. 1613), whom Holinshed mentions; and John Rothe (d. 1620) and his wife, Rose Archer. Also in St Mary's Lane may be seen the rear gable of Shee's Hospital or Almshouse (alias St Mary's Poorhouse); the front gable is in Rose Inn St. The almshouse was founded in 1582 by Sir Richard Shee and his wife. The building was restored in 1981 and now serves as the Tourist Office.

The most conspicuous building in High St is the arcaded Tholsel, erected in 1761 as the Exchange and Town Hall; the civic regalia and muniments are worth inspection. Here and there in the street the observant eye can recognize details of 16th and 17th c. houses; e.g. Crotty's premises mask a 16th–17th c. Shee house. Behind No. 15 is the ruined 'Hole in the Wall', a once-famous courtyard tavern. Between High St and St Kieran St are the Slips, old stepped lanes. St Kieran St is a narrow lane once full of old coaching inns, among them Kyteler's Inn (No. 27). A celebrated Kyteler was Dame Alice, who, in 1324, was charged by the deranged bishop, Richard de Ledrede, with witchcraft, heresy, and murderous assaults on her four husbands. She escaped to England, but her maid, Petronilla, was burned at the stake.

Parliament St, formerly Coal Market, is so called in memory of the General Assembly of the Catholic Confederation. The Assembly met in a house belonging to Robert Shee that stood at the entrance to New Market (now a car-park). On the same side of the street is the County Court House, a good Classical building of 1794. On the opposite side of the street is the Rothe House (Nat. Mon.), a fine double-court house built in 1594 for John Rothe. Restored 1965–6, it houses the museum and library of the Kilkenny Archaeological Society.

At the (Bull) Ring, ENE. of Parliament St, in the grounds of Smithwick's brewery, are the ruined choir (*c.* 1232, extended *c.* 1324) and central tower (*c.* 1350) of the Franciscan Friary (Nat. Mon.) founded by Richard the Marshal. The 13th c. font was brought there from St Kieran's Well beside Kyteler's Inn. Friar John Clyn, noted 14th c. annalist, was a member of the community.

In Abbey St, W. of Parliament St, is Black Abbey Dominican church. This is a remodelled re-edification of the church of the Dominican friary of the Most Holy Trinity, founded outside the NW. angle of the town by William the Marshal *c.* 1225. About 1780 the Dominicans demolished the choir to make way for a new convent. About 1788–93 the surviving portion of the church was re-roofed, but it was not reopened for regular public worship until 1840. The medieval remains comprise: 13th c. aisled nave, 14th c. S. transept (good windows), early-16th c. central tower, and the lower part of the W. tower. Displayed in the church are a 15th c. alabaster carving of the Blessed Trinity, a fine 16th c. Flemish statuette of the Virgin, and a crude Penal-times oak figure of St Dominic. E. and NE. of the church are fragments of the town wall, including Blackfriars (Trinity) Gate.

A short distance S. of Black Abbey, in James's St, is the Cathedral of the Assumption (1843–57), a dull building in a hard, Gothic style by 'Mr Butler, architect, of Dublin', with late-19th c. alterations by William Hague. The statue of the Blessed Virgin is by John Hogan's Italian friend, Benzoni.

In Irishtown, on the N. side of the Bregagh River, St Canice's Cathedral and a Round Tower mark the site of the ancient monastery from which Kilkenny derives its name. They may be conveniently reached from Parliament St via St Canice's Steps (1614), whose walls contain fragments of medieval carvings.

The Round Tower (101 ft) is practically the sole surviving relic of the monastery. The view from the parapet is rewarding.

St Canice's Cathedral is the second successor of the abbey church to which the see was transferred from AGHABOE by the Synod of Ráth Breasail (1111). The Gothic church – it is the second largest of Ireland's medieval cathedrals – may have been begun by Hugh de Rous, first Anglo-Norman bishop, but the major portion of the work was due to Bishop Hugh de Mapilton (1251–6), and its completion to Bishop Geoffrey St Leger (1260–86). In 1332 the lofty central bell tower collapsed, bringing down much of the choir and of the transept chapels. The reconstruction was begun by Bishop Richard de Ledrede (1316–61), but was not finished until the time of Bishop Hacket (1460–78). Bishop de Ledrede also installed the celebrated stained glass E. windows of the chancel depicting the Life, Passion, Resurrection, and Ascension of Our Lord, which fell victim to the Cromwellians, who wrecked the church. From 1661 many repairs were made before a general restoration was undertaken in 1866, the architect being Sir Thomas Newenham Deane, to whom the cathedral owes its present appearance. (Deane was responsible for the absurd treatment of the interior wall faces; for removing the screen which had carried the medieval rood-loft; and for the good, but un-Irish, hammer-beam roof.) Charles W. Harrison of Dublin (*see p. 155*) did the stone carving.

The cathedral (224 × 128 ft overall) is unusually consistent in style and unusually symmetrical in plan: a cruciform church with aisled nave of five bays, choir-cum-chancel flanked on either side by two E. chapels projecting in echelon from the aisleless transepts, low central tower, and S. porch.

The oldest part is the chancel, which may be of Bishop de Rous's time; the remainder of the E. arm, including the transepts, is probably the work of Bishop de Mapilton. All the dressings and ornamental features are of sandstone, whereas in the nave they are of limestone. The outstanding feature of the chancel is the three-light E. window, which contained Bishop de Ledrede's famous glass. The clerestory windows in the side walls, sedilia, etc., are the work of Sir Thomas Deane. In the N. wall is a tomb with a fine 14th c. episcopal effigy of Richard de Ledrede.

The transepts preserve their original features little altered, but the doorway in the N. transept seems to be a restoration. To one side of this doorway is a good 13th c. tomb niche; to the other has been placed St Kieran's Chair, a 13th c. seat which probably came from the choir. The S. choir aisle, now a vestry, served as the chapter-house until 1866. The adjoining chapel was entirely reconstructed by Deane, on the original plan and largely with original materials. 'More glass than wall', it represents a late-13th c. enlargement of the original chapel.

The NW. pier of the crossing seems to be 13th c.; the other three date from the 14th c. reconstruction. The two E. piers seem to have been designed to carry an extra inner ring to the chancel arch. The elaborate star-vaulting is part of Bishop Hacket's work.

The nave arcades are carried on quatrefoil columns with mid- and late-13th c. details. The clerestory windows, somewhat over-large, are likewise quatrefoil. Beneath the centre light of the W. window is a unique gallery with trefoil arches. The outer arch of the late-13th c. S. porch had detached nook-shafts of marble flanked by double roll mouldings. The W. doorway is (by Irish standards) elaborate. The adoring angels of the lateral roundels indicate that the central roundel had a figure of Christ or of the Virgin and Child. The stepped parapets of the cathedral, and of the Round Tower, are 14th/15th c. additions. Such parapets are a standard feature of later Irish Gothic.

Upwards of 100 funerary and other monuments have survived the cathedral's misfortunes. Some are fragmentary; some have been incorrectly assembled; all have lost their polychrome colouring, etc. The most important are: N. nave arcade: monument of . . ., son of Henry de Ponto de Lyra, 1285; James Schortals, Lord of Ballylarkin and Ballykeefe, and his wife, Katherine Whyte, 1507; armoured effigy in high relief, probably by Rory O Tunney; the side slab with Apostles belongs to another tomb; Edmund Purcell, captain of Ormond's kerns (d. 1549), and his wife, Elena Grace; fragmentary; mutilated miniature effigy of armoured knight in low relief; Sir John Grace, Baron of Courtstown, and his wife, Onorina Brenach (= Walsh), 1552; effigy of armoured knight, 'weepers' (Apostles), etc.; by Rory O Tunney (?). N. transept: canopied tomb; the three W. figures (from another tomb) are probably by Rory O Tunney. N. choir wall: effigy of Bishop de Ledrede (*c.* 1361). S. choir aisle: Bishop David Rothe. S. transept: Piers *Rúa* Butler, 8th Earl of Ormond (d. 1539), and Margaret Fitzgerald (d. 1542), his countess; effigies in high relief; the 'weepers' on the N. side and the Butler-Cantwell arms, etc., on the S. side do not belong to the mensa; James (?), 9th Earl of Ormond (d. 1546); armoured effigy; the 'weepers'. S. nave arcade: 13th c. baptismal font; S. nave aisle: Richard Butler, 1st Viscount Mountgarret (d. 1571); effigy in 'white' armour; Honorina Shortall (*née* Grace, d. 1596); effigy; the front panel of the tomb is from another monument (by Rory O Tunney?); unknown widow; effigy; the 'weepers' by the Ormond school. Among the windows on the Cathedral are *The Nativity* (1931) by A.E. Child, *The Parables of the Sower and Sheep* (1908) by Beatrice Elvery, and a war memorial *The Crown of Life* (1918) by Ethel Rhind.

N. of the cathedral are the 18th c. Bishop's Palace and St Canice's Library. The library has some interesting manuscripts including the *Red Book of Ossory*, and about 3,000 printed books which can be dated to the 16th and 17th c. SW. of the cathedral is the 18th c. Deanery.

St Patrick's Graveyard, off Lower Patrick St, at the S. end of the town, marks the site of Domhnach Mór, an early church, and of its successor, a medieval parish church; in it are some medieval and 16th and 17th c. tomb-stones. To the SW., in College Rd, is St Kieran's College (1836–9), Catholic seminary of the diocese of Ossory. Thomas Mac Donagh, poet and patriot, and Francis Sheehy Skeffington, pacifist, were students of the college; both were killed by the British during the 1916 Rising, the former after court martial, the latter without trial. The college museum has an interesting collection of medieval and other ecclesiastical antiquities, including a monstrance, vestments, etc., belonging to David Rothe, Bishop of Ossory, 1618–50. Rothe, a scholar and author of distinction, was for a time the only Catholic bishop in Ireland, and was later one of the outstanding personalities of the Catholic Confederation, which was, in large measure, due to him.

Greene's Bridge at Irishtown is a good – if rustic – Palladian essay of *c.* 1765 (parapets 1835); the bridge has been attributed to George Smith.

On the E. side of Lower John St, not far from John's Bridge, is Kilkenny College, otherwise the Grammar School, a Protestant boarding school founded there in 1666 by the first Duke of Ormond. Its roll includes the illustrious names of William Congreve, George Farquhar, Jonathan Swift, George Berkeley, and William Magee. The oldest surviving College buildings date from 1782.

On the W. side of Lower John St is St John's Protestant church, an 1817 rebuilding of the Lady Chapel (*c.* 1290; E. window *c.* 1300) of the church belonging to the New Priory and Hospital (for the poor and needy) of St John the Evangelist, founded *c.* 1211 by William the Marshal, Jun., for Canons Regular of St Augustine. From the multitude of its windows the chapel was known as the 'Lantern of Ireland'. All that survive are the roofless chancel and fragments of the nave and of the claustral buildings (Nat. Mons.). The chancel monuments include the tomb of '. . . Purcell and Joan, his Wife', 1500, with mutilated effigies of an armoured knight and his lady.

6½ m. N. is the famous Cave of Dunmore (Nat. Mon.), with a museum in the reception area.

4½ m. NE., in Sandfordscourt, formerly Cantwellscourt, is the tower of a 15th c. Cantwell castle; a wall chamber in the fourth storey was called 'Cantwell's narrow, hard bed'. There are some interesting ringforts and a number of ancient church sites in the neighbourhood.

2 m. E., in Leggetsrath East 'churchfield', is an ancient church site with an early cross.

5½ m. E., in Church Clara, are remains of St Colmán's medieval parish church. Built into the E. gable is an ogham stone. In the ruins are fragments of a Shortal tomb, etc. About 500 yds N. of the church are remains of the Archer castle of Clarabricken. Further NNW., in Clara Upper, is Clara Castle (Nat. Mon.). This small 16th c. Shortal castle is unusually well preserved, and is a very attractive example of a fortified dwelling of its period. – 2¼ m. (by road) E. of Clara church is Freestone Hill (464 ft). On the summit can be found a Bronze Age cemetery cairn. It has been subjected to considerable disturbance by an oval Iron Age hill-fort with a central enclosure. The fort was defended by a terrace bank.

The Market Cross, Dunmore Cave.

Muckross House, Killarney, Co. Kerry: exterior (top) and interior (see page 220).

$3\frac{1}{2}$ m. SE., beautifully situated on the W. bank of the Nore in Kilferagh, is Fiachra's Churchyard with 'St Fiachra's Statue', a mutilated, rudely carved, episcopal effigy. To the S. is St Fiachra's Well. Kilferagh House incorporates the tower of a Forstal castle. 500 yds downstream from Fiachra's churchyard are the beautifully situated ruins of Kilferagh parish church, Sheastown, with *antae* at the E. chancel gable and plain, round-headed N. and S. doors. The monuments include the tomb of Robert Forstal (d. 1585), his wife, Catherine (d. 1583), James Forstal and his wives, Elisia Shortal (d. 1597) and Ellen Comerford; it was made by James Conney, 1608.

5 m. SE. is Bennettsbridge, properly St Benet's Bridge. The medieval highway from Dublin to the South crossed the Nore there. 2 m. SE. is Kilbline Castle, one of the longest occupied in the county.

$\frac{1}{2}$ m. SW. is Castle Blunden (Lady Blunden), a good house of *c.* 1750.

$5\frac{1}{2}$ m. SW., at the ruins of St Nicholas's parish church, Grove (Tullaghanbrogue), are two medieval tombstones.

KILL, Co. Kildare (Map 3, I4), is a small village off the Dublin (16 m.)–Naas (5 m.) road. The motte of John de Hereford's invasion castle survives.

1 m. N., in Bodenstown, are the remains of a small, medieval, nave-and-chancel church. In the churchyard is the grave (vulgar memorial) of Theobald Wolfe Tone (1763–98).

$3\frac{1}{2}$ m. NNE. is Castlewarden motte (Adam de Hereford).

3 m. NE., in Oughterard, are remains of a hill-top Round Tower and small church (1009?). A vault off the nave is the tomb of Arthur Guinness (d. 1803), the famous Dublin brewer.

KILLADYSERT, alias **KILLDYSERTMURHULL**, Co. Clare (Map 6, F7), 14 m. SW. of Ennis and 20 m. E. of Kilrush, is a village on the N. shore of the Shannon estuary. It takes its name from a hermitage (*díseart*) of St Murthaile's. There are remains of a medieval parish church with dwelling-tower.

4 m. E., on Canon Island, in the Fergus estuary, are the remains (Nat. Mon.) of St Mary's Priory (Abbey?), a house of Canons Regular of St Augustine. They stand inside a cashel (site of an early monastery?). The friary-type, nave-and-chancel church and parts of the claustral range are early-13th c.; the remainder is 15th c.

KILLALA, Co. Mayo (Map 7, G2), a village on the W. shore of Killala Bay, $6\frac{1}{2}$ m. NW. of Ballina and 6 m. E. of Ballycastle, takes its name (Cill Alaidh) from a church founded by St Patrick and assigned to St Muireadhach. When the Irish Church was reorganized in the 12th c., Killala became the see of the diocese to which it has given its name. St Patrick's Cathedral (Protestant, *c.* 1670/80) occupies the site of the medieval church. Of the early monastery there survives only the 84 ft Round Tower (Nat. Mon.). (The Protestant diocese is now united with Tuam. The Catholic cathedral is now at Ballina.)

1 m. ESE. are the well-preserved remains of Moyne 'Abbey' (Nat. Mon.) a friary founded, *c.* 1455, by one of the Mac Williams (Burkes) for Franciscans of the Strict Observance and consecrated in 1462. The church has a wide S. aisle, a two-chapel S. transept and a chapel S. of the chancel. The tower is an insertion. Graffiti of 16th c. ships may be seen on the plaster of the W. nave wall and the respond of the aisle arcade. The Renaissance W. door appears to be an insertion. Extensive remains of the claustral building survive.

6 m. WNW., via Tonrehown bridge and Kincon, in Rooghan, is a ruined court-tomb. About 1 m. N., in Ballybeg, are the Cloghabracka, a court-tomb with curved forecourt.

4 m. NNW., 1 m. NE. of Palmerstown bridge, is Carbad More dual court-tomb, with a circular court at each end opening on to a gallery grave. Further E. are remnants of Rathfran 'Abbey' (Nat. Mon.), a Dominican friary founded in 1274 by Sir Richard de Exeter. It had two courts (cloister garth and 'domestic' court). The S. chapel was 15th c. N. of Mullaghmore crossroads, in Breastagh, is a tall ogham stone re-erected in 1853. The damaged inscription reads L[E]GG . . . SD . . . LENGESCAD MAQ CORRBRI MAQ AMMLLONGITT. It probably commemorates the grandson of the 5th c. local king, Amalngaid, whose name is embedded in that of the barony of Tyrawley (Tír Amalngaid). $3\frac{1}{2}$ m. NNE. of Palmerstown bridge, in Foghill, is a pillarstone, said to have been erected by St Patrick. Also in Foghill is a monument to the poet Micheál Mag Ruaidhri (1860–1936), friend of Padraig Pearse. $1\frac{3}{4}$ m. NE., in Ballinlena, are St Cummin's Well and the ruins of Kilcummin, a small, early church. N. of the church is St Cummin's Grave, marked by two pillarstones and an early gravestone with three 'Patrick's' crosses. It was on the seashore nearby that Gen. Humbert's French force landed, August 1798.

KILLALOE, Co. Clare (Map 6, J6), a small market town on the Limerick (13 m.)–Scarriff (11 m.) road, is beautifully situated on the W. bank of the Shannon. It is the cathedral town of the Protestant diocese (united with Clonfert, Kilfenora, and Kilmacduagh) of Killaloe. (The Catholic cathedral is now at ENNIS.)

Since the 12th c. at least, the name of the place, Cill Da Lúa, has been taken to mean the Church of Do-Lúa, alias Mo-Lúa. However, the patron of Killaloe is St Flannán, an 8th (?) c. prince of Dál gCais. The rise to power of Dál gCais in the persons of Brian Boru and his descendants (the O Briens), and the proximity of the monastery to the ancestral seat of the O Briens, combined to make Killaloe one of the leading ecclesiastical centres of Munster, and at the 12th c. reformation it became the see of a diocese corresponding to the O Brien kingdom of Thomond.

The principal feature of the town is St Flannan's Cathedral (Protestant), attributed to King Donal Mór O Brien (d. 1194). A simple, Late Transitional, aisleless, cruciform building, with tower (upper part *c.* 1800) over the crossing, it has been modified (N. transept remodelled, middle of nave reconstructed, etc.) at various dates. Noteworthy are: the rich Romanesque doorway (from an older church) which frames a window at the SE. angle of the nave; the nearby, 12th c. High Cross (removed from Kilfenora in 1821) with *Crucifixion*; the cross-fragment with the ogham and Runic inscriptions requesting a blessing for Thorgrim, who carved it; the medieval font; the Late Transitional E. window; the Transitional window in the E. wall of the S. transept. In the churchyard is St Flannán's Church (Nat. Mon.), well-preserved, stone-roofed nave of a Romanesque nave-and-chancel church.

In the Catholic parish church is a two-light window *The Presentation of Our Lord* with *The Annunciation and Flight into Egypt* (1927) by Harry Clarke. Beside the church have been re-erected the remains of St Mo-Lúa's Oratory (Nat. Mon.), removed in 1929 from Friars' Island (submerged in the course of the Shannon hydro-electric works). The stone-roofed chancel was an addition to the timber-roofed nave. The churchyard is alleged to occupy part of the site of Kincora, celebrated seat of the Kings of Dál gCais and of Thomond. In 1103 Magnus Barefoot, King of Norway, visited King Muirchertach O Brien at Kincora.

1½ m. NNW., near the W. bank of the Shannon in Ballyvally, is tree-planted Béal Boru Fort, a massive earthen ring-work. It has been heaped up over a derelict, palisaded ringfort of the 11th (–12th?) c. Brian Boru takes his sobriquet from the place.

KILLARNEY, Co. Kerry (Map 5, G4), most celebrated and commercialized of Ireland's tourist resorts, is a market town at the junction of the Limerick (67¾ m.)–Bantry (48¼ m.) and Cork (53 m.)–Tralee (20 m.) roads. It is the cathedral town of the Catholic diocese of Kerry. The romantic lake and mountain scenery of the region is world-renowned. The region is also noted for the wealth, variety, and profusion of its flora (including *Arbutus unedo* and the rare *Trichomanes radicans* fern). It also contains a number of interesting ancient monuments.

In the town itself the only building of note is St Mary's Cathedral (1842–55), by Augustus Welby Pugin (spire and nave completed by Ashlin and Coleman of Dublin); interior decoration designed by J.J. McCarthy ('the Irish Pugin'); this is one of the best Gothic Revival churches in the country. Its interior was refurbished (1973) by D.J. Kennedy, with furnishings by Ray Carroll. Martyr's Hill, College St, is a monument (by Séamus Murphy) to the most celebrated of Kerry's Gaelic poets: Goffraidh Ó Donnchadha of the Glen (d. 1677); Aodhagán Ó Rathaille (*c.* 1670–1728); Eóghan Rúa Ó Súilleabháin (d. 1784); and Piaras Feritéir (*see p. 62*), who was treacherously hanged by the Cromwellian commander, Nelson, in 1653. Nearby, on East Avenue Rd, is a Veteran Car, Cycle and Carriage Museum.

The Lakes of Killarney, to which the district primarily owes its fame, lie at the foot of MacGillycuddy's Reeks and the Mangerton Mts. They are Lough Leane ('Lower Lake', 5,000 acres), Muckross Lake ('Middle Lake', 680 acres), and the Upper Lake (430 acres.). Details of the scenic attractions of the area may be obtained from the Tourist Office in the Town Hall.

Between the town and Lough Leane is Kenmare demesne. Kenmare House, seat of the Brownes, Earls of Kenmare, was destroyed by fire in 1913. The site commands a superb view of Lough Leane. In the demesne is the beautifully sited championship course of Killarney Golf Club. On Ross Island, at the S. end of the demesne (2 m. SW. of the town by road), are the fine ruins of Ross Castle, chief seat of O Donoghue Mór. In 1652 it was held by Lord Muskerry with 1,500 men against a Cromwellian force of 1,500 foot and 700 horse, commanded by Ludlow. The defenders held out until floating batteries were brought up overland to bombard the castle from the water as well as the land. The remains comprise a massive 15th c. tower – with later additions – and a small bawn. A delightful view of Lough Leane may be had from the battlements. S. of the castle are ancient copper workings, last exploited in the 18th and early 19th c. Governor's Rock headland, noted for its native flora, is a Nature Reserve. 1 m. NW. (boats from the castle pier), is Inisfallen, a small island which, until the destruction of its trees and shrubs, was one of the gems of Killarney. A monastery was founded there in the 6th/7th c. In the 12th c. the monks became Canons Regular of St Augustine. Later in the Middle Ages they conducted a hospital there. The remains (Nat. Mons.) comprise: St Mary's Priory – small cloister garth, church with 12th c. nave (*antae* and trabeate W. doorway) and 13th c. chancel; a small, plain Romanesque oratory; a decorated Romanesque oratory; and a small stone cross which was found in the lake nearby. The celebrated *Annals of Inisfallen* are now housed in the Bodleian Library, Oxford.

1¼ m. S., on a promontory in Lough Leane, are the fragmentary remains of Castle Lough, a Mac Carthy Mór castle.

2½ m. S. is Killegy, a small, early church with bell-tower restored in the 18th c. Rudolf Ehrich Raspe (1737–94), Hanoverian scientist and embezzler, and author of *The Travels and Adventures of Baron Munchhausen*, is buried in the churchyard. He came to Killarney in 1793 as geological adviser to the Herberts, who were exploiting the copper lodes of Ross Island and the Muckross estate. – On the opposite side of the road is the magnificent, 10,000 acre Bourne-Vincent Memorial Park, formerly Muckross (Abbey) Demesne. It was presented to the nation in 1932 by Mr and Mrs Bowers Bourne of California, and their son-in-law, Senator Arthur Vincent. It is noted for its palms, bamboos, azaleas, magnolias, hydrangeas, New Zealand flax, rare ferns, etc. Since 1965 Park, gardens, and house (completed for the Herberts in 1843) have been open to the public. Muckross House has exhibitions of furniture history, natural history and folk-life relating to Co. Kerry, as well as interesting craft-making shops. Only horse-drawn vehicles are allowed in the Park. Cars must park close to Muckross House. In the demesne are the well-preserved ruins (Nat. Mon.) of Muckross 'Abbey', a friary founded in 1448 for Observantine Franciscans by (Donal) Mac Carthy Mór (d. 1468). After the Dissolution the friars clung to the place. In 1596 the heiress of Mac Carthy Mór, in defiance of the English Government, eloped from her father's castle at Pallis (*see below*) with Finghin Mac Carthy Riabhach, and married him at night in the ruined friary church. Finghin paid for his temerity with imprisonment in the Tower of London. The typical friary-type remains date for the most part to the period 1448–1500. In the chancel are the tombs of the founder and of several ancient Kerry families (O Donoghue of the Glen – including the poet Goffraidh, who died in 1677 – Mac Carthy Mór, O Sullivan Mór, Mac Gillycuddy), as well as of their upstart supplanters. The poets Aodhagán Ó Rathaille (*c.* 1670–1728) and Eóghan Rúa Ó Súilleabháin (d. 1784) are also buried at the friary. By the shore of Muckross Lake are the 'Colleen Bawn Rock', the 'Colleen Bawn Caves' and ruined 'Danny Man's Cottage'. These names, and the attendant tales, are all bogus, for the real Colleen Bawn had no connection with Killarney (*see p. 226*). When Boucicault wrote his melodrama, *The Colleen Bawn*, based on Gerald Griffin's novel, *The Collegians*, he transferred the setting to Killarney; Benedict inevitably followed suit in his opera *The Lily of Killarney*. From the latter these Killarney sites acquire their names. At Muckross village is the starting-point (signposted) for the easy ascent of Mangerton (2,756 ft). At 2,206 ft is the Devil's Punchbowl, one of the sights of Killarney.

Gap of Dunloe, Killarney, Co. Kerry (see page 222).

$4\frac{1}{2}$ m. S. is Torc Cascade, one of the best-known Killarney beauty-spots.

$2\frac{1}{2}$ m. E., in Lissyviggeen, are the Seven Sisters (Nat. Mon.), a diminutive circle of seven stones within an earthen bank, to the S. of which is a pair of outliers.

17 m. E. rise the cairn-covered Paps of Dana (2,273 ft and 2,284 ft). The mountainous country to the N. is Sliabh Luachra, famous for its 17th–18th c. school of poetry, of which Eóghan Rúa Ó Súilleabháin and Aodhagán Ó Ráthaille were the most celebrated members.

4 m. SE., in the Flesk valley, are the ruins of Killaha Castle, where the poet-chieftain Goffraidh Ó Donnchadha of the Glen (d. 1677) gave his famous feasts. Charles Lever's *The O Donoghue* is set in the district.

$2\frac{3}{4}$ m. WNW., in Parkvonear, is Round Castle (Nat. Mon.), a circular tower set in rectangular earthworks, etc. To the N. is the site of Aghadoe Monastery, founded in the 6th/7th c. by St Fíonán Lobhar. The remains (Nat. Mon.) include the stump of a Round Tower and the ruins of a small nave-and-chancel church ('Aghadoe Cathedral'). The oldest parts of the latter are the W. gable, with Romanesque doorway (incorrectly reassembled), and the E. gable (two Transitional lights). These are relics of a church commenced in 1158 by Olaf Mór O Donoghue. In the nave are an ogham stone and a medieval slab with a *Crucifixion*. The site commands a delightful view of the lakes and mountains.

1 m. W., to the N. of the Killorglin road, in Fossa, is the Church of Christ, Prince of Peace (1977), by Liam McCormick and Partners, with a lovely view behind the altar to the mountains around Killarney. Furnishings are by Helen Moloney (doors), Imogen Stuart (lectern, sedilia and altar), John Behan (tabernacle), Patrick Pye (murals in Blessed Sacrament chapel), and Nell Murphy (*Mother and Child, Good Shepherd* and Stations of the Cross).

$5\frac{1}{2}$ m. W. is Beaufort bridge. The chief seat of Mac Carthy Mór, Pallis Castle, stood close to a ringfort a few hundred yds NNE. – $1\frac{1}{4}$ m. S., in a beautiful 3,000 acre demesne with exotic trees, shrubs, and plants, is Dunloe Castle, a modernized O Sullivan Mór stronghold. In a field near the avenue, close to an ancient cemetery and Tobar Chríost, are seven ogham stones which had been used as building material by the makers of a souterrain. – 2 m. S. is the famous Gap of Dunloe, a narrow, 4 m. defile (impassable by cars) through Mac Gillycuddy's Reeks, with fine views. Ponies may be hired at Kate Kearney's Cottage, a tavern called after a celebrated local beauty of the early 19th c., who sold poteen to tourists. $4\frac{1}{2}$ m. SW. of Beaufort bridge is Gortboy school, the accepted starting-point for the ascent of Carrauntuohil, Ireland's highest mountain (3,414 ft). In clear weather the panorama from the summit is magnificent.

KILLEIGH, Co. Offaly (Map 3, E5), is a village on the Mountmellick (9 m.)–Tullamore (5 m.) road.

Killeigh takes its name from Cell Achid, a celebrated monastery founded by St Sinchell the Elder (d. 549). In the 12th c. it became a Priory of Canons Regular of St Augustine. The exterior of the Protestant Chapel-of-Ease embodies obscured medieval fragments of the nave of the Augustinian church.

It was at Killeigh that, on St Sinchell's Day, 1433, Margaret, daughter of Tadhg O Carroll of Éile and wife of An Calbhach Mór O Conor Faly, gave one of her celebrated festivals to 2,700 exponents of the 'arts of Dán or poetry, musick, and Antiquitie'. (The other was at Rathangan, Co. Kildare, 15 August 1433).

KILLESHANDRA, Co. Cavan (Map 2, C5), is a small market town and angling centre to the W. of Lough Oughter, on the road from Longford (20 m.) to Belturbet (10 m.).

The Protestant church was built in 1688 by Lord Southwell. In the S. transept is a good Jacobean-type doorway.

4 m. N., in Kildallen, on the way to Ballyconnell ($8\frac{1}{2}$ m.), was the home of the ancestors of Edgar Allan Poe (1809–49).

KILLORGLIN, Co. Kerry (Map 5, E3), a small market town and angling centre (River Laune) on the Tralee (16 m.)–Cahersiveen (25 m.) road, is best known for its annual Aonach an Phuic – Poc Fair (10–12 August inclusive). The feature of the fair is the merrymaking connected with the Poc, a large, beribboned, white, male goat. On the evening of Gathering Day (10 August), the goat is escorted with triumphant revelry to the market-square where it is hoisted aloft to preside over the trafficking in cattle, sheep, and horses until the evening of Scattering Day (12 August), when it is lowered from its perch and escorted away. The origin of the custom is uncertain.

The town grew up around Castle Conway, alias Killorglin Castle, an advance post (1215) of the Anglo-Norman Fitzgeralds confided to the Knights Hospitaller.

$1\frac{1}{2}$ m. N. is Ballykissane Pier, where, in 1916, a car with Volunteers going to meet Sir Roger Casement (*see p. 44*) and the German arms-ship *Aud*, plunged into the sea, so wrecking the enterprise. A monument commemorates those who died.

4 m. SE., close to the river, is the 16th c. tower (Nat. Mon.) of the Murray castle of Ballymalis.

3 m. SE., in Kilcoolaght, is an ogham stone (Nat. Mon.).

KILLUCAN, Co. Westmeath (Map 3, F2), is a village on the Trim (16 m.)–Mullingar (8 m.) road. St Etchenn's Protestant church stands on an ancient site and has a good medieval font basin. A two-light window *The Good Shepherd and the Good Samaritan* is by Sarah Purser (1926).

300 yds S. of the church is the shaft of a roadside, 17th c. John O Melaghlin memorial cross; and fragments of other wayside crosses of 1531 and 1604 respectively. 500 yds further S., in Rathwire (Ráth Ghúaire), is a motte-and-bailey, with considerable foundations of a stone castle in the bailey, probably built by Hugh de Lacy for his brother Robert. On 14 August 1210, King John's campaign against the de Lacys brought him to Rathwire. Cathal Crovderg O Conor of Connacht met him there by appointment, but their negotiations produced no agreement, as Cathal had failed to bring his son, Aedh, to John as a hostage.

KILLYBEGS, Co. Donegal (Map 8, C6), is a village on the Donegal (17 m.)–Glencolumbkille (13 m.) road. It is an important herring-fishing station. The well-known hand-tufted Donegal carpets are made there.

In the Catholic church is preserved the gravestone of Niall Mór MacSweeney, found near Banagh Castle (*see p. 172*).

3 m. NNE., in Carricknamoghill, is a court-tomb.

Killyleagh Castle, Co. Down.

Less than 1 m. WNW., in Cashelcummin, is another.

1½ m. S., beside the road, in Drumanoo, is a court-tomb chamber.

4½ m. WSW., in Bavan, is a remnant of a court-tomb. In Shalwy, next townland to the W., is a ruinous court-tomb. In Croaghbeg, the townland W. of that again, is a well-preserved court-tomb. Excavations at these three tombs produced Neolithic flint artefacts and pottery.

KILLYLEAGH, Co, Down (Map 1, M9), on the W. shore of Strangford Lough, 19 m. SE. of Belfast and 6 m. NE. of Downpatrick, is noteworthy for the interesting castle, belonging to the Hamilton Rowan family, which crowns the remains of an Anglo-Norman motte-and-bailey. In the 13th/14th c. the early castle was replaced by one of stone, represented by the SW. tower and adjacent parts of the existing structure. Castle and lands were sold in 1610 to Sir James Hamilton, who in 1625 enclosed the bailey by the stone wall which still stands. After damage caused by the Parliamentary forces in 1648, Henry Hamilton, 2nd Earl of Clanbrassil, restored the castle in 1666 and, extending it towards the E., built the SE. tower, his architect being James Robb. To this restoration belong also the parapet of the bailey walls, the square towers at either end of the S. bailey wall, and the subterranean dome and access-passage of the bailey draw-well. In 1850–62 the castle, having been derelict for many years, was restored and given its Rhenish aspect. Archibald Hamilton Rowan (1757–1834), a founder member of the Northern Whig Club, Belfast (1790), and Secretary of the Dublin Committee of the United Irishmen, was the son and heir of Gawin Hamilton of Killyleagh.

Sir Hans Sloane (1660–1753), a founder of the British Museum, was a native of Killyleagh.

KILMACDUAGH, Co. Galway (Map 6, G3), 3 m. SW. of Gort, was one of the greater early monasteries of Connacht (Nat. Mons.). It takes its name from the 6th c. founder, St Colmán mac Duach. According to legend, King Gúaire Aidhne miraculously discovered his kinsman saint in the Keelhilla hermitage. Impressed by his sanctity, he offered him the site for a monastery. The saint decided to leave the choice of site to Providence. One day, as he journeyed through a great wood, his girdle fell to the ground. This the saint took to be a sign from Heaven, and there he built his monastery, Kilmacduagh. At the 12th c. reformation Kilmacduagh became the see of a diocese corresponding to the lordship of Uí Fiachrach Aidhne.

The W. part of the nave of the cathedral is a small 10th/11th c. structure which was lengthened E. in the 12th c., acquired a N. transept in the 14th/15th c. and a S. transept (Lady Chapel), a new chancel, and a sacristy in the 15th. The original trabeate doorway can be discerned in the W. gable. In the N. transept are rude 17th c. carvings, *Crucifixion* and *St Colman*.

The fine 11th/12th c. belfry (112 ft), the Round Tower, inclines from the perpendicular.

Labbamacduagh, the traditional burial place of St Colmán, was SW. of the cathedral; its position is marked by the grave of Bishop French (1852).

John the Baptist's Church is a small, featureless ruin NNE. of the cathedral.

Templemurry, St Mary's Church, is a small, early-13th c. ruin ENE. of the cathedral.

The Glebe House, or the Abbot's House, is a 14th/15th c. tower-house N. of the cathedral, recently reconstructed.

O Hyne's Monastery lies NW. of the Glebe House. It was a small, late-12th c. or early-13th c. monastery of Augustinian canons, laid out on the orthodox European plan. The original Transitional features (grouped shafts and columns of chancel arch, E. window, etc.) are of the very high quality characteristic of Western Transitional work.

2¾ m. SW., by the roadside E. of Boston, Co. Clare, are the remains of Cloondooan Castle, one of the strongest in Thomond, and wrecked by the English in 1586.

KILMACRENAN, Co. Donegal (Map 1, B4), which gives its name to the parish, is now only a small village on the Leannan River, at the junction of roads from Letterkenny (7 m.) Rathmelton (16 m.), Milford (5½ m.), and Creeslough (9 m.). It derives its name, Cill mhac nÉnáin, Church of the Sons of Énán, from an early ecclesiastical foundation of which the O Friels were hereditary erenachs. St Columcille was fostered there by the priest, Cruithneachán. The saint later founded a monastery at the Termon of Kilmacrenan where Red Hugh O Donnell was elected successor to his father in 1592.

About 500 yds N. a roadway bisects an old graveyard believed to occupy the site of Columcille's monastery. To one side of the road is the site of a church; to the other, the ruins of a Franciscan Tertiary friary established, seemingly after 1536, by Manus O Donnell.

2¼ m. E., in Letter, is Giants Grave, a large court-tomb.

2 m. W. Carraig an Dúin, Doon Rock, rises from the moorland. At its S. end is the stone where, according to tradition, each succeeding O Donnell was inaugurated by the O Friel erenach of Kilmacrenan.

6 m. SW., on a hill-slope 1 m. E. of beautiful Gartan Lough, is Church Hill, a small angling resort. Gartan was the birthplace of St Columcille (A.D. 521), who is the focus of an interpretative centre there, opened in 1988. A flagstone 2½ m. W. of Church Hill, in Lacknacoo on the W. side of the lake, is said to mark the precise spot. (Nearby is a modern commemorative cross.) About 1 m. N. of the stone, in Churchtown, are remains of St Columcille's Chapel and of the 'Abbey'; also two stone crosses which mark the reputed site of Columcille's first foundation; this was one of the principal burial-places of the O Donnells of Tír Chonaill; the O Nahans were hereditary erenachs.

7 m. W. is Glenveagh National Park, an oasis in the midst of a wilderness. It is centred around a castle built by the Adair family *c.* 1870, to the design of John Townsend Trench. The castle and gardens were donated to the State by their American owner, Henry McIlhenny, in 1983. The Park, opened in 1984, has an interpretative centre and guided tour of the castle (uninspiring contents).

2 m. NW. is the Derek Hill Gallery, housing the collection of Derek Hill (b. 1916), a painter associated with TORY ISLAND. The Gallery forms part of the buildings of his former home, which he donated to the nation along with his art collection.

KILMACTHOMAS, Co. Waterford (Map 4, G5), is a village on the Waterford (16 m.)–Dungarvan (13 m.) road.

Tyrone Power (1797–1841), actor and comedian, was a native of Kilmacthomas. The poets Tadhg Gaelach Ó Súileabháin (1715–95) and Donnchadh Rúa Mac Conmara lived in the village for some years.

2 m. NE. is Newtown churchyard, burial-place of Donnchadh Rúa Mac Conmara.

KILMACTRANNY, Co. Sligo (Map 7, L3), is a village between Loughs Arrow and Skean, on the road from Ballyfarnan (3 m.) to Boyle (8 m.).

Near the ancient churchyard is a 17th c. stone cross (plain).

2½ m. NNE. are the remains of Shancoe Church. St Patrick founded a church there, and in the later Middle Ages there was a branch of the Duignans seated there. One of the sources of Mícheál Ó Cléirigh's recension of the *Book of Invasions* was *The Book of the Duignans of Shancoe*. Shancoe was the home of the eminent scribe Lame David Duignan (d. 1696), who is buried at Ballindoon (*see p. 274*). 1½ m. NW. of Shancough Church is Mounttown, formerly Knockmore, where Charles O Conor of Bellanagare, noted Irish scholar and antiquary, was born.

1½ m. NW., in Highwood, are remains of the Premonstratensian house of Athmoy, a cell of Trinity Abbey, Lough Key (*see p. 81*). 1 m. N., in Moytirra East, is a four-chambered court-tomb (Nat. Mon.). In Moytirra West are remains of the round cairn with a wedge-tomb which produced Bell Beaker pottery. The Moytirra townlands preserve the name of Magh Tuireadh, Plain of Pillars, celebrated in early Irish mythological and historical tradition as the scene of two victorious battles for the Túatha Dé Danann. The medieval literati shifted the scene of the second battle to the vicinity of CONG, Co. Mayo.

2 m. NW., in Carrickglass, is a fine portal-tomb with a 10-ton capstone.

KILMAGANNY, Co. Kilkenny (Map 4, H3), is a village on the Kells (6 m.)–Carrick-on-Suir (10 m.) road, at the foot of the Walsh Mts.

In Rossenan Demesne, to the E. of the village, are fragmentary remnants of Castle Hale, chief seat of Walsh, Lord of the Mountain, down to Cromwellian times (*see also p. 186*). Walter Walsh (d. 1619), was the subject of a well-known *caoine* by his poet son, Seán Breathnach (1580–1660).

2 m. SW., in the ancient churchyard of Lamoge, are two ogham stones.

KILMAINE, Co. Mayo (Map 7, G7), is a poor hamlet on the Headford (9 m.)–Ballinrobe (5 m.) road via Shrule. The district is rich in small tumuli and in ringforts of earth and of stone.

¾ m. N., in Raunaskeera North, is a small ringfort, Raheenagooagh, with souterrain, where, apparently, the last MacWilliam Íochtair was inaugurated, 1595.

KILMALLOCK, Co. Limerick (Map 5, L1), is a small market town on the E. road from Limerick (20 m.) to Ráthluirc, alias Charleville (6 m.).

The place takes its name from a monastery founded by St Mo-Cheallóg (d. 639/656).

The town itself was a creation of the Anglo-Normans, most notably of the White Knights and the Desmond FitzGeralds. Fortified in 1375, it was sacked for three days by Sir James Fitzmaurice and others in 1570. In 1583 the Earl of Desmond and his countess were surprised in the depths of winter by the English, and only escaped by spending the night up to their necks in the river. In 1645 Lord Castlehaven used the castle (King's Castle) as a Confederate Catholic arsenal, but the town never really recovered after the Cromwellian wars.

The modern parish church of SS Peter and Paul is a good Gothic-Revival building (1879–89) by J.J. McCarthy.

Nearby, at the junction of Sheares St and Sarsfield St, is 15th c. King's Castle (disfigured, Nat. Mon.).

In Orr St, on the N. side of the town, are the remains (Nat. Mon.) of the collegiate parish Church of SS Peter and Paul, a building of the 13th-15th c. In 1600 this church was the scene both of the humiliating submission of Hugh O Neill's 'Súgán' Earl of Desmond to Elizabeth I, and of the famous Protestant service which led to the rejection by the townsfolk of the unhappy 15th Earl, an English puppet. The belfry at the W. end of the N. aisle has been claimed as the truncated Round Tower of a pre-Norman foundation. Inside the church are interesting 17th c. monuments, including a cadaver effigy of Maurice FitzGerald (d. 1635). Aindrias Mac Craith (An Mangaire Súgach) and Séamus Ó Cinnéide, two well-known 18th c. poets, lived in the town.

The outstanding monument of Kilmallock is the Dominican Friary on the N. bank of the little Loobagh River. It was founded *c.* 1291 by one of the FitzGeralds; it was restored and enlarged in the 14th and 15th c. The remains (Nat. Mon.) include portions of the claustral buildings as well as of the fine church (choir, bell tower, nave with S. aisle, and aisled S. transept). The choir has a splendid, 13th c. five-light W. window, the transept a rich, reticulated window of the 15th c. The monuments include that (broken) of Edmund Fitzgibbon

King's Castle, Kilmallock, Co. Limerick.

(1552–1608), last of the White Knights and betrayer of the 'Súgán' Earl of Desmond.

In Emmet St is Blossom's Gate, sole survivor of the medieval town's four gates.

1 m. SW. is Ash Hill Towers (Major S. Johnson), an 18th c. house castellated in 1833. One handsome Georgian elevation survives; also some Adam-style stucco.

1 m. NW., in Tankardstown South, excavations in 1986 unearthed the foundations of Ireland's earliest-known Neolithic house, dating from the 4th millennium B.C.

KILMESSAN, Co. Meath (Map 3, I2), is a village on the Dunshaughlin (7 m.)–Bective (6 m.) road. There are remains of a motte. In the church is a 1915 window by Michael Healy. The library in the former Protestant church houses some local bygones.

KILMORE QUAY, Co. Wexford (Map 4, L6), is a seaside village near Crossfarnoge Point at the E. end of Ballyteige Bay. It is noted for its lobsters and its deep-sea fishing. It is also the port of departure for the SALTEE ISLANDS.

½ m. N. is Ballyteige Castle (15th/16th c.) with well-preserved, high-walled bawn and a tall tower (in partial use).

KILREA, Co. Londonderry (Map 1, H5), is a small town on the River Bann, 5 m. SE. of Garvagh. Although laid out and built by the Mercers' Company of London at the Plantation, the earliest surviving structures date from the 19th c.

KILRUSH, Co. Clare (Map 6, D7), is a small port and manufacturing town on the N. shore of the Shannon estuary, 27 m. SW. of Ennis.

1½ m. offshore is Scattery Island (Inis Chathaigh). In the 6th(?) c., St Seanán founded a monastery there. It suffered much from Viking raiders and 10th c. Viking settlers. At the 12th c. reformation the monastery church was made the see of a short-lived diocese. The remains (Nat. Mons.) comprise: in cemetery near landing place, 15th (?) c. Church of the Dead; 200 yds NW., the site of Seanán's monastery with: remnants of the enclosing cashel; the Collegiate Church of SS Mary and Seanán, alias the Cathedral (a much altered, pre-Romanesque church); a small church which had a rich, Romanesque chancel arch of *c.* 1180; a Round Tower; W. of the monastery, Seanán's Well; 150 yds N. of the monastery, Seanán's Church (a much altered, fragmentary, little nave-and-chancel church) and an early gravestone inscribed OR[ŌIT] DO MOENACH AITE MOGROIN and OR[ŌIT] DO MOINACH ('A prayer for Moenach, tutor of Mogrón, a prayer for Moenach, tutor of Mogrón, a prayer for Moinach'); 250 yds SW. of the monastery, fragments of pre-Romanesque Church of the Hill of the Angels. Pebbles from Scattery were believed to protect the bearer against shipwreck, and new boats were sailed *deiseal*, or sunwise, around the island.

3 m. E. is the coal-fired electricity generating station of Moneypoint.

5 m. E., in the graveyard of ruined Killimer parish church, is the grave of the Colleen Bawn (*see p. 220*) whose murdered body was washed ashore there. Gerald Griffin based his novel, *The Collegians*, on her story; and Boucicault's play and Benedict's opera, *The Lily of Killarney*, were adapted from it. – 200 yds. SW. is the car-ferry to Tarbert (sailings on the hour during daylight).

KINGSCOURT, Co. Cavan (Map 2, G6), is a village on the Navan (19 m.)–Shercock (8 m.) road.

St Mary's Parish Church has three two-light windows (*Annunciation, Crucifixion,* and *Ascension*) and one three-light window (*Apparition at Fatima*) by Evie Hone (1947–8). The *Ascension* was one of the artist's favourite works, and is an outstanding example of contemporary Irish glass. There is also a three-light rose window by Patrick Pollen, and three (*St Ernin, St Brigid* and *The Virgin and Child*, 1988) by Margaret Becker.

KINLOUGH, Co. Leitrim (Map 8, D8), is a village on the Donegal-Leitrim border, 6 m. SW. of Ballyshannon and ½ m. W. of Lough Melvin.

2 m. SE., on an island near the lake shore, are the ruins of Rosclogher Castle (late-15th c.)

8 m. SE., at the S. end of the lake, are the last remnants of the medieval parish church of Rossinver, of which St M'Aodhog is likely to have been the founder. There are two early cross-inscribed slabs there.

KINNEGAD, Co. Westmeath (Map 3, F3), is a market village at the junction of the Dublin (39 m.)–Athlone (36 m.) and Dublin-Mullingar (11 m.) roads.

5 m. NE. is the Church of the Assumption, Killyon, a student essay (1954–7) by James Fehily. The interior has been quite spoilt with bad statuary, altar cloths, etc.

1¾ m. E. are the remains of Ardnamullan Castle.

4 m. E. is Clonard. 600 yds NE. of the main road, on the E. side of the Trim road, the Protestant church marks the site of the celebrated monastery founded in 515, in what was then Leinster, not Meath, territory, by St Finnian (d. 549), bishop and abbot. Later legend made St Finnian the 'tutor of the saints of Ireland' and in particular of the 'Twelve Apostles of Ireland', i.e. of the foremost monastic founders of the 6th c. Clonard grew to be one of the pre-eminent monasteries of ancient Ireland, its school being among the first half-dozen. The episcopal monastery survived many burnings and sackings during the 9th–12th c., and *c.* 1174 became the see of the diocese of Meath, newly constituted by Bishop Echtighern Mac Maóil-Chiaráin from the ancient petty bishoprics of Clonard, Kells, Ardbraccan, Slane, Trim, and Duleek. In 1201, the first Anglo-Norman bishop transferred the see to TRIM and the ancient abbey lost its Gaelic character; but as St Peter's Priory (Augustinian) it survived until the Dissolution. The ruins were swept away centuries ago, and the sole surviving relic of medieval Clonard is the excellent 15th c. octagonal, sculptured font in the Protestant church. The figure subjects include *The Flight into Egypt, The Baptism of Christ, St Peter, St Finnian* (?), and other saints. In 1182 Hugh de Lacy built a castle near the monastery (*see p. 297*), of which the conspicuous motte survives (W. of the Trim road).

3 m. SW. of Clonard, on the left bank of the Boyne, are the remains of Ticroghan Castle, alias Queen Mary's Castle, and its 17th c., enclosing star fort. After Cromwell's sack of Drogheda in 1649, the Royalist commander in Ireland, Ormonde, retired to Ticroghan from Trim. The following year the castle was stubbornly defended by Lady Fitzgarret against the Parliamentarian colonels Reynolds and Hewson. According to legend, the attackers were about to withdraw when they noticed that the defenders, short of ammunition, were firing silver bullets. The assault was renewed and the castle captured.

3 m. W., beside the old Galway road, is the small, ancient churchyard of Clonfad (Clúain fota Baítán Aba). It marks the site of a monastery founded by St Etchen, the bishop who is said to have ordained St Columcille. In the churchyard are the upper part and socket of an unfigured High Cross and a fragment of a smaller cross. A new cross (1958) was erected at the nearby Bishop's Grave to commemorate St Etchen.

KINNITTY, Co. Offaly (Map 3, C6), is a village on the Birr (8 m.)–Mountmellick (16 m.) road. To the S. and E. rise the Slieve Bloom hills, which offer the driver delightful scenery and with the points of interest marked by special signposts. The Protestant church in the village has a curious cross-inscribed stone in the porch, and stained glass windows by Catherine O Brien (*Good Shepherd*, 1905) and Ethel Rhind (*Martha, Mary Magdalene Washing Christ's Feet; The Seven Gifts of the Holy Spirit*, all 1908).

1¼ m. NE. is 19th c. Castle Bernard, now the property of the Department of Forestry. On the terrace is the shaft of a High

Cross (Nat. Mon.) whose figure carvings include a *Crucifixion* on one face and an *Adam and Eve* on the other. The inscriptions on the base of the shaft suggest that the cross was erected by the High King Maelsechlaill (846–862), and perhaps carved by an artificer named Colman. It is probably a relic of the monastery founded in Kinnitty in the 6th/7th c. by St Finán the Crooked, a disciple of St Brendan of Clonfert.

1½ m. NNW., on the N. bank of the Camcor in Ballincur, is a fragment of the head of a High Cross, with a *Crucifixion* on one face, probably a survivor of the monastery founded by St Bárrind in the 6th c.

KINSALE, Co. Cork (Map 5, L7), is a charming, decayed, old seaport on the Bandon estuary, alias Kinsale Harbour, 16 m. SSW. of Cork and 12 m. SE. of Bandon.

The town traces its origins to the Anglo-Normans, and 1334/5 the town received its first royal charter, the so-called Constitution of Kinsale, from Edward III.

During the Middle Ages Kinsale was a place of small consequence, and not until 1601 did it achieve its place in Irish history. In September of that year a Spanish fleet, with 3,814 infantry on board, put into Kinsale. The town and the de Courcy castles of Ringrone and Castle Park were quickly seized, and the Spaniards sat down to await the arrival of Irish assistance from distant Ulster. The English Lord Deputy, Mountjoy, promptly blockaded the town and harbour, but the Spaniards held out stubbornly. Early in December O Neill and O Donnell arrived from Ulster and blockaded the English army in its turn, soon reducing it to sore straits. Pressed by the Spanish commander, Don Juan de Aguila, and by O Donnell, O Neill consented to a surprise attack at dawn on Christmas Eve. The plan was betrayed; part of the Irish army lost its way; de Aguila did nothing. Instead of attacking, the Irish army was itself attacked, and the anticipated triumph turned into an overwhelming disaster. Hugh O Neill's heroic nine-year struggle was, in effect, at an end. On 2 January 1602, Kinsale was once more in English hands.

James II landed at Kinsale, 12 March 1689, to commence his abortive campaign for the recovery of his throne. From Kinsale, too, he sailed to lasting exile after the Battle of the Boyne, the following year.

In the 17th and 18th c. Kinsale was an important British naval base. For centuries, too, it was a stronghold of the English, Protestant colony in W. Cork. (No Irish, no Catholics, were allowed to settle within the walls until the close of the 18th c., and the first post-Reformation Catholic church was not erected until 1809.)

The town is sited on the slope of Compass Hill, its attractive Georgian houses terraced into the hillside. In Church St is the Protestant parish Church of St Multo, alias Multose. This incorporates much of the fabric of an early-13th c. church, which consisted of chancel, aisled nave of four bays, short N. transept, and NW. tower. Medieval additions included the extension of the N. aisle and the addition of transepts on the N. (Southwell Aisle) and S. (Chapel of the Blessed Virgin, now roofless; built in 1550 by Geoffrey Galway, merchant) of the nave. The church suffered repeatedly from mutilation at the

Charles Fort, Kinsale.

hands of the 17th-19th c. 'restorers'. In the N. face of the tower is a fragment of a Transitional window. In the porch are preserved the town stocks (18th c.); also a wooden tablet commemorating Thomas Chudleigh of Kinsale, who made the prefabricated gunboats or floating batteries for the bombardment of Ross Castle, Killarney, 1650 (*see p. 220*). Inside the church may be seen a 17th (?) c. font and some late-medieval monuments, including a 16th/17th c. *Crucifixion* panel from the Chapel of the Blessed Virgin Mary. The church has a number of good stained glass windows by Catherine O Brien.

To the E. of St Multo's, in tiny Market Sq., is the New Tholsel or Courthouse, an interesting decayed structure of 1706, which now serves as a local museum.

In Cork St is a 16th c. tower house (Nat. Mon.) called Desmond Castle or the French Prison. (The latter name recalls that French prisoners-of-war were incarcerated there in Napoleonic times.) Above the town are Sir Robert Southwell's alms houses of 1682.

1¼ m. ESE., via Scilly (the fishermen's quarter of Kinsale), is Summer Cove, a popular bathing resort. A short distance S., on Rinncurran, are the massive ruins of Charles Fort (Nat. Mon.), principal fortification of the harbour. The fort was built *c.* 1677 to the design of Sir William Robinson, architect of the Royal Hospital, Kilmainham (*see p. 156*). Many alterations and additions were made in the course of the 18th and 19th c., and the barracks were occupied continuously down to the British evacuation in 1922. The fort was then burned down by Republican Irregulars.

Since 1977, a bridge connects the town with Ringrone, a promontory projecting from the S. side of the harbour. In 1261 (Finghin) Mac Carthy Mór, victor at the battle of Callann near Kenmare, was routed and slain at Rinn Róin by Milo de Courcy; he was thereafter known as Finghin of Rinn Róin. On the promontory are the sadly dilapidated ruins of Old Fort, alias James's Fort (Nat. Mon.), named after James I. It was built (1601–3) to the design of the celebrated English engineer Paul Ive (Ivy). Later in the c. it was remodelled by Sir William Robinson (*see* Charles Fort, *above*). At the centre of the fort are remains of Castle Park (de Courcys), which was stormed by John Churchill's Williamites, 3 October 1689. A covered way leads NE. from the castle to a ruined blockhouse battery at the tip of the promontory. William Penn of Pennsylvania was Clerk of the Admiralty at James's Fort, his father being Governor of the town and fortress, and Victualler of the Royal Navy. ¾ m. SW. of the fort, in Castlelands, are remains of Ringrone Castle (de Courcys) and church.

Kylemore Abbey, Co. Galway.

10 m. S. is Old Head of Kinsale. At the neck of the peninsula are the remains of a 15th c. de Courcy (Mac Pádraig) castle. Nearby, on the highest point of the head (259 ft), are remains of a signal station erected during the Napoleonic wars. The *Lusitania* was torpedoed 10 m. S. of the Head in 1915, with the loss of more than 1,500 lives. The sinking helped to bring the United States into the war against Germany.

7 m. SW. is Ballinspittle. Less than ½ m. W. of the village, in Ballycatteen, is a fine trivallate ringfort. Excavation uncovered traces of wooden houses, and the finds, including sub-Roman pottery from the Frankish area, dated the occupation to the period around A.D. 600.

KINVARA, Co. Galway (Map 6, G3), is a market and sea-fishing village at the SE. corner of Galway Bay, 6 m. SW. of Kilcolgan, 5 m. WSW. of Ardrahan, and 13 m. E of Ballyvaghan.

Francis A. Fahy (1854–1935), ballad writer, was a native of Kinvara. His popular *Ould Plaid Shawl* is set

Not far from old Kinvara in the merry month of May.

½ m. ENE., on an almost isolated rock, is Dungory Castle, a small 16th c. O Hynes castle with six-sided bawn (wall a 1642 re-building); it was for a time a residence of the Martyns of Tullira (*see p. 45*); refurbished by Christabel, Lady Ampthill in the 1960s, it is now owned by the Shannon Free Airport Development Co., who host banquets there.

8½ m. SW. (via Funshinmore and Cappaghmore crossroads), under the cliffs of Slievecarrin in Keelhilla, is the site of St Colmán mac Duach's hermitage. There, according to medieval legend, he spent seven years, attended only by one mass-server. At the end of that he had food for neither himself nor his attendant. He placed his trust in Providence, however, and all was well. Just at that moment the Easter banquet was being served to Colmán's kinsman, King Gúaire, in his fortress at Dungory (*above*). The dishes were miraculously borne aloft and carried away through the air. The king and his retinue followed them, and so discovered the saint. Impressed by his sanctity, Gúaire offered him the site for a monastery (*see p. 224*). In proof of the story, the 'tracks' of the royal cavalcade across the limestone survive today as Bóthar na Mias, the Road of the Dishes (weatherings in the limestone exposures). The remains at Keelhilla comprise: St Mac Duach's Bed, a 'cave' (formed by fallen blocks of limestone); St Mac Duach's Church, Tobermacduagh, and a Penitential Station, all together to the N. of the Bed, and ¼ m. SE., the Grave of St Mac Duach's Servant.

2¼ m. NW. is Durras House, now an An Óige youth hostel. It was for a time the property of Count Florimond de Basterot (1836–1904), friend of Lady Gregory and W.B. Yeats. It was there that the Gregory-Yeats project for a national theatre was born, and there too that de Basterot introduced his cousin, Edward Martyn of Tullira (*see p. 45*), to Guy de Maupassant, Maurice Barrès, and Paul Bourget.

KNOCKTOPHER, Co. Kilkenny (Map 4, H3), is a village on the Thomastown (5 m.)–Waterford (20 m.) road.

Matthew fitz Griffin, seneschal of Leinster, built a castle there at the Anglo-Norman conquest. In 1312 the place passed to the Butlers, who made it one of their principal seats.

Only the W. tower (Nat. Mon.) and a few fragments including a 14th c. double effigy survive from the medieval church of St David. SE. of the churchyard is Knocktopher Moat, motte of fitz Griffin's castle. Knocktopher House, on the opposite side of the road, incorporates the tower, kitchen, etc., of the important Carmelite friary of St Saviour; it was founded in 1356 by James Butler, 2nd Earl of Ormond.

1¼ m. SSE. is Ballyhale. The parish church of St Martin of Tours incorporates the 'Castle of Ballyhale', actually the W. tower of the medieval church of Kiltorcan; two medieval fonts serve as holy-water stoups.

1½ m. SSW. is well-preserved Kilcurl Castle, a Purcell stronghold in the 16th and 17th c. 2½ m. S., in the Kilkeasy, are the ruins of a church with remains of a fine Romanesque doorway.

1 m. SW., in Ballyboodan, is an ogham stone.

1¼ m. W., in Sheepstown, are the ruins of a 12th c. church (Nat. Mon.). 2 m. SW., in Aghaviller, the stump of a Round Tower, ruins of a church (Nat. Mons.), and a holy well mark the site of an ancient monastic foundation to St Brendan of BIRR.

KYLEMORE, Co. Galway (Map 7, C8), one of the best-known beauty spots of Connemara, is situated in a valley which is at its best when rhododendron and fuchsia are in bloom.

On the N. shore of little Pollacappul Lough, is Kylemore Abbey, a convent (with school) of Benedictine nuns (Irish Dames of Ypres) who settled there after the First World War. The nuns treasure a captured British flag entrusted to their keeping by the Irish Brigade after the battle of Fontenoy (1745). The abbey is a great Victorian 'castle' built at enormous expense by the Liverpool merchant, Mitchell Henry, M.P. (1826–1910). To the E. is a costly Gothic church which he also erected.

L

LAMBAY ISLAND, Co. Dublin (Map 3, L2), 4 m. SE. of Rush, is a well-known bird sanctuary. The island is private property (Lord Revelstoke), permission to land must be sought from the Steward (address: Lambay Island, Rush, Co. Dublin).

A Columban monastery on the island may have been destroyed by the Vikings. After the battle of Aughrim the island was used as a place of internment for Jacobite prisoners-of-war.

Lambay Castle, Lord Revelstoke's house, which was designed by Sir Edwin Lutyens, incorporates remains of a small 15th c. castle where Archbishop James Ussher (1581–1656) wrote several of his works. Roman objects unearthed in 1927 about 500 ft to the NW. of the castle may be from graves of refugees who fled from Roman Britain in the 1st c. A.D.

LARAGH, Co. Wicklow (Map 3, K6), at the junction of Glendalough, Glendasan, Glenmacnass, the Annamoe valley, and the Clara valley, is the meeting-place of roads which traverse some of the most beautiful parts of the Wicklow Mts.

Lough Fee, Connemara.

NE. of the bridge over the Glenmacnass River is Laragh Barracks, one of the posts which guarded the old Military Road from Rathfarnham. The road NE. follows the pretty Annamoe valley to Lough Dan and ROUNDWOOD. That NNW. leads up Glenmacnass, along the line of the Military Road, to the Sally Gap; 4½ m. from the bridge is the waterfall which gives the valley its name.

SE. is the beautifully wooded Clara valley, down which the lovely Avonmore tumbles its way. 2½ m. S. of Derrybawn bridge are the remains of the O Byrne castle of Knockrath.

LARNE, Co. Antrim (Map 1, L6), is a manufacturing town and seaport (car-ferry service to Stranraer) 21 m. NE. of Belfast.

Edward Bruce landed at Larne in 1315 and, in 1914, Carson's Ulster Volunteers landed a cargo of German arms there in defiance of the Liberal government and its Irish Home Rule Act. The Round Tower at the harbour commemorates James Chaine, who started the Stranraer steamer service.

On the Curran, a spit of land just S. of the town, is the fragmentary Curran Castle (in State care), a small 16th(?) c. tower.

Inver (SW. part of the town) Protestant Church has two two-light windows by Wilhelmina Geddes: *SS Patrick and Columcille* (1923) and *Christ Meets Mary and Martha* (1927).

4 m. N. is Ballygalley Head (300 ft), which offers a magnificent prospect towards Gorse Craig. ½ m. W., incorporated in a hotel, is Ballygalley Castle, Ireland's best preserved 'Scottish baronial' castle, built by James Shaw of Greenock in 1625. Inland, Sallagh Braes, W. of Carncastle village, are a magnificent amphitheatre of basalt with a safe, cliff-top path; from Knockdhu, at the N. end, there are splendid views both seaward and inland. On Knockdhu is a large earthen promontory fort. 6 m. WNW of Carncastle village is Dunteige bridge, ½ m. ENE of which is Dunteige Giant's Grave, a wedge-tomb.

LAURAGH, Co. Kerry (Map 5, E6), is a small village on Kilmakilloge Bay, Kenmare River, at the junction of the Glantrasna and Glanmore valleys, 14 m. SW. of Kenmare, 6 m. NE. of Ardgroom, and 3½ m. N. of Healy Pass in an area noted for the beauty and variety of its scenery. To the NW. is the beautiful demesne of Derreen House, with its fine gardens, open to the public on certain days.

5½ m. SW., in Ardgroom townland, is Canfea stone circle (with outlier).

2½ m. W., in Cashelkeelty, are the remains of a five-stone circle beside a short stone row and the remnants of a larger circle.

2½ m. NW., overlooking the harbour to which it gives its name, is Kilmakilloge, an ancient church-site with remains of a two-period (Romanesque and earlier) church. 400 yds NE. is the holy lake, Lough Mackeenlaun, long famous for its floating tussocks. By the E. shore are the remains of the primitive Church of St Cilian (martyred at Würzburg in 689).

LECARROW, Co. Roscommon (Map 7, M8), is a hamlet on the Athlone (11 m.)–Roscommon (10 m.) road.

2½ m. E., at the NW. corner of Rinndown (Rinn Dúin) peninsula, Lough Ree, a graveyard and remains of little St John's Church preserve the memory of the medieval Hospital of St John the Baptist (Augustinian Crucifers). A short distance S. a towered wall (564 ft), with central gateway, crosses the peninsula from shore to shore. 800 yds S. of the wall an embanked ditch cuts off the tip of the peninsula. Near the W. end of this ditch are remnants of a nave-and-chancel church. Wall, ditch, and church are the sole visible relics of a town (fortified in 1251) which had grown up in the shelter of a strong English royal castle at the E. end of the ditch. The first castle there was erected *c.* 1227 by the English Justiciar, Geoffrey de Marisco, in preparation for the invasion of Connacht. The remains – in a dense thicket and scandalously neglected – comprise a polygonal castle of stone with rectangular keep (with twin-vaulted basement) incorporated in the curtain, modified in the 16/17th c. In front of the gate are remains of a bridge across the ditch. The inner gate (with portcullis) is late.

LEENAUN, alias **LEENANE**, Co. Galway (Map 7, E7), is a hamlet at the SE. corner of beautiful Killary (Harbour), 20 m. NE. of Clifden, 9 m. NW. of Maum and 18 m. SSE. of Louisburgh. There is superb scenery in the area.

Fjord-like Killary (Harbour), 8 m. long (sometime station of the British Atlantic fleet), is the drowned lower valley of the Erriff River.

3 m. NE., on the Erriff River, is Aasleagh, a waterfall.

5 m. WSW., at the foot of Garraun (1,975 ft), is lovely Lough Fee with its rhododendron-smothered island.

LEHINCH, Co. Clare (Map 6, E5), is a small seaside and golfing resort on Liscannor Bay, 19 m. NW. of Ennis. It has a good beach with sand dunes.

At the N. end of the links are the remains of Dough Castle, the property of Daniel O Brien in the mid-17th c. The sand holes here are reputed to be the haunts of Donn, the Fairy King.

LEIGHLINBRIDGE, Co. Carlow (Map 4, I1), is a small village where the Carlow (9 m.)–Muine Bheag (5 m.) road (the old highway from Dublin to the South) crosses the Barrow.

In 1181, John de Claville, a follower of Hugh de Lacy, built a castle (*see below*) to command the river-crossing, and in 1320 a stone bridge was built by Maurice Jakis, canon of Kildare Cathedral. The English Crown managed to keep control of the river crossing, but the castle was wrecked by Rory Óg O More in 1577. Rebuilt once more, it was finally demolished by the Cromwellian Col. Hewson. The remains, a 14th c. tower (Nat. Mon.), are now known as the Black Castle.

3 m. NE., at Nurney, a granite cross (Nat. Mon.) with simple ornament marks the site of an early monastery.

3 m. E. (1¼ m. SSW. of Nurney), in Agha, the remains of a church with *antae*, trabeate door, and later features mark the site of the early monastery of Achadh Urghlais.

2 m. W. is (Old) Leighlin, where a monastic church was founded in the 5th or 6th c. Under abbot Laisrén (d. 639), 'apostolic delegate' and champion of the Roman method of computing the date of Easter (*see p. 287*), it became one of the foremost monastic churches of Leinster. And so, at the 12th c. Reformation, it became the see of the diocese to which it has given its name. (The Catholic diocese is now united with Kildare, the Protestant with Ossory and Ferns.) The only relics of the older, monastic church are St Laserian's Cross and Well (in a field W. of the cathedral), and the pedestal of a cross in the churchyard. St Laserian's Cathedral (Protestant) is one of the smaller medieval Irish cathedrals. The remains are substantially those of a late-13th c. nave and chancel church with transepts and N. Chapel added later. The few surviving features of interest include a font which probably derives from a 12th c. cathedral, and a 16th c. altar-tomb which reproduces as an ornament the elaborate ribbing of the crossing vault. The four-light window of *Christ, with SS Moling, Brigid, Fiacc, Canice, Patrick, John, Paul and Laserian* is by Catherine A. O Brien.

LEITRIM, Co. Leitrim (Map 7, M4), which gives its name to the county, is a small Shannonside village on the Carrick-on-Shannon (4 m.)–Drumshanbo (15 m.) road. Some traces remain of a medieval O Rourke castle.

LEIXLIP, Co. Kildare (Map 3, J3), is a village on the Dublin (10 m.)–Maynooth (5 m.) road, at the confluence of the Liffey and the Rye Water. It takes its name – Salmon-leap, a relic of Norse Dublinshire – from the fall on the Liffey which is now harnessed by a power station.

The Protestant parish church has a medieval W. tower.

Leixlip Castle (the Hon. Desmond Guinness), is an early-18th c. house which incorporates two much altered towers etc. of a medieval castle.

St Catherine's, on the N. side of the Liffey, was designed by Francis Johnston in 1798.

1¼ m. SW. is the Wonderful Barn, a five-storey, bottle-shaped structure with external stairway, built in 1743 by Mrs Connolly of Castletown (*see pp. 104 and 206*).

LETTERFRACK, Co. Galway (Map 7, C8), is a small village beautifully situated on the Clifden (6½ m.)–Leenaun (9 m.) road, near the SE. corner of splendid Barnaderg Bay (Ballynakill Harbour). The village was founded by a 19th c. Quaker named Ellis, as one of a series of mission settlements along the N. Connemara coast.

Good bathing may be had on Barnaderg Bay and elsewhere, and the scenery in the region is very fine.

½ m. S. is the Connemara National Park, with a reception centre and two nature trails.

LETTERKENNY, Co. Donegal (Map 1, B5), cathedral town of the diocese of RAPHOE, is situated near the head of Lough Swilly, on the Derry (20 m.)–Glenties (27 m.) road. It is one of the two administrative centres of Co. Donegal (the other being Lifford).

The only building of note is St Eunan's (= Adhamhnáin's) Cathedral (1890–1901). This is a mediocre, late Gothic Revival structure (by Hague and Mac Namara) tricked out with pseudo

Irish-Romanesque details. The ten clerestory windows (1928–9) are by Harry Clarke. In the transepts are three Michael Healy windows: *Convention of Druim Ceat* (five-light, 1910), *Dallán and Conall* (two-light, 1911), and *St Helena* (two-light, 1911). The carvings which smother the arch of the crossing depict episodes from the lives of SS Adhamhnán and Columcille. The bronze statue (1929), in the churchyard, of Cardinal O Donnell is by Francis Doyle.

2 m. W., on the Glenties road, is Conwal, site of an ancient monastery, with a very ruinous medieval parish church, a holy well, and two cross-pillars with spiral, fret, swastika, and other patterns.

3 m. SW., below New Mills, is Scarriffhollis, a ford over the Swilly where, on 21 June 1650, Sir Charles Coote's Parliamentarian army destroyed the last Royalist-Catholic army in Ulster with the loss of 1,500 lives. Those officers who surrendered on promise of quarter were butchered by Coote, including Col. Henry O Neill, son of Eóghan Rúa, who was clubbed to death outside Coote's tent. Heber Mac Mahon, Bishop of Clogher and commander of the Royalist-Catholic forces, escaped, but was wounded and captured two days later, and taken to Enniskillen, where, six months afterwards, Coote hanged him 'with all the circumstances of contumely, reproach, and cruelty he could devise'.

LETTERMULLAN, Co. Galway (Map 6, C1), is a small island to the W. of GORUMNA ISLAND, with which it is linked by a road bridge. Close to the bridge are traces of a castle which was the residence of Murchadh Mac Hugh in 1584.

LIFFORD, Co. Donegal (Map 1, C6), one of the two administrative centres of Donegal, is situated on the west bank of the Foyle opposite STRABANE, 16 m. SSW. of Derry and 17 m. SE. of Letterkenny.

7 m. WSW., in Liscooley, is Donoughmore Presbyterian Church (1977) by Liam McCormick and Partners. The Communion table and lectern are by Derry O Connell, and the stained glass by Helen Moloney, who also designed the reredos hanging *The Burning Bush*.

1½ m. WNW., at Murlough, is a noteworthy church by Corr and McCormick of Derry. The stained glass is by Patrick Pollen, the Stations of the Cross and the *Virgin and Child* by his wife Nell Murphy, and the crucifix by Imogen Stuart. The statue of St Patrick and the exterior mosaics are by Oisín Kelly, and the enamelled tabernacle by Patrick McElroy. The altar is by Ray Carroll.

LIMAVADY, Co. Londonderry (Map 1, F4), is a market and administrative town situated where the Derry (17 m.)–Coleraine (14 m.) road crosses the River Roe at the mouth of the Glengiven valley. It takes its name (properly Newtown Limavady) from Leim a Mhadaigh, 'Dog's leap', the site of the principal O Cathaín castle 2½ m. S. (now situated inside the Roe Valley Country Park, which includes a museum and relics of industrial archaeology). The town was built by Sir Thomas Phillips at the time of the Plantation.

Thackeray's 'Sweet Peg of Limavady' lived in Ballyclose St. William Massey (1856–1925), Prime Minister of New Zealand, was a native. The tune of 'The Londonderry Air' or 'Danny Boy' was first collected there, in 1851, from a travelling fiddler by Miss Jane Ross.

5½ m. NE. at Largantea is Well Glass Spring wedge-tomb and nearby round cairn.

1 m. S. in Roepark Demesne (home of 18th c. William Connolly, Speaker of the Irish Parliament) is the Mullach or 'Daisy Hill', a grassy height thought to be the site of the Convention of Druim Ceatt (575) at which, among the political issues discussed, St Columcille championed the cause of the *filid* or Gaelic literati and saved them from banishment.

3 m. W. in Ballykelly are the remains of the Fishmonger's Plantation bawn and church, at Walworth, and a number of fine 18th and 19th c. buildings.

6½ m. N. in Tamlaghtard (Magilligan) is the site of an early monastery with remains of a church, mortuary house ('St Aidan's Grave') and a holy well.

LIMERICK, Co. Limerick (Map 6, I7), capital of its county and cathedral town of the diocese of Limerick, is the fourth largest city in Ireland. Situated at the head of the Shannon estuary, 13 m. ESE. of Shannon Airport, it is a seaport and manufacturing centre, as well as an important market and communications centre.

The older city falls into three principal parts: English Town, on King's Island in the Shannon; Irish Town, on the mainland to the SE.; and Newtown Pery, to the SW. of Irish Town.

The city had its origin in a Norse settlement which was established on King's Island in A.D. 922, and rapidly became a menace to the whole of Munster. In 967 King Mahon of Thomond and his celebrated brother, Brian Boru (*see p. 220*), broke the power of the Limerick Norse at the battle of Solohead, near Tipperary. Thereafter the Norse town was sacked and survived only by the grace of the Thomond kings, who valued it as a trading centre. (Hrafn, friend and informant of Ari who made voyages from Iceland to America, was a merchant of Limerick.) Muirchertach Mór O Brien, King of Munster (1086–1118) and High-King of Ireland (1101–18) as well as King of Thomond, actually made Limerick his principal seat. His grandson, Donal Mór O Brien, King of Thomond (1168–94), made the town his undoubted capital. The first recorded Bishop of Limerick, Giolla Íosa, alias 'Gilbert' (1106/7–40), took a prominent part in the 12th c. Reformation, and was Papal Legate at the National Synod of Ráth Breasail (1111). He was an Irishman, but his immediate successors down to 1190 seem to have been Hiberno-Norse. Limerick was an early objective of the Anglo-Normans, and in October 1175 was stormed by Raymond le Gros. The following spring he had to depart, whereupon Donal Mór O Brien razed the place to the ground. Thereafter Donal was able to keep the invaders at bay, and the town was rebuilt, Donal himself founding a new cathedral. But the town fell into English hands again soon after, receiving its first charter from Prince John in 1197. In 1201 John reserved to the English Crown the city and the Cantred of the Ostmen (Norse) outside the walls. Throughout the rest of the Middle Ages Limerick remained an English trading colony directly dependent on the Crown – to which it remained inflexibly loyal – but ruled by its own freemen. Despite a sacking by the Irish in 1369, and having a tribute imposed by the King of Thomond in 1466, the town continued to prosper, and by the coming of the Reformation had no fewer than 15 parochial, monastic, and other churches. In 1642 the town was captured after a siege by a Confederate Catholic force who, however, had to surrender it to Cromwell's son-in-law, Ireton, in 1651. In 1690, William of Orange attacked the town with 26,000 men. But after Patrick Sarsfield's daring cavalry raid to Ballyneety behind the Williamite lines, to destroy the approaching siege train, and the heroic defence of a great breach in the town wall (where the Williamites lost 2,000 men), William withdrew discomfited. He was more successful the following year, and the Jacobites capitulated, 3 October 1691, on terms guaranteeing minimal civil rights to the Catholic majority and permitting the fighting men to join the French service. Two weeks later a great French fleet arrived in the estuary with strong reinforcements and abundant supplies. The Jacobites stood by their bond. Not so the victors; with the Jacobite forces (who included almost the entire surviving native aristocracy and leadership) out of the way, the civil articles of the Treaty of Limerick were soon violated. In the course of the following century the city gradually recovered from its wounds, a notable development being the laying out of Newtown Pery with its well-planned streets of Georgian brick houses.

Notable Limerick names in Anglo-Irish literature are those of Gerald Griffin (1803–40), playwright and novelist (*The Collegians, The Colleen Bawn*), and Kate O Brien (1897–1974), distinguished novelist. Francis Bindon (1690?–1765) of Clooney, Co. Clare, painter, architect, and associate of Richard Cassels, was born in Limerick.

The more important relics of medieval Limerick are in English Town. In Nicholas St, to the E. of Mathew Bridge, is St Mary's Protestant Cathedral. The church was founded by Donal Mór O Brien after the fire of 1176. The original (*c.* 1180–95?) Romanesque–Transitional church was cruciform (aisleless chancel and transepts, aisled nave of four bays), plan and certain details reflecting the influence of the Cistercian architecture (Burgundian variety) current in the Ireland of that time. To this simple, austere building a bell-tower, at least nine chantry chapels, battlements, and a S. porch were added in the course of the 13th–16th c. Thereafter the Reformation, the Cromwellians, war, and 17th, 18th, and 19th c. restorers all left their marks on the cathedral which, nonetheless, has its interesting features. In the chancel are: the alleged tombstone of King Donal Mór O Brien; a 15th(?) c. slab inscribed DONOH and alleged to commemorate Bishop Donnchadh O Brien (d. 1207); the monument erected 1678 to Donnchadh O Brien, 'Great' Earl of Thomond, in place of one wrecked by the Cromwellians (it includes the remains of the effigies of the earl and his countess from the original, 1621, monument); a fragment of the 1421 tomb of Bishop Conor O Dea whose 15th c. effigy was spared by the Cromwellians only to be destroyed by 19th c. 'restorers'. In the choir (and nave) are late 15th c. stalls whose misericords are the only carved examples surviving in Ireland. In the S. transept is an excellent 15th c. Galwey–Bultingfort tomb originally polychrome; restored by Slater, it now incorporates the mensa (episcopal effigy erased) of an older tomb. The S. aisle is flanked by four chantries, the W. one (*c.* 1480) dedicated to St George. The aisle pier second from the W. has a slab with carvings of the Crucifixion, Christ and Satan, and St Michael and Satan. The N. aisle is flanked by three chantries, the latest now serving as baptistry. The largest, St Nicholas's Chapel, possibly dating from the 14th c., was restored *c.* 1490 (and by Fuller, 1869); the 1836 Bishop Jebb statue is by Bailly. The nave piers have Transitional capitals. The Romanesque W. doorway was wantonly 'restored' by Fuller in 1895, only the hood and the innermost of its four orders being left. The cathedral was again restored in 1968. In the churchyard, at the S. side of the cathedral, is the Sexten vault with medieval *Pelican in Her Piety* (symbolic of Christ the Redeemer) and *Seven-Headed Dragon* (symbolic of Antichrist).

Georgian door, Limerick City.

Close to the cathedral, on the SW., is the riverside County Court House, a Classical building of 1809 by the Limerick architects Nicholas and William Hannan (the interior was reconstructed, 1957).

Commanding Thomond Bridge, a short distance NW. of the cathedral, are the remains of King John's Castle (Nat. Mon.), a once splendid fortress of 1200 which was an integral part of the town defences. The magnificent twin-towered gatehouse, N. curtain, NW. and SW. angle towers, and S. curtain, survive in part; at the SE. angle is a fragment of a 1611 bastion which replaced the medieval angle tower there. The medieval works show various alterations. The interior was altogether spoiled by 18th–19th c. barracks and 20th c. municipal dwelling-houses (hopefully to be demolished shortly). Fragments of the town wall survive nearby at St Munchin's Church (Protestant), Church St.

E. of the castle, in the grounds of the Convent of Mercy, Convent St, are remains of the Dominican Friary of St Saviour (1227), founded by Donnchadh Cairbreach O Brien, King of Thomond, and rebuilt by James, 6th Earl of Desmond.

At the W. end of Thomond Bridge, mounted on a pedestal, is the 'Treaty Stone', on which, according to tradition, the articles of capitulation were signed in 1691.

In the grounds of St Anne's Vocational School, W. of Mary St, are the remains (Nat. Mon.) of Fanning's Castle, a late-15th c. house.

Irish Town is connected to English Town by two bridges across the Abbey River. Beyond the SE. bridge (Ball's Bridge), Broad St and John St lead SE. towards St John's Cathedral (*see below*). At the S. end of the W. bridge (Mathew Bridge) is the Custom House, an attractive building (1769, by Davis Ducart) which is unworthily maintained. (The principal front is to the river.) Rutland St leads from the bridge to Patrick St and O Connell St, main axis of Newtown Pery, the handsome Georgian town (now in decline) laid out on Pery lands outside the municipal boundary by Davis Ducart for Edmond Sexton Pery (1719–1806; Speaker of the Dublin House of Commons, 1771–85; Viscount Pery, 1785) and the Independent Citizens – heirs of the old Merchants' Guild. At the foot of Rutland St is the Town Hall, an attractive brick house built in 1805 by the Independent Citizens as the Commercial (alias Mercantile) Buildings. O Connell St terminates in the Crescent (1857 statue of O Connell by John Hogan). Close by is the Belltable Arts Centre. Further W., in Upper Henry St, is St Alphonsus's Church, a Gothic Revival essay (1858–62) by P.C. Hardwick.

SE. of O Connell St, in Pery Sq., is the People's Park with Rice Memorial Column (by the famous engineer Alexander Nimmo) commemorating the achievements of Thomas Spring-Rice (1790–1866), 1st Baron Monteagle of Brandon. Spring-Rice was a Protestant liberal lawyer who devoted himself to civic reform and justice for Catholics; he was Chancellor of the United Kingdom Exchequer, 1835–9. Also in the park are the Public Library and Art Gallery, with a collection of modern Irish paintings. Nearby, to the N., is St Saviour's Church (Dominican), a remodelling, 1860 onwards, of an 1815–16 building. Chancel, high altar, and Lady Chapel are by J.J. McCarthy. Above the Lady Altar is a 17th c. statue of Our Lady brought from Flanders in 1640. The Savings Bank nearby in Glentworth St, a little Doric temple, is by W.H. Owen, a Welsh architect who settled in Limerick.

In Henry St (N. of O Connell St) are the Franciscan church (1876 onwards, by William Edward Corbett), the 1784 Protestant Bishop's Palace (windows spoilt), and the former town house (also 1784) of the Perys, later Earls of Limerick.

On the S. side of the city, near the site of Irish Town's John Gate, is St John's Sq, with three sides of stone-fronted houses by Davis Ducart. In one of them is a good City Museum. Nearby is St John's Cathedral, a good Gothic-Revival building (1856–61) by P.C. Hardwick. The fine tower and spire are by M. and S. Hennessy of Limerick. The statue of the Virgin and Child is by John Hogan's friend, Benzoni.

N. of the cathedral, at and near St John's Hospital, are fragments of the city walls, which the Williamites unsuccessfully tried to breach in 1690.

Sarsfield Bridge leads to the Ennis Rd, where is the Church of Our Lady of the Rosary (1949–50). This temporary wooden church, by F.M. Corr and W.H.D. Mc Cormick, is the first notable modern church to have been erected in Ireland after the Second World War. The teak statue on the tower (*Our Lady of Fatima*) is by Oisín Kelly, the nearby *Annunciation* by Imogen Stuart. Over the entrance (inside) is a *Deposition from the Cross* by Andrew O Connor; this is the plaster model for the bronze now in the Tate Gallery, London. The Sanctuary figures of the *Sacred Heart* and *Our Lady* are by Yvonne Jammet. The *St Anne* is by Éamonn Costello. In the baptistry is a single-light *Baptism of Christ* by Evie Hone (1950).

On the right bank of the Shannon (via the N. Circular Rd), in the grounds of Old Church near Barrington's Pier, is ruined St Mainchín's (Munchin's) Church, better known as Kilrush (Nat. Mon.): an early church with trabeate W. door.

3½ m. N., at Ardnacrusha, is the power station of the Shannon hydro-electric scheme (1925), first step in the development of native power resources by the new Irish state.

1¼ m. E. (via Clare St), in Singland, St Patrick's Well marks the site of an early monastery whose Round Tower and church were levelled in 1766. According to legend, St Patrick baptized Cairthenn, King of Dál gCais, at the well, which is still a place of pilgrimage on 17 March. – 2 m. E., in Plassey, is the National Institute for Higher Education, the most advanced third-level institute for technological studies in the country. It houses a part of the Hunt Museum, with an important collection of Irish and other European *objets d'art* from prehistoric times to the 19th c. In the old Plassey House on the campus is the Kneafsey Gallery, a nationally important collection of self-portraits by most of the important Irish artists of this century.

3 m. SW. is Mungret, site of a monastery founded by the deacon, Neassán (d. 551), who, according to some, was a disciple of St Patrick. The monastery was one of the greatest of the early monasteries of Ireland, and the learning of its monks was proverbial. It survived every disaster, including repeated devastation by the Norse. In its heyday it had six churches; but all that now survive are: a 12th c. church with trabeate W. door; the 'Abbey', a 13th–15th c. nave-and-chancel church with dwelling tower at the W. end; and a small 13th (?) c. chapel (all Nat. Mons.). The modern Catholic church (1978) in the village is by John Kernan, with furnishings by the monks of Glenstal. 2 m. NW. of Mungret are the shattered remains of the great rock castle of Carrigogunnel built by the O Briens *c.* 1336. In August 1691, it was surrendered to the Williamites, who blew up the defences in 1698. The lower ward had a gate on the SE., a postern to the W., and a great hall at the NE. angle. In the small, paved upper ward are the remains of a great keep, a circular bastion, a long range of buildings, and a 16th c. house.

LISBURN, Co. Antrim (Map 1, K9), on the River Lagan, is a manufacturing and commercial town 8 m. W. of Belfast. The place was granted in 1609 to Sir Fulke (later Viscount) Conway, who planted it with settlers and built a castle in 1627. The town was destroyed by fire in 1707, but was quickly rebuilt and subsequently became prosperous as a centre of the linen industry – a development already stimulated by the arrival of a colony of Huguenot refugees under the leadership of Samuel Louis Crommelin (1652–1727).

The castle has disappeared, apart from a gateway (1677) in the Castle Gardens, Castle St. Across the street, the front building of the Technical College was the home of Sir Richard Wallace (1818–90), the 19th c. owner of the town and connoisseur, whose art collection can be seen in his London home, Hertford House.

Christ Church, cathedral of the Protestant diocese of Connor, was built in 1623 as a parish church and raised to cathedral status in 1662; the spire was added in 1807. The two-light window *Ruth and David* (1939) is by Catherine O Brien. Among the memorials are one (1827) to the celebrated divine Jeremy Taylor, bishop of Down and Connor 1661–7, who is buried at DROMORE; and one to Lieut. William Smith Dobbs (1780, by Edward Smyth), killed in the encounter with Paul Jones off CARRICKFERGUS in 1778. In the churchyard are Huguenot tombs.

The 18th c. Market House, with its handsome Assembly Room, has been sympathetically adapted (architect, Robert McKinstry) for use as a museum of local history. Nearby is a statue (by J.H. Foley) to John Nicholson (1821–57), hero of the Siege of Delhi, whose family had Lisburn connections. The United Irishmen Henry Munro and Bartholomew Teeling, both hanged in 1798, were natives of Lisburn.

2½ m. WSW., via the Ballinderry Road, is Lissue, a univallate ringfort (in State care) which excavation showed to have contained, in the 10th c., one large house covering the whole interior.

LISCANNOR, Co. Clare (Map 6, E5), is a small fishing village at the N. end of Liscannor Bay, 22 m. NW. of Ennis. John P. Holland (1841–1914), patriot and inventor of the submarine, was a native of Liscannor.

The castle W. of the village was an O Brien stronghold.

1 m. NE. of the village, on the seashore, is Kilmacreehy, Mac Creiche's Church, a medieval nave-and-chancel parish church. Hugh Mac Curtin (1680–1755), the antiquarian, was born and died near there.

2½ m. NW. is a 19th c. monument to Cornelius O Brien, M.P., of Birchfield. O Brien compelled his tenants to pay for it. The festival of Lughnasa was celebrated at St Brigid's Well nearby.

3 m. NW. are the Cliffs of Moher (highest point 668 ft), which rise sheer from the Atlantic. There is a magnificent view from O Brien's Tower (a disused tea house erected in 1835), 587 ft above the sea.

LISCARROLL, Co. Cork (Map 5, J2), is a village on the Buttevant (7 m.)–Drumcolliher (7 m.) road.

There are remains (Nat. Mon.) of the third largest 13th c. castle in Ireland: a quadrangular court with cylindrical angle-towers, a strong rectangular gatehouse (upper storey 15th c.) in the S. curtain, and a rectangular tower in the N. curtain. The castle was probably built by the Anglo-Norman Barrys.

LISDOONVARNA, Co. Clare (Map 6, E4), is a 'spa' (sulphur and chalybeate springs) and popular holiday resort set 400 ft above sea level in the bleak uplands of W. Clare, 8 m. N. of Ennistimon and 10 m. SW. of Ballyvaghan.

3½ m. N., in Slieve Elva, is Pollnagollum, entrance to one of the longest (4½ m.) caves in the country.

3 m. NW. is the interesting rock castle of Ballynalackan, a 15th c. O Brien stronghold: tower and well-preserved bawn.

Lismore Castle, Co. Waterford (see page 237).

Lough Gur, Co. Limerick (top, see page 239) and Croagh Patrick, Co. Mayo (see page 241).

LISMORE, Co. Waterford (Map 4, D6), is a market town beautifully sited in the celebrated Blackwater Valley, at the S. foot of the Knockmealdown Mountains. It is 13 m. S. of Clogheen, 4 m. W. of Cappoquin, 18 m. NNW. of Youghal, and 16 m. E. of Fermoy.

Lismore is famous in Irish history as the site of a double monastery founded towards the close of his life by St Carthage (d. 637/8) of Rahan (*see p. 298*). The famous Welsh saint Cadoc of Llan Carvan, and St Cathaldus, 7th c. Bishop of Tarentum in S. Italy, are said to have been trained there. Lismore was one of the strongholds of the 8th–9th c. *céle Dé* movement (*see p. 287*). In the 12th c. it was one of the leading monasteries of Munster, figured prominently in the reform movement, and, *c.* 1120, became the see of a diocese. Henry II paid a two-day visit to the Papal Legate, Bishop Gilla Críst Úa ConDoirche of Lismore, in 1171, and picked the site for an English castle. Two years later Lismore was pillaged by Anglo-Normans led by Raymond le Gros. In 1185 Prince John of England, as Lord of Ireland, erected a castle (*see below*) beside the river. In 1363 the diocese was united by Pope Urban V with that of Waterford, but it retained its own cathedral until the Reformation. (The Church of Ireland diocese is united with those of Waterford and Cashel and Emly.) In 1589 the bishop's castle was presented to Sir Walter Ralegh by the notorious pluralist, Miler Mac Grath (*see p. 77*). Ralegh sold it to Richard Boyle, 'Great' Earl of Cork (*see p. 307–8*), in 1602. In 1753 the castle passed, with the Boyle estates, to the 4th Duke of Devonshire on his marriage to Lady Charlotte Boyle.

In its heyday Lismore had, it is said, no fewer than 20 churches. Today only a few scraps remain to recall ancient greatness. Greatly altered St Carthage's Cathedral (Protestant) dates from 1633, when it was erected by the notorious Richard Boyle on the site of the ruined pre-Reformation cathedral, some fragments of which (chancel arch, S. transept windows, etc.) it incorporates. It was much rebuilt by William Robinson *c.* 1680. In it may be seen an elaborate Mac Grath tomb of 1557, with figures of *The Crucifixion, Ecce Homo, Apostles, SS Gregory the Great, Cárthach, Catherine of Alexandria, Patrick*, etc.

The imposing 'Castle', superbly sited above the Blackwater, was built by Joseph Paxton, of Crystal Palace fame, for the 6th Duke of Devonshire, but it incorporates fragments of the medieval episcopal castle. The Romanesque gateway has been purloined from some other 12th c. church. In 1814 the 'Lismore Crozier' (National Museum) and the 15th c. manuscript known as the *Book of Lismore* – an important collection of Irish saints' lives and much secular material – were discovered hidden in one of the castle walls. Richard Boyle's sons, Robert (1627–91), the chemist (formulator of 'Boyle's Law'), and Roger (1621–79), later Earl of Orrery, were born in old Lismore Castle. Adele Astaire, the dancer, who married the late Lord Charles Cavendish, lived in the existing castle for some years.

St Carthage's Church (1881–4) is a Lombardo-Romanesque structure by W.G. Doolin.

6 m. W. is Ballyduff Castle, an interesting fortified house erected in 1628 by the 'Great' Earl of Cork. 2 m. W. are the ruins of Mocollop Castle, with circular keep and square flankers. James, 6th Earl of Desmond and son of Gearóid *file* (Earl Gerald, the Gaelic poet), died there in 1462.

3 m. WNW. is Ballysaggartmore, where two romantic Gothic gateways (one a bridge over a stream) represent the only completed part of a grandiose residence planned, it is said, by Mrs Keily (alias Ussher) to outdo the castle of a brother-in-law, but which went no further when the money ran out.

LISNASKEA, Co. Fermanagh (Map 2, C4), is a village on the Clones (11 m.)–Enniskillen (11 m.) road. In the Protestant churchyard S. of the village are the ruins of Castle Balfour (Hist. Mon.), a Plantation castle with Scottish architectural details built by Sir James Balfour in 1618, and partly dismantled in 1689. In 1821 the town was bought by the 1st Earl of Erne for £82,500. In 1841 the 2nd Earl of Erne built the Cornmarket and erected there the base and part of the shaft of a High Cross brought from an early monastery; on one face is a weathered *Fall of Adam and Eve*.

½ m. NNE., in Cornashee, is the Moat, a large earthen mound probably covering a passage-tomb, where the Maguire kings were inaugurated.

5 m. NE. is Colebrooke, Brookeborough, a Classical house of 1825 by William Farrell, and ancestral home of Field Marshal Lord Alanbrooke.

1¾ m. S. in Aghalurcher, on the site of an early foundation of St Ronan's, are remains of a medieval parish church (Hist. Mon.), patronized by the Maguires. There are interesting 17th and 18th c. gravestones. Two stones from there (one showing a bishop with book and crozier) are in the Fermanagh County Museum.

LISTOWEL, Co. Kerry (Map 6, D9), is a market town on the Tarbert (11 m.)–Tralee (16 m.) road.

Bryan Mac Mahon, writer of distinction, was a schoolmaster there, while John B. Keane, the dramatist, runs a pub.

There are remains (Nat. Mon.) of a castle of the Fitzmaurices, Lords of Kerry.

5¾ m. ENE. is Knockanure. Corpus Christi Church (1963–4) is by Michael Scott and Associates. It has three works by Oisín Kelly: *Last Supper* (porch screen), *Virgin and Child*, and *Crucifix*. The tapestry Stations of the Cross were designed by Leslie Mc Weeney.

4 m. NW. is Gunsborough, birthplace of Lord Kitchener of Khartoum (1850–1916).

LIXNAW, Co. Kerry (Map 6, C9), is a village 6 m. SW. of Listowel. There are remains of The Court, a castle of the Knights of Kerry which surrendered to the Elizabethan commander, Sir Charles Wilmot, in 1602. E. of the village is a monument to John, 3rd Knight of Kerry.

3¼ m. SW., in Tonaknock, is a plain, sandstone cross (defective, Nat. Mon.).

LONGFORD, Co. Longford (Map 2, B8), on the Edgeworthstown (8¼ m.)–Strokestown (12 m.) road, is the county town of Co. Longford and the cathedral town of the Catholic diocese of Ardagh and Clonmacnois.

St Mel's Cathedral, a Classical church which Pugin denounced as 'a bad copy of that wretched compound of pagan and Protestant architecture, St Pancras New Church in London', is one of the better post-Emancipation churches in Ireland. The original architect was Joseph B. Keane. It was built intermittently between 1840 and 1893; the final form of the belfry (about 1860) being due to John Burke, that of the portico (1889–93) to George C. Ashlin. It was refurbished (1976) by Richard Hurley and Wilfrid Cantwell, with furnishings by Ray Carroll (including a fine tapestry of *The Second Coming* behind the bishop's throne) and Imogen Stuart (*The Holy Ghost* on a pillar above the baptismal font). Behind the church is St Mel's Diocesan Museum, containing a small collection of local antiquities, including the remains of St Mel's enshrined bachall.

5½ m. SW. (2¾ m. NW. of Killashee), in Ballynakill graveyard, are a number of early cross-inscribed slabs (Nat. Mons.) of the Clonmacnois type, indicating that this is the site of an early monastery.

LORRHA, Co. Tipperary (Map 6, L3), is a small village situated 6 m. N. of Borrisokane, 5 m. E. of Portumna, and 8 m. W. of Birr.

St Rúán (d. 584), disciple of Finnian of Clonard (*see p. 226*), founded a monastery there, which became one of the foremost in Munster. One of its 'wonders' was a food-giving tree, perhaps a sacred tree in heathen times. The celebrated 9th c. Stowe *Missal* (Royal Irish Academy) belonged to the old monastery of Lorrha, where it was probably written. Its metal shrine is now in the National Museum. When the *Missal* was found secreted in a wall of the O Kennedy castle of Lackeen (*see below*) *c.* 1735, no local scholar could read it. So Aindrias Mac Cruitín (*see p. 247*), the West Clare poet and *seanchaí*, was brought over for the purpose (having been first provided with a new suit, a horse, and ample 'expense' money). St Rúán's Bell is now housed in the British Museum.

The Protestant church and churchyard, at the E. end of the village, occupy the site of St Rúán's monastery. In the churchyard are the stumps and bases of two 8th/9th c. High Crosses. The church has a two-light window (*The Holy Women at the Tomb of Christ*) by Michael Healy (1918); the roofless nave has a 13th(?) c. S. doorway, inset in which is a smaller, 15th c. doorway with interesting details.

NW. of the Protestant church is the ruined church of the Augustinian priory Beatae Mariae Fontis Vivi (Nat. Mon.), with an interesting, Perpendicular doorway.

SW. of the village is the ruined church (Nat. Mon.) of a Dominican friary founded in 1269 by Walter de Burgo. The adjacent parish church occupies the site of the conventual buildings; in the gable may be seen some medieval fragments. The church was refurbished (1977) by Anthony and Barbara O Neill, with altar, ambo and sedilia by Imogen Stuart, tabernacle by Niall O Neill and wooden cross by Michael Killeen.

2¾ m. E. is the 16th c. O Kennedy castle of Lackeen: tower and large bawn (Nat. Mon.).

3 m. NNW. is the 15th c. Mac Egan Castle of Redwood, burned in 1640 (recently restored).

4 m. NE., in Rathcabbin, is the Church of Our Lady Queen of Ireland (1984) by Anthony and Barbara O Neill, with murals and stations by David King, a wooden statue of *Our Lady* by Imogen Stuart, another by Bríd ní Rinn, and ambo falls as well as a wall-hanging by Sadhbh O Neill.

LOUGH CORRIB, Co. Galway (Map 7, F–G–H 8–9), second largest lake (27,000 acres) in Ireland, is a beautiful, island-studded sheet of clear water, some 27 m. long from near Galway in the S. to the Galway-Mayo border in the N. It is famous for its large trout (Mayfly 'dapping' is a speciality).

The shores and islands abound in monuments of all periods, which are referred to under ANNAGHDOWN, CONG, GALWAY, HEADFORD, MAUM, MOYCULLEN, and OUGHTERARD.

LOUGH DERG, Co. Donegal (Map 8, F7), is a small, lonely lake in the mountains of S. Donegal. It is most readily reached from PETTIGOE, 5 m. to the S.

Lough Derg was internationally celebrated in the later Middle Ages as the place of St Patrick's Purgatory, a cave where Patrick was said to have fasted for 40 days and to have had a vision of the Otherworld. It was believed that any properly disposed pilgrim entering the cave might, by St Patrick's help, himself behold the horrors of purgatory and hell. Pilgrims came to Lough Derg for this purpose even from distant lands. After the cave was blocked up in the 17th c., the site of the pilgrimage was moved to Station Island (½ m. offshore in the S. part of the lake). Pilgrims still flock there between 1 June and 15 August. They travel from and to their homes fasting, and spend two nights on the island, one of them keeping vigil in the basilica. By day they perform the 'stations', or traditional exercises, their only food being a single meal each day of dry bread and black tea. The penitential exercises include a barefoot circuit of the basilica, the Crosses of St Patrick and St Brigid, and six other 'stations' ('beds') marked by remains of ancient monastic huts. The basilica is a fine octagonal building by William A Scott. It has a notable series of windows (1927–8), *Apostles and Saints Holding Stations of the Cross*, by Harry Clarke, and a crucifix (1988) by Imogen Stuart, as well as a tabernacle etc. by Patrick McElroy (1988).

¾ m. NW. of Station Island is Oileán na Naomh (Saint's Island), actual site of St Patrick's Purgatory.

LOUGH DERG (Map 6, J–K3–4–5), largest of the Shannon lakes, is some 25 m. long, and reaches from Portumna in the N. almost to Killaloe in the S. *See further pp. 219, 250, 256, 266, and 278.*

LOUGH ERNE, LOWER, Co. Fermanagh (Map 8, F–G 7–8–9), is a beautiful sheet of water stretching for 18 m. from Enniskillen to Belleek, which has much to offer both fishermen and antiquarians alike.

3 m. NNW. of Enniskillen is Devenish Island with its early and medieval ecclesiastical remains (Hist. Mons.) on and near the site of a monastery founded in the 6th c. by St Molaise. The earliest surviving buildings are 12th c. – the small oratory called St Molaise's House (originally stone-roofed) with its Romanesque angle pilaster bases; the complete Round Tower, 81 ft high, with its Romanesque cornice carved with four human heads. Beside the tower are the foundations of another Round Tower. St Molaise's Church was begun in the early-13th c. and extended E. *c.* 1300. There is a late medieval residential annexe to the N. and a Maguire Chapel to the S. with 17th c. heraldic slabs, and a two-sided bullaun originally used for grinding food

and other materials. The base of a sarcophagus inside the W. end of the church is called St Molaise's Bed and was associated with a cure for back ache. In the surrounding graveyard are many fine gravestones. St Mary's Priory was a house of Canons Regular of St Augustine and was built in the mid-15th and early-16th c. The E. window was removed to the Protestant parish church at Monea (*see p. 179*) in 1804. In the N. wall of the chancel is a fine 15th c. sacristy door and there is a small cloister and traces of surrounding buildings to the N. of the church. In the graveyard is an elegant 15th c. High Cross, unparalleled in Ireland, and a weathered coffin lid of *c.* 1300. In the thatched site museum are many decorated stones, including a limestone head finial from the W. door of St Mary's Priory. It was to Devenish that the Early Christian Soiscél Molaise (a book shrine), now in the National Museum, originally belonged.

Access by ferry May to Sept.

4½ m. N. of Devenish (7½ m. NNW. of Enniskillen) in Killadeas graveyard on the E. shore of the lake are two Early Christian carved stones and a pillar. The Bishop's stone (9th–10th c.) shows a bishop or abbot in profile bearing the episcopal emblems of bell and crozier. On its narrow side is a face in high relief above a band of interlacing. The second stone bears a relief carving of a Greek cross in a circle on a forked stem with interlaced knots on each arm. The name Killadeas suggests that there may have been a foundation of céli Dee or Culdees there.

9 m. NNW. of Devenish, in Castle Archdale (*see p. 207*) Bay, is White Island, with ruins of a church with a Romanesque S. door. Into the N. wall have been built a carved head and six stone figures whose original function was architectural. Access by ferry from Castle Archdale Marina May to September.

5½ m. NW. of Devenish (2½ m. W. of Killadeas), close to the W. shore near Blaney, is Inishmacsaint, site of an island monastery founded in the 6th c. by St Ninnidh (*see p. 178*). Surviving from it are remnants of a church (W. end early) and a tall undecorated High Cross. 3 m. WNW. at Benmore, is the present parish church (1831) which contains a Wilhelmina Geddes window, *Angel of Resurrection*.

LOUGH GUR, Co. Limerick (Map 6, I–J8), is a small lake 2½ m. NNE. of Bruff and 12 m. SSE. of Limerick. Gerald the Rhymer, Earl of Desmond, who disappeared in 1398, is said to sleep beneath its waters. Every seventh year he emerges to ride the moonlit ripples of the lake. His wife, Eleanor Butler, was famous in poetic tradition for her gallantries.

The light limestone soil of the district attracted Neolithic cultivators, and they and their successors have left many monuments in the area. For convenience, Holycross crossroads on the main Limerick (12¼ m.)–Bruff (2¼ m.) road is here taken as the starting-point of a circuit of the lake (proceeding sunwise, in the traditional manner). A good interpretative centre explaining the history of the area stands close to the lakeside car park.

½ m. N. of the crossroads, to the E. of the Limerick road, in Grange, is the Lios (Nat. Mon.), largest stone circle in Ireland, built at the transition from the Stone Age to the Bronze Age. In the next field to the N., a circle of 15 stones within a slight bank encloses a low mound (Nat. Mon). To the SW. are nine surviving stones of a circle of 69 stones (Nat. Mon.). On the opposite side of the Limerick road are remains (Nat. Mon.) of a court-tomb.

In the fields between the Lios and the lake shore are traces of an ancient roadway.

400 yds NE. of the Lios, at the foot of Ardaghlooda Hill, is a pillarstone (Nat. Mon.). On the hill are ancient field walls and a circular enclosure (summit). 300 yds N., in swampy ground, is Crock Island, a crannóg. By the lake shore, 300 yds SE. of Loughgur House, is a stone circle (Nat. Mon.). E. of this is a platform ringfort with attached enclosures, 300 yds N. of which, on Knockfennell, is a stone ringfort. On the summit of Knockfennell (531 ft) is a small cairn; in the valley below, to the E., are Red Cellar Cave and ancient cultivation terraces. Some 400 yds ESE. of these is a group of ancient house and hut sites with their fields, etc. (Nat. Mons.). 440 yds E. of these is Leagaun, a pillarstone; 200 yds N. of this is a hill-top pillarstone; some 200 yds SE. of the first pillarstone is a third. 400 yds SE. of this last is an undateable stone circle which had an internal fosse; nearby, to the SE., is a flat, kerbed cairn which contained Urn burials. On Carraig Aille, the ridge to the S., are two 8th–10th c. stone ringforts, ancient fields and stone enclosures (all Nat. Mons.).

At Loughgur crossroads, SE. of Carraig Aille, is a large, slab-like standing stone (Nat. Mon.). The road to the SW. leads back to Holycross crossroads (1½ m.). ¾ m. WSW., on the S. side of this road, in Loughgur townland, is a wedge-tomb (Nat. Mon.) in which were buried more than 12 individuals, along with decorated Neolithic ware, as well as Beaker and Early Bronze Age pottery. 400 yds. N., at the foot of Knockadoon, are the ruins of 15th c. Black Castle. Some 400 yds. WNW. of the castle, on Knockadoon, is a circular Neolithic cemetery (Nat. Mon.) surrounded by a double-kerbed bank. On the S. and W. slopes of the hill were found many Neolithic and Bronze Age habitation sites (including a rectangular, aisled, Neolithic house site). At the NE. foot of the hill is the fine 15th c. tower of Bourchier's Castle, one of the chief seats of the Earls of Desmond. To the NE., in a corner of the lake, is Bolin Island, a crannóg.

¼ m. SW. of Loughgur gallery grave are the ruins of Teampall Nua, a simple, 15th c. church. 300 yds SE. is Carriganaffrin, a rock where Mass was said in Penal times. 440 yds SW., to the S. of the road in Ballynagallagh, is Leaba na Muice, a ruined wedge-tomb (Nat. Mon.).

LOUGHLINSTOWN, Co. Dublin (Map 3, L4), is a suburban village on the Dublin (9 m.)–Bray (3 m.) road.

The windows in the Protestant church at Rathmichael include A.E. Child, *The Nativity* (1939), Catherine O Brien, *The Crucifixion* (1938), and Sarah Purser, *The Good Samaritan* (1903).

1½ m. SE., near the E. side of the road, are the remains of Kiltuck Church. A 15th/16th c. granite cross from there has been re-erected in the grounds of the Catholic church at Shankill.

1¼ m. SSW. are the fragmentary remains (Nat. Mon.) of the early monastery of Rathmichael; St Comgall of BANGOR is said to have been the founder. The remains include part of the enclosing ring-wall of earth and stone; the stump of a Round Tower; fragments of a 12th/13th c. nave-and-chancel church and several early gravestones with concentric-circle and/or herring-bone patterns, and, ½ m. SE., in the lane to the S. of Shankill House, a granite cross with a *Crucifixion*.

1½ m. SW. is Puck's Castle, a ruined 15th/16th c. fortified house of the Dalkey type.

Loughrea Cathedral, Co. Galway.

LOUGH NEAGH, (Map 1, H–I 7–8), is the largest lake in either Great Britain or Ireland, being 153 sq. m. in area. It receives the waters of the Upper Bann and is drained by the Lower Bann. It takes its name, Loch nEachach, from the horse-god, Eochu, Lord of the Otherworld beneath its waters.

Here, the principal antiquities of the lake shore are listed under the nearest town or village.

LOUGHREA, Co. Galway (Map 6, I2), a market town on the S. or main road from Ballinasloe (19 m.) to Galway (22 m.), is pleasantly situated beside the small lake which gives it its name. In the Middle Ages it was the principal seat of the Mac William Uachtair Burkes (Earls of Clanricarde). Today it is the cathedral town of the diocese of Clonfert. Seamus O Kelly (1880–1918), journalist, Abbey Theatre playwright, and author (*The Weaver's Grave, Wet Clay*, etc.), was born at Mob Hill.

The principal medieval monument is the interesting church of the Carmelite friary founded *c.* 1300 by Richard de Burgo (unfortunate modern 'pointing').

The glory of Loughrea is St Brendan's Cathedral (1897–1903). The dull exterior of this insignificant, uninspired, Gothic-Revival essay by William Byrne suggests nothing of the riches within. The interior, completed and furnished under the direction of Professor William A. Scott of University College, Dublin, epitomizes the development of the ecclesiastical arts and crafts in Ireland from 1903 to 1957. John Hughes was the sculptor of the excellent *Virgin and Child* in the Lady Chapel. A.E. Child (*see p. 45*), Sarah Purser, Hubert McGoldrick, Michael Healy, Evie Hone, and Patrick Pye did the windows, which admirably illustrate the beginnings and development of the Dublin school of stained glass. The windows are as follows in order of date: 1903: Child, *Annunciation, Agony in the Garden, Resurrection* (all two-light). 1904: Healy, *St Simeon*; Purser, *St Ita* (painted by Catherine A. O Brien); Child, *Baptism of Christ* (two-light). 1907: Healy, *Holy Family, Virgin and Child with SS Patrick, Brendan, Colman, Iarlaith, Columcille, Brigid* (in Lady Chapel). 1908: Healy, *St Anthony*. 1908–12: Purser, *Childhood of Christ, Passion Cycle* (two three-light, in E. transept, painted by Child; Purser herself painted the little *St Brendan* of the porch, undated). 1925: McGoldrick, *Sacred Heart*. 1927: Healy, *St John the Evangelist*. 1929: Child, *SS Clare and Francesca* (two-light). 1930: Healy, *Tu Rex Gloriae Christe*. 1933: Healy, *Regina Coeli*. 1934: Child, *Centurion*. 1935: Healy, *St Joseph*. 1936: Healy, *Ascension* (three-light). 1937: Child, *St Patrick*. 1936-40: Healy, *Last Judgement* (three-light, beside his *Ascension* in W. transept). 1942: Hone, *St Brigid* (features 'sweetened' to order). 1950: Hone, *Creation* (rose). 1957: Pye, *St Brigid* (porch). Healy's *Ascension* and *Last Judgement* are among his finest works. The altar rails, font, and all the stone carvings are by Michael Shortall. Scott designed the sanctuary pavement and all the ironwork and wooden furnishings. The *opus sectile* Stations of the Cross are by Ethel Rhind. Jack B. Yeats was one of those who designed embroideries for the cathedral.

In a separate building to the W. of the cathedral is a museum of ecclesiastical art (some noteworthy chalices, medieval figures, and vestments of the Dun Emer Guild, etc.), from the diocese.

4 m. NNE., in Turoe (NW. of Bullaun), is the Turoe Stone (Nat. Mon.), a remarkable phallic stone of the 1st c. B.C. or A.D., covered with three-plane, abstract, curvilinear ornament in the Celtic style. It formerly stood close to a nearby ringfort.

LOUGH REE, Cos. Roscommon – Westmeath – Longford (Map 3, B2), one of the great lakes of the Shannon, stretches for 16 m. above Athlone. Several of the islands contain interesting antiquities.

Close to the Westmeath shore, 4 m. NNE. of Athlone, is Hare Island, where St Cíarán founded a monastery before founding CLONMACNOIS.

2 m. further N., on Inchmore, the ruins of a church mark the site of an early monastery founded by St Líobán.

2 m. NE. of Inchmore is Inchbofin. A monastery was founded there by St (Mo-)Rí-óg (d. 588). The remains (Nat. Mons.) include an enclosing cashel and two small churches.

In the N. half of the lake is Inchcleraun, where St Díarmaid, teacher of Cíarán of Clonmacnois, founded a monastery in the 6th c. The remains (Nat. Mon.) comprise: remnants of an enclosing cashel which had a Romanesque gateway (voussoirs in Teampall Mór, *below*); diminutive, once stone-roofed, Teampall Dhíarmada, 'Dermot's Church', with gable *antae* and trabeate doorway; Teampall Mór, 'Great Church' (with Transitional and later features), and the E. cloister range of the priory; Teampall

Mhuire, 'St Mary's Church', a nave-and-chancel stucture; Teampall na Marbh, 'Church of the Dead'. NW. of the enclosure, on the highest point of the island, is Clogás an Oileáin, 'Bell-tower of the Island', a church (Nat. Mon.) with W. bell-tower.

LOUISBURGH, Co. Mayo (Map 7, D6), is a village on the Westport (14 m.)–Leenaun (18 m.) road.

2½ m. E., at Old Head, is a pleasant little beach dominated by Croagh Patrick.

1 m. E. are the remains of Kilgeever Church and Tobar Rí an Domhnaigh where some Croagh Patrick (*see p. 305*) pilgrims complete their penitential exercises.

6 m. S., in Srahwee, to the NE. of Lough Nahaltora, is a wedge-tomb, regarded locally as a holy well.

7 m. S., via the Leenaun road, are the romantic solitudes of Glencullen and Doo Lough. At the S. end of the glen, by Owengar and Fin Lough, is a fishing lodge to which one of the Lords Sligo, overcome by the Grand Tour, gave the name Delphi!

7½ m. SW., in Cloonlaur, is the Killeen, an ancient churchyard with a great cross-pillar (incised 'marigold' cross). At the head of a grave between this cross-pillar and the gate is an early cross-slab. 3 m. N., in the Dooghmakeon sandhills, is a cross-pillar.

4 m. W. is Roonah Quay, starting-point for CAHER ISLAND, CLARE ISLAND, and INISHTURK.

LOUTH, Co. Louth (Map 2, H6), which gives its name to the county, is a village 7 m. SW. of Dundalk and 5 m. N. of Ardee.

St Mochta (d. 535), 'a British pilgrim, a holy man, a disciple of the holy bishop Patrick', founded a church there, precursor of a flourishing monastery. About 1135/40 the king (Donnchadh O Carroll) and bishop of Uriel transferred the diocese from CLOGHER to St Mary's Church, Louth, where it remained for some 60 years.

The sole relic of the early monastery is St Mochta's House (Nat. Mon.), a small, stone-roofed, 12th/13th c. church; door and windows modern. Nearby are remains of Louth 'Abbey', a long, 14th(?) c. friary-type church.

2 m. NE., in Rathiddy, to the E. of the Dundalk road, is Cloghfarmore (Nat. Mon.), a fine pillarstone, in modern times identified as the pillar to which the mythical Cuchulainn was said to have bound himself in his last combat.

4 m. NNW. is Inishkeen. The scant remains (Nat. Mon.) of the early monastery founded by St Daig mac Cairill (d. 587) include the stump of a Round Tower. The disused church on the site now houses a folk museum. Inishkeen is the native place of Patrick Kavanagh (1904–67), poet and novelist, whose *The Great Hunger* and *Tarry Flynn* reflect aspects of local life. He is buried in the local churchyard.

1 m. E. is the Church of Our Lady of Mercy (1974) by Carr, Sweeney, O Farrell (the Stations of the Cross by Charles Cullen have already been removed!).

LUCAN, Co. Dublin (Map 3, J3), a suburban village on the Dublin (8¾ m.)–Maynooth (8 m.) road, is situated on a beautiful reach of the Liffey. In the 18th c. it was a fashionable spa.

Adjoining the village on the W. is beautiful riverside Lucan Demesne. In the 1670s it was the home of the great soldier Patrick Sarsfield. At the Williamite Revolution the property passed (by marriage) to Agmondisham I Vesey, whose son, Agmondisham II, designed Palladian Lucan House in 1772. The house, which was later remodelled, has stucco by Michael Stapleton and medallions possibly by Angelica Kauffmann. The house (restored by Brendan Ellis) is now the residence of the Italian Ambassador. In the grounds are the ruins of a late medieval church and castle.

2 m. NNE., to the N. of the Liffey, in the magnificent demesne of Woodlands, is Luttrelstown Castle, a 19th c. castellated mansion incorporating portions of a medieval castle.

½ m. NE. is St Edmondsbury, now the convalescent home of Swift's Hospital, Dublin. The original house was built by Edmund Sexton Pery, Speaker of the Irish House of Commons, 1771–85, and afterwards Viscount Pery (*see p. 234*). He was an opponent of the Union.

LURGAN, Co. Armagh (Map 1, I9), is an important centre (now part of the Borough of CRAIGAVON) on the Portadown (5 m.)–Belfast (21 m.) road, 2½ m. SE. of Lough Neagh. It was founded by the Brownlows (English Planters) in the reign of James I. The broad main street dates from the late 17th c.

George W. Russell (1867–1935), better known as 'A.E.', journalist, poet and painter, was born in William St James Logan (1674–1751), one of the founders of Pennsylvania, was also a native of Lurgan.

The Turoe Stone, near Loughrea, Co. Galway.

3 m. SE., at Waringstown, are a charming house (1667) and the parish church (1681, but the chancel, aisle and transept are 19th c. additions). The interior presents perhaps the best surviving example of late-17th c. Protestant architecture in the country.

LUSK, Co. Dublin (Map 3, L1), is a village on the Dublin (14 m.)–Skerries (5 m.) road.

Bishop St Cuindid, alias Mac Cuilinn (d. 497), founded a monastery there. When he died he was buried in the cave (*lusca*) from which the place takes its name. The monastery suffered severely at the hands of the Vikings. After the Anglo-Norman invasion the monastery and its possessions were granted to St Mary's Abbey, Dublin.

The Protestant parish church (1847; now the Willie Monks Museum) and churchyard occupy portions of the site of the monastery founded by St Mac Cuilinn (d. 497), of which the only surviving relic is the Round Tower (Nat. Mon., capping modern). To it has been attached the square tower (*c.* 1500) of a large church demolished in the 19th c. In the medieval tower are housed the effigy tombs of James Bermingham of Ballough (probably 1637) and of Sir Christopher Barnewall of Turvey and his wife, Marion Sharl. The Bermingham effigy is the only armoured effigy of the English Pale with Irish-style harness. The Barnewall tomb, erected in 1589, is an elaborate Renaissance work of Italian (?) and Kilkenny marble. It was erected by Dame Marion Sharl and her second husband, Sir Lucas Dillon of Moymet.

The Church tower at Lusk, Co. Dublin.

St Maculind's Church at the other end of the village is an Irish Romanesque essay (*c.* 1924) by John J. Robinson. It has windows (1924) by Harry Clarke: *St Mac Cuilinn* and three three-light symbolic windows. The Baptistry window is by Patrick Pollen.

M

MACROOM, Co. Cork (Map 5, I5), is a market town in the picturesque Sullane valley, 23 m. W. of Cork, 31 m. SE. of Killarney, and 34 m. NE. of Bantry. The surrounding countryside has a number of megalithic tombs and standing stones.

The town has some good late-Georgian houses, a Protestant church by George Richard Pain of Cork, and a pleasant, small, early-19th c. Market House. The latter is the successor of the market house beside which Eileen Dubh O Connell of Darrynane met and loved the ill-fated Art O Leary in 1768 (*see p. 54*). In the town is a small museum with folk material.

Macroom Castle, which stood by the E. bank of the Sullane, was one of the principal seats of the Mac Carthys of Muskerry (the others being Blarney and Kilcrea). In 1654 Cromwell granted the castle and manor at Macroom to Admiral Sir William Penn, father of William Penn of Pennsylvania.

4 m. NE. is Rusheen crossroads. 2 m. NW., in a farmyard in Caherbaroul, are an early cross-pillar and a bullaun found ¼ m. N. of Parknalicka.

2¾ m. SE., in Mashanaglass, are remains of a 16th c. castle with two angular projections. It was the sole Mac Carthy Mór stronghold in the territory of the Mac Carthy of Muskerry, and was confided to the keeping of the Mac Swineys, a family of professional mercenaries (galloglas).

3½ m. W., on the N. side of the Sullane, is the tower (Nat. Mon.) of the rock-castle of Carrigaphooca, an early-15th c. stronghold of Mac Carthy of Drishane (*see p. 246*). It was stormed by O Sullivan Beare and Cormac Mac Carthy of Muskerry in 1602. The rock, says tradition, was the haunt of a *púca* or malicious sprite; hence its name. Some 200 yds NE. is a small circle of five stones, remnant of a stone circle (Nat. Mon.).

10 m. WNW., where the main Cork–Killarney road penetrates the Derrynasaggart Mts (Mullaghanish, 2,133 ft), is Ballyvourney village, formerly a noted resort of students of Irish. 1 m. SE. is the parish church. In a nearby school is a small museum with folk material. A much worn, 13th c. wooden figure of St Gobnat is preserved by the parish priest. It is displayed to pilgrims on the saint's day (11 February) and on Whit Sunday. Some still make use of the traditional Tomhas Ghobnatan, a length of woollen thread, or of ribbon, measured against the statue and used for curative purposes. ¾ m. W. of the church, in Glebe, is the site of a nunnery founded in the 6th/7th c. by St Gobnat. Tigh Ghobnatan (St Gobnat's House), alias An Ula Uachtarach, is outside the churchyard gate. It was a small, circular, dry-masonry hut, with thatch (?) roof supported by a central post. Excavation has shown that the occupants were smelters of iron and workers in bronze. The house itself was the

successor of a rectangular timber house (or houses) used for the same purposes. Outside the door is the house well. (The 1950 statue to the S. of the house is by the Cork sculptor Séamus Murphy.) Inside the churchyard gate is St Gobnat's Grave, alias An Ula Láir, a small mound on which rest three bullauns, discarded crutches, etc. Teampall Ghobnatan incorporates some fragments of an earlier church, including An Gadaí Dubh, alias Gadaí Ghobnatan. This is a human-mask voussoir from a Romanesque arch. Its name arises from the legend that one of the masons of the church stole his fellows' tools; his likeness was carved in stone as a reminder of the crime. Over one of the church windows is a sheila-na-gig. Outside the SE. angle of the church is the Priest's Grave. The traditional pilgrims' rounds follow the order: An Ula Uachtarach, An Ula Láir, An Tríu Ula (outside the W. end of the church), Chancel, Priest's Grave, Holy Well. ¾ m. E. of the well are St Abbán's Grave and Well. St Abbán is said to have given Gobnat the site for her nunnery. The grave is a small cairn with a short cist, and is set about by three ogham stones. On it lies a bullaun. Pilgrims make their rounds here also. – ½ m. NE. of Ballyvourney church, in Killeen, is St Gobnat's Stone, an interesting early cross-pillar. On each face is a Greek cross inscribed in a double circle. The cross on one face is surmounted by a small staff- or crozier-bearing figure. The stone was found at the site of a dried-up well nearby.

6 m. NW is Carriganimmy village, birthplace (1839) of Canon Peadar Ó Laoghaire, noted Irish writer. It was at Carriganimmy that Art Ó Laoghaire (O Leary) was killed 1773 (*see p. 54*).

MAGHERA, Co. Londonderry (Map 1, G6), is a town off the Derry (35 m.)–Belfast (39 m.) road at the E. foot of the Sperrins.

Charles Thompson (1730–1824) who, as Secretary of the United States Congress, wrote the manuscript of the American Declaration of Independence, was born at Gorteade 4 m. NE.

On the E. edge of the town is the ancient monastic site (Hist. Mon.) said to have been founded in the 6th c. by St Lurach, now occupied by a graveyard and ruined church. The nave, with traces of *antae*, may be 10th c. The W. door, similar to that at Banagher (*see p. 243*) has an elaborate *Crucifixion* scene carved on the lintel and probably dates to the second half of the 12th c. when this church was the seat of the diocese of Cenel Eoghain (later Derry). Later additions include the chancel (*c.* 1200) and the 17th c. tower. W. of the church is the saint's 'grave' marked by a crude cross-inscribed pillar.

St Mary's Catholic church (1973) is by Liam McCormick and Partners. The aluminium doors, stained glass and sanctuary cross are by Helen Moloney, the Stations and narthex panel by Nell Murphy, the gargoyles by Imogen Stuart, the exterior metal sculpture by Barry Orr, and the vestments were designed by Joy McCormick.

3 m. NE., at Upperlands, Clarke's Linen Manufacturers maintain a small museum of artefacts associated with the linen industry.

2 m. NW. is the Tirkane sweat-house (Hist. Mon.) and, 1 m. SE. of this, Tirnony portal-tomb.

MAGHERAFELT, Co. Londonderry (Map 1, H7), is a market and administrative centre on the Bellaghy (5 m.)–Moneymore (5 m.) road. It was founded by the Salters' Company of London at the time of the Plantation. The ruins of the old parish church (built 1664) survive.

7 m. SE. on the shores of Lough Neagh is Salterstown, the abandoned site of what, unsuccessfully, was to have been the Company's major settlement. The ruins of the bawn are preserved in a modern farmyard.

MAGHERY, Co. Armagh (Map 1, H9), is a village at the mouth of the River Blackwater.

1 m. NE in Lough Neagh is Coney Island (Nat. Trust). Excavations in 1962–4 showed human activity dating from Stone Age times with an Anglo-Norman fort and later military occupation.

MALAHIDE, Co. Dublin (Map 3, K2), is a rapidly expanding seaside resort and dormitory suburb at the mouth of the Broad Meadow Water, 9 m. NE. of Dublin and 3 m. ESE. of Swords. The Protestant church has a two-light window *Our Lord Blessing Children* (1950) by Catherine A. O Brien.

SW. of the village are Malahide Demesne and Castle (the latter with admission charge and guided tour). With the exception of a brief interval during the Cromwellian period, the castle was owned by the Talbot family from the time of the Norman invasion until the Hon. Rose Talbot felt forced to sell it in 1973, as the Government of the day was not prepared to accept the castle and contents in lieu of death duties. Fortunately, interested public and private parties combined to buy

Carrigaphooca Castle, Co. Cork.

back much of the furniture and some of the paintings at auction, and the castle is now owned by the Dublin County Council, and leased to Dublin Tourism. It is for the most part post-medieval (it has good rococo plaster of the Robert West school), and has lost its outworks, though traces of the moat can be recognized. The 6th Lord Talbot was a great-great-grandson of James Boswell (1740–95), biographer of Dr Samuel Johnson. The castle treasures formerly included a great collection of Boswell's private papers. The Great Hall still houses one of the largest collections of family paintings left in Ireland, and these form the core of a National Portrait Gallery in the castle. E. of the castle are the ruins of the 'abbey', a 15th–16th c. manorial, nave-and-chancel church with priest's dwelling over the sacristy. In the nave is the fine 15th c. effigy tomb, said to be that of Maud Plunket, heroine of Gerald Griffin's ballad *The Bride of Malahide*. Her first husband, Lord Galtrim, was slain in battle on their wedding day. She subsequently married the owner of Malahide. The Cottage Museum at the main entrance gate to the Castle houses a collection of local antiquities.

1 m. SE., by the shore, is Robswalls Castle, a 15th c. Bermingham castle which passed to the Barnewalls.

MALIN, Co. Donegal (Map 1, D2), is a village on Inishowen, 4 m. N. of Carndonagh. It still retains its 17th c. (Plantation) layout and triangular village green.

8½ m. NW. is Malin Head, most northerly point of Ireland.

MALLARANNY, alias **MULRANNY**, Co. Mayo (Map 7, D5), is a delightful little resort, with sandy beaches, on the N. shore of Clew Bay, 11 m. WNW. of Newport, 8 m. SE. of Achill Sound, and 20 m. SSW. of Bangor Erris. It has a mild climate.

8 m. SSW. is Curraun. The new church has a 1924 *St Brendan* window designed by Wilhelmina Margaret Geddes (1888–1955), painted by Ethel Mary Rhind, and presented to the church in 1943 by Sarah Purser.

MALLOW, Co. Cork (Map 5, K3), a market and sugar-manufacturing town on the N. side of the beautiful Blackwater, is an important road and rail junction, 21 m. NNW. of Cork, 8 m. S. of Buttevant, and 17 m. W. of Fermoy.

The Geraldines of Desmond were the real founders of the town. In 1584, following on the attainder of the 15th Earl of Desmond, the place was granted to Sir Thomas Norreys, English Lord President of Munster. Subsequently it passed by marriage to the Jephsons. Castle Garr (Short Castle), at the W. end of the town, was taken by Castlehaven's Confederate Catholics in 1642, the town itself in 1643, Mallow Castle (*see below*) in 1645. In 1650 Cromwell captured the castle. Thereafter the town remained a typical 'New English', Protestant, settlement. In the 18th and early-19th c. it was a watering place of the Anglo-Irish gentry of Co. Cork, and the 'Rakes of Mallow' acquired considerable notoriety.

Thomas Davis (1814–45), Young Ireland leader and a founder of the *Nation* newspaper, was born at 72 Thomas Davis St. P.A. (Canon) Sheehan (1852–1913), novelist, was born in O Brien St. William O Brien (1852–1928), Nationalist leader, was also a native of the town.

Apart from the Court House, Market House, and some good dwelling houses, the only relics of Mallow's fashionable heyday are original little Spa House (now a private dwelling) and the fine race-course.

At the SE. end of the town are the ruins (Nat. Mon.) of Mallow Castle, built by Sir Thomas Norreys before 1598 and burned by the Jacobites in 1689. After the Williamite victory the Jephsons converted the 17th c. stables into a residence (altered and enlarged in 1837, completed 1954).

5 m. SSE. is Ballynamona Protestant church (1717).

5¾ m. SSE. are the extensive, but fragmentary, ruins (Nat. Mon.) of Mourne 'Abbey', a preceptory of the Knights Hospitallers of St John of Jerusalem. Founded before 1216, probably by Alexander de Sancta Helena, its defences – a strong curtain with two towers and a keep – enclosed an area of several acres. The church was 180 ft long, its tower sited in unusual fashion over the W. end of the choir. Not far ESE., in Greenhill, is an ogham stone; some 40 yds away, by a fence, is a fragment of a second. 2 m. SE. is Ráth an Tóiteáin, alias Burn Fort, a ringfort which gives its name to the townland; in the souterrain was found an ogham stone. 1 m. NE. of Burnfort village, in Island, are remains (Nat. Mon.) of a wedge-tomb set in a heel-shaped cairn. Tomb and cairn were partly restored following excavation in 1957. – 1¼ m. NW. of the preceptory are the ruins (Nat. Mon.) of Castlemore, alias Barrett's Castle.

7½ m. SSW., in Carrigcleenamore, is Carraig Chlíodhna, Cleena's Rock. A great rock at the SE. end is traditionally the door to the Otherworld seat of the goddess Clíodhna (*see p. 276*).

4½ m. W., on a lofty rock by the S. bank of the Blackwater, is Dromaneen Castle (Nat. Mon.), a large O Callaghan strong-house of the 16th and 17th c., in a bawn of 6 acres.

4 m. W., to the N. of the Blackwater, is Longueville, formerly Garrymacony. O Callaghan lands here, confiscated by the Cromwellians, were purchased by the Longfields in 1698. They built the beautifully sited house, 1700–40. (It was enlarged early in the 19th c.) Richard Longfield was created Baron Longueville in 1795, whence the change of the place name. For supporting the Union he was rewarded with a viscountcy. Arthur O Connor, the Republican leader, was his nephew, and might have been his heir but for refusing to forswear his principles. Longueville is now once more O Callaghan property, being a fine hotel.

MANOR CUNNINGHAM, Co. Donegal (Map 1, B5), is a village on the Derry (15 m.)–Letterkenny (6½ m.) road, close to the head of Lough Swilly.

½ m. S. is the ancient church site of Raymoghy, where St Columcille came to be instructed by Bishop Brugach. ¾ m. SSE., in Carrickballydooey, is a pillarstone with an incised cross.

2½ m. NNE., on Lough Swilly, are the ruins of Balleeghan 'Abbey', a 15th c. Franciscan Tertiary church.

MANORHAMILTON, Co. Leitrim (Map 7, L1), is a strategically sited Border village in the beautiful Bonet River valley, near the head of lovely Glencar. It is the junction of roads from Dromahaire (10 m.), Bundoran (16 m.), Belcoo (14 m.), and Garrison (8 m.).

The surrounding hills are rich in archaeological remains, including chamber-tombs.

A short distance N. are remains of a stronghouse built in 1638 by Sir Frederick Hamilton, grantee of confiscated Irish lands.

2½ m. SSE., in Tullyskeherny, are the remains of two court-tombs. One has six or more subsidiary chambers, as well as a two-segment gallery grave.

3 m. NW., on the N. side of Glenade in Barracashlaun, is a dual court-tomb.

MARKETHILL, Co. Armagh (Map 2, H3), is a little market town on the Armagh (7 m.)–Newry (11 m.) road.

Gosford Castle, a great Norman-style fantasy, was commenced by Thomas Hooper in 1819 for Archibald Acheson, the 2nd Earl of Gosford. Dean Swift was a frequent visitor to the earlier Acheson residence here, hence his 'well', 'chair', etc., in the demesne which is now a forest park (Dept of Agr.) with a walled garden, arboretum, walks and camping and caravan facilities.

MAUM, alias **MAAM**, Co. Galway (Map 7, E8), is an angling (salmon, sea trout, brown trout) centre in the magnificent Maum valley which climbs for some 8 m. from the NW. arm of Lough Corrib to the saddle overlooking the head of Killary (Harbour).

3 m. NW., in Kilmeelickin Church, is a single-light window (*St Brendan*) by Evie Hone (1950).

3 m. SE., in Lough Corrib, are the 13th c. keep and curtain (Nat. Mon.) of the O Conor island castle, Caisleán na Circe, Castlekirke.

2 m. WNW., at Cur, a footpath climbs SW. to Maumeen (3 m.), a mountain saddle associated with St Patrick, where Patrick's Bed (a rock recess) and Well mark a place of pilgrimage and Lughnasa celebrations, still visited on the last Sunday of July. The well was believed to cure murrain in cattle, as well as human ills.

MAYNOOTH, Co. Kildare (Map 3, I3), is a village beside the Royal Canal, on the main Dublin–Galway road, between Leixlip (5 m.) and Kilcock (4 m.).

At the W. end of the main street is St Patrick's College (*see below*). Inside the gate is St Mary's Protestant church, which incorporates the tower and fabric of a manorial church associated with the great castle of the Earls of Kildare, whose massive ruins (Nat. Mon.) are to the right of the gate. The earliest castle there was, doubtless, constructed for Gerald fitz Maurice (d. 1203), 1st Baron O ffaly and ancestor of the Fitz Geralds, Earls and Marquesses of Kildare and Dukes of Leinster. The ruins include fine gatehouse, massive keep, great hall, etc. The keep probably dates from the 13th c.; the other works are of various dates. Stronghold of the rebel Silken Thomas, the castle was taken after a week's siege in March 1535, by Henry VIII's deputy, Sir William Skeffington. Skeffington bombarded the castle with the first siege guns used in Ireland. Re-edified in 1630, the castle was pillaged in 1641. In 1647 it was dismantled by order of Eóghan Rúa O Neill and was thereafter abandoned. In the church ('restored', 1770) is buried the noted German-born architect Richard Cassels, who died in 1757 while working at Carton (*see below*).

St Patrick's College is the greatest Catholic seminary in these islands. It was founded in 1795 by the English authorities, who had become alarmed by the Revolution in France, where so many Irish priests had had till then to seek their education by reason of the Penal Laws. In 1896 it was accorded the status of a Pontifical university, with faculties of Philosophy, Theology, and Canon Law. In 1908 the Senate of the new National University of Ireland accorded it the status of a Recognized College of the University, with faculties of Arts, Celtic Studies, Philosophy, and Science. It was visited by Pope John Paul II in October 1979.

The great complex consists primarily of two large courts or squares. The nucleus of it all was the stark Classical residence known as Stoyte House (central block of the E. range), to which harmonizing N. and S. wings were added. Early-19th c. additions included the N. and S. sides of St Joseph's Sq. and the Junior House. No architect appears to have been employed as such, but prominent among the builders were Michael (designer of the chapel about 1796) and Francis Stapleton, members of a Dublin family of distinguished architect-builders and stuccoers. Their work has been appreciably modified of late.

In 1845 extensive additions were entrusted to the celebrated English Gothic-Revival Architect Augustus Welby Pugin. 'The architect wanted one thing, the (college) authorities another, the builder had his own view, and the presiding genius, the Board of Works, wanted something else.' The result was the great, and in many respects admirable, though still incomplete, Gothic quadrangle (1845–50) which contains St Mary's and St Patrick's Houses. The College Chapel (1875–1902), by Ireland's foremost Gothic Revivalist, J.J. Mc Carthy, is one of the major departures from Pugin's plan. Mc Carthy in his turn died before the completion of his design (the Chapel being finished by his pupil, William Hague), and his white marble high-altar was replaced in 1911 by the existing, inferior, if more pretentious, work. Since Mc Carthy's time there have been many unfortunate departures from the architectural tradition of the college. By and large, the college mirrors the 19th–20th c. rise and fall of the artistic standards of the resurgent Catholic Church in Ireland.

In a corridor may be seen Viavicenzi's *Flight into Egypt* (formerly at Carton; presented by Hermione, Duchess of Leinster) and a limestone head of St Patrick by the Cork sculptor Séamus Murphy. The library has a large collection of late manuscripts and early printed books in the Irish language; these are housed in the John Paul Library (1983), opposite the entrance to which is Imogen Stuart's bronze statue of Pope John Paul II (1987), commemorating his visit in 1979. To the N. of the Maynooth – Kilcock road, and joined to it by a footbridge, is the modern University campus, of which the most noteworthy feature is the chapel of the Society of African Missions (1972) by Bailey and Johnson, with most of the metal furnishings by Benedict Tutty.

The college museum contains a small, but interesting, collection of antiquities and works of art, mainly ecclesiastical. Among the vestments are those of Geoffrey Keating (*see p. 87*) as well as vestments presented to the Irish College of Salamanca by Queen Maria Barbara of Spain (1746–59), to the Irish College of Nantes by Queen Marie Antoinette, and to Maynooth College by the Empress Elizabeth of Austria. The museum also contains early electrical apparatus invented or used by the Rev. Nicholas Callan (1799–1864), who was Professor of Science at Maynooth, 1826–64, where he discovered the principles of the self-induced dynamo (1837).

At the E. end of the main street is the 1,000 acre demesne of Carton (now owned by a consortium), where the Rye Water feeds an artificial lake. The mansion was remodelled (*c.* 1739–47) by Richard Cassels for the 19th Earl of Kildare. The superb state apartments include a saloon with a coved stucco ceiling by Paul and Philip Franchini; the organ (1839) is by Lord Gerald Fitzgerald. The dining room (1815) is by Sir Richard Morrison. In the grounds is the Shell Cottage made by the 3rd Duchess of Leinster.

2 m. ESE., on the S. side of the canal, is Donaghmore, site of an early monastery, with an ancient field-system, and the ruins of a small nave-and-chancel church. ¾ m. S. is 140 ft Carton Obelisk, alias Conolly's Folly, erected in 1740 (to the design of Cassels?) by Speaker Conolly's widow to close a 2½ m. vista from the back of Castletown (*see p. 102*).

3 m. S. the ruins of Taghadoe (locally Taptoo) Round Tower (65 ft, Nat. Mon.) and church mark the site of a monastery founded by St Túa.

7 m. SW. is Donadea. In the Protestant church is a fine, Renaissance, canopied tomb (1626) with kneeling effigies of Sir Gerald Aylmer (d. 1634) and his wife, Dame Julia Nugent (d. 1617), as well as figured panels (*Crucifixion, Blessed Virgin, SS Jerome, Gregory, Ambrose, Augustine*); the tomb was brought there from the pre-Reformation church. The Aylmers, who remained Catholics until the 18th c., lived at Donadea from the 15th to the 20th c.

MELLIFONT ABBEY, Co. Louth (Map 2, H7), 4½ m. WNW. of Drogheda, was the first Cistercian abbey in Ireland. The Cistercians of Mellifont were among the first Irish representatives of a great European order; their monastery one of the first Irish representatives of the classic, integrated, monastic architecture of medieval Europe.

The lavabo, Mellifont, Co. Louth.

The abbey was founded in 1140 by Donchadh O Carroll, King of Uriel, at the instance of the celebrated reformer, St Malachy Ó Morgair, Bishop of Down (he had resigned the archbishopric of Armagh in 1137). Impressed by his experience of St Bernard's rule at Clairvaux, St Malachy had had some Irish novices trained there. These, accompanied by a number of French Cistercians, came to Mellifont in 1142. Soon afterwards St Bernard sent a skilled master-mason, Robert by name, to aid them in the building of the new-style abbey. By 1148 four daughter houses had been founded: Bective, Co. Meath; Boyle, Co. Roscommon; Monasternenagh, Co. Limerick (*see p. 123*); and Baltinglass, Co. Wicklow. By 1272 these in turn had sent out 20 other offshoots, mostly in Munster and Leinster.

The first church of Mellifont was consecrated in 1157, on the occasion of a national synod presided over by Cardinal Paparo, the papal legate. Rich donations were made to the abbey by the High-King and others, including the famous Dervorgilla, wife of Tiernan O Rourke of Breany, who subsequently retired to the abbey, and died there in 1193. That same year St Malachy's relics were brought from Clairvaux and deposited in the abbey.

After the abbey was suppressed in 1539 it was turned into a fortified house of the Moore family, where the great Hugh O Neill submitted to the English Lord Deputy in 1603. Nothing remains of the house.

The ruins (Nat. Mon.) are highly interesting, though very fragmentary, consisting for the most part of little more than foundations. The plan is the normal Cistercian one: on the N., a cruciform church; on the S., chapter-house, refectory, kitchen, dormitories, etc., ranged in integrated order round a cloister. The church had an aisled nave of eight bays, aisleless chancel, transepts with E. chapels; noteworthy is the unique pseudo-crypt at the W. end. In the course of the 13th, 14th, and 15th c. many alterations and extensions were carried out. Thus, the first church was smaller than the second; instead of three square-ended E. chapels in each transept, it had one square-ended chapel flanked by two apsidal chapels. Conspicuous among the ruins are: the reconstructed fragments of the Romanesque cloister arcade; the remnant of the unique octagonal Transitional lavabo or washing-place (*c.* 1200) on the S. side of the cloister, facing the door of the refectory; and the 13th c. E. extension of the chapter-house. In the floor of the latter have been set encaustic tiles from the church. N. of the abbey are the remains of the 15th c. castle-like gatehouse. The small, plain church NE. of the precincts is probably post-Reformation.

MIDLETON, Co. Cork (Map 4, C8), is a market town where the Cork (14 m.)–Youghal (17 m.) road crosses the head of the Owenacurra estuary, near the NE. corner of Cork Harbour. Founded by the Brodericks, later Earls of Midleton, *c.* 1670, it now has the largest distillery of Irish whiskey in the country.

Sir Richard Morrison (1767–1849), architect, a pupil of Gandon's and father of William Vitruvius Morrison (1794–1838), was a native of Midleton.

The Protestant parish church was built in 1825 to the design of the brothers Pain, pupils of John Nash (*see p. 118*). It occupies part of the site of the Cistercian Abbey of Monasterore, which was colonized from Monasternenagh (*see p. 123*) in 1180.

John Philpot Curran (1750–1817, *see p. 258*) went to school at Midleton College, founded in 1696 as a free grammar school by Elizabeth Villiers (Countess of Orkney), mistress of William of Orange. The building was remodelled on ponderous Georgian lines in 1829.

10½ m. NNE. (via Clonmult), in Garryduff, is a small ringfort (originally bivallate), with stonefaced earthen rampart. Excavated finds included sub-Roman pottery of Rhenish types and a unique, gold 'wren' (now in Cork Public Museum), and date the two-phase occupation of the fort to the 7th and 8th c.

1¾ m. ENE. are the remains of Cahermone Castle, a Fitzgerald (Knights of Kerry) stronghold.

MILLFORD village, Co. Donegal (Map 1, B4), is an angling centre (Lough Fern and Leannan River) near the head of Mulroy Bay, on the Rathmelton (4 m.)–Carrigart (10 m.) road.

Local beauty spots are the Fairy Glen, and secluded Bunlin Glen (1 m. NW.) with its two waterfalls, the Grey Mare's Tail and Golan Loop.

St Peter's Church (1961), by McCormick and Corr, is a good, simple essay with stained glass by Patrick Pollen (*SS Columcille, Adamnan, Comgall*), Patrick Pye (*SS Patrick, Brendan, Eunan – sic*), Phyllis Burke (*SS Malachy, Brigid, Attracta*), and Imogen Stuart (*St Garvan*). The tapestry altar dorsal (*The Miraculous Draught of Fishes*) was designed by Colin Midleton of Belfast. The carved wooden door and the ceramic Stations of the Cross are by Imogen Stuart. The *St Peter* over the door is by Oisín Kelly. The sacristy weathervane is by Ian Stuart.

3½ m. NNE. (1¼ m. S. of Carrowkeel village), in Gortnavern, is a good portal-tomb.

MILLSTREET, Co. Cork (Map 5, I4), a village of the upper Blackwater valley, is situated on the Macroom (13 m.)–Kanturk (12 m.) road. It is the site of an important annual horse-show. There is a small museum in the Carnegie Hall. The nearby Boggeragh Mts are rich in megalithic remains.

1¾ m. NNE., in Drishane, is the tower (Nat. Mon.) of a castle built in 1436 by Dermot Mac Carthy. The fireplaces and armorials were inserted by the Walls family in the 17th c. Nearby are remains of a church.

5¾ m. SE., in Knocknakilla, on the upper slope of Musheramore, is a stone circle (Nat. Mon.) accompanied by a low cairn and a pair of monoliths, one prostrate.

5¼ m. SSE., in Glentane East, are remains of a wedge-tomb; also a stone circle enclosed by a fosse, outside which is a prostrate monolith (there is another in the fosse).

MILLTOWN MALBAY, Co. Clare (Map 6, E5), is a small market town 20 m. W. of Ennis (via Inagh) and 7 m. SW. of Lehinch.

2 m. SW. is the seaside resort of Spanish Point, which takes its name from the Armada Spaniards shipwrecked thereabouts in September 1588, and later butchered at the command of Sir Richard Bingham, English Governor of Connacht.

2 m. NE. are remains of Kilfarboy, a late-15th c. parish church on the site of a foundation (*c.* 740) attributed to St Laichtín. In the churchyard are buried Andrias Mac Cruitín (d. 1749) and Mícheál Ó Coimín (d. 1760), Gaelic poets, writers, and scholars.

3½ m. SW. is Quilty, a fishing village. The ugly, 1909–11 church commemorates the valour of the 12 men who, in four currachs, tried to rescue the crew of the French ship *Leon XIII*, wrecked offshore in the great storm of October 1907. 1½ m. S. is Kilmurry, with remnants of the late-medieval parish church. – 2½ m. SW. (by currach) is Inis Chaorach, alias Mutton Island, with traces of an anchoritic settlement attributed to St Seanán (*see p. 226*).

MITCHELSTOWN, Co. Cork (Map 4, B5), is a market and creamery town on the main Dublin (126½ m.)–Cork (32 m.) road, 7 m. N. of Fermoy.

Creation of the King family (Earls of Kingston), the town is a good example of early-19th c. planning. At the N. end is College Sq., with Main St opening off the S. side. The vista at the S. end of the street is closed by the Protestant parish church erected in 1823 to the design of George Richard Pain, a pupil of John Nash, who settled in CORK.

College Sq. takes its name from Kingston College, an asylum for decayed Protestant gentlefolk. A statue of John Mandeville and three crosses in the pavement commemorate a Land League meeting held there in 1887, in the course of which three men were killed by the police. At the W. side of the square is the entrance to Mitchelstown Castle demesne. The 'castle', seat of the Earls of Kingston, was burned down in 1922, and the stones were taken away to build the new abbey church at Mount Melleray (*see p. 89*). An ancient graveyard in the demesne marks the site of the hermitage or monastery of Brigown, whose founder, St Fionn-Chú(a), died of the Yellow Plague in 664. He was noted for his austerities. Legend asserts that, having surrendered his assured place in Heaven to a king of the Déise, he had seven smiths make him seven sickles, on which he mortified his flesh for seven years, so as to win a new place for himself. The Round Tower of Brigown remained standing until 1720.

4 m. NE., in Co. Tipperary, is the ruined church of Kilbeheny. John O Mahony (d. 1877), co-founder with James Stephens of the Fenians, was born nearby.

4 m. SSW. is the ruined hill-top castle of Caheradriney, a stronghold of the Condons.

5 m. NW., in Labbamolaga Middle, is the ancient monastic site of Leaba Mo-Laga (Nat. Mon.). It takes its name from St Mo-Laga, disciple of St David of Wales. The remains there include ancient dry-masonry enclosing wall, scant fragments of a small Romanesque or Transitional church (it had quoin shafts), and remains of a diminutive oratory with *antae* and architraved, trabeate W. door. At the S. side of the oratory is Mo-Laga's *leaba* ('bed', 'tomb'); to spend a night under the limestone slab cures rheumatism. In the enclosure is a small, early cross-slab.

MOATE, Co. Westmeath (Map 3, C3), a village on the Kilbeggan (9 m.)–Athlone (9½ m.) road, takes it name from the earthwork, Moatgrange, to the SW.

3½ m. NW. is Mount Temple, alias Ballyloughloe. Built into a wall in an old graveyard is an early cross-inscribed stone bearing the inscription OR[ŌIT] DO MAELMAIRE ('A prayer for Máel-Maire'), which is said to have come originally from Calry churchyard. Nearby is an Anglo-Norman (de Lacy?) motte.

MOIRA, Co. Down (Map 2, J1), is a former linen and market village on the Belfast (12 m.)–Lurgan (5 m.) road. Thereabouts was fought, 24 June 637, the battle of Mag Roth (Moira), in which the King of Tara, Domnall II, defeated his rebel foster-son, Congal Clóen, son of the King of Dál Áraide, and the latter's allies, the Kings of Scottish Dál Ríada (Argyllshire) and of Ulster. The battle was one of the most celebrated in Gaelic literary legend, having caused, among other things, the madness of Suibne Gelt, which inspired a long poem by the modern Irish poet Seamus Heaney.

From Moira the Rawdon family, who lived to the NW. of the village, takes its title (Earls of Moira). The Protestant church is a good example of early-18th c. Gothick. It was erected by Lord Hillsborough and Sir John Rawdon. Berwick Hall, ½ m. E., is a 17th c. Plantation farm-house (altered).

1¾ m. SW. is Magheralin, an early monastery founded by 7th c. St Rónán Fionn. The site is marked (Hist. Mon.) by the remains of a 15th c. parish church (residential tower, 17th c. and later additions), dismantled in 1845. The 1845 Protestant church has two-light windows (1908) by A.E. Child (*SS Comgall and Finnian*), Lady Glenavy (*SS Gall and Columbanus*), and Michael Healy (*SS Patrick and Columcille*), and a three-light window *The Institution of the Eucharist; Judas, John and the Virgin*, and *The Miraculous Draft of Fish* by Ethel Rhind (1915).

MONAGHAN, Co. Monaghan (Map 2, F3), on the Clogher (15 m.)–Castleblayney (15 m.) road, is the capital of the county to which it gives its name, and also the cathedral town of the Catholic diocese of Clogher. In 1462 Felim Mac Mahon, the local lord, founded a friary for Conventual Franciscans, some fragments of which survive near the Diamond.

The good Market House, built in 1792 for Gen. Robert Cuningham, afterwards 1st Baron Rossmore, is now a tourist office. The dull Court House is by John Bowden. In Hill Street is the award-winning County Museum. St Mac Cartan's Cathedral (1861–92) is a very fine Gothic-Revival church by J.J. Mac Carthy (only five of his seven planned bays built). The exterior has been marred by incongruous Carrara marble statues, the interior by bad glass, but there are fine interior furnishings by Michael Biggs (stonework and round confessional) and his wife Frances (tapestries – *St Macartan, Baptism* and *The Eucharist*), with a tabernacle by Richard King. In the bishop's house are two two-light windows (*SS Mac Cartan, Brigid; SS Patrick, Damhnat;* 1911–12) by Michael Healy. In the Louis Convent is a Heritage Centre, concerned with the history of Monaghan and of the St Louis order of nuns.

Sir Charles Gavan Duffy (1816–1903), founder-editor of the epoch-making *Nation* newspaper and one of the leaders of the Young Ireland movement, who afterwards became Prime Minister of Victoria, was born in Dublin St. One of his sons was Mr Justice Gavan Duffy (d. 1951), an Irish signatory of the 1921 Anglo-Irish Treaty, and later President of the High Court.

6 m. NE., overlooking the lake of Glaslough, is Glaslough House, former home of the late Sir Shane Leslie, Bt, author (1885–1971). The house (1878) is by Lanyon, Lynn, and Lanyon and is now occupied by Sir John Leslie; one gate-lodge is by John Nash. 1¼ m. WSW. is the ancient church site of Donagh. The 17th c. ringed cross with rude *Crucifixion*, was found in Donagh Bog, and, in 1911, was erected there by Sir Shane Leslie and F.J. Bigger.

7 m. SE. is Clontibret, where, in 1595, Great Hugh O Neill sharply defeated Sir Henry Bagenal as he returned to Newry after revictualling the fort at Monaghan.

5 m. SW., in Tiredigan, is a court-tomb (Nat. Mon.).

5 m. WSW., near Smithborough, is Drumsnat (Druim Sneachta). Mo-Lúa of Clonfertmulloe (*see p. 80*) had a monastery there. One of the earliest Irish literary codices was *The Book of Drumsnat* (8th c.).

4½ m. NW. is Tedavnet where, in the 6th c., St Damhnat founded a monastery for women. Her name being Latinized as Dymphna, she has been unjustifiably identified with the saint of that name long venerated at Gheel in Flanders as patroness of the insane. St Damhnat's enshrined bachall, or staff, is now in the National Museum.

MONASTERADEN, Co. Sligo (Map 7, K4), is a village on the W. shore of Lough Gara. Many of the islands of the lake are crannógs dating back to prehistoric and early Christian times.

2 m. NNE., overlooking the NW. corner of Lough Gara, are the ruins of Moygara Castle, chief seat of the O Garas. The remains are probably 16th c., and comprise a large square tower and a rectangular bawn with square corner towers.

¾ m. SW. is St Áracht's Well; there is a *Crucifixion* carving of 1662 there. On the Opposite side of the road is Coolavin (Madame Mac Dermot), built in 1897–8 to the design of J.F. Fuller of Tralee. In the grounds, close to the road, in Clogher, is Cashelmore, a restored stone ringfort (Nat. Mon.) with two accessible souterrains.

MONASTERBOICE (Mainistear Bhuíthín), Co. Louth (Map 2, I8), in Newtown Monasterboice, to the W. of the Drogheda (5¾ m.)–Dunleer (5¼ m.) road, is an early monastic site celebrated for its High Crosses. The monastery is attributed to St Buíthe who is said to have died in 521. The most celebrated name in its history is that of Flann Mainistreach, Flann of Monasterboice (d. 1056), Latin master of the monastery, and reputed author of versified treatises on the Túatha Dé Danann, the Kings of Tara, etc. In 1097 the belfry (Round Tower) was destroyed by fire, and with it books and other treasures.

The remains (Nat. Mons.) at the site comprise two churches, a pre-Gothic sundial, an early cross-decorated slab, a Round Tower, and three High Crosses.

The churches are small, simple, rectangular structures of minor interest.

The Round Tower, or cloigtheach (belfry of the monastery), though shorn of its uppermost part, is still about 100 ft high.

Towards the NE. corner of the graveyard is the imperfect North Cross. The head has a simple *Crucifixion*, and a fine spiral composition. The shaft is modern. In an enclosure nearby is the early sundial.

The West Cross, to the S. of the North Church, is traditionally St Bween's Cross. It is exceptionally tall (21 ft 6 in.). The subjects figured are not all intelligible. They include: E. face: *David Killing the Lion, Abraham's Sacrifice of Isaac, David with the Head of Goliath, David Anointed by Samuel, The Three Children in the Fiery Furnace, Christ in Majesty*; W. face: *Resurrection, Baptism of Christ, Crucifixion, Peter Drawing His Sword at Gethsemane, The Kiss of Judas.*

The South Cross, traditionally St Patrick's Cross, is now commonly called Muiredach's Cross by scholars because of the inscription, at the bottom of the W. face of the shaft, which Macalister reads: OR[ŌIT] DO MUIREDACH LASNDERNAD I[N] CHROS ('A prayer for Muiredach by whom the cross was made'). The Muiredach named in the inscription cannot be positively identified. The cross (17 ft 8 in.) is the finest of the remarkable Irish series of early figured crosses. (These were essentially 'picture books' of Scriptural and other edifying stories for the unlettered. In their original condition they were almost certainly picked out with polychrome painting.) The figure subjects on this splendid cross include: Base: *Animal Figures*; E. face: *The Fall, The Murder of Abel, David and Goliath, Moses Smiting the Rock, Epiphany, Last Judgement, SS Anthony and Paul in the Desert*; W. face: *The Second Mocking of Christ, The Raised Christ, The Ascension, Christ Presents a Key to St Peter, A Gospel to St Paul, The Crucifixion*. The summit of the cross is fashioned in the shape of a shingle-roofed church with gable-finials.

Muiredach's Cross, Monasterboice, Co. Louth.

MONASTEREVAN, Co. Kildare (Map 3, G5), is a village where the Kildare (7 m.)–Port Laoise (13 m.) road crosses the River Barrow and the Grand Canal. The cross in the Market Place commemorates Father Prendergast, who was hanged there for his part in the insurrection of 1798.

To the S. of the village is Moore Abbey, sometime seat of the Moores, Earls of Drogheda. It occupies the site of the early monastery founded by St Eimhíne, who was of royal Munster stock. In the 12th c. this monastery was refounded as a Cistercian abbey (Ros Glas, alias de Rosea Valle), dedicated to SS Mary and Benedict, by Dermot O Dempsey, King of Uí Fáilghe. The mansion was remodelled in 1767 and Gothicized in 1846. For some years it was the residence of the celebrated singer John McCormack, and is now a home for epileptics.

MONEYMORE, Co. Derry (Map 1, G7), is a small market town on the Maghera (12 m.)–Cookstown (5 m.) road. It was founded by the Drapers Company of London which, by 1619, among other amenities, had provided piped water to the town.

1 m. SE. is Springhill, built by the Conyngham family in the late 17th c., with later 18th and 19th c. additions. It is now maintained by the National Trust and houses a fine collection of family furniture and mementoes, as well as a costume museum.

2¾ m. S. in Tamlaght (½ m. W. of Coagh) is the fine Cloghtogle portal-tomb.

MONKSTOWN, Co. Cork (Map 4, B9), is a small residential suburb and resort at the NW. corner of Cork Harbour, some 7 m. SW. of Cork city.

Castle Mahon, alias Monkstown Castle, now Monkstown Golf Club, is a strong-house of 1636. It was built by Anastasia Archdeacon for a net cost – so the tale asserts – of 4d.; i.e. after she had deducted the cost of the workmen's keep from their wages. And her husband was dissatisfied! In the main hall is a good fireplace of 1636.

The Church of the Sacred Heart (1867–73) is by Edward Welby Pugin and George C. Ashlin.

MOUNTMELLICK, Co. Laois (Map 3, E6), is a market town where the Tullamore (15 m.)–Port Laoise (7 m.) road crosses the Owenass to the E. of Slieve Bloom. The town, like CLARA, originated as a Quaker settlement and in 1677 the first Quaker school in Ireland was opened there. Later the town was a prosperous linen-spinning centre, shipping its goods by the Grand Canal. The principal streets are still essentially 18th c. in character and have some good houses.

4 m. WNW. is the village of Rosenallis, which, like Mountmellick, was a Quaker colony and linen centre.

MOUNTRATH, Co. Laois (Map 3, E7), is a small, now decayed market town on the Port Laoise (8 m.)–Roscrea (16 m.) road, to the SE. of Slieve Bloom. In the 17th and 18th c. the town had a thriving linen industry, which was fostered by the Cootes, Earls of Mountrath.

St Fintan's Church is a Gothic-Revival essay by John S. Butler.

5 m. NNE., on the slope of Conlawn Hill (1,004 ft), is Ballyfin House, now the Patrician College. Sir Charles Henry Coote built the house to the designs of Sir Richard Morrison (1767–1849), a pupil of Gandon's. Morrison was assisted by his son, William Virtruvius Morrison. Lack of funds has caused sad deterioration of the once fine glass-houses. The gardens were laid out by Sir Edwin Lutyens. The Tower of Ballyfin is said to command a view of seven counties.

1½ m. E. is Clonenagh, where St Fintán moccu Echdach (d. 603), patron of the O Mores, founded a monastery. Famous for his asceticism and manual labours, Fintan is said to have numbered St Comgall of Bangor among his disciples. Óengus the Culdee (*see pp. 124, 285 and 287*) was a member of the community there before going to Tallaght. Only a few mounds mark the site of the monastery today.

3 m. NW., on the slope of the mountain, is Roundwood House, probably by Francis Bindon. It now offers guests accommodation in Palladian style.

MOUNTSHANNON, Co. Clare (Map 6, J5), is a village and angling centre delightfully situated on the Clare side of Lough Derg, on the road from Portumna (16 m.) to Limerick (30 m.). 1½ m. SE., beautifully situated in Lough Derg, is Inis Cealtra, alias Holy Island, with its monastic ruins. The monastery's origins are associated in legend with the fabulous St Mac Creiche, with St Colm of Terryglass (*see p. 266*) and with the 7th c. St Caimin, reputedly half-brother of Guaire Aidhne, King of Connacht. It suffered Norse raids but in the later 10th c. came under the patronage of the rising Dál gCais dynasty of east Clare. Brian Boru is said to have built there, and his brother Marcán, who held the abbacy (as well as those of Killaloe and Terryglass), died there in 1010. Conn Ua Sinnaig, 'anchorite of Ireland', died on the island in 1033 and Cathasach, 'head of the piety of Ireland', in 1111. The site was excavated, 1970–80.

The main group of buildings centres on 'St Caimin's Church', with *antae*, possibly the work of Brian Boru towards the end of the 10th c. A Romanesque chancel and W. doorway were inserted in the late-12th c., and these have been rebuilt by the Office of Public Works in 1879 and 1979 respectively. W. of this building is a Round Tower, topless and possibly never complete, which appears to be contemporary with St Caimin's. Between the two there is the shaft of a 9th c. High Cross, the head of which is affixed to the interior of St Caimin's, along with other carved or inscribed stones. Among these carvings are two other crosses, one of which bears the inscriptions: OR[OIT] DO ARDSENOIR HERENN .I. DO CATHASACH ('A prayer for the archsenior of Ireland, i.e. for Cathasach') and: O[ROIT] DO THORNOC DO RINGNI IN CROIS ('A prayer for Tornóg who made the cross'). To the E. of St Caimin's lies the burial ground known as 'the saints' graveyard', which has a rebuilt ancient boundary wall. Within it are recumbent grave-slabs of the 12th c., with inscriptions in Irish (there are earlier inscribed slabs in St Caimin's), and, near the SW. corner, a structure inscribed ILAD I[N] DECHENBOIR ('The grave of the ten'). There is also in the graveyard a small ruined building which is recorded as *Teampal na bhFear nGonta* ('the church of the wounded men'). This was extensively rebuilt *c.* 1700, but the original structure dates from *c.* 1200. Just to the NE. of the Saints' Graveyard is a diminutive stone structure, known as 'the Confessional', of masonry enclosing two pairs of inward-inclined rude orthostats, with an E. entrance, within a small enclosure. Excavation has shown that this was rebuilt many times (the last *c.* 1700), and that there had been an earlier timber structure within a rectangular fenced enclosure. It appears to have been a shrine. A large slab, with ringed cross in relief, was set to the E. of the stone shrine, probably in the 10th c., and, farther to the E., there is the base of a High Cross.

Inis Cealtra, Co. Clare.

St Caimin's stands at the E. edge of a complex of earthworks, consisting of low banks forming small enclosures, with roads or paths between them. Excavation showed these to be post-monastic, formed in the Middle Ages and later to cater for the growing annual Whitsuntide pilgrimage or 'patron', which brought huge numbers of people to the island before the custom was suppressed in the 19th c. Part of this complex, a D-shaped enclosure at the highest point of the island, was an infants' burial ground, in use since the 15th c. The enclosure was known as *Garraí Mhichíl* ('Michael's Garden'). 280 yds. S. of this is another small enclosure within which stands a small ruin known as the 'Baptism Church'. The minute building has a Romanesque W. doorway of the middle of the 12th c., rebuilt in 1879. The Baptism Church was not in use as a place of worship for long, being replaced early in the 13th c. by St Mary's, just to the S., a larger structure which is post-monastic and which served as a parish church in the Middle Ages. St Mary's, a featureless building, was much rebuilt at various periods. Within the building are some inscribed grave slabs and a rustic Baroque O Brien tomb. Just SE. of St Mary's is a 'Lady Well'. There are several bullaun stones on the island.

Excavation on Inis Cealtra produced material ranging from the beginning of the 7th c. to the present day. Traces of the early monastery (a very small community) and its graveyard were found in the area around the Round Tower. There had been a very small, mud-walled, oratory, built in the 7th or 8th c., and some large round huts with internal subdivisions. The community may have been founded to tend the shrine which, although Christian, was possibly pagan originally. After *c.* 1200 the island ceased to be monastic, but a small secular community lived in

Greencastle, Co. Donegal.

the area SE. of St Caimin's and conducted some manufacture, of querns and bone objects, as well as metal-working. The Baptism Church was used for burial at this time.

MOVILLE, Co. Donegal (Map 1, E3), is a seaside resort on the W. shore of Lough Foyle, 19 m. N. of Derry. Before the Second World War it was a port of call for transatlantic liners.

3½ m. N., in Carrowblagh, alias Leckemy, on the road to Culdaff, is a sweat-house.

3 m. NE., is Greencastle, with the overgrown ruins of the great castle (Nat. Mon.) of Northburg, alias Greencastle, built in 1305 by Richard de Burgo, 'Red' Earl of Ulster. In 1316 it was captured by Edward Bruce and his Irish adherents, but was recovered by de Burgo in 1318. It fell into Irish hands in 1333. In 1555 An Calbhach O Donnell revolted against his father and wrecked the castle. Until the end of the 19th c. the castle was included in the defences of Lough Foyle. The medieval remains include a 14th c., twin-towered, residential gate house giving entry to a small yard, beyond which was the upper ward with large NE. tower; the rectangular tower at the N. curtain was a 15th c., O Doherty addition. East of the castle is a 19th c. battery.

1 m. W., in Carrownaff, are the remains of an ancient church, a plain monolithic High Cross, and the 'Skull House'. The latter is a small, stone-roofed mortuary house.

3½ m. NW. is Kinnagoe Bay where the wreck of the *Trinidad Valencera*, one of the largest ships of the Spanish Armada, was discovered in 1971. The finds from the vessel are now in the Ulster Museum in Belfast.

MOY, Co. Tyrone (Map 2, G2), is a small town on the River Blackwater, on the Dungannon (6 m.)–Armagh (8 m.) road. The town, with its tree-lined 'square', was laid out after the plan of the Italian town of Marengo by Lord Charlemont, the Volunteer Earl. The place is known to the locals as 'The Moy', and probably derives from its great horse fair in the 19th c. called by that name.

The parish church in the square dates from 1819. Only the entrance gates (Hist. Mon.) survive of Roxborough Castle, a French-style château built in 1865 by a later Lord Charlemont.

1½ m. N., at Grange, is the old Quaker Meeting House, founded in 1660, but reconstructed to its present form in 1816.

MOYCULLEN, Co. Galway (Map 6, F1), is a hamlet on the Galway (7 m.)–Oughterard (10 m.) road.

4½ m. NNE., to the E. of Ross Lake (Lough Lonan), is St Annin's Well. ½ m. NW. are the featureless ruins of Killannin, a medieval parish church dedicated to St Annin; in the tomb of the Martins of Ross is buried Major Poppelton, Napoleon's esteemed custodian on St Helena, whose wife was a Martin of Ross House (*see below*). ¼ m. NW. of Killannin are the ruins of Templebegnaneeve, a diminutive oratory with trabeate W. door.

2½ m. S., in Killagoola townland, are remnants of Templeany, 'Enda's Church', a small nave-and-chancel structure.

3½ m. NW., on the W. side of the main road in Rosscahill, are the remains of Temple Brecan, a small, early church.

4 m. NNW., to the E. of the main road, is Ross House, former home of the Martins and birthplace of 'Martin Ross' (Violet Martin, 1862–1915), who collaborated with her cousin, Dr Edith Oenone Somerville (*see p. 101*), in the celebrated 'Somerville and Ross' series of novels and tales.

MUFF, Co. Donegal (Map 1, D4), is 6 m. NNE. of Derry, on the Moville (13 m.) road.

1½ m. NNE., in Ardmore, is a massive pillarstone with cup-and-circle devices.

2 m. NNW., at the foot of Eskaheen Mt (1,377 ft), are the ancient monastic (Columban) site and holy well of Eskaheen. Somewhere thereabouts is the grave of Eógan, son of Niall

Nine Hostager and eponymous ancestor of Cenél Eóghain (Tír Eóghain, Tyrone). On the hillside overlooking the church are the pillarstones called Niall's Rocks.

MUINE BHEAG, Co. Carlow (Map 4, J1), a small market town on the E. bank of the Barrow $9\frac{3}{4}$ m. S. of Carlow and 16 m. NE. of Kilkenny, was founded towards the close of the 18th c. by Walter Bagenal of Dunleckny Manor, who intended it 'to be of considerable architectural pretensions and to bear the name Versailles'. Re-routing of the coach road disappointed Walter's ambitions and left the place with no prouder name than Bagenalstown, which it kept until the present century.

The court house has a good Doric portico.

$2\frac{1}{4}$ m. E. are the ruins of Ballymoon Castle (Nat. Mon.), a unique castle consisting of a square enclosure without angle towers, but having rectangular towers projecting from the faces of three of the walls. Inside there were buildings against all four walls.

$3\frac{3}{4}$ m. SE., in Lorum, is a small granite cross (Nat. Mon.), relic of a monastery founded by St Laisrén of Leighlin. $1\frac{1}{2}$ m. ENE. is the fragmentary Kavanagh Mac Murrough Castle of Ballyloughan (Nat. Mon.), a keepless castle (*c.* 1300) with twin-towered gatehouse, towers at the SW. (hall-tower) and NE. angles, and a turret at the NW. angle.

2 m. S., in Ballinkillen, the interesting Catholic church (1793) still retains some original fittings, and has some fine modern (1980) stonework by Michael Biggs, and metal- and enamel-work by Richard King.

MULLINAVAT, Co. Kilkenny (Map 4, H4), is a village pleasantly situated in the Black Water valley, 17 m. SSW. of Thomastown and 8 m. NNW. of Waterford.

$2\frac{1}{2}$ m. SE. is Tory Hill (966 ft), called after the outlaw Eamonn Denn (*fl. c.* 1688). Lughnasa was celebrated there on Fraochán Sunday (second Sunday of July).

5 m. NW., in Kilmogue, is Leac an Scáil (Nat. Mon.), a magnificent portal-tomb.

MULLINGAR, Co. Westmeath (Map 3, E2), county town of Westmeath and cathedral town of the diocese of Meath (*see p. 295*), is situated on the Dublin (50 m.)–Longford (24 m.) road. It is the market centre of Ireland's premier cattle county, and is the junction of the Dublin–Sligo and Dublin–Galway railways.

Mullingar was a manor granted by Hugh I de Lacy to William le Petit. The town is dominated by the disappointing Cathedral of Christ the King, erected in 1936 to the design of Ralph Byrne. The only pleasing features are the mosaics by the Russian artist Boris Anrep, in the chapels of SS Anne (*St Anne Presents the Virgin Mary in the Temple,* 1954) and Patrick (*St Patrick Lights the Paschal Fire at Slane,* 1949). The pediment sculpture (*The Blessed Virgin Presents the 1831–6 Cathedral of the Immaculate Conception to Christ the King*) is by Albert Power. The cathedral museum has vestments which belonged to St Oliver Plunkett (1629–81), Archbishop of Armagh.

The Town Museum in the old Market House displays a collection of local antiquities and bygones. The Military Museum in Columb Barracks (open by appointment with the curator) houses items of military interest from home and overseas. The Church of St Paul, Bellview, on the Delvin Road (1987) is by Meehan, Levins, Delaney, Kavanagh and Associates, with unusual Stations of the Cross by Elizabeth Ryan, and the tabernacle and sanctuary cross by her husband Christopher.

3 m. NE., on the Delvin road, is the Pass of Rathconnell, alias 'Pass if you can'. In 1642 the English garrison and colonists withdrawing from Athlone had to fight through the pass.

3 m. SSW. is pretty Lough Ennell. Near the NE. corner of the lake the fragmentary ruins of Lynn Church mark the site of a monastery founded by Colmán, son of Lúachán. In 1394 the monastery, church and the shrine with the saint's relics were destroyed by Muirchertach Óg Mac Eochagáin. 1 m. S. of Lynn is Belvedere, the good 18th c. house and gardens (open to the public) from which Robert Rochfort (1708–72) took his title, Earl of Belvedere. The nearby Jealous Wall, a Gothick 'ruin' by Barradotte, is supposed to have been erected so as to shut out the sight of the nearby home of the earl's brother, Arthur, whom his lordship accused of being the paramour of Lady Belvedere (*see p. 274*).

4 m. WNW. is Slanemore Hill (499 ft), with three tumuli on the summit. Slanemore and adjoining Slanebeg are doubtless the Slemain Mide where the Ulster forces are described as camping in *Táin Bó Cúalnge*. $5\frac{1}{2}$ m. NNW. of the hill, near the W. shore of Lough Iron, is Tristernagh House. It occupies the site of a priory of Canons Regular of St Augustine founded by the Anglo-Norman Geoffrey de Costentin, *c.* 1200. All that survives of the priory are two 14th c. arcades embedded in post-Dissolution work. W. of the house is the small, late-15th c., parochial church of Templecross, with priest's residence at the W. end. 2 m. N. of Templecross is the site of the former Baronstown House. Just inside the entrance gate are remains of the medieval town of Kilbixy. Edmund Malone (1741–1812), Shakespearean scholar, was a member of the Baronstown family.

5 m. NW., near the W. shore of Lough Owel, are the ruins of Portloman Castle. $\frac{3}{4}$ m. N., on the shore of the lake, are the remains of Portloman 'Abbey', a medieval parish church on the site of a monastery founded by St Patrick's disciple, Lommán. There is a decorated medieval gravestone in the cemetery.

3 m. NNW. is Lough Owel. In 845 Melaghlin, King of Meath, drowned the notorious Viking Thorgestr (Turgesius) in the lake.

MULTYFARNHAM, Co. Westmeath (Map 2, D9), is a village 2 m. to the NE. of the Mullingar (9 m.)–Edgeworthstown (12 m.) road.

The Franciscan church incorporates parts of the church of a Franciscan friary founded before 1272 by William Delamere (*hibernicé* Mac Herbert) and sacked by English troops in 1601. The interior was refurbished (1976) by Wilfrid Cantwell, with altar and ambo by Ray Carroll, and tabernacle and Stations of the Cross by David King.

$1\frac{1}{2}$ m. SW. is Wilson's Hospital, a school with good 18th c. buildings. The United Irishmen of Westmeath, mustered to assist Humbert's Franco-Irish army, had their headquarters there 5–7 September 1798, but were subsequently routed at Bunbrosna, 1 m. to SW.

Malahide Castle, Co. Dublin: exterior (top) and interior (see page 243).

The heritage centre at Nenagh.

N

NAAS, Co. Kildare (Map 3, I5), county town of Kildare, is a small garrison town and marketing centre, now by-passed by the Dublin (21 m.)–Kildare (13 m.) road.

As its Irish name (Nás na Ríogh) denotes, the place was one of the royal seats of Leinster in early times. At the Anglo-Norman invasion Maurice fitz Gerald, ancestor of the Fitzgeralds, was granted the surrounding cantred of O ffelan by Strongbow, and it is he, presumably, who built the castle represented by the North Moat (W. of Main St). In 1534 the castle was taken from Silken Thomas's garrison by Sir William Skeffington (*see p. 245*). In 1577 the town was sacked by Rory Óg O More of Laois. In 1650 it was captured by the Cromwellian Col. Hewson. It also figured in the 1798 insurrection.

The dull Court House is by Sir Richard Morrison.

St David's Church, Main St, incorporates the great W. tower (much altered, 1781) and two window embrasures of the medieval parish church. The baptismal font has a handsome medieval basin.

The parish church of SS Mary and David, Sallins Rd, is an 1827 'Carpenter's Perpendicular' structure by Thomas A. Cobden. The 1858 Gothic-Revival tower and spire were modelled on those of St Andrew's Church, Ewerby, Lincolnshire. The 1954 Mortuary Chapel is by A.D. Devane with crucifix by Laurence Campbell. The church itself was refurbished (1986) by Richard Hurley, with strikingly coloured tabernacle by Benedict Tutty, and batik behind the sedilia by Bernadette Madden, stone altar by Michael Biggs, and lectern by Lua Breen.

3 m. E. is Furness (Forenaghts). Furness House (Mr Synnott) is a good small house of *c.* 1730–40. In Forenaghts Great is Longstone Rath (543 ft, Nat. Mon.), a prehistoric ritual enclosure surrounded by a great earthen ring in which are two openings. At the centre is a 17 ft granite pillarstone. Excavation revealed a large, roofless cist at the W. side of the stone. Behind Furness House are the ruins (Nat. Mon.) of a small nave-and-chancel manorial church with Romanesque doorway, windows, and chancel arch.

3 m. SE. is Punchestown, celebrated in horse-racing circles as the place of the annual three-day Kildare and National Hunt Race Meeting. On the E. side of the Woolpack Road (the medieval highway from Dublin to Kilkenny – via Rathcoole, Kilcullen, Athy) is the Long Stone of Punchestown Great (Nat. Mon.), a tapering granite monolith $19\frac{1}{2}$ ft high, which was found to have a cist near the base. $\frac{1}{2}$ m. SW., to the W. of the road, in Craddockstown West, is another Long Stone of Co. Wicklow granite. $2\frac{1}{2}$ m. SSE., in Sillagh, is The Ring, half of a great bivallate earthwork (an uncompleted hill-fort ?).

$2\frac{1}{2}$ m. S. is Killashee, a church founded by Bishop Auxilius, a 5th c. missionary bishop. The derelict Protestant church incorporates the unusual 15th/16th c. tower (square below, circular above) of a medieval church.

1 m. SW., beside the old road to Kildare, are the massive, overgrown remains of Jigginstown House (Nat. Mon.), a huge, palatial brick building begun, 'and in a manner finished', by Lord Deputy Thomas Wentworth, Earl of Strafford, for the entertainment of Charles I and for use as a country residence for the English Lord Deputy. Had it been completed, it would have been the largest unfortified residence ever built in Ireland (390 120 ft). The designer/builder is said to have been John Allen 'of great skill in architecture'. The house was one of the earliest brick buildings in Ireland. On 15 September 1643 the Confederate Catholics signed a 'Cessation' with Charles I's Lord Deputy, Ormonde, at Jigginstown.

NARAN and **PORTNOO**, Co. Donegal (Map 8, C5), are twin little resorts on Gweebarra Bay, 7 m. NNW. of Ardara and 7 m. WNW. of Glenties.

Less than $\frac{1}{2}$ m. offshore (reachable on foot at low tide) is Inishkeel, still a place of popular pilgrimage by reason of its associations with St Conall Caol (feast day, 2 May), who founded a monastic retreat there in the 6th c. Dallán Forgaill, author of *Amra Choluim Chille*, the celebrated (A.D. 597) elegy on St Columcille, is buried there. There are remains of two churches, an early cross-slab with figure subjects, part of a cross with broad ribbon interlacing, etc.

2 m. SSE. of Naran, in Kilclooney More, are a court-tomb and, nearby, twin portal-tombs in the remains of a long cairn.

2 m. S. of Naran is Doon Lough, with a well-preserved stone ringfort on one of the islands.

$2\frac{1}{2}$ m. SW. is Kiltooris Lough; on the SW. shore a low cross-pillar and remains of a church mark an ancient site; on O Boyle's Island are remains of a castle.

NAVAN, Co. Meath (Map 2, G9), officially An Uaimh, the county town of Meath, is a prosperous, small-scale industrial and mining (zinc) centre at the confluence of the Boyne and Blackwater, on the Dublin (28 m.)–Kells (11 m.) road.

Jocelin de Angulo, to whom Hugh I de Lacy granted Navan and the lands of Ardbraccan (*see below*), built a motte which is still to be seen near the railway on the W. side of the town. Francis Beaufort (1774–1857), inventor of the wind-scale which bears his name, was a native of Navan.

The simple, tasteful, Classical church of 1836 was designed by the parish priest, Archdeacon O Reilly, who modelled the plan on that of Francis Johnston's St George's Church, Dublin. Many years ago the building was ruthlessly transformed into a pseudo-Romanesque affair and furnished with vulgar marble altars. More recently the Classical reredos (with painted *Jerusalem* background) of the High Altar was veiled from sight and the excellent *Christ Crucified*, designed specifically for it by the Co. Meath sculptor Edward Smyth (1749–1813; of Four Courts, Dublin, fame), was mounted on a barbarous cross. (Earlier this century the *Christ*, Smyth's only religious work, had been supplied with a plaster beard!) The bust of Archdeacon O Reilly is by Terence Farrell.

4 m. N. are the remains of Kilberry Church and motte-castle.

1½ m. NE., at Donaghmore on the W. bank of the Boyne, the fragments of a small 16th c. church and a Round Tower (Nat. Mon.) mark the site of a 'great church' built by St Patrick and entrusted to the care of Cassán, a priest. St Cassán's wonder-working relics were venerated there for centuries. The tower has a Romanesque doorway, with a *Crucifixion* above and a human mask on either side of the architrave. 1¼ m. E., near the river, are the ruins (Nat. Mon.) of the 16th c. D'Arcy castle of Dunmoe. It was burned down in 1799. 2½ m. NE. of the castle is Broad Boyne bridge. 450 yds below the bridge is the King's Hole, where, on the first Sunday of Harvest, used to be held a *pátrún* at which people swam their cattle across the river to guard them against 'the good people' as well as against certain diseases.

3 m. NE., on the S. side of the Boyne, is Ardmulchan, with the remains of the medieval parish church of St Mary.

½ m. SE., beside the Duleek road, are the ruins of Athlumney Castle (Nat. Mon.), a 15th c. Dowdall castle with 17th c. house attached. Tradition asserts that the last occupier, Sir Launcelot Dowdall, set fire to it with his own hand rather than have it shelter the usurping William of Orange.

7 m. ESE., in Kentstown Protestant church (1797), is the mensa (with flat-relief effigy) of the tomb of Sir Thomas de Tuite (d. 1363).

1¾ m. SSE. is Kilcarn bridge. ¾ m. ENE. is Johnstown church. Built into a face of the tower is a figure (archbishop with right hand raised in blessing) from Bective Abbey. Against an inner wall has been mounted a noteworthy 15th/16th c. font basin (*Twelve Apostles, Coronation of the Virgin*) from the medieval church of Kilcarn (½ m. S., fragments only).

2¾ m. S., in Ardsallagh, are the ruins (Nat. Mon.) of St Brigid's Church (parochial), a nave-and-chancel building erected by the de Angulos in the 12th/13th c. and rebuilt in the 15th.; 2¼ m. S. of the church, on the S. side of the Boyne, is Ballinter House, built by Richard Cassels for John Preston, M.P. (1700–81) and grandfather of the 1st Baron Tara. It is now an adult education centre conducted by the community of Our Lady of Sion.

3 m. WNW. is Ardbraccan, which takes its name from St Breacán, founder of a monastic church there in the 7th c. St Ultán (d. 657/63), Bishop of Ardbraccan, was one of the first two men known to have concerned themselves with recording the acts of St Patrick. Bishop Tírechán (*fl.* 670), author of a celebrated memoir of St Patrick, was a disciple of Ultán's. Ultán is also honoured as a patron of sick children; he is said to have set up a hospital at Ardbraccan for infants whose mothers had been killed by a great plague. Cathal Crovderg O Conor of Connacht made formal submission to John of England at Ardbraccan in July 1210. The Protestant parish church (1777) has a medieval bell-tower; Bishop Pococke (1704–65), the historian, is buried in the churchyard.

2½ m. NW., close to the Kells road and the W. bank of the Blackwater, are the ruins of 15th c. Liscartan Castle and manorial church.

NENAGH, Co. Tipperary (Map 6, K5), is a market town and small-scale manufacturing centre on the Roscrea (20 m.)–Limerick (25 m.) road.

The name of Nenagh (An Aonach; anciently Óenach Téite) recalls that this was the meeting-place of one of the principal public assemblies of Munster. At the Anglo-Norman invasion this part of Munster, Ormond, belonged to the O Brien Kingdom of Limerick, otherwise Thomond, and the N. portion was allotted by the invaders to Theobald Walter, 'Butler of Ireland' and ancestor of the great house of Butler. Theobald came to Nenagh *c.* 1200, fixed on it as the *caput* of his chief manor, and built (*c.* 1217) the great castle whose fragmentary remains still dominate the town. The castle remained the chief seat of the Butlers until the second half of the 14th c., when the Earls of Ormond transferred to GOWRAN. For nearly 150 years thereafter Nenagh remained in the possession of the O Briens of Ára, but in 1533 it was recovered by Gaelicized Sir Piers Rúa Butler, Earl of Ossory (Earl of Ormond, 1537). In 1548 O Carroll of Éile burned the place. It changed hands three times during the Cromwellian period, and twice during the Williamite wars, when it was slighted. In 1703 the Butler connection with Nenagh was severed by the sale of manor and town to pay the Duke of Ormond's debts.

The principal feature of the town is the Butler castle (Nat. Mon.). This was a pentagonal fortress with twin-towered gatehouse on the SW., strong towers at the NW. and SE. angles, and a mighty circular donjon on the NE. The latter, the most remarkable structure of its kind in Ireland, is now 100 ft high; but the uppermost 25 ft date from *c.* 1860, when the ruin was 'castellated after the manner of Windsor' by the Catholic Bishop of Killaloe. Nearby is the parish church of St Mary of the Rosary, a large and costly Gothic-Revival edifice (1892–1906) by W.G. Doolin; details poor. Close by is Nenagh Heritage Centre, with displays of local bygones in the heptagonal Governor's House and gatehouse of the former gaol.

In Abbey St are remains (Nat. Mon.) of the church, etc., of a Franciscan friary founded about 1250 by Bishop Donal O Kennedy of Killaloe and his kinfolk. This was one of the most important Franciscan houses in the country, particularly after the failure of the late-13th c. English plan to segregate the English and Irish elements of the Order in Ireland. The final destruction of the friary was due to the Cromwellians.

4 m. ENE. is Rathurles, a remarkable trivallate ringfort whose noteworthy stone gateposts lie prostrate in the field on the NE.

Inside the fort are the ruins of a plain 15th c. church. $\frac{1}{4}$ m. S. are the ruins of a small, 16th c., round castle (O Kennedy Donn).

1 m. SE. are the battered remains of Tyone (Teach, alias Tigh, Eóin), a priory and hospital of the Augustinian Crucifers, dedicated to St John (Eóin) the Baptist and founded *c.* 1200 by Theobald Walter.

3 m. SE., in Ballynaclough, are remains of a church and of a 13th c. castle (motte, fragment of great hall, etc.), relics of the manor of Weyperous (Gué Pierreux) granted to the de Mariscos by Theobald Walter.

$4\frac{1}{2}$ m. S. are the ruins of Kilboy House, built in the 18th c. by William Leeson for Henry Prittie, 1st Baron Dunalley, and restored by Mr Tony Ryan. $\frac{1}{4}$ m. SE. are the remains of Dolla medieval church, privately conserved in 1988.

$6\frac{1}{2}$ m. SSW. is Silvermines, a village at the foot of the Silvermine Mts (1,609 ft). The silver, lead, and zinc ores thereabouts have been exploited from time to time throughout the centuries.

$7\frac{1}{2}$ m. W., in the Ara Mts (Tountinna, 1,517 ft), is the village of Portroe, best known for its proximity to the great 'Killaloe' slate quarries. $2\frac{1}{2}$ m. S. of the village, in Lackamore, is a wedge-tomb. $3\frac{3}{4}$ m. SW., on the slope of Tountinna in Coolbaun, are some stones called the Graves of the Leinstermen; fine view.

$5\frac{3}{4}$ m. NW. is pretty Dromineer Bay, one of the favourite fishing resorts on Lough Derg with angling, boating, and bathing. By the lake shore are the ruins of a medieval church with Romanesque fragments. The castle, an early-16th c. structure, was built by the O Kennedys, who gave it and its manor to the Earl of Ormond in 1556 in exchange for other property.

7 m. NNW., in Johnstown, are the ruins of Killodiernan, a Romanesque church, which local initiative recently prevented from collapsing.

NEWBLISS, Co. Monaghan (Map 2, E4), is a village on the Clones (5 m.)–Ballybay (11 m.) road.

$2\frac{3}{4}$ m. NE., in Garran, is Giant's Grave, a portal-tomb. $\frac{3}{4}$ m. NE., in Tiredigan, is a court-tomb. $1\frac{1}{2}$ m. NW. of Lecklevera road-junction, in Cloghernagh, is a second court-tomb. $1\frac{1}{4}$ m. SE. of Lecklevera road-junction, in Carn, is a third.

2 m. SE. is Annaghmakerrig House, former home of Sir Tyrone Guthrie, theatre director, and now a centre for artists, writers and musicians.

NEWBRIDGE, alias **DROICHEAD NUA**, Co. Kildare (Map 3, H5), is a small manufacturing, maket and former garrison town of no antiquity, where the Naas (8 m.)–Kildare (5 m.) road crosses the River Liffey.

The church of Cill Mhuire, Ballymany, at the W. end of the town is by Meehan, Levins, Delaney and Associates, with Stations by Elizabeth Ryan, and stone statuary by Henry Flanagan, O.P.

N. of the town is Newbridge Dominican College, a boarding-school for boys. Nearby, on the E. bank of the Liffey, in Oldconnell, is a fine motte.

$1\frac{1}{2}$ m. SE., in Great Connell, are the remains of the Augustinian Priory of Our Lady and St David, founded in 1202 by Myler fitz Henry as a cell of Llanthony Prima in Wales. In the Middle Ages this was one of the most important of Anglo-Irish monasteries, and the prior was a Lord Spiritual of Parliament. The effigy of Walter Wellesley and other pieces of medieval sculpture from there have been moved to Kildare Cathedral (*see p. 212*).

NEWCASTLE, Co. Down (Map 2, K4), is a small port and well-known seaside and golfing resort delightfully situated on Dundrum Bay, 31 m. S. of Belfast and 25 m. E. of Newry. It takes its name from a late-16th c. castle of the Magennises.

Immediately S. and SW. of the town Slieve Donard (2,796 ft) rises from the sea. It is named after St Domangard of Ráth Murbhuilg (*see below*), son of Echu (last pagan king of the region) and immortal guardian of the mountain, who died *c.* 506 (?).

3 m. N., in Carnacavill, is the circular (cashel) churchyard, Ráth Murbhuilg, with remains of a church, the stump of a Round Tower, and two early cross-slabs (Hist. Mons.); these are relics of an early monastery founded by Bishop Domhanghard. A 13th c. tombstone marks a modern grave.

2 m. NW., to the W. of Priest's Bridge on the Bryansford road, is Barbican Gate, entrance to Tollymore Forest Park.

NEWCASTLE, alias **NEWCASTLE-LYONS**, Co. Dublin (Map 3, J4), is a small village on the Rathcoole (3 m.)–Celbridge (5 m.) road, 12 m. SW. of Dublin. It takes its name from an English royal castle and manorial village erected there, at the time of the Anglo-Norman invasion. In 1641 Newcastle was the headquarters of the Catholic forces operating in Co. Dublin. When abandoned by them the following year it was pillaged by an English force, which returned to Dublin rich in plate and cattle. In the 16th c. the place contained six 'castles', i.e. fortified town houses, of which two survive, one in the rectory grounds, the other in a field among the houses of the village. Near the gate of St Finian's Protestant Church is the motte-and-bailey of the 12th c. royal castle. The church is an early-15th c. nave-and-chancel structure with a dwelling tower added (as often in the Pale) at the W. end. The chancel was callously unroofed about 1724, the chancel arch blocked up, and the excellent curvilinear E. window re-erected in the blocking. The nave, relentlessly modernized, has some good wood-carving dating from 1724. In the graveyard, on the S. side of the church, is an early granite cross with traces of a raised cross-in-a-circle on the E. face and of a raised cross on the W. face.

NEWCASTLE WEST, Co. Limerick (Map 6, F9), is a small market town on the Limerick (25 m.)–Abbeyfeale (13 m.) road.

The Gothic-Revival parish church is by J.J. Mc Carthy.

Partly incorporated in a modern residence are remains of a great castle of the Earls of Desmond, viz. water fosse, bastion, part of the curtain, rectangular tower, circular keep, and two 15th c. halls. One of the latter, Desmond's Hall (Nat. Mon.), is complete, and has a fine vaulted basement. It changed hands many times in the course of its history before Confederate Catholics besieged it from December 1641 until the following Easter Monday, when it surrendered and was burned. On the town square side of the castle is a bronze equestrian figure (1978) of Gerald, Earl of Desmond (1337–98) by Cliodna Cussen, a native of the town.

Three well-known 17th-18th c. poets have associations with Newcastle West or its vicinity: Dáibhidh Ó Bruadair was born in the vicinity; Dáibhidh Ó Cléirigh lived in the town; Father Liam Inglis, O.S.A. (d. 1778), whose *Caiseal Mumhan* was translated by Sir Samuel Ferguson, is buried in St John's Church.

6 m. E. are remnants of nave-and-chancel St M'Aodhóg's Church, possibly the site of a monastery founded by St M'Aodhóg of FERNS.

3½ m. SE., in Mahoonagh Beg, are remains of a church with simple, Romanesque S. window; the church was restored in 1410.

6 m. S., in Killeedy (Cill Íde) churchyard, St Ida's Well and fragmentary remains of a church mark the site of a nunnery founded by St Íde ('Fostermother of the Saints', d. 570/77), who 'succoured many grievous diseases' and is mentioned in one of Alcuin's poems. According to legend, she was privileged to suckle Jesus, who came to her in the form of an infant. The nunnery seems early to have been replaced by a monastery for men, which was several times plundered by the Norse. At the junction of nave and chancel (S. side) is St Íde's Grave; in summer pilgrims strew it with flowers. Also in Killeedy townland, on a motte, are the remains of a Desmond castle.–1½ m. W. of Killeedy is the tower (repaired 1840, Nat. Mon.) of the Desmond castle of Glenquin.

NEWGRANGE, Co. Meath (Map 2, I8), 5 m. E. of Slane and 7 m. SW. of Drogheda, is the most famous of the many prehistoric monuments in the 'Bend of the Boyne'.

Newgrange (Nat. Mon., admission charge, guided tours) is a great chambered mound of turves and stones about 280 ft in diameter and about 44 ft high, constructed *c.* 3100 B.C. The body of the mound is bounded by a retaining kerb of large, horizontally laid stones, some bearing spirals, lozenges, zigzags and other splendidly carved prehistoric motifs. The white quartz wall surmounting them on the SE. sector of the mound is modern, backed by a reinforced cement wall to prevent further slipping of the mound behind it. The controversial reconstruction is based on the position of the layers of white quartz stones found outside the kerb during the excavations on the site between 1962 and 1975. Some distance outside the kerb are 12 roughly hewn standing stones, the survivors of a circle of stones, originally numbering more than 35, encircling the great mound, but dating at earliest from the Beaker period, 1000 years after the construction of the mound. At the SE. side of the mound, the kerb dips slightly inwards to a superbly decorated kerbstone with triple spiral ornament, which now stands in front of the entrance to the tomb and the slab which acted as a blocking door of the tomb. The wall around the entrance is an unashamedly modern reconstruction. Above the entrance to the passage leading to the tomb is an opening, known as the 'roof-box', designed to allow the rays of the sun rising above the horizon on the days around the winter solstice (21 December) to penetrate at a sufficiently high level along the passage so that they can fall on the ground at the very centre of the tomb. The passage, which is 62 ft long, follows the rising slope of the hill on which the mound was built, and many of the upright stones forming its walls bear geometrical decoration. The chamber is roughly cruciform in plan, with one recess to the right and left respectively, and a third at the rear. Its roof, rising to a height of 19 ft, is built on the beam-wall principle, so that each horizontal stone rests roughly on the mid-point of two stones adjoining one another beneath it. A number of the stones in the chamber, including the capstone of the right-hand recess, are decorated with a variety of geometric motifs. Resting on the floor of the recesses are great stone basins, one each in the left-hand and rear recess, but two superimposed in the right-hand recess, where the upper basin has two saucer-like depressions. Excavations in the chamber produced remains of two inhumed and at least three cremated individuals, as well as 'marbles', pendants and beads of stone, together with a variety of bone pins.

Two further 'satellite' tombs were found respectively E. and W. of the entrance. Modern cement stakes to the SE. of the entrance mark the post-holes of a remarkable double circle of upright wooden posts, a kind of 'Woodhenge', containing cremation pits of the Beaker period. Outside the Tourist Office are two decorated megalithic stones from Dowth, and just inside the car-park fence is a third (from Ballinacrad, nr Dowth).

Some 500 yds SSE. of the great cairn is a tumulus, 220 ft in circumference and 20 ft high. About 450 yds SE. of the tumulus, by the river, is a mound 90 ft in diameter and 20 ft high. Some 450 yds. NNE. is a 10 ft high pillarstone. About ¼ m. NNW. is a stone-kerbed tumulus, 280 ft in circumference.

400 yds. NE. of these (1¾ m. NE. of Newgrange) is the great chambered cairn of Dowth (Nat. Mon., admission charge), which has suffered severely from the attentions of antiquarians and others. The mound is 280 ft in diameter and 47 ft high. Some of its kerbstones bear prehistoric scribings. At the W. perimeter is the entrance to the principal tomb. Passages to the left and right lead to the chambers of a 70 ft long souterrain, with a beehive chamber at either end, and dating from the early historic period. Straight ahead is the tomb passage, 27 ft long, lined with uprights which support a lintelled roof, and segmented by three sill-stones, one of which bears scribings of Newgrange type. The cruciform chamber, with further decorated stones, contains the re-assembled fragments of a stone basin. An opening at the SW. corner leads to a unique additional series of small chambers. Just inside the tumulus kerb, on the SW., is the entrance to a second tomb, with a circular chamber having one side-chamber. Some of its stones bear decoration.

About 150 yds E. of the mound are the ruins of a small medieval church and a castle. ¼ m. ENE. of the castle is Dowth House (built for Viscount Netterville *c.* 1780), which has good ceilings. SW. of the house is a mound with a small, corbel-roofed hexagonal chamber with five peripheral cells. ¼ m. E. of the house is a large, circular, ritual enclosure surrounded by a great earthen bank. John Boyle O Reilly (1844–90), poet and Fenian, was a native of Dowth.

1¾ m. NW. of the great Newgrange cairn is Knowth (closed to the public, viewing platform beside road), the third of the three great passage-tombs in the Bend of the Boyne, and roughly contemporary with Newgrange. It is 280 ft in diameter and 40–50 ft high. Surrounding it are the remains of at least 17 'satellite' tombs, two of which had to be partially removed to enable the building of the main mound. Unusually, the great mound contained two tombs, each of a different type, which almost meet at the centre of the tumulus. Of these, the W. tomb, discovered in 1967, is just over 100 ft long, consisting of a lintelled passage which veers slightly to the right about three-quarters of the way along its length, before rising to the chamber, which also has a lintelled roof. In contrast, the E. tomb, discovered in 1968, is, like that at Newgrange (*see above*), cruciform, but with a corbelled roof, the combined length of passage and tomb being about 120 ft. In the right-hand recess is a highly decorated stone basin. With few exceptions, the burials in this tomb were cremations, and the grave goods included stone pendants and bone pins. In the right-hand recess was found a unique ceremonial flint macehead. A number of stones in both tombs bear decorative motifs, and the kerbstones of the mound have proved to bear a very considerable amount of further ornament. Iron Age burials came to light at Knowth, and at the top of the mound a souterrain was discovered, dating from the early historic period. During the Iron Age, the mound was fortified by two penannular ditches, one at the base of the mound, the other around the top. Foundations of 13 rectangular houses show Knowth to have been a settlement around A.D. 800, and during the following two c., Knowth was the residence of the Kings of Northern Brega. Hugh de Lacy granted it to one of his barons, Richard de Flemming, *c.* 1175, and the site would appear to have been abandoned about a century later.

1¾ m. ENE., in Monknewtown, are the remains of a large circular henge, dating from the Beaker period, and a 17th (?) c. cross with *Crucifixion*.

NEWMARKET, Co. Cork (Map 5, I2), is a village on the Kanturk (5 m.)–Abbeyfeale (22 m.) road, founded by the Aldsworths in the time of James I. John Philpot Curran (1750–1817), father of Sarah Curran, Robert Emmet's betrothed, was a native of the place. He treated Sarah very badly for her association with a rebel. She later married an English officer, but Thomas Moore's

> She's far from the land
> Where her young hero sleeps

has assured her an unmerited reputation for fidelity to Emmet's memory. She died young, and is buried in Newmarket churchyard, as is also Mrs Aldworth, the woman mason (*see p. 131*).

NEWMARKET-ON-FERGUS, Co. Clare (Map 6, G6), is a village on the Ennis (7½ m.)–Limerick (23 m.) road, near Shannon Airport. The Catholic church (1970) is by John Thompson, with furnishings by Ray Carroll and decorative concrete by Robin Costello.

¾ m. W., in Kilnasoolagh Protestant church, is the recumbent effigy of Sir Donough O Brien (1642–1717) by William Kidwell (d. 1736), the Dublin statuary.

3 m. N., in a well diversified demesne of 1,500 acres, is Dromoland Castle, until 1962 seat of Lord Inchiquin, but now a luxury hotel with golf course, etc. The Leamanch (*see p. 212*) O Briens moved to Dromoland at the end of the 17th c., but the present house, a 'baronial castle' by Pain of Cork, dates from *c.* 1826. In the garden are a gateway from Leamaneh and an 18th c. temple. William Smith O Brien (1803–64), younger brother of the 13th Baron Inchiquin and leader of the Young Irelanders, was born at Dromoland. 2 m. NNE., inside the SE. entrance to Dromoland Demesne, is Mooghaun, a trivallate, stone hill-fort of 27½ acres, with two ringforts.

4 m. NE., in Finlough, is Tomfinlough, site of a monastic or anchoritic foundation (*c.* 550) by St Luchtighern. The remains comprise a holy well, the W. gable of a tiny oratory with trabeate W. doorway beneath three Romanesque masks, and the ruins of a Western Transitional church, which was subsequently Gothicized. Built into the S. wall of the churchyard is the Plague Stone, and early cross-slab.

NEWPORT, Co. Mayo (Map 7, E5), is a village and angling centre near the NE. corner of Clew Bay, 8 m. N. of Westport and 12 m. W. of Castlebar, on the road to Achill (19 m.).

The parish church (1914) is an interesting essay in the Irish Romanesque style, by Rudolph M. Butler. Its E. window (*Last Judgement*) was designed by Harry Clarke and painted under his supervision the year he died (1930). From Cortoon, 2½ m. E. came the family of the late Princess Grace of Monaco.

3 m. W., on the shore of Clew Bay, is the tower of Carrigahooley (Carraiglan Chabhlaigh), alias Rockfleet, Castle (Nat. Mon.), a Burke stronghold. The famous Gráinne Ní Mháille (*see p. 104*) beat off an English attack in 1574. In 1583, after the death of her second husband, Richard *an Iarainn* Burke, she took up her residence in the castle, the only one that can be positively associated with her.

2 m. NW., to the S. of the Achill road, are the ruins of Burrishoole 'Abbey' (Nat. Mon.), a Dominican friary founded by Richard Burke of Turlough, MacWilliam *Íochtair*, who retired to the friary in 1469 and died there in 1473.

NEWPORT, Co. Tipperary (Map 6, J7), is a village on the Limerick (11 m.)–Thurles (29 m.) road through the Slieve Felim–Mauherslieve Mts.

Outside the parish church is a stoup from Kilcommenty.

3 m. NNW., in Ballyard, is the ancient church-site, Kilcommenty. St Cominad's Bed there is a boulder with bullauns and the 'prints of the saint's ribs and hands'. St Cominad's Well still attracts devotees.

NEW ROSS, Co. Wexford (Map 4, J4), is a busy little port as well as a manufacturing, marketing, and communications centre on the E. bank of the tideway of the Barrow, where the Waterford (15 m.)–Enniscorthy (21 m.) road crosses the river. In the Middle Ages it was an important seaport, rivalling Waterford.

The town was the creation of William the Marshal, Earl of Pembroke, and his wife, Isabella, heiress of Strongbow and Díarmait Mac Murrough's daughter, Aoífe. In 1265 it was walled by the townsfolk.

In October 1394 Art Óg Mac Murrough, King of Leinster, attacked and destroyed the town, and then retired to his forest fastnesses when assailed by Richard II and the feudal might of England. He later made the town his own, and died there in 1418. In 1649 the Catholic garrison, overawed by the fate of Drogheda and Wexford, surrendered to Cromwell, who had crossed the Barrow by a bridge of boats (the permanent bridge having been destroyed in 1643). On 4 June 1798 a large

Insurgent force, led by Bagenal Harvey, made an unsuccessful effort to seize the town and river-crossing, with a loss of 2,000 lives. In the course of the fighting much of the town was destroyed by fire.

The principal monument in the town (Church Lane) is the roofless chancel and transepts (Nat. Mon.) of St Mary's, the parish church of the 'new town of Ross' founded by William the Marshal and his wife, Isabella. Dating from *c.* 1210–20, they are among the earliest examples of pure Gothic work in Ireland. In the older, roofless, part of the church (locked) there is a fine collection of medieval tombstones. The site of the crossing and of the aisled nave is occupied by the early-19th c. Protestant church, which also contains interesting tombs and memorials.

Of the walls of the town only a few fragments now remain.

The Tholsel, in Irishtown, is a good building of 1749, rebuilt in 1806. (As so often, the ground-floor loggia has been blocked up.) There may be seen the civic insignia and muniments, including the maces and James II's charter.

5½ m. NNE. is Pollmounty. According to tradition, it was to Eibhlín Kavanagh of Pollmounty that Cearbhall Ó Dálaigh sang his celebrated elopement song, *Eibhlín a Rúin (Eileen Aroon) c.* 1600 (*see p. 196*).

4¾ m. E., at Old Ross, is a fine motte, perhaps constructed by Strongbow.

4½ m. S. is Slievecoilta (888 ft), where the Kennedy Park with arboretum commemorates John F. Kennedy, President of the United States. The granite fountain is by Michael Biggs.

4½ m. SSW., in Dunganstown, are remains of the family home of Patrick Kennedy, great-grandfather of President Kennedy. The farm is still the home of his kinsfolk and was twice visited by President Kennedy.

4 m. SW., on the Barrow, is the 15th–16th c. tower of Annaghs (Co. Kilkenny) Castle.

The Kilnasaggart stone, Co. Armagh.

NEWRY, Co. Down (Map 2, I4), is a seaport and manufacturing town on the main Dublin (65 m.)–Belfast (38 m.) road, a few miles N. of the strategically important Gap of the North, of the Border, and of Carlingford Lough. It is also the cathedral town of the Catholic diocese of Dromore. About 1144 the great St Malachy and Donnchad Mac Cearbhaill, King of Uriel, founded an abbey which was subsequently (1153) colonized by Cistercians from Mellifont. In 1156 the High-King, Muirchertach Mac Lochlainn (of Cenél Eóghain) took the abbey under his protection and endowed it, and so is usually reckoned as the founder. No trace of it survives.

Because of its strategic position, Newry suffered repeatedly in the wars for control of the N. in the Middle Ages. About 1575 Sir Nicholas Bagenal built hill-top St Patrick's Church (the first Protestant church in Ireland built as such). In 1689 the retreating Jacobites under Berwick fired the town, and only the tower of Bagenal's church survived; in the porch is a 1578 tablet with Bagenal's arms.

St Colman's Cathedral, Hill St, is a dull 19th–20th c. Perpendicular building; the original architect was T.J. Duff of Newry. At the N. end of the street the Town Hall is built across the little Clanrye River. The nearby Court House is a simple Classical building of 1843.

John Mitchel (1815–75), celebrated Republican, journalist, and author, is buried in the Unitarian (First Presbyterian) churchyard, Old Meetinghouse Green, High St. The 1962 memorial to him in St Colman's Park, Hill St, is by Donal Murphy. The present Unitarian Church (1853) was Ulster's first Gothic-Revival church; architect, 23-year-old W.J. Barre of Newry.

Newry's link with Lough Neagh was the first (1730–41) major canal to be constructed in the British Isles. Richard Cassels was engineer until 1736, when the work was entrusted to Thomas Steers of Liverpool.

6 m. NNE., on the Banbridge (14 m.) road, the churchyard of Donaghmore marks the site of a 5th/6th c. monastery founded by St Mac Erca, brother of Mo-Chaoi of Nendrum (*see p. 114*). In the churchyard stands a figured High Cross (Hist. Mon.) dating from the 9th/10th c. The much weathered sculptures represent subjects from the Old and New Testaments (*The Fall, Noah's Ark, The Crucifixion, The Last Judgment,* etc.). The cross, which had long lain overthrown, was set up in its present position in 1891 above a souterrain (closed).

5½ m. S., near Killeen, Co. Armagh, is Clontygora (Hist. Mon.), a two-chamber court-tomb. Close by are remains of a second court cairn.

2 m. SW., on the SE. slope of Camlough Mountain (1,385 ft), in Ballymacdermot, is a court-tomb (650 ft, Hist. Mon.), excavated in 1962.

8 m. SSW., in Edenappa, Co. Armagh, ¼ m. ESE. of Kilnasaggart railway bridge, is the Kilnasaggart Stone (Hist.

Mon.), an early Christian pillarstone with ten cross-inscribed circles on the N. face, another on the E. angle of the head, and a Latin cross and a large cross-inscribed circle on the S. face. Between these last is the inscription IN LOC SO TANIMMAIRNI TERNOHC MAC CERAN BIC ER CUL PETER APSTAL (thus Macalister; some of his readings are doubtful): 'This place did Ternóc son of Ciarán bequeath under the protection of Peter the Apostle'. Ternóc died *c.* 714/16, and the stone is the earliest securely dated Christian field-monument in Ireland. At the foot of the stone are four early cross-slabs. ¼ m. SW. of Kilnasaggart railway bridge, in Carrickbroad, is Moyry Castle (Hist. Mon.), built in 1601 by Lord Mountjoy to secure the Moyry Pass, gateway to the Fews and the heart of the still Gaelic North.

2½ m. NW. is Derrymore House (Nat. Trust), an interesting thatched villa built by Isaac Corry, M.P. for Newry (1776–1806), and last Chancellor of the Irish Exchequer. In the drawing-room the Act of Union is said to have been drafted.

NEWTOWNARDS, Co. Down (Map 1, L8), is a neat and well-planned town near the head of Strangford Lough, 10 m. E. of Belfast and 5½ m. S. of Bangor. It was founded by Hugh Montgomery, laird of Braidstone in Scotland, who, with James Hamilton (*see p. 202*) and Sir Moyses Hill (*see p. 70*), between 1605 and 1616 contrived to get hold of the lands of Upper Clannaboy and Great Ardes at the expense of feckless, alcoholic Conn O Neill of Castlereagh.

In Castle Place are the remains of the prominent Market Cross (Hist. Mon.) designed by Sir James Montgomery and erected in 1635.

At the E. end of Court St is the ruined church (Hist. Mon.) of a 13th c. Dominican friary, founded probably by the Savage family. In the great Market Place is a fine Market House and Town Hall of *c.* 1770. It has an interesting lock-up.

1 m. E., on the Millisle road, is the site of the celebrated abbey of Movilla (Magh Bhile), funded *c.* 540 by St Finnbarr ('Finnian the Younger'), patron of Ulaid, who introduced the Vulgate to Ireland. Several famous 6th c. saints and scholars were trained at Movilla, among them Columcille, who was ordained deacon there. The monastery was an important centre of Gaelic scholarship. There are remnants (Nat. Mon.) of a 13th c. church extended W. in the 15th c. In the E. gable are an inserted 12th (?) c. window and four human masks. On the N. side of the chancel are an early grave-slab inscribed OR[ŌIT] DO DERTREND and eight 13th c. gravestones.

1 m. SW. is Scrabo Hill (307 ft), with traces of ancient hut-circles, earthworks, etc. (Hist. Mon.). Many others were destroyed in the making of the golf-course and of the memorial tower to the 3rd Marquess of Londonderry (1857), which is the focal point of Scrabo Country Park.

NEWTOWNBUTLER, Co. Fermanagh (Map 2, D4), is a Border village on the Clones (6 m.)–Lisnaskea (8 m.) road.

3¾ m. S., in Annaghmore Glebe, is the Druid's Temple, a circle of enormous stones which formed the kerb of a large mound removed in 1712, when several Bronze Age burial chambers or cists were found.

3¼ m. SW. in the churchyard on Galloon Island, Upper Lough Erne, is the site of a 6th c. monastery founded by St Tighernach, who also founded Clones monastery. Within the graveyard are the remains of two scripture High Crosses and 18th c. gravestones with emblems of mortality.

4 m. WSW. by Upper Lough Erne, is Crom Castle, seat of the Earls of Erne, built by Blore (1834–40). On the lakeshore, ½ m. SSE. of the house, are the remains of Crom Old Castle, a Plantation castle built in 1611 by Michael Balfour, Lord of Mountwhany in Fifeshire, who sold it in turn in 1655 to Abraham Crichton, ancestor of Lord Erne. In March 1689 it was besieged by Jacobites under Lord Galmoy; in July, by Jacobites under Gen. Mac Carthy. It remained the home of the Crichtons until its accidental destruction by fire in 1764. Only the outer bawn wall and two flankers survive. Nearby is an enormous yew, reputedly the largest in Ireland. The grounds are owned by the Nat. Trust and are open to the public.

NEWTOWN CUNNINGHAM, Co. Donegal (Map 1, C4), is a village on the Derry (9 m.)–Letterkenny (15 m.) road.

2 m. NNE., on the summit of Castle Hill, are the battered ruins of Burt Castle, a late-16th c. O Doherty fortress which changed hands many times in the O Dohertys' struggle against the English between 1601 and 1607.

3¾ m. NNE. is the Church of St Aengus by Corr and McCormick (1967), its round shape reflecting that of the great stone fort of Grianán of Aileach (*see below*) on the hill-top nearby. It has interior furnishings by Imogen Stuart (crucifix, altar and font), Patrick McElroy (tabernacle), Veronica Rowe (ambo tapestry), and Helen Moloney (stained glass and vestments), and the story of the site is described on an external concrete wall-plaque by Oisín Kelly. 5 m. ENE. on Greenan Mt (803 ft) is the fortification known as the Grianán of Aileach (Nat. Mon.). This consists of a massive stone fort or cashel, with two galleries in the thickness of the walls, which stands at the centre of a series of three eroded earthen banks together enclosing about 4 acres. This large enclosure is probably a hill-fort of the late Bronze or early Iron Age. The cashel was probably built in the early Christian period as the chief fort of the northern Uí Néill (descendants of Niall Nine Hostager), whose power extended from there over all of Donegal and eventually over much of Cos. Derry, Tyrone and Armagh, the so-called over-kingdom of Aileach. The site figures frequently in the mythological and historical literature of ancient Ireland. In 1101, though by then presumably only of symbolical significance, it was wrecked by Muirchertach O Brien, King of Munster, in revenge for the destruction of Kincora (*see p. 220*) in 1088 by Domnal Mac Lochlainn, King of Aileach. Although legend says that O Brien's men carried away the stones so that it could not be rebuilt, enough survived for the cashel to be restored in the late-19th c.

NEWTOWN FORBES, Co. Longford (Map 7, N6), is a village on the Longford (3 m.)–Carrick-on-Shannon (20 m.) road. The Catholic church of the Immaculate Conception was refurbished (1974) by Robinson, Keefe and Devane, furnishings by Ray Carroll. Just W. of the village is 19th c. Castle Forbes, seat of the Earl of Granard. Permission to visit must be obtained in advance.

4½ m. NNW., in Co. Leitrim, is the ancient churchyard of Cloonmorris. Inside the gate is an ogham stone.

NEWTOWNHAMILTON, Co. Armagh (Map 2, H4), a village (dating from 1770) on the main Dundalk (16 m.)–Armagh (12 m.) road, lies in the heart of the picturesque Fews (Na Feadha, The Woods) of Armagh.

3½ m. NE., in Ballymoyer Demesne, are the remains of a church built in the time of Charles II. In the churchyard is buried Florence Mac Moyer (d. 1713), last hereditary keeper of *The Book of Armagh,* one of the treasures of Trinity College Library, Dublin (*see p. 146*).

MacMoyer pledged the book to raise funds for a journey to London for the purpose of giving perjured evidence against Archbishop Oliver Plunkett. It was recovered by Arthur Brownlow of LURGAN and passed into the possession of Archbishop Lord John George Beresford who, in 1858, presented it to Trinity College in Dublin.

NEWTOWN MOUNTKENNEDY, Co. Wicklow (Map 3, L6), is a village on the Bray (10½ m.)–Wicklow (8 m.) road.

½ m. N. is Mount Kennedy House (Mr Quinn), built *c.* 1785–6 by Michael Stapleton (?; by Thomas Cooley after designs of James Wyatt?) for Col. Cuningham, the basement being constructed as a fort. It has good stucco by Stapleton and chiaroscuro paintings by Peter de Gree. Adjoining the house is a fine motte. Mount Kennedy is called after Sir Robert Kennedy, who was granted the property in 1671.

2 m. NE. is Woodstock House (Mr William Forward), a good 18th c. mansion.

2 m. SE., 1 m. from the sea, is the quiet little resort of Newcastle. It derives its name from an English royal castle of *c.* 1200, which was taken more than once by the O Byrnes, and finally destroyed by them in 1405. In 1542 they surrendered the manor to the Crown, and a new royal castle was built. A fragment of the gatehouse of this castle remains on a circular mound. The St Francis door and tympanum of the Protestant church (1979) is by Imogen Stuart.

2½ m. S. are Dunran Demesne – with a pretty glen – and a fake 'castle' of *c.* 1770.

NEWTOWNSTEWART, Co. Tyrone (Map 1, D7), is a market town on the Strabane (10 m.)–Omagh (10 m.) road.

The town takes its name from Sir William Stewart (ancestor of Lord Mountjoy) who, through marriage *c.* 1628, acquired the place, then called Lislas. It was burned by Sir Phelim O Neill in 1641, and by James II in his retreat in 1689. It lay in ruins until 1722, when the Stewarts rebuilt most of the town. The castle at the foot of Main St was built at the Plantation by Sir Robert Newcomen, Stewart's father-in-law. Little beyond the crow-stepped gables now remains intact. The town's old six-arch stone bridge dates from 1727. St Eugene's Protestant parish church stands at the head of Main St. It was rebuilt in 1724, and a spire was added in 1806.

¾ m. SW. is Harry Avery's Castle (Hist. Mon.), which is said to take its name from Henry O Neill who died in 1392. The castle, which appears to be of a later date, was destroyed in 1609, and little remains beyond the twin towers.

3 m. SW. is Baronscourt, the seat of the Hamiltons, Dukes of Abercorn. The house dates from 1741, but was much altered in 1791–2 by Sir John Soane, and again in the early-19th c., when William Vitruvius Morrison was employed to complete the work and to re-model the interiors. The Agent's House, to the SE. of the main house, dates from 1741. Nearby Derrywoone Castle is a good example (though now just a shell) of a Scottish Planter's stronghouse. The demesne contains three partly artificial lakes, Mary, Fanny and Catherine. In Lough Catherine is the crannóg

Harry Avery's Castle, Newtownstewart, Co. Tyrone.

of Island MacHugh, on which stands a small castle said to date from the time of King John, though probably of much later date.

3¾ m. WNW., at Ardstraw, are the remains of a medieval church and of a late-17th c. Protestant church. Ardstraw was a bishop's see in the days of the early Church, but at the 12th c. reformation, the see was transferred to MAGHERA in Co. Derry, and no trace survives now of the ancient monastic episcopal foundation. 1 m. NNW. of Ardstraw bridge, in Clady Halliday, is Carnmore, a three-chamber court-tomb.

NOBBER, Co. Meath (Map 2, G7), is a small village on the Navan (13 m.)–Kingscourt (8 m.) road.

Before 1196 Gilbert de Angulo built a castle (An Obair?) there: the motte survives. In 1201 John de Courcy was treacherously trapped in the castle by Hugh II de Lacy for delivery to King John. In the old village churchyard, on the opposite side of the road to the Catholic church, are three 17th c. effigies, one (mounted in a modern wall) of Gerald Cruice (1619), and another, nearby, of the Rev. Murtagh Carolan. A more famous Carolan, the celebrated blind harper and songwriter Turloch O Carolan (1670–1738), was born not far away, at Spiddal.

5 m. NE., at Drumcondra, alias Drumconrath, is a motte. In Woodtown, 2 m. S. of Drumcondra, is a well-preserved section of the Pale (earthworks).

2 m. SW., in Cruicetown, is an early monastic site with remains of a simple Romanesque church (Nat. Mon.) containing a 1688 double-effigy tomb and other Cruice memorials. The 1688 cross (Nat. Mon.) with *Crucifixion* and *Virgin and Child* is also a Cruice memorial. Nearby is Robertstown Castle (Nat. Mon.), a 17th c. embattled house.

½ m. WSW. is Moynagh Lough crannóg, where excavations in the 1980s uncovered workshop evidence for the manufacture of fine metalwork during the 8th c.

O

O BRIENSBRIDGE, Co. Clare (Map 6, I6), is a decayed village at the only crossing of the Shannon between Killaloe (5 m.) and Limerick (9 m.). It was there that Ireton's Cromwellians forced a crossing of the river in 1651.

The picturesque river has been much altered thereabouts by the Shannon Electricity scheme (*see p. 234*).

OLDCASTLE, Co. Meath (Map 2, E8), is a small market town on the Kells (16 m.)–Ballinagh (17 m.) road.

There is a motte W. of the town.

To the SE. rises the 4 m. ridge of Slieve na Cailliighe (sometimes called the Loughcrew Hills). On the three main heights, Carnbane West (842 ft), Carnbane East (911 ft), and Patrickstown Hill, are the remains (Nat. Mons.) of 30 chambered cairns and tumuli, a ringfort, a rectangular earthwork, a pillarstone, a stone cross, and other ancient monuments. The cairns and related monuments are the survivors of a remarkable passage-tomb cemetery, which is particularly noteworthy for the wealth of its hieratic 'art'. The tomb types themselves present a series of variations on the cruciform plan, of which that on the summit of Carnbane East (locked) is probably the classic example of an Irish cruciform passage-tomb. The Hag's Chair, a massive kerbstone on the N. periphery, bears scribings.

Very inadequate 'excavations' in the last century recovered cremated bones from many of the tombs, along with sherds of coarse, crudely ornamented pottery, bone pins, stone beads and pendants, etc. – About 2 m. E. of Slieve na Cailliighe, on King's Mountain, a large stone with Newgrange-type spirals has been set up as a rubbing stone for cattle. It is all that survives of a chambered tumulus which stood on the spot. At the SW. foot of Slieve na Cailliighe stood Loughcrew House. The Loughcrew estate belonged to a branch of the great Plunkett family (*see p. 133*) until the Cromwellian conquest, and his father's home here was the birthplace of St Oliver Plunkett (1629–81), Archbishop of Armagh, who was unjustly executed at Tyburn. There are ruins of a medieval church WNW. of the house.

OMAGH, Co. Tyrone (Map 1, D8), the county town of Tyrone, is a market town on the Strabane (20 m.)–Monaghan (24 m.) road. The town has a good Classical courthouse built in 1814, as well as several interesting churches.

4¾ m. N., in Dunmullan townland, are the ruins of Cappagh old church. The present Cappagh parish church, with its impressive spire, dates from 1768. It lies 2½ m. S. of the old site.

12 m. NE. is Aghascrebagh ogham stone. Nearby, in Crouch townland, is Dun Ruadh multiple-cist cairn.

6 m. SE. is Seskinore Forest, where a game farm and sanctuary for rare breeds of poultry has been established in the outbuildings at Seskinore House (now demolished).

4½ m. NW., at Camphill, is the Ulster-American Folk-Park, constructed around the old single-storey farmhouse of the Mellon family, which they left on emigrating to Pennsylvania in 1818. The house was opened to the public in 1968, having been presented to the Scotch-Irish Trust by the Mellon family. Since then, additional land adjoining the farm has been acquired, and an extensive folk park set up illustrating the buildings of the old world which Thomas Mellon left (forge, school, church, etc.) and the new to which he emigrated (log cabin, barn, smokehouse, etc.). The park, which concentrates on the theme of emigration, has an interesting interpretative centre and exhibition area. The boyhood home of John Hughes, Roman Catholic Archbishop of New York, has been removed from Dernaved (N. Monaghan) and re-assembled in the park.

OOLA, Co. Limerick (Map 4, C3), is a village on the Tipperary (6 m.)–Limerick (20 m.) road. There are ruins of a 16th c. gabled tower-house; an O Brien residence, it was blown up by Patrick Sarsfield in 1690.

ORAN, Co. Roscommon (Map 7, K7), is on the Roscommon (9 m.)–Ballymoe (6 m.) road. There was an early monastery there, of which there remain the stump of a Round Tower, a scrap of a church, and a holy well.

The Pennsylvania farmhouse in the Ulster-American Folk Park at Camphill, Co. Tyrone.

4 m. S., on the Suck, is Dunamon Castle, which resembles that at Bunratty; it is now the novitiate of the Society of the Divine Word for Foreign Missions.

ORANMORE, Co. Galway (Map 6, G2), is a small village at the junction of the Galway–Dublin and Galway–Limerick roads, 5½ m. E. of Galway. By the shore of Galway Bay stands the massive tower of a 16th c. Clanricard Burke castle. It was re-edified for occupation by Anita Leslie, the author.

3 m. ENE., in Mountain West, is Lisroughan, a henge-type circular earthwork. The entrance is flanked by two large stones.

OUGHTERARD, Co. Galway (Map 7, F9), is a market village and well-known angling centre where the main Galway (17 m.)–Clifden (33 m.) road crosses the little Owenriff near the beautiful upper end of Lough Corrib.

2 m. SE., to the E. of the Galway road, are the ruins (Nat. Mon.) of the once fine O Flaherty castle of Aughnanure (16th c.). At the Cromwellian period, this was one of the outposts guarding Galway from attack around the head of the lake. In the midst of the alarms Lame David Duignan was working on Royal Irish Academy manuscript 24 P 9 in the castle. The remains (well restored by the Office of Public Works) comprise fragments of two bawns (the inner with corbel-roofed angle turret), a fine tower, and one wall of a beautiful hall (note window embrasures); the rest of the hall has been eroded.

P

PALLAS GREEN, NEW, Co. Limerick (Map 4, B2), is a village on the Tipperary (10 m.)–Limerick (13 m.) road.

1¾ m. SW. is Pallas Green (Old). The name preserves that of Grían (*see p. 204*), a sun-goddess whose Otherworld seat was in nearby Cnoc Gréine. There is a fine motte there; also remains of an Anglo-Norman manorial church, established by Geoffrey fitz Robert. 3 m. NW., in Longstone, is a ringfort with a 9 ft 6 in. pillarstone which gives its name to the townland.

PALLASKENRY, Co. Limerick (Map 6, H7), is a village 2 m. N. of the Limerick (12 m.)–Askeaton (7 m.) road. There are remains of a Desmond rock-castle and of a bawn.

2¼ m. SE., on the road to Kildimo, are remains (Nat. Mon.) of Killulta, reputed to be the oldest church in the county (9th/10th c.?). 3 m. E., in Ballyculhane, are remains of a Purcell castle.

3 m. SSW., in (Killeen) Cowpark, are the well-preserved remains of a small 15th c. church.

PASSAGE EAST, Co. Waterford (Map 4, I5), is a village and port on the W. side of Waterford Harbour, 7 m. ESE. of Waterford. There is a ferry to the villages of Ballyhack and Arthurstown.

Double-headed stone, Boa Island, Co. Fermanagh.

Strongbow landed at Passage, 23 August 1170, with 200 knights and 1,000 other men. Next day he was joined by Raymond le Gros with 40 knights, and on 25 August took Waterford by storm. On 17 October 1171, Henry II of England arrived at Passage with 4,000 men in 400 ships. In 1649 Cromwell's son-in-law took the fort by storm.

1 m. S., at Crooke, are remains of a nave-and-chancel church and of a castle (Nat. Mon.) of the Knights Templar.

2 m. S. are the ruins of Geneva Barracks, remnant of an abortive 1782–4 project to found a city there for emigré intellectuals and watchmakers from Geneva. The city was to have had a university to attract scholars from all parts of Europe.

3 m. S. is Woodstown House, where Jacqueline Kennedy spent an undisturbed holiday with her children in 1967.

2 m. NW., at Faithlegg, are the ruins of a nave-and-chancel church (medieval font). Nearby are remains of Ailward castles.

PETTIGOE, Cos. Donegal–Fermanagh (Map 1, A8), is a market village and angling centre on the Donegal (17 m.)–Enniskillen (20 m.) road, near the N. shore of LOWER LOUGH ERNE.

The Border follows the Termon River through the middle of the village, which lies in two counties, and in two states.

3 m. N., in Templecarne graveyard, is a ringed cross brought there from Saints Island in Lough Derg.

2 m. SW., on Lough Erne, is Termon Mac Grath Castle, seat of the Mac Graths, hereditary coarbs of St Davoge's monastery, Lough Derg. A notorious member of this family was Myler Mac Grath, the Elizabethan pluralist (*see p. 77*). John Kells Ingram (1823–1907), scholar and auther of *Who Fears to Speak of Ninety-Eight?*, was born at Aghnaboo nearby. 5 m. (by road bridge) SW. of the castle is Boa Island. In Dreenan (at the W. end of the island) is Caldragh, an ancient churchyard. There is a (pagan?) stone (Nat. Mon.) with twin cross-armed figures set back to back. Another effigial stone (Nat. Mon.) has been brought there from nearby Lusty More island.

PILTOWN, Co. Kilkenny (Map 4, H4), is a village on the Waterford (12 m.)–Carrick-on-Suir (4 m.) road.

In 1462 took place the battle of Piltown between Thomas, Earl of Desmond, and the Lancastrian Butlers led by John, 6th Earl of Ormond, and Émonn mac Risderd Butler, who was captured. His ransom was two great Irish literary codices, one now in Oxford, one in the British Museum (*see p. 89 and 198*).

The village has a good, early-19th c. Market House (now the police station) built by Lord Bessborough. In the Catholic churchyard is the fragment of a 16th c. tomb surround with *The Virgin and Child*. The sham castle is the monument of a Ponsonby killed in the Napoleonic wars. Bessborough House, seat of the Ponsonbys, Earls of Bessborough, was a fine mansion of 1744 by Francis Bindon of Clooney, Co. Clare. Burned down in 1922, it is now an agricultural and horticultural college.

2 m. SSE., on a beautiful reach of the Suir, is Fiddown. The 1747 Ponsonby mausoleum is an adaptation of the chancel of a 13th c. church demolished about 1870; in the E. gable is the head of a *Blessed Virgin Mary* slab; the Mary, Countess of Bessborough (d. 1713) monument and the William Ponsonby, Viscount Duncannon (d. 1724) monument are by William Kidwell of Dublin (d. 1736); the monument to the 1st Earl of Bessborough (d. 1758) and his wife is by Sir William Atkinson.

1¼ m. WSW., close to the Suir in Tibberaghny, is the site of an early monastery whose patron was St Mo-Dhomnóg of Lambecher (*see p. 52*). The remains include part of a carved cross-shaft (?) removed from its socket *c.* 1860, an early stone trough, and remains of a church with early chancel and 13th/14th c. nave; the cross-shaft carvings include figures of hieratic beasts, spirals, etc. SW. of the churchyard is St Faghtna's Well, after which the place is called. Tibberaghny Castle incorporates the tower of a 15th/16th c. castle which belonged to the Mountgarret Butlers in the 17th c.

3 m. NW. the Protestant church of Whitechurch stands in a large, ancient, circular enclosure divided into three parts by the modern roads. Castletown House, to the NE., was built about 1767–70 for Michael Cox, Protestant Bishop of Ossory.

3½ m. NNW., at the little village of Owning, are remains of a medieval parish church (Assumption of the Blessed Virgin Mary); the chancel, an addition to the simple nave, has a beautiful S. door. The district was rich in prehistoric chamber tombs, some of which survive.

PLUMB BRIDGE, Co. Tyrone (Map 1, D6), is a little village at the junction of roads from Dunnamanagh (10 m.), Draperstown (21 m.), Omagh (via Gortin, 14 m.) and Newtownstewart (6 m.). The road to Draperstown climbs Glenelly via Cranagh and Sperrin at the foot of Sawel, to Glengomna and Labby.

3 m. N., ¼ m. E. of the Dunnamanagh road, in Clogherny, is Meenerrigal Rocks (800 ft), a wedge-tomb at the centre of a ring of stones. In the same townland, close to Butterlope Glen (700 ft), are the remains of five stone circles. 1½ m. NNW., 300 yds W. of the by-road, is Balix Lower court-tomb (Hist. Mon.).

3½ m. ENE., to the E. of Glensass Burn (800 ft), in Castledamph, is part of a double stone circle with central cairn and cist, and a double alignment. 100 yds. N. are two contiguous stone circles and remains of another double circle.

4 m. E., on the N. side of Glenelly, just N. of St Patrick's Church, in Glenroan, is a large stone with a cup mark which local legend regards as the imprint of St Patrick's knee. In the churchyard is a stone with four cup marks. – 8 m. E., in Cranagh townland, is the Sperrin Heritage Centre (opened in 1987), where the natural history, history and wildlife of the area are interpreted. The centre has a craft shop and tea room.

3½ m. SW. is Corrick Abbey, a 15th c. Franciscan friary.

1 m. W. is Letterbrat portal-tomb (500 ft, ruined); 1½ m. W., to the S. of the Strabane road, is Meenagorp chambered cairn.

POMEROY, Co. Tyrone (Map 1, F8), is the highest village in the county. It lies at the junction of the Stewartstown (10 m.) and Cookstown (10 m.) roads to Omagh (19 m.). The area round about is particularly rich in chamber tombs, stone circles and other megalithic remains (*see also pp. 94 and 116–7*). In the village square stands Altdesert parish church (1841), built largely at the expense of the Lowry family of Pomeroy House (now a forestry school), who did much to develop the village.

2 m. NNE., in Moymore, are the remains of seven low stone circles, six of them with tangential alignments.

2½ m. SSW. is Altmore, the birthplace of General James Shields (1806–79), the only American general to defeat Stonewall Jackson. All his life he promoted the cause of Irishmen and, as Governor of Oregon, was responsible for Irish immigration to the American North West, and for the many Ulster names given to towns and townships there. 1½ m. SE. of Altmore is King James's Well, where James II halted in 1689.

3 m. WNW., in Tremoge, are two stone circles, one of which has an alignment of massive stones. 1 m. NE of Lough Mallon, and ½ m. SE. of Evishatrask school, is Cregganconroe court-tomb (Hist. Mon.), with a huge capstone still partly in place.

PORTADOWN, Co. Armagh (Map 2, H2), is a manufacturing centre on the Armagh (11 m.)–Belfast (26 m.) road. The town is a creation of the late-18th c. and, like Lurgan, is now incorporated in the Borough of CRAIGAVON.

7 m. NW., in Derryhubbert, is the Birches Peatland Park (D.O.E. Conservation Service). A country park on the theme of Irish peat (or turf) with a visitor centre and narrow-gauge railway. Access from the M1.

2 m. S. is Brackagh Moss (D.O.E. Conservation Service), a National Nature Reserve of wetland interest (botany and entomology).

PORTAFERRY, Co. Down (Map 2, M2), is a small port and resort beautifully sited on the E. side of the entrance to Strangford Lough, opposite Strangford, with which it is connected by a twice-hourly ferry. It is 29 m. from Belfast.

In Meetinghouse Lane is the Presbyterian church, a good Doric building.

On the W. side of Church Street are some fragments of the ancient parish church (Temple Cranny). In Castle St are the ruins of a 15th c. castle (Hist. Mon.). Next to it is the Northern Ireland Aquarium (1985).

4 m. N., on Castle Hill, Ardkeen, is a motte-and-bailey erected *c.* 1180 by John de Courcy. Nearby St Mary's is a much altered manorial church, containing a simple medieval grave-slab. 3½ m. E. is Kirkistown Castle (Hist. Mon.), built by one of the Savages in 1622.

1½ m. NE., in Derry, are the ruins of two small, early churches whose masonry is bonded with clay. One or both was dedicated to the virgin, Cumain. Under them runs an extensive 7th/8th c. cemetery with long cist graves.

6½ m. NE., in Ballyspurge (to the SE. of Cloghy village), are the ruins of the White House, a 1½-storey, Plantation house (*c.* 1640–50) with pistol-loops; fragments of the bawn survive.

2¼ m. ESE. in Keentagh, by the shore of Millin Bay, is a unique Neolithic long cairn (Hist. Mon.). Sixty-four stones bore passage-grave and other devices.

PORTARLINGTON, Co. Laois (Map 3, F5), is an 18th c. town on the Tullamore (17 m.).–Kildare (13 m.) road, beside the River Barrow and near the Grand Canal. It takes its name from Sir Henry Bennet, afterwards Lord Arlington, an Englishman who introduced Protestant French and German settlers, but himself returned in the end to Catholicism. William III granted the estate to the Huguenot Gen. Henri de Massue, Marquis de Ruvigny, Earl of Galway, who settled Huguenot refugees on the lands and in the town; among them Jean Cavalier, the Camisard leader from the Cevennes. St Paul's Protestant Church is the 1851 successor of de Ruvigny's Calvinist Église Française de St Paul (1696). The Act of Resumption, 1699, terminated de Ruvigny's ownership of Portarlington, which was eventually acquired by Ephraim Dawson, ancestor of Lord Portarlington. The Dawsons did much to improve the town, which still has many good, 18th–19th c. houses.

2½ m. E., between the canal and the Barrow, are the remnants of the Castle of Lea, a stronghold of the FitzGerald barons of Offaly. It had a fine keep (*c.* 1250?) at the centre of an inner, oval ward. The twin-towered gatehouse of the outer ward suggests a date of *c.* 1297 for the latter. Silken Thomas stored his treasure there when he rebelled in 1534. The Cromwellians wrecked the castle in 1650.

PORT LAOISE, Co. Laois (Map 3, F6), county town of Co. Laois, is situated on the main Dublin (53 m.)–Limerick (70 m.) road, between Monasterevin (14 m.) and Mountrath (8 m.). It traces its origin to the Plantation of Laoighis and Uí Fáilghe under Mary Tudor, whence its former name, Maryborough. The town itself is noteworthy merely as the location of the Republic's only male convict prison. The Court House is by Sir Richard Morrison (1767–1849), a pupil of Gandon's. The

Protestant church has a 1938 window by A.E. Child: *Christ Blessing Little Children.*

Dr Bartholomew Mosse (1712–59), philanthropist and founder of Dublin's celebrated Rotunda Hospital, was born there; his father was the rector.

4 m. SSE. is the Pass of the Plumes, where Eóghan, son of Rúairí O More, defeated Essex in 1599. The name derives from the helmet-plumes which strewed the ground after the battle.

PORTLAW, Co. Waterford (Map 4, H5), is a village set where the S. road from Waterford (10 m.) to Carrick-on-Suir (7 m.) crosses the little Clodiagh River. The pioneer model village built by the Quaker Malcolmsons for the workers of their cotton-spinning mills (1825–1904) has been vulgarized out of recognition. The parish church (1859, tower completed 1910) is a characteristic piece by J.J. McCarthy, 'the Irish Pugin'. Adjoining the village to the W. is the beautiful demesne of Curraghmore. 1½ m. from the entrance gate is Curraghmore House, splendid 18th c. seat of the Marquess of Waterford (Beresford). It incorporates an older de la Poer castle. The 18th c. decorations include excellent stucco, wood-carving by John Houghton, and paintings by Peter de Gree and Antonio Zucchi. The family portraits include works by Sir Thomas Lawrence, Sir Joshua Reynolds, and Thomas Gainsborough. The courtyard is noteworthy. In the demesne is a Shell House made by Cáitlín Paor; it has a statue of her by J. van Nost, Jun.

1½ m. SE., at Kilbunny, called after St Munnu (of Taghmon), are remains of a church with rebuilt Romanesque doorway, over-restored in 1987.

1½ m. NW., on Clonagam Hill, is a bogus 18th c. Round Tower.

PORTMARNOCK, Co. Dublin (Map 3, L3), is a village and seaside resort 8 m. NE. of Dublin with fine beach and 18-hole championship golf course.

The ruins of St Marnock's Church and St Marnock's Well preserve the memory of St Ernín, alias M'Earnóg, founder of an early church thereabouts. His name is preserved in the Scottish churches of Kilmarnock and Inchmarnock.

1½ m. SSE., in Seagrange, Baldoyle, is the church of St Laurence O Toole (1981) by Scott, Tallon, Walker with wooden cross by Michael Warren.

3¼ m. SW. are St Doolagh's Church and Well (Nat. Mons.), and an ancient granite cross. The stone-roofed church (E. end mid-12th(?) c.) includes an anchorite's cell with St Doolagh's Tomb, a chapel, and a 15th c., battlemented, square tower, the living quarters of the successors of the 6th/7th c. hermit who gave his name to the church. The 19th c. Protestant church (by Sloane) occupies the site of the medieval parish church. St Doolagh's Well (alias the Baptistry) is enclosed by a stone-roofed octagon; it is said to have been decorated with paintings. St Doolagh's Lodge nearby was long the home of Nathaniel Hone (1831–1917), friend of Corot (with whom he lived at Barbizon) and Ireland's greatest landscape and seascape painter.

PORTRUSH, Co. Antrim (Map 1, G3), is a popular seaside resort beautifully situated on Ramore Head promontory, 6 m. W. of Bushmills, 4 m. E of Portstewart, and 6 m. N. of Coleraine. It has two good beaches and two golf courses (Royal Portrush enjoys an international reputation). The town is within easy reach of the Bann and the Giant's Causeway (*see p. 85*).

1 m. SE., in Ballywillin, are the remains of a church with Transitional and later features.

PORTSALON, Co. Donegal (Map 1, B3), is a little resort superbly situated at the N. end of Ballymastocker Bay on Lough Swilly, 10 m. NE. of Milford and 6 m. S. of Fanad Head. There are five beaches to the N. and NW.

Another excellent beach runs 2 m. SE. to Saldhanha Head (frigate *Saldanha* wrecked, 1811) where the Knockalla Mts (1,203 ft) terminate in steep cliffs (19th c. battery) opposite Dunree Head.

2 m. NNE. are the spectacular Seven Arches (sea tunnels).

5 m. N. are the cliffs and Great Arch of Doagh Beg.

PORTSTEWART, Co. Derry (Map 1, G3), is a beautifully situated, popular little seaside and golfing (two courses) resort, 5 m. N. of Coleraine and 4 m. W. of Portrush. 1½ m. SW. beautiful Crossreagh beach (sandhills) runs 1½ m. W. to the mouth of the Bann.

Thackeray went there in 1842 and visited Charles Lever (1806–72), the novelist, who practised as a physician.

PORTUMNA, Co. Galway (Map 6, K3), is a small market town at the head of Lough Derg.

Adjoining the town on the S. is the quondam demesne of Portumna Castle, sometime seat of the earls and marquesses of Clanricarde. The last marquess was a notorious miser and landlord. On his death the direct line of the ancient house of Mac William *Úachtair* Burke became extinct; the earldom passed to the Marquess of Sligo; the estates to the Earl of Harewood, who sold them. In the demesne are the ruins of the Clanricarde 'castle' and of a Dominican friary (Nat. Mons.). The 'castle', a semi-fortified house of 1609, was accidentally destroyed by fire in 1826, and has recently been conserved. In 1634 the notorious Earl of Strafford held an inquisition at the Burke castle to establish the title of the English Crown to the land of Connacht. To the SE. are the interesting ruins (*c.* 1426–1500) of the Dominican Observant friary (Ireland's first house of the Observance), founded *c.* 1425 by the O Maddens on the site of a chapel belonging to Dunbrody Abbey (*see p. 89*).

3½ m. NNE., to the E. of the Eyrecourt road, are the remains (tower and bawn) of the small castle of Derryhiveney (Nat. Mon.). Erected by Donal O Madden in 1643, it was one of the very last true castles built in Ireland. It has Jacobean and other interesting details.

7 m. SE., near the E. shore of Lough Derg, is Terryglass, Co. Tipperary, site of a celebrated Leinster monastery on Munster soil. Its founder was St Colm(án) moccu Cremthainn Áin (d. 549/552; *see p. 249*), who was of Leinster royal stock and one of the principal disciples of Finnian of Clonard (*see p. 226*). The monastery was intimately associated with TALLAGHT and Clonenagh in the céle Dé movement, and with LORRHA. Terryglass had important literary associations: it is said to be the burial place of

Flann, son of Lonán (slain *c.* 893), ollamh of Ireland, one of the three principal poets of Connacht, and the earliest Irish professional poet of whom any definite tradition survives. He was called 'Devil's Son because he was so satirical and burdensome', and it was believed he went to Hell for his avarice. Sometime between 1151 and 1224 Áed Úa Cremthainn, coarb of Colm moccu Cremthainn Áin and 'prime historian of Leinster in wisdom, and knowledge, and book-lore, and science, and learning', compiled and wrote the so-called *Book of Leinster* (more correctly the *Book of Novghaval*, *see p. 285*), which 'sums up all the learning of the monastic period of Irish writing'. Few remains of the Abbey survive. Beside the former Protestant church are two walls of a relatively large church. There are also some fragments (including a cross-base) in the Catholic churchyard, ½ m. NE. – ½ m. NW., by the lake shore, are the truncated ruins of Old Court, keep of a 13th c. castle of Irish type which was probably built (by John Marshall?) at the time of the Anglo-Norman (Butler) conquest of Ormond. This, despite its quite insignificant history and its fragmentary condition, has been taken into State care, while illustrious Terryglass Abbey is consigned to oblivion! To the N. of the village is a 1983 sculpture by Gerard Fox.

POYNTZPASS, Co. Armagh, (Map 2, I3), is a village (dating from 1790) on the Portadown (11 m.)–Newry (9 m.) road, where Lieut. Poyntz fought desperately to prevent Hugh O Neill from entering Down.

½ m. SE., in Killysavan, Co. Down, and 1 m. NE., in Loughadian, are portions of the Dane's Cast (Hist. Mon.), a great travelling earthwork defending the frontier of the kingdom of Ulaid in protohistoric times (*see p. 278*).

2 m. S., in the demesne of Drumbanagher House, are Tyrone's Ditches earthworks constructed by Hugh O Neill in the course of the Nine Years' War.

Q

QUIN, Co. Clare (Map 6, H5), a village 3 m. E. of the Ennis (4 m.)–Limerick (11 m.) road, is noted for its Franciscan friary (Nat. Mon.), founded by Mac-Con MacNamara *c.* 1433, allegedly the first Observantine house in Ireland.

The ruins, E. of the River Rine, illustrate the architecture and arrangements of the medieval friaries. They incorporate part of an earlier castle built by Thomas de Clare, Anglo-Norman invader of Thomond, and destroyed by the Irish in 1286.

On the W. side of the river is St Finghin's Church (Nat. Mon.), a plain, aisleless, parish church of the early-13th c.

¾ m. ENE., in Danganbrack, is a lofty, gabled, 16th c. tower with angle machicolations and tall chimneys.

Portumna Castle, Co. Galway.

2½ m. NE., in Toonagh (N. of Hell Bridge), is Magh Adhair, inauguration place of the Kings of Dál gCais and their descendants, the O Brien Kings of Thomond. A flat-topped, ditched mound (Nat. Mon.) is probably the scene of the ceremony. A small tumulus and a pillarstone (W. of river, survivor of two) proclaim the pre-Christian sanctity of the place.

3 m. ESE. is Craggaunowen, where a castle houses a part of the collection of the late John and Putzel Hunt (*see p. 234*), including a number of medieval European *objects d'art*. In the grounds are a modern crannóg and ringfort, to show what these typically Irish habitations might have looked like in their heyday, more than 1,000 years ago. In a glass house designed by Liam McCormick is preserved the modern currah in which Tim Severin crossed the Altantic in 1976–7, to show how it would have been possible for the 5th/6th c. St Brendan to have discovered America.

R

RAGHLY, Co. Sligo (Map 7, J1), is a hamlet at the neck of a low promontory of the same name, on the W. side of Drumcliff Bay, some 9 m. W. of Drumcliff.

¾ m. NE. are the ruins of Ballymuldorry, alias Ardtermon, Castle, a 17th c. fortified house with flanking towers (restored) and traces of a bawn, recently excavated. It was built by Sir Nathaniel Gore, ancestor of the Gore-Booths of Lissadill (*below*).

4½ m. ENE. is beautifully situated Lissadill Demesne (open to the public). Lissadill House (Miss A. Gore-Booth), a good Classical house of the 1830s, was the birthplace of the Arctic explorer Sir Henry Gore-Booth (1843–1900), and of his remarkable daughters, Eva Gore-Booth (1870–1926), poetess, and Constance Gore-Booth, Countess Markievicz (1884–1927), who was condemned to death for her part in the 1916 Rising, but was spared. In 1918 she was elected the first woman member of the British House of Commons, but took her seat in Dáil Éireann instead. At the turn of the 12th/13th c. Lissadill was the home of the celebrated poet, Muireadhach Albanach ('Scottish') O Daly, brother of the even greater poet, Donnchadh Mór O Daly (*see p. 81*) and ancestor of the Mac Vurich (Mac Mhuireadhaigh) family 'who more than any other race of bards maintained the Irish tradition in Scotland'. Fearing for his life after he had murdered a tax-collector, he fled to Scotland, where his art found fruitful patronage and his devotion a wife. During his exile he seems to have gone with a Scottish contingent on the Fifth Crusade (1217), and poems written by him in the Adriatic survive. In one of them he still sighs for Lissadill:

> How peaceful would my slumbers be
> In kind O Conor's fair demesne,
> A poet in good company
> Couched upon Éire's rushes green.
>
> (*trans.* Robin Flower)

1½ m. NW., overlooking the Yellow Strand, is Knocklane Hill (189 ft), which is reputed to be haunted by the Baintighearna Bhán or White Lady, i.e. the white-robed ghost of the wife of Sir Nathaniel Gore of Ardtermon, which rides in a chariot drawn by golden-shod horses.

RAHENY, Co. Dublin (Map 3, K3), is a suburban village on the Dublin (5 m.)–Howth (4 m.) road.

The Catholic church (1960–2) is by Louis Peppard and Hugo Duffy; the porch echoes the Romanesque pediment at CLONFERT.

St Assam's Church (Protestant) was Patrick Byrne's last work (1863–4).

2 m. NNE. is Belcamp Hall, now the College of Mary Immaculate. The chapel has 12 windows by Harry Clarke (1925): *SS Columcille, Dúileach, Damhnait, Brigid, Brendan, Maol M'Aodhóg, Lorcán O Toole, Eithne and Fedhlim, Gobnait, Patrick, Oliver Plunkett,* and *Kevin.*

1¾ m. NE., by the seashore, are the scant remains of Kilbarrack church. Mariners imperilled by the treacherous sands of Dublin Bay used to make their votive offerings there. In the church are buried James McNeill (1869–1938), second Governor-General of the Irish Free State, and his brother, Eoin Mac Neill (1867–1945), founder of the Gaelic League, founder and Commander of the Irish Volunteers, first Free State Minister of Education, and an eminent historian.

RANDALSTOWN, Co. Antrim (Map 1, I7), is a village N. of Lough Neagh, on the Belfast (22 m.)–Antrim (5 m.)–Derry (43 m.) road. The old Presbyterian church (1790) is oval in plan, with a hexagonal cupola. The Catholic church (1972) is by Laurence McConville; metalwork by Ray Carroll, sanctuary window by Helen Moloney.

4 m. SW., in Churchtown, are the remains (in State care) of the small 13th c. church of Cranfield. Close by is St Colman's Well; its 'pebbles' (crystals of gypsum) were said to protect men from drowning and women from death in childbirth.

RAPHOE, Co. Donegal (Map 1, C6), is a village on the Stranorlar (10 m.)–Derry (16 m.) road.

Raphoe's place in history is due to a monastery associated with the name of the celebrated scholar and ecclesiastical statesman St Adomnán (*c.* 624–704), ninth abbot of Iona and author of a famous *Life* of his kinsman, St Columcille, who appears to have been the founder of the monastery. At the 12th c. reformation Raphoe became the see of the diocese which still bears its name. In 1835 the Protestant diocese was united with Derry. The post-Penal Catholic cathedral is at Letterkenny.

Nondescript St Eunan's (= Adomnán's) Cathedral (Protestant), a 17th c. structure re-edified in 1892 by Sir Thomas Drew, occupies the site of the medieval cathedral and its predecessors. In the tower (1737) porch is a fragment of a lintel *Crucifixion* from a doorway; another fragment is built into the outer face of the N. wall of the church. In the S. wall of the chancel are 13th c. sedilia. In the S. porch are some carved fragments. SE. of the cathedral is the ruined bishop's palace, a stronghouse erected *c.* 1636 by Bishop John Lesley. Fire destroyed it in 1839.

2 m. S., on the summit of Tops Hill, is Beltany (*sic*) Ring (Nat. Mon.), a stone circle with 64 stones.

Lissadill House, Co. Sligo.

RATHCONRATH, Co. Westmeath (Map 3, D2), is a small village on the Mullingar (7 m.)–Ballymahon (10 m.) road. The neighbouring townlands (particularly Milltown, Ballyglass, Rathtrim, and Kilpatrick) to the NW., N., and NE. are rich in ringforts and other ancient remains.

1½ m. SSW. is Mount Dalton, birthplace of Gen. James D'Alton, and his brother, Count Richard D'Alton, Governor of the Austrian Netherlands (d. 1790), members of a landed Anglo-Noman family. The General built a new house there in 1784, at the back of which he and his brother erected a pyramidal monument ('Loughan Spire') with marble profiles of the Empress Maria Theresa, the Emperor Joseph II, and George III.

2 m. WNW. is Skeaghmore Hill (426 ft), assembly point of a body of the United Irishmen of Westmeath in September 1798. On the summit is Carraig na Muice, an outcrop with 'two marks on it made by the Black Pig' to which is attributed the Black Pig's Dyke (*see p.198*).

RATHCOOLE, Co. Dublin (Map 3, J4), is a village off the Dublin (11m.)–Naas (9 m.) road. In the old churchyard at the E. end of the village is an ancient granite cross carved from a cross-inscribed slab.

4 m. SW. is Kilteel, Co. Kildare. Close to the S. side of the by-road leading SE. are scant remains (Nat. Mon.) of the early monastery, Cill tSiaghail, including remnants of a nave-and-chancel church with fragments of a Late Romanesque chancel arch (figurations of *The Fall, Samson and the Lion, David with Goliath's Head*, etc.); in the nave is a cross-inscribed stone and the lintel of a trabeate doorway. SW. of the road-junction, and close to the E. side of the Rathmore road, are fragments (Nat. Mon.) of a High Cross. SSE. is 'Kilteel Castle' (Nat. Mon.): a gateway with flanking tower. This, and the other medieval fragments to the N. of the church (*above*), are relics of a commandery of the Knights Hospitaller of St John of Jerusalem, an important border fortress of the English Pale, founded by Maurice FitzGerald, 2nd Baron Offaly (d. 1257).

RATHCORMACK, Co. Cork (Map 4, B7), is a village on the Fermoy (5 m.)–Cork (16 m.) road, 2 m. SW. of Castelyons.

1½ m. S. is Kilshanning House (Mr D. Merry), a good Palladian house by Davis Ducart (*c.* 1766).

2 m. SW., near Kildinan, are the remains of Shanaclogh, a castle of the Earls of Desmond.

RATHCROGHAN, Co. Roscommon (Map 7, L6), to the W. of the Bellanagare (4½ m.)–Tulsk (3 m.) road, preserves the name of Cruachain, in Heroic epic and other early tales the seat of Ailill mac Máta who was King of Connacht by virtue of his marriage to 'Queen' Medb (Meadhbh, Maeve; cf. English 'Queen Mab'). Medb had previously been 'wife' of King Conor mac Nessa of Ulster and of Tinne and Eochaid Dála of Connacht. She had a double in Medb Red-side, 'wife' in turn of a King of Leinster and of three Kings of Tara. Medb Red-side 'would not allow a king in Tara without his having herself to wife; and by her was built the royal rath on the side of Tara, viz. Rath Maeve' (*see p. 288*). Plainly there was only one Medb, a goddess, whose name signifies intoxication. The reign of each Irish pagan king was inaugurated by a mystic marriage to a goddess. The 'marriage' may have taken the form of a ritual beer-banquet which induced a 'divine' intoxication of the new king.

As the seat of 'sacred' kings, Cruachain had a religious significance which is exemplified by ancient references to its royal cemetery and to its Otherworld entrance.

In early literature the name Cruachain can refer to the great limestone plain of the Roscommon – Elphin – Strokestown – Castlereagh area, seat in protohistoric and early historic times of the Uí Briúin kings of Connacht descended from Brión, allegedly a half-brother of Niall Nine Hostager of Tara. The Uí Briúin still dominated the plain in the 12th–13th c., the ruling family being the O Conors of Connacht.

The Rathcroghan countryside is still rich in field monuments, of which only a selection can be offered here. Rathcroghan crossroads provide a convenient focal point for the visitor.

½ m. SSE. of the crossroads, in Toberrory, to the W. of the Tulsk road, is Rathcroghan itself, a large mound crowned with a small, degraded ring-barrow. 120 yds NNE. is Misgaun Meva, 'Medb's Lump', a prostrate pillarstone. The field fence S. of Rathcroghan follows the line of an ancient roadway.

½ m. ESE. of Rathcroghan a bohereen leads S. from the Tulsk road. About 750 yds S. of the junction a field path leads W. for ¼ m. to Knockannagorp, 'Hillock of the Corpses', alias Dathi's Grave, a partly artificial mound (non-burial) enclosed by a bank and surmounted by a pillarstone. Less than 300 yds W. are remnants of a stone ringfort with a souterrain. 240 yds N. of this is a ruinous circular enclosure identified as Reilig na Ríogh, 'The Cemetery of the Kings', by Charles O Conor of BELANAGARE, but shown by excavation not to be a burial-place. 300 yds NW. is Oweynagat, 'Cave of the cats', a limestone fissure with souterrain 'vestibule', two of whose lintels bear ogham inscriptions. This is generally taken to be the Otherworld entrance ('Cave of Rathcroghan') of mythological literature. 60 yds NW. is a ring-barrow and 600 yds NNW. is Rathnadarve (*see below*). 400 yds SW of Oweynagat are Mucklaghs, two bivallate linear earthworks, one of which continues 600 yds SW. to the remnants of Cashelmanannan, 'Manannán's Fort', a stone ringfort.

180 yds SSW. of Rathcroghan crossroads, on a roadside knoll, is Rathbeg, a bivallate ring-barrow. 600 yds SSW. is roadside Rathnadarve, a large univallate ringfort; an ancient roadway led E. past Rathcroghan.

Further earthworks of various kinds are to be found in a wide arc from the NE. to the NW. of the crossroads.

RATHDOWNEY, Co. Laois (Map 3, D8), is a small market town, on the Abbeyleix (12 m.)–Templemore (11 m.) road.

4½ m. W. is Errill, where the ruins of St Kieran's Church (Nat. Mon.) and a monastic site preserve the memory of a foundation by St Ciarán of Saighir (*see pp. 78 and 299*). At the nearby crossroads are portions of a cross (Nat. Mon.) erected in 1622 to the memory of Florence Mac Gillapatrick (Fitzpatrick), baron of Upper Ossory, and of Katherine O More, his wife. They had both died in 1613.

RATHDRUM, Co. Wicklow (Map 3, K7), is a village perched above the Avonmore, at the SE. end of the Vale of Clara. The parish church of SS Mary and Michael (1856–60) is by J.J. McCarthy.

1½ m. S. is Avondale (1779), birthplace and home of Charles Stewart Parnell (1846–91), the great Home Rule leader; it is now a State forestry school. Noteworthy features are: the Parnell museum, the Professor Henry memorial grove, the arboretum, the trial plots, and the seed-extraction nurseries.

3½ m. S. the Avonmore is joined by the Avonbeg in that 'Meeting of the Waters' made famous by Thomas Moore's song. Beside the Meeting is the skeleton of a tree in whose shade the poet is said to have dreamed away many an hour. Close by is a monument to the poet (stone lettering by Michael Biggs). The valley there is still charming, despite the scars of the railway and the many copper pyrites mines. It is dominated from the E. bank by the beautifully timbered demesne of Castle Howard. Behind Castle Howard is Cronebane (816 ft), worth climbing for the view; on the summit is the Mottha (Mottee) Stone, legendarily the hurling stone of Finn Mac Cool. From the 'Meeting of the Waters' to ARKLOW, the Avonmore nowadays goes by the name Avoca (Ovoca), given it by a pedant who identified it with Ptolemy's *'Οβοκα*.

RATHFARNHAM, Co. Dublin (Map 3, K4), is a village and suburb at the foot of the Dublin mountains, 4 m. SW. of the city.

Beside the village is Rathfarnham Castle. Since 1913 a Jesuit House of Studies, but bought by the State in 1986, currently unoccupied and looking desolate in the midst of a modern housing estate, this massive Elizabethan castle was built *c.* 1585 by Archbishop Loftus, who had acquired an estate there. During the 17th and 18th c., the castle and lands passed through various hands (including those of Speaker Conolly of Castletown, CELBRIDGE). In 1767 they were bought by Nicholas Loftus, 2nd Earl of Ely, descendant of Archbishop Loftus. The Jesuits magnanimously transferred the six Harry Clarke windows from here to the Catholic church in Tullamore.

½ m. SE. is Loreto 'Abbey', which incorporates a good early Georgian house built for William Palliser and recently well restored. The convent chapel has sculptures by John Hogan (1800–58). ¾ m. E. of the 'abbey' is Hall's Barn, erected *c.* 1742 by a Major Hall; this curious structure was probably modelled on the Wonderful Barn at Castletown, Celbridge. – ½ m. S. of the 'abbey' is Hermitage, where Robert Emmet courted Sarah Curran; in 1910 Patrick Pearse transferred the famous Coláiste Éinne (St Enda's College) there from Cullenswood, Ranelagh. St Enda's is now a Pearse Museum. ½ m. ESE. of Hermitage is Marlay, sometime residence of David La Touche, the 18th c. banker; it has stucco by Michael Stapleton. 1 m. S. is St Columba's College, a Church of Ireland boarding school run on English public school lines; the nucleus of the school is Holly Park, built *c.* 1780 by tobacco manufacturer Lundy Foot. There are two windows by Catherine O Brien and two by Sarah Purser in the College.

1½ m. S., at Whitechurch, are the remains of a small, medieval, nave-and-chancel church, with cross-inscribed slab. By the roadside is The Wartstone, base of an ancient cross.

4 m. SSE., via Whitechurch, is Larch Hill (Kilmashogue) chamber tomb (ruined).

Tacumshin (or Tacumshane) windmill, Co. Wexford (see page 276).

Roundstone, Co. Galway (see page 276).

3½ m. SSW., via Rockbrook, in Mount Venus demesne, Woodtown, is a ruined portal-tomb with enormous granite capstone.

3¾ m. SSW., via Ballyboden and Woodtown, on the summit of Mountpelier (1,271 ft), are the ruins of a massive, 18th c. sporting lodge, popularly, but erroneously, called Hell Fire Club. The road to the S. via Killakee Mountain is the N. end of the Military Road constructed after 1798 to control the mountain fastnesses. Noted for its scenery, it leads via Glencree – Sally Gap – Cloghoge – Glenmacnass – Laragh – Glenmalure – Aghavanagh to within 4 m. of Tinahely, keeping for much of the way to a great height.

1 m. SW., in Ballyroan, is the church of the Holy Spirit (1967) by Raymond Mc Donnell, with furnishings by Imogen Stuart (note the door handles) and Seán Keating. – 2 m. SW. is St Columcille's church, Knocklyon (1981), by Tyndall, Hogan, Hurley, with metal furnishings by Seán Adamson, and batiks by Bernadette Madden.

RATHFRYLAND, Co. Down (Map 2, J3), on the Newry (11 m.)–Downpatrick (21 m.) road, is a village set on a conspicuous hill (506 ft) dominating the plain anciently called Magh Cobha. It takes its name from the large, but defaced, *ráth* or ringfort which lies towards the E. This was for long a seat of the petty kings of Iveagh, whose descendant, Art Magennis, 1st Viscount Iveagh, built (*c.* 1611) the castle represented by the scant remains on the hill-top.

The Rev. Henry Boyd (d. 1832), translator of Dante, was rector of Rathfryland.

5½ m. NE. is Ballyroney motte, with three extensive baileys. ½ m. SSE., on a hillock on the opposite bank of the Bann, is Seafin Castle, built in 1252 by the English Justiciar Maurice fitz Gerald. Captured and wrecked the following year by Brian O Neill, King of Tír Eóghain, it was not restored until 1260.

RATHKEALE, Co. Limerick (Map 6, G8), is a small market town on the Limerick (18 m.)–Newcastle West (6½ m.) road.

The Desmond FitzGeralds had a castle there; only fragments survive. There are remains of St Mary's Augustinian priory founded in the 13th c. by Gilbert Harvey. The Protestant church has a 1676 Southwell monument, and a window *The Sower* by Catherine O Brien. The Gothic-Revival parish church is by J.J. McCarthy.

1 m. W. is Castlematrix. The tower was repaired early in the 19th c. James, 9th Earl of Desmond, was murdered there by his servants in 1487.

In 1709 the Rathkeale neighbourhood was settled by Lord Southwell with Calvinist refugees from the Rhenish Palatinate. Descendants of these Palatines are still to be found thereabouts, but they have been absorbed by the native population and most of them are now Catholics.

3 m. NNE., in Cappagh, are the remains of Kilmacluana, a small, plain, Gothic church. ¾ m. WSW. are the remains of a late-15th c. castle of the Knights of Glin.

4 m. ENE., at Croagh, are remains of a medieval church (cruciform; collegiate) and tower; in the neighbourhood are several ruined Geraldine castles.

RATHLIN ISLAND, Co. Antrim (Map 1, I–J2), lies 5 m. off the coast from BALLYCASTLE, from which (weather permitting) a motor-boat service runs to Church Bay. The spectacular coast, most of it cliff-bound, is the haunt of great numbers of sea birds.

St Comgall is said to have visited the island; St Columcille to have founded a monastery there. Rathlin was the first place in Ireland to be attacked by the Vikings (in 795). Robert Bruce, King of Scotland, found refuge from the English in 1306 (in Ballycarry is Bruce's Castle, a high promontory defended by a wall on the landward side, the setting of the story of Bruce and the spider; nearby is Bruce's Cave, a basalt cavern). In 1597 the islanders, and the dependants of the MacDonnells who had been taken there for safety, were all slaughtered by English forces.

RATHLUIRC, Co. Cork (Map 5, K1), for long Charleville, is a market town at the intersection of the Limerick (22 m.)–Mallow (18 m.) and Kilmallock (6 m.)–Drumcolliher (11 m.) roads. It was founded by Roger Boyle (1621–79), Lord Broghil, later Earl of Orrery, who named the place after Charles II.

¼ m. SSE., in the ruined church of Ballysallagh, is the grave (Latin epitaph) of Seán Clárach Mac Domhnaill (1691–1754), noted Gaelic poet; his works included a translation of Homer. His farm in Kiltoohig, to the W. of the town, was the meeting place of a 'Court of Poetry' frequented by Liam Dall Ó Hiffearnáin, Seán Ó Tuama (1706–75), and Eóghan Rúa Ó Súilleabháin (d. 1784)

2½ m. SSE., in Ballyhay, are remains of a church with a gabled Romanesque doorway in the S. wall. The sole ornaments of the doorway are two 'ox-head label-stop' masks.

4¼ m. SE. are fragments (Nat. Mon.) of the 12th c. church of Ardskeagh.

7½ m. WSW., in Kilbolane, are remains (Nat. Mon.) of a late 13th c. Cogan – later Desmond – castle of Liscarroll type.

RATHMELTON, Co. Donegal (Map 1, B4), is a village on the Letterkenny (8 m.)–Milford (4 m.) road, where the Leannan River flows into Lough Swilly. Francis Mackemie, founder of the Presbyterian church in North America, was born there in 1658.

The ruined church has an interesting, degenerate, perpendicular E. window (17th c.?); built into the wall above it is the head of a decorated Romanesque window from Aughnish, an island in Lough Swilly, 4 m. (by road) NE. The Protestant church has a three-light window (*Benedicite Psalm*) by Patrick Pollen.

2¾ m. SE. are the ruins of Killydonnell Franciscan Tertiary Friary, founded by the O Donnells in 1471.

RATHMULLAN, Co. Donegal (Map 1, C4), is a small port and holiday resort on the W. shore of Lough Swilly, 7 m. NE. of Rathmelton.

In 1587 the 15-year-old Red Hugh O Donnell was lured from Mac Sweeny of Fanad's Castle, which stood by the beach, on to an English merchantman and taken to Dublin Castle. This act of treachery towards a family friendly to the English was one of the causes of the great war (1595–1603) between the still Gaelic North and the English Crown. In 1591 Red Hugh contrived a daring escape and the following year succeeded to the lordship of

Tír Chonaill (*see p. 224*). On 14 September 1607, the Earls of Tyrone (Great Hugh O Neill) and Tyrconnell (Rúairí O Donnell, Red Hugh's successor) sailed away to the Continent from Rathmullan. This tragic Flight of the Earls marked the final overthrow of the Gaelic order in its last great stronghold, and cleared the way for the Plantation of Ulster. In 1798 Wolfe Tone and the other prisoners from the French warship *Hoche*, crippled in a desperate fight with a superior English force off Lough Swilly, were landed near Rathmullan (*see p. 83*).

At Rathmullan are remains of a Carmelite friary of the Blessed Virgin Mary, built by Eóghan Rúa Mac Sweeny in 1516. The church was adapted as a stronghouse (1617–18) by Bishop Knoxe, second Protestant bishop of Raphoe, who converted the choir into a domestic chapel. In the grounds of the Catholic church is a cross-inscribed slab from Killycolman, 3 m. N.

Near the pier is a 19th c. battery, one of the series built to defend Lough Swilly when it was a British naval station.

3½ m. NNW., in Drumhallagh Lower is St Garvan's Grave, a small cairn with an 8th c. cross-slab on which is carved a plaited cross with two angels (?) above and two ecclesiastics below the arms.

RATHVILLY, Co. Carlow (Map 3, I8), is a village beside the Slaney, on the Baltinglass (10 m.)–Tinahely (8 m.) road.

There is a large motte just beside the village. The pleasant little d'Israeli School was built (1826) by Joseph Welland for Benjamin d'Israeli of nearby Beechy Park.

1½ m. N., to the E. of the Baltinglass road, is Broughillstown grooved pillarstone.

4½ m. ESE. is Tombeagh grooved pillarstone.

2 m. SE. is Williamstown Gallan, alias The Six Fingers, a grooved pillarstone. Fionn Mac Cumhaill threw it, 'tis said, from Eagle Hill, Hacketstown. According to another story it rolls down to the nearby Derreen for a drink from time to time.

3½ m. SE., on the E. bank of the Derreen near Acaun bridge, is Haroldstown portal-tomb (Nat. Mon.).

RATOATH, Co. Meath (Map 3, J2), is a village between Ashbourne (4 m.) and Dunshaughlin (5 m.). Before 1186 Hugh I de Lacy built a castle there, now represented by a very fine motte-and-bailey. In the grounds of the ruined Protestant church is the effigy of a knight of *c.* 1300.

2 m. S. is Fairyhouse Race-course, where the Irish Grand National Steeplechase is run.

REAR CROSS, Co. Tipperary (Map 4, C1), is a road-junction on the Limerick (18½ m.)–Thurles (21½ m.) road. There are numerous megalithic monuments in the hills thereabouts.

1½ m. NE., in the roadway in Baurnadomeeny, is Cloghfadda, a fine pillarstone (survivor of a pair). 150 yds S. is a Late Neolithic/Bronze Age wedge-tomb.

1½ m. S., in Shanballyedmond, is an excavated court-tomb which had a unique peristyle of 34 timber posts which linked up with the 'horns' of the funnel-shaped paved court in front of the two-segment gallery. There were six cremations in the tomb.

3¾ m. E. (1½ m. SW. of Kilcommon village) is Anglesey Bridge. – 1½ m. SW. of the bridge, in Knockshanbrittas, is a ruined wedge-tomb; nearby to the N. is a second. – 2 m. NE. of the bridge, in Loughbrack, is a roofless wedge-tomb; this was much the largest chamber tomb in the whole area. – 3 m. ENE. of Anglesey Bridge is Inch. ½ m. E., in Knockcurraghbola Crownlands, are the remains of a wedge-tomb. – 3 m. E. of Inch is Shevry crossroads. 2 m. NW., in Knockcurraghbola Commons, is a very fine wedge-tomb.

RINVYLE, Co. Galway (Map 7, C7), is a promontory on the lovely N. coast of Connemara, 5 m. NNW of Letterfrack and 16 m. W. of Leenaun. Rinvyle House Hotel, which stands close to a small beach, belonged for many years to Oliver St John Gogarty, surgeon, author, poet, and wit.

1½ m. W. of the hotel are the ruins of the 15th c. O Flaherty castle of Rinn Mhíl. To the E. of the castle, in Ardnagreevagh, is a prehistoric chamber-tomb. 250 yds SW. of the castle, in Kanrawer, is the Well of the Seven Daughters, called after the saintly daughters of a British (= Welsh) king. SSW. of the well, in Cashleen, is the Church of the Seven Daughters.

2 m. SSE. of Rinvyle House Hotel, in Derryinver (on the high ground SW. of Tully Lough), is an alignment of six pillarstones; to the SW. is a fragment of a small stone circle.

2½ m. SE. is Tully Cross. The church has three windows by Harry Clarke (1926): *St Barbara*, *Sacred Heart*, *St Bernard*.

RIVERSTOWN, Co. Sligo (Map 7, K3), is on the Collooney (7 m.)–Kilmactranny (8 m.) road, to the N. of Lough Arrow.

2 m. E. are the remnants of Drumcolumb (Druim Choluimcille) church and the broken ring-head of a plain, stone cross. Columcille is said to have placed his disciple, Finnbárr, in charge of a monastery there.

3¼ m. SE., in Heapstown, is the great kerbed cairn (Nat. Mon.) which has given its name to the townland. It is traditionally the grave of Ailill (brother of Niall Nine Hostager) who gave his name to Tirerrill. 2 m. NE. is Lough Nasool ('of the eyes'), traditionally associated with Balor of the Baleful Eye (*see p. 294*). It is reputed to dry up every 100 years, and last did so in 1933. 5 m. SE., in Ballindoon, are the ruins of a Dominican friary founded in 1507 by the Mac Donaghs, the site of whose castle is ½ m. SSE. of the friary. The church has a singular belfry cum rood screen (magnified) at the junction of nave and choir. In the cemetery lie buried Lame David Duignan (d. 1696) and, nearby, the celebrated Great Counsellor Terence Mac Donagh (d. 1717), patron of Roderick O Flaherty (*see p. 284*).

ROCHFORTBRIDGE, Co. Westmeath (Map 3, E3), is a hamlet on the Kinnegad (10 m.)–Tyrrelspass (4 m.) road. It is called after Dean Swift's friend, political renegade Robert Rochfort (1652–1727), M.P. for Westmeath and Speaker of the Dublin House of Commons. It was in Gallstown House, 1¾ m. NE., that Robert Rochfort (1708–72), 1st Earl of Belvedere, imprisoned his wife (*see p. 252*).

1 m. NW., at Castlelost, a motte-and-bailey and a fragment of a stone castle mark the seat of the Anglo-Norman Tyrrels from the 13th c. to the Cromwellian conquest. 400 yds N. are remains of a semi-fortified, manorial church.

ROSCOMMON, Co. Roscommon (Map 7, L7), capital of the county to which it gives its name, is a small town on the main Athlone (20 m.)–Sligo (53 m.) road.

The place takes its name from the abbot-bishop St Commán, who founded a monastery there in the 6th c., of which not a trace survives. There are, however, remains (Nat. Mon.) of the church of the Dominican Friary of the Assumption founded in 1253 by Felim O Conor, King of Connacht. After a fire in 1308, it was rebuilt in 1453 (N. transept, traceried windows, etc.), and the surviving fragments date from then. The most interesting feature is Felim O Conor's Tomb, in a canopied niche in the chancel. The effigy may be dated to *c.* 1300, and is possibly that of King Felim; but the eight weepers (galloglas) are late-15th c., and may belong to the tomb of Tadhg O Conor (d. 1464).

The Court House is by Sir Richard Morrison (1767–1849).

W. of the town, on the Tulsk road, are the ruins (Nat. Mon.) of the great castle built in 1269 by the English Justiciar, Roger d'Ufford, as a Crown fortress. The fortifications were dismantled by the Cromwellians in 1652. The remains are those of a splendid, 13th c. keepless castle which had an unusually fine twin-towered gatehouse on the E., a subsidiary gate on the W., and four great D-shaped corner towers. About 1580 the interior was remodelled and large windows were inserted in the towers and in the curtain.

5 m. NE., in the grounds of Holywell House, are the remains of Kilbride (St Brigid's Church) and St Brigid's Well. The Gunning sisters, celebrated 18th c. beauties, are said to have owed their complexions to the waters of this well.

4½ m. E. are the ruins of Kilteevan Church. It has an unusual small E. window (15th/16th c.). Nearby is a holy well.

4 m. WSW. is Fuerty, where an ancient churchyard and two early gravestones (built into the wall of a church tower) mark the site of a Patrician foundation confided to Justus, baptizer and tutor of Cíarán of CLONMACNOIS. The early monastery there was closely associated with Clonmacnois. One of the gravestones bears a fish symbol – rare in Ireland – and the inscription OR[ŌIT] AR ANMAIN AIDACAIN ('A prayer for the soul of Aidacán') possibly refers to the Aeducán, 'tanist-abbot of Clonmacnois and abbot of many churches', who died in 865. The other has the inscription OR[ŌIT] AR MOR ('A prayer for Mór'). ½ m. NE., to the E. of the Ballymoe road, is Dermot and Grania's Bed, a ruined wedge-tomb. – 1 m. W., on the River Suck, is Castlecoote, celebrated in the 18th c. for its flour mills. Castlecoote was the home of John Gunning, father of the celebrated Gunning sisters.

ROSCREA, Co. Tipperary (Map 3, C7), is a manufacturing and market town where the Dublin–Limerick road crosses the gap between Slieve Bloom and Devilsbit Mts, 12 m. SE. of Birr.

In the 6th/7th c. Cronan of Éile founded a monastery on a desert promontory (Ros Cré) of a nearby lake (Loch Cré). Before his death he founded a second monastery on a site more convenient for travellers, from which grew the town of Roscrea. (To this monastery belonged the so-called *Book of Dimma*, an 8th c. illuminated manuscript now in the library of Trinity College, Dublin.) Later a subsidiary foundation, on an island (Monaincha *below*) in the lake, was prominent in the *céle Dé* movement (*see p. 287*).

On the E. side of town the main road cuts through the site of St Cronan's second monastery. The remains comprise a Round Tower, 12th c. figured High Cross, and the W. gable of a Romanesque church demolished in 1812. The gable, which has projecting *antae*, has a porch under a tangent gable with an ecclesiastic in the pediment, and is flanked by a blind arcade of four bays. Much-repaired St Cronan's cross stands to the S., adorned with interlacing, an *Adam and Eve*, a *Crucifixion* and an ecclesiastic on the W. and E. faces. The Round Tower has a carving of a one-masted sailing ship on the E. window.

About 1212, Roscrea's strategic importance forced the Anglo-Normans to erect a motte to command the pass. In 1280 this was replaced by a stone castle, later granted to the Butlers. This irregular, polygonal structure in Castle St has a gate-tower, curtain wall and two D-shaped corner towers; the gables and chimney stacks are 17th c. additions.

On the south side of the courtyard is a good Queen Anne house, built by the Damers. It has been undergoing restoration since the early 1970s when the house was saved from demolition. It now houses Roscrea Heritage Centre with its exhibitions and displays of local archives and artefacts. The centre has pioneered genealogical research into parish records, and has undertaken a wide range of archaeological and environmental surveys over the SW midlands of Ireland.

On the S. side of the town are the remains (E. and N. walls of the chancel, bell-tower, part of N. nave arcade, etc.) of a Franciscan friary, founded before 1477 by an O Carroll of Éile. The surviving ruin serves as gateway to the Catholic church, an imposing Gothic-Revival building, erected (1844 and after 1866) to the design of William Deane Butler. Facing the W. door is a pillarstone (8th/9th c.?) with weathered figure and other carvings, brought there from Timoney Park, 5 m. SE.

5 m. N. is Leap Castle, burned in 1922.

2½ m. SE. is Monaincha Abbey, once a little island (*Inis na mBeo*, Giraldus' *Insula Viventium*) in the now-drained Loch Cré. A céle Dé community flourished there. In time the Augustinian canons joined the community, building the beautiful little Romanesque church (the surviving ruins have later alterations and additions) in the 12th c. The ruins comprise a small stone cross, church and a two-storey annexe of later date. The W. door (restored) has an inscription and, like the chancel arch, is in three orders with much decoration. The 12th c. cross (the cement shaft is 20th c.) bears a figure of Christ.

5¾ m. SE., in Timoney and Cullaun, are almost 300 standing stones (Nat. Mon.) with one group of eight forming part of a circle; the rest are in no coherent order. Excavation is necessary to show whether these date to the Bronze Age or are – as local tradition asserts – the result of medieval land clearances.

4 m. SW. is Ballinakill Castle, a 17th c. stronghouse of the Butlers with a huge bawn.

2½ m. W. is the Cistercian abbey of Mount St Joseph with guest house and college.

ROSMUCK, Co. Galway (Map 6, D1), is a parish in the heart of the Connemara Gaeltacht, 36 m. W. of Galway. In Turlough is the cottage (Nat. Mon.; much restored) which was used as a summer home by Patrick H. Pearse (1879–1916), poet and author, who commanded the Dublin insurgents in 1916. His writings in Irish and English drew much of their inspiration from the Rosmuck country and its people.

ROSS CARBERY, Co. Cork (Map 5, I8), is a quiet, picturesquely sited, little resort at the head of a shallow, landlocked inlet of Ross Carbery Bay, 10 m. WSW. of Clonakilty and 9 m. ENE. of Skibbereen. The tides rushing into the sea caves of the bay produce a peculiar, melancholy roar. Hence Tonn Chlíodhna (Cleena's Wave), one of the three magic waves of Irish mythology (*see p. 244*).

The place was anciently known as Ros Ailithir, the Pilgrim's Promontory, after a pilgrim named Colmán. In the 6th/7th c. Bishop-Abbot St Fachtna mac Mongaigh of Dairinis (*see p. 308*) founded a monastery there, which became the principal monastery of Corca Loígde and was famous for its school. One of its teachers, Airbertach, was ransomed by Brian Boru after he had been captured on one of the Norse raids on the monastery. Some time before 1197 the Irish Benedictines of Würzburg established a priory at Ross. It survived until the 16th c. At the Synod of Kells, 1152, Ros Ailithir was chosen to be the see of a diocese, which maintained its separate jurisdiction until recently.

At the S. end of the village, St Cummin's Well and the scant remains of Ross 'Abbey' mark the site of the Benedictine Priory of Our Lady. At the E. side of the village is little St Fachtna's Cathedral (Protesant, diocese united to Cork and Cloyne since 1617). It incorporates fragments of the pre-Reformation, cruciform cathedral whose nave and tower were levelled in the 17th c. The existing tower probably dates from 1696; the capping and spire date from 1806. The rest of the church is almost entirely 19th c., but the N. transept is probably largely medieval.

1½ m. E., in Burgatia, are the remains of diminutive Teampaillín Fhácthtna (St Fáchtna's little church); ¼ m. E. of the church is Toberfaughtna, where pilgrims still make their rounds. ¼ m. ENE. of the latter, in Bohonagh, is a stone circle; a shallow grave at the centre held a cremation. SE. of the circle is a displaced stone with seven cup marks. 20 yds ESE. of the circle is a low tomb whose capstone has seven or more cup marks. – 500 yds S. of the well is Callaheenacladdig, a fine portal-tomb.

2 m. SE. is Inch Strand. At the SE. end is Cloghna Head. Offshore is Cleena's Rock, said to be haunted (by the goddess; *see above*). Between the strands is Castlefreke Demesne, formerly seat of Lord Carbery. In the demesne are the ruins of Rathbarry castle (motte nearby) and church.

2¼ m. WSW., in Ballyvireen, is Coppinger's Court (Nat. Mon.), a large 17th c. stronghouse.

2m. W. are the remains of Benduff Castle, alias Castle Salem, an O Donovan stronghold.

3 m. NW., in Reanascreena South, is a stone circle. 1¾ m. NNW. of this circle, in Carrigagrenane, is another stone circle. 1½ m. NNE. of the latter, in Maulatanvally, is a third (with a white quartz boulder inside it).

ROSSLARE, Co. Wexford (Map 4, M5), is a village and resort (4 m. sandy beach) on Rosslare Bay, 11 m. SE. of Wexford.

3 m. SE. is Rosslare Harbour: passenger and car-ferry service to Fishguard, Cherbourg and Le Havre.

6 m. SE., near the coast, is Ballytrent House, birthplace of John Redmond (1856–1918), leader of the Irish Party in the House of Commons. Beside the house is a large bivallate ringfort.

5 m. S., at the head of Lady's Island Lake – a saltwater lagoon – is Lady's Island, for centuries a place of pilgrimage. Near the ruins are the remains of a granite castle of *c.* 1237 with, adjoining it, a leaning tower of limestone. 2 m. SSE., in Clougheast, is the 15th c. tower of a Codd castle. 2 m. S. of this is sandy Carnsore Point: ¼ m. N. are remains of a primitive monastery with cashel, small church, holy well, and large cross-inscribed boulder. The patron is St Vogue, usually identified with St Véoc (Béóc), who died at Lanvéoc, in Brittany, in 585. Excavations in advance of an abortive attempt to build a nuclear power station on the site uncovered a small wooden structure (shrine?) of the 6th or 7th c. 7 m. ENE. of the Point is the famous Tuskar Rock, with a lighthouse built in 1815 and improved in 1885.

4 m. SW., in Ballysampson, is the birthplace of Commodore James Barry (1745–1803), 'father of the American navy'.

7 m. SW., in Tacumshin, alias Tacumshane, is one of the last Irish windmills (Nat. Mon.). Tacumshin Lake is a salt pill, or lagoon, cut off from the open sea by a storm beach.

ROSTREVOR, Co. Down (Map 2, J5), is a small seaside resort on Carlingford Lough. It lies 2½ m. E. of Warrenpoint, on the delightful Newry (8½ m.)–Newcastle (22¼ m.) road.

W. of the town is an obelisk commemorating General Ross (1766–1814), a former proprietor of the town. He died of wounds received in the British attack on Baltimore, U.S.A., after the capture of Washington and Bladensburg.

1 m. NE., on the Hilltown road, is Kilbroney (Brónach's Church). The church is called after its founder, the Virgin Brónach, a patron of seafarers, but the remains are those of a much later parochial church. SE. of the ruins is a large cross (Hist. Mon.) with all-over ornament on the W. face. Between it and St Brónach's Well is a small cross (Nat. Mon.) with crude conventionalized *Crucifixion* on the E. face. St Brónach's enshrined staff, now in the National Museum, was long venerated in the church. The bell from the monastery is preserved in the Catholic church at Rostrevor. In the graveyard is the grave of Paddy Murtagh (d. 1861), in his day – at 8 ft 1 in. – the tallest man in the world.

1 m. SE., 300 yds W. of Causeway Water and 500 yds N. of the Kilkeel road, is Kilfeaghan Cromlech (Nat. Mon.), a portal-tomb with a 40 ton capstone and traces of a cairn.

ROUNDSTONE, Co. Galway (Map 7, C9), is a decayed fishing village, 7 m. SW. of Ballynahinch and 14 m. SE. of Clifden. The village was built in the 1820s by the Scottish engineer Alexander Nimmo, and settled with Scottish fisherfolk. It was to Roundstone Court that Thackeray came with Richard Martin (son of 'Humanity Dick') to hear him dispense justice. Kate O Brien (1897–1974), the novelist, lived for some years at the Fort, overlooking the harbour.

2½ m. SW., at the foot of Errisbeg, are Dog's Bay and Gorteen Bay, with fine beaches. The tides and winds there have piled up great dunes of fine white sand between the mainland and a small island, ½ m. offshore.

ROUNDWOOD, Co. Wicklow (Map 3, K6), is a small village beside the Vartry, at the junction of main roads from Bray (12½ m.), Glendalough (7 m.), and Ashford (7 m.), with lesser roads from Newtown Mountkennedy (6½m.), Enniskerry (10 m.), and Glencree (11½ m., *see p. 177*) via the Sally Gap.

2 m. SSW. is Annamoe bridge. It was there that the novelist Laurence Sterne (1713–68) fell into the mill race.

3 m. S., 1 m. SE. of Annamoe bridge, is Castlekevin, built *c.* 1214 by Henry de Londres, English archbishop of Dublin. But it became an O Toole stronghold in the 14th c. In 1591 Red Hugh O Donnell sought refuge there with Felim O Toole, after escaping from Dublin Castle, and there he was recaptured. In 1597 the castle passed again into English control, but by the early 17th c. it had fallen into ruin. All that survive today are a square motte (formerly revetted with masonry) with a long bailey (on the E.) and the scant remains of the gate tower and of the NE. angle tower.

9¾ m. NW., in a deep, cliff-girt corrie, is romantic Luggala (Hon. Garech Browne) with its little lake (Luggala Lake, alias Lough Tay). The lodge by the shore was built for Sir Philip Crampton (1777–1858), the celebrated surgeon. In the grounds has been erected (1950) a garden temple originally at Templeogue House and afterwards at Santry Court. 3 m. NW. is Sally Gap (1,631 ft), from whence there is a very fine drive (through some of the loveliest solitudes of the Wicklow massif) to or from Glendalough.

RUSH, Co. Dublin (Map 3, L2), is a fishing village and small seaside resort on the Dublin (18 m.)–Skerries (5 m.) road, 4 m. E. of Lusk. The light, sandy soil in the vicinity is particularly favourable for market gardening, and the bulb farms are very attractive in spring.

¾ m. N. is Kenure Park. A giant granite portico standing in a housing estate is all that remains of a Classical house of *c.* 1830, which was the home of the Palmers until 1964. NE. of the house are the ruins of medieval St Catherine's Church.

2 m. NE., in Drumanagh, to the SE. of Loughshinny, is a very large promontory fort.

1 m. SW. is Rogerstown, point of departure for LAMBAY ISLAND.

S

SAGGART, Co. Dublin (Map 3, J4), is a small village, 8¼ m. SW. of Dublin and 1 m. ESE. of Rathcoole. It takes its name, Saggart, alias Tasagart, from an early monastery founded by St Sacru. Of the monastery the sole surviving relics are a cross-pillar, a cross fragment, a finial and a cross socket (the Wart Stone) in the old graveyard. In the Middle Ages Saggart was an English border strongpoint against the O Tooles and O Byrnes.

1 m. S. is the Slade of Saggart, a narrow defile by which the Dublin-Blessington road penetrates the W. end of the Dublin mountains. On the NE. part of Saggart Hill, in Lugg (1,000 ft.), are a semi-denuded small cairn and a complex Iron Age ritual monument (Nat. Mon.) enclosed by two ramparts with intervening ditch and having at the centre a mound with surrounding bank and ditch.

SAINTFIELD, Co. Down (Map 2, L1), is a small linen town on the Belfast (11 m.)–Downpatrick (11 m.) road.

1 m. S. is Rowallane (Nat. Trust) whose 50 acre gardens, laid out by Hugh Armytage Moore between 1903 and 1955, are noted for their landscaping and for their rhododendrons, magnolias, cherries, wall plants, Chinese and Chilean shrubs, etc. The gardens are at their best in spring and autumn.

ST JOHNSTOWN, Co. Donegal (Map 1, C5), is a small Border village on the Derry (7 m.)–Raphoe (6 m.) road.

3 m. S. are the remains of Mongavlin 'castle', a Plantation stronghouse built 1619–22 by Sir John Stuart; it was James II's headquarters during the Siege of Derry.

ST MULLIN'S, Co. Carlow (Map 4, J3), is a little village charmingly situated on the Graiguenamanagh (7 m.)–New Ross (8¾ m.) road through the lovely Barrow valley.

The place takes its name from the important monastery founded here by St Mo-Ling, a patron of South Leinster. (He is said to have secured a remission of the notorious Bórama tribute for the Leinstermen.) Teach Mo-Ling, Moling's House, was his principal foundation, and there he was buried *c.* 697. It long remained an important place of pilgrimage. It was also the burial-place of the South Leinster kings and of their medieval representatives, the Mac Murroughs Kavanagh (including the celebrated King Art, 1417), who were long the custodians of the enshrined gospel book called the *Book of Mulling* of c. 800, now in Trinity College, Dublin. The remains (Nat. Mons.) of Teach Mo-Ling are close to the Protestant church. They include remains of a small nave-and-chancel church and of a two-apartment building ('St Mullin's Abbey') attached to a Round Tower (stump only). Close to the SE. corner of the church ruin is a figured High Cross (*Crucifixion,* etc.); part of the shaft is missing. E. of this are remains of a diminutive oratory ('St James's Chapel'). NE. of the Protestant church are remnants of St Mo-Ling's Mill. 150 yds N. of the monastery are St Mo-Ling's Well and remains of a bath house *(antae)*. WNW. of the monastery is a motte. S. of the monastery are remains of Caisleán Maol, built *c.* 1581 to enable a Mac Murrough who had thrown in his lot with the English to keep his kinsfolk in check. There are some attractive 19th c. tombstones in the churchyard.

2 m. SE. is Drummin, where the Catholic church has been tastefully refurbished (1975) by Ray Carroll.

SALROCK, Co. Galway (Map 7, D7), is a small hamlet beautifully situated at the head of Little Killary Bay, 9 m. E. of Rinvyle and 8 m. W. of Leenaun. Close to the hamlet is an ancient church-site, traditional burial place of St Roc (after whom the place is named). Coffins are borne three times round the graveyard before burial. The road to the NW. leads to the mouth of Killary Harbour (1 m.) and a magnificent view of that fjord-like inlet (*see p. 231*).

SALTEE ISLANDS, Co. Wexford (Map 4, K6), lie 2-4½ m. off the coast, to the S. of KILMORE QUAY. The Great Saltee is Ireland's most important bird sanctuary.

After the defeat of the Wexford insurgents in 1798, their leaders, Bagenal Harvey (*see p. 83*) and John Colclough, sought temporary refuge here, but were tracked down, discovered in a cave, and taken to Wexford, where they were beheaded.

SANTRY, Co. Dublin (Map 3, K3), is a village 4 m. from Dublin and 5 m. from Swords, which is now engulfed in the Dublin suburbs. St Papán's Protestant church (1709) occupies the site of the 13th c. successor of a monastery founded in the 6th c. by St Papán. In it are a hexagonal 14th c. font, a handsome reredos of 1709, an interesting pulpit, and the pew of the Domville family. Near the churchyard door is the tomb of Richard Barry, 2nd Lord Santry (d. 1694), and his wife (d. 1682); it was restored in 1847. In the church there is one window (*St Michael*, 1929) by Hubert McGoldrick, and another (*Fortitude and Justice, with Job and St John the Baptist*, 1935) by Catherine O Brien.

2 m. N. is Dublin Airport. The scale of its growth in recent decades is best seen by comparing the original passenger terminal building, built by Desmond Fitz Gerald *c.* 1940, with its enormous successor of 1969–72 by L.M. Carroll. The interesting airport church with atrium (1962–3) is by A.D. Devane, with stained glass by Michael Dunne. The Madonna figure and the fountain by Imogen Stuart are 1969 additions.

SCARRIFF, Co. Clare (Map 6, I5), is an angling and market village on the Clare side of Lough Derg, 10½ m. N. of Killaloe.

2 m. S. is the village of Tuamgraney, where the interesting Protestant parish church incorporates the remains of a pre-Romanesque church (with *antae* and trabeate W. door), to which a Transitional chancel was added in the later 12th c. A monastery was founded here in the 6th c. by a St Crónán. The nave of the present church is alleged to represent a rebuilding by Abbot Cormac O Killeen (d. 969). In the church are preserved some Romanesque fragments.

SCARVA, Co. Down (Map 2, I3) is a 1756 village on the Newry canal, between Tanderagee (8 m.) and Loughbrickland (3 m.). It was the rallying-place of the Williamite forces on their advance to the South in 1689. The event is commemorated by the mimic battle enacted in front of Scarva House on 13 July, a major, popular, rural occasion for Unionist Protestants of all denominations. Scarva House (1717) has a strong 17th c. flavour. A large Spanish chestnut tree is said to have shaded King William's tent.

The course of the Newry River southwards represents the line of the W. frontier of Ulster as it was at some undetermined date, usually thought to be the 4th c. Considerable stretches of the frontier defences, popularly called the Dane's Cast (Nat. Mon.), survive. These consist of banks and ditches constructed wherever there was no natural obstacle to stay an enemy. One such stretch may be seen in the demesne of Scarva House, where it turns NE. away from the river and towards Lisnagade House. Another long stretch is to be seen to the E. of Poyntz Pass, 3 m. S. of Scarva (*see also p. 267*).

2 m. E. is Lisnagade, a trivallate ringfort (Hist. Mon.), which has been described as 'the largest and most strongly entrenched rath in Ireland'.

3 m. SE. is Loughbrickland village, founded *c.* 1585 for English Protestant settlers by Sir Marmaduke Whitechurch, purveyor of clothing to the Elizabethan army.

SHANAGOLDEN, Co. Limerick (Map 6, F8), is a village on the Foynes (3 m.)–Newcastle West (10 m.) road.

2 m. E., at Old Abbey House, are remains of Monasternagalliaghduff, the Augustinian nunnery called St Catherine's of Uí Conaill. The 13th c. church (some 15th c. details) opens off the E. side of a cloister court which had the refectory and kitchen on the S. and domestic buildings (with undercrofts) on the W. Remains of gatehouses, fish pond, and columbarium survive.

2 m. SSW. is Shanid. There are fragmentary remains of Shanid Castle, 'Desmond's first and most ancient house', which suggested the famous Desmond war-cry and motto: *Shanid aboo.* The motte-and-bailey are relics of the first Geraldine castle here, built by Thomas fitz Maurice. The motte is crowned by curtain walls (a shell-keep?), within which are remains of a polygonal keep. The castle first figures in history in 1230. It was captured by Red Hugh O Donnell of Tyrconnell in 1600.

SHANNONBRIDGE, Co. Offaly (Map 3, B4), is a village on the Cloghan (8 m.)–Ballinasloe (10 m.) road. Nearby is a power station fired by milled peat. On the W. bank of the Shannon is a small, well-preserved, early-19th c. fort, built to secure the Connacht bridgehead.

SHERCOCK, Co. Cavan (Map 2, F6), is a village on the Bailieborough (7 m.)–Carrickmacross (9 m.) road.

3 m. NNW., in Corgreagh, Co. Monaghan, is Labbyfirmore, a long cairn containing a megalithic chamber with a large roof-stone, now displaced.

SHILLELAGH, Co. Wicklow (Map 3, J9), is a small village where the Carnew (4½ m.)–Tullow (10 m.) road crosses the wooded valley of the Shillelagh River. The local woods are the modern representatives of a once great oak forest which, it is claimed, supplied roof timbers in the Middle Ages for Westminster Hall, London, as well as for St Patrick's Cathedral, Dublin.

1½ m. E. is Coolattin Park, former seat of the Earl of Fitzwilliam, now largely despoiled of its fine oaks.

5 m. WNW. (1¾ m. SW. of Coolkenna crossroads), in Aghowle Lower, are the ruins of an early-12th c. church (Nat. Mon.), St Finden's (*sic*) Cross (Nat. Mon.), a bullaun and a stone basin. The celebrated St Finnian of Clonard founded his first monastery there. The church has a noteworthy trabeate W. door with double-faced architrave, bosses, etc.; also two small Romanesque windows. 2 m. S. of the church, in Moylisha, is Leaba na Saighe (800 ft), a roofless, wedge-tomb (Nat. Mon.).

3 m. NW., in the second field E. of Kilquiggin churchyard, are the head and socket of an early cross.

SHRULE, Co. Mayo (Map 7, H8), is a village where the Ballinrobe (9 m.)–Headford (5 m.) road, via Kilmaine, crosses the Shrule or Black River.

Commanding the river crossing is the tower (Nat. Mon.) of a Burke castle, unsuccessfully besieged by the English President of Connacht and the Earl of Clanricard in 1570. In a house in the grounds is a family-owned folk museum.

2 m. NW. are the ruins of Kill 'Abbey' ('St Brendan's little church'), first (before 1426) Irish house of the Third Order Regular of St Francis. By 1536 it had some 46 dependencies.

SIXMILEBRIDGE, Co. Clare (Map 6, H6), is a village on the Tulla (9 m.)–Limerick (9 m.) road. Mount Ievers (private) is a fine Georgian house, built about 1730 for the Ievers family by John and Isaac Rothery(?); (noteworthy drawing-room.)

2 m. N. are remains of Ballymulcashel (Mountcashel) castle, built by Conor na Sróna O Brien, King of Thomond (1466–96).

1¼ m. NNW., in Ballysheen, are remains of Kilfinaghta, a 12th c. Western Traditional church.

2 m. NNE., in Knopoge, is a wedge-tomb. Nearby is Knappogue Castle (Hon. Mark Andrews), an O Brien castle, open to the public in summer, when banquets are held.

SKELLIGS, THE, Co. Kerry (Map 5, A6), are a group of rock islets – Little Skellig, Great Skellig, Washerwoman's Rock – 7 m. W. of Bolus Head. They can be reached, in calm weather, from Portmagee, Ballinskelligs or Waterville.

The Little Skellig is the most southerly of the few breeding places of the gannet in these islands.

The Great Skellig (Sceilg Mhichíl, Skellig Michael) is a huge rock rising to twin peaks, 715 and 650 ft above the Atlantic. It was one of Europe's many ancient lofty places associated with the cult of St Michael (as Mont St Michel in Brittany and St Michael's Mount in Cornwall), and is famous for well-preserved remains (Nat. Mons.) of an austere anchoritic settlement attributed to one of the SS Fíonán. The settlement was raided by the Vikings in 823, and disappears from history after 1044. (The monks are said to have removed to BALLINSKELLIGS, in the 12th c.) From East Landing a flight of ruined steps marks one ancient ascent to the main settlement. The modern approach is via the lighthouse road along the SE. cliffs. Some 500 yds SW. of the landing, steps and a path climb towards the monastery. On the sheer slopes NE. of the path is a cross carved in the round from the natural rock. 200 yds from the road the path reaches Christ's Valley, a saddle with two rude stone crosses on the S. side. To the W. rises South Peak with Needles Eye, a rock-chimney (714 ft); near the peak is a platform with remains of a small oratory (access difficult). Half-way up the peak is another ruin; there are artificial terraces on the steep slopes to the NE., W. and S. On the N. side of Christ's Valley the path to the monastery is joined by a flight of steps from North Landing. A flight of steps and a path lead NE. to the remains of the settlement proper, which consists of a series of enclosures set on steep terraces 550–600 ft above the ocean.

In the main enclosure are five dry masonry, corbel-roofed, stone huts (clocháns), and another in ruins, a small oratory of Gallarus (*see pp. 61–2*) type, the remains of little St Michael's Church, and the cemetery. In the latter are 22 early gravestones. On a platform W. of the oratory is a stone cross; near its SE. corner is a cross-inscribed slab, and nearby a stone cross. To the NE. of the clocháns is a small, isolated oratory. To the S. of them

The Little Skellig, Co. Kerry.

is the 'Monk's Garden', below which are a ruined structure and the ancient stairway from East Landing. The monastic area has recently been cleaned up by the Office of Public Works, who have had to carry out extensive conservation works because of the excessive number of visitors to the island.

SKERRIES, Co. Dublin (Map 3, L1), is a popular small seaside resort on the Rush (5 m.)–Balbriggan (5 m.) road.

1¼ m. ENE. is St Patrick's Island (Inis Phádraig), where Patrick is said to have landed on his way from Wicklow to Ulster. An early monastery on the island was plundered by the Vikings in 795, and the Shrine of St Do-Chonna was carried off. In 1148 a national reform synod assembled at the monastery to make formal application to the Pope for palls for the first Irish archbishops, and sent St Malachy to Rome as its spokesman. (He died en route, at Clairvaux, 2 November 1148.) On the island are fragments of a tufa-roofed nave-and-chancel church.

At the S. end of the town is Holmpatrick, where the Protestant church occupies part of the site of the priory transferred from St Patrick's Island in the 13th c. In the churchyard are the tombstones of the last prior, Richard de la Hoyde of Loughshinny (d. 1587), and of Elizabeth Finglas (d. 1577).

2 m. SSW, at Baldongan, are the ruins (Nat. Mon.) of a nave-and-chancel church with massive W. tower. To the NE. stood formerly Baldongan Castle, whose garrison of 200 Confederate Catholics was slaughtered by the Parliamentarians in 1642.

SKIBBEREEN, Co. Cork (Map 5, H8), is a small market town and fishing port where the Clonakilty (20 m.)–Ballydehob (10 m.) road crosses the Ilen, 8 m. S. of Drimoleague and 7 m. NE. of Baltimore.

4 m. SW. is lovely, almost completely landlocked, Lough Hyne (Ine). On Castle Island are the remains of Cloghan Castle (O Driscolls). At the S. end of the lough are a well and church dedicated to St Brigid. The Marine Biology station of University College, Cork, is on Lough Hyne.

1 m. W., on the N. side of the Ilen, are the remains of Abbeystrowry, a cell of the Cistercian abbey of Maune (*see p. 122*).

3 m. SW. are Creagh Gardens (open to the public in summer).

6½ m. WNW., in the church of Kilcoe, is a window designed by A.E. Child and executed by Catherine O Brien in 1905 (*Crucifixion, SS Patrick and Brigid*). The rose window *Virgin and Child with the Three Magi* (1905) is also by Catherine O Brien. 1 m. SW. are the remains of the medieval church of Kilcoe. Some 500 yds SW. of the latter, on an offshore islet of Roaring Water Bay, are the ruins of a 1495 Clann Diarmada Mac Carthy castle. After the 17th c. English plantation it was held by the Coppingers.

SKREEN, Co. Sligo (Map 7, J2), is on the Ballysadare (10 m.)–Ballina (23 m.) road. An old churchyard and overgrown fragments of a medieval church mark the site of an early Columban monastery which acquired the name Scrín Adhamhnáin because St Adhamhnán (locally pronounced Awnawn), biographer of Columcille, deposited there a reliquary (Latin *scrinium*, whence Irish = Skreen) containing a collection of miscellaneous relics. E. of the churchyard is roadside St Adhamhńan's Well, with a pillar erected in 1591 by Eóghan Mac Domhnaill, Vicar; the Annals state that it was erected in 1599 by his widow Bean-Mhumhan Óg Duignan. On the lower slope of Knockachree (1,766 ft) is Loch Achree, 'Ireland's youngest lake'. It was formed by an earthquake in 1490.

1½ m. NE, in Ardabrone, are the remains of the great castle of Ardnaglass, one of the chief strongholds of the O Dowds of Tireragh; later of their Mac Swiney galloglas.

3 m. SE. is Longford House (1782), where Lady Morgan (Sydney Owenson, *c.* 1783–1850) wrote her first novel, *The Wild Irish Girl.* Near the site of Longford castle (O Dowds) are the ruins of an 18th c. chapel with figure carvings.

1½ m. W. is Doonflin, where An Dubhaltach Óg Mac Fhirbisigh (*see p. 205*) was murdered (1671) in an inn by Thomas Crofton. 2 m. WSW. is Grangebeg, with remains of a medieval parish church and adjacent tower house.

SKULL, Co. Cork (Map 5, F8), is a fishing village on Skull Harbour, an inlet of Roaring Water Bay, 14 m. W. of Skibbereen and 8¾ m. NE. of Crookhaven.

3 m. NE. the road to Bantry makes its way through a wild pass on the E. side of Mount Gabriel (1,339 ft). In the valley to the N. are Bronze Age copper mines.

3¾ m. W., in Carriganine, Aderawinny, is a portal-tomb. 1¼ m. SW., close to the E. shore of Toormore Bay in Altar townland, is a wedge-tomb. 2¾ m. SSW. of Carriganine, at Castle Point (Léim Chon), is Black Castle, a late-15th c. castle of the O Mahonys. It was taken by the English in 1602, following on the capitulation of Kinsale.

5 m. W. is Toormore. 2¼ m. N., on Dunmanus harbour, are the remains of Dunmanus castle. Not far away, in a swampy, tide-covered field, is a boulder-burial.

7½ m. SW. is Goleen, where there is a good small beach. There are a number of wedge-tombs in the area.

13 m. SW. is Mizen Head (765 ft). 5 m. N. (7 m. WSW. of Goleen) is Three Castles Head (private). E. of the Head, between the SW. end of little Doo Lough and the low cliffs of Coosnaronety, are remains of Dún Locha, a promontory fort. In the Middle Ages the O Mahonys erected a tower on the highest knoll on the line of the rampart. Subsequently the rampart was demolished, and fosses and a mortar-built wall were constructed to close the gap between the sea-cliff and the lake. At the same time a gatehouse was built beside the lake, and a turret between this and the main tower.

SLANE, Co. Meath (Map 2, H8), is now the name of a small village on the Drogheda (9 m.)–Navan (8 m.) road, just NW. of the bridge which carries the old Dublin – Ashbourne – Collon – Ardee turnpike road across the Boyne.

Francis Ledwidge (1887–1917), the gifted young poet killed in Flanders, was a native of Slane. His home, a cottage on the Drogheda road, is now a Ledwidge museum. The Rev. Mervyn Archdall (1723–91), antiquary, was Rector of Slane. At the Protestant parish church are a 15th c. doorway and armorial panel recently extracted from Stackallen church, 4 m. W.

N. of the village rises Slane Hill (529 ft). It was on this hill, legend asserts, that St Patrick kindled his first Paschal Fire in breach of King Loígaire's decree. In early historic times there was an episcopal-monastic church there, associated with the Patrician bishop St Earc (d. 512/14). In 948 the Round Tower, together with 'the best of bells' and St Earc's enshrined crozier, was destroyed by Norse raiders. In 1170 it was ravaged by Diarmait Mac Murrough and Strongbow. In 1512 Sir Christopher Fleming and his wife, Elizabeth Stuckley, founded a college of four priests, four clerks, and four choristers, to serve the church. In 1631, the anti-Catholic laws being relaxed, the Flemings installed Capuchins in the college, but these were expelled by Cromwell. The church was finally abandoned in 1723. The remains (Nat. Mons.) comprise a church and, NE. of it, the College, a courtyard residential building with 16th c. windows and other details. The church ruins comprise nave, later S. aisle, and a fine W. tower of *c.* 1500 which offers a magnificent prospect of the Boyne valley from Trim to the sea. S. of the church are the gable ends of an early tomb (St Earc's?). Coffins brought to the cemetery for burial used formerly to be set down for a brief space at this ancient tomb. At the W. end of the hill is the motte of a castle built in 1175 by Richard le Fleming and destroyed the following year by Melaghlin of Cinéal Eóghain.

The Boyne bridge crosses the river near the place where Williamite infantry made their surprise crossing, 12 July 1690 (*see p. 133 and 167*). On the N. bank of the river, in a dense thicket to the W. of the bridge (Slane Castle demesne), are the tumbledown remains of late-15th/16th c. St Earc's Hermitage. They consist of a little church or chapel, with an earlier low tower and dwelling intervening between nave and chancel.

Fragmentary sculptures surviving include figures of St Catherine and an angel. W. of the church is the Apostles' Stone, a medieval tomb-rest with figures of the Crucifixion and the Twelve Apostles. Further W., by the river, is Lady Well, to which pilgrims resort on 15 August, 'Lady Day in Harvest'. ¼ m. S. of the bridge is Fennor Castle, a 17th c. house.

3 m. SE., on the S. bank of the Boyne, is Rosnaree, traditionally the burial place of King Cormac, son of Art. It was by surprise crossings at Rosnaree ford and Slane, on 12 July 1690, that the Williamites turned the Jacobites' left flank and made their positions in front of Donore untenable (*see p. 133 and 167*).

3½ m. SW., on the S. bank of the Boyne, is Beauparc House (Lord Mountcharles), a good Georgian mansion of 1755.

2 m. WSW., by the roadside in Carrickdexter, is Baronstown Cross, the shaft (with long inscription) of a cross erected about 1590 by Dame Ienet Dowdall for herself and her deceased husband, Oliver Plunkett, fourth Baron of Louth (*see p. 42*); the figures represent SS Peter and Patrick.

1¼ m. W. is Slane Castle, seat of Lord Mountcharles, who stages massive pop-concerts in the field in front of the house. The architect was James Wyatt (1785), but Francis Johnston later carried out a number of alterations. Built into a wall near the entrance to the basement restaurant is the effigy of a 14th c.(?) bishop.

5½ m. NW., in Rathkenny, is a chamber-tomb with one end of the capstone fast in the ground. There are many inscribed devices on the capstone.

SLIEVE GULLION (1,894 ft), Co. Armagh (Map 2, I4), to the W. of the Dundalk (8 m.)–Newry (7 m.) road, dominates the Gap of the North, gateway into Ulster from the South. It is now the centre of a Forest Park. On the S. summit is Calliagh Birra's House (Nat. Mon.), a cruciform passage-tomb. On the NE. side of the mountain, in Ballintemple, is Killevy Old Church (*Cill Shleibhe Cuilinn*, Hist. Mon.). The ruin comprises two joined, but not intercommunicating, plain rectangular churches. The W. church is pre-Romanesque (10th/12th c.), the E. church medieval with a 15th c. E. window. There was formerly a round tower to the S. of the W. church. Killevy was one of the most important early nunneries in Ireland, founded in the 5th c. by one of Ireland's traditional patrons of seafarers (*see p. 276*), St Darerca, alias St Monenna. ½ m. SE. is Clonlum North Cairn (Hist. Mon.) a court-tomb. ½ m. S. of this is Clonlum Cromlech or South Cairn (Hist. Mon.), an open cist in a round cairn.

1¼ m. E. of the church, in Aghayalloge, are portions of the S. angle of the Dane's Cast (*see p. 267*). On the W. flank of the mountain, ½ m. S. of the Camlough–Crossmaglen road and 4 m. NNW. of Forkill, in Ballykeel, is a tripod dolmen or portal-tomb set in the end of a long cairn (Nat. Mon.) and excavated in 1963.

SLIGO, Co. Sligo (Map 7, K1), second largest town in Connacht, is the cathedral town of the Catholic diocese of ELPHIN and, since 1962, of the Protestant diocese of Elphin and Ardagh. It is one of the most beautifully sited of Irish towns, straddling the Garavogue River.

Sligo first came into prominence with the de Burgo invasion of Connacht (1235), when, together with extensive territories, it was granted to Maurice FitzGerald, Lord of Naas and Baron of Offaly, ancestor of the Earls of Kildare (*see p. 245*). FitzGerald built a castle there in 1245 and founded (1253) a Dominican friary close by. Between 1245 and 1295 the castle was destroyed four times. In 1310 a new castle was built, and a new town laid out, by Richard III de Burgo, Red Earl of Ulster. In 1315 this castle was demolished by O Donnell. Thereafter the effective control of Sligo passed to the Carbury branch (later known as O Conor Sligo) of the ancient royal house of Connacht. This branch usually acknowledged the overlordship of O Donnell, who always endeavoured to keep Sligo out of menacing hands. In 1414 town and friary were destroyed by fire. In 1595 English besiegers of the castle, under George Bingham, severely damaged the friary. In 1641 town and friary were sacked by the Parliamentarian Sir Frederick Hamilton (*see p. 245*). In 1645 the town was captured by the notorious Sir Charles Coote. In 1689 it was seized by Williamite rebels under Lord Kingston, but was retaken by Patrick Sarsfield for King James.

Of the castle nothing at all remains, but a substantial portion (Nat. Mon.) of the once beautiful Dominican Friary of the Holy Cross, popularly known as the 'Abbey', survives in Abbey St. The friary had a chequered history, and suffered much from accident, as well as from the English Reformation and the wars of the 16th and 17th c. After the fire of 1414, it was largely rebuilt *c.* 1416 by Friar Brian Mac Donagh, scion of the Mac Donaghs of Tirerrill. The Sligo O Conors made it their family burial place, and were thus able, for a time, to stave off its dissolution.

The remains of the friary comprise the choir (or chancel) and part of the nave of the original 13th c. church, the 15th/16th c. bell-tower, parts of the 15th/16th c. S. aisle and S. transept, and of the 15th c. cloister and claustral buildings. Among the features of interest are: the 15th c. E. window: the well-preserved 15th/16th c. high altar – the only sculptured example to survive in any medieval Irish monastic church; the fragments of the tasteful 14th/15th c. rood screen; the remains of the simple, but beautiful, cloister arcade; the reader's desk in the refectory (on the upper floor on the N. side of the cloister); and the interesting series of 16th and 17th c. tombs and monuments. Of these last the most important are the O Craian (Crean) tomb of 1506 in the N. wall of the nave, and the O Conor Sligo monument of 1624 in the S. wall of the chancel. (Both have lost their polychrome colouring.) The O Craian tomb is surmounted by the remains of an excellent traceried canopy, while the front of the chest is divided into nine beautifully canopied niches with figures (left to right) of SS Dominick and Catherine, an unidentified saint, the Virgin, the Crucifixion, SS John, Michael and Peter, and an archbishop. The Latin inscription may be rendered: 'Here lie Cormac O Craian and Gehonna Nic Aengusa (Magennis) his wife. A.D. 1506.' The O Conor Sligo monument is a Renaissance piece of remarkable quality, with three Latin inscriptions. Above a boldly moulded cornice are the arms of O Conor Sligo, flanked by figures of SS Peter and Paul and surmounted by a crucifix. Below the frieze are two arched recesses with kneeling effigies of Sir Donnchadh O Conor Sligo and his wife.

The modern Dominican church (High St) is by Pearse McKenna (1973). It has retained a two-light window (1911) by Michael Healy: *SS Raymundus, Antoninus*, from its 19th c. predecessor, and the slab-glass is by Murphy Devitt Studios.

Sligo 'Abbey'.

The ceramic Stations are by Christopher Ryan, the sanctuary furnishings by Ray Carroll, and the marquetry mural of Our Lady and St Dominic is by Oisín Kelly. In Stephen Street is the County Library and Museum (converted from a church of 1850), which contains memorabilia of W.B. Yeats, paintings by his father John and his brother Jack B., and others by a variety of 20th c. Irish artists.

$\frac{1}{2}$ m. E. of the medieval friary, close to the Garavogue in the uninspired municipal housing of Abbeyquarter North, are the weed-covered kerb and other remains of a prehistoric cairn; a shoddy Calvary group was erected there in 1950.

The Catholic Cathedral (Temple St) is a dull Romanesque essay (1869–75) by George Goldie of London. Not far away (John St) is the cathedral (since 1962) of the Protestant dioceses of Elphin and Ardagh. This is an unfortunate 1812 Gothicization of the Church of St John the Baptist and St Mary the Virgin erected, to the design of Richard Cassels, on the site of Sligo's first (17th c.) Protestant church. Built into the W. wall of the nave is the mensa (defective) of the tomb of Sir Roger Jones of Banada (d. 1637), English Governor of Sligo; it has low-relief effigies of Sir Roger and his wife. In the N. transept is a brass tablet to Susan Mary Yeats, mother of William Butler and Jack Butler Yeats. The reredos *Creation*, in the chancel, was painted by Percy Francis Gethin (1874–1916) in memory of his brother, Reginald Owen Gethin (d. 1899).

The Town Hall (Quay St, 1865) is by Hague.

Boats are available on the Garavogue, which offers the pleasantest and most beautiful approach to Lough Gill, $2\frac{1}{2}$ m. SE. of the town. Lough Gill itself (5 m. by $1\frac{1}{2}$ m.), in its ring of wooded hills, is one of the loveliest and most romantic of Irish lakes, and a delightful circular tour of the lake can be made. The largest island is Inis Mór, alias Church Island. At the N. end of the island some remains (Nat. Mon.) of a medieval church mark the site of a 6th c. foundation of St Lommán's. Near the door is Our Lady's Bed, a cavity in the rock; women who pray there are said not to die in childbirth. The illustrious family of Ó Cuirnín, hereditary poets and historiographers to O Rourke of Breany (*see p. 134*), had its chief seat here in the Middle Ages. A fire which destroyed the church in 1416 burned all Ó Cuirnín's books, including a *Lebor Gerr*. $1\frac{1}{4}$ m. SE. of Church Island is 'the lake isle of Inisfree' sung by W.B. Yeats. Towards the SW. end of the lake is Cottage Island, alias Gallagher's Island, with remains of an ancient church. S. of the island, in Aghamore Far on the S. shore, the heights of Dooney (Doonee) Rock offer an excellent vantage point; the name, of course, recalls Yeats's *Fiddler of Dooney*.

4½ m. ENE. (½ m. S. of the Manorhamilton road beyond Colgagh church), in Magheranrush (Magheraconrish), alias Deerpark, are the remains (Nat. Mon.) of the central court-tomb. There the ritual court is an oval, or subrectangle, with the entrance at the middle of the S. side. At the W. end is a roofless, segmented gallery; at the E. end, a pair of similar galleries side by side. The tomb is in a clearing in the midst of a forestry plantation. In the next field to the S. are remains of a stone ringfort (Nat. Mon.) with a small, L-shaped souterrain. In the field S. of this are remains of a wedge-tomb (Nat. Mon.). Other National Monuments in Magheraconrish are a stone circle, a small cairn (ruined), and remains of a stone hut. – About 2 m. N. of Magheranrush in Formoyle, is Giants Grave, remnant of a court-tomb.

2 m. SSE. is Cairns (alias Belvoir) Hill (404 ft), easily climbed and offering delightful views. On the hill are two stone ringforts, two prehistoric cairns, and a 'stone circle' (the remains of a third cairn?). At the SE. foot of the hill, near the lakeshore, 2½ m. from Sligo, are Tobarnalt(ha), alias Tobar an Ailt, holy well and Penal-times altar, where 'stations' are made on Garland Sunday, alias Tobernalt Sunday (last Sunday of July).

3½ m. SE. (via the Manorhamilton road), between the Garavogue and Lough Gill, is Hazelwood House, formerly home of the Wynnes, for whom it was designed by Richard Cassels *c.* 1731. It is one of the finest of the smaller 18th c. country houses of Ireland. The once lovely demesne is now derelict.

2 m. WSW. are the outliers of the important, but shamefully neglected, 'Carrowmore' Group (Nat. Mons.) of tombs and other monuments. The main concentration of these will be found in Tobernaveen, Carrowmore, Graigue, and Knocknash-ammer, alias Cloverhill. More than 85 tombs are said to have survived down to the 19th c., when they were rifled by amateur antiquarians or demolished by 'improving' landowners, to the great loss of science. Today only about 35 tombs are worth visiting. Several of them belong to the passage-grave family, and some were excavated by a multi-disciplinary Swedish team in 1977–81. One of the most interesting is a small, horseshoe chamber, now roofless, in Cloverhill some 200 yds E. of Laghtareel Hill; four of the nine uprights bear curvilinear devices. In addition to chamber-tombs and cairns, the Carrow-more area contains a number of pillarstones, ringforts, etc.

4 m. WSW. is conspicuous, isolated Knocknarea (1,083 ft), whose summit (easily reached via Primrose Grange) rewards the climber with a superb view that includes the mountains of Donegal, to the N., and Croagh Patrick and Nephin, to the SW., as well as Sligo Bay and the hills beyond Lough Gill. It is crowned by Miosgán Meabha (*see pp. 202, 270–1 and 288*) 'Maeve's Lump' (Nat. Mon.), a cairn, 200 ft in diameter, and 34 ft high. Nearby are the remains of seven satellite tombs, one of them a cruciform passage-tomb. In Grange North, on the E. spur of the mountain, are the remains of another passage-tomb.

2½ m. W., in Cummeen, are two roofless, opposed, galleries of a court cairn in an earthen ring (Nat. Mon.), cairns, other antiquities, and 19th c. follies. Cummeen Strand figures in Yeats's early poetry.

5 m. W., at the foot of Knocknarea, is the seaside village and resort of Strandhill, more properly Larass (two good beaches). ½ m. NNW., in Killaspugbrone townland, is Labbynawark, rem-nant of a court-tomb. ½ m. further NNW., near Killaspug Point, are the ruins of the church of Killaspugbrone which gives its name to the townland and parish. It is called after Bishop Brón (d. 510/11), whom St Patrick is said to have placed in charge of a church here. St Patrick, we are told, shed a tooth, which fell on the threshold of the church. The tooth was enshrined and kept there. The reliquary, known as the Fiacal Pádraig, was re-edified at the expense of Thomas Bermingham, Lord of Athenry, who died in 1376. It is now in the National Museum. Killaspugbrone was a simple, rectangular, small church with trabeate W. doorway and a small, plain, Romanesque E. window. It had a Romanesque doorway (inserted) of two plain arches in the S. wall. Nearby is Sligo airport.

5 m. NW., in 'the Green Lands' sung by Yeats, is beautifully situated Rosses Point, a noted golfing resort (championship links) with good sea bathing.

SNEEM, Co. Kerry (Map 5, D5), is a village where the Kenmare (16 m.)–Waterville (20 m.) road crosses the head of the Sneem estuary.

The Italianate parish church (1865) was the gift of the 3rd Earl of Dunraven (*see p. 35*), an Oxford Movement convert to Catholicism; the parish priest at the time was Father Michael Walsh (1829–66), the 'Father O Flynn' of Alfred Percival Graves's well-known ballad; the W. window is a memorial to the poet Aubrey de Vere (1814–1902; also an Oxford Movement convert; *see p. 48*). The Protestant parish church dates from the 17th c.; much altered.

In the centre of the village is a controversial sculpture (1983) by Vivienne Roche, commemorating Cearbhall Ó Dalaigh, Pre-sident of Ireland 1974–6. In the old Courthouse, in North Square, is a small folk museum.

2 m. SSE., in Derryquin, is Parknasilla, noted alike for its genial winter climate and its beauty. The Great Southern Hotel

Deerpark court-tomb, Co. Sligo.

is successor to the residence of Charles Graves (1812–99), Protestant Bishop of Limerick and distinguished scholar, father of Alfred Percival Graves (1846–1931), and grandfather of Robert Graves, poet and novelist. The lovely gardens and woods are a maze of salt-water channels. On the W. side of the bay is beautiful Garinish (Mr Browne), with its gardens, woods, and sandy coves (*not* open to the general public).

SPIDDAL, Co. Galway (Map 6, E2), is a small seaside resort and market village 12 m. W. of Galway city.

In the village is St Éanna's Church (1904), an excellent little building by Professor William A. Scott. It has four windows by the Sarah Purser studio and *opus sectile* Stations of the Cross by Ethel M. Rhind. In the adjacent graveyard are fragmentary remains of the 'abbey', a medieval parish church.

Adjoining the village is the demesne of Spiddal House (former home of Lord Killanin). The house is a partial reconstruction of one by Prof. Scott (1910), burned down in 1922; the carvings are by Michael Shortall of Loughrea (*see pp. 45 and 240*).

2 m. E., in Park, was the home of Roderick O Flaherty (1629–1718), an antiquary of note (*Ogygia* and *A Chorographical Description of West or Iar Connacht*) and a great collector of manuscripts. He ended his days in extreme poverty, bereft of all his literary treasures.

8 m. W., in Tully, St Colmcille's Church (1963–4; by Daniel Kennedy) is noteworthy for the effective simplicity of the interior and for the works in copper and enamels by Benedict Tutty, O.S.B., of Glenstal Abbey: font cover, Stations of the Cross, altar crucifix, tabernacle, and sanctuary lamp. The stained glass windows are by Margaret Becker.

STEPASIDE, Co. Dublin (Map 3, K4), is a mountainside hamlet on the Dublin (8 m.)–Enniskerry (5 m.) road.

½ m. NNW., close to the remains of the 18th c. Protestant church of Kilgobbin, is a 12th c., granite High Cross (Nat. Mon.) with *Crucifixion* in low relief. There was an early monastery, Cell Gobbán, there.

2¼ m. SSW., 350 yds W. of the Glencullen road, on the SE. slope of Two Rock Mountain in Ballyedmunduff, is Giants Grave (1,100 ft, Nat. Mon.), a wedge-tomb.

STEWARTSTOWN, Co. Tyrone (Map 1, G8), is a village 6 m. from Cookstown and 5 m. from the shores of Lough Neagh.

2 m. N. is the early Protestant church of Ballynaclog, where Rev. Charles Wolfe (1791–1823) had his first curacy (*see p. 170*).

3 m. ENE. is Stuart Hall, a fine Georgian house built about 1760 by Viscount Castlestuart. About 1 m. SW. is Drumcairne Forest Park, formerly the demesne of the Earl of Charlemont. The Charlemont house there dates from the early 19th c.

4 m. ESE. is Mountjoy Castle (Hist. Mon.), built inside a star-shaped campaign fort by a Dutch engineer for Lord Mountjoy's campaign against Hugh O Neill. It was burned just after the 1641 rising, and the remains today are those of a square stone and brick building with four projecting, rectangular loop-holed towers.

3 m. SW., in the grounds of Roughan House, are the ruins of a small Plantation castle with round angle-turrets, built by Sir Andrew Stewart in 1618. It was burned by Sir Phelim O Neill in 1641. 1 m. further SW. is Newmills village, and old Tullaniskin Protestant church, built in 1793.

STILLORGAN, (Map 3, K3), is a village on the Dublin (5 m.)–Bray (7 m.) road, and now a suburb of Dublin. Stillorgan Castle is now a hospice of the Order of St John of God. Obelisk House takes its name from a mausoleum built by Sir Edward Lovett Pearce for the Allen family. He died at Tighlorcain House (then The Grove on the Allen estate), 7 December 1733. The 1st Viscount Allen of Stillorgan was a grandson of the builder of Jigginstown House (*see p. 254*). The 2nd was satirized by Swift. Oriel was the birthplace of the celebrated painter Sir William Orpen, Bt (1870–1931). The Esso Petroleum Company's office (by J.E. Collins, 1961) has a courtyard sculpture by Ian Stuart.

2¼ m. SE., on Brighton Rd, Foxrock, is Tullow Protestant parish church, by Welland and Gillespie (1864). Oisín Kelly designed the sanctuary cross, Beatrice Elvey (Lady Glenary) the *art nouveau* lectern. She also executed two two-light windows. Other windows are by Catherine O Brien.

STRABANE, Co. Tyrone (Map 1, C6), is a market town at the centre of a rich agricultural district 14 m. from Derry and 20 m. from Omagh. It was the Abercorns who developed the town and introduced the linen trade during the 18th c. In 1755 they had the Lifford bridge rebuilt. A new town around the canal basin – the four-mile canal capable of taking small sailing vessels was one of the earliest in the British Isles – was laid out in the early years of the 19th c.

The principal buildings of the town are its churches. The Protestant parish church of Camus-juxta-Mourne dates from 1874. The Catholic church of St Mary's, Melmount, is by Patrick Haughey (1971). One of the oldest shopfronts is Gray's at 49 Main Street, a late Georgian bow-fronted façade which once adorned the front of a printer's works. Here John Dunlap (1747–1812), who printed the American Declaration of Independence, learned his trade before emigrating to Pennsylvania. He founded one of the first daily newspapers in America, and published *The Pennsylvania Packet*.

Among other distinguished natives of the town and district were Sir Guy Carleton, Lord Dorchester (1724–1808), who defended Quebec against the United States; Dr George Sigerson, the poet and nationalist, and Mrs Frances Alexander, the prolific hymn writer, who was born at Milltown House. It was the view from her bedroom window there which inspired the words of 'There is a green hill far away'. In this century, Strabane was the home town of author Brian O Nolan, alias Flann O Brien (*At Swim Two Birds*), alias Myles na gCopaleen (1911–66).

2 m. ESE is Dergalt (Nat. Trust), the home of James Wilson, who emigrated to America in 1807. His grandson, Woodrow, became the 28th President of the United States in 1913.

3 m. S. is Sion Mills village, with its large spinning mill established by the Herdman family in the 1840s. There is an Elizabethan air about the black and white half-timbered houses and cottages that they built for themselves and for their workers. The architect W.E. Unsworth was responsible for much of this,

and for the Church of the Good Shepherd (1909), which is said to be modelled on a church at Pistoia near Florence. The big modern Catholic church of St Teresa was built in 1963 by Patrick Haughey. It has a very impressive façade with Oisín Kelly's beautiful *Last Supper* above the entrance. Kelly also did the font in the church. The windows are by Patrick Pollen.

$3\frac{1}{2}$ m. SW. is Urney Presbyterian church, said to be the oldest Presbyterian church in the Foyle valley (built in 1654 and reconstructed in 1695). Little of the original now remains.

STRADBALLY, Co. Laois (Map 3, F6), is a village on the Athy (9 m.)–Port Laoise (7 m.) road. It stands in the heart of the historic territory of the O Mores of Laois. The O Mores of Noughaval, $\frac{1}{2}$ m. SE., were for centuries the owners of the so-called *Book of Leinster* (*see p. 266*), which was known as *Leabhar na Núachongbhála* (Book of Noughaval) down to the 18th c. In 1447 O More of Noughaval founded a Franciscan friary at Stradbally (on the site of the modern Presentation Convent).

During the annual midsummer steam rally a number of steam-driven vehicles can be seen.

Kevin O Higgins (1892–1927), revolutionary leader and Cabinet Minister, who contributed so much to the Statute of Westminster, was a native of Stradbally, where his father, Dr T. O Higgins, practised as physician.

$5\frac{3}{4}$ m. NE., beyond Vicarstown, on the bank of the Barrow, is the great ringfort of Dunrally. Henry Grattan built a residence in the enclosure.

$2\frac{1}{4}$ m. SSW. Timogue Protestant church is an interesting 18th c. re-edification of an earlier church; restored 1964; there is a medieval font.

$2\frac{3}{4}$ m. WNW., to the N. of the Port Laoise road, is the great Rock of Dunamase (150 ft), crowned by the shattered remains of a large castle (Nat. Mon.). Díarmaít Mac Murrough gave the place to Strongbow as part of Aoífe's dowry. William Marshall, heir of Strongbow, had a motte castle here, with a ditch and rampart dividing the slope into two or three baileys. About 1250 his son-in-law and heir, William de Braose, rebuilt and enlarged the castle. Conall O More of Laois (d. 1497) wrested the castle from the English, and rebuilt it to be the chief stronghold of his house, which it remained until the Plantation of Laois. In 1641 the Parliamentarian Sir Charles Coote I took it from the insurgent O Mores. In 1646 Eóghan Rúa O Neill recovered it for the Catholic Confederates, who held it until 1650, when it was attacked and destroyed by Cromwellians under Hewson and Reynolds. The ruins are those of a complex fortress. On the SE. is a D-shaped outer bailey. Behind this is a triangular walled courtyard entered by a twin-towered drawbridge gateway. Beyond this again, on the summit of the rock, is the heart-shaped inner ward. It is entered by a badly wrecked central gateway, and enclosed by an irregular, towerless curtain. Inside it, on the highest point of the rock, are the remains of a rectangular 13th c. keep, altered at various dates; it may have been cut off from the rest of the inner ward by a cross-wall. – $\frac{1}{4}$ m. E. are Cromwell's Lines (a bivallate ringfort); S. of and below the Lines, and above the road through the gap, is the Cromwellian gun platform. – $1\frac{1}{2}$ m. SW. of the Rock, on the W. slope of Hewson's Hill, are the ruins of Dysert(enos) (*Dísert Óengusa*), which takes its name from the 9th c. retreat of Óengus the Culdee (*see pp. 249–50*).

The Fiddler of Dooney, *by Imogen Stuart, Stillorgan.*

STRADBALLY, Co. Waterford (Map 4, G6), is a village near the sea, on the Dungarvan (8 m.)–Bunmahon (4 m.) road. There are remains of a medieval nave-and-chancel church.

NE. of the village, at Toberkillea (holy well), Ballinvoony, are two ogham stones.

2 m. N., in Drumlohan, is an early church site. In the enclosing rampart is a celebrated souterrain ('the ogham cave of Drumlohan'; Nat. Mon.) incorporating ten ogham stones.

2 m. SW., in Island townland, is a fine ringfort-type enclosure (site of an early monastery?), formerly revetted with stone. The gateway, facing W., was of large blocks. Inside is a bullaun and an ogham stone (prostrate).

STRANGFORD, Co. Down (Map 2, M2), is a small fishing port on the W. side of the entrance to Strangford Lough, 9 m. NE. of Downpatrick, and $\frac{3}{4}$ m. SSW. of Portaferry, with which it is connected by a half-hourly car-ferry. Several of the castles in the locality are said to owe their origin to John de Courcy or other of the earliest Anglo-Normans who seized lands in Ulster. The foreshore of Strangford Lough is protected by the Nat. Trust, and the N. half of the Lough is designated as a National Nature Reserve.

In the town itself is Strangford Castle (Hist. Mon.), a much altered late-16th(?) c. fortified town house; perhaps the best example in Ulster (entrance a reconstruction).

Teak Stations by Imogen Stuart, Firhouse, Tallaght.

3 m. S. is Kilclief Castle (Hist. Mon.), attributed to John Cely, or Seely, Bishop of Down (1412–41). Some of the windows have elaborate details. This castle seems to have served as a model for several 15th and 16th c. Co. Down castles.

3½ m. SW. is Raholp Church (Hist. Mon.). Legend asserts that the original church here was entrusted by St Patrick to his artificer, Bishop Tassach. The ruins, which stand inside an earthen rath, have suffered from over-restoration. There are several genuine early gravestones.

2 m. W. is Castleward House, built *c.* 1765 for Benjamin Ward, 1st Viscount Bangor; one front is strictly Palladian, the other Gothick. The interior has excellent stucco (Gothick as well as rococo) and panelling. The house and 600 acres of the beautiful demesne have been given to the Nat. Trust by Viscount Bangor, who has lent the period furniture. Just below the mansion, the Nat. Trust have created a Victorian laundry, tea-room and small theatre. ½ m. NNE. of the house, in Audleystown, is Castle Ward (Hist. Mon.), a small, well-preserved Plantation castle built about 1610 by Nicholas Ward. ½ m. further NNE., is Audley's Castle (Hist. Mon.), a well-preserved 15th/16th c. stronghold of the Audleys, seemingly modelled on Kilclief. To the WNW. are the remains of Templecormick, a small dry-masonry church set inside a dilapidated cashel. ½ m. further W. is Audleystown double-court cairn (Hist. Mon.). Its eight chambers contained 34 burials, mostly uncremated, which were accompanied by Western Neolithic pottery, etc. 2 m. W. (by the main road) is 16th c. Walshestown castle (Nat. Mon.).

STROKESTOWN, Co. Roscommon (Map 7, M6), is an 18th and early-19th c. village on the Longford (15 m.)–Elphin (7 m.) road. It was laid out for Maurice Mahon (1738–1819), who was created Baron Hartland in 1800: two streets intersecting at right angles, the broader terminating on the E. at his lordship's gate, on the W. at an octagonal church, now St John's Heritage Centre. Strokestown Park House, sometime seat of the Mahons, who acquired the property late in the 17th c., is a great 18th c. mansion, which was opened to the public in 1987. The ruins of a nearby medieval church were turned into a Mahon mausoleum.

SUMMERHILL, Co. Meath (Map 3, H2), is a small village on the Trim (6½ m.)–Kilcock (7 m.) road. It was a good example of an 'improving' landlord's planning: a tree-lined mall leading to the principal avenue to Lord Langford's great mansion, which was sadly bulldozed in 1961–2. Today little more remains than two monumental flanking gateways. The radiating avenues of trees too are gone, save only that (renewed) leading from the village. NE. of the house-site is Knock (Linch). In a grove near the NW. foot of the hill are the ruins of a 16th/17th c. Lynch stronghouse (Knock Castle), defended in June 1642 for five days and nights by Barnaby Geoghegan of Ballynagreine against Charles II's Lord Lieutenant, Ormonde. On the village green is the shaft of a 1554 Peter Lynch memorial cross.

4 m. NE., in Galtrim, is the motte of a castle constructed by Hugh de Hose, to whom Hugh de Lacy had granted the land *c.* 1172, but it was abandoned by the Normans after the destruction of Slane in 1176.

3½ m. ESE., in Kilmore churchyard, is the gravestone of scribe Rughraidhe Buidhe Mhag Mhaghamhna of Kilmeague, Co. Kildare: *Crucifixion* and inscriptions in Irish and Latin.

2 m. SE. are remains of Drumlargan church. Drumlargan is the Dungan Hill where, on 8 August 1647, Jones and the Parliamentarian army of Dublin destroyed the Confederate Catholic field army of Leinster ineptly commanded by Thomas Preston (*see p. 295*), who lost half his army in the encounter.

3½ m. NW. are remains of Dangan Castle, sometime home of the Wellesleys (*see also pp. 175 and 295*). The Duke of Wellington is said to have spent much time there as a boy. Dangan was the birthplace of Don Ambrosio O Higgins (1720?–1801), Spanish Viceroy of Chile and Peru and father of Bernardo O Higgins, Liberator of Chile.

SWINEFORD, Co. Mayo (Map 7, H4), is a market town on the Charlestown (7 m.)–Foxford (9 m.) road, 7 m. NE. of Kiltimagh.

3 m. SW., in Meelick, a Round Tower (Nat. Mon.) marks the site of an early monastery attributed to St Broccaidh. There is an early gravestone there, with a crudely interlaced cross and border. It is inscribed OR[ŌIT] DO GRIENI ('A prayer for Griene').

SWORDS, Co. Dublin (Map 3, K2), a village on the Dublin (8 m.)–Drogheda (22 m.) road, is threatened with early engulfment by the city. It takes its name, Sord Cholaim Chille, from a pure well *(sord)* said to have been blessed by St Columcille. There was a monastery there in the 9th/10th c. In 1014 the bodies of Brian Boru and his son, Murchad, rested overnight at the monastery on their way to solemn burial at Armagh. A fire in 1130 destroyed the churches and their relics. Before the Anglo-Norman invasion the monastery and its possessions had been transferred to the Archbishop of Dublin, and Swords subsequently became one of the principal archiepiscopal manors. In 1219 the church was made a prebend – the 'Golden Prebend of Swords' – in St Patrick's Cathedral, Dublin. (In 1366 the prebend was held by no less a person than the celebrated William of Wykeham, Bishop of Winchester and Chancellor of England.) Today the only relic of the ancient monastery is the Round Tower; it has a pre-Romanesque doorway. Adjoining it is the 14th c., square steeple of the medieval prebendal church.

At the N. end of the main street are the ruins (Nat. Mon.) of the archbishop's manorial castle. It was begun *c.* 1200, but was modified in the 13th and 15th c. In plan it is an irregular, 1½ acre pentagon. (The stepped battlements are typical of 15th c. Irish work.) Its interior structures have disappeared. The principal remaining building is the gatehouse, with warden's quarters, etc. (modified in modern times), on the W. side, and a chapel with 13th c. W. tower (containing porter's lodge below and chaplain's rooms above) on the E. side. Excavations in the chapel uncovered medieval paving tiles *in situ.* There are a number of towers in the curtain walls. The castle ceased to be an archiepiscopal residence in the 15th c. (*see right*), and the constableship ultimately became hereditary in the Barnewall family.

The Borough School was designed by Francis Johnston (1761–1829), and is now a restaurant.

1 m. ENE. on the seashore are the remains of Seatown castle.

2 m. W., by the roadside to the N. of Knocksedan bridge, is Brazil Moat, a large tumulus. Brackenstown House nearby was the home of Robert Molesworth, 1st Viscount Swords, to whom Swift addressed his *Drapier's Letters.*

T

TAGHMON, Co. Wexford (Map 4, K4) is a village on the New Ross (13 m.)–Wexford (8 m.) road. It takes its name, Teach Munnu, Munnu's house, from a monastic church of some consequence founded in the 7th c. by St Munnu, son of the druid Tailchán. At the Synod of Magh Ailbhe, which met *c.* 630 to consider the problem of the date of Easter, Munnu was the spokesman of the recalcitrant traditionalists against St Laisrén of Leighlin (*see p. 231*). Surviving from the monastery are the head and base of St Munna's Cross in the graveyard. The Talbots had a castle there, of which a tower survives.

H.F. Lyte (1793–1847), author of the well-known hymn 'Abide With Me', was for a time Protestant curate of Taghmon.

5 m. W. is Foulkesmill, where battles took place in 1798. Longgraigue House, to the SW., was the headquarters of Gen. Sir John Moore.

TALLAGHT, Co. Dublin (Map 3, J4), is a village at the foot of the Dublin Mts, on the Dublin (7½ m.)–Blessington (12½ m.) road.

The place is celebrated in Irish history as the seat of a monastery founded by St Máel-Rúáin (d. 792), leader of the anchoritic (*célé Dé* 'culdee') movement (*see p. 15*). Among his disciples were Máel-Díthruib of Terryglass (*see p. 266*), Óengus of Clonenagh (*see p. 249–50*), and Dysertenos (*see p. 285*), author of the earliest Irish martyrology (*below*). Closely associated with Tallaght in the *céle Dé* movement were Terryglass (*see p. 266*) and FINGLAS. So high indeed stood the fame of Tallaght and Finglas in the 9th c., that the *Triads of Ireland* call them 'The Two Eyes of Ireland'. The prestige of Tallaght itself was such that in 811 the monks were able to prevent the King of Tara, Áed, son of Niall, from holding the great Assembly of Teltown (Aonach Tailteann), because the sanctuary of their monastery had been violated by the Uí Néill. From this monastery came two celebrated documents, the *Martyrology of Óengus* (*c.* 800) and the *Martyrology of Tallaght* (early-10th c.). Its proximity to Norse Dublin exposed Tallaght to the Vikings, and the monastery appears to have decayed relatively early. After the Anglo-Norman invasion the church became parochial, and the abbey lands became an archiepiscopal manor. A small tower in the grounds of the Dominican friary remains of the archiepiscopal castle, which was a bulwark of the English Pale in the 15th c.

St Maelruan's Protestant church stands on the site of the medieval parish church, which occupied part of the site of the ancient monastery. The bell-tower is that of the medieval church. In the churchyard are St Mulroon's Losset, a large, granite basin, and St Mulroon's Stone, a small, plain, granite cross.

1 m. E. is Firhouse. The church of Our Lady of Mount Carmel is by De Blacam and Meagher (1979), with unusual Stations of the Cross by Imogen Stuart.

1 m. W., in Fettercairn, is the Church of the Incarnate (1983) by Don Henihan.

TALLOW, Co. Waterford (Map 4, D7), a village on the Lismore (5 m.)–Youghal (12 m.) road, was the birthplace of the sculptor John Hogan (1800–58), as also of his weaver-poet namesake, John Hogan (1780–1858), Bard of Dunclug. The Tallow district was planted with English Protestants in the early 17th c. by Richard Boyle, Great Earl of Cork (*see p. 308*).

2¾ m. W., near the Bride in Co. Cork, are the ruins of Mogeely Castle, favourite residence of Thomas, 11th Earl of Desmond, whose wife was the celebrated 'Old Countess' of Desmond (*see p. 307*). The castle was acquired by Sir Walter Ralegh at the Plantation of Munster. From Ralegh it passed to Richard Boyle.

2½ m. further W., on a rock over the Bride, are the ruins of Conna castle (16th c., Nat Mon.), birthplace of the 'Súgán', Earl of Desmond. It was stormed by Confederate Catholics under Lord Castlehaven in 1645, bombarded without success by Cromwell in 1650, burned in 1653, and in part restored in the last century.

TANDRAGEE, Co. Armagh (Map 2, I2), is a small industrial town on the Portadown (6 m.)–Poyntzpass (4 m.) road. In 1641 the O Hanlons, dispossessed by the St John family at the

Conna Castle, Co. Cork.

Plantation, captured the castle (now a factory) and destroyed it. In the second half of the 17th c. the outlaw Redmond O Hanlon, hero of popular song and story, terrorized Armagh and neighbouring counties. He is buried in the ancient graveyard of Relicarn.

TARA, Co. Meath (Map 3, I1), a low hill 1 m. W. of the Dublin (23 m.)–Navan (6 m.) road, is one of the most famous places in Ireland. Its fame, however, may be due to the fantasies conjured up by Thomas Moore's ballad, rather than to appreciation of its ancient significance, or of its monuments (which are not spectacular), or of its delightful prospects over the rich, rolling Midlands – 'Gentle Midhe of the corn measures'.

At the dawn of Irish history Tara was an important centre of paganism – associated particularly with the goddess Medb (Maeve; the Queen Mab of English fairy lore; *see also p. 270*). It was the seat of priest-kings who, in addition to being over-kings of Meath, were also heads of the Uí Néill federation, and thus the most powerful kings in Ireland. The apotheosis of each King of Tara was his symbolic mating (at a ritual banquet, *Feis Temrach*, which was attended by all the Uí Néill kings as well as by his vassals) with the local earth goddess.

The Uí Néill descended from Niall Nine Hostager, who seized Tara in the 5th c. and whose sons partitioned the Midlands (*Midhe,* Meath) and most of the ancient Fifth of the Ulaid between them. The dispersal of Niall's descendants over so much of the North, as well as the Midlands, was to affect the future of Tara, for the law of succession favoured collaterals rather than sons. In the event, the title 'King of Tara' passed to rulers whose seats were elsewhere, often, indeed, far off in the North-West, so that the political significance of Tara withered away. (After 727–8 it was only a titular royal seat, though occasionally the venue for important gatherings.) The final victory of Christianity also contributed to the decline of Tara by depriving it of its religious significance, and Díarmait mac Cerrbeóil was the last King of Tara to celebrate the heathen Feis (560). Medieval Christian writers could hardly confess the true nature of the Christian impact on Tara. They therefore invented a legend to the effect that the hill was abandoned because Díarmait mac Cerrbeóil had been cursed by St Rúadhán of Lorrha and the 'Twelve Apostles of Ireland' for slaying an outlaw who had sought ecclesiastical sanctuary.

The ancient remains (Nat. Mons.) at Tara, though not spectacular, are very extensive. Their official names are not necessarily genuine. (They derive from medieval documents as interpreted by modern scholars.)

The circuit of the monuments may conveniently commence at the churchyard, which encroaches on the ancient site. In the church is a two-light E. window (*Pentecost*, 1936) by Evie Hone.

W. of the church is Adamnán's Cross, a broken pillar with a much-weathered figure. Nearby is a prehistoric standing stone(?).

Adjoining the churchyard on the W. is the Fort of the Synods (Nat. Mon.), a trivallate earthwork savagely mutilated some 60 years ago by British Israelites in a quest for the Ark of the Covenant. On the W. a small, earlier, burial mound (the King's Chair) has been brought within the ambit of the outer bank. Excavations showed that the fort proper had had four structural phases between the 1st and 3rd c. A.D. At the centre had stood timber houses. The defences had included timber palisades.

S. of the Fort of the Synods is the Fort of the Kings (Nat. Mon.), an oval hill-fort, 950 ft × 800 ft, enclosed by a ditch with remains of a bank on its outer margin. Excavation has shown the ditch to have been cut into the underlying rock to more than 11 ft below the present surface. Near the N. end of the enclosure is the Mound of the Hostages (Nat. Mon.), alleged site of Lia Fáil, the inauguration stone of the King of Tara. Excavation has shown this to cover the stone cairn or a small passage grave dating from *c.* 2100 B.C. Towards the centre of the enclosure are two conjoint earthworks (Nat. Mon.): the Royal Seat on the E., Cormac's House on the W. On the N. of Cormac's House the outer bank bends around a pre-existing burial mound. A shoddy modern statue commemorates St Patrick's legendary visit to the court of King Loígaire. A pillarstone marks the grave of insurgents killed in the battle of Tara, 1798. It is said to have lain near the Mound of the Hostages, and so is now labelled Lia Fáil.

S. of the Fort of the Kings are the remains of Loígaire's Fort (Nat. Mon.), a large, univallate ringfort.

NW. of the Fort of the Kings, on the flank of the hill, are the Sloping Trenches (Nat. Mon.), two unusual ring-earthworks.

E. of the Sloping Trenches is Gráinne's Fort (Nat. Mon.), a burial mound enclosed by a ditch and bank. Gráinne was a goddess.

Further E. is the Banqueting Hall (Nat. Mon.), a rectangular earthwork some 750 ft × 90 ft. which may, however, have been the ritual entrance to the Hill. Medieval accounts describe the Banqueting Hall (Tech Midchuarta) of Tara as a great hall of five aisles. The central aisle was a circulation passage with hearths, cauldrons, lights, etc. The others were divided into booths, or cubicles, allocated according to the social precedence of those feasting with the King of Tara. Near the Hall are small burial mounds.

½ m. S. of Tara, on the next hill-top, is Rath Maeve (Nat. Mon.), a univallate hill-fort 750 ft in diameter.

4 m. E. of Tara is the Hill of Skreen (507 ft), whose name preserves the memory of Scrín Choluim Chille, 'Columcille's Shrine', a monastery to which the great saint's relics were brought in 875. In 1127 the Dublin Norse carried off the shrine, but it was restored to its house inside a month. In 1185–6 the new, Norman, proprietor, Adam de Feipo, bestowed the church on St Mary's Abbey, Dublin. Crowning the hill are the ruins (Nat. Mon.) of a manorial church. In the massive 14th/15th c. tower are stored a font basin, a tomb slab, and other medieval fragments. NE. of the church is a stone cross (Nat. Mon.) with rude *Crucifixus* (17th? c.). Skryne Castle, on the SE. slope of the hill, incorporates medieval work (largely obscured). 1¼ m. S. (via Obertstown crossroads), on the Drogheda road, is St Columcille's Church. Built into a low wall in the churchyard (to which it was brought from Trevet church N. of Dunshaughlin), is the frontal of a 1571, Renaissance-style tomb of Sir Thomas Cusack (Lord Chancellor of Ireland under Henry VIII and Mary Tudor), his wife, four sons and six daughters. In the SW. corner of the churchyard is a 16th c. wayside cross from Lismullin, 2 m. NW.

TARBERT, Co. Kerry (Map 6, E7), on the Glin (4 m.)–Ballylongford (5 m.) road, is a quiet village overlooking a beautiful reach of the Shannon estuary. A car-ferry operates from there (on the half-hour during daylight hours) to Killimer on the Clare side of the estuary.

¾ m. N. is Tarbert House, a Georgian residence. On Massy's Hill, ½ m. N., is a 17th c. star fort. Nearby is a large electricity generating station.

1½ m. N., on Tarbert Island (road-bridge), is an early-19th c. battery.

TEMPLEMORE, Co. Tipperary (Map 3, C8), a small market town on the Roscrea (12 m.)–Thurles (9 m.) road, lies at the E. foot of the Devil's Bit (1,577 ft).

The former British Military Barracks is now the training centre for the Garda Siochána.

The town takes its name from a 'great church' whose remains may be seen in the Town Park. George Borrow, whose father and brother were stationed at Templemore for some months in 1816, describes the district in *Lavengro* (*see p. 112*).

3¼ m. S. are the ruins of Loughmoe Court (Nat. Mon.). The S. end is the tower of a 15th c. castle; the remainder is a 17th c. embattled house. Home of the Purcells, Loughmoe Court gave his title to Nicholas Purcell, Baron Loughmo[r]e, one of the Jacobite signatories of the Treaty of Limerick, 1691. W. of the railway are the ruins of a church with Purcell monuments.

Templemore, Co. Tipperary.

Jerpoint Abbey, Co. Kilkenny.

2½ m. SW., near the Borrisoleigh road, are the remains of the five-storey keep of Knockagh Castle.

4 m. SW., in Drom, are remains of a church and, nearby, a ringfort. According to some, this was the meeting-place of the celebrated Synod of Rath Bréasail, 1110, though others claim the location of the synod was near Banteer in Co. Cork.

TEMPLEPATRICK, Co. Antrim (Map 1, J7) is a village on the Belfast (1 m.)–Antrim (6 m.) road.

Its most celebrated native is James Hope (1764–1843), an organizer of the United Irishmen and lifelong Republican, who took part in the battle of Antrim, 1798, and was also involved in Emmet's rebellion, 1803. He is buried at Mallusk, on the old Belfast road.

Castle Upton (Sir Robin Kinahan), an early-17th c. castle which incorporated remains of a monastery, was extended and redecorated for the 1st Viscount Templetown by Robert Adam in 1783. Adam was also responsible for the Upton mausoleum (Nat. Trust) and the battlemented stable block (1788).

3 m. ESE, in Craigarogan, is Granny's alias Carngraney, a passage-tomb.

2 m. SSE, is Lyle's Hill (753 ft). 12½ acres of hill-top are enclosed by a degraded Neolithic bank. At the summit is a low, round Bronze Age cairn. The sill-stone (Ulster Museum) from the 'entrance' in the kerb bears chevrons and hatched triangles.

TEMPO, Co. Fermanagh (Map 2, C2), is a village on the Enniskillen (7 m.)–Fintona (10½ m.) road. Tempo manor was built in the Jacobean manorial style by Sir Charles Lanyon in 1862–7 on the site of an earlier Maguire house.

4½ m. E. are the remains of Tullyweel Castle.

½ m. SE. (to the E. of the Enniskillen road), in Doon, are the Grey Stones (300 ft), two stones now superimposed. The lower boulder contains depressions, the upper is inscribed with two concentric circles and a curvilinear motif.

¾ m. SSW. and ¾ m. NE. of Coolbuck Church, 450 ft in Cloghtogle, is a chamber-tomb, possibly a wedge-tomb. ¼ m. NW. of the church is Coolbuck wedge-tomb (650 ft). ¾ m. SW. of the church is Mountdrum wedge-tomb (550 ft).

2¾ m. SW. is Mullyknock, alias Topped Mt (910 ft), with a cairn on the summit. A secondary cist contained remains of an adult male skeleton accompanied by a gold-mounted bronze dagger, traces of a cremation, and a Food Vessel.

3½ m. NW., in Ballyreagh, is a dual court-tomb (Hist. Mon.).

TERMONFECKIN, Co. Louth (Map 2, J8), is a small village on the Drogheda (5 m.)–Clogherhead (2¾ m.) road.

It takes its name from the celebrated 6th c. saint, Féichín of Cong, Co. Mayo, and Fore, Co. Westmeath, who founded a monastery there also.

The Anglo-Norman conquest of SE. Uriel split the primatial diocese of Armagh into two parts: one – including the primatial see – 'among the Irish', where the English king's writ did not run; the other (Co. Louth) 'among the English'. After 1346 the primates, approved by the English Crown, resided of necessity 'among the English', principally at Termonfeckin, and made St Peter's Church, Drogheda, their pro-cathedral. After the Reformation the Protestant primates continued to reside at Termonfeckin until 1613. The primatial manor was destroyed at the 1641 insurrection.

The Protestant churchyard occupies the site of the ancient abbey, whose only relics are: an early gravestone (in the church porch) inscribed OROIT DO ULTAN ET DO DUBTHACH DO RIGNI IN CAISSEL ('A prayer for Ultán and Dubhtach who made the cashel'); a High Cross (Nat. Mon.); a medieval *Crucifixion* slab; the base of a small early cross. On the E. face of the High Cross is a carving of the *Crucifixion:* on the W. face, one of the *Last Judgement* (*Christ in Majesty*?). The base of the cross is modern.

Termonfeckin Castle (Nat. Mon.) is a small, 16th c. tower (relic of a Dowdall castle?).

Grianán, formerly Newtown House, S. of the village, is a training centre of the Irish Countrywomen's Association, to which it was presented by the Kellogg Foundation, U.S.A.

2¾ m. NNE. is Clogherhead, a fishing village and small resort. The country round about has many associations with St Oliver Plunkett.

THOMASTOWN, Co. Kilkenny (Map 4, I3), formerly Grenan, is a small market town beautifully situated on the Nore, at the junction of the Kilkenny (11 m.)–New Ross (16 m.) and Carlow (24 m.)–Waterford (21 m.) roads.

The town takes its name from Thomas fitz Anthony, Anglo-Norman seneschal of Leinster, the motte of whose castle survives. In the Middle Ages it was a walled town, but the only remains of the fortifications are Sweetman's Castle and Low St 'Castle' by the bridge. The principal feature of the town is the remnants (chancel arch, N. arcaded wall, fragment of W. wall; Nat. Mon.) of the parish church of the Assumption of the Blessed Virgin Mary ('St Mary's'), founded by fitz Anthony late in the 13th c. In the churchyard are the head of a cross, two badly weathered effigies of ecclesiastics, and some 16th and 17th c. tombstones.

½ m. SE., on a wedge-shaped earthwork, on the W. bank of the Nore, are the well-preserved remains of Grenan Castle, which was for centuries a stronghold of the Dens.

2½ m. NNE., at Kilfane (site of an early monastery), are the ruins and churchyard (Nat. Mons.) of an early-14th c. church which served as the Protestant parish church until 1850. The sedilia show traces of polychrome painting. The tower on the N. side was the priest's residence. There is a magnificent, Cantwell, armoured effigy of *c.* 1260.

2 m. SSE., near the W. bank of the Nore in Dysart, are remains of a fortified church. Nearby to the S. was Dysart Castle, alleged birthplace of the celebrated philosopher George Berkeley (1685–1753), Bishop of CLOYNE.

1½ m. SW., on the little River Eoir, are the fine ruins (Nat. Mon.) of the Cistercian abbey of Jerpoint (Eoiripons, de Jeriponte). The abbey was founded by Donal Mac Gillapatrick, King of Ossory, and was colonized from BALTINGLASS in 1180. In 1184 it, in turn, sent colonies to Kilcooly (*see p. 300*) and Kilkenny. In 1227, like Baltinglass, it was affiliated to Fountains Abbey, Yorkshire, in accordance with the anglicizing policy of the Anglo-Norman colony, but 160 years later the abbot was fined for contravening the notorious Statutes of Kilkenny by accepting Irish monks. The abbey was largely rebuilt in the 15th c. The ruins are perhaps the most interesting Cistercian remains

Effigy of a Cantwell knight at Kilfane, Co. Kilkenny.

in Ireland. The original church (*c.* 1180–1200) closely resembled that of Baltinglass, but had a barrel-vaulted presbytery and transept chapels. It followed the normal Cistercian plan: cruciform, with aisled nave (six bays) and E. chapels (two) in each transept. In the E. part of the nave the piers are alternately cylindrical and square, and the capitals have Irish Romanesque details. There was a low screen (perpyn) wall between the piers of the arcade. The crossing and the three E. bays of the nave were screened off, to form the choir, by a pulpitum with two recessed chapels on its W. face. These served the lay brothers' choir, which occupied the W. part of the nave. The large E. window is a 14th c. replacement of a 12th c. triplet; the central tower dates from the 15th c.; the N. wall of the nave is a 15th c. rebuilding. The S. arcade of the nave was blocked up, seemingly in the 15th c., and the S. aisle taken into the cloister. Fragmentary frescoes of unidentified armorial shields have recently been discovered on the N. wall of the chancel. Despite its 13th c. appearance the cloister arcade is probably 15th c. work; the carvings, of unusual interest, include an armoured knight and his lady. In the E. cloister range are the sacristy, chapter-house, and day room; the monks' dormitory was above; the S. range contained the refectory. A number of interesting monuments survive: the effigy of Felix O Dulany, Bishop of Ossory, 1178–1202, in the E. niche on the N. side of the chancel; the tombstone (*c.* 1275) with very fine engraved effigies of 'The Brethren', two mailed knights, in the S. chapel of the S. transept; the Robert Walsh (d. 1501)–Katerine Poher tomb (beneath the tower), and the effigy of a harper and his wife (in a room beside the chapter house), both by Rory O Tunney. – ¼ m. NW., in Newtown Jerpoint, are the site of a medieval town and the ruins of its little parish church (St Nicholas's). In the graveyard is a 14th c. tomb mensa with the effigy of an ecclesiastic in low relief; nearby are the base and socket of the town market cross. The town was founded in 1200 by William the Marshal, and fell into complete ruin in the 17th c.

2 m. NW., at Legan 'Castle', is a cross-inscribed ogham stone.

THURLES, Co. Tipperary (Map 4, E1), is a market and sugar-manufacturing centre on the Suir, 9 m. S. of Templemore and 13 m. N. of Cashel. Since Penal times it has been the cathedral town of the archdiocese of Cashel and Emly.

The town was a creation of the Butlers.

Between West Gate and Parnell St are remains of Black Castle (1493?).

At the W. end of the bridge across the Suir is Bridge Castle, a tower of 1453(?).

Further E., on the site of a medieval friary, is the Cathedral of the Assumption, a pedestrian essay (1865–72) by J.J. McCarthy in an Italianate Romanesque style. The high altar tabernacle was designed by the celebrated Baroque architect and painter Andrea Pozzo, S.J. (1642–1709), for the Gesu in Rome. The interior decoration was designed by J.C. Ashlin. The side-altar statues of the Sacred Heart and Our Lady are by Benzoni.

Opposite the cathedral is the entrance to St Patrick's College for the education of priests, chiefly for dioceses overseas. The National Synod of 1850 which, among other things, condemned the Queen's Colleges, was held there. E. of the cathedral, in St Mary's Avenue, is St Mary's Protestant Church. There may be seen the tomb of Edmund Archer, a 1520(?) monument which includes figures of saints and the effigies of an armoured knight and his lady.

2 m. N. is unfinished Brittas Castle. Projected as a large-scale copy of Warwick Castle, complete wih water moat, the building of this 19th c. extravagance came to a sudden stop when the proprietor was killed by a falling piece of masonry.

6½ m. E., to the E. of the Urlingford–Cashel road, in Leigh(more), two ruined churches (Nat. Mons.) mark the site of a monastery founded in the 7th c. by St Mo-Chaomhóg. The larger church has a simple Romanesque N. door and chancel arch, but the church was much altered and added to subsequently. The smaller church, to the N., is a simple, single-chamber structure with *antae* and trabeate W. doorway. Foundations of a Round Tower were found during excavations in 1971.

6 m. SE., via Horse-and-Jockey, are the ruins of Grallagh Castle (Nat. Mon.): 16th c. tower and traces of the bawn.

8½ m. SE., via Littleton, on a 20 acre island emerging from a bog in Lurgoe, is the ancient monastic site of Derrynavlan, founded by Rúadhán of LORRHA. The Gobaun Saer's Grave (a small mound), the 'Abbey' (remnants of a 13th c. nave-and-chancel church), and some medieval carved slabs (Nat. Mons.) can be found there. In unlicensed digging near the church in 1980, the most significant Irish hoard of ecclesiastical silver vessels came to light – a chalice, a paten and 'stand', as well as a strainer, dating from the 8th/9th c. After a long legal wrangle over ownership, the Supreme Court finally adjudged the hoard to belong to the State, and it is now on display in the National Museum in Dublin.

4¼ m. SW., beside the Suir, are the interesting ruins (Nat. Mon.) of Holy Cross Abbey. It was founded in the 12th c. for the Order of Tiron, Donal Mór O Brien, King of Limerick (Thomond), being an important patron. It passed to the Cistercians before the close of the century, but was colonized from Monasternenagh (*see p. 123*). It took its name from a relic of the True Cross. The relic made the abbey a noted place of pilgrimage, and about the 15th c. the buildings were extensively remodelled. (The work of this phase includes outstanding examples of the distinctly Irish style of Gothic, as well as of 15th c. craftsmanship.) The remains comprise a well-preserved church, remnants of the cloister and its ranges, and – to the SE. – ruins of the infirmary and guest-house (abbot's lodging?). The church is typically Cistercian: cruciform with E. chapels (two) in each transept, low central tower, and aisled nave. At the 15th c. rebuilding, the N. aisle, choir (including the two E. bays of the nave), tower, transepts, and presbytery (chancel) acquired their existing form; but the S. aisle and the four W. bays of the nave (the lay brothers' choir) were left unaltered (windows and door excepted). Noteworthy features of the church are: the vaulting of the E. arm; the varied 15th c. windows; the excellent 15th c. sedilia in the presbytery, with the arms of England (first escutcheon) and Butler (third and fourth escutcheons); the mural painting (a hunting scene) in the N. transept; the unique 15th c. shrine(?) between the chapels of the S. transept; the Transitional doorway (rebuilt) from the S. aisle to the E. walk of the cloister; and the living quarters over the E. end of the church. The church was restored (1971–5) under the direction of Percy LeClerc, and parts of the cloister and adjoining buildings were subsequently reconstructed. The modern altar and sedilia are by Michael Biggs, and the Stations of the Cross in batik are by Bernadette Madden. The Abbey now houses two relics of the True Cross, one in a modern reliquary in the N. chapel of the N. transept, the other (presented by the Ursuline nuns in Cork) is placed in the O Fogarty tomb-niche in the N. wall of the chancel, with a metal setting by Richard Enda King. The new tabernacle with *Twelve Apostles* in the S. chapel of the N. transept is also by King. The incongruous drapes, pictures and candles which have recently crept in detract from the purity of the 1975 restoration, but may give us some idea of the interior of the church when it was a place of pilgrimage in the Middle Ages. The fragments of the cloister arcade (*c.* 1450) have some interesting carvings, e.g., the arms of Abbot Donnchadh Ó Conghail (*c.* 1448–55) with inscription recording the erection of the arcading (*me fieri fecit*).

3 m. WNW., in Ballynahow, is the circular tower (Nat. Mon.) of a Purcell castle.

TIMAHOE, Co. Laois (Map 3, F7), is a village 7½ m. SE. of Port Laoise and 5 m. SW. of Stradbally.

It takes its name, Teach Mo-Chúa, from the monastery founded there by St Mo-Chúa (d. 657). Of this monastery there survive fragments of a church and a very fine 12th c. Round Tower (Nat. Mons.). The tower has a beautiful Romanesque doorway. The 15th c. church, to the E. of the tower, was converted into a small castle in the 17th c.

In the Catholic church are two single-light windows (*Immaculate Conception* and *Sacred Heart*) by Michael Healy (1921).

½ m. W. of the village is the Rath of Ballynaclogh, motte and bailey of a castle built in 1182 for Meiler fitz Henry by Hugh de Lacy.

TINAHELY, Co. Wicklow (Map 3, J8), is a village on the Aughrim (8 m.)–Shillelagh (6 m.) road. Rebuilt by Earl Fitzwilliam after destruction in the 1798 rebellion, it has a good Court/Market House (now a furniture saleroom). Nearby, in Coolruss, are Black Tom's Cellars, remains of a large house begun by Lord Deputy Strafford *c.* 1639, but never completed.

5¾ m. N. is Moyne, birthplace of Edward L. Godwin (1831–1902), founder of the New York *Nation* (1865).

TIPPERARY, Co. Tipperary (Map 4, C3), which gives its name to the county, is a market town and manufacturing centre of the fertile Golden Vale, 26 m. SE. of Limerick, 12 m. WSW. of Cashel, and 14 m. NW. of Cahir.

The town, an Anglo-Norman creation, figured in the 19th c. Land War when it was the scene of the abortive New Plan of Campaign: the tenants of the Smith Barry estate abandoned their homes for a time and moved to New Tipperary, situated outside the town.

John O Leary (1830–1907), Fenian leader, was a native of the town. Liam Dall Ó hIfearnáin, 18th c. poet, was a native of Shronell, 3 m. W. James O Neill, father of Eugene O Neill, the American playwright, was born near Tipperary.

In Main St is a good statue (by John Hughes, 1898) of Charles T. Kickham (1828–82), the novelist and Young Irelander (*see p. 293*).

4¼ m. ENE., in Moatquarter, is Kilfeakle Moat, remains of a motte-and-bailey castle built in 1192 by William de Burgo during a Norman attempt on Donal Mór O Brien's kingdom (*see p. 232*); there are also traces of a later stone castle and a church in the area.

5 m. SE., at the mouth of the beautiful Glen of Aherlow, is the small village of Bansha where Darby Ryan (1770–1855), poet, is buried.

8½ m. W. is the little village of Emly. St Ailbe, that 'other Patrick of the island of Ireland', who died in 527, founded a church there which was the principal church of Munster prior to the rise of Cashel, and which became the see of a diocese which survived until 1718. The parish church occupies the site of the medieval cathedral: in the churchyard are St Alby's Well and a rude stone cross.

4 m. NNW. is Solloghodbeg (Soloheadbeg). The first ambush of the Anglo-Irish guerrilla war (1919–21) took place near the quarry, 21 January 1919; a monument at Solloghod (Solohead) hamlet, 4 m. W. of Tipperary, commemorates the event.

7 m. WNW., in Longstone, is a ringwork with central pillarstone.

TOBERCURRY, Co. Sligo (Map 7, J3), is a market town on the Sligo (23 m.)–Collooney (14 m.) road.

3 m. NE. is Achonry, where St Nath-Í, disciple of St Finnian of Clonard, founded, *c.* 530, a monastery which in the 12th c. became the see of the diocese to which it has given its name. The medieval cathedral is represented, however, only by some shapeless ruins. The Catholic Cathedral is now at Ballaghaderreen.

5¼ m. NE. (3½ m. N. of Achonry), to the E. of the Coolaney road in Lavagh, are the tower and S. transept chapels of Abbey Court, a friary built in the 15th c. for Franciscan Tertiaries (brethren and sisters) by the O Haras.

5 m. WSW., in Banada, are the remnants of Corpus Christi Priory, first Irish house of Augustinian friars of the Regular Observance. It was founded by Donnchadh Dubh O Hara in 1423, but was still incomplete in 1460. 2 m. WSW. of Banada bridge is Coolrecuill, where the celebrated poet Tadhg Dall Ó Huiginn (1550–91) made his home. He satirized the O Haras of Castle Carragh, 3 m. N., and paid for it with his life.

TOOMYVARA, Co. Tipperary (Map 3, B8), is a small village on the Nenagh (8 m.)–Roscrea (13 m.) road. In the 7th c. St Donnán founded a monastery there, which later became an Augustinian priory (dedicated to the Blessed Virgin) dependent on Monaincha (*see p. 275*). In the 15th and 16th c. the wardenship of the priory was held by the O Mearas, who made the priory their place of sepulture. Near the Catholic church is the 'Abbey', ruined church of the 15th c. priory; in the priests' burial plot in the grounds of the Catholic church is a fragment of the 15th c. effigy of Joannes O Meara.

2½ m. E. are the ruins of Aghnameadle church. SE. are the remains of a castle and of Aghnameadle Court, sometime homes of a branch of the celebrated Mac Egans, hereditary jurists to the O Kennedys of Ormond.

TORY ISLAND, Co. Donegal (Map 8, D1), lies 7½ m. NW. of Horn Head. It is best reached by boat from Magheraroarty, Gortahork. It has a school of local primitive painters, encouraged by the artist Derek Hill, who often went to paint there.

A monastery founded there by St Columcille in the 6th c. was raided in 1595 by the English garrison of Sligo, led by George Bingham and Ulick Burke.

The scanty monastic remains (Nat. Mon.) are situated in West Town. They comprise the ruins of a Round Tower, portions of a sculptured High Cross, a number of carved fragments, a plain, T-shaped, stone cross, and two early grave-slabs. There are also 'cursing stones' said to have been effectively used in 1884, when the gunboat *Wasp* endeavoured to land police and troops to collect rates from the islanders. (The *Wasp* was wrecked with loss of life.)

Balar's Fort, a quadrivallate promontory fort at the E. end of the island, takes its name from Balar of the Baleful Eye, the mythological Fomorian associated with the island (*see p. 197*).

TRALEE, Co. Kerry (Map 5, F2), the county town, is situated at the head of Tralee Bay and the NE. corner of the magnificent Corcaguiney peninsula ('Dingle Peninsula'), 16 m. SW. of Listowel, 20 m. NNW. of Killarney, and 31 m. ENE. of Dingle.

The palatine earls of Desmond had their principal castle at Tralee. Town and castle suffered severely during the rebellion of the 15th earl, and were granted thereafter to Sir Edward Denny, an English newcomer. In 1641 they were captured after a siege by Confederate Catholics led by Sir Piaras Feritéir (*see p. 62*), but fell two years later to the notorious renegade Murrough the Burner O Brien. In 1691 the Jacobites fired the town on the approach of superior Williamite forces.

St John's Church, Castle St, is a good Gothic-Revival essay (1870) by J.J. McCarthy. It has two windows (1957) by Patrick Pollen: two-light *Four Evangelists* and rose *Trinity*.

The Court House, Ashe St, is by William Vitruvius Morrison (1794–1838). It has a good Ionic portico.

The 1798 memorial in Denny St is by Albert Power.

The church of St Brendan (1971) is by D.J. Kennedy, with furnishings by Benedict Tutty, Ray Carroll, Brian Clarke, Ian Stuart and Seán Adamson.

In Abbey St is the graveyard of the Dominican friary of the Holy Cross, founded in 1243 by John fitz Thomas, ancestor of the Earls of Desmond. Thirteen earls were buried in the friary, of which little remains but a few carved stones preserved at the modern Dominican priory. The priory church was built by George Ashlin to the design of his master (and partner), Edward Welby Pugin. In the sacristy are stained glass panels by Michael Healy (1912).

3 m. ENE., in the grounds of Chute Hall, are two ogham stones taken from Kilvickillane, Smerwick Harbour (*see p. 61*), in 1848.

1 m. E. are the ruins of Ratass church (Nat. Mon.), a nave-and-chancel structure with *antae,* trabeate W. door (architrave), and simple Romanesque E. window. Inside is a cross-inscribed ogham stone.

8 m. E. is Glanageenty, a defile in the Glannaruddery Mts (Knight's Mt, 1,097 ft) where the unfortunate 15th Earl of Desmond was slain in 1583 when he sought refuge from the English. The cuckoo called that winter's night at Ardmhic-Ghráinne. A low, coffin-shaped mound near the head of the glen is the Desmond's Grave of local tradition.

3¼ m. S., in Glanaskagheen, alias 'Scota's Glen', a bogus ogham inscription and a flagstone mark 'Scota's Grave'. Scota, according to a pedantic fiction, was the widow of Mil (Milesius), whose people – the prehistoric Gaelic invaders of Ireland – waged a great battle with the mythological Túatha Dé Danann at the foot of Slieve Mish. Scota and another Milesian princess, Fais, were among the slain.

3 m. SW., in the ruined medieval church of Annagh (Nat. Mon.), is a 13th c. carving (armed horseman).

10 m. SW. is Camp village. – Some 400 yds SE., on the lower slopes of Caherconree Mt, is a great ogham stone, to which a forger has added FECT CONURI. – 4 m. SE., via the Finglas valley, is Caherconree Mt (2,715 ft). It takes its name from Cathair Chon-Raoí, a great promontory fort whose remote remains (Nat. Mon.) lie at 2,050 ft. The fort itself is called after the mythological Cú-Raoí mac Dáire. A legend explains the name of the Finglas, 'white stream': Cú-Raoí's faithless wife turned its waters white with milk to inform her husband's enemies of his presence; they climbed the mountain, took him unawares, and slew him. – 1¾ m. WSW., in Scrallaghbeg, is Tobernagalt. Nearby, in Foilatrisnig, is Clochnagalt (a pillar-

stone) and a ringfort; S. of the latter, in Glannagalt, is another pillarstone; to the W. is a third; ¾ m. SE., in Doonore South (500 yds W. of the main road), is a second Tobernagalt. Glannagalt, and Clochnagalt take their names (Gleann na nGealt, etc.; 'Valley of the Lunatics', 'Stone of the Lunatics'), from the insane who allegedly went there in search of a cure. – 2 m. SSW., in Maumnahaltora, are two prehistoric chamber-tombs and penitential stations.

TRAMORE, Co. Waterford (Map 4, I6), on Tramore Bay, 7 m. SSW. of Waterford, is one of Ireland's most popular seaside resorts.

The sculptor John Edward Carey (*c.* 1785–1868) was a native of Tramore.

The Church of the Exaltation of the Holy Cross (1856–71) is a good Gothic-Revival building by J.J. McCarthy.

5 m. ENE. the dilapidated remains of Kilmacleague church, a bullaun, and a medieval font, mark the site of a monastery founded by St Mac Líag, disciple of Déaghlán of Ardmore. 1 m. NNW. of Clohernagh bridge, and close to Waterford airport, is Ballyganner Kill(eenagh), an ancient bivallate church-site of one acre. The enclosure is divided by a drystone wall. Excavation revealed the post-holes of a timber structure (church?). The only surviving monuments are an early cross-slab and a small cross-pillar.

3 m. N., in Carricklong, is a V-shaped passage grave. 1 m. W., in Munmahoge, is a ruinous V-shaped passage-tomb.

3½ m. W. is Fennor. The Church of the Immaculate Conception (1894) is by Doolin. 2 m. W., at Woodtown bridge, are the remains of the rock castle of Dunhill, a Power stronghold. 1¼ m. N. of the castle is The Church of the Sacred Heart (1884), also by Doolin. In the adjoining townland of Ballynageeragh is a portal tomb (Nat. Mon.). 2 m. WNW. is Savagetown portal dolmen. – 1½ m. N. of Fennor church, in Matthewstown, is a V-shaped passage-tomb (Nat. Mon.).

2 m. WNW. is Carrickavantry wedge-tomb.

TRIM, Co. Meath (Map 3, H2), since 1955 the cathedral town of the Protestant diocese of Meath, is a small market town where the Dublin (28 m.)–Athboy (8 m.) road crosses the Boyne. In the Middle Ages it was one of the principal strongholds of the English Pale, with a great castle, an Augustinian priory, Dominican and Franciscan friaries, a nunnery-cum-hospital, and a parish church. Nearby were the cathedral of the diocese of Meath and an Augustinian hospital-friary.

According to ancient tradition, the Trim country was converted to Christianity by Bishop Lommán, a British disciple of St Patrick's. Patrick built a church which subsequently acquired a monastic character, and Lommán's successors came to combine the offices of bishop and abbot. In 1152 the Synod of Kells decreed the amalgamation of the little diocese with those of Ardbraccan, Slane, Duleek, and Clonard (*see p. 226*) to form the diocese of Meath. In 1206 Simon de Rochfort, first Anglo-Norman bishop of the new diocese, transferred the see from Clonard to Newtown Trim (*see below*).

At the Norman invasion Hugh I de Lacy set up the chief manor and castle of his lordship of Meath at Trim. In time a town grew up in the shelter of the castle; it was re-walled in 1393. Several Anglo-Norman parliaments met there in the 15th c. Among the enactments of the parliament of 1447 was one to the effect that every man wishing to be accepted as English should abandon his Irish-style moustache and shave both lips. At the beginning of August 1647, Preston (*see p. 52*), Confederate Catholic commander for Leinster, unsuccessfully laid siege to Trim, and in 1649 a Confederate Catholic force occupied the town, but was driven out by the Parliamentarian, Sir Charles Coote II, who lost his life in the fighting.

The town is dominated by the Castle (Nat. Mon.) on the S. bank of the Boyne. This is one of the finest surviving examples of medieval military architecture in Ireland. The square keep, 75 ft high, with a tower projecting from the middle of each face, dates from *c.* 1200. On the ground floor are the Great Hall and a small chamber; in the E. tower is a small chapel. Of the curtain wall, which enclosed about two acres, considerable stretches (of various dates) remain. These include the gatehouse and eight flanking towers, of which the most interesting are the circular tower with a barbican (on the S.) and the square tower with a sallyport (on the N.). SE. of the latter is a crypt. The moat was fed by the Boyne. King John's expedition of 1210 against the de Lacys brought him to Trim in July of that year. He confiscated the castle, but gave it back in 1215. In 1399 Richard II of England left his cousins, Humphrey of Gloucester and Henry of Lancaster (afterwards Henry V), in ward in the castle. Richard of York, heir (through the Mortimers) to the de Lacys and to the de Burgo earls of Ulster, and Lieutenant of Ireland since 1447, spent the winter of 1449–50 at the castle, and may have been there repeatedly in 1450 and again in 1459–60. The castle was

Trim Castle, Co. Meath.

taken, together with the town, by Silken Thomas in 1537. In 1647 the castle was refortified by the Confederate Catholics, but was captured, after bombardment, by Sir Charles Coote II. Opposite the entrance to the castle is the County Library, where local bygones are displayed.

W. of the castle, between Castle St and Emmet St, and again W. of Emmet St, are fragments of the town wall. The Court House occupies the site of the medieval Franciscan friary. Arthur Wellesley, later Duke of Wellington, lived as a boy in Emmet St (*see also p. 286*). At the S. end of the street is a column raised in his honour in 1817. Nearby St Patrick's Church (1902) is by Hague.

On the N. side of the Boyne (Abbey Lane off High St) are the remnants of St Mary's Priory of Canons Regular (Victorine Congregation) of St Augustine: beneath Talbot Castle, the undercroft of the refectory; a part incorporated in fragmentary Nangle Castle (a late stronghouse; Nat. Mon.); E. of the latter, the Yellow Steeple (Nat. Mon.), a magnificent 14th c. seven-storey (125 ft), bell-tower blown up by command of Ormonde in 1649. Its miraculous statue of the Blessed Virgin, 'the Idol of Trim', was wantonly destroyed at the Reformation. Talbot Castle, a late stronghouse (modernized) with the arms of Talbot, served for a time as the Protestant diocesan school (Arthur Wellesley was a pupil). 150 yds SE. are the remains (Nat. Mon.) of little Sheep Gate, survivor of the town's five gates.

Towards the N. end of the town is the small St Patrick's Protestant Cathedral (until 1955 the parish church). Built in 1802, it incorporates the tower and maltreated parts of the nave walls of the medieval parish church. The 19th c. W. window has 15th c. human masks. High above the 19th c. doorway of the tower are the arms (impaling Mortimer and de Burgo) of Richard of York. In the porch are miscellaneous tomb and cross fragments, etc. Built against the W. wall of the nave is a medieval font. E. of the church are remains of the medieval chancel: excellent three-light, 15th c. S. window, one of whose human-mask label stops wears a ducal coronet (Richard of York?).

1 m. E., on the N. bank of the Boyne at Newtown Trim, are the ruins (Nat. Mon.) of the beautiful Cathedral of SS Peter and Paul and its priory. The see was set up there in 1206 by Bishop Simon de Rochfort, who confided the services and fabric to a community of Augustinian canons of the Congregation of St Victor of Paris. The ruins represent, in the main, the choir (which was vaulted) and a short portion of the nave of de Rochfort's church. In the N. wall is a weathered episcopal 13th c. effigy. The fragments of the Victorine priory include the chapter house and the refectory (which stands on an undercroft). E. of the cathedral are the ruins of the medieval parish church. A tomb fragment with small *Coronation of the Virgin* has been mounted in the outer face of the S. wall. In the church is the excellent, if weathered, altar tomb of Sir Luke Dillon of Moymet and his wife, Jane Bathe (1586); Sir Luke's effigy has Renaissance armour. Nearby is St Peter's Bridge, partly ancient. On the S. side of the river are the remnants (Nat. Mon.) of the Friary and Hospital of St John the Baptist (Augustinian Crucifers) the E. end of the church is 13th c.; the residential tower to the W. is 15th.

1½ m. SSE., in Knightsbrook, are the remains of 'Stella's House'. It occupies the site of the house where Dean Swift's 'Stella' (Esther Johnston) lived with Mrs Dingley. ¾ m. SSE. is Laracor (Lethercor) Protestant church, successor of the church to which Swift ran the race with Delaney and in which his 'dearly loved Roger' officiated as clerk; the altar plate used by Swift survives. 140 yds NW. of the church, opposite Knightsbrook motte, is the site of Swift's residence (Glebe House) when incumbent of Laracor (1700–14; he was often an absentee).

8 m. SW., ½ m. W. of Inchamore bridge, is the tower (square with round angle-turret) of Donore Castle (Nat. Mon.).

TUAM, Co. Galway (Map 7, I8), is a small market and manufacturing centre at the intersection of the Galway (21 m.)–Dunmore (10 m.) and Athlone (42 m.)–Ballinrobe (21 m.) roads. It is the see of the archdiocese to which it has given its name; also of a Protestant diocese united with Killala and Achonry. The surrounding countryside is very rich in prehistoric and historic remains, notably so in ringforts, many of which have souterrains.

The first and second Protestant archbishops, Nehemiah Donnellan (1595–1609) and William O Donnell (1609–28), were associated with the production of the first translation of the New Testament into Irish (1602).

Henry Mossop (1729–74), actor and founder of Dublin's Smock Alley Theatre, was the son of Prebendary John Mossop.

The story of Tuam commences in the 5th/6th c. with the foundation of a monastery by St Jarlath, disciple of St Benignus (*see* Kilbannon, *below*). In the 12th c. the expanding power of the O Conor Kings of Connacht added the Tuam district to their territories, and Tuam itself became one of their principal seats. It is not surprising, therefore, that the 12th c. reformers should have chosen Tuam as the metropolitan see of Connacht. By the time of the Anglo-Norman invasion the place was well on the way to becoming the capital of Connacht. Thereafter, however, its importance was primarily ecclesiastical. Prior to the Reformation it had three churches and two monasteries: the Cathedral, St Íarlaith's Church, Holy Trinity Abbey (Premonstratensian), St John's Abbey (Augustinian Canons Regular), and Teampall na Scríne (where St Íarlaith's relics were enshrined); also a nunnery-cum-hospital.

The Protestant cathedral, Galway road, is a dull Gothic-Revival building (1861–3), by Sir Thomas Deane. It incorporates the barrel-vaulted chancel of a small nave-and-chancel cathedral of about the 1180s, and the chancel (choir) added to it *c.* 1312 as the first stage of an ambitious building project never carried further. The 12th c. nave was destroyed by fire in 1787. For nearly 100 years thereafter the Romanesque chancel served as a porch, to the further detriment of its fire-damaged arch. This splendid six-order arch and the triple E. window of the chancel are among the outstanding relics of the Irish Romanesque style, and reflect the Scandinavian (Urnes-style) influence so marked in 12th c. Connacht art. Near the W. door is the shaft of a 12th c. High Cross with interlaced and other ornament. It is inscribed OR[ŌIT] DON RIG DO THA[I]ṘDELBUCH Ú CHONCHOBAIR OR[ŌIT] DON THAER DO GILLU C[H]R[ĪST] U THUATHAI[L] ('A prayer for the king, Turloch O Conor. A prayer for the craftsman, Giolla-Críst O Toole'); and OR[ŌIT] DO CHOMARBA IARLAITHE .I. DO AED U OSSIN [LAS]IN DERNAD AN CHROS-SA ('A prayer for the successor of Íarlaith, i.e. for Áedh O Hession for whom this cross was made'). (Turloch O Conor reigned 1106–56; Áedh O Hession was Abbot of Tuam 1126–51, Archbishop of Tuam 1152–61.) The factory windows of the aisles present some pathetically funny examples of late Victorian art. The ugly parapet of the 14th c. chancel is a 19th c. 'restoration', and the building itself was restored again in 1987.

NE. of the cathedral are the fragmentary remains of Temple Jarlath, with an interesting Transitional three-light E. window; also some Romanesque fragments.

At the centre of the town is the imperfect 'Market Cross', assembled from scattered pieces, one of which came from the Protestant churchyard. It is very unlikely that head and shaft belonged to the same cross originally. On the W. face of the head is a *Crucifixion*. The shaft and base have an elaborate, all-over, Urnes-style, interlaced ornament very lightly carved. On the base are the inscriptions: E. face: [ORŌIT] DO THAIRDELBUCH U CHONCHUBUIR DOND RĪG [OCUS DO . . .] RAFLATH . . . SIN . . . DO RIGNE I[N] SAETHAR-[SA] ('A prayer for Turloch O Conor, for the king; and for . . . raflath O Hession(?) . . . who made this work'); W. face: [ORŌIT DO AED] Ū OSSIN DOND ABBAID . . . ('A prayer for Áedh O Hession, for the abbot. . .').

The Cathedral of the Assumption, Bishop St, is an early post-Emancipation (1827–37) structure in the Gothick style by Dominic Madden. The statue of Archbishop Mac Hale (1791–1881) is by John Henry Foley.

In Shop St is a restored mill and Mill Museum.

2 m. N. is Fairy Mill Bridge. Close by to the E. is Muileann an Liupracháin, alias the Fairy Mill, a limestone cave with subterranean watercourse; an unbelieving generation no longer leaves corn to be ground by the leprechaun.

2½ m. N., to the W. side of the road, is the 1673 monument of James Lally of Tullinadaly. He was great-grandfather of the illustrious Marshal of France Lally-Tollendal (Thomas Arthur Lally, Baron de Tollendal, Count de Lally, 1702–66), who very nearly drove the British from India, and whom an ungrateful Louis XV 'murdered with the sword of justice'. (His name is now inscribed along with those of France's greatest soldiers on the Arc de Triomphe.)

6 m. SE. are the ruins of Barnaderg Castle, a 16th c. O Kelly stronghold.

4 m. S. is Ballinderry Castle, well designed for defence against firearms.

2½ m. NW., at Kilbennan in Pollacorragune, a ruined Round Tower and fragmentary church (Nat. Mons.) mark the site of a foundation by St Benignus (Beannán), disciple of St Patrick and his successor at Armagh. St Íarlaith of Tuam is said to have been a disciple of St Benignus here. NW. of the church is Tobar Bannon, alias St Benen's Well. A medieval tale recounts how Patrick and Benignus called forth the spring by lifting the sod. Here they baptized and healed nine lepers. A great *pátrún* was held at the well (on the last Sunday of July) until well into the 19th c. when the parish priest, scenting pagan practices (he was of those who thought Round Towers were pagan fire-temples!), set about suppressing it.

5½ m. NW., in Castlegrove East, is F(e)artagar Castle (Nat. Mon.).

9 m. NW. (via Milltown) is Millbrook House, home of John Bermingham (1816–74), the astronomer.

TULLA, Co. Clare (Map 6, H5), is a small town picturesquely sited on high ground 9 m. E. of Ennis. There are remains of a barrel-vaulted 17th c. church, and the area still preserves several O Brien and Mac Mahon castles. In the surrounding countryside are preserved a good number of wedge-tombs.

TULLAMORE, Co. Offaly (Map 3, D4), county town of Offaly, is a prosperous market and manufacturing town at the junction of roads from Birr (23 m.). Mountmellick (15 m.), Portarlington (17 m.), and Clara (9 m.)

The town is the creation of the Burys, a Co. Limerick family which (*c.* 1750) succeeded the Moores, Earls of Tullamore, who had obtained the confiscated lands of the O Molloys in the 17th c. In 1785, still a mere village, it was destroyed as a result of an accident to a great balloon. Rebuilt on a much more ambitious scale, it supplanted DAINGEAN as the county seat in 1833.

In the town are several good late Georgian houses, and the Court House (*c.* 1840) has a good Ionic portico.

The Presbytery, Canal Harbour, was built as a hotel by the Grand Canal Company (defunct).

On the E. side of the town is St Catherine's Church (Protestant), a fine example (1815) of Francis Johnston's Gothick; several windows retain their original clear glass.

The Catholic church went up in flames in 1982, but has since been restored by E. Smith, with the inestimable addition of the following windows by Harry Clarke, formerly at Rathfarnham Castle, Co. Dublin: *SS Peter and Paul, Brendan, Patrick and Benignus, Ignatius, Sacred Heart, Joseph and Our Lady* (all 1928) and *Christ's Wounds* (1927).

4½ m. N. (Kilbeggan road), in Durrow Abbey demesne, is the site of one of the earliest (551) and most important of St Columcille's monasteries. The site was given to Columcille by Áed mac Bréanainn, King of Tethba. Of the ancient abbey the only certain remains surviving on the site are: a fine 9th/10th c. High Cross (Nat. Mon.), a fragment with interlacing, and five early gravestones of Clonmacnois type, all W. of the derelict, early-18th c. Protestant church (which may incorporate something of the fabric of a pre-Norman church). The subjects on the High Cross include: W. face: *Crucifixion, Soldiers Guarding the Tomb of Christ*, etc.; E. face: *Last Judgement, Sacrifice of Abraham, King David;* N. side: *Joachim, Anne and John the Baptist* and (?) *John the Baptist Greeting Christ*; S. side: *The Fall*, etc. Of the five commemorative slabs (one very large), two are inscribed OR[ŌIT] DO AIGIDIU and OR[ŌIT]DO CHATHALAN respectively. The head of another early cross with a *Crucifixion* was apparently removed to Durrow Abbey nearby in 1974. NE. of the churchyard is Columcille's Well, resorted to on the saint's festival, 9 June. SE. of the churchyard is the Headache Stone, the base of a stone cross. The celebrated *Book of Durrow*, now in the library of Trinity College, Dublin, belonged to the abbey.

5 m. NE., on the Tyrrelspass road, is Rahugh, which takes its name from the 6th c. St Áed ('Hugh'), son of Bric, founder of a monastery there (*see also pp. 64, 93 and 193*). 250 yds E. of the church is St Hugh's Well. 200 yds SW. of the churchyard is St Hugh's Stone, a boulder with weathered ring-cross. It is reputed to cure headaches. Rahugh was for a time the seat of a Cromwellian Anabaptist colony.

2 m. SW. is Charleville Forest, sometime seat of the Burys, Earls of Charleville. This is a fine Gothick house by Francis Johnston (1801).

4 m. WSW., beyond Charleville Forest demesne, is Lynally, site of Lann Elo, an important monastery founded *c.* 580 by

Church with Romanesque doorway at Rahan, Co. Offaly.

Bishop Colmán Elo (d. 611), patron of churches in Scotland as well as second patron of CONNOR, on land near the River Ela given him by the King of Meath. Apart from *antae* at the W. gable and an inserted 15th/16th c. window, the church is featureless. It seems to have been rebuilt for Protestant use in the 18th c. On the S. are fragments of claustral buildings. Two 8th/9th c. gravestones found nearby are in the National Museum.

4 m. W., on the N. bank of the canal, are the ruins of Ballycowen castle, a fortified horse built 1626 by Sr Jasper Herbert.

7 m. W., between the canal and the Clodiagh River, are the remains of the great monastery of Rahan, founded, it has been claimed, by the Patrician bishop Camelacus, author of a Latin hymn in praise of St Patrick. The most famous name associated with Rahan is that of St Cárthách (Mo-Chuda). At Easter, 636, Mo-Chuda was expelled by King Bláthmac of Tara, at the instance of the monks of Durrow (possibly for abandoning the traditional Irish dating of the festival), and withdrew to LISMORE, Co. Waterford. Thereafter the history of Rahan is obscure. The remains comprise earthworks and three small churches. The largest of the churches (tastelessly cemented) serves as the Protestant parish church (nave rebuilt in the 18th c.); the stone-roofed chancel was originally flanked by a pair of transept-like chambers; between the chancel and nave is a very fine and unusual Romanesque arch; in the chancel is a unique, circular, Romanesque E. window. The other two churches (Nat. Mons.) are roofless ruins. One of them incorporates a beautiful Romanesque W. doorway, but the church was substantially rebuilt in the 15th(?) c. The other was a simple, primitive structure. $\frac{3}{4}$ m. N., in Tullabeg, is St Stanislaus College, a Jesuit house of retreat. The chapel has five Evie Hone windows (1946): *Nativity, The Beatitudes, Last Supper, Pentecost, The Sacred Heart with Jesuit Saints*. The three first named are superb.

$3\frac{1}{2}$ m. NW. is Tihilly, which takes its name (Teach Theille) from St Teille, son of Seigín. St Munnu of TAGHMON is said to have given the place to the virgin Cera (d. 670?). In the later 9th c. the monastery was subject to the abbot of Castledermot. It disappears from history after 936. Besides remnants of a church, there survive an early gravestone and a High Cross (Nat. Mons.). The unusual cross has figurations of *The Fall* and *The Crucifixion*, as well as panels of beautiful zoomorphs, etc.

TULLOW, Co. Carlow (Map 3, H8), is a pleasant, small market town set in attractive country where the Carlow (10 m.)–Shillelagh (10 m.) and Castledermot (17 m.)–Bunclody (15 m.) roads cross the Slaney.

The Protestant parish church has a Clement Nevil memorial (1745) by David Sheehan.

The Butlers built a castle at Tullow to command the important river-crossing. The successor of that castle was stubbornly but unsuccessfully held against the Cromwellians in 1650. There was an early monastery at Tullow; also an Augustinian friary founded in 1314. Nothing survives of either, save a stone cross in the graveyard and the name of St Austin's Abbey.

It was in a field near Tullow that, on 7 January 1395, Art Óg Mac Murrough, King of Leinster, made formal submission to Richard II's representative, and undertook to leave Leinster together with his subordinate lords.

4 m. E., on high ground beside the old Shillelagh road in Rath East, Co. Wicklow, is Rathgall (Nat. Mon.), a four-ring, stone hill-fort about 18 acres in total area. At the centre is a citadel, or strong ringfort, of dry masonry, 150 ft in diameter; the enclosing rampart is 18 ft thick at the base. Excavations revealed traces of Bronze Age occupation *c.* 700 B.C., including the first known Irish metal workshop of the period. 200 yds N. is the ruin of an 8¼ acre fort; only one ring survives, but traces of a second are discernible.

1¾ m. SE., on a long, low mound in Rathglass, are two pillarstones; one has an ogham inscription.

5½ m. S. is Altamont House, whose formal and informal gardens are open to the public in summer.

3 m. SSW., in adjacent fields in Ardristan, are two pillarstones, one of them grooved. In Aghade, next townland to the S., is Cloch an Phoill, Cloghaphile (Nat. Mon.), a perforate pillarstone legendarily associated with Niall Nine Hostager. In Aghade fox covert is a ruined portal-tomb. The ancient churchyard ½ m. NW. of Aghade bridge probably marks the site of a church founded by St Iserninus (d. 468), disciple of St Patrick. In Ballynoe, alias Newtown, on the E bank of the Slaney, are a grooved pillarstone and a small portal-tomb.

6 m. SW. is Kellistown, site of an early monastery whose Round Tower survived until 1807. Muirchertach mac Erca, King of Tara, routed and slew Oengus mac Nat Fraích, King of Cashel, in Kellistown, A.D. 490/491, while O Byrne and Mac Davy there routed and slew Roger Mortimer, Earl of March, Lord of Carlow, Richard II's Lieutenant in Ireland, and heir to the English throne, 10 July 1398.

1½ m. WNW. is Castlemore Mote, the motte of a castle erected by Raymond le Gros. The early cross-slab was originally situated in an adjoining field.

3½ m. NNW., in Straboe, are the remains of Templeboy, a church; there is an early gravestone (Nat. Mon.) here from nearby Killerig where, besides the early monastery, there was also a preceptory of the Knights Hospitaller of St John of Jerusalem.

TULSK, Co. Roscommon (Map 7, L6), is a village on the Roscommon (12 m.)–French-park (10 m.) road. Beside the Strokestown road is a fragment of a Dominican friary founded in 1448 by the Mac Dowells. The parish church has a four-light window (1913) by A.E. Child: *Baptism of Christ, Ecce Homo, Resurrection,* and *Ascension.*

1 m. N. is Clooneyquin, where Percy French (1854–1920), artist, entertainer and songwriter, was born. A monument marks the spot.

3 m. SSW., is Carnfree (alias the 'Hill of Carns'), which was the inauguration place of the Kings of Connacht. 300 yds SE. of Carnfree is Dumha Shealga, a tumulus associated in heroic and early religious literature with the Connacht dynasts (Uí Briúin).

TYNAN, Co. Armagh (Map 2, G3), 7 m. SW. of Armagh is a village on the site of an early monastery. Beside the church is a 9th/10th c. High Cross (Nat. Mon.) which formerly stood in the churchyard. The cross is decorated with bosses on the head, and *Adam and Eve* in a panel near the foot. A second cross (Nat. Mon.) in the churchyard was removed *c.* 1844 to Tynan Abbey demesne where it stands on the terrace close to the ruins of the house. Also in the demesne are two High Crosses from Glenarb (*see p. 88*); one (Nat. Mon.) is on an island in Corfehan, the other in Fairview or Mucklagh, ½ m. WSW. of the village. The Fairview cross has a very weathered *Crucifixion.*

TYRRELSPASS, Co. Westmeath (Map 3, E3), is a small village on the Rochfortbridge (5 m.)–Kilbeggan (6 m.) road. It takes its name from the strategically important way through the bogs where, in July 1597, Piers Lacy and Capt. Richard Tyrrel ambushed and cut to pieces an English force commanded by Christopher Barnewall. The village was laid out as a crescent around the village green in the late 18th c. by the Countess of Belvedere. In the crescent is a cast stone group of three children by Imogen Stuart (1970) – an inspired IRA memorial which looks forward with hope to the future, rather than heroically back to the past. At the W. end of the village is the tower of a 15th c. Tyrell castle.

U

URLINGFORD, Co. Kilkenny (Map 4, F1), is a village on the Durrow, Co. Laois (20 m.)–Cashel (14 m.) road, close to the Tipperary border.

NNW. of the village are the ruins of a nave-and-chancel church, and of a castle which belonged to the Mountgarret Butlers (*see* Clomantagh, *below, and p. 66*) in the 16th c.

2 m. NE. is Johnstown. In St Kieran's Church (1832) are a window and a richly carved baptismal font from Fertagh (*see below*). Built into the churchyard wall is a superbly carved, highly stylized crucifix, also from Fertagh. The Protestant church (1799) incorporates the W. doorway and Perpendicular E. window from Fertagh church. 2 m. NW. are the ruins of a 15th c. Purcell castle and an ancient church; an early church bell found in the nearby Decoy Well is in the National Museum.

4½ m. NE. are Fertagh Round Tower (Nat. Mon.) and fragmentary 'Abbey'. St Cíarán of Saighir (*see pp. 78 and 270*) founded a monastery at Fertagh. In 861 it was attacked by a Viking raiding party, and in 1156 the monastery and its Round Tower were burned. In the 13th c. the monastery was refounded by the Norman Blanchevilles (Blanchfields) as a priory

Kilcooly Abbey, Co. Tipperary.

of Canons Regular of St Augustine. The ruined 'abbey' was the priory – later parochial – church (*see* Johnstown, *above*). It is a structure of various dates, and was used as a Protestant church until 1780. On the N. side is the 15th/16th c. 'Kilpatrick' Chapel, built as their burial place by the Mac Giolla Phádraig (Mac Gillapatrick, Fitzpatrick) lords of Upper Ossory. In it is situated the tomb (1540) of John Mac Gillapatrick of Upper Ossory (d. 1468), and his wife; and effigies of an armoured knight and his lady, which are probably by Rory O Tunney. – 1 m. NE. is Glashere Castle, which in the 16th and 17th c. belonged to the Ormond Butlers.

3 m. E., in Upper Balief, are the ruins of a Shortall castle with a circular tower. 1¼ m. E. of Balief crossroads are Clomantagh Church (with sheila-na-gig) and Castle. The church, a 13th/14th c. structure, was dedicated to the Nativity of the Blessed Virgin Mary.

4 m. S., in a private estate (Mr P.D. Ponsonby) in Co. Tipperary, are the very interesting remains of Kilcooly Abbey (Nat. Mon.), a small Cistercian abbey in honour of the Blessed Virgin Mary and St Benedict, which was founded for the monks of Magh Airbh (*see below*) about 1182 by Donal Mór Ó Brien, King of Thomond, and was colonized from Jerpoint (*see p. 291*) about 1184. It was destroyed by armed men about 1445, and restored by Abbot Philip O Mulwardayn. The church (*c.* 1200) was a variant of the normal Cistercian cruciform plan, with aisled nave and E. chapels (two) in each transept. The 1445 disaster occasioned extensive reconstruction about 1445–70, in the course of which the E. window triplet was replaced by the existing large traceried window; the chancel vaulted; the central tower built over the crossing; the transepts rebuilt and vaulted; the nave arcades blocked up; the S. aisle thrown into the cloister; rooms built over the chancel, crossing, and transepts; and both nave and chancel propped with ungainly buttresses. The church has two unique features: the pair of stalls (for abbot and prior ?) in the responds of the W. tower-arch, and the sculptured screen between the S. transept and the sacristy. The figure subjects on the screen include the *Crucifixion* and *St Christopher*. The monuments, etc., in the church include: in front of the altar, the tombstone of the restorer of the abbey, Abbot Philip (d. 1463), and his parents; and the tomb of Piers fitz James Óg Butler of Clonamicklon (d. 1526), his parents, and his son, James; it has the high-relief effigy of an armoured knight and panels of 'weepers' (apostles, etc.), and is signed by the maker, Rory O Tunney (RORICUS OTUYNE SCRIPSIT); the effigy is the earliest signed example by O Tunney. In addition there are two other tombstones by Rory O Tunney, one by Patrick O Tunney (1587), and another by Patrick Kerin (1608). There is also a carved font. The claustral buildings were considerably altered in the 15th and 16th c., and again in more recent times. To the NE. is a corbel-vaulted, circular dovecot. – 1¾ m. S. of the abbey are the ruins of the Butler castle of Clonamicklon. – 7 m. SW. of the abbey, in Derryvella bog, is an ancient oval churchyard enclosed by an earthen vallum. This is probably the site of the monastery of Daire Mór, whose foundation is ascribed to St Colmán (son of King Nat Fraích of Cashel), which was later known as St Mary's of Magh Airbh (de Arvicampo), and which was ultimately replaced by Kilcooly Abbey.

V

VALENCIA ISLAND, Co. Kerry (Map 5, B5), close to the mainland, lies 3 m. SW. of Cahirsiveen. Its Spanish-looking name is an English corruption of Béal Inse, the name of the adjacent sound; its proper name is Oileán Dairbhre. A bridge at Portmagee connects the island to the mainland. Knightstown, at the E. end of the island, is the 'capital' and the principal resort.

It was the E. terminal station of the first Transatlantic cable (cable station closed 1965). The basic mileages below are reckoned from Knightstown.

1 m. W. are remains of the medieval church of Kilmore. ¾ m. further W. is the beautiful demesne of Glanleam, formerly home of the FitzGeralds, Knights of Kerry. ¾ m. N. of Glanleam, at Fort Point, are the remains of Cromwell's Fort; inside it is a pillarstone.

2½ m. WSW., in Feaghmaan West, are remains of an ancient anchoritic enclosure with ruins of an oratory, a clochán, etc. At Kildreenagh, in Cool East, is an ancient anchoritic enclosure with remains of three clocháns and of three small rectangular structures; also the overgrown remains of an ancient tomb and a cross-inscribed ogham stone. The graves here are arranged radially about the pillarstone. S. of the road, in Cool 'village', is another ogham stone.

4½ m. SW., in Coarhabeg, are Tobar Ula Bhréanainn (a holy well dedicated to St Brendan) and three rude stone crosses.

7 m. SW. is Bray Head; the cliffs rise to 800 ft. On the S. slope are remains of five clocháns; the site commands lovely views.

¾ m. NW. is the little island, Beginish. It preserves an ancient system of small fields and remains of eight scattered small houses, two of which (Nat. Mons.) have been dated to the period 1100–1200. A stone with a Runic inscription and an incised cross had been appropriated for use as a door-lintel in one house. The Runic inscription – the fifth found in Ireland – reads: LIR. RISTI. STIN. THINA [MUNUIKL?]. RISTI. [RUN] ('Lir erected this stone; M ... carved the runes'). Close to Beginish on the E. (accessible on foot at very low tide) is tiny Church Island. Remains of a cashel, of an oratory of Gallarus (*see pp. 61–2*) type, and of clocháns (Nat. Mons.), show that it was the site of a diminutive anchoritic settlement. A fine early cross-pillar found here (now in the Public Museum, Cork) has an ogham inscription imposed on the incised cross.

VENTRY, Co. Kerry (Map 5, B3), is a small village 6 m. WSW. of Dingle, 4½ m. SE. of Ballyferriter, and 5 m. E. of Dunquin. It takes its name from the lovely sandy beach called Fionn Traigh, setting of the early Fionn mac Cumhail tale, *The Battle of Ventry* (*Cath Fionntrágha*). The countryside thereabouts is almost embarrassingly rich in ancient remains, of which only a very limited selection can be mentioned here.

½ m. NE., on Caherard Hill, is Leaba an Fhir Mhuimhnigh (Labbanirweeny), a wedge-tomb.

1 m. NNE., at the ancient church site of Kilcolman (Nat. Mon.), Maumanorig, is a rock with ogham inscription and incised cross. Nearby is St Brendan's Well, where 'stations' are made. 1 m. W., in Rahinnane, are ruins of a late castle (Nat. Mon.) which uses a ringfort (with souterrain) as bawn.

To the W. of Ventry Harbour rises Sliabh an Iolair, alias Mount Eagle (1,695 ft). The lower slopes are strewn with the wreckage of the past. Some 60 years ago a survey of these townlands recorded two promontory forts, 22 ringforts, 414 clocháns, 12 stone crosses, 18 pillarstones (two with ogham inscriptions), 19 souterrains, and 29 miscellaneous structures and enclosures. Since then many have been cleared away by farmers, local authorities, and other vandals. The more important monuments are listed below, townland by townland.

3¼ m. SW. of Ventry is the ancient burial ground of Kilvickadownig. In it are a cross-slab and remains of a ringfort-type enclosure. Inside the latter are remains of a clochán. In the next field to the S. is Leac na Rae, a large stone with a cross inscribed in a spiral-ended 'omega'. – ¼ m. S. of Kilvickadowning 'village' is a good univallate ringfort. 600 yds WSW., in Páirc na Croise, is a heap of stones with a small stone cross. 500 yds WNW. of Páirc na Croise is Fahan 'village'. Bóthairín na Maoilinne leads NNW. up the slope. NE. of the end of this bohereen, in Kilvickadownig, is Cathair na Maoilinne, remains of an oval enclosure with the dilapidated ruins of diminutive clocháns. Some 700 yds NW. is interesting Clochán an Ardáin (1,000 ft), a circular enclosure with three clocháns, the largest of which had a lintelled entrance passage. – ¼ m. S. of Fahan 'village' is a fine promontory fort, Dún Beag (Nat. Mon.). It has quadrivallate earthworks in front of the main, dry-masonry, rampart. The latter is terraced, and has guardrooms flanking the entrance. A souterrain passes under this rampart and the path through the outer defences. Inside the fort are remains of a large clochán, for which excavations in 1977 suggested a date between the 8th and 11th c. (The seaward edges of the fort have been greatly eroded by the sea, and the inturned ends of the stone rampart are by the Board of Works, which did much unrecorded restoration there.) – ¾ m. WSW. of Fahan 'village', in Glanfahan, is Caher Conor (Nat. Mon.), a ruined stone ringfort with clocháns (secondary?), wall-chamber, souterrain, etc. Some 400 yds NNW. is a double clochán with remains of a forecourt. ¼ m. W. of Caher Conor is Cathair na Mairtíneach (Nat. Mon.), an interesting stone ring-fort with 'gate-lodge', clocháns (secondary?), etc. Some 600 yds WNW. of this fort is Glanfahan 'village'. 200 yds N. is Clochán Ais, a four-chamber clochán with open forecourt. 250 yds W. is Cathair Bán, a clochán complex. – 600 yds SSW. of Glanfahan 'village' is Caher Murphy (Nat. Mon.), a unique stone ringfort, unfortunately much restored. In it is a five-chamber clochán complex; in the second-largest (or S.) chamber is the entrance to a souterrain. A pillarstone, found here in the last c., is now in the National Museum. Some 400 yds W. is Cathair Sayers (Nat. Mon.), a three-chamber clochán with external chamber flanking the entrance. In the main chamber is the entrance to a souterrain. A short distance NE. is An Clochán Mór, a large double clochán. 170 yds NW. of Cathair an dá Dhorus is Clochán Sileóid, alias Clochán Sgológa (Nat. Mon.), a quadruple clochán.

VIRGINIA, Co. Cavan (Map 2, E7), a market village – full of flowers – on the Kells (11 m.)–Ballyjamesduff (6 m.) road, stands on the N. shore of lovely Lough Ramor. It dates from the Plantation of Ulster and is called after Elizabeth I, the 'Virgin Queen'.

1½ m. NE. is the site of Cuilcagh House, home of the Rev. Thomas Sheridan (1687–1738), schoolmaster, friend of Swift, and author of a charming translation of Persius. He was father of Thomas Sheridan (1719–88), author, lexicographer, actor, manager of Smock Alley Theatre, Dublin, and grandfather of Richard Brinsley Sheridan (1751–1816), the playwright. Swift wrote *Gulliver's Travels* at Cuilcagh House, 1726.

2½ m. ESE., in Cloughballybeg, is St Kilian's Well, where, traditionally, St Kilian was born *c.* 640. The saint went on a mission to Franconia, but was martyred in 689 for meddling in the marital affairs of the local duke, Gozbert. His tomb in

Wiirzburg became a famous centre of pilgrimage in the Middle Ages. – 2 m. E., the church dedicated to St Kilian, in Mullagh, has a tabernacle and crucifix by Benedict Tutty.

W

WARRENPOINT, Co. Down (Map 2, J5), is a seaside resort very beautifully situated on the N. shore of Carlingford Lough, between Newry (6 m.) and Rostrevor (3 m.). The Catholic church has a three-light window (*The Annunciation*, *Christ the King*, *The Ascension*) by Michael Healy (1928).

2 m. NW., on the lough, is very attractively maintained Narrow Water Castle (tower and small bawn, Hist. Mon.), built by one of the Magennises of Iveagh *c.* 1560.

WATERFORD, Co. Waterford (Map 4, I5) on the tideway of the Suir is the regional capital of the south-east. Meat-processing, glass-making, brewing and ironfounding are the traditional manufacturing industries. Today the city also makes pharmaceuticals, optical products, electronics and aerospace components. It is 14 m. SW. of New Ross, 17 m SE. of Carrick-on-Suir and 29 m. NE. of Dungarvan. It is the cathedral town of the Diocese of Waterford and Lismore and of the Church of Ireland dioceses of Cashel, Waterford and Lismore.

Like several other Irish seaports, it traces its origin to the Vikings, whose fleets appeared in the harbour in the early 10th c. and who made a settlement there about this time. The English name of the city preserves the Norse name of the harbour, Vethrafjorthr (the ford of Father Odin). The Irish name is Port Láirge. By the end of the 11th c. the Scandinavians had become Christians, but rejecting the authority of the Irish See of Lismore they had established their own diocese. Their first bishop was Malchus OhAinmire, an Irish Benedictine of Winchester, whom they had consecrated in 1096 at Canterbury with the approval of High-King Muirchertach O Brien. Earlier, in 1050, they had built the Christ Church as the Cathedral Church of their new diocese in what is now Cathedral Square.

On 25 August 1170 Waterford was taken by Strongbow and Raymond le Gros, the leaders of the Norman invasion. Strongbow, Earl of Pembroke, was married to Aoife, daughter of Diarmuit Mac Murrough, King of Leinster in Christ Church Cathedral. In 1171 Henry II, King of England declared Waterford a Royal City and throughout the Middle Ages it remained inflexibly loyal to the English Crown. In 1487 the city withstood a six-week siege by the supporters of Lambert Simnel, and in 1495 the citizens were so enraged with Perkin Warbeck, another pretender to the throne, that they repulsed his forces for 12 days, sank most of his ships and pursued him to Cornwall. Henry VII promptly rewarded Waterford with the motto *Urbs Intacta Manet Waterfordia.*

Waterford had by this period become one of the chief ports in the country. Subsequently, however, the prosperity of the city declined, largely as a result of the adherence of its citizens to the Roman Catholic faith during the Reformation era. During the period of the Confederation of Kilkenny, Waterford was one of the Catholic strongholds and on 24 November 1649 Cromwell ranged his forces against its walls.

The city was ably defended by Ulster troops under Lieut. Gerald OFarrell and after eight days Cromwell withdrew, having made no impression on the defences. He returned on 29 May 1650, but the city held out until 10 August when it was surrendered to Cromwell's son-in-law, General Ireton, on honourable terms. In the 16th and 17th c. Waterford produced a remarkable group of gifted men who played significant roles in the Catholic struggle for survival. Among them were Father Luke Wadding (1588–1657), Franciscan scholar and historian, professor of theology at Salamanca and agent of the Confederate Catholics at the papal court; Michael Wadding, alias Miguel Godinez (1591–1644), Jesuit theologian and missionary to Mexico; Peter Lombard (1554–1625), Franciscan professor of philosophy and theology at Louvain, member of the celebrated papal *Congregatio de Auxiliis,* and Archbishop of Armagh.

Other natives of Waterford include the Rev. Francis Hearn (d. 1801), Professor of Rhetoric at Louvain and 'saviour of the Flemish language'; Thomas Francis Meagher (1823–67), Young Ireland leader who was condemned to death in 1848 and escaped from Van Diemens Land to America where he fought with distinction at Fort Sumter and Fredericksburg and became Governor of Montana; Dorothea Jordan (1762–1816), actress; Charles Kean (1811–68), actor; William Vincent Wallace (1813–68), composer of *Maritana, Lurline*, etc; and Robert West (d. 1770), artist.

In the 18th c. Waterford was one of the leading centres of the famous Irish glass industry and its products made at that time are largely sought after by connoisseurs. The industry was revived in 1951 and Waterford now has the largest crystal factory of its kind in the world.

The major feature of Waterford is the great quay which stretches for 1 m. E. of Edmund Ignatius Rice Bridge. Edmund Rice (1762–1844, *see p. 88*), a native of Callan, was a wealthy merchant in Waterford who devoted his life to the cause of the education of the poor and founded the Irish Christian Brothers. The bridge which bears his name in Waterford was opened in 1984.

Grey Friars (Nat. Mon.) was founded for the Franciscans *c.* 1240 by Sir Hugh Purcell. The remains comprise nave, chancel, tower and Lady Chapel of the austere Friary Church. At the Dissolution the friary passed to the Crown and in 1545 was sold to Patrick Walsh, who founded the Holy Ghost Hospital. In 1695 the Corporation assigned the Choir to Huguenot refugees to serve as their parish church: hence the popular name of the ruin 'The French Church'.

At the junction of the Quay and the Mall is Reginald's Tower, allegedly built by Reginald the Dane in 1003 and reputed to be the oldest tower of mortared stone in Europe. The tower marks the NE. angle of both the Norse and medieval towns and was the strongpoint in the city's ancient defences. It houses a fine civic museum where Waterford's remarkable collection of charters, and the ceremonial swords of King John and Henry VIII, and a unique Charter Roll of Richard II are displayed.

The City Hall, incorporating the beautiful Victorian Theatre Royal in the same building, was erected as Assembly Rooms in 1788 to the design of John Roberts (1749–94). John Roberts was a native of Waterford and was great-grandfather of the Victorian Field Marshal Lord Roberts of Waterford and Kandahar. The Luke Wadding centenary statue (1958) on the Mall is by Gabriel Hayes. The Classical Court House (1849) in the People's Park is by Sir Richard Morrison. It occupies the site of St Catherine's Priory of Canons Regular of St Augustine. It takes the place of a court house in Broad St by James Gandon.

Cathedral Square is dominated by the Protestant Cathedral, Christ Church, built in 1770–9 to the design of John Roberts. It was partly destroyed by fire in 1815 and restored in 1818. In 1891 it was re-edified under the direction of Sir Thomas Drew. It occupies the site of the old Viking Cathedral and its medieval enlargement which survived until 1770. Of the medieval Cathedral only a small crypt and some miscellaneous fragments survive. The medieval monuments in the Cathedral include a tomb of James Rice, of *c.* 1490, and an early-16th c. tomb with the effigy of an armoured knight.

Near the Cathedral is the former Bishop's Palace, now housing the City Engineering Department. This was the former residence of the Protestant Bishops and was later the Bishop Foy school. This fine building has been attributed to Richard Cassels, but is probably by John Roberts. Near the Cathedral is also the former Deanery, now a Waterford Corporation office and restored. Under the Deanery garden is a medieval crypt. West of the Cathedral are the graveyard and Clergymen's Widows Apartments (1902), now unfortunately coated with cement.

In Lady Lane the Franciscan Friary (1834) occupies the site of the medieval St Mary's Chapel. The water font (1626) inside has the arms of White and Walsh and comes from the 'French Church'. A short distance away is the former St Olave's Church, now a youth centre. This was formerly a Viking foundation and the west wall of the original building survives. Its 18th c. furnishings were sadly dispersed in the 1970s. Excavations nearby in 1987 uncovered traces of the medieval Church of St Peter, with the earliest known example of an apse in Ireland.

Near Barronstrand St is Blackfriars, called after St Saviour's Dominican Priory founded in 1226. The church tower and other fragments survive. North of Blackfriars, on the east side of Barronstrand St, is the Catholic Cathedral of the Holy Trinity. It was erected in Penal Times (1793–6): the site was granted by the Corporation, at that time a Protestant body. The building was one of the last works of John Roberts. The Cathedral has some interesting 17th and 18th c. altar plate, including a chalice which belonged to Seathrún Céitinn (*see p. 87*) and also a throne monstrance of 1729.

At the south end of Barronstrand St is Broad St and nearby George's St. The Chamber of Commerce and Harbour Commissioners occupy the charming town house (noteworthy staircase, stucco work and oval dome light) of the Morris family of Rosduff. It was built *c.* 1795 by John Roberts. St Patrick's Church, off George's St, is the oldest church in Waterford. It originated as a Penal Chapel in a corn store in Jenkins Lane. In Bridge St is situated St Saviour's Church (Dominican) by Goldie, Child and Goldie of London (1874–8). A small oak figure of Our Lady (17th c. Seville school) which is preserved there is thought to have reached Waterford during the reign of the Stuarts.

The Waterford city walls have been restored by the city's Corporation. Waterford claims to have more of its ancient walls extant than any other city in Ireland (except Derry). A fine tower may be seen in St Stephen's school grounds in Patrick St. Other towers may be seen at Railway Square, Jenkins Lane and Castle St. In Barrack St is Mount Sion Christian Brothers Schools and Chapel of Edmund Ignatius Rice, the latter with a stone crucifix (1980) by Ken Thompson (b. 1936).

In Manor St are the remains of the Benedictine priory of St John, once a dependency of Bath Abbey, England. Further along the Cork Road is the former Holy Ghost Hospital which was transferred there from the 'French Church', along with some medieval statuary. The building retains the handsome façade which dates from 1888.

John St ends at John's Bridge, across the St John's River. On John's Hill is the former Infirmary (by John Roberts, 1780). This was the former Leper Hospital, the lineal descendant of the medieval Leper Hospital of St Stephen which stood in Stephen Street. St John's College, on John's Hill (1867–71), by Goldie, is nearby. On Passage Rd is the splendid Newtown School (Quakers). The nucleus is the Georgian residence of the Wyse family. Sir Thomas Wyse (1791–1862) married Letitia Bonaparte, niece of Napoleon.

Churches built in Waterford city during the recent past include St Saviour's, Ballybeg (Dominican), by O Dwyer & Co.; St Paul's, Lisduggan, by Chris Harvey Jacob, and Sacred Heart Church, The Folly and St Joseph's and Benildus, Lower Newtown, by Don O Neil Flanagan.

3½ m. NE. is Slieveroe, Co. Kilkenny. The Catholic church is a Gothic-Revival building by Ashlin and Coleman. 1 m. N., in Smiths-Nicholastown, are the Three Friars, a row of three pillarstones. In nearby Attateemore was the birthplace of the great Irish scholar, John O Donovan (1806–66; *see* Dunkitt, *below*).

6 m. NE. are the remains of Kilcolumb (Co. Kilkenny) Church. 50 yds N. is Cloch Cholaim (Colm's Stone), a boulder with bullauns locally believed to be the imprint of the saint's head and knees. Persons subject to headaches resort to the bullauns.

2⅓ m. S., in Ballindud, is a collapsed portal-tomb.

4 m. SSW, in Knockeen, is a magnificent portal-tomb (Nat. Mon.)

5½ m. SW., in Gaulstown, is a splendid portal-tomb (Nat. Mon.). In adjoining Pembrokestown is a motte. 2½ m. ESE. of Gaulstown is Munmahoge (*see p. 295*). 1 m. S. of Pembrokestown are Ballymoat 'Moat' and pillarstone.

10½ m. SW., via the Bunmahon road, in Savagetown, is a ruined portal-tomb.

5 m. WSW., by the Suir, are Mount Congreve House and demesne. The house dates from the early-18th c. The dining-room, originally the entrance hall, is decorated with chiaroscuro paintings on canvas pasted to the walls. Some of these may have come from Whitfieldcourt (Whitfieldstown), a small Georgian house 2m. SW. The Mount Congreve gardens and woodlands are open to the public only on demand (enquire at tourist office). NW. of Mount Congreve House are the remains of Kilmeedan Castle, a Power stronghold taken by Cromwell in 1649.

2½ m. WNW., on the N. bank of the Suir in Granny, Co. Kilkenny, are the ruins (Nat. Mon.) of a le Poer castle granted to James, Earl of Ormond, in 1375 following the attainder of Eustace fitz Arnold le Poer. It had two wards, a 13th c.(?) curtain with four circular flankers, and a later square tower to which a 16th c. hall was attached; one wall (with small oriel window) of the hall survives. In 1650 the Ormondist garrison surrendered to the Cromwellian regicide, Col. Axtel. 3 m. SW. is the five-storey tower of Curluddy castle, a Grant stronghold. 2 m. WNW. of Curluddy is the well-preserved motte-and-bailey of Portnascully, erected probably by Strongbow's follower, Milo, son of Bishop David of St David's in Wales.

3½ m. NW. is Dunkitt (Co. Kilkenny), a village which takes its name from a nearby ringfort, the Ráth of Dunkitt. There are remains of a medieval nave-and-chancel church, at the S. side of which are the graves of the father (Edmund O Donovan 'de Ata-Temoria', d. 1817) and other ancestors of the great Irish scholar John O Donovan (*see* Attateemore, *above*).

WATERVILLE, Co. Kerry (Map 5, C6), is a beautifully situated angling resort 8¾ m. NNW. of Caherdaniel and 11 m. S. of Cahersiveen.

2 m. NNE., in Termons, to the W. of Termons Lake, are remains of a small, ancient, anchoritic enclosure with a cross-slab (incised crosses on both faces) and the ruins of a clochán. ½ m. ENE. is a tall pillarstone, ¾ m. NE. of which, in Caherbarnagh, are remains of another anchoritic enclosure, with an early cross-slab and a ruinous clochán. ¼ m. S. of this is St Fíonán's Well. ¾ m. E. of the well, in Dromkeare, is an unenclosed, ancient burial ground; there is a cross-inscribed ogham stone here. ¾ m. ENE. of Dromkeare bridge, on the S. side of the road, is Cahersavane, a stone ringfort (with rampart terrace) which gives its name to the townland.

1 m. NE., by the lakeshore in Beenbane, is Lisoven, a 'horse-shoe' ringfort with a system of souterrains; outside it is a ruined clochán (Nat. Mons.). The fields to the N. are littered with ancient remains.

2 m. ENE., in Lough Currane, is Church Island. The remains (Nat. Mons.) of St Fíonán's Church, of three clocháns (one called St Fíonáns Cell), and of an enclosing cashel, represent a monastery allegedly founded by St Malachy after his expulsion from BANGOR in 1127. The church is a small, nave-and-chancel, Romanesque building; doorway very much restored. In the graveyard are two pillarstones and eight early gravestones and cross-slabs, two with inscriptions.

¾ m. ESE., in Eightercua, is the ancient church site, Templenakilla. NNE. fourth tall pillarstones stand close together on the perimeter of a small ruined fort. – 5 m. E., in Inchfarrannagleragh Glebe (S. of the road and SE. of Iskanagahiny Lough), is a small, unenclosed burial ground; there is an early cross-pillar there.

2¾ m. further S., in Loher (60 yds W. of the old road to Darrynane), is Kildreenagh, an oval enclosure with remains of a small oratory (on a platform) and of a clochán. S. of the oratory are three early cross-pillars; the W. pillar has A and Ω under the arms of the cross. There are several stone ringforts thereabouts; one excavated in the 1980s showed a series of round houses beneath rectangular ones.

WELLINGTON BRIDGE, Co. Wexford (Map 4, K5), is a village on the Bridgetown (11 m.)–New Ross (17 m.) road. It is named after the Iron Duke (*see p. 296*). 1¼ m. W. is Nelson's Bridge. – 1½ m. SE., at the head of Bannow Bay, is the site of the medieval town of Clonmines. There are remains of four castles and three churches. The latter include St Nicholas's Church – a unique, castle-like parish church – and the choir, S. aisle, and tower (inserted) of a late-14th c. friary of Austin Hermits.

3½ m. SE., in Coolehull, is an unusual, small, late-16th c. castle.

5 m. SSW. (on the E. side of Bannow Bay) are Bannow Island and Bannow Strand. About 1 May 1169, the first Norman invaders, Robert FitzStephen, Hervey de Montmorency, uncle of Strongbow, and Maurice de Prendergast, together with an army of more than 400 armed men, landed on Bannow Island, at that time still cut off from the mainland. When later joined by Díarmait Mac Murrough, King of Leinster and the Danes, with 500 men, they combined forces and marched to attack Wexford. On the mainland are the ruins of St Mary's, a simple, 13th c., nave-and-chancel church with later N. and S. porches. This and the remains of a small chapel are all that survive of the 'lost city of Bannow', the first Anglo-Norman corporate town in Ireland. Though subsequently covered by sand, it continued to return two members to the Dublin House of Commons until the Union, though all they had to represent in the end were the church and a chimney.

3 m. WNW. is Ballycullane. The Church of the Holy Spirit, St Leonard's (1971) is by Wilfrid Cantwell, with furnishings by Benedict Tutty, O.S.B.

WESTPORT, Co. Mayo (Map 7, E6), is a market town and small seaport on the Ballinrobe (20 m.)–Newport (8 m.) road, at the head of Westport Bay (SE. corner of Clew Bay).

It is a well laid-out little town (planned by James Wyatt *c.* 1780), with a pleasant tree-lined Mall. The Catholic church has *opus sectile* Stations of the Cross by Hubert McGoldrick (*c.* 1930). The stained glass windows in the sanctuary end of the church are by Patrick Pye (1979), *Madonna* and *Child Enthroned* and *Christ Enthroned*. The Protestant church (*c.* 1880) is a good period piece with *art nouveau* carvings and other noteworthy details; 'George A. Bermingham' (Canon J. Hannay, 1865–1952), the novelist, was rector there for many years.

Adjoining the town (entrance from the Quay) is the mutilated demesne (open to the public, with zoo and recreation park) of Westport House (Lord Altamont), with ornamental waters achieved by controlling the tides of an inlet of Clew Bay. The house (*c.* 1730) is by Richard Cassels; 1778 additions and alterations by James Wyatt (windows mutilated). Among its former treasures were the ornamental pillars from the so-called Treasury of Atreus, alias the Tomb of Agamemnon, at Mycenae. They had been brought home by the 2nd Marquess (1788–1845) and erected at a side-door of Westport House. Their fate remained a mystery to archaeologists until 1910, when they were sold to the British Museum.

2½ m. ENE., close to the Castlebar road and commanding a very fine view, is Sheeaun, a hill-top (382 ft) tumulus. Daniel O Connell's great meeting here still lives in folk memory. 2 m. SE., in Dooncastle, are the ruins of a castle of the Mac Philbin branch of the Mac William *Iochtair* Burkes. 3 m. SE. of this, in Aille, are remains of Mac Philbin's Castle. Less than ½ m. S. Tóchar Phádraig – an ancient pilgrims' road to Croagh Patrick (*see below*) via Aghagower, 1½ m. W. (*see below*) – led W. from the Aille River.

4½ m. SE. on Tóchar Phádraig (*above*), is Aghagower. St Patrick is said to have founded a church here, which he confided to Bishop Seanach. Later there was a monastery here. There are ruins (Nat. Mons.) of a 12th(?) c. Round Tower and of a 12th/13th c. church with 15th c. features. 'Stations' are made to the various enclosures outside the churchyard on Crom Dubh's (Garland) Friday and Sunday; *see* Croagh Patrick pilgrimage (*below*). Tóchar Phádraig continued W. of Aghagower via Lahardaun ford to Cloghan bridge (1¾ m. SW.), thence through Lankill, Lanmore, and Boheh to the Owenwee and so to Croagh Patrick. ¾ m. SW. of Cloghan bridge, in Lankill, is a 7 ft pillarstone (Nat. Mon.) with incised cross and concentric circles (fake?). Nearby is an ancient churchyard with Toberbrendan, 'Brendan's Well'.

2¾ m. SSW., in Knappamanagh, is an ancient circular churchyard. A small stone here has an incised anthropomorphic cross design and other devices.

4½ m. SSW., in Boheh, are St Patrick's Chair and Killeen. St Patrick's Chair is a heap of stones with concentric-circle cup marks, etc. The killeen is an ancient churchyard. Tóchar Phádraig continues W. past them to the Owenwee.

5½ m. WSW., to the N. of the Louisburgh road, are the remains of Murrisk 'Abbey' (Nat. Mon.), a small Augustinian friary founded in 1457 by Tadhg O Malley, 'Captain of his nation.'

6 m. WSW. is Croagh Patrick (2,510 ft), Ireland's Holy Mountain. A beautiful quartzite ridge and cone, it rises steeply from the S. shore of Clew Bay, and in clear weather offers magnificent views. St Patrick is said to have fasted on the mountain top for 40 days, and every year thousands of devout pilgrims climb to the summit (some before dawn) on Domhnach Chrom Dubh, 'Crom Dubh's Sunday' (last Sunday of July; down to the early part of the last c. the pilgrimage took place on Aoine Chrom Dubh, *i.e.* the preceding Friday). The ascent is begun in Murrisk; the final climb is over the bare scree of the upper cone, or *crúach* proper. At the base of the upper cone is the first pilgrim's 'station', Leacht Mhionnáin, 'St Benignus's Monument', where seven *deiseal* praying circuits are made. The climb continues W. up Casán Phádraig 'Patrick's Path' to the summit, where the pilgrims kneel and pray. At the last traces of Teampall Phádraig, 'Patrick's Church', further prayers are said, followed by 15 *deiseal* circuits (over 2 m.) of a circular path around the summit. The next 'station' is Leaba Phádraig, 'Patrick's Bed', now a mere heap of stones NE. of the modern chapel. Prayers are said inside it, after which seven *deiseal* circuits are made. The last 'station' is Roilig Mhuire, 'St Mary's Cemetery', alias An Garraí Mór, 'the Great Garden', with its three mounds of stones, ½ m. WSW.; seven circuits are made at each mound, followed by seven circuits around the *roilig*.

WEXFORD, Co. Wexford (Map 4, L4), the county town, is attractively situated at the mouth of the Slaney in Wexford Harbour, 24 m. E. of New Ross and 11 m. NW. of Rosslare. Once a busy seaport, it is today a manufacturing and marketing centre.

Preceded by a Gaelic settlement, Loch Garman, the Viking town (Weissfjord) owes its origin to the Norse, who founded a trading settlement there in the 9th or early-10th c. In May 1169 it was captured by Díarmait, King of Leinster, and his Norman allies, the first town in Ireland to fall into Norman hands. Díarmait promptly granted it to Robert FitzStephen and Maurice FitzGerald. On Díarmait's death in 1171 the townsfolk burned the town, and FitzStephen fled to Carrick-on-Slaney. In 1172 Henry II reserved the town to the Crown, but subsequently assigned it to Strongbow. In the 14th c., having outgrown its old defences, the town was enclosed by a new towered wall with five gates. In 1649, Cromwell massacred the inhabitants in breach of the agreed terms of surrender. In 1798 the town was stormed and held for nearly a month by the Insurgents.

Wexford is a town of quaint, but inconveniently narrow, streets. Of the town wall, however, only some fragments and the West Gate remain (near the principal railway station).

Near the West Gate are the ruins (Nat. Mon.) of the 13th c. church of the Augustinian Priory of SS Peter and Paul, commonly called Selskar (*i.e.* Holy Sepulchre) Abbey. The priory – not far from where Henry II of England spent the Lent of 1172 doing penance for the murder of St Thomas à Becket – was founded by the local branch of the Flemish Roches. At the W. side of the churchyard is a fragment of the town wall (Nat. Mon.).

At the intersection of Abbey St, Main St, and Quay St is the Bull Ring, scene of one of the worst episodes of the Cromwellian massacre. Its name recalls the once popular pastime of bull-baiting. The 1798 memorial (1905) is by Oliver Sheppard, R.H.A.

On the Crescent (Quay), east of Main St, is a 1956 statue (by the American sculptor Wheeler Williams) of Commodore John Barry (1745–1803), 'father' of the United States Navy. Barry was a native of Ballysampson (*see p. 276*).

The interesting small early-19th c. theatre in High St (extended in 1987) has been restored, and is now the focus of the famous annual Wexford Opera Festival of music, drama, and the arts (a fortnight in late October/early November).

In the Franciscan church, School St, are the enshrined remains of the Roman boy-martyr, St Adjutor. The church occupies the site of a Franciscan friary founded in 1242 by Strongbow's grandson, William the Marshall II, replaced in the 17th c. by a Franciscan Mass house which served as the parish church from 1690 to 1858.

At the S. end of McSweeny St–Patrick St are the remains of St Patrick's Church, a double-nave edifice. A short distance SE., between Main St and Bride St, is a fragment of St Mary's Church.

The Church of the Assumption, Bride St (two-light 1919 window by Harry Clarke: *Our Lady, SS Aiden and Breen*), and the Church of the Immaculate Conception, Rowe St, are called the Twin Churches because built at the same time (1851–8) to the designs of the same architect, Robert Pierce, pupil and assistant of Augustus Welby Pugin. Pugin himself designed the excellent Chapel of St Peter's College, Summerhill Rd, and the pretty, suburban church of St Alphonsus, Barntown, on the New Ross road.

Wexford was the birthplace or the home of several famous or interesting persons. Jane Frances Elgee, Oscar Wilde's eccentric mother, better known as Speranza, was born (1826) at the old rectory in South Main St. Sir Robert Mac Clure (1807–73), who discovered the North-West Passage (1851), was born in North Main St in the house next to White's Hotel. The mother of Thomas Moore, the songwriter, lived in the Cornmarket.

Outside the town, on the New Ross road, a copy of Pompey's Pillar at Alexandria commemorates the British conquest of Egypt. It was erected in 1841 by Gen. Brown-Clayton, who took part in the campaign.

4 m. NE., in Wexford Harbour, is Beggerin Island, now joined to the mainland as a result of reclamation works. The name is a corruption of Beag Éire, Little Éire. There was an early monastic church here, attributed to a 'pre-Patrician' Bishop Ibar. Despite the Viking settlement nearby, it survived, and in 1182 was granted by the Wexford Roches to St Nicholas's Monastery, Exeter. The remains include the ruins of a small church and some early gravestones. In 1171 the Wexford folk took refuge on the island, bringing with them FitzStephen and their other Norman prisoners, and forced Strongbow to withdraw by threatening to behead the captives.

6 m. NE. is the quiet little family resort of Curracloe with a 6 m. sandy beach.

3¾ m. S. are the interesting tower and bawn of Killiane Castle. 3 m. SW. (½ m. NW. of the Kilmore road) is the picturesque Rosseter Castle of Rathmacknee (Nat. Mon.), one of the best preserved of the many 15th c. castles of S. Wexford. The remains comprise a well-preserved tower and a five-sided bawn.

4½ m. SW. is Johnstown Castle, an excellent 19th c. Gothic mansion which incorporates the remains of an Esmonde castle. The castle was presented to the nation in 1944, and it is now a research station of the Agricultural Institute. There is a well-presented Agricultural Museum there. The grounds and gardens are open to the public.

3 m. W. is Three Rock Hill, site of one of the principal insurgent encampments in 1798.

2½ m. WNW. is Ferrycarrig, where the Slaney forces its way through a narrow gorge. On a spur of rock on the N. bank is the tall tower of a 15th c. castle built by the Roches to defend the river crossing. The tower on the S. bank commemorates the Wexfordmen who fell in the Crimean War. The high earthen bank and broad ditch nearby, which cut off a level space on the riverside rock, almost certainly represent FitzStephen's fort of Carrick on Slaney, that 'first Norman castle in Ireland', in which FitzStephen took refuge when forced to abandon Wexford on the death of Díarmait, King of Leinster, in 1171. On the W. side of the Slaney is the Ferrycarrig Heritage Park, with a number of reconstructed examples of Irish buildings from the Stone Age to the 13th c.

WHITEABBEY, Co. Antrim (Map 1, K7), lies on the N. outskirts of Belfast on the loughshore road to Carrickfergus (4½ m).

1 m. N., at Jordanstown, St. Patrick's Church (1866, by W.H. Lynn) is the earliest 'whole-hearted and scholarly' essay in the Celtic-Revival style, complete with round tower. Nearby, the University of Ulster, Jordanstown campus (1970, by Building Design Partnership), is a well-planned if distinctly unattractive building in extensive grounds.

WHITEHEAD, Co. Antrim (Map 1, L6), is a seaside resort on the N. shore of Belfast Lough, 5 m. NE. of Carrickfergus and 9 m. SE. of Larne. It is the most convenient place for exploring ISLAND MAGEE. The poetess Amanda McKittrick Ross (1860–1939) was the wife of the station master there.

2½ m. NW., in Ballycarry village, are the ruins of Templecorran Church, with a memorial (*c.* 1720) to the Rev. Edward Brice, the first Presbyterian minister ordained (1613) to preach in Ireland. In the churchyard is the grave of James Orr (1770–1816), 'Bard of Ballycarry', and a member of the United Irishmen. ½ m. N. is Red Hall, a Clannaboy O Neill castle which passed in 1609 to Sir William Edmonston, who remodelled it. The interior has interesting 17th c. stucco ceilings.

WICKLOW, Co. Wicklow (Map 3, L7), county town of the county to which it gives its name, is a small seaport and seaside resort at the mouth of the Vartry, 32 m. SE. of Dublin.

The town takes its English name from a 9th c. Norse settlement (Vikingaló); its Irish name (Cill Mhantáin) from a church founded by St Mantán, reputedly a disciple of St Patrick. Both Palladius and St Patrick are said to have landed at the mouth of the Vartry, only to be driven away by the local ruler.

At the Anglo-Norman conquest the town and district were granted to Maurice FitzGerald, ancestor of the barons of Naas, who remained nominal lords of the place until 1350, when the castle became an English royal fortress. Nevertheless, from *c.* 1430 to 1542 town and castle lay at the mercy of the O Byrnes, who exacted 'Black Rents' from the English townsfolk. In 1542 the O Byrnes indentured with Henry VIII to cease to exact their tributes, but they razed both castle and town in 1580, though losing their power in the area not long afterwards.

The 18th c. Protestant church occupies the site of the medieval parish church of St Patrick. Built into the S. porch are fragments of a 12th c. Romanesque doorway. The *Ascension* window is by Catherine O Brien (1929), and the ship and lifeboat windows by Patrick Pollen. To the N. is the Round Mount, a motte.

In the garden of the parish priest's residence is the Abbey, remnant of a small, poor, Franciscan friary founded, presumably by the Naas FitzGeralds, in the 13th c., and extended or rebuilt by the O Byrnes in the 15th.

In the Market Sq. is a 1798–1867 memorial (statue of the valiant Billy Byrne of Ballymanus); in Fitzwilliam Sq. a monument to Capt. Robert C. Halpin (1836–94) of Wicklow, captain of the *Great Eastern,* which laid the first successful Transatlantic cable in 1866.

On a cliff-promontory E. of the town are the ruins of Black Castle, successor to Maurice FitzGerald's castle of 1178.

4 m. S., by the little Three Mile Water, is Ennisboyne. There was an early ecclesiastical foundation there, which legend associates with St Patrick's landing. At the close of the 6th c. the relics of SS Sylvester and Solinus were brought there.

5½ m. SSW., by the roadside in Castletimon townland, is an ogham stone (Nat. Mon.). 1¼ m. WNW. are the ruins of Dunganstown Castle.

6½ m. S. is Brittas Bay; its lovely 2¼ m. beach backed by sand dunes has been spoiled by modern tourist development.

WOODFORD, Co. Galway (Map 6, J4), is a village at the intersection of the Portumna (9 m.)–Ennis (36 m.) and Loughrea (14 m.)–Mountshannon (10 m.) roads. It was there that

Johnston Castle, Co. Wexford.

Wilfred Scawen Blunt (1840–1922), English author, politician, and champion of the oppressed, was arrested in October 1887, after organizing a Mass Protest Meeting of the tenants on the Clanricarde estates (*see p. 266*). He was imprisoned for two months in Galway and Kilmainham gaols. His *In Vinculis* (1889) describes his experiences.

Y

YOUGHAL, Co. Cork (Map 4, E8), is an interesting old market town, fishing port and seaside resort at the W. side of the Blackwater estuary, 17 m. E. of Midleton, 18 m. S. of Lismore, and 19 m. SW. of Dungarvan.

Nothing is known of the history of Youghal prior to the foundation of a baronial town by the Anglo-Normans in the 13th c. After its foundation by the Anglo-Normans in the 13th c., the town changed ownership several times in the 13th, 14th, and 15th c. Subsequently the town passed to the Earls of Desmond. On 15 November 1579, the Rebel Earl of Desmond sacked and burned the town. At the Plantation of Munster the town was included in the vast grant made to Sir Walter Ralegh. Local 'tradition' notwithstanding, Ralegh spent little time in the place. He neither built nor lived in Ralegh's House (*see below*); nor did he plant the first Irish potatoes in its garden. In December 1602 he sold out to the notorious Richard Boyle, afterwards Earl of Cork (1566–1643). Boyle built a new College House (*see below*) and made it his residence. When Cromwell reached New Ross in November 1649, the English garrison of Youghal went over to the Parliamentarian side, and on 6 December Cromwell laid up his army in winter quarters in the town.

South Abbey St, at the S. end of the old town, preserves the memory of vanished 'South Abbey', the first Franciscan friary in Ireland, founded in 1224 by Maurice FitzGerald, 2nd Baron Offaly.

The Clock Gate, South Main St, is a 1777 replacement (architect, William Meade) of the medieval Iron Gate, between the upper and lower towns. It served as the town gaol until 1837. The Water Gate ('Cromwell's Arch'), nearby in Quay Lane, is an early-19th c. 'restoration'.

On the E. side of North Main St is Tynte's Castle, a much-altered, ruinous, 15th c. tower-house. On the opposite side of the street is the Red House, a brick building with Dutch Renaissance details. It was built (1706–15) for the Uniackes by a Dutch builder named Leuventhen.

Also on the W. side of North Main St, S. of the Post Office, is the much-altered gable of St John's House, a hospital (founded

The Clock Tower, Youghal, Co. Cork.

1360) belonging to the Benedictine priory-hospital of St John the Evangelist, Waterford. Also in North Main St are almshouses for six poor Protestant widows, founded in 1634 by Richard Boyle and re-edified early in the last century.

To the W. of North Main St is St Mary's Church (Protestant), erected about 1250 on the site of an older edifice. Partly wrecked by Desmond's followers in 1579, neglected by Richard Boyle in breach of his covenant, savaged by 18th c. churchwardens, and unhappily 'restored' (1852–4) by a local architect and antiquary, Edward Fitzgerald (1820–93), it remains, for all that, a building of interest. It is a cruciform structure with aisled nave of five bays, aisled N. transept, aisleless S. transept, long chancel, and massive bell-tower at the NW. angle of the N. transept. The ugly candle-snuffer roof, which smothers nave, transepts, and aisles, is the work of Edward Fitzgerald, who swept away the battlemented parapets of the nave walls. Nave, transepts, and tower are basically mid-13th c. work, but the nave walls were considerably modified in the 15th c., probably around 1464, when Thomas, 7th Earl of Desmond, established a college (warden, eight fellows, and eight singing men) to supply the church services. The church has a good 14th/15th c. font and a number of interesting tombs and monuments, including 14th and 15th c. effigies. Of particular interest are the monuments in the S. transept (Cork Transept), founded by Richard Benet and his wife, Ellis Barry, as the chantry of St Saviour. Wrecked by Desmond's men in 1579, it was tardily re-edified by Richard Boyle in 1619. Boyle restored the tomb of the 13th c. founders, and furnished it with the polychrome effigies in 17th c. costume. He also erected the grandiose Renaissance monument (by Edmund Tingham of Chapelizod?; restored 1848) to himself, his wives, his mother, and nine of his children; the effigies are very good. (Another Tingham monument was erected by Boyle in St Patrick's Cathedral, Dublin, *see p. 161.*) The churchyard is partly enclosed by a portion of the town wall (repaired more than once in the 17th and 18th c. and again in the 20th c.). The grave of the well-known writer Claude Cockburn in the graveyard is marked by a good tombstone by Ken Thompson.

E. of the church is New College House, 1781–2, successor of Richard Boyle's house of 1608. The flanking towers are relics of the defences constructed by Boyle, 1641–2; the only other relic of Boyle's house is an elaborate chimney-piece.

NE. of St Mary's Church is Myrtle Grove, alias Sir Walter Ralegh's House, a much-altered Elizabethan house (*not* open to public).

Near the N. end of North Main St are the remnants (Nat. Mon.) of North Abbey, church of a Dominican friary founded in 1268 by Thomas FitzGerald.

2 m. N., at Rinncrew, magnificently sited above the confluence of the Blackwater and Tourig, are the fragmentary remains of a cell of the Knights Hospitaller preceptory of Mourne Abbey, Co. Cork (*see p. 244*). On an island in the Blackwater (causeway approach), are the ruins of Dairinis Augustinian priory. St Máel-Anfaidh ('Molana'), abbot of Lismore, founded an anchoritic settlement there in the 6th/7th c. A charming anecdote is told of the saint in the *Félire* of Oengus the Culdee. 'Máel-Anfaidh, abbot of Dairinis, a cell of Mo-Chuda's Lismore . . . This is the Máel-Anfaidh who one day saw a little bird weeping and lamenting. "O my God", said he, "what has happened to that creature? I swear", said he, "that I will eat no food until it is revealed to me." So abiding there he beheld an angel approaching. "Hail, cleric," said the angel, "let the trouble of this vex you no longer. Mo-Lúa, son of Oche, has died. And the creatures lament him because he never killed any creature, little or big. And men bewail him no more than do the other creatures, including the tiny bird you see."' Fer-dá-chrích (d. 747), Abbot of Dairinis, was one of the leaders of the 8th c. reform movement. At the 12th c. reformation, Dairinis adapted the Rule of the Augustinian Canons Regular. Raymond le Gros is believed to have been a patron of the reformed foundation, and to have been buried there. The remains comprise a ruined church and fragments of the claustral buildings. The church consisted of short, early nave and later (*i.e.* early-13th c.) chancel. The chancel, in Augustinian fashion, is longer than the nave. Opening off the N. side of the chancel is the later, two-storeyed, prior's lodging(?).

1 m. S., at Kilcoran, was the home of Edmund Spenser's wife, Elizabeth Boyle, golden-haired daughter of a kinsman of Richard Boyle's. It was for her that Spenser wrote his *Amoretti* sonnets and *Epithalamium*. After Spenser's death she married Sir Robert Tynte of Ballycrenane.

6 m. WSW. are remnants of the 13th c. circular keep of Inchiquin Castle, *caput* of the Anglo-Norman barony to which it gave its name.

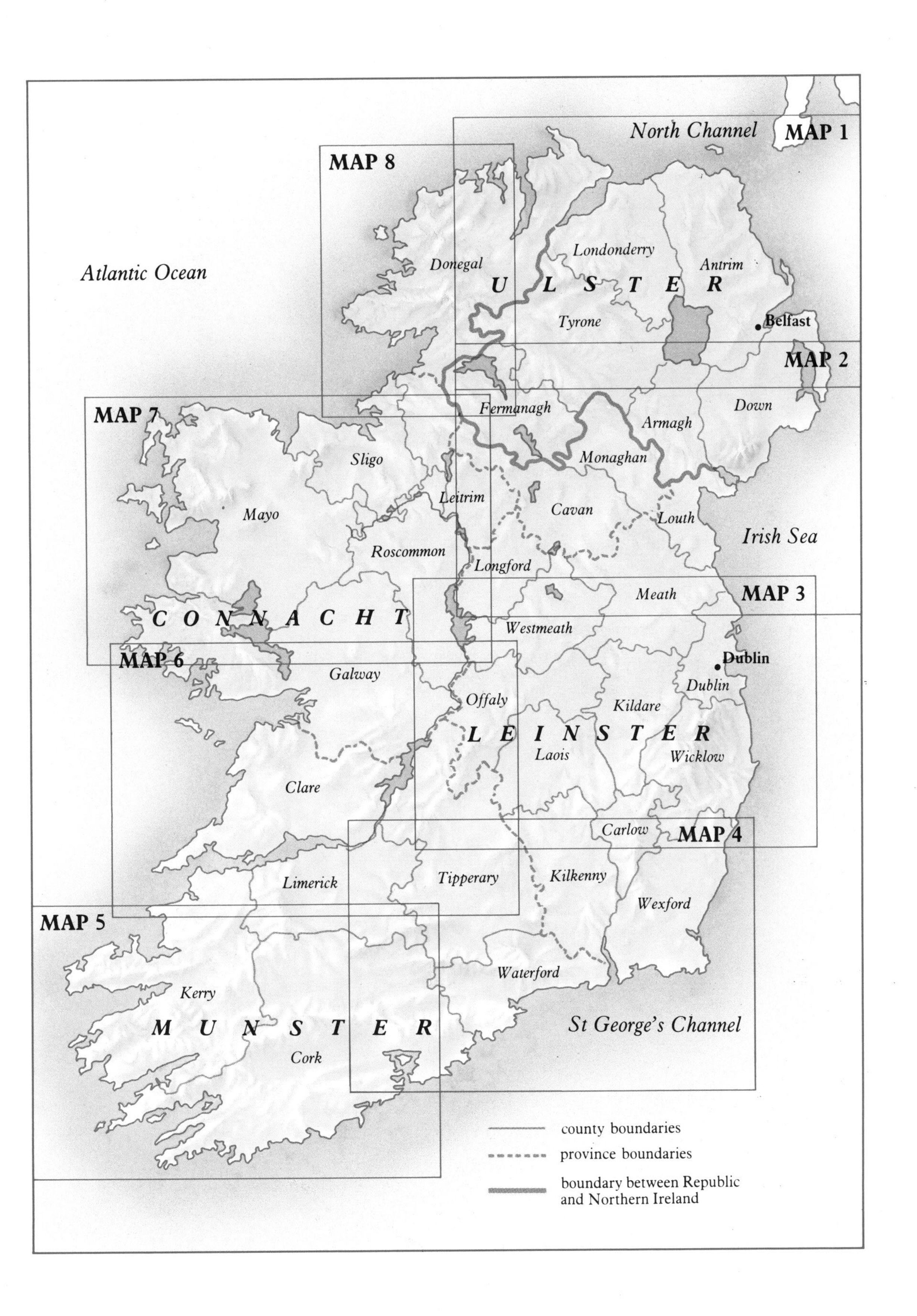
MAP 1
MAP 2
MAP 3
MAP 4
MAP 5
MAP 6
MAP 7
MAP 8
North Channel
Atlantic Ocean
Irish Sea
St George's Channel
U L S T E R
C O N N A C H T
L E I N S T E R
M U N S T E R
Donegal
Londonderry
Antrim
Tyrone
Belfast
Fermanagh
Armagh
Down
Monaghan
Sligo
Leitrim
Cavan
Louth
Mayo
Roscommon
Longford
Meath
Westmeath
Dublin
Dublin
Galway
Offaly
Kildare
Laois
Wicklow
Clare
Carlow
Limerick
Tipperary
Kilkenny
Wexford
Waterford
Kerry
Cork
county boundaries
province boundaries
boundary between Republic and Northern Ireland

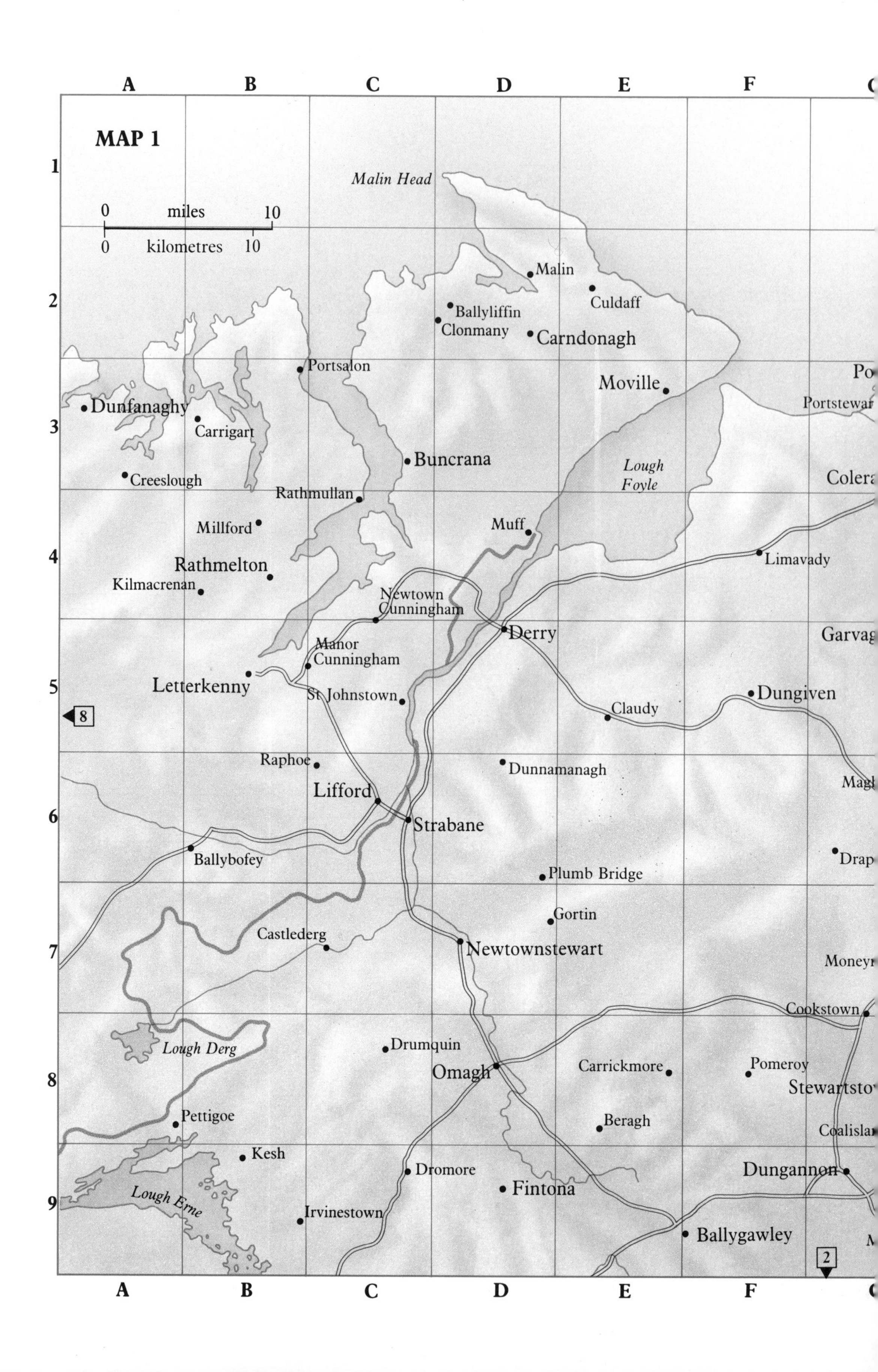
MAP 1
A
B
C
D
E
F
1
2
3
4
5
6
7
8
9
0 miles 10
0 kilometres 10
Malin Head
Malin
Culdaff
Ballyliffin
Clonmany
Carndonagh
Portsalon
Moville
Dunfanaghy
Carrigart
Portstewart
Buncrana
Lough Foyle
Creeslough
Rathmullan
Millford
Muff
Rathmelton
Kilmacrenan
Limavady
Newtown Cunningham
Derry
Manor Cunningham
Letterkenny
St Johnstown
Claudy
Dungiven
8
Raphoe
Dunnamanagh
Lifford
Strabane
Ballybofey
Plumb Bridge
Gortin
Castlederg
Newtownstewart
Cookstown
Lough Derg
Drumquin
Omagh
Carrickmore
Pomeroy
Pettigoe
Beragh
Kesh
Dromore
Fintona
Dungannon
Lough Erne
Irvinestown
Ballygawley
2

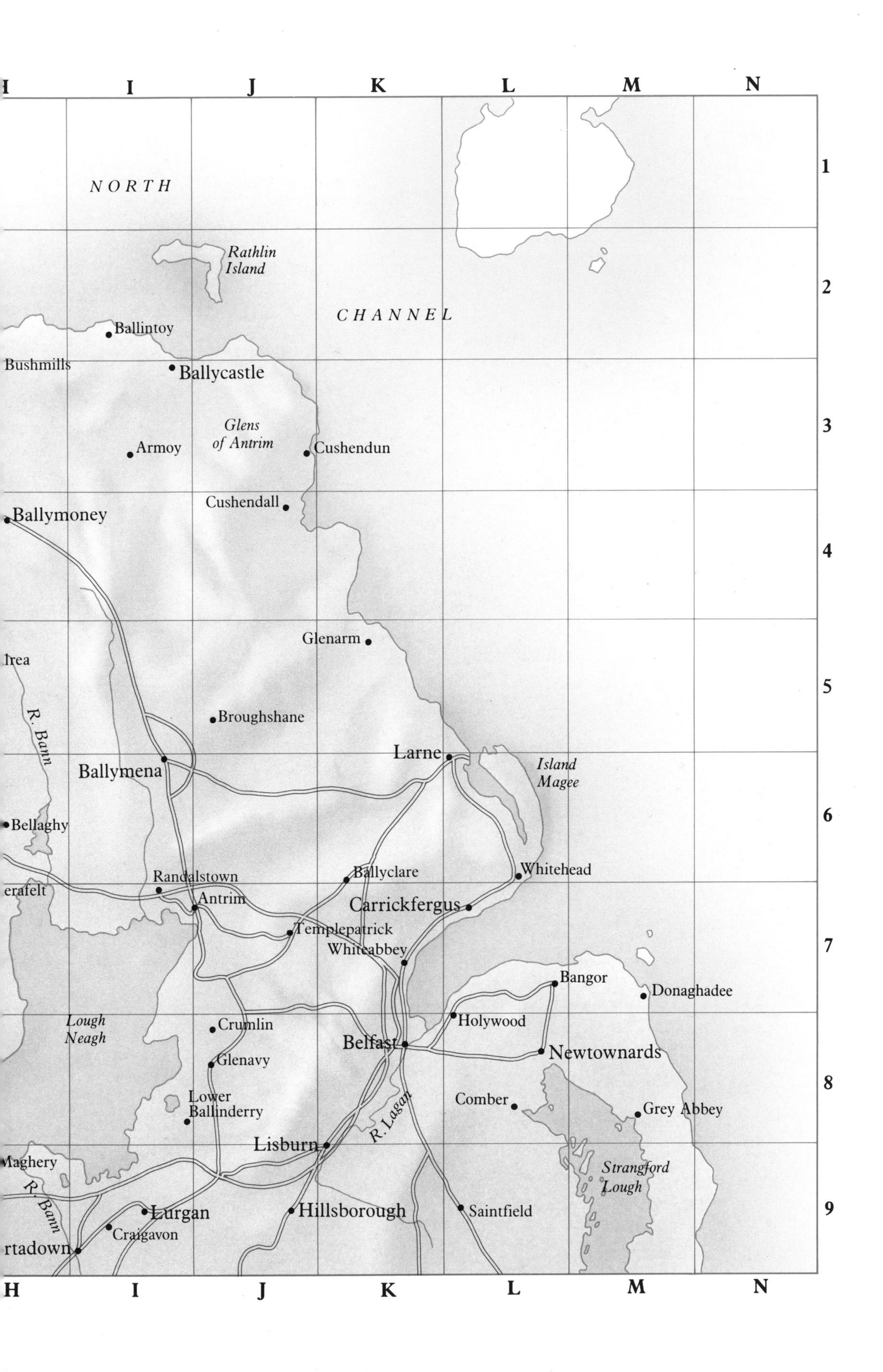

H
I
J
K
L
M
N
1
2
3
4
5
6
7
8
9
NORTH
CHANNEL
Rathlin
Island
Ballintoy
Bushmills
Ballycastle
Glens
of Antrim
Armoy
Cushendun
Cushendall
Ballymoney
Glenarm
lrea
R. Bann
Broughshane
Larne
Island
Magee
Ballymena
Bellaghy
Whitehead
Ballyclare
Randalstown
erafelt
Antrim
Carrickfergus
Templepatrick
Whiteabbey
Bangor
Donaghadee
Holywood
Lough
Neagh
Crumlin
Belfast
Newtownards
Glenavy
Lower
Ballinderry
Comber
Grey Abbey
R. Lagan
Lisburn
Maghery
Strangford
Lough
R. Bann
Lurgan
Hillsborough
Saintfield
Craigavon
rtadown

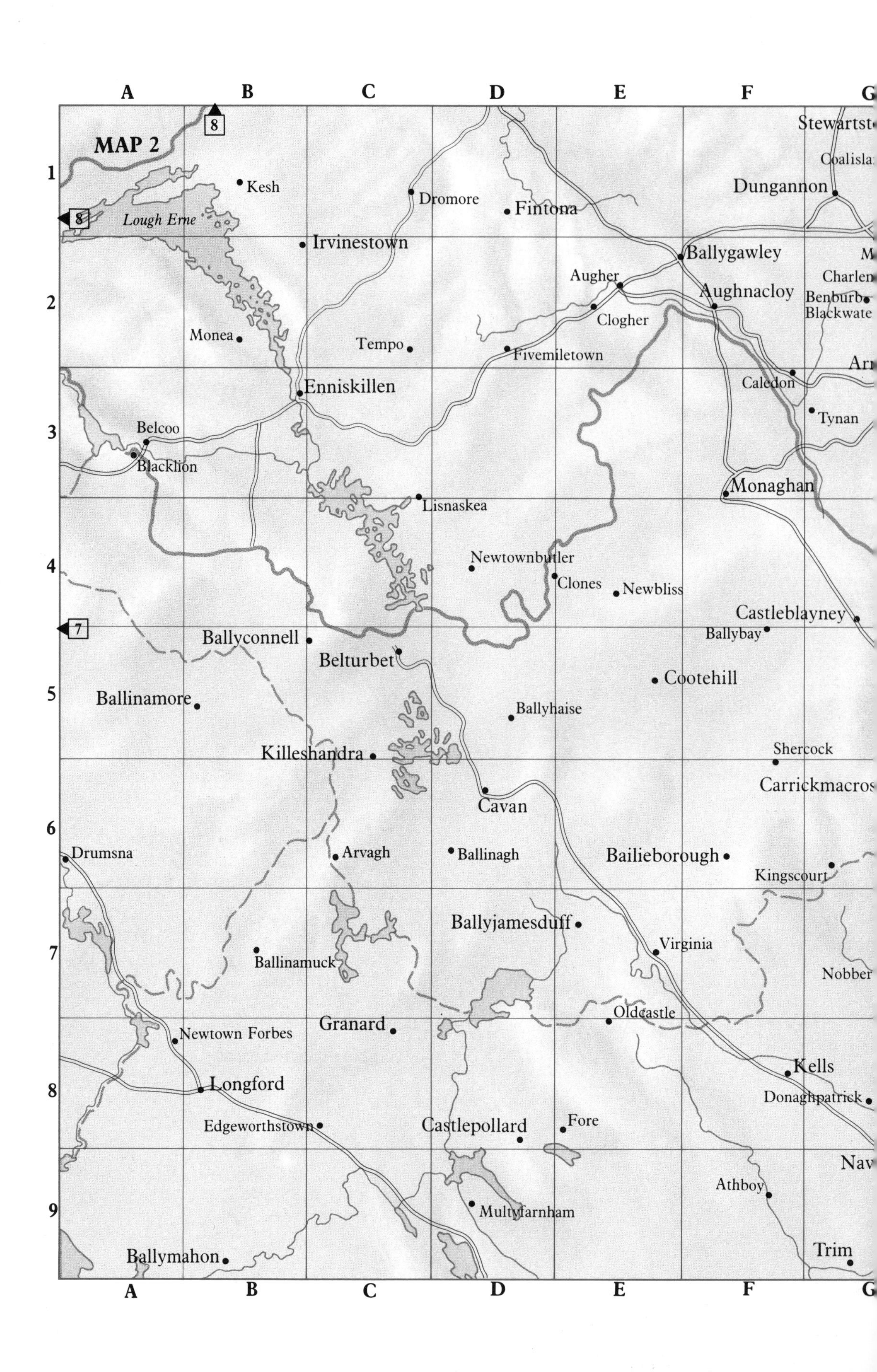

MAP 2
A
B
C
D
E
F
G
1
2
3
4
5
6
7
8
9
8
8
7
Kesh
Lough Erne
Dromore
Fintona
Dungannon
Coalisla
Stewartst
Irvinestown
Ballygawley
Augher
Aughnacloy
Clogher
Charlen
Benburb
Blackwate
Monea
Tempo
Fivemiletown
Enniskillen
Caledon
Tynan
Belcoo
Blacklion
Monaghan
Lisnaskea
Newtownbutler
Clones
Newbliss
Castleblayney
Ballybay
Ballyconnell
Belturbet
Cootehill
Ballinamore
Ballyhaise
Killeshandra
Shercock
Carrickmacros
Cavan
Drumsna
Arvagh
Ballinagh
Bailieborough
Kingscourt
Ballyjamesduff
Virginia
Ballinamuck
Nobber
Granard
Oldcastle
Newtown Forbes
Longford
Kells
Donaghpatrick
Edgeworthstown
Castlepollard
Fore
Athboy
Multyfarnham
Ballymahon
Trim

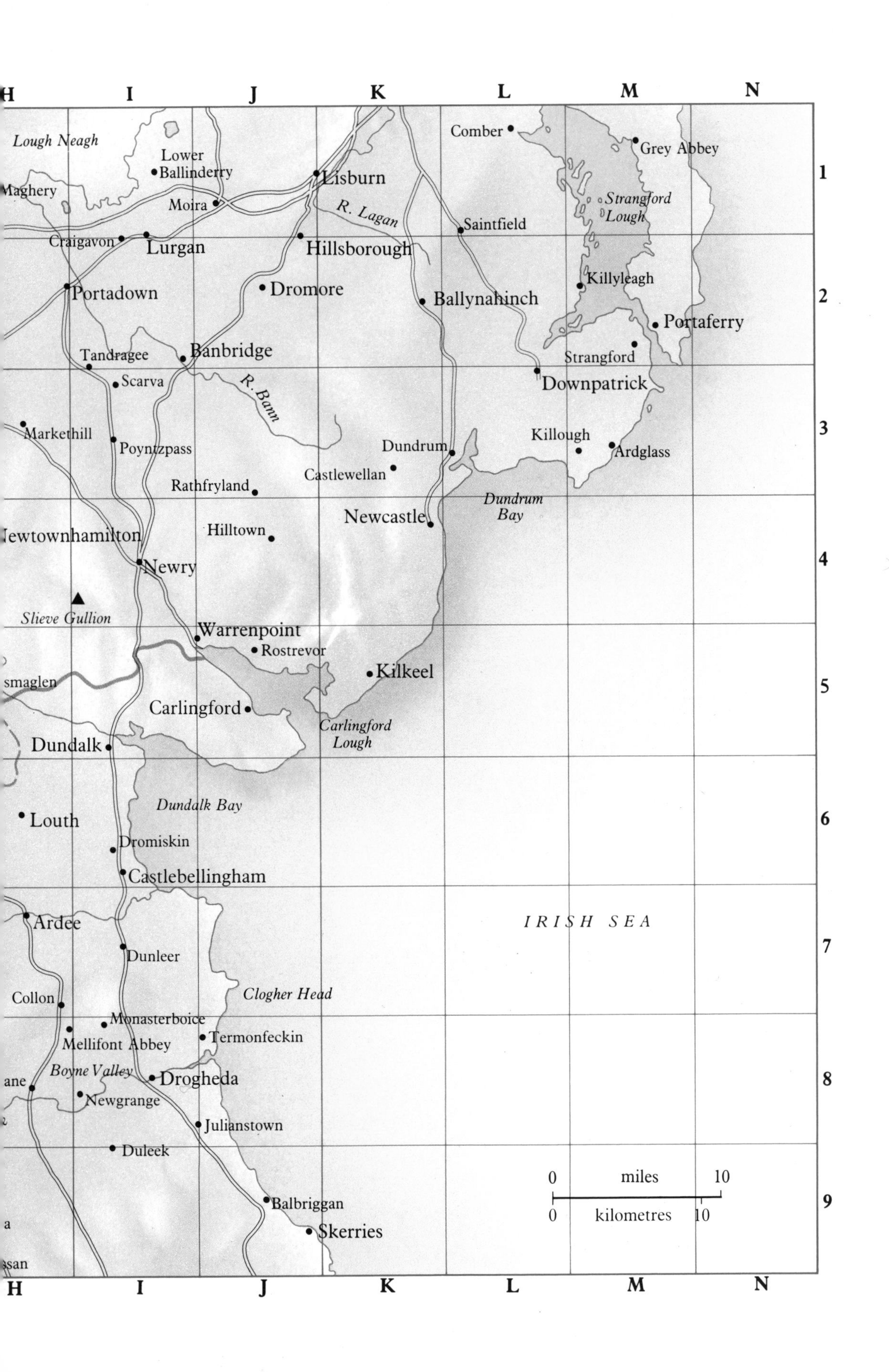
H
I
J
K
L
M
N
1
2
3
4
5
6
7
8
9
Lough Neagh
Lower
Ballinderry
Maghery
Moira
Lisburn
R. Lagan
Comber
Grey Abbey
Strangford
Lough
Saintfield
Craigavon
Lurgan
Hillsborough
Portadown
Dromore
Ballynahinch
Killyleagh
Portaferry
Strangford
Tandragee
Banbridge
Scarva
R. Bann
Downpatrick
Markethill
Poyntzpass
Dundrum
Killough
Ardglass
Castlewellan
Rathfryland
Dundrum
Bay
Newcastle
Newtownhamilton
Hilltown
Newry
Slieve Gullion
Warrenpoint
Rostrevor
Kilkeel
Crossmaglen
Carlingford
Carlingford
Lough
Dundalk
Dundalk Bay
Louth
Dromiskin
Castlebellingham
Ardee
IRISH SEA
Dunleer
Collon
Clogher Head
Monasterboice
Termonfeckin
Mellifont Abbey
Boyne Valley
Slane
Drogheda
Newgrange
Julianstown
Duleek
0
miles
10
0
kilometres
10
Balbriggan
Skerries
H
I
J
K
L
M
N

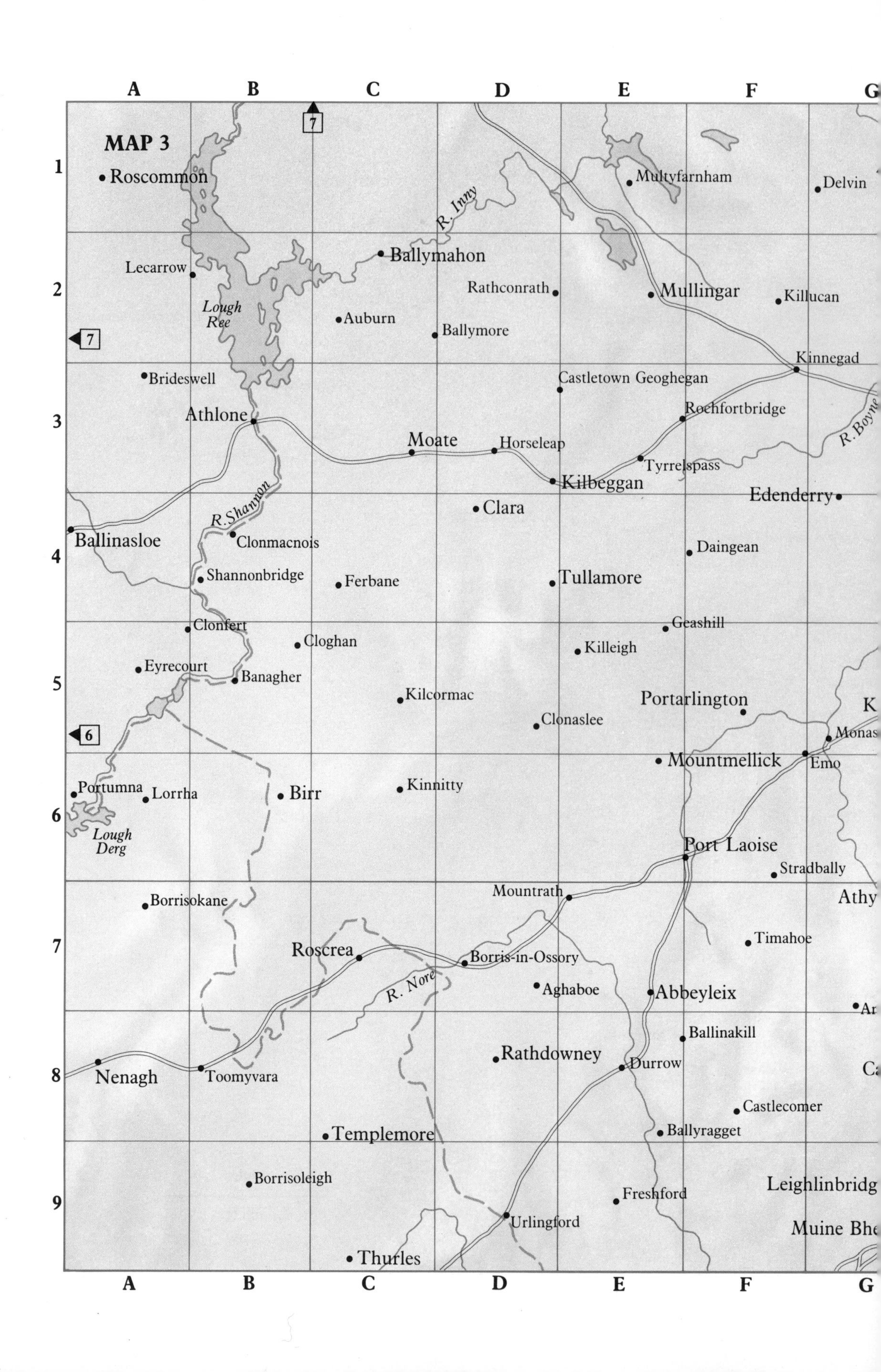

MAP 3
A
B
C
D
E
F
G
1
2
3
4
5
6
7
8
9
7
6
Roscommon
Multyfarnham
Delvin
R. Inny
Ballymahon
Lecarrow
Lough Ree
Rathconrath
Mullingar
Killucan
Auburn
Ballymore
Kinnegad
Brideswell
Castletown Geoghegan
Athlone
Rochfortbridge
R. Boyne
Moate
Horseleap
Tyrrelspass
Kilbeggan
Edenderry
R. Shannon
Clara
Ballinasloe
Clonmacnois
Daingean
Shannonbridge
Ferbane
Tullamore
Clonfert
Geashill
Cloghan
Killeigh
Eyrecourt
Banagher
Kilcormac
Portarlington
Clonaslee
Emo
Mountmellick
Portumna
Lorrha
Birr
Kinnitty
Lough Derg
Port Laoise
Stradbally
Borrisokane
Mountrath
Athy
Timahoe
Roscrea
Borris-in-Ossory
R. Nore
Aghaboe
Abbeyleix
Ballinakill
Rathdowney
Durrow
Nenagh
Toomyvara
Castlecomer
Templemore
Ballyragget
Borrisoleigh
Freshford
Urlingford
Thurles

H
I
J
K
L
M
N
1
2
3
4
5
6
7
8
9
2
Navan
Duleek
Julianstown
Balbriggan
Skerries
Bective
Tara
Trim
Kilmessan
Lusk
Rush
Dunshaughlin
Ratoath
Ashbourne
Ballyboghill
Lambay Island
Donabate
Summerhill
Swords
Malahide
Portmarnock
nnfield
Kilcock
Castleknock
Santry
Finglas
Raheny
Howth
Maynooth
Leixlip
R. Liffey
Clontarf
Dublin Bay
Lucan
Celbridge
Clondalkin
Chapelizod
Dublin
Newcastle
Rathfarnham
Stillorgan
Dun Laoghaire
Clane
Tallaght
Dundrum
Dalkey
wood
Rathcoole
Saggart
Cabinteely
Stepaside
Golden Ball
Loughlinstown
Kill
Naas
Enniskerry
Bray
Droichead Nua
Newbridge
Blessington
Greystones
Delgany
Kilcullen
Ballymore Eustace
Newtown Mountkennedy
Hollywood
Roundwood
Dunlavin
Ashford
Donard
Glendalough
Laragh
Ballitore
Wicklow
Wicklow Head
Glenmalure
Baltinglass
Rathdrum
Aghavannagh
Castledermot
Rathvilly
Hacketstown
Aughrim
Tullow
Tinahely
Arklow
Shillelagh
R. Slaney
Clonegall
Carnew
Gorey
0 miles 10
0 kilometres 10

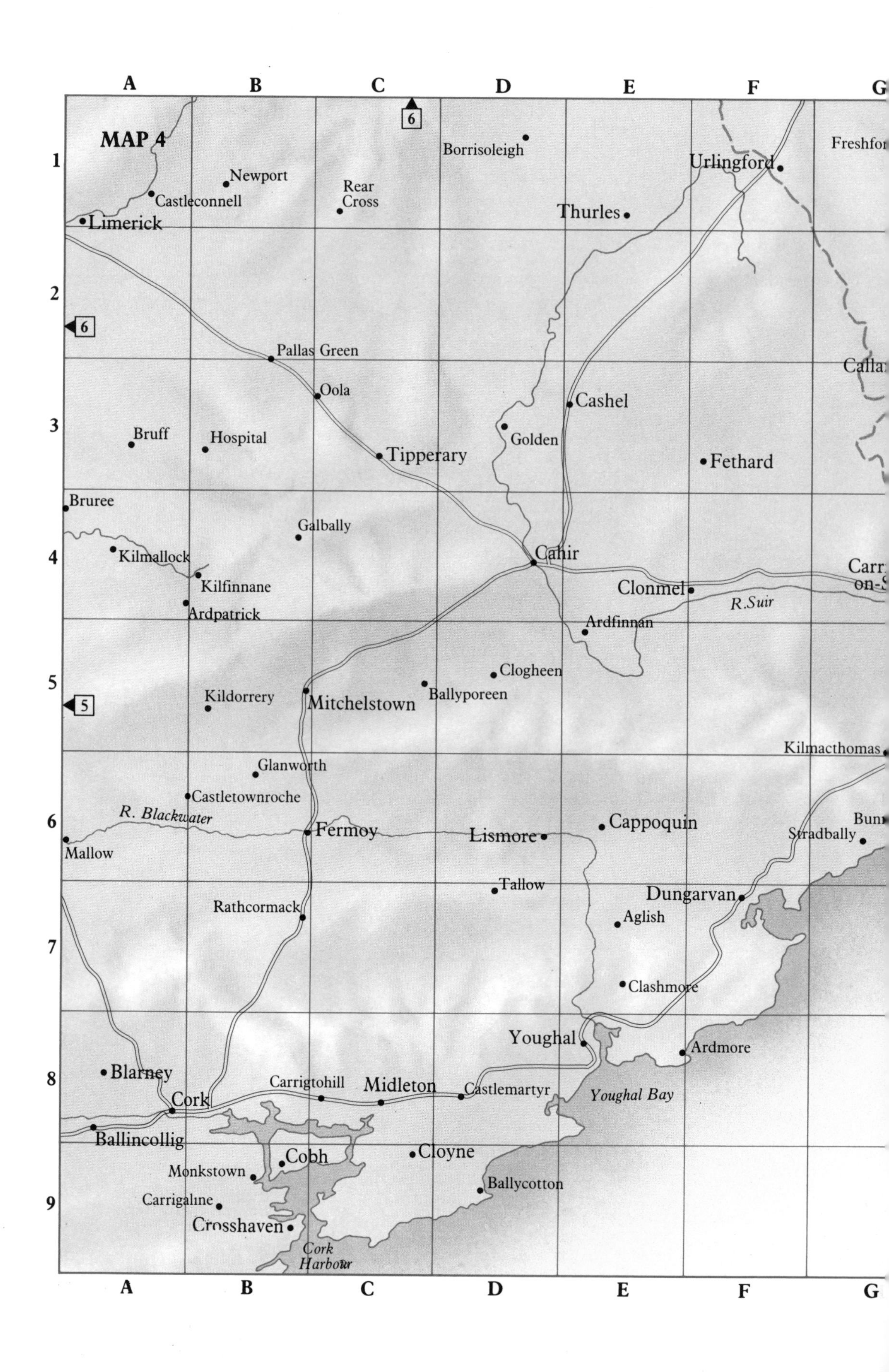

MAP 4
A
B
C
D
E
F
G
1
2
3
4
5
6
7
8
9
6
5
Borrisoleigh
Urlingford
Newport
Rear Cross
Castleconnell
Limerick
Thurles
Pallas Green
Oola
Cashel
Bruff
Hospital
Golden
Tipperary
Fethard
Bruree
Galbally
Kilmallock
Cahir
Kilfinnane
Clonmel
Ardpatrick
R.Suir
Ardfinnan
Clogheen
Kildorrery
Ballyporeen
Mitchelstown
Kilmacthomas
Glanworth
Castletownroche
R. Blackwater
Cappoquin
Fermoy
Lismore
Stradbally
Mallow
Tallow
Dungarvan
Rathcormack
Aglish
Clashmore
Youghal
Ardmore
Blarney
Carrigtohill
Midleton
Castlemartyr
Youghal Bay
Cork
Ballincollig
Cobh
Cloyne
Monkstown
Ballycotton
Carrigaline
Crosshaven
Cork Harbour

H
I
J
K
L
M
N
1
2
3
4
5
6
7
8
9
Shillelagh
Leighlinbridge
Carnew
Muine Bheag
Clonegall
Gorey
Kilkenny
Goresbridge
Gowran
R. Nore
Ferns
Borris
R. Barrow
Bunclody
Graiguenamanagh
Thomastown
Enniscorthy
Inistioge
St. Mullin's
Knocktopher
ganny
R. Slaney
New Ross
Mullinavat
Wexford
Wexford Harbour
Taghmon
Campile
Wellington Bridge
Rosslare
Waterford
Bridgetown
Passage East
Duncannon
Fethard
Kilmore Quay
Tramore
Dunmore East
Saltee Islands
Waterford Harbour
ST. GEORGE'S CHANNEL
0
miles
10
0
kilometres
10

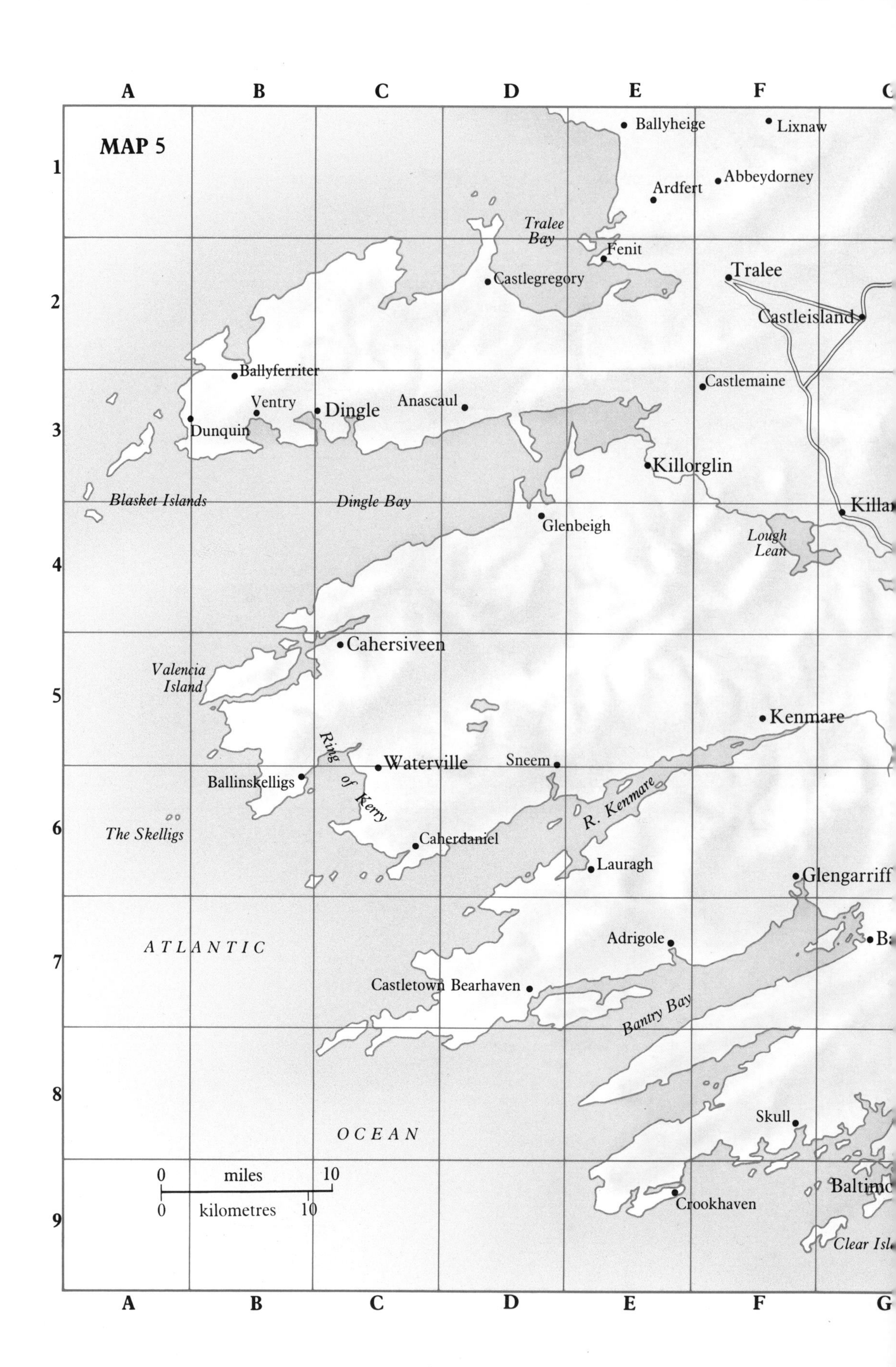

A
B
C
D
E
F
MAP 5
1
2
3
4
5
6
7
8
9
Ballyheige
Lixnaw
Abbeydorney
Ardfert
Tralee Bay
Fenit
Castlegregory
Tralee
Castleisland
Ballyferriter
Castlemaine
Ventry
Dingle
Anascaul
Dunquin
Killorglin
Blasket Islands
Dingle Bay
Glenbeigh
Lough Lean
Cahersiveen
Valencia Island
Kenmare
Ring of Kerry
Waterville
Sneem
Ballinskelligs
R. Kenmare
The Skelligs
Caherdaniel
Lauragh
Glengarriff
Adrigole
ATLANTIC
Castletown Bearhaven
Bantry Bay
Skull
OCEAN
0
miles
10
0
kilometres
10
Crookhaven
Clear Isl

H
I
J
K
L
M
N
1
2
3
4
5
6
7
8
9
Kilmallock
Galbally
beyfeale
Rathluirc
Kilfinnane
Drumcolliher
Ardpatrick
Ballyporeen
Liscarroll
Kildorrery
Mitchelstown
Buttevant
Newmarket
Doneraile
Glanworth
Kanturk
Castletownroche
R. Blackwater
Mallow
Fermoy
4
Rathcormack
Millstreet
Blarney
Coachford
Dripsey
Midleton
Cork
Macroom
Carrigtohill
Ballincollig
Cloyne
R. Lee
Monkstown
Cobh
Crookstown
Carrigaline
Inchigeelagh
Crosshaven
Cork Harbour
Bandon
Dunmanway
Ballineen-Enniskean
Kinsale
Drimoleague
Clonakilty
Courtmacsherry
Ross Carbery
Glandore
Skibbereen
Castletownsend

A
B
C
D
E
F
G
MAP 6
1
2
3
4
5
6
7
8
9
0
miles
10
kilometres
Carna
Rosmuck
Lettermullan
Moycullen
Lough Corrib
Claregalwa
Galway
Oran
Spiddal
Gorumna Island
Galway Bay
Inishmore
Aran Islands
Inishmaan
Inisheer
Corcomroe Abbey
Ballyvaghan
Kilmacduag
Lisdoonvarna
Carran
Doolin
Kilfenora
Liscannor
ATLANTIC
Ennistimon
Lehinch
Corrofin
Dysert O Dea
Milltown Malbay
Ennis
OCEAN
Clarecastle
Newmarket-on-Fe
Kilkee
Killadysert
R. Shannon
Kilrush
Carrigaholt
Foynes
Aske
Tarbert
Glin
Shanagolden
Ballylongford
Mouth of the Shannon
Ballybunnion
Rathkeale
Ardagh
Listowel
Newcastle West
Ballyheige
Lixnaw
Abbeyfeale
5

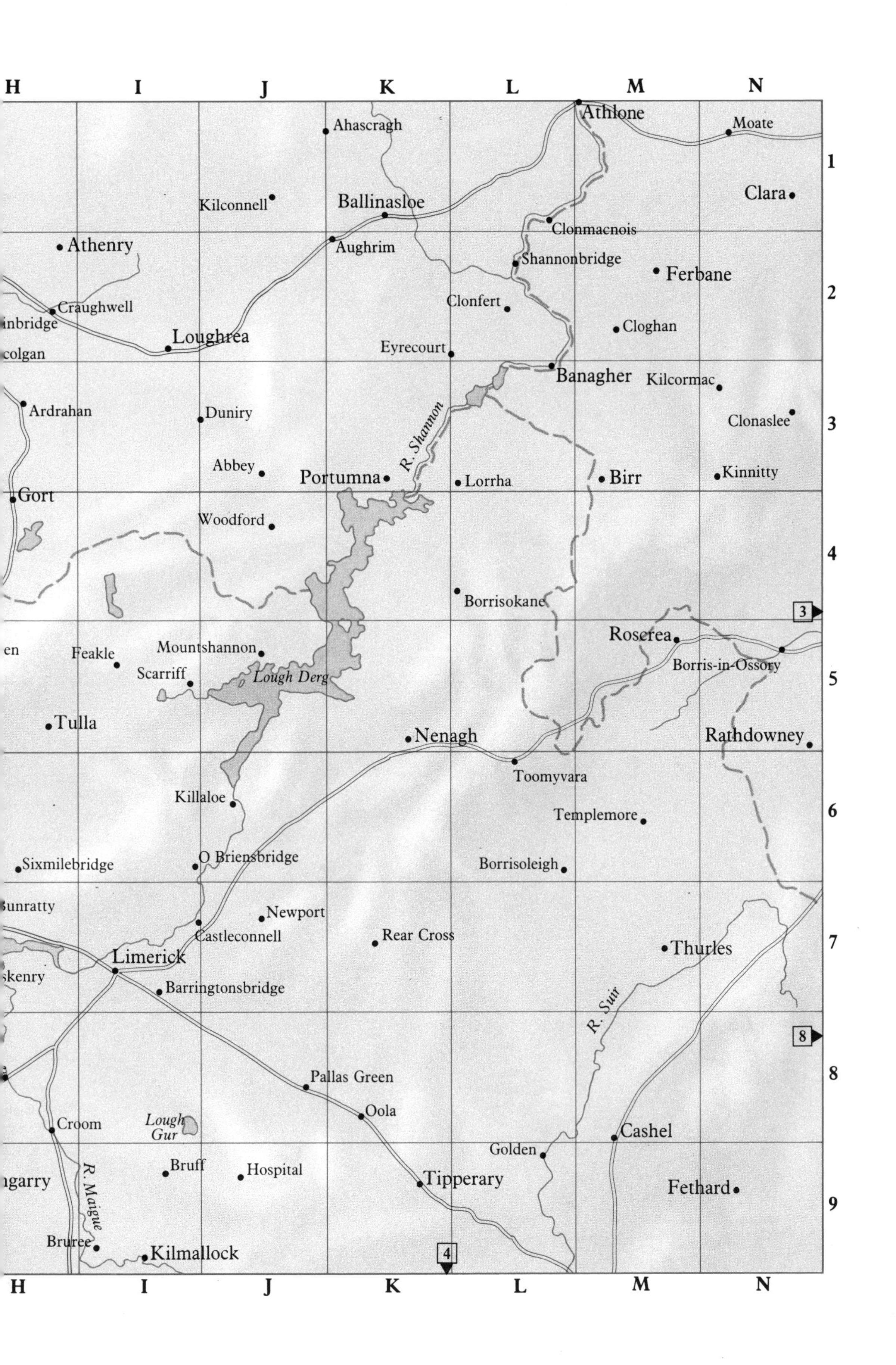
H
I
J
K
L
M
N
1
2
3
4
5
6
7
8
9
Athlone
Moate
Ahascragh
Clara
Kilconnell
Ballinasloe
Clonmacnois
Athenry
Aughrim
Shannonbridge
Ferbane
Craughwell
Clonfert
Cloghan
Loughrea
Eyrecourt
Banagher
Kilcormac
Ardrahan
Duniry
R. Shannon
Clonaslee
Abbey
Portumna
Lorrha
Birr
Kinnitty
Gort
Woodford
Borrisokane
3
Roscrea
Feakle
Mountshannon
Borris-in-Ossory
Scarriff
Lough Derg
Tulla
Nenagh
Rathdowney
Toomyvara
Killaloe
Templemore
Sixmilebridge
O Briensbridge
Borrisoleigh
Newport
Castleconnell
Rear Cross
Thurles
Limerick
Barringtonsbridge
R. Suir
8
Pallas Green
Oola
Croom
Lough Gur
Cashel
Golden
Bruff
Hospital
Tipperary
Fethard
R. Maigue
Bruree
Kilmallock
4
H
I
J
K
L
M
N

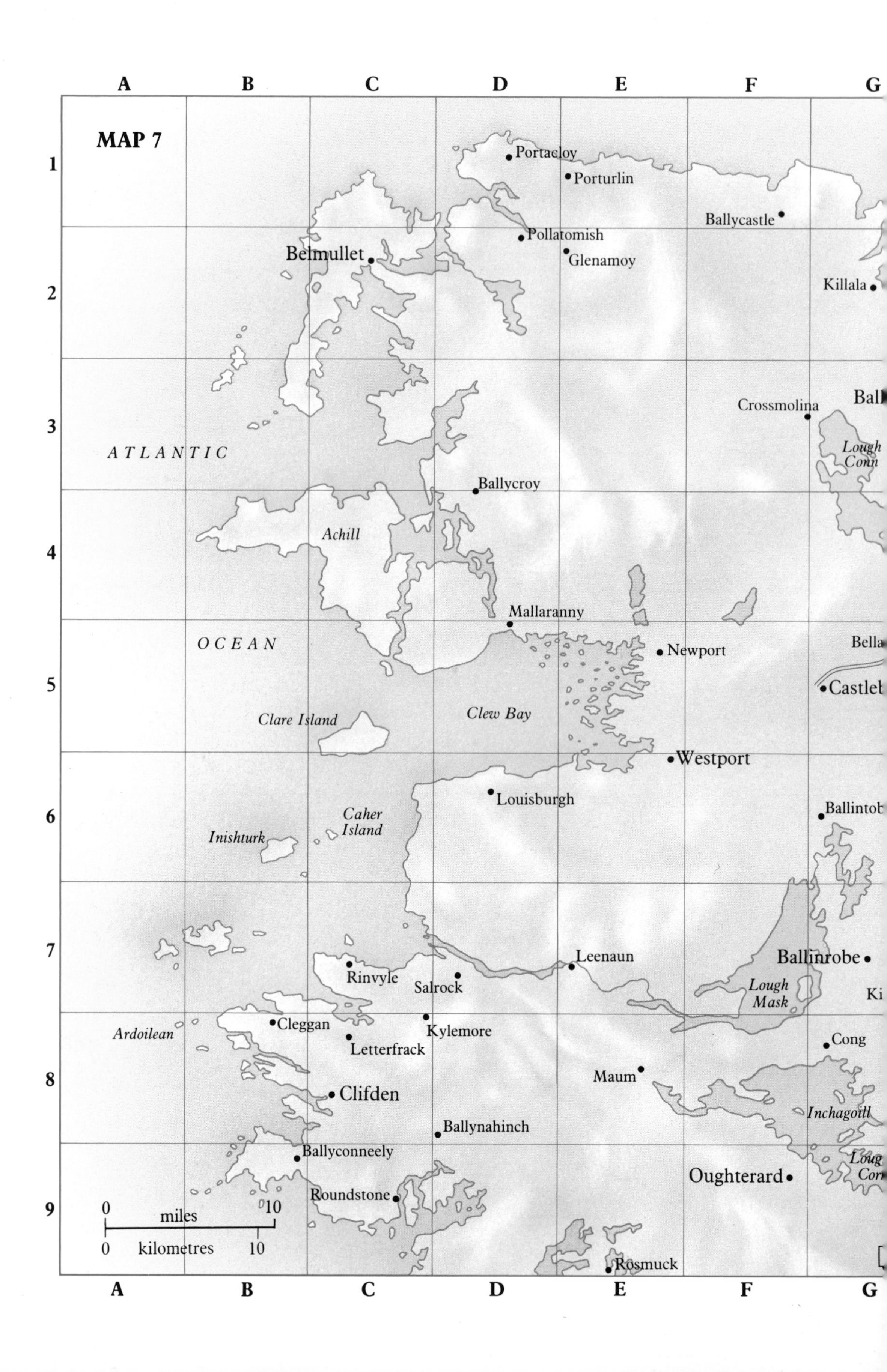

MAP 7
A
B
C
D
E
F
G
1
2
3
4
5
6
7
8
9
Portacloy
Porturlin
Ballycastle
Pollatomish
Belmullet
Glenamoy
Killala
Crossmolina
Ball
Lough
Conn
ATLANTIC
Ballycroy
Achill
Mallaranny
OCEAN
Newport
Bella
Castlet
Clare Island
Clew Bay
Westport
Louisburgh
Caher
Island
Inishturk
Ballintob
Leenaun
Ballinrobe
Rinvyle
Salrock
Lough
Mask
Ki
Cleggan
Kylemore
Ardoilean
Letterfrack
Cong
Maum
Clifden
Inchagoill
Ballynahinch
Ballyconneely
Loug
Cor
Oughterard
Roundstone
0
miles
10
0
kilometres
10
Rosmuck

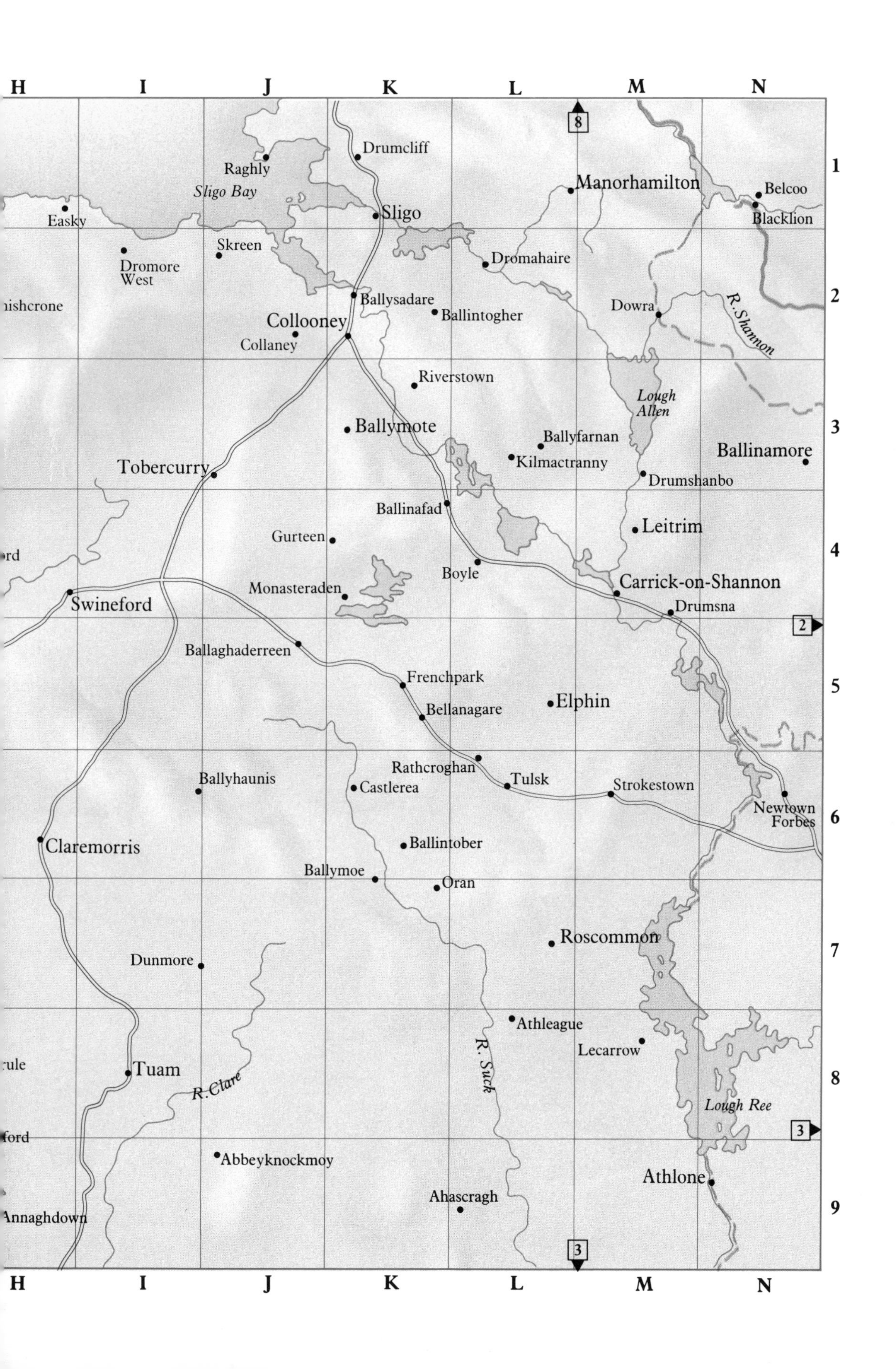

H
I
J
K
L
M
N
8
1
2
3
4
5
6
7
8
9
Raghly
Sligo Bay
Drumcliff
Manorhamilton
Belcoo
Blacklion
Easky
Sligo
Skreen
Dromore West
Dromahaire
Ballysadare
Ballintogher
Dowra
R. Shannon
nishcrone
Collooney
Collaney
Riverstown
Lough Allen
Ballymote
Ballyfarnan
Kilmactranny
Ballinamore
Tobercurry
Drumshanbo
Ballinafad
Leitrim
Gurteen
rd
Boyle
Carrick-on-Shannon
Monasteraden
Drumsna
Swineford
2
Ballaghaderreen
Frenchpark
Elphin
Bellanagare
Rathcroghan
Tulsk
Strokestown
Ballyhaunis
Castlerea
Newtown Forbes
Claremorris
Ballintober
Ballymoe
Oran
Roscommon
Dunmore
Athleague
R. Suck
Lecarrow
rule
Tuam
R. Clare
Lough Ree
ford
3
Abbeyknockmoy
Athlone
Ahascragh
Annaghdown
3

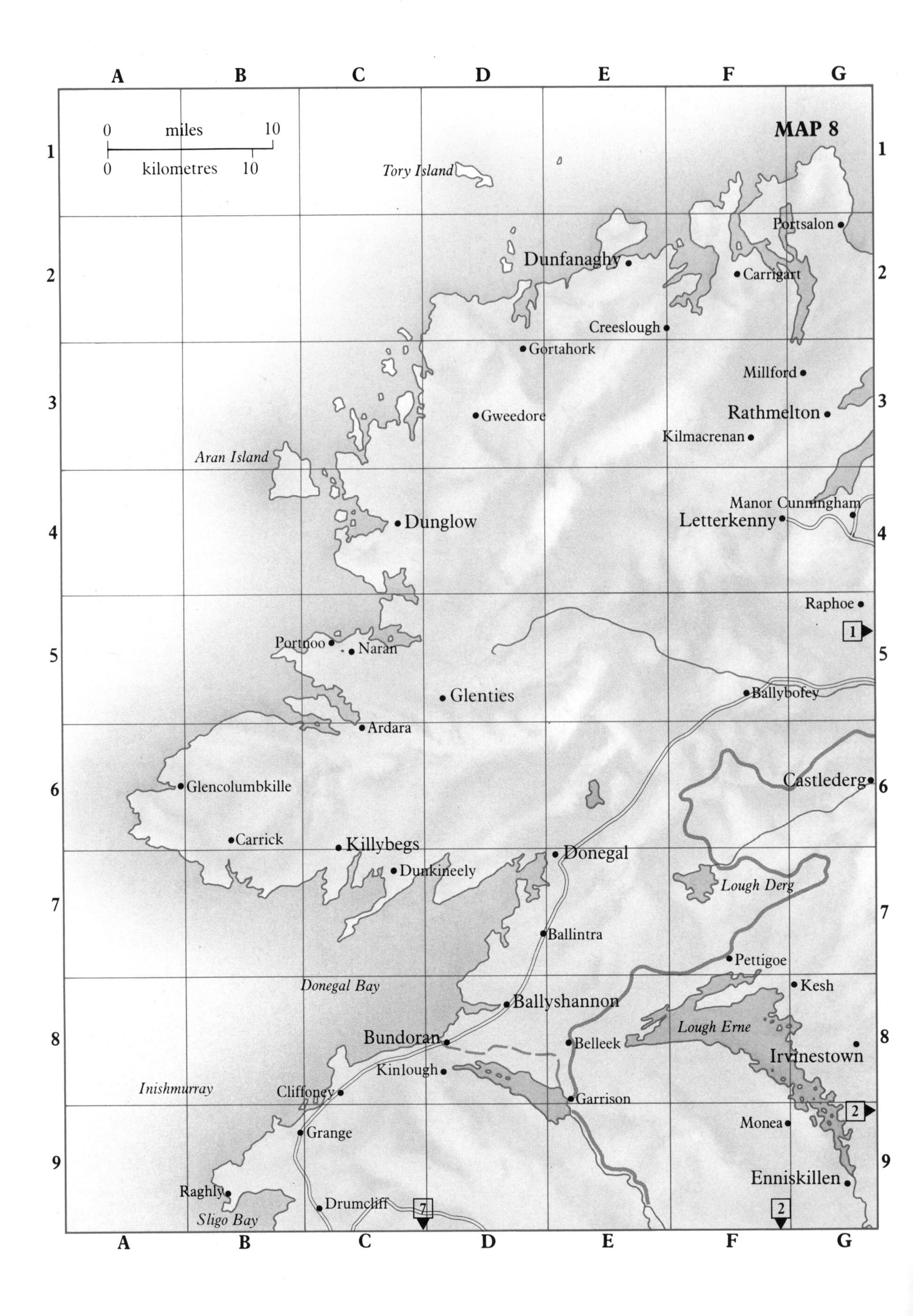

MAP 8
A
B
C
D
E
F
G
1
2
3
4
5
6
7
8
9
0
miles
10
0
kilometres
10
Tory Island
Portsalon
Dunfanaghy
Carrigart
Creeslough
Gortahork
Millford
Gweedore
Rathmelton
Kilmacrenan
Aran Island
Manor Cunningham
Dunglow
Letterkenny
Raphoe
1
Portnoo
Naran
Glenties
Ballybofey
Ardara
Glencolumbkille
Castlederg
Carrick
Killybegs
Donegal
Dunkineely
Lough Derg
Ballintra
Pettigoe
Kesh
Donegal Bay
Ballyshannon
Lough Erne
Bundoran
Belleek
Irvinestown
Kinlough
Inishmurray
Cliffoney
Garrison
2
Monea
Grange
Enniskillen
Raghly
Drumcliff
7
Sligo Bay

INDEX

A

B

C

D

E

F

G

H

I

K

L

M

N

P Q

R

S

T

U

V

W

Y Z

BIBLIOGRAPHY

The Gill History of Ireland, Dublin 1972–5, 11 vols
The Helicon History of Ireland, Dublin 1981, 7 vols (continuing)
The New Gill History of Ireland, Dublin, 2 vols (continuing)
A New History of Ireland, Oxford, 5 vols (continuing)
L. Barrow, *The Round Towers of Ireland*, Dublin 1979
T. B. Barry, *The Archaeology of Medieval Ireland*, London 1987
M. Bence-Jones, *Burke's Guide to Country Houses Vol 1: Ireland*, London 1978
P. Bowe and M. George, *The Gardens of Ireland*, London 1986
H. Boylan, *A Dictionary of Irish Biography*, Dublin 1988 (2nd ed.)
M. Craig, *Classic Irish Houses of the Middle Size*, London 1977
M. Craig, *Irish Architecture from the Earliest Times to 1880*, London 1982
A. Crookshank and the Knight of Glin, *The Painters of Ireland*, London 1978
K. Danaher, *The Year in Ireland*, Cork 1972
L. de Paor, *The Peoples of Ireland*, London 1986
M. and L. de Paor, *Early Christian Ireland*, London 1958
R. de Valera and S. O Nualláin, *Survey of the Megalithic Tombs of Ireland*, Dublin 1961, 5 vols (continuing)
C. Fitz-Simon, *The Arts in Ireland: A Chronology*, Dublin 1982
C. Fitz-Simon, *The Irish Theatre*, London 1983
N. Gordon-Bowe, D. Caron and M. Wynne, *Gazetteer of Irish Stained Glass*, Blackrock 1988
A. Gwynn and R. N. Hadcock, *Medieval Religious Houses: Ireland*, London 1970
P. Harbison, *Pre-Christian Ireland*, London 1988
P. Harbison, *The High Crosses of Ireland*, Mainz (forthcoming), 3 vols
P. Harbison, H. Potterton, and J. Sheehy, *Irish Art and Architecture*, London 1978
R. J. Hayes (Ed.), *Sources for the History of Irish Civilisation (Persons, Places, Dates)*, Boston 1970, 9 vols
F. Henry, *Irish Art during the Early Christian Period*, London 1965–7, 3 vols
K. Hughes, *The Church in Early Irish Society*, London 1966
J. Hunt, *Irish Medieval Figure Sculptures*, Dublin and London 1974, 2 vols
R. Hurley and W. Cantwell, *Contemporary Irish Church Architecture*, Dublin 1985
Lord Killanin, *My Ireland*, London 1987
H. G. Leask, *Irish Churches and Monastic Buildings*, Dundalk 1955–61, 3 vols
H. G. Leask, *Irish Castles and Castellated Houses*, Dundalk 1964
P. MacCana, *Celtic Mythology*, London 1983
M. MacNeill, *The Festival of Lughnasa*, Oxford 1962
F. Mitchell, *Shell Guide to Reading the Irish Landscape*, Dublin 1987
E. R. Norman and J. K. St Joseph, *The Early Development of Irish Society*, London 1969
T. P. O'Neill, *Life and Tradition in Rural Ireland*, London 1977
S. P. Ó Ríordáin, *Antiquities of the Irish Countryside*, London 1979 (5th ed.)
M. Ryan (Ed.), *Treasures of Ireland: Irish Art 3000 B.C.–1500 A.D.*, Dublin 1983
P. Shaffrey, *Irish Countryside Buildings*, Dublin 1985
R. Stalley, *The Cistercian Monasteries of Ireland*, London and New Haven 1987

CONVERSION CHART

Miles	1	2	3	4	5	10	20	25	50	100	200
Kilometers	1.6	3.2	4.8	6.4	8	16	32	40	80	160	320